The Concept of Necessity in International Law and the World Trade Organization

World Trade Institute Advanced Studies

Series Editor

VOLUME 17

The titles published in this series are listed at *brill.com/wtia*

The Concept of Necessity in International Law and the World Trade Organization

History, Lessons and Prospects

By

Senai W. Andemariam

BRILL | NIJHOFF

LEIDEN | BOSTON

Library of Congress Cataloging-in-Publication Data

Names: Andemariam, Senai W., author.
Title: The concept of necessity in international law and the World Trade Organization: history, lessons, and prospects / by Senai Andemariam.
Description: Leiden; Boston: Brill/Nijhoff, 2024. | Series: World Trade Institute advanced studies; volume 17 | Includes bibliographical references and index. | Summary: "This book aims to make the three contributions mentioned above by responding to the following key question: can the concepts of necessity in WTO law and CIL influence each other to achieve a more coherent concept of necessity across different fields of international law? The main reasons for focusing on these two concepts of necessity in this book are: (a) the clarity of their respective definitions; (b) their extensive application in the respective fields of international law where they operate; and (c) their potential to influence the development of the concept of necessity in other fields of international law. Since the gist of this book is to finally discuss the concept of necessity in the broader context of fragmentation and coherence of international law, it is requisite to analyze in detail the relationship between these two relatively elucidated concepts of necessity in international law. Analysis of this relationship must culminate in identifying the possibility for these two differing concepts of necessity to learn from (i.e., influence) each other so that a more coherent concept of necessity can develop in international law"– Provided by publisher.
Identifiers: LCCN 2024010488 | ISBN 9789004699991 (hardback) | ISBN 9789004700000 (ebook)
Subjects: LCSH: World Trade Organization. | Customary law, International. | Necessity (International law) | General Agreement on Tariffs and Trade (Organization) | General Agreement on Trade in Services (Organization) | Foreign trade regulation.
Classification: LCC K4610 .A957 2024 | DDC 341–dc23/eng/20240310
LC record available at https://lccn.loc.gov/2024010488

Typeface for the Latin, Greek, and Cyrillic scripts: "Brill". See and download: brill.com/brill-typeface.

ISSN 2405-9331
ISBN 978-90-04-69999-1 (hardback)
ISBN 978-90-04-70000-0 (e-book)
DOI 10.1163/9789004700000

Contents

PART 2
The Concept of Necessity in International Law

PART 3
The Concept of Necessity in WTO Law

Foreword

Through the intricate tapestry of international law, the concept of necessity runs as a common thread, a principle that both binds states and frees them to pursue their interests in the exercise of sovereign autonomy. This book, a meticulous exploration of the concept of necessity in the law of the World Trade Organization (WTO), delves into the heart of this concept, examining its emergence and evolution through history, unravelling its implications across key WTO agreements and exploring its reflection within the broader realm of international law. In doing so, it searches for coherence in the understanding of this key concept across various fields of international law.

The importance of the study of necessity goes beyond understanding its theoretical contours. The concept of necessity has significant practical implications. It shapes the boundaries of permissible state action in the pursuit of legitimate policy objectives, such as climate change mitigation and health protection. By doing so, it seeks to balance the competing interests of security and predictability in international relations and regulatory autonomy, a delicate but crucial endeavor. This book, through its nuanced exploration, seeks to demystify the multifaceted nature of necessity, highlighting its importance and influence on the fabric of international trade governance.

A valuable aspect of this exploration is the historical lens through which necessity is viewed. The author carefully traces the evolution of the concept, examining its roots and its gradual crystallization into a distinct legal principle. The understanding of necessity is greatly enhanced by this journey through time, unpicking the threads of decisions, disputes, and negotiations that have woven its contemporary meaning.

At the core of the analysis in this book is the investigation of how necessity is given shape within the specific context of various WTO agreements. The author skillfully navigates through the text of these agreements, exploring necessity in the exceptions provisions of the General Agreement on Tariffs and Trade (GATT), the General Agreement on Trade in Services (GATS) and the Agreement on Trade-Related Aspects of Intellectual Property Rights (TRIPS), before turning to necessity as a substantive obligation in the Agreement on Technical Barriers to Trade (TBT) and the Agreement on the Application of Sanitary and Phytosanitary Measures (SPS). By examining the interpretative nuances of necessity within these agreements, the book offers a comprehensive understanding of how necessity functions as a balancing principle in different areas of WTO law, distilling the commonalities but also reflecting on divergences.

The analysis in this book leads us beyond the confines of WTO law, discussing the concept of necessity also in other international law regimes. By analyzing the perspectives of international tribunals in interpreting necessity, the author offers valuable insights into the interconnectedness of the understanding of necessity as a legal principle across various regimes. The question at the heart of this exploration is whether the concept of necessity in WTO law is an isolated thread or part of the broader fabric of customary international law. The answers lie in the rigorous analysis of decisions by international tribunals, providing guidance for understanding the interplay between necessity in WTO law and in the wide tapestry of international legal norms.

As the author crosses this extensive legal landscape, he is guided by a critical question: has the concept of necessity in WTO law influenced, or been influenced by, its counterpart in customary international law? The author's insightful analysis traces the threads connecting these two regimes. The book engages in a comparative study, exploring the relationship between necessity in WTO law and its evolution within the broader context of customary international law. This examination sheds light on the cross-fertilization of understandings, case law developments, and normative frameworks that have shaped the concept of necessity on the global stage.

In the often fraught relationship between state regulatory sovereignty and global trade governance, necessity emerges as a pivotal arbiter. This excellent book, with its interdisciplinary approach, offers a very useful panoramic view of the concept of necessity in WTO law, capturing its essence, delving into its historical roots, and laying bare its harmonies and dissonances with customary international law.

Denise Prévost
Maastricht University

Peter Van den Bossche
Word Trade Institute, Bern

Acknowledgments

This book is the culmination of my doctoral research at the Faculty of Law of Maastricht University (MU), The Netherlands. The support of many individuals and institutions made possible the success of preparing it.

My foremost appreciation goes to my supervisors Prof. dr. Peter L. H. Van den Bossche, Director of Studies at the World Trade Institute (WTI) and Professor of International Economic Law at the University of Bern and Dr. Denise Prévost, Associate Professor of International Economic Law at MU. They have also graciously written the foreword to this book.

From the first day we met in person in his Appellate Body office, when he was a member of the Appellate Body of the World Trade Organization (WTO), Prof. Van den Bossche's belief in my capacity to successfully complete my doctoral research kept me going. I will always be grateful for his paying, out of his book royalties, for my attendance in two, one-week long courses offered at the WTI which provided be with important insights in some areas of the research. He also arranged a two-week visiting fellowship at the WTO where I was able to consult references and interview people. His kind lunch and dinner invitations over which we discussed my dissertation remind me that the doctoral dissertation road is also human, not merely intellectual.

I equally appreciate Dr. Prévost for her kindness and ever readiness to quickly respond to any and all questions that I had. She read and meticulously commented on the dissertation twice. Her insightful comments kept the dissertation in focus. She put her office at the Faculty of Law of MU at my disposal during the few summers I came for research at MU.

I give thanks to the administration and support staff of the Faculty of Law of MU for all administrative support they gave me and for hosting me during my numerous visits to prepare my dissertation.

I am grateful to the four members of the dissertation Assessment Committee whose perceptive comments/critiques and unanimous approval of the dissertation to be defended confirmed to me that I made the right choice in pursuing academic career in international law in general and international trade law in particular. Thank you: Prof. dr. Anselm Kamperman Sanders (*chair*) (Faculty of Law, MU); Prof. dr. Malgosia Fitzmaurice (Queen Mary, University of London); Prof. dr. Liesbeth Lijnzaad (MU and Judge at the International Tribunal for the Law of the Sea); and Prof. dr. Gabrielle Marceau (WTO and Université de Genève).

I thank the National Higher Education and Research Institute of Eritrea for providing full funding for the completion of my doctoral study. Special thanks go to Dr. Mengsteab Negash, the former head of the Department of Law of the College of Business and Social Sciences (Eritrea), where I teach, and to the entire faculty of the Department for their unwavering support and encouragement.

Special thanks are also reserved for Prof. dr. Thomas Cottier, Series Editor of the World Trade Institute Advanced Studies Series (WTIAS) at Brill, who read the manuscript with great detail and, upon review by, and in consultation with, fellow editors at Brill, decided to take up the manuscript for publication in the WTIAS. I thank him for his comments which were important in giving this book the final substance and structure it now has.

I also thank Ms Beth Derr, Associate Editor for International Law at Brill, for diligently following up the process of publishing this book and her timely responses to any questions that I had. I also appreciate Marie Sheldon, Publishing Director of International Law at Brill and Martin Banigan, my production editor, for their invaluable contributions.

I dedicate this book to all members of my family, especially my wife Ellen Estifanos and our children, and my close friends who gave me enough support and patiently let me take as much time as I needed throughout the years of preparing my doctoral dissertation and this book. I could not have achieved this much without their constant encouragement.

Thank you all!

Senai W. Andemariam
Asmara, 26 January 2024

Tables

Acronyms

ARSIWA	Articles on Responsibility of States for Internationally Wrongful Acts
BITS	bilateral investment treaties
CIL	customary international law
CPW	circumstances precluding wrongfulness
DARIO	Draft Articles on the Responsibility of International Organizations
DSU	Understanding on Rules and Procedures Governing the Settlement of Disputes
ECCC	Extraordinary Chambers in the Courts of Cambodia
ECHR	European Convention on Human Rights
ECJ	European Court of Justice
EU	European Union
GATS	General Agreement on Trade in Services
GATT	General Agreement on Tariffs and Trade
GIL	general international law
GP Agreement	Agreement on Government Procurement
HALB	Libyan Arab Republic-Burundi Holding Company
IACHR	Inter-American Convention on Human Rights
ICC	International Criminal Court
ICCPR	International Covenant on Civil and Political Rights
ICJ	International Court of Justice
ICL	international criminal law
ICRC	International Committee of the Red Cross
ICSID	International Centre for Settlement of Investment Disputes
ICTR	International Criminal Tribunal for Rwanda
ICTY	International Criminal Tribunal for the Former Yugoslavia
IEAS	international environmental agreements
IEL	international economic law
IEnL	international environmental law
IHL	international humanitarian law
IHRL	international human rights law
IIAS	international investment agreements
IIL	international investment law
ILC	International Law Commission
ILO	International Labour Organization
ITL	international trade law
ITLOS	International Tribunal for the Law of the Sea
ITO	International Trade Organization

LAFICO	Libyan Arab Foreign Investment Company
L.N.T.S.	League of Nations Treaty Series
MPIA	Multi-Party Interim Appeal Arbitration Arrangement
NIMT	Nuremberg International Military Tribunal
NPMS	non-precluded measures
PCA	Permanent Court of Arbitration
PCIJ	Permanent Court of International Justice
PIL	public international law
SCM Agreement	Agreement on Subsidies and Countervailing Measures
SCR	self-contained regime
SPS	sanitary and phytosanitary
SPS Agreement	Agreement on the Application of Sanitary and Phytosanitary Measures
TBT Agreement	Agreement on Technical Barriers to Trade
TRIMS Agreement	Agreement on Trade-Related Investment Measures
TRIPS Agreement	Agreement on Trade-Related Aspects of Intellectual Property Rights
UAE	United Arab Emirates
UK	United Kingdom
UN	United Nations
UNCLOS	UN Convention on the Law of the Sea
US	United States
USSD	US State Department
VCDR	Vienna Convention on Diplomatic Relations
VCLT	Vienna Convention on the Law of Treaties
WTO	World Trade Organization

Introduction

> Necessity has no law.[1]
>
> OLIVER CROMWELL

•••

> Mighty is law, mightier necessity![2]
>
> PLUTUS

•••

> [Necessity] has the almost mystical power to transform what would otherwise be illegal or immoral into a justified or excused act, all because the action was 'necessary'.
>
> OHLIN and MAY

∴

Background

From Cicero's *salus populi est suprema lex* ("public safety is the supreme law") to Gratian's *quod non est licitum lege, necessitas facit licitum* ("what is not licit in law, necessity makes licit") and Thomas Aquinas' "necessity is not subject to the law", from the 5th century AD Germanic maxim *noth und tod hat kein gebot* ("necessity and death have no command") to the Islamic maxim "necessity renders prohibited things permissible", from German Chancellor Theobald von Bethmann-Hollweg's "necessity knows no law!"[3] to Oscar Schachter's

1 William Harris, *An Historical and Critical Account of the Life of Oliver Cromwell, Lord Protector of the Commonwealth of England, Scotland, and Ireland: After the Manner of Mr Bayle, Drawn from Original Writers and State Papers to Which is Added an Appendix of Original Papers, now First Published* (London: Printed for A. Millar, 1962), p. 236.

2 Plutus in Johann Wolfgang von Goethe, *Faust: Parts 1 and 2* (Bayard Taylor trans., Dover Thrift editions) (Mineola: New York: Dover Publications, Inc., 2018), p. 175 (Part 2).

3 All discussed in further detail in Sub-section 2.1.10.

 | DOI:10.1163/9789004700000_002

"[international law] rejects the idea that necessity knows no law",[4] the concept of necessity has been at the heart of the debate on the limits of human and state obligation to be bound by law. Ohlin and May have called necessity "quite possibly the most powerful concept in law".[5] By its very nature, necessity, unless limited by a legal instrument that recognizes it, carries the inherent capacity to be balanced against all obligations contained in that same legal instrument.

The evolution of the concept of necessity shows that the scope of discussions on it expanded with the development of societal and national structures. It was, as will be shown in Chapter 2, at the time around the conclusion of the Peace of Westphalia that the old concept of necessity – hitherto limited to relations between individuals as well as between individuals and social, religious or political entities – started to be discussed in relation to the legal relations between nation states, i.e., necessity in the realm of international law. This book focuses on the concept of necessity as developed in one specific field of international law, ITL, and within ITL, in WTO law, although the context to be provided for the concept of necessity in WTO law is the concept of necessity as contained in the wider area of international law.

Brief Literature Review

In the first two decades of the 20th century, the concept of necessity started to be clearly distinguished from similar concepts such as self-preservation, self-defense as well as *force majeure* and has since then attracted increasing scholarly attention. Works of some of the more notable authors on the subject can be mentioned here. Arrigo Cavaglieri's *Lo Stato di Necessità nel Diritto Internazionale*, published in 1917, can be referred to as the first work to introduce, in detail, necessity as a recognized concept in international law. Cavaglieri formulated in general the issues on the subject of necessity for further debates. Rodick's *The Doctrine of Necessity in International Law* has also been hailed as probably one of the first comprehensive works on the subject of necessity in international law. Rodick covered the subject of necessity in much detail and identified a list of limitations that necessity should be subjected

4 Oscar Schachter, *International Law in Theory and Practice* (Dordrecht: Martinus Nijhoff Publishers, 1991), p. 173.

5 Jens David Ohlin and Larry May, *Necessity in International Law* (New York: Oxford University Press, 2016), p. 1.

to in the sphere of international law.[6] Paul Weidenbaum's article, *Necessity in International Law* (1938), masterfully summarized the philosophical origins and the then contemporary debates on necessity including the debate on whether necessity exists in international law.[7] Professor Roberto Ago, chairing the ILC's study group on state responsibility, can take the credit for discerning a pattern out of state and tribunal practices since the 18th century and laying out the rules for the defense of necessity in international law.

Sarah Heathcote's works, starting from her doctoral thesis, *State of Necessity and International Law* (2005), should be recognized for their extensive analyses of the CIL status of the plea of necessity. Yamada's study in 2005 of necessity in international law which examined the practice of international tribunals from the *Neptune* case (1797) up to the ICJ's advisory opinion in *Legal Consequences of the Construction of a Wall in the Occupied Palestinian Territory* (2004) is a reliable source as well.[8] Ohlin and May's 2016 book, *Necessity in International Law*, has well-clarified the contemporary concept of necessity specifically as it applies to domestic criminal law, the law of use of force and international humanitarian law. Diane Desierto's book, *Necessity and International Emergency Clauses: Sovereignty in Modern Treaty Interpretation* (2012), discusses in detail the historical genesis of the necessity doctrine and its development in municipal and international legal orders (such as IIL, ITL, *jus ad bellum* and *jus in bello*). Desierto also discusses substantive and methodological issues that must be considered in interpreting necessity clauses in treaties.[9] Federica Paddeu's book, *Justification and Excuse in International Law: Concept and Theory of General Defenses* (2018), has also dedicated nearly one hundred pages to the philosophical origins of the concept of necessity (from the 17th century until the mid-20th century) and on the works of the ILC rapporteurs in developing and refining the concept.[10] Parts 1 and 5 of this book especially benefitted from the works of the scholars mentioned above.

As this book will show, however, the publications on the subject have mainly focused either on: (a) the existence of necessity in international law in general;

6 Burleigh Cushing Rodick, *The Doctrine of Necessity in International Law* (New York: Columbia University Press, 1928).

7 Paul Weidenbaum, 'Necessity in International Law', *Transactions of the Grotius Society*, Vol. 24, Problems of Peace and War, Papers Read before the Society in the Year 1938, pp. 105–132.

8 Yamada, Takuhei, 'State of Necessity in International Law: A Study of International Judicial Cases', *Kobe-Gakuin Law and Politics Review*, 34(4): 2005, pp. 107–158.

9 Diane A. Desierto, *Necessity and National Emergency Clauses: Sovereignty in Modern Treaty Interpretation* (Leiden: Martinus Nijhoff Publishers, 2012).

10 Federica Paddeu, *Justification and Excuse in International Law: Concept and Theory of General Defenses* (Cambridge: Cambridge University Press, 2018), pp. 334–429.

(b) how the concept has been defined by the ILC; (c) how necessity has been formulated or understood by international tribunals since the 18th century; (d) how necessity is related to, or can co-operate with, other defenses (such as self-defense and *force majeure*); or (e) on how the concept of necessity operates in specific fields of international law, including WTO law. The cumulative sound of all these works is, however, loud and clear: necessity has asserted its own place in international law and can be invoked in any area of international law which lays out state obligations.

Contributions of This Book

This book joins the stream of publications on the concept of necessity in international law in general and in WTO law in particular. There is no dearth of works discussing the concept of necessity in WTO law, of course. However, the corpus of publications produced to-date in this area could be enriched by three contributions that this book intends to make.

Firstly, this book aims to systematically dig into the evolution of the concept of necessity in bilateral and multilateral trade treaties from the 18th century until the drafting of the legal texts of the WTO Agreement and identify the lessons that can be learned from that evolution.

Secondly, since most of the works on necessity in WTO law have largely focused on how the concept has been understood in the different WTO agreements, this book will inquire if there is a pan-WTO Agreement concept of necessity (called the 'concept of necessity in WTO law' in this book) presented as a substantive obligation and/or an affirmative defense. It will also examine if the so-called 'weighing and balancing' interpretation of necessity which has been applied to a number of WTO agreements to interpret the necessity provisions therein can also be applicable to the necessity element in the Security Exceptions of the WTO agreements, the interpretation of which has largely remained sealed until the disputes which discussed necessity in the context of national security (such as the *Russia – Traffic in Transit* (*2019*) and *Saudi Arabia – Measures Concerning IP Rights* (*2020*) disputes).

Thirdly, and this is the main focus of this book, a whole part (Part 4) has been dedicated to discuss the concept of necessity in WTO law in the context of the broader discussion on the fragmentation and coherence of international law by interrelating the concept of necessity in WTO law with the concepts of necessity in other fields of international law, particularly the concept of necessity in CIL as now codified in Article 25 of the ARSIWA which were endorsed by the UN General Assembly in 2002. Given the increasing importance of the concept of necessity in international law, it is important to examine if a more coherent[11] concept of necessity can be developed across the different fields of international law.

But why separately discuss and focus on the concept of necessity in WTO law among the different fields of PIL? It will be shown that until the early 1980s, the works on the concept of necessity mainly focused on distinguishing it from other defenses in international law and, thanks to Ago and his colleagues,[12] this was achieved in the early 1980s. Interestingly, however, at about the same time as the ILC refined the concept of necessity as a secondary norm of international law, a different definition started to develop for the defense of necessity in one particular field of PIL: ITL as embodied in the GATT 1947. The foundation for the concept of necessity in WTO law, arguably laid in the *US – Section 337* dispute in 1989, was built upon by the Appellate Body of the WTO and we now have a well-refined and consistently applied definition of necessity in WTO law: the 'weighing and balancing' test. This book will show that while the concepts of necessity in different fields of international law particularly the concept of necessity in CIL (which has largely influenced the concepts of necessary in the other fields of international law) share significant similarities, the concept of necessity in WTO law is different in many aspects. This book will, therefore, pay attention to comparing the elements of the concept of necessity in WTO law with those in other fields of international law, particularly the concept of necessity in CIL (as now codified in the ARSIWA) which arguably 'represents', or has largely influenced, the concepts of necessity in other fields of international law.

Key Question, Methodology and Structure of the Book

The Key Question

This book aims to make the three contributions mentioned above by responding to the following key question: *can the concepts of necessity in WTO law and CIL influence each other to achieve a more coherent concept of necessity across different fields of international law*?

The main reasons for focusing on these two concepts of necessity in this book are: (a) the clarity of their respective definitions; (b) their extensive application in the respective fields of international law where they operate; and

11 This book does not argue that there should be a single concept of necessity in international law.

12 See Section 5.4.

(c) their potential to influence the development of the concept of necessity in other fields of international law. Since the gist of this book is to finally discuss the concept of necessity in the broader context of fragmentation and coherence of international law, it is requisite to analyze in detail the relationship between these two relatively elucidated concepts of necessity in international law. Analysis of this relationship must culminate in identifying the possibility for these two differing concepts of necessity to learn from (i.e., influence) each other so that a more coherent concept of necessity can develop in international law.

Methodology Used to Respond to the Key Question

The history of the concept of necessity in international law shows that initially there was a common concept of necessity applicable in international law but that with the development of the different fields of international law varying concepts of necessity started to develop. We are now at a stage where we can argue that there are two most discernible concepts of necessity in international law: the concept of necessity in WTO law and the concept of necessity in CIL as codified in Article 25 of the ARSIWA. To keep pace with the contemporary need to seek for coherence in international law, this book inquires the possibility for the development of a more coherent concept of necessity in international law by examining the interoperability between these two concepts of necessity.

The final analysis of the interoperability between the concepts of necessity in WTO law and CIL must, therefore, be preceded by two earlier stages of discussions: presenting the long evolution of the concept of necessity until the development of international law and its different areas (particularly CIL) (Parts 1 and 2 of this book); and the separate evolution of the concept of necessity in ITL (particularly WTO law) (Part 3 of this book). Bifurcation of the narration of the evolution of the concept of necessity is necessary to identify the specific elements of the two concepts of necessity in international law which must be examined for the potential to influence each other. The subsequent process of *interoperability* (*interface*) between the concepts of necessity in WTO law and CIL (Part 4 of this book) is based on identifying their similarities and differences (especially their inherent differences).

Structure of the Book

This book is divided into four parts.

Part 1, covering Chapters 1–3, traces the historical origins of the concept of necessity from around the 1st millennium BC to the Middle Ages until its near refinement by the middle of the 20th century. It aims to show that until the Middle Ages the distinction between necessity as a *justification* and necessity as an *excuse* was not very clear (Chapter 1). It will also show that state experiences and international tribunals between the 18th century and the 1930s largely contributed to the refinement of the various elements of necessity as we know them today and to distinguish necessity from related defenses such as self-defense, self-preservation, self-protection and *force majeure*. Part 1 explain how the scope of the application of necessity slowly expanded from war and national security to the realms of international investment and trade (Chapter 2). By way of reflecting on the long evolution of the concept of necessity and how it affects the national and international domains, Part 1 ends with a brief discussion on how the concept of necessity feeds the discussion on the relationship between treaty law and the contemporary notion of state sovereignty (Chapter 3).

Part 2, covering Chapters 4–6, introduces the concept of necessity in international law by discussing how the concept has developed in different fields of international law and how international tribunals since the establishment of the establishment of the PCIJ contributed to the development of the concept in international law.

After discussing the concept of necessity in international law in general (Chapter 4), the concepts of necessity in eight different fields of international law other than WTO law (which is the focus of Part 3) will be presented (Chapter 5). These fields are: the law of use of force; IHL; IEnL; the law of state responsibility as codified in the ARSIWA; IIL; IHRL; ICL; and the law of responsibility of international organizations as codified in the DARIO. Chapter 5 will show that while, on the one end of the spectrum, there is little or no practice or interpretation of the concept of necessity in some fields of international law, there is, on the other end, a relatively advanced set of practices and interpretations of necessity in other fields of international law. In the fields where adequate source of practice and interpretation can be found, two trends appear. While some fields strive to develop their own concepts of necessity, others have largely relied, or can rely, on the two most recognizable concepts of necessity to-date: the concept of necessity in CIL as codified in Article 25 of the ARSIWA or the concept of necessity in WTO law. The lessons learned here will be used in Part 4 to interrelate the concept of necessity in WTO law with the concept of necessity in CIL and, through the CIL, the other fields of PIL. After presenting the concepts of necessity in the eight fields of international law, the experience of the interpretation of necessity by international tribunals since the establishment of the PCIJ will be presented (Chapter 6).[13] The

13 However, owing to the contexts of the respective parts, the interpretations of GATT/WTO organs will be discussed in Part 3.

analyses of the PCIJ, it will be observed, laid the ground for the steady process of distinguishing necessity from other defenses (particularly *force majeure*) and for identifying its elements. As a result of the interpretations developed by the PCIJ and the other tribunals to be mentioned in Chapter 6, not only were the elements of the plea of necessity slowly identified, but the scope of its application was also expanded to spheres beyond the traditional situations of war or public emergency (such as finance, investment, the environment, law of the sea and diplomacy). This experience culminated in the eventual drafting of the defense of necessity in the ARSIWA and its final declaration by the ICJ as constituting CIL.

Part 3, covering Chapters 7–9, focuses on the development of the concept of necessity in one special field of PIL: ITL, and more particularly WTO law. This part highlights the concept of necessity in WTO law and compares it, in Part 4, with the lessons learned in Part 2, particularly Chapters 5 and 6. Although the development of the concept of necessity in trade treaties dates back to the early decades of the 19th century,[14] the main focus of Part 3 will be on the drafting of the necessity provisions in the General and Security Exceptions of the GATT 1947 (Chapter 7) and on how these, mainly the General Exceptions, were progressively interpreted by the dispute settlement organs of the GATT and the WTO to finally introduce the so-called 'weighing and balancing' interpretation of necessity (Chapter 8). Part 3 will show that the 'weighing and balancing' test that was initially developed within the context of the General Exceptions (i.e., necessity as an affirmative defense) has also been adopted for interpreting necessity as found (in the form of substantive obligation) in other WTO agreements such as the TBT Agreement and the SPS Agreement. Part 3 will also discuss whether this test can also be adopted to interpret similarly-worded necessity provisions in other WTO agreements, particularly the Agreement on Trade-Related Aspects of Intellectual Property Rights, so that a 'concept of necessity in WTO law' can be identified and be compared with concepts of necessity in other fields of international law (discussed in Part 2) (Chapter 9).

---

14 John M. Leddy, the economist who was the main draftsman of the GATT 1947 (Petros C. Mavroidis, *The Regulation of International Trade* (*Vol. 1: GATT*) (Cambridge, MA: MIT Press, 2015, p. 20), admitted later that: "Well, let's put it this way, I guess I was the guy who sort of pulled together and helped to guide through the interagency executive committee the old multilateral convention on commercial policy ... We had in the U.S. Government worked on these provisions *drawing them from the old bilateral trade agreements, as well as various multilateral instruments that had existed* ... In other words, we drew from both U.S. and international sources (*emphasis added*)". Douglas A. Irwin *et al.*, *The Genesis of the GATT* (Cambridge: Cambridge University Press, 2008), p. 80, f.n. 106.

Part 3 will argue that there is enough ground to respond to this question in the affirmative.

Part 4, covering Chapters 10–12, begins with the premise, resulting from the discussions in Parts 1–3, that there are at least two distinctly identifiable concepts of necessity in international law: the concept of necessity in CIL as codified in Article 25 of the ARSIWA and the concept of necessity developed in WTO law. After dwelling on the issue of the place of WTO law in the universe of international law (Chapter 10), it lays the ground for the subsequent discussion on the interoperability between WTO law and other fields of international law by focusing on the similarities and differences between these two concepts and the potential for conflict between them (Chapter 11). The final step of the analysis will be to conduct the exercise for interoperability between WTO law and CIL concepts of necessity (Chapter 12). This part aims to answer the following questions asked in different forms:

(a) Do the similarities between the two concepts of necessity warrant the conclusion that the concept of necessity has now been crystalized into one concept for purposes of international law?

(b) Or do the differences warrant the conclusion that there is a 'conflict' in the concepts of necessity?

(c) Can the differences be reconciled? Are the two fields within which the two concepts of necessity operate (i.e., WTO law, on one hand, and the other fields of PIL where the concept in CIL has been influential, on the other hand) 'closed' to any influence from each other?

(d) More specifically, is the WTO-regime a self-contained regime and, hence, does the principle of *lex specialis* govern the relationship of the legal texts of the WTO Agreement with the other fields of international law?

(e) If one accepts that the two concepts of necessity can (have to) continue to develop in their respective spheres of influence, is there room for interoperability between the two, i.e., can the concept of necessity in WTO law benefit from some of the elements of the concept of necessity in CIL and *vice versa*?

(f) If so, what are the grounds for such interoperability?

After addressing these questions, Part 4 will conclude by providing an answer to the key question asked in this book, namely that the concepts of necessity in WTO law and CIL can, while maintaining their respective uniqueness and applying within their respective fields in international law, further enhance and crystallize their substance by the process of interoperability examined in Chapter 12.

Limitations, Key Terminologies and Citation of GATT and WTO Panel/Appellate Body Reports

Limitations

A few words on what issues are not dealt with in this book. Firstly, the concepts of necessity in WTO law and in CIL have been taken 'at face value' without any criticism of the interpretations respectively developed for them mainly because the aim of this book is to interrelate them not to analyze or critique their respective elements. Secondly, it needs to be remembered that both the GATT/WTO law interpretation of necessity and the ARSIWA definition of necessity (which codified the concept of necessity in CIL) started to develop in the 1980s. However, the reason why the dispute settlement organs of the GATT and the WTO have developed an interpretation of necessity for GATT/WTO law different from the ARSIWA definition of necessity has not been examined in detail. This could be due to a lack of clear information on how the GATT/WTO adjudicators developed the concept of necessity in GATT/WTO law. Thirdly, this book does not discuss in depth – but makes a recommendation to study – whether the rules and limitations utilized in the exercise of interoperability between the concepts of necessity in WTO law and CIL can also be extended to potential interoperability between other rules and principles existent in WTO law and other fields of international law (for example, the precautionary principle) or between rules and principles existent in other fields of PIL.

Key Terminologies

International law and the different fields in it are referred to in different contexts in this book. The terms 'international law', 'fields of international law', 'PIL', 'fields of PIL', 'CIL', 'GIL' and 'WTO law' are frequently used in this book. In this book, the term:

(a) 'international law' refers to the area of law encompassing PIL (as distinguished from private international law), GIL and CIL;
(b) 'fields of international law' refers to PIL, GIL or CIL;
(c) 'fields of PIL' refers to the ensemble of areas of PIL (such as WTO law and those fields discussed in Chapter 5);
(d) 'GIL' refers to the sum of CIL and general principles of law;
(e) 'CIL' refers to the international custom evidenced by actual and general practice of states and its acceptance by states as law (*opinio juris*); and

(f) 'WTO law' refers to the legal texts of the WTO Agreement as explained below.[15]

Please note that this book distinguishes 'fields of international law' or 'fields of PIL' from 'sources of international law' or 'sources of PIL'. The terms 'sources of international law' or 'sources of PIL' refer to the sources of international law/PIL such as those listed in Article 38 of the Statute of the ICJ (international conventions, international custom, the general principles of law and judicial decisions and the teachings of the most highly qualified publicists). Thus, a 'field' of PIL may have developed out of one or a combination of some of these 'sources'.[16] The focus of this book is to examine the concepts of necessity contained in some 'fields' of international law (regardless of the 'sources' of the respective concepts of necessity in these 'fields' of international law) and compare them with the concept of necessity in WTO law.

The term 'concept of necessity' has been frequently used in this book to refer to necessity whether presented as a substantive obligation or an affirmative defense. Use of the term 'plea of necessity' is intended to convey the same meaning as the 'concept of necessity'. The term 'defense of necessity' is used to refer to the use of necessity as an affirmative defense, although within the larger context of the 'concept of necessity'.

The terms 'interoperability', or its equivalents such as 'interface' and/or 'interaction' define this book. They have been used interchangeably to refer to the possibility and the process for varying definitions or interpretations of the same concept found in different fields of international law to learn or benefit from each other for purposes of coherence of in international law. This book conducts this exercise of interoperability between the varying definitions or interpretations of the concept of necessity in WTO law on the one hand and

15 For the definition of international law and PIL as used in this book, see, Malcolm N. Shaw, *International Law* (8th ed.) (Cambridge: Cambridge University Press, 2017), pp. 1–2; Sir Robert Y. Jennings, 'International Law', in Rudolf Burnhardt (ed.), *Encyclopedia of Public International Law* (Vol. 7) (Amsterdam, New York and Oxford: Elsevier Science Publishers, 1984), pp. 278–297; Donald McRae, 'International Economic Law and Public International Law: The Past and the Future', *Journal of International Economic Law*, 17(3): 2014, pp. 627–638. For the definition of GIL and WTO law as used in this book, see, Joost Pauwelyn, 'The Role of Public International law in the WTO: How Far Can We Go?' *American Journal of International Law*, 95(3): 2001, p. 536.

16 See Peter Malanczuk, *Akehurst's Modern Introduction to International Law* (7th revised ed.) (New York: Routledge, 1997), pp. 35–62; James Crawford, *Brownlie's Principles of Public International Law* (8th ed.) (Oxford: Oxford University Press, 2012), pp. 20–47; Shaw, ibid, pp. 51–95.

the other fields of international law (especially CIL as codified in the ARSIWA) on the other.

The term 'WTO Agreement' refers to the Marrakesh Agreement Establishing the WTO (i.e., the charter that established the WTO and the texts annexed to it). Whenever there is a need to refer to a specific agreement in the WTO Agreement it is referred to as, for example, the 'TBT Agreement', the 'SPS Agreement', or the 'TRIPS Agreement' after first introducing the acronym. When reference is made to these agreements together, the term used is 'agreements' instead of 'Agreements'. For example, the term 'the TBT and SPS agreements' is used instead of 'the TBT and SPS Agreements'.

'Dispute settlement organs' of the GATT/WTO is meant to refer to the GATT Contracting Parties, the GATT panels, the WTO panels, the Appellate Body and the WTO's Dispute Settlement Body, as applies.

The works of the study groups of the ILC have been identified as, for example, 'Ago's report/work', 'Crawford's text/work', 'Koskenniemi's study/work' etc. only to identify the works through the respective rapporteurs. The works and contributions of the colleagues of these rapporteurs are duly recognized.

Citation of GATT and WTO Panel/Appellate Body Reports

In the text, the year indicated inside a parenthesis in the short form for the title of a GATT or WTO panel/Appellate Body report is the year the report was adopted or a mutually agreed solution was notified. In case of the recent WTO panel reports currently under 'hanging appeal' despite the absence of the Appellate Body, the year of the circulation of the panel report is indicated inside the parenthesis.

PART 1

History of the Concept of Necessity in Law

CHAPTER 1

Evolution of the Concept from the 1st Millennium BC to the 20th Century

The concept of necessity, rooted in ancient legal traditions, has developed through an evolution of philosophies as well as domestic and inter-state practices. Part 1 aims to show how ancient and modern thinkers, scholars, governments and legal practitioners rationalized the concept of necessity under natural, social, political and/or divine underpinnings. It also aims to show that necessity, initially linked to the limitations of human nature or divine permissions, was later explained in its relation with society's (and its leaders') need to establish harmony among its members and with other societies (states). With the emergence of sovereign states along the lines of the Peace of Westphalia (see, Section 1.3), necessity would be invoked as *raison d'état* to allow states to take otherwise unlawful domestic and international measures to ensure their survival (self-preservation).

In its purpose to lay a ground for the subsequent three Parts, Part 1 aims to present the following key points.

Firstly, Part 1 will present the development of the different elements of necessity from around the 1st millennium BC until their near refinement by the middle of the 20th century. The narration will include how the concept expanded from domestic application (in the private law and public law spheres) to the sphere of inter-state relations. Sections 1.1–1.2 are limited *mainly* to continental Europe because of two reasons: lack of availability of references on the development of the concept of necessity in other parts of the world; and the need to gear the narration toward the Peace of Westphalia which is essential to the narrative in Part 1 (the transition from domestic to inter-state application of necessity).

Secondly, Part 1 aims to show that since the early days until the Middle Ages, the distinction between necessity as a *justification* and necessity as an *excuse* was not clear.[1] Since the 17th century, however, philosophers began to assert

1 The difference between *justification* and *excuse* in the context of defense of necessity or self-defense originates from criminal law. Whereas *justification* removes the unlawfulness of an otherwise unlawful act, *excuse* simply means that a wrongful act shall not be punished. Marcelo G. Cohen, 'The Notion of "state survival", in International Law', in Laurence Boisson de Chazournes and Philippe Sands (eds.), *International Law, the International Court*

 DOI:10.1163/9789004700000_003

their understanding of necessity in various circumstances either as a justification or an excuse.

Thirdly, Part 1 will show that the frequent use of the defense of necessity in various state and tribunal practices (from the 18th century until the 1930s) contributed to further refinement of the elements of necessity – hitherto identified by jurists and philosophers – as well as to distinguishing it from related defenses such as self-defense, self-preservation, self-protection and *force majeure*. Moreover, these practices, especially the later of the tribunal practices, slowly expanded the application of necessity – hitherto limited to war and national security – to the realms of international investment and trade.

1.1 Early Period

1.1.1 *The Old Testament*

One of the enduring examples of an act of necessity is theft committed due to extreme hunger. Such act of necessity has been recognized in the Old Testament. The book of Proverbs, said to have been compiled sometime between the 10th and 6th centuries BC,[2] in Part 6, verses 30 through 33 (English Standard Version) reads:

of Justice and Nuclear Weapons (Cambridge: Cambridge University Press, 1999), p. 309; Albin Eser, 'Justification and Excuse', *American Journal of Comparative Law*, 24(4): 1976, pp. 621–637; Winfried Hassemer, 'Justification and Excuse in Criminal Law: Theses and Comments', *Brigham Young University Law Review*, 3: 1986, pp. 573–609; Khalid Ghanayim, 'Excused Necessity in Western Legal Philosophy', *Canadian Journal of Law and Jurisprudence*, 19(31): 2006, p. 31. In a more precise manner, Paddeu presents the difference between justification and excuse as follows: "There is conduct that is unlawful, there is conduct that is justified, and there is conduct for which, despite being unlawful, the actor is excused. This ... captures the distinction between justifications and excuses: justifications exclude the wrongfulness of conduct; excuses preclude the responsibility of an actor for wrongful conduct. The former concern the conduct, the latter the actor." Federica Paddeu, *Justification and Excuse in International Law: Concept and Theory of General Defenses* (Cambridge: Cambridge University Press, 2018), p. 23. Paddeu provides an extensive critique of the dichotomy in pp. 23–129. Owaydhah also describes the difference between justification and excuse as follows: "a justification is the statement that the conduct in question is not illegal due to the elimination of the legal elements, whereas the concept of excuse is conceived to show justice for some unlawful conduct. Thus, as far as the concept of necessity is concerned, the doctrine of necessity prescribes that the act, which otherwise would be considered unlawful, must be recognized as lawful if it is conducted in good faith under the pressure of necessity". Khalid A. Owaydhah, 'Justifications and Concept of Criminal Liability in Shari'ah', *Humanities and Social Sciences Review*, 3(2): 2014, p. 62.

2 *An Introduction to the Book of Proverbs*, available at, https://bible.org/article/introduction-book-proverbs.

30. People do not despise a thief if he steals to satisfy his appetite when he is hungry,
31. but if he is caught, he will pay sevenfold; he will give all the goods of his house.
32. He who commits adultery lacks sense; he who does it destroys himself.
33. He will get wounds and dishonor, and his disgrace will not be wiped away.

These verses differentiate between sins (theft and adultery in this case) depending on whether the sins were committed out of necessity. Theft committed due to hunger is viewed more lightly and its punishment is extenuated whereas adultery, not resulting out of necessity, is punished.[3] Another Old Testament example of necessity is the story of the future King David and his men to whom the priest Ahimelech gave hallowed bread (shewbread), only allowed to be eaten by the priests, because they were very hungry (1st Samuel 21:2–7). During one of his confrontations with the Pharisees who challenged him and his disciples for plucking and eating heads of grain on a Sabbath, Jesus referred to David's story and said "I tell you, something greater than the temple is here. And if you had known what this means, 'I desire mercy, and not sacrifice', you would not have condemned the guiltless" (Mathew 12:1–8).

It may be noted here that the Proverbs example presents necessity (hunger necessitating theft) more along the lines of an excuse (unlawfulness of the act is not removed, only the punishment is reduced)[4] whereas the 1st Samuel story as interpreted by Jesus presents necessity (hunger necessitating breach of the law of holy bread) as a justification, i.e., unlawfulness of the act is removed.

1.1.2 *The Talmud*

The Talmud has a record of a debate between two sages, Rabbi Akiva and Ben Petura. They were asked to debate on a situation where two persons are lost in a desert and one of them has a canteen full of water just enough for only one person until the next source of water. Whereas Ben Petura argued that they should share the water and try their luck, Rabbi Akiva argued that the

3 *Proverbs 6 Bible Commentary*, available at, http://www.christianity.com/bible/commentary.php?com=mh&b=20&c=6; http://biblehub.com/commentaries/proverbs/6-30.htm.

4 This verse would have been cited as an example of full excuse if Solomon had recommended no punishment for the act of theft. See, definition of excuse in above note 1. On the other hand, it would have been cited as an example of justification if Solomon had not considered the act sinful.

owner, by his mere ownership, should drink alone and save his life because the certainty of saving one life is preferred to the uncertainty of saving two lives. Normative Jewish law follows Rabbi Akiva[5] whose opinion, just like in the case of the Plank of Carneades which will be mentioned in Sub-section 1.1.6, is more along the lines of justification than excuse.

1.1.3 *The Chinese*

In his compilation of the anecdotes and conversations of the ancient Chinese philosopher Mengzi (Mencius) (372–298 BC), James Legge presents a conversation between Shun-yu K'wăn and Mencius:

> Shun-yu K'wăn said, "Is it the rule that males and females shall not allow their hands to touch in giving or receiving anything?"
>
> Mencius replied, "It is the rule."
>
> "If a man's sister-in-law be drowning," asked K'wăn, "shall he rescue her by the hand?"
>
> [Mencius] said, "He who would not [so] rescue his drowning sister-in-law would be a wolf. For males and females not to allow their hands to touch in giving and receiving is the [general] rule; to rescue by the hand a drowning sister-in-law is a peculiar exigency."[6]

In this narration Mencius lays out a rule which would in contemporary terms is equivalent to the notion of justifiable, not excusable, necessity defense where the act committed under exigent circumstances causes no liability on the author of the act.

1.1.4 *The Law Code of Manu*

Formulated in about 200 BC, or 100 BC by some other accounts,[7] the *Manusmriti* (*Laws of Manu* or *The Remembered Tradition of Manu*) also called *Manava-dharma-shastra* (*The Dharma Text of Manu*) is the most authoritative of the

5 Halley S. Faust, Paul T. Menze, *Prevention vs. Treatment: What's the Right Balance?* (Oxford: Oxford University Press, 2012), p. 286; Ghanayim, above note 1; *Who Drinks the Water?*, available at, http://www.jewishtreats.org/2010/05/who-drinks-water.html.

6 James Legge, *The Chinese Classics: Vol. 2, The Life and Works of Mencius* (London: Trübner & Co., 57 & 59: Ludgate Hill, 1875), p. 151, available at, http://www.rosenfels.org/pll-v5/pdf/Legge_1430-02_EBk_v5.pdf.

7 Charles J. Naegele, *History and Influence of Law Code of Manu* (unpublished SJD Thesis at Golden Gate University School of Law), p. 3:, available at, http://digitalcommons.law.ggu.edu/cgi/viewcontent.cgi?article=1004&context=theses.

books of the Hindu code, the *Dharma-shastra*, in India. Verses 282 and 283 of the book, as put in George Bühler's translation, read:

> 282. But he who, except *in a case of extreme necessity*, drops filth on the king's high-road, shall pay two karshapanas and immediately remove (that) filth (*emphasis added*).
>
> 283. But a person *in urgent necessity*, an aged man, a pregnant woman, or a child, shall be reprimanded and clean the (place); that is a settled rule (*emphasis added*). [8]

Verse 282 would be an example of excuse. Dropping filth on the king's high-road is an offense at all times; however, persons who commit the offense under *extreme* necessity are spared the penalty. Verse 283 refers to *urgent* necessity which, like the Proverbs verse mentioned above, is used only to reduce the penalty. Both verses do not view necessity as justification in which case the act would not have been considered a crime at all.

1.1.5 *Lex Rhodia*

The *Lex Rhodia*, the ancient ancestor to modern maritime law, said to have developed in Rhodes around 800 BC,[9] provided that in time of distress the captain of ship can authorize the jettisoning of cargo to lighten the ship and save the ship and the other cargo, provided that the owners whose cargoes have been rescued will compensate the owner of the sacrificed cargo. Accordingly, the act of jettison becomes excusable rather than justifiable.[10] *Lex Rhodia* also provided that provisions owned by private individuals can be made available to people on board the ship in times of necessity.[11]

1.1.6 *The Greeks*

The Greek concept of necessity was described more along the lines of justification than excuse. One of the earliest Greek contributions to the concept of necessity was the hypothetical thought experiment called the Plank of Carneades attributed to its originator, the academic sceptic Carneades of

---

8 George Bühler (translator), *The Laws of Manu* (Sacred Books of the East, Vol. 25), Part IX, available at, http://www.sacred-texts.com/hin/manu/manu09.htm.

9 *Lex Rhodia: The Ancient Ancestor of Maritime Law – 800 BC*, available at, https://insuranceranked.com/business-insurance/lex-rhodia-rhodian-sea-law.

10 Robert D. Benedict, 'The Historical Position of the Rhodian Law', *Yale Law Journal*, 18(4): 1909, pp. 223–242.

11 Sarah Heathcote, *State of Necessity and International Law*, Thesis no. 772, submitted to the University of Geneva for PhD in Law (Geneva: 2005), p. 320.

Cyrene (214/3–129/8 BC). Carneades presented a situation where two persons are stranded in the middle of an ocean and the only way to safety is by sailing on board a plank fit to sit only one of them. To avoid certain death, one of them pushes the other into the ocean and saves himself by sailing on board the plank. The story, with a message similar to that of the Akiva-Ben Petura debate mentioned in Sub-section 1.1.2, has hitherto been recurrently cited to describe a situation of necessity where unlawful acts (in this case murder) can be justified in exceptional circumstances where the unlawful act was the only option to save an interest of equal or higher value.[12]

While discussing responsibility in his *Nicomachean Ethics*, Aristotle (384–322 BC) referred to the Rhodian law of jettison of cargo as an example of justifiable actions taken to avoid a threat.[13] In his record of the life and laws of the Athenian statesman Solon (*c*. 638-*c*. 558 BC), the Greek biographer and essayist Plutarch (*c*. 46–120 AD) refers to a water law set out by Solon that carries elements of a justifiable act in case of absolute impossibility.[14]

1.1.7 *The Romans*

The concept of necessity got more clarified along the justification-excuse divide during the Roman era. Various positions were held by the legal scholars and philosophers on the concept of necessity. One of the earliest thinkers on the subject was Marcus Tullius Cicero (106–43 BC).

Cicero divided necessity into three distinct categories: necessity premised on honorable conduct as the greatest of necessities;[15] necessity based on safety; and necessity related to usefulness. For the first type of necessity, Cicero cites the example of a general who surrenders his arms and equipment in exchange for safe passage of his troops.[16] For the second category, Cicero

---

12 Chazournes and Sands, above note 1.

13 Gerard J. Hughes, *The Routledge Guidebook to Aristotle's Nicomachean Ethics* (London and New York: Routledge, 2013), pp. 150–151; Michael Pakaluk, *Aristotle's Nicomachean Ethics: An Introduction* (New York: Cambridge University Press, 2005), p. 125.

14 *Plutarch: The Parallel Lives* (*The Life of Solon*), available at, https://penelope.uchicago.edu/Thayer/E/Roman/Texts/Plutarch/Lives/Solon*.html; Alan E. Samuel, *Plutarch's Account of Solon's Reforms*, f.n. 5, available at, https://grbs.library.duke.edu/article/viewFile/12021/4037; Heathcote, above note 11, p. 309.

15 According to Cicero, if: "[T]hat slight diminution of honesty [for the sake of safety that may be] caused by our conduct may be hereafter repaired by virtue and industry, then it seems proper to have regard for our safety. But when that does not appear possible then we must think of nothing but what is honorable". Eugene R. Milhizer, 'Justification and Excuse: What They Were, What They Are, and What They Ought To Be', *St. John's Law Review*, 78(3): 2012, p. 768.

16 Ibid.

gives the example of a ship's captain who commits otherwise unlawful acts if compelled by forces of nature. According to Cicero, the captain, if prosecuted, could assert that he was not responsible for causing conditions and that "the judges should consider his intentions, and not the result".[17]

The subsequent Roman law contribution towards the development of the concept of necessity can best be viewed in light of the private law-public law distinction which distinction was first introduced by the Roman jurist Domitus Ulpianus (*c.* 170–223 AD).

Roman private law did not introduce the defense of necessity until the 3rd century AD. When the concept was introduced, numerous provisions, such as those related to burning houses, superior order and easements etc., recognized situations in which a person could raise the defense of necessity. Most of the defenses were, however, presented more in the form of justification than excuse. The most notable of these situations is the case where a person destroys another person's burning house to stop the spread of the flames to his house or the village at large.[18] As recorded in the *Digest* (also called the *Pandectae*, the collection of passages from the writings of Roman jurists, arranged in 50 books and published in 533 AD under the authority of Emperor Justinian), when such cases were brought before the Roman judges or when the legal thinkers of the day analyzed the situation, the judges and thinkers did not only consider the rationale for the act of necessity but also whether compensation is due to the person whose house was destroyed, hence triggering the application of the law of responsibility, the *Lex Aquila*.[19] The element of compensation means that the unlawfulness of the act is not removed; hence, necessity was seen as an excuse (necessity *exceptio*) rather than a justification. Under Roman private law, whereas it was clear that for the necessity *exceptio* to apply there had to be grave and imminent threat and that the action taken was the sole possible means of averting the danger, it was not clear whether there was the need to compare the value of the sacrificed interest (the burnt house in this case) with the value of the rescued interest (the actor's house or the other village houses).[20] The examination and balancing of interests, otherwise

17 Ibid, p. 769.

18 Another recurrently discussed scenario was a situation where a boat by force of storm finds itself caught in the cables and nets of another vessel and the crew of the latter vessel cut the cables and nets to save themselves and leave the other vessel in real danger. In some circles, the tangled net case is considered as a clear case of *force majeure* than necessity. Heathcote, above note 11, p. 317.

19 Ibid, pp. 314–317.

20 Ibid, p. 316.

known as the proportionality test, would later be developed and become a key element of the necessity test. Other Roman private law situations which involved acts of necessity were presented more in the form of justification than excuse.[21] The contribution of Roman law toward the development of the concept of necessity is attributed more to its private law than its public law. Whereas Roman private law contributed to the development of the elements of necessity, Roman public law (or constitutional law in today's parlance) contributed to the development of the concept of *rationales of state* which is similar to the modern-day concepts of public safety or public health exceptions. In the realm of Roman public law, we once again meet Cicero who, in his treatise *De Legibus* (Book III, Part III, sub. VIII), reflected on the notion of *ollis salus populi suprema lex esto*, translated as: "[t]he health of the people is (should be) the supreme law". Cicero repeats the phrase *salus populi* eighteen times in his treatise as he discusses government actions taken for the safety of the community.[22] This is because for Cicero, good governance stems from two principles: *ratio reipublicae* which we can associate with the Middle Ages principle of *raison d'état*; and *honestas* which essentially refers to a superior moral law, the latter serving as a limit to the acts of the republic.[23] Thus, although the impact of Roman public law in the development of the concept of necessity is not as strong as that of Roman private law, its most important contribution is that the maxim *salus populi suprema lex esto*, which embodies the later concept of *reason of state*, found its way in such documents as the Justinian *Digest* and the political reflections of later writers such as Rousseau.[24]

1.2 Medieval Period (5th to 15th Centuries)

The period we now know as the Middle Ages (medieval period) begins in the early-to-middle of the 5th century, spans over the Dark Ages for around a thousand years and ends with the spread of renaissance in the 15th century.[25] This

21 Ibid, pp. 318–319.

22 Andrew Roy Dyck, *A Commentary on Cicero, De Legibus* (Ann Arbor: The University of Michigan Press, 2004), p. 459.

23 Gaines Post, *Studies in Medieval Legal Thought: Public Law and the State 1100–1322* (Clark: The Law Exchange, Ltd., 3rd print, 2008), pp. 253–255.

24 Heathcote, above note 11, p. 313. Rousseau refers to the maxim in his letter to Mirabeau. Victor Gourevitch (ed. and trans.), *Rousseau: The Social Contract and Other Later Political Writings* (Cambridge: Cambridge University Press, 1997), p. 319.

25 Peter Stein, *Roman Law in European History* (Cambridge: Cambridge University Press, 1999), pp. 29–30; *Depth Study Option: Medieval Europe*, available at, https://www.oup.com.au/__data/assets/pdf_file/0027/58068/03_OBI_H8_TB_76962_SPREADS.pdf; *Middle*

section will discuss how the concept of necessity developed in different fields of private and public law during the Middle Ages.

1.2.1 *Private Law of Necessity during the Middle Ages*

This section briefly presents the development of the concept of necessity in private law during four eras of the Middle Ages: the era of the Germanic rulers during the early Middle Ages; the Middle Age Christian writers and the Canon Law; Islam; and the Glossators.

Following the demise in 476 AD of the Western Roman Empire, the Germanic ruler Euric, the king of the Visigoths, decreed that Roman and Visigothic subjects should be governed by separate laws. The legislation for his Visigoth subjects was influenced by Roman laws, principles and legal maxims of necessity (i.e., necessity more as a justification than an excuse).[26] The *Lex Romana Burgundionum* issued by King Gundobad of the Burgundians had a provision which stated that a person who placed a trap in an uncultivated field to ensnare an animal for food would not be liable for damages. Another provision allowed people to help themselves to the goods of others in times of need. Visigoth laws also foresaw easements of necessity in the case of a closed or blocked path.[27]

Throughout the centuries of the expounding of Christian teachings, the element of necessity was raised *vis-à-vis* the obligation to keep God's commandments. In fact most scholars agree that the famous phrase *necessitas legem non habet* (necessity knows no law) can claim its origins to a 12th century text – the *Decretum Gratiani* (also known as the *Concordia Discordantium Canonum* or *Concordantia Discordantium Canonum*) – which was the codification of Canon Law by the Benedictine monk and jurist Gratian around 1140 AD. Gratian, who, drawing from and influenced by Roman law, incorporated a number of principles into his texts including the concept of necessity.[28]

Ages, available at, https://www.britannica.com/event/Middle-Ages; *Middle Ages*, available at, https://www.encyclopedia.com/history/modern-europe/ancient-history-middle-ages-and-feudalism/middle-ages.

26 For list of the maxims, see, Paul Moariaud, *De la Justification du Délit par L'état de Nécessité*, Thesis submitted to the University of Geneva for PhD in Law (Geneva: 1889), p. 81, digital scan available at, https://archive.org/details/delajustificatiooomori; Heathcote, above note 11, p. 322.

27 Heathcote, ibid.

28 Diane A. Desierto, *Necessity and National Emergency Clauses: Sovereignty in Modern Treaty Interpretation* (Leiden: Martinus Nijhoff Publishers, 2012), p. 63 (f.n. 2). Gratian's exact maxim was *quia enim necessitas non habet legem, set ipsa sibi facit legem* (necessity knows no law, but makes law). Kristian Cedervall Lauta, *Disaster Law* (London and New York: Routledge, 2015), p. 57. Aquinas also used the maxim *necessity knows no law.*

Probably influenced by Augustine of Hippo's (354–430 AD) understanding of just war, Gratian, in Canon III of his *Decretum*, stated: "[w]e should wish for peace and make war only because of necessity, in order that God may deliver us from this necessity and preserve us in peace ... Let it then be necessity and not the will which overthrows the enemy who we fight."[29] With this, Gratian is credited to have broadly introduced the concept of just war in international law.[30] Gratian and his followers recognize necessity as a naturally acceptable ground to breach the law, including the law of celebrating mass and other religious laws. to describe this notion, they use the maxim *quod non est licitum lege, necessitas facit licitum* (what is not licit in law, necessity makes licit).[31] Thomas Aquinas (1225–1274 AD) later added and expounded on the Gratian concept of necessity[32] by, for instance,[33] using the example of a person stealing food because of hunger. When we move to examining Canon Law, the body of laws and regulations made or adopted by ecclesiastical authority of the Catholic Church for the government of the Christian organization and its members, we see that it played a crucial role in the later development and legitimization of principles such as necessity because it gave them a moral footing. By way of an example, Canon Law incorporated the concept of necessity in the book of sacraments, the *Penitential* which provided that if violations such as eating prohibited food, perjury, blasphemy, apostasy, heresy and homicide of an innocent third-party during self-defense were committed under necessity, there would be no penance. In the subsequent centuries, non-application

Jens David Ohlin and Larry May, *Necessity in International Law* (Oxford: Oxford University Press, 2016), p. 148.

29 Lauta, ibid, pp. 63–64. Augustine had made the statement that is today referred to as an embodiment of the concept of just war/military necessity: "Let necessity, therefore, and not your will, slay the enemy who fights against you." John Mark Mattox, *St. Augustine and the Theory of Just War* (New York: Continuum, 2006), p. 61.

30 Wendy Marie Hoofnagle, *Creating Kings in Post-conquest England: The Fate of Charlemagne in Anglo-Norman Society*, Thesis no. 3313279, submitted to the University of Connecticut for PhD (2008), p. 98, f.n. 192. Kantorowicz states that Canonists "ever since the twelfth century, pointed out that war was justified, in case of 'inevitable and urgent necessity'" Ernst H. Kantorowicz, *The King's Two Bodies A Study in Mediaeval Political Theology* (Princeton, New Jersey: Princeton University Press, 1957), p. 236.

31 Desierto, above note 28, p. 64 (f.n. 4).

32 Giorgio Agamben, *State of Exception* (translated by Kevil Attell) (Chicago: The University of Chicago Press, 2004), pp. 24–25.

33 Milhizer, above note 15, p. 785, f.n. 340, taken from Aquinas' *Summa Theologiae*: Volume 38, Injustice (2a2æ, Questions 63–79), Responses to question 66 (theft and robbery with violence). Aquinas' quoted statements are respectively contained in articles 7 [is theft justifiable in cases of necessity?] and 2 [is it legitimate for individual men to possess anything as their own?] of his responses to question 66.

of penance for acts committed in cases of necessity was extended to.[34] When Gratian's *Decretum* and different papal decisions were finally compiled into a voluminous package that was printed in Paris in 1500 AD as the *Corpus Juris Canonici*, the position of the church on the *penitential* was summarized in one phrase: *quod non est licitum lege, necessitas facit licitum* (what is not licit in law, necessity makes licit). Although this maxim seems to view the said acts of necessity as justifiable acts, the fact, however, that only the penance (i.e., penalty) was waived made the acts look more like excusable acts. Accordingly, the specialists of Canon Law, the Canonists, gave the concept of necessity a general acceptance.[35]

Necessity and other defenses (duress, self-defense, age etc.) are well-rooted concepts in Islamic law (which started to expand from the early 7th century).[36] Regarding necessity (*darūrah*, from the Arabic word *darar* which means injury that cannot be avoided), Surah Al-Baqarah (Surah 2, verse 173) of the Quran, for instance, states that "there is no sin upon him" who consumes prohibited food and drinks forced by necessity, without desiring them and without exceeding the limit. Not only the Quran, but also the traditions of the Prophet Muhammad (the Hadith) cite many stories where the prophet endorsed otherwise prohibited acts of necessity.[37] These stories present necessity as justification, but Al-Muntari, who conducted a thorough investigation of the history and development of necessity in Islamic jurisprudence, includes compensation as an element of necessity in Islamic law, hence some notion of excuse. The Islamic concept and maxims of necessity found themselves in subsequent imperial and national laws which were based on Islamic law. The *Majalla* (*Mecelle*), the Ottoman Civil Code,[38] the criminal laws of Saudi Arabia (uses the Shari'ah), Afghanistan (Article 95 of the Afghani Penal Code of 1976) and Iran (Article 55 of the Iranian Penal Code of 1996), basing themselves essentially on Islamic law, preserved necessity either as a justification (Saudi Arabia

---

34 Heathcote, above note 11, p. 324.

35 Ibid. In his collections of the works of Erasmus, McGinness refers to acts of excusable necessity under the Church's laws such as the sacrament of baptism conducted by a lay person in time of necessity. Frederick J. McGinness (ed.), *Collected Works of Erasmus: Spiritualia and Pastoralia* (Vols. 67 & 68) (Toronto: University of Toronto Press, 2015), p. 401.

36 Mansour A. Al-Muntari, *Necessity in Islamic Law*, Thesis submitted to the University of Geneva for PhD in Law (Edinburgh: 1997), pp. 1–273; Owaydhah, above note 1, pp. 55–71.

37 From the list at Al-Muntari, ibid, pp. 32–33.

38 *Al-Majalla Al-Ahkam Al-Adaliyyah*: *The Ottoman Courts Manual* (*Hanafi*), available at, http://legal.pipa.ps/files/server/ENG%20Ottoman%20Majalle%20(Civil%20Law).pdf.

and Afghanistan) or excuse (Iran, although there are some who consider it as justification).[39]

Moving to the late Middle Ages, we see that the glossators, scholars of Roman law from the 11th to the 13th centuries in Italy, France and Germany, reduced the concept of necessity to specific exceptions, the two notable ones being 'necessary' theft of food and homicide of a third party in the face of threat of death. Thus, unlike the canonists,[40] the glossators deprived necessity of the status of a general application.[41] The works of the glossators on necessity had two distinct impacts: firstly, they influenced generations of commentators after them to develop theories on necessity; secondly, they introduced, or rather expounded, the idea of morality-based proportionality test in evaluating necessity in criminal law.[42]

1.2.2 *Public Law of Necessity during the Middle Ages*

Compared to private law, the public law side of necessity during the Middle Ages was not refined. In public law, necessity was related to the measures that the papal or temporal authorities could take in times of necessity, i.e., danger to the very existence of the Church or the empire.

In the sphere of public law, the early Middle Ages witnessed the blurring of the line between the secular and temporal authorities, hence constant friction between the Church and the imperial government to extend influence over each other.[43] At the heart of this papal-imperial controversy was the definition and limit of the respective powers (papal and imperial) and the grounds for intervening in the other's sphere of influence. And here is where intervention based on necessity comes into the picture. As observed by Hugoccio, the pope considered himself as having divine mandate to intervene in imperial authority and even depose the emperor when it was necessary to do so.[44] Pope Innocent III, followed also by Pope Innocent IV,[45] continued the

39 Owaydhah, above note 1, p. 62; Kevin Heller and Markus Dubbe (eds.), *The Handbook of Comparative Criminal Law* (Stanford: Stanford University Press, 2011), pp. 332–333. When summing up the medieval Christian and Islamic views on necessity, Desierto holds that necessity in these two religions was viewed as an indispensable excuse to mitigate *dura lex sed lex* (The law is harsh, but it is the law). Desierto, above note 28, pp. 63, 68–69.

40 Heathcote, above note 11, p. 324.

41 Ibid.

42 Ibid, p. 325.

43 Danuta M. Gorecki and Arnold Wajenberg, 'Canon Law: History, Sources, and a Proposed Classification Scheme', *Law Library Journal*, 75: 1982, p. 385.

44 Heathcote, above note 11, p. 329.

45 Ibid, p. 329–330; *Innocent IV*, available at, https://en.wikisource.org/wiki/1911_Encyclop%C3%A6dia_Britannica/Innocent/Innocent_IV. For more on the tension between

Gregorian practice[46] and believed that papal intervention could be based on two grounds: when an urgent cause (*causa urgenta*) arises; and when the very existence of Christianity was at stake.[47]

A notable development related to necessity in the public sphere during the Middle Ages was the rise of the practice of representatives of communities to consent to the acts of the kings or princes during times of emergency or cases of necessity (*cassus necessitatis*) and thereby bind their communities.[48]

Whereas, until the Peace of Westphalia in mid-17th century, necessity had been viewed as an appendix – in the form of justification or excuse – to the obligation to abide by law no matter how harsh the law is (*dura lex sed lex*), the emergence, following the Westphalian treaties, of nation states as sovereign entities elevated necessity, as we will see in Section 1.3, into a "'right' of the state to act in order to ensure its own survival".[49] With the creation of nation states came recognition of the states' (their leaders') sovereign power to take otherwise illegal measures during times that threaten the survival of the state, i.e., measures necessary for *reason of state*. With such recognition also came debates on whether there are moral or other limitations on the exercise by the sovereign of reason of state powers. Section 1.3 will discuss these issues in further detail.

1.3 The Westphalian Concept of Necessity and the Aftermath (17th to 20th Centuries)

Section 1.3 discusses the development of the concept of necessity from the Peace of Westphalia up to the middle of the 20th century. It will be shown that the concept of necessity began to appear in the new field of the law of nations (international law) following the Peace of Westphalia in mid-17th century. This section divides the narration into three temporal sub-sections: the 17th and 18th centuries; the 19th century; the first half of the 20th century.

Innocent IV and Frederick IV, see, David G. Terrell, '*Pope Innocent IV and Emperor Frederick II:* Auctoritias *and* Potestas *in Conflict*', available at, https://www.scribd.com/document/31886312/terrell-dg-first-council-of-lyons-scribd.

46 Gorecki and Wajenberg, above note 43, pp. 391–392.

47 Heathcote, above note 11, p. 329.

48 Gaines Post, '*Plena Potestas* and Consent in Medieval Assemblies: A Study in Romano-Canonical Procedure and the Rise of Representation, 1150–1325', *Traditio*, 1 (1943), pp. 355–373; Heathcote, above note 11, pp. 330–337; Post, above note 23, pp. 27–162.

49 Desierto, above note 28, p. 69.

1.3.1 17th and 18th Centuries

Although the concepts of *raison d'état* (reason of state) and *self-preservation* as discussed in light of acts of necessity by kings and princes (or nation states) during the 17th and 18th centuries are the main focus of Section 1.3, the Peace of Westphalia (1646–1648) has been included in the title since it is an important transition for the narration in this book: from an era of understanding territories as the *dominus* of the monarchs to their creation and recognition as sovereign states. The Peace of Westphalia asserted not only the internal dominion of nation states within their territories but also their autonomy in the choice of their relations with other nation states and thereby consolidating the beginning of modern era of international relations. This sub-section will discuss the concept of necessity as it was practiced by nation states and as commented on by philosophers on how necessity should be viewed and on its constituent elements.

The concept of necessity as practiced by sovereigns during the three centuries from the days of Niccolò Machiavelli (1469–1527) is intertwined with the concept of *raison d'état* (reason of state), the idea that the well-being and stability of the state takes precedence over all other interests and that the government should take all measures towards securing it.[50] The first writer to discuss the concept was not, as widely believed,[51] Machiavelli but the Roman senator and historian Publius (or Gaius) Cornelius Tacitus (*c.* 56–*c.* 120 AD) who produced two major works – *Annals* and *Histories* – in examining the reigns of the Roman emperors Tiberius, Claudius and Nero.[52] Giovanni Botero (*c.* 1544–1617), who first coined the phrase 'reason of state' in his *Della Ragione di Stato* (1589), understands it as "the knowledge of the means appropriate to founding, preserving, and extending the State".[53] *Raison d'état* is generally understood as allowing the taking of actions that would be considered illegal or immoral

50 *Niccolò Machiavelli* in *Stanford Encyclopedia of Philosophy*, available at, http://plato.stanford.edu/entries/machiavelli/; *The Prince: Machiavelli, Critical Essays: Reason of State*, available at, https://www.cliffsnotes.com/literature/p/the-prince/critical-essays/reason-of-state.

51 In fact, Machiavelli never used the phrase in *The Prince*. Victoria Kahn, 'Machiavelli's afterlife and reputation to the eighteenth century', in John M. Najemy (ed.), *The Cambridge Companion to Machiavelli* (Cambridge: Cambridge University Press, 2010), p. 247; *The Prince: Machiavelli, Critical Essays Reason of State*, ibid.

52 Jan Waszink, 'Lipsius and Grotius: Tacitism', *History of European Ideas*, 39(2): 2013, pp. 156–157.

53 Kahn, above note 51 pp. 247–248. Giovanni Botero, *The Reason of State*: Book One, available at, http://www.nlnrac.org/critics/machiavelli/primary-source-documents/the-reason-of-state.

under ordinary circumstances.[54] For this reason, the term is associated to concepts such as public reason, emergency and state of necessity.[55]

The authors who, between the first half of the 15th century and the end of the 19th century, commented on the notion of *raison d'état* did not question the right of the state to take otherwise illegal measures during circumstances of necessity. Their differences were, however, centered on two perceptions: (1) the relationship between morality and sovereign acts taken during times of necessity (i.e., acts for reason of state); and (2) on the limitations on reason of state powers.

Regarding morality, Tacitus, Machiavelli and later David Hume (1711–1776) detach acts taken in preservation of the state from their moral dimensions, whether these are of social, legal or religious nature.[56] Botero, Jean Bodin (1530–1596) and Thomas Hobbes (1588–1679), among others, on the contrary, consider, or appeal to, morality to limit the sovereign's actions taken for reason of state.[57]

The views on the limitations on the powers exercised under reason of state widely differ and at least five patters appear. Machavelli believes in no limitation of the exercise of these powers and wanted his sovereign to be "bound by any considerations whatsoever except sentiments for the love of the state".[58] Among the second group, Botero, opposing Machavelli's version of the prince, believed that the prince's use of acts of necessity is limited by his "benevolent self-restraint and moral nature" because nation states are created by the pact between the sovereign and the subjects according to which the subjects pledge to obey the sovereign who displays his "outstanding excellence" to govern them at all times.[59] Johannes Althusius (*c.* 1563–1638), Bodin and Hobbes, constituting the third group, pursue the opinion that within the internal dynamics of the state there are divine and/or state-level communitarian

54 *The Prince: Machiavelli*, above note 50.

55 Desierto, above note 28, p. 69. It is known as *la raison d'état*, *ragione di stato* or *Staatsräson* in French, Italian and German respectively.

56 Waszink, above note 52, p. 158; Frederick G. Whelan, *Hume and Machiavelli: Political Realism and Liberal Thought* (Lanham, Maryland: Lexington Books, 2004), pp. 200–208.

57 Desierto, above note 28, pp. 71–72, 76–77. Kahn, above note 51, p. 248; Whelan, ibid, pp. 202–203; Thomas Hobbes, *Leviathan* (*or the Matter, Form, & Power of a Commonwealth Ecclesiastical and Civil*), Part XXII, p. 218 (on pdf version available at, http://socserv2.socsci.mcmaster.ca/econ/ugcm/3ll3/hobbes/Leviathan.pdf).

58 Urmila Sharma and S. K. Sharma, *Western Political Thought* (*Vol. 1*): *From Plato to Burke* (New Delhi: Atlantic Publishers and Distributors, 2006), p. 369. See also, Desierto, ibid, pp. 70–71.

59 Desierto, ibid, pp. 71–72.

forces that in effect limit the exercise of reason of state powers by the sovereign.[60] The fourth group of thinkers like Baruch Spinoza (1632–1677), Baron de Montesquieu (1689–1755) and James Harrington (1611–1677) sought for structural or institutional limitations. While Spinoza stressed on the individual rights of freedom and thought of all members of the polity as limitations to the authority of the sovereign in the use of reason of state powers,[61] Montesquieu laid his trust on the constitutional foundations of states which regulate power to be exercised by the sovereign including in times of emergency.[62] Harrington "advocated a form of constitutional dictatorship, but with an additional check on the exercise of emergency powers"[63] and provided details on the establishment of a constitutional organ that would oversee the exercise of power of the sovereign during times of emergency.[64] The fifth group constitutes thinkers like John Locke (1632–1704), Jean Jacques Rousseau (1712–1778) and Immanuel Kant (1724–1804) who, writing in the second half of the 18th century, relied on social contract as the limitation to the powers of the sovereign.[65]

It may be observed that these early discussions on the limitation of the power of the states in times of emergency can be related to the continuing debate, relevant to this book, on the security exceptions in the WTO Agreement,[66] as to the precise meaning of the clause "to prevent any Member from taking any action *which it considers necessary* for the protection of its essential security interests (*emphasis added*)". This issue is further discussed in Part 2.

With the proliferation of nation states, the constant rise of forces influencing the shape of these states and the increase in inter-state relations, necessity attracted the continuous attention of writers who commented on the subject from angles different than those mentioned above (morality and limitation). These writers, with differing stances on whether necessity should be raised as a justification or an excuse, further refined the concept by detailing, in their

60 Ibid, pp. 75–77.

61 Benedictus de Spinoza, *Tractatus Theologico-Politicus: A Critical Inquiry into the History, Purpose, and Authenticity of the Hebrew Scriptures; with the Right to Free Thought and Free Discussion Asserted and Shown to be Not Only Consistent but Necessarily Bound Up with True Piety and Good Government* (translated by Robert Willis) (London: Trübner & co., 1862), pp. 342–353; ibid, pp. 72–73.

62 Desierto, ibid, pp. 73–74.

63 Ibid, p. 74.

64 Ibid, pp. 74–75.

65 Ibid, pp. 78–81.

66 As contained, for instance, in Article XXI(b) of the General Agreement on Tariffs and Trade (1994), Article XIV *bis* (1)(b) of the General Agreement on Trade in Services and Article 73 of the Agreement on Trade-Related Aspects of Intellectual Property Rights.

respective opinions, the elements of necessity. There are many similarities and differences in the approaches of these writers and, therefore, clustering their perspectives is difficult. One may classify the varying perspectives based on:

(a) the status, and conditions for application, of necessity measures in domestic law and international law;
(b) whether the determination of necessity rests on the rulers or the people;
(c) whether acts taken under necessity carry the obligation of paying damages; and
(d) the legal system within which the concept of necessity was developed (civil or common law, for example) etc.

Heathcote's classification appears to be more comprehensive. Building on the division of rationales among the judges and thinkers of the *Digest*, she classifies the perspectives on the basis of how they rationalize the use of necessity at domestic and international levels. Glimpses of these rationales are scattered throughout the development of the concept of necessity. It is during the 17th and 18th centuries, however, that a clear pattern of distinction starts to appear. The jurists and philosophers of these two centuries mostly used ancient examples (hunger-induced theft, destroying of a burning house, declaration of war etc.), but they provided more crystalized theoretical analyses of the concept of necessity and the rationale for the act.

Heathcote divides the rationales into three groups: objective, subjective and mixed strands of thought.

The *objective or natural law strand* is premised on the idea that acts of necessity such as hunger-induced theft are founded and recognized in the community of goods (folk life), i.e., in nature. Thus, the focus is on the act, not the actor. It is accordingly assumed that there is a public understanding, including consent of the proprietor of the damaged interest, that preservation of human life or property during emergency-like situations is more important than continuing to keep the law, i.e., not violating the interests of others. Natural lawyers of the 17th and 18th centuries developed this rationale and, basing their theory on natural law, found it easy to extend the scope of necessity from domestic law to international law.[67] Foremost among these were Hugo Grotius (1583–1645),[68]

67 Paul Weidenbaum, 'Necessity in International Law', *Transactions of the Grotius Society*, Vol. 24, Problems of Peace and War, Papers Read before the Society in the Year 1938, 1938, p. 113.

68 Heathcote, above note 11, p. 343–347; Desierto, above note 28, pp. 81, 83–84; Weidenbaum, ibid, pp. 113–114; Paddeu, above note 1, pp. 339–340; Hugo Grotius, *The Rights of War and Peace*, 1625 (translated by A. C. Campbell, 1901 ed.), available at, http://oll.libertyfund.org/titles/grotius-the-rights-of-war-and-peace-1901-ed, Book II, Part II, paras. VII–VIII, X.

Samuel von Pudendorf (1632–1694),[69] Christian Wolff (1679–1754),[70] Emmerich de Vattel (1714–1767)[71] and Jean Barbeyrac (1764–1744). Although they differed on the issue of whether acts of necessity carry the duty to compensate, these philosophers agreed that necessity embodies the right to self-preservation and that it should apply under prescribed conditions.[72] Thus, depending on the duty to compensate, necessity may be viewed as a justification or an excuse.

The *subjective strand* bases necessity on lack of free will, such as in the case of superior order and duress, and hence the focus is on the actor, not on the act. It is accordingly believed that depending on the extent of free will that the actor was able to exercise, the act may later be used as ground for total exemption from responsibility (i.e., justification) or as a ground for attenuation of punishment (i.e., excuse).[73] The main impact of this strand of thought was in domestic criminal laws, especially as necessity is related to crimes committed under duress, rather than in international law. The jurists who wrote on necessity along this line of thought, such as Julius Clarus (Giulio Claro) (1525–1573) and the French jurist André Tiraqueau (1488–1558), mainly discussed acts committed under superior orders (a concept that developed into duress in the Middle Ages), hence the impact of this school of thought is mainly on domestic laws. The subjective test school, therefore, accommodates necessity both as a justification or an excuse, but mainly as an excuse, depending on the circumstances of the commission of the act.

The *hybrid or mixed strand*, which is essentially the creation of the works of the legal theorist Antonius Matthäus (1601–1654) on necessity, believes that in an act of necessity the act needs to be deemed voluntary, but that the actor should be excused. In other words, "the act [is] considered imputable, the

69 Weidenbaum, ibid, p. 114; Desierto, ibid, pp. 86, 88; Heathcote, ibid, pp. 134, 348–350, 352–353; Milhizer, above note 15, p. 768; Paddeu, above note 1, p. 340.

70 Heathcote, ibid, pp. 348, 353–354; See, Christian Wolff, *Jus Gentium Methodo Scientifica Pertractatum*, § 3, pp. 9–10; § 273, p. 139 (Joseph H. Drake trans., Oxford University Press, 1934) (1764), as cited in Jens David Ohlin, 'The Doctrine of Legitimate Defense', *International Law Studies*, 91: (2015), p. 129, f.n. 37.

71 Emer de Vattel, *The Law of Nations, Or, Principles of the Law of Nature, Applied to the Conduct and Affairs of Nations and Sovereigns with Three Early Essays on the Origin and Nature of Natural Law and on Luxury (edited by Béla Kapossy & Richard Whatimite, 2008), Book II, Part IV, para. 50, Book II, Part IX, paras. 117–121 (online English version available at, http://oll.libertyfund.org/titles/vattel-the-law-of-nations-lf-ed)*; Desierto, above note 28, p. 88; Weidenbaum, above note 67, p. 115; Heathcote, ibid, pp. 354–355; Robert D. Sloane, 'On the Use and Abuse of Necessity in the Law of State Responsibility', *The American Journal of International Law*, 447 (2012), p. 455; Paddeu, above note 1, p. 340.

72 Heathcote, ibid, pp. 339, 341–343, 355.

73 Ibid, pp. 339, 355–357.

question of free will not being in doubt, and yet the sanction would be attenuated on ostensibly subjective grounds".[74] So here necessity is viewed as an excuse rather than a justification. It is the process of mixing the objective and subjective perspectives that the theorists of this mixed school, such as Joachim (Johann) Georg Darjes (Daries, as he is commonly known, 1714–1791),[75] Kant[76] and Friedrich von Gentz (1764–1832)[77] refined the difference between justification and excuse.[78]

It can be summarized, therefore, that the writers of the 17th and 18th centuries further refined the concept of necessity, with more emphasis on states as the subject of discussion, not only by respectively listing the elements of necessity but also by rationalizing it by focusing either on the actor (subjective test), the act (objective test) or both (mixed test) and by refining the difference between necessity as a justification and necessity as an excuse. Another notable contribution of the 17th and 18th century writings on necessity was the attempt to identify the source of necessity (nature, human weakness, community of goods etc.) both in domestic and international law. We now move to the 19th century.

1.3.2 *The 19th Century*

The 19th century discussions on necessity were dominated by the writings of German philosophers, such as Johann Gottlieb Fichte (1762–1814) and Georg Wilhelm Friedrich Hegel (1770–1831), who viewed necessity, in their reflections of German criminal law, from the objective test point of view mentioned in Sub-section 1.3.1 above with the tendency to view necessity more as a justification than an excuse.

Fichte, who considered events of necessity as "natural casualty" rather than a person attacking another to save an interest,[79] reflected on the Carneades'

74 Ibid, pp. 357, 340.

75 Joachim Hruschka, 'Imputation', *Brigham Young University Law Review*, 3: 1986, pp. 676–680; ibid, pp. 357–358.

76 Immanuel Kant, *The Metaphysics of Morals: Texts in German Philosophy* (introduction, translation and notes by Mary Gregory) (Cambridge: Cambridge University Press, 1991), pp. 60–61; Heathcote, ibid, p. 359.

77 Heathcote, ibid.

78 Ghanayim, above note 1, p. 34. It should be noted at this level, however, that it is a mix of philosophers on the other strands as well who contributed to the development of the concept of imputation and application of the law in times of necessity. Hruschka, for example, gives equal credit to Pufendorf, Wolff, Daries, Kant, Koch and Feuerback, among others, in influencing German criminal law notion of imputation. Hruschka, above note 75, pp. 669–704.

79 Heathcote, above note 11, p. 365.

plank situation and argued that since the functioning of the law presupposes coexistence of humans, a Carneades situation eliminates the presupposition and creates a situation beyond the law. Thus, the killer is neither subject to any obligation of compensation nor can it even be said that there is a right of necessity for rights exist only in the universe of the law.[80] In effect, Fitche's line of argument would accept the act as a justification rather than an excuse.

Hegel reflected on necessity only as it applied to domestic law, yet he had a tremendous influence on German 19th century thought and practice. Although he admits that there is a state of necessity, he approaches it from another point of view: comparison of the interest sacrificed vs. the interest saved. For Hegel, the contention in a situation of necessity is between personal liberty (saved interest) and appropriation of property (interest sacrificed) and that "personal liberty is anterior to property and in a state of necessity, the absolute right of life takes pre-eminence over property". Hegel engages in this comparison of interests because it is impossible to erode human will by any situation; therefore, both human interests (saved and sacrificed) have to be compared and placed in a hierarchy.[81] It is this objective 'balancing of interests' test that would ultimately find a place in the 20th century cases before the ICJ and other tribunals as well as the ARSIWA.[82]

Mention should also be made of mostly 19th century Swiss, Italian, Belgian and French thinkers and legal philosophers who contributed to the development of the concept of necessity. Weidenbaum succinctly summarizes their positions as follows:

> Less significant, but still noticeable, is the influence of the early authorities on French and Italian modern writers. French and Italian writers are, in their majority, opposed to a right of necessity. Only the Swiss-Belgian writer [Alphonse] Rivier [1835–1898][83] recognizes the right of necessity. Even military necessity may be sufficient. Most French writers are, however, of the opinion that the whole doctrine of necessity is nothing but a subterfuge for illegal acts. 'The so-called 'right of necessity', remarks [Laurent Basille] Hautefeuille [1805–1875] 'is the power given to

80 Ibid.

81 Ibid, pp. 366–367.

82 Ibid, pp. 371–373.

83 In his *Principes du Droit des Gens*, 1896. On self-preservation, he stated that it is "le premier des droits essentiels il les résume tous right." (p. 257) as quoted in, Marco Roscini, 'On the "Inherent" Character of the Right of States to Self-defense', *Cambridge Journal of International and Comparative Law*, 4(3): 2015, p. 638, f.n. 31.

each belligerent to take all kinds of measures against all kinds of people with the sole exception of their respective enemies'.[84] These ironic words are essentially true. Highly theoretical are [Paul-Louis-Ernest] Pradier-Fodéré's [1827–1904] objections. The law is based on the doctrine of freedom of determination; it cannot or ought not, in his opinion, to recognize the influence of force. This view begs the question. International Law as well as municipal accepts as basic principle the doctrine that each individual – person or State – is free to decide his actions and is therefore responsible for them. But the question has to be considered whether and in how far limitations exist to this principle. Pradier-Fodéré maintains, furthermore, that no right of 'necessity' can exist in a sphere where another one has obtained a right, as there cannot be a 'collision of rights'. But there is no collision of rights. In so far as the right of necessity exists any other is excluded. It is true that Wolff has spoken of a collision of rights, but this must be understood as a term of legal philosophy and not of law.

Among Italian writers it is especially Fior[e] [1837–1914] who recognizes necessity. A right exists in all cases in which the State cannot protect its 'natural sphere' in any other way. The State has, if possible, to compensate the damage done. [Giuseppe] Cavarretta, on the other hand, acknowledges only a necessity of a sudden and morally irresistible character. It is not possible to give a definition which applies to all cases. [Arrigo] Cavaglieri denies the relevance of necessity altogether, which, in his view, is neither recognized by State practice nor as a desirable legal doctrine. He especially objects to the role of each State as judge *in rem suam*.[85]

1.3.3 *The First Half of the 20th Century (1900–1945)*

The following brief presentation of the development of the defense of necessity is based largely on Paddeu's work on the subject.[86] Paddeu states that parallel developments in domestic and international law underpin the doctrinal

---

84 He also called military necessity "an utter juridical nullity". Gregory A. Raymond, 'Military Necessity and the War against Global Terrorism', in Howard M. Hensel (ed.), *The Law of Armed Conflict: Constraints on the Contemporary Use of Military Force* (Hampshire: Ashgate Publishing Limited, 2007), p. 1, f.n. 3.

85 Weidenbaum, above note 67, pp. 117–118. Desierto attributes this wariness by these civil law-trained jurists in accepting the defense of necessity to the absence of "[express codification of the concept] with predefined qualification, conditions, and limitations". Desierto, above note 28, pp. 92–93.

86 Paddeu, above note 1, pp. 363–386.

elaboration of the defense of necessity in the first half of the 20th century (1900–1945). The development of the defense of necessity from the second half of the 20th century, when the General Agreement on Tariffs and Trade was established, until the present day will be covered in Parts 2 and 3.

In the first half of the 20th century, domestic law witnessed a proliferation of codes and legislation (for instance the domestic penal laws of Brazil, Germany, Austria-Hungary, Portugal, Italy, Japan and China) which incorporated the late 19th century concept of the defense of necessity. These domestic law provisions were related to such theoretical underpinnings as the wisdom of punishing individuals who commit crimes, or cause damage, out of necessity or the idea of moral constraint.

In international law, the growing influence of positivism as the foundation of international law eclipsed the hitherto overarching doctrine of fundamental rights of states and, with it, the doctrine of the right of self-preservation. The abuses perpetrated throughout the 19th century by invocation of the right of self-preservation also made the right of self-preservation unpopular. Even the use of the term 'self-preservation' was slowly abandoned. To fill the jurisprudential space left by the abandonment of the concept of self-preservation, an abstract and general rule of necessity, whose characterization varied, was developed by legal writers. Some writers, such as Jean Pierre Adrien François (1889–1978), Karl Strupp (1886–1940) and Karl Wolff (1890–1963) argued for the existence of a *right of necessity*. Others recognized only a *defense of necessity*. Among those who accepted necessity as a defense, one group (such as Emanuel Ullmann (1841–1913) and Arrigo Cavaglieri (1880–1936) who, as did Fiore and Rivier in the 19th century, would later become a foremost critic of the rule of necessity) argued that necessity operated as an excuse while another group (including Roberto Ago (1907–1995), Dionisio Anzilotti (1867–1950), Scipione Gemma (1867–1951), Franz von Holtzendorff (1829–1889), Paul Heilborn (1861–1932) and Franz von Liszt (1851–1919)) accepted it as justification. Whether necessity was accepted as a right, a justification or an excuse, the differences were, however, not rigorously maintained; the common context appeared to be that necessity was a doctrine accepted within the then developing notion of state responsibility. A more common theme in the writing of these legal scholars was that necessity inherently reflected a clash of two interests: the interest of the invoking state and the interest of the injured state (previously it used to be comparison between two *rights*: a state's right to self-preservation and the right of the other state). The writers were divided on which interest should prevail and why.

International lawyers also debated on the theories underlying the rule of necessity. In a fashion similar to that mentioned in Sub-section 1.3.1, they viewed necessity either from the objective or subjective points of view. The objective view focuses on analyzing the act *vis-à-vis* the position of the state at that time. This analysis leads to exclusion of the legal consequences of the wrongful act (responsibility) only, but not its attribution or wrongful character, i.e., excuse. The subjective view focuses on the state and the notion of state will which gets excluded in times of necessity. If a state's will is so excluded, then the act cannot be imputed to the state and leads to the conclusion that no wrongful act had been committed – i.e., justification.

Paddeu then identifies four tenets of the theories of the rule of law (or objective rationales, as she calls them) as elaborated by the legal writers of this era. Firstly, international law remained simply 'neutral' to the act adopted in a situation of necessity. In other words, international law 'had no interest' in either imposing fulfilment of the invoking state's obligations or in granting the state the right to infringe the law. Secondly, a situation of necessity temporarily suspends international law in the sense that the necessitated act does not breach the state's international obligations as long as the situation of necessity continues. Thirdly, it was argued that a situation of necessity limits the binding force of all international obligations because it was assumed that states could not be understood to have agreed to be bound by international obligations as far as self-destruction. Fourthly, it was maintained that the interest of the necessity-invoking states rests superior to legitimate interests of third states.

One incident, though, continued to deeply divide opinions on the rule of necessity, even to the point of rejecting the existence of necessity: the invasion of Belgium and Luxembourg by Germany in 1914 and Chancellor von Bethmann-Hollweg's defense of the invasion with the words "necessity knows no law". Even Cavaglieri, an ardent supporter of the plea of necessity since at least 1906, deeply affected by the German invasion, turned against the plea arguing that if recognized, the plea could at most exclude the responsibility of the actor without affecting the wrongfulness of the conduct. During the first half of the 1940s, critics of the plea of necessity launched three main objections against the plea of necessity: (a) the plea was not recognized by positive international law; (b) the structure of international law could not support its recognition; and (c) the defense of necessity could only lead, as in 1914, to anarchy, chaos and the demise of international law by legitimizing might over right. Some scholars of the period went as far as referring to the state of necessity as a 'German notion' and argued that, by invoking this defense in 1914, Germany improperly transposed its domestic law to the international field. Even (at least two judges of) the ICJ, in its first case, the *Corfu Channel* (1949), seriously questioned the existence of the defense of necessity. In that case the United Kingdom defended its mine-sweeping operation of November 1946 in the

Corfu Channel as an act of self-help. Judge Krylov, in his dissenting opinion where he rejected the defense of the United Kingdom, wrote that:

> It should be observed that the British argument on this point, i.e., their defense of the alleged right of self-help – which is nothing else but intervention – relied on assertions *which have already been outstripped by the further development of international law, especially since the ratification of the Charter of the United Nations*. Since 1945, i.e., after the coming into force of the Charter, *the so-called right of self-help, also known as the law of necessity* (*Notrecht*), *which used to be upheld by a number of German authors, can no longer be invoked. It must be regarded as obsolete.* The employment of force in this way, or of the threat of force, is forbidden by the Charter (para. 4 of Art. 2) (*emphasis added*).[87]

Moreover, another dissenting member of the Court, Judge Azevedo, in respect of the disputed, earlier passage in October 1946 of two British cruisers and two destroyers also opined that the situation in question was not considered "a state of necessity".[88] while reflecting on the dispute, Yamada argues that the judges did not mean that the defense of necessity does not exist at all in international law, but that it is not applicable to violations against the principle of prohibition of use of force under Article 2(4) the UN Charter (Krylov) and that it did not specifically apply to the case of the passage of British ships northward through the North Corfu Channel (Azevedo).[89]

Furthermore, state practice showed that countries were reluctant at this time, especially after the 1914 German invasion of Belgium and Luxembourg, to make use of the plea of necessity. This is partly reflected in the arguments of the parties in notable international disputes litigated during the first half of the 20th century (disputes such as *French Company of Venezuelan Railroads, Russian Indemnity, S.S. Wimbledon, Serbian Loans, Société Commerciale de Belgique* etc. – discussed in Chapters 2 and 6) where, regardless of the similarity of the substance of the respective defenses to the plea of necessity, the

87 *Corfu Channel case* (*United Kingdom v. Albania*), Judgment (Merits), 9 April 1949, ICJ Rep. 1949, pp. 76–77. It is mainly for the reason of the United Kingdom's relying on the doctrine of self-help or referring to necessity only as part of other defenses that the *Corfu Channel* case has not been selected for discussion in Chapters 2 and 6 for its contribution to the development of the plea of necessity in international law. See, Paddeu, above note 1, p. 410, f.n. 510 for the same reasoning.

88 *Corfu Channel* case, ibid, p. 109, para. 38.

89 Takuhei Yamada, 'State of Necessity in International Law: A Study of International Judicial Cases', *Kobe-Gakuin Law and Politics Review*, 34(4): 2005, pp. 130–131.

defenses were mainly identified by the defendants as *force majeure*. For more on this, see, Sections 6.1 and 6.7.

Rehabilitating the plea of necessity, which was seriously damaged after the First World War, was left to the ILC's study group on state responsibility. The credit goes especially to Special Rapporteur Roberto Ago (1969–1972, 1976–1980) who, by clearly distinguishing the defense of necessity from self-preservation, prepared extensive, comprehensive and analytical reports on the defense. He distinguished the development of the concept to such level where the ICJ finally recognized the plea as a customary international law.[90]

The proliferation of post-Westphalian inter-state relations and, thus, many incidents of tension led nation states to look for defenses to justify/excuse actions that they would not take in times of normal, peaceful relations. Most of the times these defenses were presented in communications between the conflicting states, but often they were – until the establishment of an international tribunal to settle state conflicts under international law, the PCIJ – brought before tribunals explicitly established to settle the disputes. Chapter 2 will briefly present these state and tribunal practices from the 18th century until the 1930s.

---

90 *Case Concerning the Gabčíkovo-Nagymaros Project* (*Hungary v. Slovakia*), Judgment, 25 September 1997, ICJ Rep. 1997, pp. 40–41, paras. 51–52; *Legal Consequences of the Construction of a Wall in the Occupied Palestinian Territory*, Advisory Opinion, 9 July 2004, ICJ Rep. 2004, pp. 194–195, para. 140.

CHAPTER 2

State and Tribunal Practices until the 1930s

It is difficult to categorize the many state and tribunal practices where otherwise unlawful measures were defended under a number of grounds including necessity. These practices can be categorized either chronologically, by the nature of the incidents that gave rise to the act of necessity (war situation, financial situation, economic emergency, natural disaster etc.), by the source of obligation whose breach was in dispute (general custom, treaty etc.) or by the nature of the act intended to preclude wrongfulness (self-defense, self-preservation, necessity etc.). Chapter 2 focuses on presenting state and tribunal practices from mid-18th century until the establishment of the PCIJ. The establishment of the PCIJ (set up in 1921 and became operational in 1922) has been used as the cut point because the establishment of the PCIJ may rightfully be considered as the turning point towards the settlement in international tribunals of disputes under international law.[1] Section 2.1 chronologically presents 11 select state practices before the establishment of the PCIJ. Only two incidents (the Japanese invasion of Manchuria (1931) and the Italian invasion of Abyssinia (1935)) have been added for the purpose of convenience. Section 2.2 chronologically presents four tribunal practices before the establishment of the PCIJ. Tribunal practices after the establishment of the PCIJ, with the exception of the *Russian Indemnity* case (1912) will be presented in Chapter 6. Section 2.3 addresses the often-arising issue of conflating, and presents points for distinguishing between, the concept of necessity with other defenses. Section 2.4 presents the lessons learned from these state and tribunal practices.

1 A brief history of the PCIJ is available at, http://www.icj-cij.org/court/index.php?p1=1&p2=1 and http://opil.ouplaw.com/view/10.1093/law:epil/9780199231690/law-9780199231690-e72. For a detailed contribution of the PCIJ to development of international law, see, Malgosia Fitzmaurice and Christian J. Tams (eds.), *Legacies of the Permanent Court of International Justice* (Leiden and Boston: Martinus Nijhoff Publishers, 2013); Malcolm N. Shaw, *International Law* (8th ed.) (Cambridge: Cambridge University Press, 2017), p. 23.

 | DOI:10.1163/9789004700000_004

2.1 State Practices

2.1.1 *Frederick the Great's Passage through Saxony (1756)*

Since Frederick the Great's (1712–1786) ascension to the Prussian throne in 1840, Prussia and Austria had been in constant tension over the control of Prussia proper. With tensions mounting, on 28 August 1756, Frederick led his army on a three-pronged crossing into the territory of neutral Saxony and occupied Leipzig on 29 August.[2] In his communications with the Saxon elector (king), Augustus III, and his messages to the Saxon people as well other to other countries, Frederick stated that his actions, widely considered at that time a flagrant breach of international law,[3] were necessary for the purpose of self-defense (self-preservation or necessity in other writings, hence the interchangeable use of the defenses).[4] In his six-volume book, *The History of England: From the Invasion of Julius Caesar to the Revolution in 1688*, David Hume reflected on the Saxon invasion of 1756 which was fresh on his mind at the time he wrote the book, and he also believed that the Prussian attack was justified on grounds of self-preservation *and* self-defense.[5]

2.1.2 *Destruction of Danish Fleet (1807)*

When, following the Treaties of Tilsit that France signed with Russia and Prussia (which would allow the Danes to allow the French to seize their fleet to attack Britain), the British navy made a pre-emptive attack on the Danish fleet in August 1807,[6] the debates before the British Parliament raised the question of justifying the attacks on Denmark. It was argued during the debates that "[t]he right in this case blended itself with the policy since in fact necessity was only a superior ground of policy … Was it politic to a degree of necessity? The

2 For more on the seven years' war, see, Franz A. J. Szabo, *The Seven Years War in Europe: 1756–1763* (London and New York: Routledge, 2013); Herbert J. Redman, *Frederick the Great and the Seven Years' War, 1756–1763* (Jefferson, North Carolina: McFarland & Company, 2015); Daniel Marston, *Seven Years' War* (Oxford: Osprey Publishing Limited, 2001).

3 Sarah Heathcote, *State of Necessity and International Law*, Thesis no. 772, submitted to the University of Geneva for PhD in Law (Geneva: 2005), p. 203.

4 Redman, above note 2, p. 7; Szabo, above note 2, pp. 36–40; Paul Weidenbaum, 'Necessity in International Law', *Transactions of the Grotius Society*, Vol. 24, Problems of Peace and War, Papers Read before the Society in the Year 1938, 1938, p. 122.

5 David Hume, *The History of England: From the Invasion of Julius Caesar to the Revolution in 1688, Continued to the Death of George the Second* (all in one volume compiled by T. Smollett) (London: Joseph Ogle Robinson, 1833), p. 1178.

6 For a brief narration of the 1807 battle, see, Hans Christian Bjerg, '"To Copenhagen a Fleet" The British Pre-emptive Seizure of the Danish-Norwegian Navy International', *Journal of Naval History*, 7(2): 2008.

character of this important transaction must stand upon its necessity."[7] British Foreign Minister George Canning asked in return:

> Was it to be contended that in a *moment of imminent danger and impending necessity* we should have abstained from the course which prudence and policy dictated in order to meet *those calamities that threatened our security and existence* because if we fell under the pressure we should have the consolation of having the authority of Pufendorf to plead? (*emphasis added*).[8]

Regarding the incident, Weidenbaum commented that "...this was only an additional defense of the Government. Mr. Canning's policy was not attacked as illegal under all circumstances. The opposition admitted that *in a case of genuine necessity the action was justifiable by International Law* (*emphasis added*)."[9] The British government stated that the danger it faced was "certain, urgent and extreme, as to create a case of urgent, paramount necessity, leaving His majesty's ministers no choice," an expression similar to that used in the *Caroline* incident in 1837 (see, Sub-section 2.1.6).[10] Thus, the British government seems to have viewed its actions as acts of necessity. However, scholars of the use of force refer to the 1807 bombardment of Copenhagen as an example of "anticipatory self-defense to thwart discernible impending attacks".[11]

2.1.3 *Response to the Neapolitan Revolt (1820)*

Alerted by the so-called Neapolitan revolt of July 1820 against King Ferdinand I of the Two Sicilies (i.e., Sicily and Naples), the Quintuple (Austria, Russia, Prussia, Britain and France) met, on 20 October 1820, in Troppau (Austrian Silesia) to enforce a September 1815 agreement to quash revolutions against their monarchies. A split of ideas between Britain and the trio of Austria, Russia and Prussia became visible about the nature of intervention against the revolutions. After a series of meetings among the trio the Troppau Protocol was signed on 19 November 1820 to quash administrations which come to

---

7 Referred to in Weidenbaum, above note 4, p. 122.

8 Ibid, p. 123.

9 Ibid.

10 Gregory A. Raymond and Charles W. Kegley, Jr., 'Pre-emption and Preventive War', in Howard M. Hensel (ed.), *The Legitimate Use of Military Force: The Just War Tradition and the Customary Law of Armed Conflict* (London and New York: Routledge, 2008), pp. 100–101.

11 Ibid, p. 100.

power through Neapolitan-like revolutions.[12] British foreign minister Robert Stewart (Lord Castlereagh) made known his government's opposition to the Troppau Protocol through a circular dispatch of 19 January 1821. In the circular, Castlereagh distinguished between the Troppau Protocol principle and the particulars of the Naples insurrection:

> [i]t should be clearly understood that no government can be more prepared than the British government is to *uphold the right of any state or states to interfere, where their own immediate security or essential interests are seriously endangered by the internal transactions of another state.* But as they [in the Protocol] regard the assumption of such right as only to be justified by the strongest necessity, and to be limited and regulated thereby, *they cannot admit that this right can receive a general and indiscriminate application* to all revolutionary movements without reference to their immediate bearing upon some particular state or states, or be made prospectively the basis of an alliance. *They regard its exercise as an exception to general principles of the greatest value and importance,* and as one that only properly grows out of the circumstances of the special case; but they at the same time consider that *exceptions of this description never can, without the utmost danger, be so far reduced to rule as to be incorporated into the ordinary diplomacy of States, or into the institutes of the law of nations (emphasis added).*[13]

Castlereagh, in terms close to our contemporary understanding of the concepts of necessity and self-preservation, laid out some interesting ideas. Firstly, he appeared to recognize that interventions arising out of necessity are the exception to the general principles (such as the right of the people to establish a government of their own). Secondly, such right of intervention must be exercised in extreme situations. Thirdly, the intervention cannot be equally applied to all insurrections; it has to be assessed on a case-by-case basis. Fourthly, interventions are secondary rules in international relations and international law.

---

12 For a more detail on the Troppau Congress, see, Paul W. Schroeder, *Metternich's Diplomacy at its Zenith, 1820–1823: Austria and the Congresses of Troppau, Laibach, and Verona* (Austin: University of Texas Press, 1962), chap. III.

13 Lassa Oppenheim (ed.), *The Collected Papers of John Westlake on Public International Law* (Cambridge: Cambridge University Press, 1914), p. 125.

2.1.4 *Anglo-Portuguese Dispute (1832)*

The led to eight years of chaos (the Portuguese Civil War) and also affected the interests of Britain.[14] Under the Treaty of Windsor the Portuguese government had an obligation to respect the property of British subjects in Portugal. In 1832 the Portuguese authorities, as part of its measures to quell the chaos that started following the death of Portuguese King João VI in 1826, appropriated property of British subjects in Portugal. The British government then consulted its Advocate-General, Sir Herbert Jenner-Fust (1778–1852), to give his opinion on the matter. In a reflection that echoes a number of the contemporary elements of self-preservation and necessity and in one of the few instances where both sides agree on the existence of necessity/self-preservation, Jenner-Fust stated:

> In a case, therefore, *of pressing necessity* I think that it would be competent to the Portuguese Government to appropriate to the use of the Army such Articles of Provisions etc., etc., as may be *requisite for its subsistence* even against the will of the Owners, whether British or Portuguese; for I do not apprehend, that the Treaties [of perpetual alliance] between this Country and Portugal … ought to be so *strictly adhered to, as to deprive the Government of Portugal of the right of using those means, which may be absolutely and indispensably necessary to the safety, and even to the very existence of the State* [echoing self-preservation].
>
> The *extent of the necessity*, which will justify such an appropriation of the Property of British subjects, must depend upon the circumstances of the particular case, but it must be *imminent and urgent* (*emphasis in cited reference*).[15]

2.1.5 *Occupation of Nacogdoches (1836)*

Convinced that the Mexican government was not honoring the treaty they signed in April 1821 to maintain peace and harmony among the Indians who inhabit the lands adjacent to the borders of the two countries, the US government ordered General Edmund Pendleton Gaines to move his troops closer to

14 For more on the Portuguese Civil War, see, Paulo Jorge Fernandes, 'The Political History of Nineteenth Century Portugal', *e-Journal of Portuguese History*, 1(1): 2003, pp. 4–5.

15 A/CN.4/318/Add.5–7, *Addendum – Eighth Report on State Responsibility* by Roberto Ago, Special Rapporteur – the Internationally Wrongful Act of the State, Source of International Responsibility (part 1), Extract from the *Yearbook of the International Law Commission* (1980), p. 30, referring to A. D. McNair, *International Law Opinions* (Cambridge: Cambridge University Press, 1956), vol. II, pp. 231 *et. seq.*

the border. On the grounds for taking action inside Mexican territory, President Andrew Jackson wrote to Gaines that:

> unless the *necessity exists*, unless there are actual disturbances of the peace on the frontier, or a moral certainty that the Indians in hostile array for the purpose are drawing the means of operation from the territory of Mexico, the occupation of an advanced post in that territory by our troops must be avoided (*emphasis added*).[16]

Finally convinced that the raids would not stop and Mexico was not going to keep its promise, the US government allowed Gaines' army to cross the imaginary border between the two countries and enter into the small Texan city of Nacogdoches to curb the alleged Indian raids. This incident sparked a series of diplomatic exchanges between the two governments and it is in these exchanges that the US' understanding of necessity in the situation is made clear. In his 3 May 1836 letter to Manuel Eduardo de Gorostiza, the Mexican Minister to the US, John Forsyth, the Secretary of State, mentioned that:

> Except in cases of *necessity* General Gaines will not occupy ground not indisputably within the limits of the United States. In cases of *necessity*, whether the possession of the ground he may occupy is now claimed by Mexico, cannot be made a question by that officer ... The just and friendly purposes being explained ... it will prevent suspicion of any ... equivocal design on his part ... (*emphasis added*).[17]

Forsyth elaborately discussed his point of view in a subsequent 10 December 1836 letter to Gorostiza where he distinguished necessity from self-defense:

> [O]ur action ... rests upon *the principle of the law of nations, entirely distinct from those on which war is justified upon the immutable principle of self-defense* ... upon *the principles which justify decisive measures of precaution to prevent irreparable evil to our own or to a neighboring people* [i.e., necessity] (*emphasis added*).[18]

16 Letter from Jackson to Gaines cited at Robert L. Jones and Pauline Jones, 'Occupation of Nacogdoches', *East Texas Historical Journal*, 50(2): 2012, pp. 33–34.

17 Cited in Weidenbaum, above note 4, p. 124.

18 Cited in ibid, pp. 124–125.

2.1.6 *Destruction of the Caroline (1837)*

The *Caroline Affair* (or the *Schlosser Incident* as it is also called) of 29 December 1837 is one of the most important incidents in the development of the concepts of necessity and self-defense in international law. Jennings claimed that "[i]t was in the *Caroline* case that self-defense was changed from a political excuse to a legal doctrine."[19] A group of people rebelled against the British Government in Canada and, stationing themselves in Navy Island on the Canadian side of the Niagara River, started to prepare themselves to invade the Canadian mainland. There they proclaimed a Provisional Government of Upper Canada and prepared to invade the Canadian mainland. As part of their preparation, they employed the services of the *Caroline*, a privately owned US steamboat, to convey men and materials to the rebel forces. At the end of its first day of service, the *Caroline* was docked for the night at Schlosser, in New York State, directly across from Navy Island. Knowing this, the British sent troops to Schlosser who forcibly seized the ship, towed it into the current of the Niagara River, and destroyed it by fire. Two Americans were also killed. The event angered the US government which arrested a suspect on the murder of the two Americans. Henry Fox, the British Minister in Washington, in condemning the arrest, asserted that the attack on the *Caroline* was a public act [of force in self-defense][20] and therefore the US could not proceed against individuals engaged in the incident.[21] When Mr. Forsyth, the American Secretary of State, wrote to Mr. Fox that his government would demand redress, Mr. Fox responded that that the destruction of the *Caroline* was an act of necessary self-defense [and self-preservation, according to other sources[22]].[23]

It is the communications that Mr. Daniel Webster, the US Secretary of State, exchanged with Mr. Fox and Lord Ashburton, special British representative to the US, in 1841 and 1842, that arguably contain clear definitions for the modern concept of self-defense and necessity.[24]

---

19 Robert Y. Jennings, 'The Caroline and McLeod Cases', *American Journal of International Law*, 32(1): 1938, p. 82.

20 *British-American Diplomacy: The Caroline Case*, available at, http://avalon.law.yale.edu/19th_century/br-1842d.asp.

21 Martin A. Rogoff and Edward Collins, Jr., 'The Caroline Incident and the Development of International Law', *Brooklyn Journal of International Law*, 16(3): 1990, pp. 493–496.

22 Sharon Korman, *The Right of Conquest: The Acquisition of Territory by Force in International Law and Practice* (Oxford: Clarendon Press Oxford, 2003 (reprint)), p. 103.

23 *British-American Diplomacy: The Caroline Case*, above note 20. Other narrations may be read at Howard Jones, 'The Caroline Affair', *The Historian*, 38(3): 1976, pp. 485–502; Jennings, above note 19, pp. 82–99.

24 The paragraphs containing the communications are available at *British-American Diplomacy: The Caroline Case*, above note 20.

Webster to Fox (April 1841)

> The Undersigned has now to signify to Mr Fox that the Government of the United States has not changed the opinion which it has heretofore expressed to Her Majesty's Government, of the character of the act of destroying the '*Caroline*'. It does not think that that transaction can be justified by any reasonable application or construction of *the right of self-defense under the laws of nations*. It is admitted that a just right of self-defense attaches always to nations, as well as to individuals, and is equally necessary for the preservation of both. But the extent of this right is a question to be judged of by the circumstances of each particular case; and when its alleged exercise has led to the commission of hostile acts, within the territory of a power at peace, *nothing less than a clear and absolute necessity can afford ground of justification* ...
>
> Under these circumstances, and under those immediately connected with the transaction itself, it will be for Her Majesty's Government to show, upon what state of facts, and what rules of national law, the destruction of the '*Caroline*' is to be defended. *It will be for that Government to show a necessity of self-defense, instant, overwhelming, leaving no choice of means, and no moment for deliberation*. It will be for it to show, also, that the local authorities of Canada,- *even supposing the necessity of the moment authorized them to enter the territories of the United States at all,-* did nothing unreasonable or excessive; *since the act justified by the necessity of self-defense, must be limited by that necessity*, and kept *clearly within it*. It must be strewn that admonition or remonstrance to the persons on board the '*Caroline*' was impracticable, or would have been unavailing; it must be strewn that daylight could not be waited for; that there could be no attempt at discrimination, between the innocent and the guilty; that it would not have been enough to seize and detain the vessel; but that there was a *necessity, present and inevitable*, for attacking her ... A necessity for all this, the Government of the United States cannot believe to have existed (*emphasis added*).

Ashburton to Webster (July 1842)

> Every consideration therefore leads us to set as highly as your Government can possibly do *this paramount obligation of reciprocal respect for the independent territory of each. But however strong this duty may be it is admitted by all writers, by all Jurists, by the occasional practice of all nations, not excepting your own, that a strong overpowering necessity may arise, when*

> *this great principle may and must be suspended. It must be so for the shortest possible period, during the continuance of an admitted overruling necessity, and strictly confined within the narrowest limits imposed by that necessity. Self-defense is the first law of our nature and it must be recognized by every code which professes to regulate the condition and relations of man …*
>
> Agreeing therefore on the general principle and on the possible exception to which it is liable, the only question between us is whether this occurrence came within the limits fairly to be assigned to such exception, whether, to use your words, there was 'that *necessity of self-defense, instant, overwhelming, leaving no choice of means*' which preceded the destruction of the *Caroline*, while moored to the shore of the US (*emphasis added*).

Webster to Ashburton (August 1842)

> The President sees with pleasure that your Lordship fully *admits those great principles of public law … respect for the inviolable character of the territory of independent States is the most essential foundation of civilization*. And while it is admitted, on both sides, that there are exceptions to this rule, he is gratified to find that your Lordship admits that such exceptions must come within the limitations stated and the terms used in a former communication from this Department to the British Plenipotentiary here. *Undoubtedly it is just, that while it is admitted that exceptions growing out of the great law of self-defense do exist, those exceptions should be confined to eases in which the 'necessity of that self-defense is instant, overwhelming, and leaving no choice of means, and no moment for deliberation'.*
>
> Understanding these principles alike, the difference between the two Governments is only whether the facts in the case of the '*Caroline*' make out a case of such necessity for the purpose of self-defense (*emphasis added*).

The principles laid out in these communications by Webster are now known as the *Caroline Doctrine* and they are hailed for laying the foundation for defining the elements of self-defense in international law. Unlike in the law of state responsibility (ARSIWA) where necessity and self-defense are distinct concepts, in a number of literatures, including the Webster-Ashburton/Fox communications, necessity is here considered as an element of self-defense[25] and

25 The other elements in contemporary law of self-defense are proportionality, imminence and existence of armed attack. See, for instance, Daniel Bethlehem, 'Self-Defense against

this idea originates in Webster's communications.[26]

2.1.7 *The Russian Fur Seals Controversy (1893)*

In 1892, a Russian cruiser named *Zabraka* seized three British sealing vessels more than 40 miles from the Commander Islands which are well beyond Russia's territorial waters.[27] Eventually, the Russian government issued a Decree which stated that "for the ensuing reason, and pending the adoption of international regulations Russia would, *as a measure of legitimate self-defense*, prohibit sealing within ten miles of all her coasts, and within thirty miles of the Commander Islands and Robben Island (*emphasis added*)".[28] In response to a concern by the British government, the Russian Foreign Minister Chickline sent a letter to the British Ambassador in February 1893 referring to a provisional measure of absolute necessity, adopted under pressure of exceptional circumstances.[29] The Minister "identified an 'absolute necessity of immediate

an Imminent or Actual Armed Attack by Nonstate Actors', *The American Journal of International Law*, 106(4): 2012, pp. 769–777 and Dapo Akande and Thomas Liefländer, 'Clarifying Necessity, Imminence, and Proportionality in the Law of Self-Defense', *The American Journal of International Law*, 107(3): 2013, pp. 563–570; Daniel Bethlehem, 'Principles of Self-Defense – A Brief Response', *The American Journal of International Law*, 107(3): 2013, pp. 579–585; M. A. Weightman, 'Self-Defense in International Law', *Virginia Law Review*, 37(8): 1951, pp. 1095–1115; J. L. Taulbee, 'Retaliation and Irregular Warfare in Contemporary International Law', *The International Lawyer*, 7(1): 1973, p. 202, f.n. 19; Harold S. Quigley and Kenneth W. Colegrove, 'Enforcement of Treaty Obligations by Self-help and Self-defense', *Proceedings of the American Society of International Law at its Annual Meeting* (1921–1969), 26 (April 28–30 1932), pp. 92, 95. Uniacke, however, separates self-defense from necessity and argues that the proportionality needed in the two defenses is different. Suzanne Uniacke, 'Proportionality and Self-Defense', *Law and Philosophy*, 30(3): 2011, pp. 253–272. Alhoff, in discussing the difference between necessity and self-defense as grounds for torture holds (p. 227) that "To be sure, self-defense and necessity are closely related – I think of self-defense as a limiting case of necessity". Fritz Allhoff, 'Torture Warrants, Self-Defense, and Necessity', *Public Affairs Quarterly*, 25(3): 2011, pp. 217–240.

26 Anthony Clark Arend, 'International Law and the Preemptive Use of Military Force', *The Washington Quarterly*, 26(2): 2003, p. 91.

27 Robert D. Sloane, 'On the Use and Abuse of Necessity in the Law of State Responsibility', *The American Journal of International Law*, 447 (2012), pp. 466–467.

28 Maria Agius, *The Invocation of Necessity in International Law*, p. 10, f.n. 20, available at, https://www.uppsalajuristernasalumnistiftelse.se/wp-content/uploads/2014/11/Maria-Agius.pdf.

29 Maria Agius, 'The Invocation of Necessity in International Law', *Netherlands International Law Review*, 56(2): 2009, pp. 99–100. See also, Malgosia Fitzmaurice, 'Necessity in International Environmental Law', in Ige F. Dekker and E. Hey (eds.), *Netherlands Yearbook of International Law: Necessity across International Law*, Vol. 41 (The Hague: T.M.C. Asser Press, 2010), p. 164.

precautionary measures' and underlined 'the essentially precautionary character of the above-mentioned measures, which were taken under the pressure of exceptional circumstances"[30] and "proposed that Russia's seizure of the vessels 'may be regarded as a case of force majeure and assimilated to cases of self-defense'".[31] Professor Roberto Ago took note of the case and reflected on its impact on the concept of necessity in international law as follows:

> This position is therefore interesting as an affirmation of the validity of the plea of necessity in international law, and also because it brings out several of the conditions enumerated above as having to be fulfilled before one can even consider whether a situation of '"necessity" justifies action by a state which is not in conformity with an international obligation: namely, the absolutely exceptional nature of the alleged situation, the imminent character of the danger threatening a major interest of the state, the impossibility of averting such a danger by other means, and the necessarily temporary nature of this "justification", depending on the continuance of the feared danger.[32]

Surely, the Russian Foreign Minister's letter refers to situations of self-defense, necessity and *force majeure*. Examining the Minister's letter through the contemporary test makes it hard to identify the nature of Russia's defense. Sloane rightly noted:

> But the foreign minister's use of the word 'necessity' does not appear to have indicated, expressly or implicitly, a claim of legal necessity. Insofar as Russia defended its conduct in legal terms at all, the foreign minister ascribed Russia's seizures to 'the pressure of exceptional circumstances'. Implicitly conceding that it lacked a viable legal defense, the foreign minister proposed that Russia's seizure of the vessels 'may be regarded as a case of *force majeure* and assimilated to cases of self-defense'. It is true, as we have seen, that *force majeure and necessity were sometimes conflated at the time of that incident*. But necessity, force majeure, and self-defense all would have failed to provide a viable defense for Russia's conduct in the *Russian Fur Seals* incident ... More to the point, no evidence suggests that either state regarded this incident as involving a plea of necessity.

30 Gebhard Bücheler, *Proportionality in Investor-State Arbitration* (Oxford: Oxford University Press, 2015), p. 268.

31 Sloane, above note 27, p. 467.

32 A/CN.4/318/Add.5–7, above note 15, pp. 26–27.

> Depending on one's methodological views, the incident might nonetheless be viewed as a form of state practice that contributes to the modern customary law of necessity. But if so, it is not especially helpful support for Article 25 [of the Articles on Responsibility of States for Internationally Wrongful Acts (ARSIWA) titled *necessity*]. Unlike that article, the conception of necessity at issue in the *Russian Fur Seals* incident did not involve any consideration of the competing 'essential interests' of Russia and Britain (*emphasis added*).[33]

2.1.8 *Japanese Occupation of Korea (1904)*

On 8 February 1904 Japan began naval war on Russia[34] and crossed into Korea. For the Japanese, full annexation of Korea was imperative "from the standpoint of Japan's self-preservation."[35] The then Japanese Prime Minister Katsura Taro stated that "on the political side we are fighting for political self-preservation and national existence."[36] Commenting on the incident, Weidenbaum states that "Japan invoked the right of necessity when it occupied, in 1904, neutral Korea under the pretense of acting in self-preservation and in a state of emergency."[37]

2.1.9 *Austrian Annexation of Bosnia and Herzegovina (1908)*

With the aim of restoring the Ottoman Constitution of 1876 which was suspended in 1878, a Committee of Union and Progress (so called Young Turks) took the Ottoman Empire authorities by surprise and controlled the government in a revolution in July 1908.[38] Concerned that the Turkish revolution may galvanize the Muslims of Bosnia and Herzegovina to claim autonomy, Emperor Franz Joseph (1830–1916) announced the annexation of Bosnia and Herzegovina on 5 October 1908. Vehement opposition followed, but

---

33 Sloane, above note 27, p. 467.

34 More detail available at, Rotem Kowner, 'Becoming an Honorary Civilized Nation: Remaking Japan's Military Image During the Russo-Japanese War, 1904–1905', *Historian*, 64(1): 2001, pp. 19–38; Katō, Yōko, 'What Caused the Russo-Japanese War: Korea or Manchuria?', *Social Science Japan Journal*, 10(1): 2007, pp. 95–103.

35 Toyokichi Iyenaga, 'Japan's Annexation of Korea', *The Journal of Race Development*, 3(2): 1912, p. 204.

36 Kim Ki-Jung, 'The War and US-Korean Relations', in John W. Steinberg, Bruce W. Menning, David Schimmelpenninck van der Oye, David Wolff and Shinji Yokote (eds.), *The Russo-Japanese War in Global Perspective: World War Zero (Vol. 2)* (Leiden and Boston: Brill, 2007), pp. 480–481.

37 Weidenbaum, above note 4, p. 125.

38 Eugene Rogan, *The Fall of the Ottomans: The Great War in the Middle East* (New York: Basic Books, 2015), pp. 3–6.

Austria-Hungary defended its action as an act of 'urgent necessity'. A few days before the annexation Joseph sent a letter to Wilhelm II (German Emperor (Kaiser) and King of Prussia (1859–1941)): "I am reporting this matter to you immediately since I owe that to the close relationship which unites us as friends. I am certain that you will judge this with friendly good-will and that you will not fail to understand that we are acting *under the pressure of urgent necessity* (*emphasis added*)."[39]

2.1.10 *German Invasion of Neutrals Luxembourg and Belgium (1914)*

As part of the build-up to attack France during the First World War, on 1 August 1914 German troops moved into neutral Luxembourg. On 2 August, Germany gave neutral Belgium an ultimatum for Belgium to allow German troops to pass through the land over to attack France. When this proved unsuccessful, German troops invaded Belgium.[40] In one of the clearest presentations of the necessity and self-defense justifications made before a national assembly,[41] German Chancellor Theobald von Bethmann-Hollweg stood before the Reichstag and said: "Gentlemen, *we are now [acting] in self-defense; and necessity knows no law! … Gentlemen, this is against the rules of international law* (*emphasis added*)."[42] In a 2 December 1914 speech before the Reichstag, Dr. Hollweg reiterated his August statement that "We notified Belgium that the necessities of self-defense would compel us to march through Belgium."[43] Moreover, he added: "The German government, in answering the charges of the violation of her treaty engagements, sets up two kinds of defenses. On one hand … the Imperial Chancellor and the Secretary of State for Foreign Affairs, tries to justify its unlawful actions, 'on the ground of supreme necessity', and 'high military reasons'"[44] Although it may be debated whether Hollweg's

39 Available at, https://wwi.lib.byu.edu/index.php/The_Annexation_of_Bosnia_and_Herzegovina_by_Austria-Hungary.

40 William Kelleher Storey, *The First World War: A Concise Global History, 2nd ed.* (London: Rowman & Littlefield, 2014), pp. 29–34; Samuel R. Williamson, Jr., 'The Origins of the War', in Hew Strachan (ed.), *The Oxford Illustrated History of the First World War* (Oxford: Oxford University Press, 1998), pp. 9–25.

41 The sources on the date of Hollweg's statements differ: Heathcote, above note 3, p. 211 (4 August); Partem, below note 42 (5 August).

42 As cited in Michael Greenfield Partem, 'The Buffer System in International Relations', *The Journal of Conflict Resolution*, 27(1): 1983, p. 11.

43 Theodore P. Ion, 'The International Status of the Grand Duchy of Luxemburg and the Kingdom of Belgium in Relation to the Present European War', *Michigan Law Review*, 13(5): 1915, f.n. 10.

44 Ibid, p. 369.

defense passes muster,[45] or whether his statements were a "moral middle term",[46] or whether this was an extreme logical application of the term 'necessity',[47] he clearly acknowledged that:

(a) international law forbids an attack against neutral countries in time of war;
(b) only extreme situations which can cause fatality to a country's survival justify an attack;
(c) the attack/occupation is the only available means to avert the extreme situations;
(d) the attack/occupation must end as soon as the military objective is met; and
(e) any damage that the said attack/occupation caused must be reasonably made good.

2.1.11 *Japanese Invasion of Manchuria (1931) and Italian Invasion of Abyssinia (1935)*

In response to the wide opposition that its invasion in 1931 of Manchuria was contrary to League of Nation's Covenant and the Kellogg-Briand Pact, Japan argued that it acted in "defense of rights and interests on which her very existence depends" and in self-defense against the threat from a disorganized and civil war-torn China.[48] In fact, Brownlie cites the statements of the Japanese representative before the League's Council who described his government's action as "justifiable measures of self-protection on the standard principle laid down in the Caroline case, that every act of self-defense must depend for its justification on the importance of the interests to be defended, on the imminence

45 Heathcote, above note 3, pp. 211–212. For detailed discussion on whether Germany violated the neutralities of Belgium and Luxembourg, and through that the Hague Conventions, see, Editorial Comment of the American Society of International Law, 'The Hague Conventions and the Neutrality of Belgium and Luxemburg', *The American Journal of International Law*, 9(4): 1915, pp. 959–962.

46 Nomi Claire Lazar, *States of Emergency in Liberal Democracies* (Cambridge: Cambridge University Press, 2009), p. 89.

47 Gaines Post, *Studies in Medieval Legal Thought: Public Law and the State 1100–1322* (Clark: The Law Exchange, Ltd., 3rd print, 2008), p. 8.

48 Kinga Tibori Szabó, *Anticipatory Action in Self-defense: Essence and Limits under International Law* (The Hague: T.M.C. Asser Press, 2011), pp. 88–93. Heathcote adds that Japan's political arguments "rested on the idea of *Lebensraum* [the territory which a state or nation believes is needed for its natural development.]: necessity to find markets for its excess production; the necessity to gain access to food ... and the necessity of ensuring the protection of the island (Japan)". Heathcote, above note 3, p. 213.

of the danger, and on the necessity of the act".[49] There is even another reference where the Japanese Foreign Minister, in his 20 January 1933 speech before the Japanese Diet (national parliament), referred to 'necessity'.[50] Thus, in the various Japanese statements (or views of scholars), self-preservation (self-protection),[51] necessity and self-defense were raised as justifications for the invasion, although most of the literature on the subject focuses on the self-defense argument. A September 1932 Lytton Commission report, an official narration of the Manchurian incident, endorsed a stance already taken by the League Council that Japan's act was not based on legitimate self-defense. Brownlie mentioned that the Council's reference to self-defense was not clear because while the Council's wording seemed to refer to military necessity, Japan reiterated self-defense on non-military grounds as well (i.e., the purpose of protecting the lives and property of its nationals).[52]

The opportunity for Mussolini's ambition to occupy Abyssinia, now Ethiopia, and declare an east African colony came on 5 December 1935 (although the war started on 3 October elsewhere) when a skirmish arose in the Ogaden region in the town of WelWel between Somali soldiers, who were under Italian pay, and Ethiopian soldiers. When in December 1935 its troops invaded Abyssinia, now Ethiopia, the Italian government claimed that "it was forced by Ethiopian hostility to exercise legitimate self-defense."[53] Szabó commented that:

> As with the Japanese invasion of Manchuria, the Italian claim of self-defense against Ethiopia was far from meeting the requirements of the narrow, natural-law concept of self-defense. There was no evidence of an attack, imminent or in preparation. The clashes that occurred in the disputed area were far from qualifying as an attack that created an immediate need for action or, in Webster's words, 'a necessity, present and inevitable'. Moreover, the full-scale invasion of Ethiopia and the use of chemical weapons could hardly be justified as a moderate use of self-defense.[54]

49 Ian Brownlie, *International Law and the Use of Force by States* (2002 re-print of 1963 edn.) (Oxford: Oxford University Press, 2002), p. 242.

50 Heathcote, above note 3, p. 213.

51 Winfield, for instance, viewed the Japanese argument as a gross abuse of the right of self-preservation. P. H. Winfield, *The Foundations & the Future of International Law* (Cambridge: Cambridge University Press, 1941), p. 31.

52 Brownlie, above note 49. See also, Szabó, above note 48, p. 93 on Japan's failure to demonstrate "the existence of an immediate need for action against an imminent attack, let alone an attack in progress".

53 Szabó, ibid, p. 94.

54 Ibid, p. 95.

2.2 Tribunal Practices

2.2.1 *Case of the Neptune* (1797)

In June 1795, *The Neptune*, an American vessel laden with cargo including rice, tobacco and indigo, was, *en route*, captured by the British navy and its cargo was, following proceedings before High Court of Admiralty, sold to the British Government. Unhappy with the valuation of the cargo for sale,[55] the owners of the cargo aboard the *The Neptune* appealed to a panel of five Commissioners as it was their right to do so under the Jay Treaty signed between the British and US governments in 1795.[56] Explaining why it paid the amount set by the registrar and the buyers, the British government stated that "the seizure was lawful, provisions being, under the circumstances of the case, liable to be treated as contraband of war; and that at any rate its conducts were justified by necessity since Great Britain had been threatened with a scarcity of the seized articles [resulting from the war between Britain and France which started in 1793]".[57] The Commissioners ruled in favor of the claimant and rejected the British plea that the seizure was justified by the necessity of scarcity of foodstuffs at the time. The opinions of the Commissioners in rejecting the necessity plea – they also referred to 'self-preservation' – are relevant to this book. Commissioner William Pinkney stated that:

> I shall not deny that *extreme necessity* may justify such a measure [seizure of foodstuffs]. It is only important to ascertain whether that extreme necessity existed on this occasion and upon what terms the right it communicated might be carried into exercise.
>
> We are told by Grotius that the necessity must not be imaginary, that it must be real and pressing, and that even then it does not give a right of appropriating the goods of others until all other means of relief consistent with the necessity have been tried and found inadequate (*emphasis in cited reference*).[58]

---

55 Takuhei Yamada, 'State of Necessity in International Law: A Study of International Judicial Cases', *Kobe-Gakuin Law and Politics Review*, 34(4): 2005, pp. 111–112; Roman Boed, 'State of Necessity as a Justification for Internationally Wrongful Conduct', *Yale Human Rights and Development Law Journal*, 3(1): 2000, p. 8; Bücheler, above note 30, p. 282; Bin Cheng, *General Principles of Law as Applied by International Courts and Tribunals* (Cambridge: Cambridge University Press, 2006 edn.), p. 70.

56 Text of Jay Treaty is available at, http://avalon.law.yale.edu/18th_century/jay.asp.

57 Yamada, above note 55, p. 112.

58 Ibid, pp. 112–113; Boed, above note 55, pp. 8–9.

Commissioner Christopher Gore quoted Grotius:

> The necessity must be really extreme to give any right to another's goods; second, it should be requisite that there should not be the like necessity in the owner; third, when absolute necessity urges us to take, we should then take no more that it requires.[59]

Commissioner John Trumbull joined:

> The necessity which can be admitted to supersede all laws and to dissolve the distinctions of property and right must be absolute and irresistible, and we cannot, until all other means of self-preservation shall have been exhausted, justify by the plea of necessity the seizure and application to our own use of that which belongs to others (*emphasis in cited reference*).[60]

The analysis of the concept of necessity in *The Neptune*, when read now, is very detailed. Ago referred to it in his *Addendum – Eighth Report on State Responsibility*[61] and Bin Cheng deduced six rules out of it, rules which have remained common to the decisions of international tribunals of the 20th and 21st centuries: (1) when the existence of a state is in peril, the necessity of self-preservation may be a good defense for certain acts which would otherwise be unlawful; (2) this necessity "supersedes all laws," "dissolves the distinctions of property and rights" and justifies the "seizure and application to our own use of that which belongs to others"; (3) this necessity must be "absolute" in that the very existence of the State is in peril; (4) this necessity must be "irresistible" in that all legitimate means of self-preservation have been exhausted and proved to be of no avail; (5) this necessity must be actual and not merely apprehended; and (6) whether or not the above conditions are fulfilled in a given case, is a proper subject of judicial inquiry. If they are not, the act will be regarded as unlawful and damages will be assessed in accordance with principles governing reparation for unlawful acts.[62]

---

59 Yamada, above note 55, p. 113.
60 Ibid, pp. 113–114; Bücheler, above note 30, p. 282.
61 A/CN.4/318/Add.5–7, above note 15, p. 34.
62 Cheng, above note 55, p. 71.

2.2.2 *The Bering Fur Seals Fisheries Jurisdiction Arbitration (1893)*

In 1893, the US government, in implementing its claim that it could extend the application of its fisheries regulations beyond its territorial waters up to the high seas of the Bering Sea (a claim triggered by excessive hunt of fur seals by Canadian sea hunters on the high seas), seized British fishery ships. The British Government objected to the application of US' regulations on the high seas and that Canadian sealers were operating only on the high seas. To solve the dispute, both governments submitted to arbitration under a February 1892 Treaty.[63] Although the thrust of the issue before the tribunal was the exercise of regulatory power on the high seas, self-defense was raised by the US to justify its action and was given proper attention by the Tribunal. The agent for the US argued:

> While conceding and interested to maintain the general rule of the freedom of the sea, as established by modern usage and *consensus* of opinion, [the US] asserts that … *the right of self-defense on the part of a nation is a perfect and paramount right to which all others are subordinate, and which upon no admitted theory of international law has ever been surrendered; that it extends to all the material interests of a nation important to be defended* … that … wherever an important and just national interest of any description is put in peril for the sake of individual profit by an act upon the high sea, … the right of the individual must give way, and the nation will be entitled to protect itself against the injury, *by whatever force may be reasonably necessary, according to the usages established in analogous cases* … All rights of self-defense are the result of necessity.[64]

When asked by the president of the Tribunal to further describe the rationale for the US' disputed measure, he replied, in a way that, seen today, mixed three justifications in one sentence: "It was simply an exercise of self-defensive power, standing upon the principle of necessity, and limited by the principle of necessity … I refer to the case of the *Caroline* … [and] a celebrated instance of the seizure by Great Britain of the Danish fleet in the harbor of Copenhagen."[65] In response, the agent of the British government responded that in time of peace a state cannot have a right to self-defense or self-preservation in the high seas and that most cases which raised these defenses were related to curbing belligerents in times of genuine emergency. Finally, the Tribunal found that the

63 Fitzmaurice, above note 29; A/CN.4/318/Add.5–7, above note 15, p. 27.

64 A/CN.4/318/Add.5–7, ibid; Yamada, above note 55, pp. 114–115.

65 Yamada, ibid, pp. 115–116.

US could not exercise the right in the high sea and "rejected proposed amendments to the award submitted by the United States member of the Tribunal, the most important of which would have recognized the rights of all nations, under international law, in respect of self-protection and self-defense".[66]

Both in this case and the *Russian Fur Seals Controversy* case (1893) (see Sub-section 2.1.7), the US government invoked necessity and/or self-defense to justify the exercise of its fisheries regulations it the high seas. Ago, who referred to these two cases as part of his drafting process of the Articles on State Responsibility, made an interesting distinction and concluded that based on the draft Articles – which distinguished different forms of defense – the US' measures cannot be considered an act of necessity or self-defense, but one of self-protection.[67]

2.2.3 *Company General of the Orinoco Case (1905)*

In the 1880s Venezuela granted concessions to the French company, Company General of the Orinoco. Much of the area covered by the concession contracts was, however, in areas that Venezuela believed it had sovereignty on but was in fact claimed by Colombia. To avert the threat of severe conflict with Colombia, Venezuela rescinded the contract with the French company and the company's liquidators, through the French government, brought a claim against Venezuela before the France-Venezuela Mixed Claims Commission. When the Commissioners for France and Venezuela found themselves in serious disagreement, the claim was decided by Umpire Frank Plumley.[68] In a careful balance of Venezuela's right to preserve itself against a potential conflict and the right of compensation to the French company, Plumley held:

> As the Government of Venezuela, *whose duty of self-preservation rose superior to any question of contract*, it had the power to abrogate the contract in whole or in part. It exercised that power and cancelled the provision of unrestricted assignment. *It considered the peril superior to the obligation* and substituted therefor the duty of compensation. Had

66 A/CN.4/318/Add.5–7, above note 15, p. 28.

67 Ibid.

68 Shabtai Rosenne, *The International Law Commission's Draft Articles on State Responsibility*, Part 1, Articles 1–35 (Dordrecht: Martinus Nijhoff Publishers, 1991), pp. 356; Yamada, above note 55, p. 116; Bücheler, above note 30, p. 290. Full text of the 31 July 1905 award can be read at *Company General of the Orinoco Case*, United Nations, Reports of International Arbitral Awards (Vol. x, pp. 184–285), available at, http://legal.un.org/riaa/cases/vol_X/184-285.pdf.

> there been no other troublesome question of State entangled with the contracts of the Company General of the Orinoco, it is quite possible that this governmental surgery would not have taken the life of the claimant company. Such entanglements, however, existed (*emphasis added*).[69]

Plumley stated that although the Venezuelan government committed a grave error in signing the contract in full knowledge of its dispute with Columbia,[70] it nevertheless found itself in a situation where it could legitimately take actions for its self-preservation.[71] He finally awarded the company compensation for its loss. Yamada observes that Plumley, who, as in the *Caroline* case, referred to self-preservation in crafting the base of his judgment, indicated that he would have exonerated the Venezuelan government from responsibility had it not contributed to the occurrence of the crisis. The element of contribution would later on be included in the definition of necessity in Article 25 of the ARSIWA.[72]

2.2.4 *French Company of Venezuelan Railroads Case (1905)*

This case is similar to the *Orinoco* case. The Venezuelan government awarded concessions to a company named the *French Company of Venezuelan Railroads* to build railroads. An emergence of revolutionary movements and the outbreak of the civil war, however, made it impossible for the company to continue working and for the government to pay its dues to the company. When the case was brought before the France-Venezuela Mixed Claims Commission, the umpire Plumley exonerated Venezuela from any responsibility because he saw neither fault nor contribution (unlike in the *Orinoco* case) of the government. His reasoning was, however, based on a mix of *force majeure* and self-preservation:[73]

> The claimant company was *compelled by force majeure* to desist from its exploitation in October, 1899; the respondent Government, from the same cause, had been prevented from paying its indebtedness to the claimant company. The umpire finds no purpose or intent on the part of the respondent Government to harm or injure the claimant company in any way or in any degree. Its acts and its neglects were caused and incited by entirely different reasons and motives. Its first duty was to itself. *Its*

69 *Company General of the Orinoco Case,* ibid, p. 280.

70 Ibid, pp. 282–283.

71 Ibid, pp. 281–282.

72 Yamada, above note 55, p. 119.

73 Ibid, pp. 119–120.

> *own preservation was paramount*. Its revenues were properly devoted to that end. The appeal of the company for funds came to an empty treasury or to one only adequate to the demands of the war budget (*emphasis added*).[74]

2.3 Avoiding the Conflation

It has been observed above that at least since the 18th century the concept of necessity was often conflated with other defenses, particularly self-preservation, self-defense and *force majeure* until the ILC's study group on state responsibility distinguished it from the other defenses. The following is a brief summary of the key differences between necessity and those defenses.

As to the difference between necessity and self-preservation, for instance, Agius states that "[s]elf-preservation is a notion that can only by invoked in cases where the very existence of the State is in danger, which is not the case with necessity."[75]

Paddeu distinguishes necessity from distress and *force majeure*. As far as the relationship between necessity and distress is concerned, she states that the two defenses (as they have also been articulated in the ARSIWA) share more similarities than they have differences. Their key difference lies in their respective scopes. Necessity applies to protect the interests of the defending state and other states as well as the international community, while distress is limited only to protecting the interests of an individual state agent, or individuals entrusted to his care.[76]

As to the relationship between necessity and *force majeure* (Articles 23 and 25 of the ARSIWA respectively) Paddeu states that the two defenses "differ in some fundamental aspects" and then discusses three fundamental differences between them. The differences lie in:

---

74 *French Company of Venezuelan Railroads Case*, United Nations, Reports of International Arbitral Awards (Vol. X, pp. 285–355), p. 353 available at, http://legal.un.org/riaa/cases/vol_X/285-355.pdf.

75 Agius, above note 28, p. 12. Agius admitted that 'Necessity has previously been subsumed under the now widely rejected notion of self-preservation, and is closely intertwined with this concept. Still, the link between the modern concept of necessity, as codified by the ILC, and self- preservation, is not indissoluble. Agius, above note 29, pp. 97–98. See also, Agius, above note 28, p. 11.

76 Federica I. Paddeu, 'A Genealogy of *Force Majeure* in International Law', *British Yearbook of International Law*, 82(1): 2012, pp. 461–462.

(a) the cause that triggers the situation of either defense (i.e., the cause of *force majeure* is an irresistible force or unforeseen event, beyond the control of the state, whereas Article 25 makes no such qualifications);
(b) the temporal element of the triggering causes of both defenses (i.e., while *force majeure* is invoked as a reaction against a past or, at the very least, a currently-occurring event and cannot accommodate future events, in the case of necessity the triggering cause is the anticipation of a future harm (imminent peril) caused by a past or a future event); and
(c) the relationship between the defending state and the origins of the cause that triggered the defense (i.e., whereas *force majeure* arises out of a situation outside the control and will of the state and, therefore, nullifies its freedom to comply with its international obligation, necessity involves a deliberate or intentional measure taken by the state to defend an essential interest).

Paddeu next identifies two elements that only these two defenses share as well as a number of other elements that these two defenses share with the other defenses contained in the ARSIWA.[77]

2.4 Lessons Learned from the State and Tribunal Practices

The state and tribunal practices dating back to the 18th century show that the increase in disputes between nation states contributed to the use and development of a number of defenses to otherwise unlawful state acts. These defenses, other than necessity (reason of state), include self-defense, self-protection, self-preservation and *force majeure*. In state and tribunal practices, these various defenses, now generally known as circumstances precluding wrongfulness, were: (a) used mainly to justify politico-military decisions; (b) not, as we understand them today,[78] clearly distinguished from each other; (c) often used interchangeably; (d) generally raised without providing an exhaustive list of the constituent elements of the respective defenses (although the tribunal practices provided better detail than the state practices); and (e) raised

77 Ibid, pp. 462–467.

78 For instance, Articles 20–25 of the ARSIWA which clearly distinguish consent, self-defense, countermeasures, *force majeure*, distress and necessity from each other.

without much clarity, unlike in the developments discussed in Sections 1 and 2, on whether they provided justifications or excuses.

Necessity, like all these defenses, was initially mentioned and discussed under such lack of clarity.[79] Moreover, in these practices, necessity was raised with qualifying terms such as 'urgent', 'extreme', 'paramount', 'impending', 'strongest', 'absolute', 'irresistible', 'overriding' 'supreme', 'overruling' etc. It appears, however, that these qualifying terms were used more for the purpose of emphasis than for the purpose of referring to different classes of necessity with respective rights and responsibilities for the defending state.

The analyses of the tribunals mentioned in Section 2.2 above, were, as we will see in Section 5.4, helpful to the five special rapporteurs of the ARSIWA in refining and developing distinct definitions for the various circumstances precluding responsibility, necessity being one of them.

In a specific relation to this book, it can be observed that the nature of disputes brought before the tribunals mentioned in Section 2.2 above shows that the debates on, and practices of, necessity (self-preservation) which were initially limited to territorial, war and national emergency situations slowly moved into fields of international trade and investment (e.g., the *Fur Seals*, *Orinoco* and *Venezuelan Railroads* cases).

79 In the words of Jennings: "There is probably no branch of international law which is so calculated to encourage the skeptic as that mass of contradictory precedents, dogmatic assertions, and vague principles which are collected under the common head of 'intervention,' and perhaps there is no more potentially dangerous ground of intervention than that which is variously described as 'self-preservation' and 'self-defense.'" Jennings, above note 19, p. 82.

CHAPTER 3

Placing Necessity in the Context of the Relationship between Sovereignty and Treaty Law

Since the Peace of Westphalia, which is identified as the marker for the formation of nation states (and hence the creation of the notion of state sovereignty), a balance has always been sought to be maintained between the sovereignty of nation states and the systems created by the numerous (now thousands of) supra-nation state treaties and other forms of binding agreements between nation states. To this can be added the phenomenon of CIL which, frequently discussed in this book, may have a binding effect even on states which may not have participated in its formation through continuous state practice and, as "holdout" states, oppose the *opinio juris* (i.e., acceptance of the practice as law).[1] The Peace of Westphalia can be also be viewed as the landmark event for the parallel development of the notion of state sovereignty (via the creation of modern states) and the proliferation of treaties as the main source of international law (via the creation of modern states with the power to conclude treaties). This parallel development of state sovereignty and international law naturally demands maintaining the balance between the powers exercised by states and the system created by the agreement of states (mainly treaties and CIL). It is within this context that the exercise of powers of necessity by states, as an exception to their obligations under treaties and CIL should be viewed.

3.1 How the Exercise of Powers of Necessity Evolved since the Peace of Westphalia

It was mentioned in Section 1.3 that the Peace of Westphalia gave birth to the notion of *raison d'état* (reason of state), i.e., that the well-being and stability of the state takes precedence over all other interests and that the government should take all measures towards securing it. In the nearly three centuries following the Peace of Westphalia the creation of nation states continued with the constant battles for them to assert and consolidate their territories and

1 John H. Jackson, *Sovereignty, the WTO and Changing Fundamentals of International Law* (Cambridge: Cambridge University Press, 2006), pp. 58–59.

 | DOI:10.1163/9789004700000_005

their subjects. It may be observed that despite the growth of international law and proliferation of treaties as main components of international law in these three centuries, states saw no need to consider powers of necessity as an exception to their obligations under international law (treaties); they viewed necessity powers simply and extension or manifestation of state authority. This is what Prof. Jackson calls "traditional Westphalian sovereignty",[2] and in another publication, the "antiquated version of sovereignty".[3]

As mentioned in Sub-section 1.1.3, however, the growing influence, since the early 20th century, of positivism as the foundation of international law and the series of abuses perpetrated throughout the 19th century by invocation of the right of self-preservation (or necessity), demanded a natural shift on how the concept of necessity should be viewed in the context of the *then dichotomy* of state sovereignty and international law obligations. As international law – hitherto viewed within the confines of traditional state sovereignty as a mere extension of the exercise of state powers – started to be considered in the early 20th century as an 'autonomous' system with direct impact on the exercise of domestic powers by sovereign states, in the context of treaty law necessity started to be viewed not as an inherent exercise of state sovereignty, but as an exception to the obligations under treaties. The hitherto undivided, Westphalian state authority had to therefore be 'divided' into authority that remained under the will and dominion of states (such as the choice of states with which to establish diplomatic relations, the decision to join or withdraw from a treaty etc., the exercise of emergency or national security measures) and an authority to be exercised only if recognized and allowed under relevant treaties occur. The exercise of powers of necessity became one of the latter authorities of states. This meant that in the second-half of the 20th century, states parties to treaties should primarily carryout their obligations under the treaties; they could take measures of their own choice contrary to their obligations under the treaties only if the sole choice for them to preserve essential state values (which must also be recognized by the treaties) is to act inconsistency with their treaty obligations, i.e., necessity measures. The exercise of emergency and national security measures, as will be detailed in Chapter 8, however, remained mainly within the preserve of state authority (sovereignty), i.e., states could almost always invoke emergency and national security situations if they acted contrary to their treaty obligations.

---

2 Ibid, pp. 62 *et seq*.

3 John H. Jackson, 'Sovereignty: Outdated Concept or New Approaches', in Wenhua Shan *et al.* (eds.), *Redefining Sovereignty in International Economic Law* (Oxford and Portland: Hart Publishing, 2008), p. 11.

As Parts 3 will show in further detail, however, we can say we are now in the third stage of the concept of necessity in international law as seen in the context of the sovereignty-treaty obligation *interface* (as opposed to the earlier view as a *dichotomy*). We now have reached, as a result of the very active progress of international law and its institutions as well as the voluminous body of jurisprudence[4] in multiple fields of international law, a stage where, even if necessity is essentially a 'reserve' of state authority, its exercise is also being limited or monitored by 'outside' institution (i.e., the various dispute settlement organs which examine whether the measures taken as 'necessary' by a state party are valid under the relevant treaty or CIL). Jackson calls this phase the era of "sovereignty-modern". As will be discussed in detail in Section 8.3, even the exercise of necessary security exceptions (at least in WTO law) is not entirely left to the mere invocation of the state; there are some steps in the proves of the invocation of necessary security exceptions that will be scrutinized by the dispute settlement organs. Jackson succinctly describes this era of sovereignty-modern as: "most (but not all) of the time that 'sovereignty' is used in current policy debates, it actually refers to questions about the allocation of power; normally 'government legal decision-making power."[5]

IIAS (bilateral or otherwise) are a good example of the sovereignty-limiting power of treaties. Karl, who begins his argument with the idea that "[a]ny treaty limits the sovereignty of the contracting parties, and IIAS are no exception to this rule",[6] tries to show the wide-ranging limiting impact that the proliferation of IIAS and their numerous obligations have on parties to them. he continues that since IIAS cover "every kind of asset",[7] the extensive obligations that come with them affect numerous policy areas;[8] hence, "[o]bviously, the more IIAS a country concludes, the greater the number of states to which the sovereignty constraints apply."[9] One can imagine Karl's argument in light of the impact of the sheer size of BITS. The UN Conference on Trade and Development which keeps track of BITS counted, as at December 2023, 2,831 BITS out of which

4 For instance, Jakson refers to "the now extraordinarily elaborate jurisprudence of the WTO" in showing the "many of the tensions between internationalism and national government desires to govern and deliver to their democratic constituencies". Jackson, above note 1, p. 60.

5 Jackson, above note 3. See also, ibid, p. 72.

6 Joachim Karl, 'International Investment Arbitration: A Threat to State Sovereignty?' in Shan *et al.*, above note 3, p. 230.

7 Ibid.

8 Ibid, pp. 231–232.

9 Ibid, p. 231.

2,200 are in force.[10] Almost all BITs have provisions that keep limits on the exercise of necessity/security powers by the host states, powers which have been scrupulously examined, interpreted and their limitations determined by dispute settlement organs (see, Section 5.5). So why do states enter into IIAs if the latter have such constraining effect on their sovereignty? Karl responds as follows:

> It should not be forgotten that IIAs leave considerable regulatory freedom for contracting parties. The majority of them leave it up to the host countries to decide whether they want to admit foreign investment or not. With regard to the protection of established investment, the IIAs are confined to a relatively small – albeit important – number of core obligations. Countries concluding IIAs consider that these limitations on sovereignty are more than compensated by the positive impact, which these treaties may have on improving the investment climate and on making countries more attractive to foreign investors. Another explanation could be that many countries have not (yet) been involved in investment disputes, and have therefore not (yet) experienced the effects of the sovereignty restraints.[11]

3.2 Consent as the Binding Element in the Sovereignty-Treaty Obligation Interface

Karl's quoted note above embodies a crucial elaboration of why states allowed increased limitation of their sovereignty by the system and institutions of international law: consent. As modern states saw the increased benefits of international law, they consented to 'sharing' their traditional authority, even the authority to finally determine whether a certain measure is 'necessary' to preserve an important social value, with the system and institutions of international law. One cannot, therefore, see international law and as having 'eroded' state sovereignty;[12] there is no need to consider the *interface* between state sovereignty and the international law system as a "dilemma of absolute

10 UNCTAD, *International Investment Agreements Navigator*, available at, https://investmentpolicy.unctad.org/international-investment-agreements.

11 Karl, above note 6, p. 232.

12 Martin Loughlin, 'The Erosion of Sovereignty', *Netherlands Journal of Legal Philosophy*, 45(2): 2016, pp. 57–81.

state sovereignty versus the absolute validity of international law"[13] because whatever these two systems have to 'sacrifice' to exist is the result of one common source: consent of states. The paramount role played by states (and their sovereignty) cannot, accordingly, be undermined as Heller put it as follows:

> International law exists only as long as there are at least two universal and effective territorial decision-making units. The sovereign state is a necessary part of juristic thought but international law is not. The 'world state' and the state that isolates itself behind a Chinese wall would exist as sovereign decision-making units even without international law; international law without sovereign states, however, is a conceptual impossibility. A universal-planetary, effective decision-making unit would change any international law into state law – and would be sovereign in the most eminent sense. The following will show that the sovereignty of the state is not an obstacle to international law, but an essential requirement for it.[14]

Jackson adds that the system of balance between state sovereignty and treaty obligations are based on consent, although it is true that dispute settlement organs created by the treaties may, in the process of settling disputes by interpreting treaty terms, often impose on state-parties treaty obligations in a way not originally understood by the states:[15]

> one can easily see the logical connection between the sovereignty concepts and the very foundations and sources of international law. If sovereignty implies that there is 'no higher power' than the nation-state, then it is argued that no international law norm is valid when applied to such state unless that state has somehow 'consented' to the norm. Of course, treaties (or 'conventions') almost always imply, in a broader sense, satisfactory consent of the nation-states which accepted the treaty. However, important questions are raised in connection with many treaty details, such as (for example) when a treaty-based international institution sees

13 Hermann Heller, *Sovereignty: A Contribution to the Theory of Public and International Law* (edited and introduced by David Dyzenhaus and translated by Belinda Cooper) (Oxford: Oxford University Press, 2019), p. 141.

14 Ibid, p. 140.

15 The case of the persistent objection of the US government, *inter alia*, against some interpretive practices of the WTO Appellate Body, objections which largely contributed to the demise of the Appellate Body is, as briefly raised in Section 11.2, a relevant example.

> its practice and 'jurisprudence' evolve over time and purports to obligate the nation members even when they opposed such evolution.[16]

It may be argued therefore that in the three stages of development mentioned above (the Westphalian era, the intermediate era between the 1920s and the proliferation of treaties and the current era) the nature of the relationship between state sovereignty and the system of international law progressed from a *dichotomy* to a *connection* to an *interface*. We are at an era where these two systems can (and should) be viewed as operating in one sphere of co-existence. Relevant to this book, the concept of necessity in international law cannot (should not) be understood as a 'vestige' of sovereignty. The WTO trading system and, more generally, the other treaty systems and CIL as discussed in this book should not be 'divided' into spheres where states divide their sovereignty between the powers that they wish to preserve for themselves (such as necessity and Security Exceptions) and those that they agree to cede for purpose of establishing a system of international law (for instance treaties). State sovereignty and treaty must be viewed as one package where states create a space for operation of their 'individual' (i.e., national) and 'group' (treaty members') interests through amalgamation of their state sovereignty with the system they create through treaties or CIL. In this regard, the rule-exception scenario, discussed throughout this book to explain the concept of necessity, should be not viewed in terms of what is left for the powers of states and what they give to the treaty/CIL system, but simply as an arrangement where space is given for the 'community' of treaty partners (the rules) and the individual state (the exceptions). In other words, seeing this from the angle of the treaty community, carrying out state obligations is the rule and the exercise of state sovereignty is the exception; reversely, looking at it from the angle of the states, the exercise of state sovereignty is the rule and carrying out treaty obligation is the exception. The factor that makes the operation of this interface possible is the consent of states.

3.3 Lessons from the History, Practices and Presentation of Necessity since the 1st Millennium BC

By way of concluding Part 1, therefore, a nearly three-thousand-year history of the development and gradual refinement of the concept of necessity has

16 Jackson, above note 3, p. 58.

been summarized starting from the era of King Solomon. However, some of the issues in, or elements of, the concept have remained constant throughout this continuum of three millennia. These include, particularly, the justification/excuse divide, the obligation to seek alternatives, balancing between the protected and harmed interests as well as compensating the party whose interests have been harmed by the measure at hand. Religious pioneers (Moses, Jesus, Mohammed, etc.), philosophers and state leaders invoked divine, natural, social or political reasons to accept the taking of 'necessity' measures.

The Peace of Westphalia and its consequent notion of reason of state (self-preservation) expanded the application of necessity from domestic relations to the sphere of international relations. With this came the debates on the limitations of the defense measures taken by states and the conflation – continuing at least until the mid-20th century – of the concept of necessity with other defenses especially *force majeure*, self-defense and self-preservation.[17]

However, as the subsequent chapters (especially Chapters 4–6) will show, owing mainly to the works of the ILC study group on state responsibility, necessity can now be distinguished from other defenses, although all these defenses including necessity share a number of similar elements. Not only has necessity been distinguished from other defenses (particularly the two defenses with

17 Paddeu has provided us with an interesting narration of the development of the historically inter-linked concepts of self-preservation, self-defense and necessity. Federica Paddeu, *Justification and Excuse in International Law: Concept and Theory of General Defenses* (Cambridge: Cambridge University Press, 2018), pp. 345–363. Referring to scholarly writings and disputes of the 19th century (covered in detail in Part 1) which dwelt on these three concepts, often by apparently conflating them, Paddeu concluded (p. 363):

> There seems to [or should] have been, at the very least, some basic distinctions between these notions [in the 19th century]:
>
> – *Necessity*: When used in connection with the rights of self-preservation and self-defense [especially in disputes such as *the Caroline* where the terms 'the necessity of self-preservation and self-defense' or 'the necessity of self-defense' were used], the term 'necessity' referred to the factual condition for the exercise of those rights. 'Whenever the necessity arises, the right [to self-defense] arises', would claim the US before the Tribunal in *Fur Seals* [1893].
>
> – *Right of self-preservation*: It was a very broad right concerning the protection of the continued existence of the state as a political entity as well as its self-perfection having internal and external manifestations, entitling the state to precautionary and reactive measures, which could be both forcible and non-forcible.
>
> – *Right of self-defense*: It is a corollary of the right of self-preservation, usually concerned solely with external and forcible aspects of self-preservation, though sufficiently broad to include both precautionary and reactive measures.

which it has been confused – *force majeure* and self-preservation), but also the other defenses have been clearly distinguished from each other.[18]

It has also been mentioned that state and tribunal practices from the 18th century until the 1930s, extended the debates on, and application of, necessity to the fields of international trade and investment. Such extension, it can be concluded, was, however, made without making any distinction on necessity as it applies to different areas such as national security and war *vs* international investment and trade. For the early writers and in the later state/tribunal practices, the concept of necessity and its elements were uniformly understood or applied in all these areas whether domestic or international. This becomes interesting in light of this book which identifies the existence of *different* concepts of necessity in different fields of international law, i.e., as it has developed in WTO law differently from other key fields of international law especially in the law of responsibility as codified in the ARSIWA.

Part 1 has shown that while necessity was considered an exception to obligations in some fields, it was considered part of the general rules in other fields. For instance, early Roman law considered necessity as an exception, the Canonists later placed it as a general rule and the glossators subsequently reduced it to specific exceptions.

Finally, the place of the concept of necessity in the interface between state sovereignty and obligations emanating from international law was discussed to show that the consent of states is at the epicenter of this interface and that there is no contradiction of the exercise of state sovereignty and meeting of obligations under international law, particularly those based on treaties and CIL.

The narration of the development of the concept of necessity (1st millennium BC up to the 19th century) has been combined in Part 1 with state and tribunal practices up to the 1930s because, for the purposes of this book: (a) by the 1930s (before the outbreak of the Second World War) necessity was, after a long history, beginning to be distinguished from the other defenses; and (b) it was after the Second World War (after the end of the 1930s) that necessity as it specifically, and separately, applied to international trade (the discussions

18 A more recent and comprehensive read in this regard is Federica Paddeu, *Justification and Excuse in International Law: Concept and Theory of General Defenses* (Cambridge: Cambridge University Press, 2018). See also, Lorand Bartels and Federica Paddeu (eds.), *Exceptions in International Law* (Oxford: Oxford University Press, 2020); Phoebe N. Okowa, 'Defenses in the Jurisprudence of International Tribunals', in Guy S. Goodwin-Gill and Stefan Talmon (eds.), *The Reality of International Law: Essays in Honour of Ian Brownlie* (Oxford and New York: Clarendon Press, 1999), pp. 389–411.

on the GATT) and other fields of PIL (use of force under the UN Charter, state responsibility etc.) started to be regulated. Part 2 (particularly Chapter 5) will discuss necessity as it applies to other fields of international law and Part 3 (particularly Chapters 8 and 9) will discuss necessity as it applies to international trade, particularly WTO law.

This book mainly focuses on seeking interaction between the concepts of necessity in WTO and other key fields of international law especially the law of state responsibility as codified in the ARSIWA. It will be observed that concepts of necessity in WTO law and the other fields of international law have neither significantly departed from nor have added many novel elements to the definitions and interpretations of the concept as refined by philosophers and state practices since the Roman era. Key issues (elements) of the concept of necessity such as: (a) the existence of a grave and imminent evil; (b) the justification/excuse divide; (c) the obligation to seek otherwise lawful alternative measures; (d) assessing and weighing the 'saved interest' *vis-à-vis* the 'harmed interest'; (d) compensating persons/states whose interests have been harmed and; (e) the discretion in invoking, and selecting measures for, a state of necessity had been debated since the early days and have not been significantly modified in WTO law or in other fields of international law. Since WTO law is part of PIL, it becomes logical to first begin the synthesis by first looking into the concept of necessity in different fields of international law (Part 2) and then look into the peculiarities of the concept of necessity in WTO (Part 3). With these two categories of the concept of necessity laid out in Parts 2 and 3, Part 4 will then present the exercise of interoperability between the concepts of necessity in WTO and other key fields of international law especially the law of state responsibility as codified in the ARSIWA.

PART 2

The Concept of Necessity in International Law

CHAPTER 4

Preliminary Issues

Part 1 presented the development of the concept of necessity from historical, philosophical as well as intra/inter-state practice viewpoints. The narration in Part 1 highlighted how early and medieval thinkers understood necessity from natural, social, political and/or divine underpinnings in both private and public law spheres. The emergence of sovereign states and the Westphalian doctrine of sovereignty gave birth to the doctrine of *raison d'état* and related necessity to the concepts of self-preservation (self-help), self-defense, self-protection and *force majeure*. Relevant state and tribunal practices where necessity was invoked were also briefly presented covering the time span between the mid-18th century and the 1930s. It was observed that by the 1930s most elements of necessity were identified and that the defense of necessity, hitherto limited to national security, emergency and public order, started to be used in international trade and investment disputes. It was also noted that the consent of nation states remained a constant as powers reserved to states under traditional (Westphalian) sovereignty started to be shared with the supra-national, treaty-based systems that states established for their progress and common purposes.

Part 2 picks up from the narration in Part 1 and focuses on the development of the concept of necessity in the second-half of the 20th century which witnessed proliferation of the different fields of international law. This book intends to study the concept of necessity in different fields of international law, viz PIL, GIL and CIL,[1] and see if a general pattern can be identified in these concepts. It will be shown that one particular field of PIL, WTO law, has developed a different concept of necessity from that extant in a number of fields of international law, most of which are influenced by the concept of necessity in

1 For definition of international law, PIL, GIL and WTO law as used in this book, see, Malcolm N. Shaw, *International Law* (6th ed.) (Cambridge: Cambridge University Press, 2008), pp. 1–2; Sir Robert Y. Jennings, 'International Law', in Rudolf Burnhardt (ed.), *Encyclopedia of Public International Law* (Vol. 7) (Amsterdam, New York and Oxford: Elsevier Science Publishers, 1984), pp. 278–297; Donald McRae, 'International Economic Law and Public International Law: The Past and the Future', *Journal of International Economic Law*, 17(3): 2014, pp. 627–638; Joost Pauwelyn, 'The Role of Public International law in the WTO: How Far Can We Go?' *American Journal of International Law*, 95(3): 2001, p. 536. For an explanation of how these and related terms such as 'fields of international law' and 'fields of PIL' have been used in this book, see the sub-heading of the introduction to this book entitled "key terminologies".

 DOI:10.1163/9789004700000_006

CIL, as codified in the ARSIWA. Thus, a comparison needs to be made between the concept of necessity as contained and interpreted in the various legal texts of the WTO Agreement with the concept of necessity as contained and interpreted (applied) in the other fields of international law. Any similarity and difference in content and interpretation of these two types of the concept of necessity demands not only an inquiry as to why there is, or should be, such difference, but also examining whether there is a possibility for these concepts to learn from, i.e., interact with, each other. This exercise will be conducted in depth in Part 4. Thus, the first step to conduct the exercise of interoperability is to study the concept of necessity in different fields of international law – Part 2 (Chapters 4–6) does this – and then move to the more specific WTO law in Part 3 (Chapters 7–9). Chapter 4 will briefly introduce necessity as it exists in international law. It will first show that necessity is widely recognized in international law and then discuss some issues related to the concept of necessity in international law.

4.1 Necessity: A Widely Represented Concept in International Law

Sloane lists different instances where necessity has been raised by states in defense of their actions or analyzed by tribunals:

(a) humanitarian intervention or responsibility to protect in violation of an orthodox reading of the UN Charter;
(b) violation of the *jus ad bellum* by Israel's constructing a security barrier or wall in the West Bank;
(c) a hypothetical breach of the *jus in bello* by the threat or use of nuclear weapons in what the ICJ characterized as "an extreme circumstance of self-defense, in which the very survival of a state would be at stake";
(d) breaches of the arbitral award that settled the *Rainbow Warrior* affair;
(e) international trade disputes;
(f) seizure of foreign vessels in violation of the UNCLOS;
(g) a conceptual justification for the doctrine of preventive war;
(h) closing borders to refugees in circumstances that might violate the customary principle of *non-refoulement*; and

(i) suggestions by European states that they might justifiably suspend the Schengen regime because of the influx of refugees from Libya, Tunisia, and elsewhere following the Arab Spring.[2]

The 41st volume of the *Netherlands Yearbook of International Law* (2010) was dedicated to analyzing the doctrine and practices of necessity across international law. It covered such fields of international law as the law of the use of force, the law of armed conflict and ICL, state responsibility, human rights, IEL, investment arbitration, IEnL and the law of the EU. Experts in these fields of international law were asked to reflect on four questions related to the concept of necessity. One of the four questions was whether there exists any cross-reference between different fields of international law in which the concept of necessity is recognized. The conclusion of the study was that:

> International decisions related to measures adopted on grounds of necessity remain rather sparse and in the last few years concerned essentially foreign investment disputes. These decisions contain a significant amount of cross-references to the case law of the International Court of Justice (*Nicaragua, Oil Platforms* and *Gabčíkovo-Nagymaros Project*) and more recently to cases before WTO panels and the WTO Appellate Body.[3]

The conclusion indicates two facts. Firstly, the concept of necessity exists in many fields of international law. Secondly, the concept of necessity in these fields has been rather sparse as a result of their interpretation by international tribunals. This could be because, as in the words of Ohlin and May, "necessity means different things in different contexts [i.e., fields of international law]" and that "[n]ecessity is not a one-size-fits-all concept"[4] or, as in the words of Sloane, "[t]he meaning of necessity, like many legal terms of art, differs 'greatly in color and content according to the circumstances and the time in which it is used'".[5]

---

2 Robert D. Sloane, 'On the Use and Abuse of Necessity in the Law of State Responsibility', *American Journal of International Law*, 106(3): 2012, pp. 447–448.

3 Tarcisio Gazzini, Wouter G. Werner and Ige F. Dekker, 'Necessity across International Law: An Introduction', in Ige F. Dekker and E. Hey (eds.), *Netherlands Yearbook of International Law: Necessity across International Law*, Vol. 41 (The Hague: T.M.C. Asser Press, 2010), p. 8.

4 Jens David Ohlin and Larry May, *Necessity in International Law* (New York: Oxford University Press, 2016), pp. 121, 273.

5 Sloane, above note 2, p. 448.

The concept of necessity in the fields of international law discussed in Chapter 5 has a common denominator, i.e., it allows states to breach their international obligations should imminent and perilous circumstances that endanger their essential interests occur and they can only be removed by breach of the obligations.[6] Despite such commonality, basic differences have been discerned on how these fields of international law describe necessity including the purpose of necessity in the respective fields.[7] This does not mean, however, that there is no interoperability on the interpretation of necessity across these various fields of international law. Gazzini *et al.* observed that:

> The concept of necessity … differs in [different branches of international law] in some important respects. *Each sub-regime has evolved its own principles, norms and rules and developed its own management and enforcement mechanisms. The general picture is thus one of fragmentation in the sense of a varied set of legal regimes of necessity that are connected by the fact that they are all part of the international legal system but are different regarding their substantive and institutional content as well as their operation in practice …*
>
> However, it seems that in some instances judicial bodies are willing to mitigate these differences in that *they are broadening their interpretive guidelines by looking at the interpretation of the requirements of necessity given in the case law of other areas of international law* (*emphasis added*).[8]

6 Attila Tanzi, 'Necessity, State of', in Rüdiger Wolfrum (Gen. ed.), *Max Planck Encyclopedia of International Law* (Oxford: Oxford University Press, 2013), pp. 583–588.

7 Gazzini *et al.*, for example, state that: "Necessity is [accepted] as a basic legal concept in all the covered areas – conflict and security law, humanitarian law, human rights law, economic law, investment law, environmental law, and European law. Its main function is that it regulates claims that a situation is beyond the boundaries of the normal operation of the legal regime concerned. In the areas of law of collective security and the law of armed conflict, this function is *the* rational – or at least one of the main sources – of the legal sub-regime as such. In other words, the regulation of the use of armed force, whether in the context of the *jus ad bellum* or the *jus in bello*, is fundamentally governed by the concept of (military) necessity and by that giving these regimes their very special character. In all other areas necessity only functions as a possible ground for the justification [or excuse] of measures that are normally unlawful within the legal sub-regime". Gazzini *et al.*, above note 3, p. 9.

8 Ibid. For a good summary of the history and current jurisprudence on necessity in international law, see, Alexander J. Poblador, 'The Defense of Necessity in International Law', *Philippine Law Journal*, 57(3): 1982, pp. 332–370.

4.2 Issues on the Concept of Necessity in International Law

A number of points have been raised in discussing necessity across the different fields of international law. Sub-sections 4.2.1–4.2.5 will briefly present the main points.

4.2.1 *Does Necessity Exist in International Law?*

For a long time, there have been debates on the existence and nature of necessity defense in international law stemming, as narrated in Part 1, mainly from the historical link that necessity has had with self-help (self-preservation) and self-defense. Some writers expressed their reluctance in recognizing the existence of necessity. Crawford, for instance, observed that:

> It has been doubted whether necessity exists as an omnibus category, and in any event its availability as a defense is circumscribed by rigorous conditions. While necessity has been argued before a number of tribunals in a diversity of situations, its recognition as a possibility is usually followed by a denial of its applicability.[9]

De Aréchaga, who investigated the history of invocations of necessity, argued that such invocations actually pointed at self-defense or another form of defense in international law, hence his doubt of the existence of necessity.[10]

---

9 James Crawford, *Brownlie's Principles of Public International Law* (8th ed.) (Oxford: Oxford University Press, 2012), p. 546. Okowa, writing in 1999, also stated that "[m]any present-day writers are opposed to the existence of any general defense of necessity, arguing not only that it is open to the risk of abuse, but also that it is incompatible with the objective character of international law." Phoebe N. Okowa, 'Defenses in the Jurisprudence of International Tribunals', in Guy S. Goodwin-Gill and Stefan Talmon (eds.), *The Reality of International Law: Essays in Honour of Ian Brownlie* (Oxford and New York: Clarendon Press, 1999), p. 398. As Chapter 6 as well as Parts 3 and 4 will show, it appears that arguing in support of this stance in 2024 would be difficult because of the large number of disputes that involved interpreting the plea of necessity by the adjudicators of the WTO and other international tribunals.

10 He states: "The enumeration of situations where the doctrine of necessity has been invoked forms either a catalogue of serious breaches of international law or of cases susceptible of being explained without an appeal to the doctrine of necessity. Thus, cases invoked to illustrate the doctrine of necessity are sometimes really based on the concept of self-defense, the action taken being a reply to an unlawful act and directed not against innocent third parties but against those who committed or supported that act. On the basis of such a contradictory and controversial practice of states, the partisans of this doctrine derive the customary rule from the tenuous fact that although the interested states have in every instance opposed the theory of necessity, they have always done so *in concreto*

Agius reasons that the reluctance to recognize necessity in international law emanates from the concern that recognition of necessity, which for a long time did not fully distinguish itself from self-preservation or self-defense, would "entail that other states owed the fulfilment of an obligation to the state invoking that right". She adds that subjecting the legitimate interests of states to the overriding interests of the state invoking necessity, especially when the plea of necessity is not related to an unlawful behavior on the part of the former (as is the case with self-preservation or self-defense), may not be acceptable.[11]

Other writers dissociate necessity from self-preservation. True to the history of the development of the concept of self-preservation, necessity and self-defense, Special Rapporteur of the ILC Roberto Ago was emphatic in his view that "the concepts of self-preservation and state of necessity are in no way identical, nor are they indissolubly linked in the sense that one is merely the basis and justification of the other."[12] In a similar fashion, other writers have regarded necessity as a "unique type of self-defense" when danger to a state presents itself not through the use of armed force, but through, for instance, neglect in relation to shared resources, natural disasters etc.[13]

Others scholars have observed a paradigmatic shift in international law regarding [military] necessity (along with self-preservation and self-defense) towards constitutional models which seek to incorporate emergency powers into the legal system and regulate those powers within a legal framework.[14]

A final group of authors have been willing to recognize that some element of a right for states to ignore international obligations if their vital interests

---

but never *in abstracto* ...". Eduardo Jiménez de Aréchaga, 'International Responsibility', in Max Sørensen (ed.), *Manual of Public International Law* (London: Macmillan, 1968), p. 542.

11 Maria Agius, 'The Invocation of Necessity in International Law', *Netherlands International Law Review*, 56(2): 2009, p. 98.

12 Roberto Ago, 'The Internationally Wrongful Act of the State, Source of International Responsibility', *Eighth Report on State Responsibility*, Addendum (1980), ILC, 32nd sess., UN Doc. A/CN.4/318/Add.5–7, p. 8, para. 8. For a detailed story of the separate evolution of the different types of defenses in international law, see, Federica Paddeu, *Justification and Excuse in International Law: Concept and Theory of General Defenses* (Cambridge: Cambridge University Press, 2018). See also, Lorand Bartels and Federica Paddeu (eds.), *Exceptions in International Law* (Oxford: Oxford University Press, 2020); Phoebe N. Okowa, 'Defenses in the Jurisprudence of International Tribunals', in Guy S. Goodwin-Gill and Stefan Talmon (eds.), *The Reality of International Law: Essays in Honour of Ian Brownlie* (Oxford and New York: Clarendon Press, 1999), pp. 389–411.

13 Maria Agius, *The Invocation of Necessity in International Law*, available at, https://www.uppsalajuristernasalumnistiftelse.se/wp-content/uploads/2014/11/Maria-Agius.pdf, p. 9.

14 Oren Gross and Fionnuala Ni Aolain, 'Emergency, War and International Law – Another Perspective', *Nordic Journal of International Law*, 70(1): 2001, p. 31.

are at stake seems to have endured in practice.[15] In reference to necessity and distress, both of which share similarities in their respective definitions under the ARSIWA, Crawford and Olleson, for example, argued that "[A] State is not required to sacrifice human life or to suffer inordinate damage to its interests in order to fulfil its international obligations."[16]

As will be detailed in Chapter 6, the contemporary view of necessity in international law began with the *Rainbow Warrior* case (1990). The Arbitral Tribunal in that case, after analyzing the distinctions among the pleas of distress, *force majeure* and state of necessity as defined by the ILC, concluded that the existence of a general defense of necessity as then contained in the draft ARSIWA was "still controversial" and did not in fact reflect a rule of CIL.[17] Only seven years later did, the ICJ, in the *Gabčíkovo-Nagymaros Project* dispute, by referring to Article 33 of the draft ARSIWA, hold to the contrary that the defense of necessity was in fact recognized by CIL and was available to states to evade international responsibility for wrongful acts.[18] The approval of the draft ARSIWA by the UN General Assembly emboldened the ICJ to once again confirm the separate existence of the necessity defense in the *Construction of a Wall* case (2004)[19] after which "there seems to be a reasonable basis for the conclusion that the defense of necessity today is a valid and accepted plea [in international law]".[20]

4.2.2 *Is Necessity a Justification, an Excuse or an Exception in International Law?*

Ohlin and May introduce their book *Necessity in International Law* with the following opening statements: "Necessity is quite possibly the most powerful concept in the law. It has the almost mystical power to transform what would otherwise be illegal or immoral into a *justified* or *excused* act, all because the action was 'necessary' (*emphasis added*)."[21] The debate on whether the defense of necessity is a justification or an excuse has long occupied domestic law

15 Agius, above note 11.

16 James Crawford and Simon Olleson, 'The Nature and Forms of International Responsibility', in Malcom D. Evans (ed.), *International Law* (3rd ed.) (Oxford: Oxford University Press, 2003), p. 464.

17 *Rainbow Warrior* case (*New Zealand v. France*) (1990), 20 *RIAA*, Vol. XX, p. 254, para. 78.

18 *Case Concerning the Gabčíkovo-Nagymaros Project* (*Hungary v. Slovakia*), Judgment, 25 September 1997, ICJ Rep. 1997, p. 40, para. 51.

19 *Legal Consequences of the Construction of a Wall in the Occupied Palestinian Territory*, Advisory Opinion, 9 July 2004, ICJ Rep. 2004, pp. 194–195, para. 140.

20 Agius, above note 11, p. 99.

21 Ohlin and May, above note 4, p. 1.

scholarship[22] and has been transplanted into debates in international law. Referring to J. L. Austin, Johnstone presents a simplified definition for the two concepts as follows:

> 'In the one defense [justification], briefly, we accept responsibility but deny that [it] was bad; in the other, [excuse], we admit that it was bad but don't accept full, or even any, responsibility'. ... In other words, a claim of justification concedes that the elements of the offense for which necessity is invoked are satisfied, but that the act is not wrongful; a claim of excuse concedes that the act is wrongful, but seeks to avoid the attribution of the act to the actor.[23]

Thus, whereas justification removes the unlawfulness of an otherwise unlawful act, excuse simply means that a wrongful act shall not be punished.[24] In the sphere of CIL, there has been a debate on whether necessity (Article 25), as included in the list of six CPW (Articles 20–25)[25] in the 2001 ARSIWA, is a justification or an excuse when a state takes the action allowed in Article 25. It has been noted that throughout the eras of the ILC special rapporteurs on state responsibility (Francisco V. Garcià Amador (1956–1961), Roberto Ago (1969–1972, 1976–1980), Willem Riphagen (1980–1986), Gaetano Arangio-Ruiz (1988–1995) and James Crawford (1997–2001)), the understanding on necessity shifted from an unclear stand, toward a stand that edges on identifying necessity as justification and finally toward a stand that is close to recognizing necessity as an excuse.[26] There are scholars who have been willing to go

22 Ian Johnstone, 'The Plea of Necessity in International Legal Discourse: Humanitarian Intervention and Counter-Terrorism', *Columbia Journal of Transnational Law*, 43(2): 2002, p. 349.

23 Ibid, p. 350.

24 Marcelo G. Cohen, 'The Notion of "state survival" in International Law', in Laurence Boisson de Chazournes and Philippe Sands (eds.), *International Law, the International Court of Justice and Nuclear Weapons* (Cambridge: Cambridge University Press, 1999), p. 309; Albin Eser, 'Justification and Excuse', *American Journal of Comparative Law*, 24(4): 1976, pp. 621–637.

25 They are: consent (Article 20); self-defense (Article 21); countermeasures (Article 22); *force majeure* (Article 23); distress (Article 24); and necessity (Article 25).

26 For a brief summary, see, Andreas Laursen, 'The Use of Force and (the State of) Necessity', *Vanderbilt Journal of Transnational Law*, 37(2): 2004, pp. 490–494. See also, Sloane, above note 2, pp. 482–484. In its ruling in *CMS Gas Transmission Company v. Argentina* (ICSID Case No ARB/01/8) (Annulment Proceeding), 25 September 2007 ("*CMS Annulment*"), the annulment *ad hoc* committee, where James Crawford was a third Member, stated that (in para. 129) "Article 25 *is an excuse* which is only relevant once it has been decided that there has otherwise been a breach of those substantive obligations (*emphasis added*)."

beyond the 'intentionally' cloudy wording of the ARSIWA and its commentary and conclude that necessity as presented in the ARSIWA is clearly an excuse, not a justification, and that it is raised as an excuse, not as a right.[27] Others believe that the CPW are justifications, not excuses.[28]

A different form for necessity is its use as an exception. Exception in this case allows the use of necessity, unlike in the case of justification or excuse, only against those provisions of a legal instrument that allow necessity to be invoked under certain circumstances. Necessity as an exception, therefore, has a narrower scope than in the case of justification or excuse. We will see in Section 5.2, for instance, that necessity is invoked only as an exception to certain specified rules of IHL.

Thus, it can be concluded that there is no consensus in international law scholarship on whether necessity, at least as contained in the ARSIWA, is a justification or an excuse.

4.2.3 *Form of Its Presentation*

Despite the general understanding on the substance of necessity, the text, context and/or object/purpose of necessity as it is scattered throughout various fields of international law has possibly resulted in different presentations of the concept. Ohlin and May studied these 'kinds' or 'uses' of necessity and came up with three such 'uses' (which they called exception, license and constraint) with the caution that necessity is a cluster concept and that sometimes the different uses may overlap with one another.[29]

Firstly, necessity can take the form of an exception to an otherwise binding obligation in the sense that if it is necessary for one to act, for example to avoid one's death, one would be entitled to use means that would not be normally permissible. Secondly, necessity may take the form of a license to act in certain ways once it is shown that the action is part of a role and to satisfy this role it becomes necessary for one to act in this way. Thirdly, necessity can take the form of a constraint that blocks a form of activity due to the lack of necessity of the activity sought to be engaged in.[30]

The annulment ruling is available at, https://www.italaw.com/sites/default/files/case-documents/ita0187.pdf.

27 Roman Boed, 'State of Necessity as a Justification for Internationally Wrongful Conduct', *Yale Human Rights and Development Law Journal*, 3(1): 2000, pp. 1–45; Johnstone, above note 22, pp. 352–354; Vaughan Lowe, 'Precluding Wrongfulness or Responsibility: A Plea for Excuses', *European Journal of International Law*, 10(2): 1999, pp. 405–411; Agius, above note 11, pp. 95–135 (although she often uses 'justification' in reference to Article 25).

28 Gross and Aolain, above note 14, pp. 43–44.

29 Ohlin and May, above note 4, pp. 2–6.

30 Ibid, p. 3.

From another angle, Tsagourias distinguishes between three functions that necessity has been observed to have in international law: (1) necessity as a source of international rules; (2) necessity as a condition for the application of certain international rules; and (3) necessity as a circumstance precluding the wrongfulness of certain acts.[31]

4.2.4 *Operation of Necessity as Primary or Secondary Rule of International Law*

Hart early on argued that every legal system is a union of primary and secondary rules. He defined the former as rules that are "concerned with the actions that individuals must or must not do" and that the latter are "all concerned with the primary rules themselves" in that they "specify the ways in which the primary rules may be conclusively ascertained, introduced, eliminated, varied, and the fact of their violation conclusively determined."[32] Others have, by reference to the civil law system, simply defined primary rules as the substantive part of the law and secondary rules as the procedural part.[33]

Roberto Ago, who had since 1962 written on the primary-secondary rules bifurcation in international law,[34] introduced the said bifurcation into ILC's work on state responsibility[35] as he expanded the scope of the earlier work by Amador which had focused only on the responsibility of states for injuries to aliens and their property (i.e., the substantive rules of the international law of diplomatic protection).[36] Crystallizing the distinction he received from Ago's works, Crawford defines primary and secondary rules of state responsibility as:

> The law relating to the content and the duration of substantive State obligations is determined by primary rules [of international law]. The law of State responsibility as articulated in the Draft Articles provides the

31 Nicholas Tsagourias, 'Necessity and the Use of Force: A Special Regime', in Dekker and Hey, above note 3, p. 12.

32 H. L. A. Hart, *The Concept of Law* (3rd ed.) (Oxford: Oxford University Press, 2012), p. 94. See also, the distinction between the two in p. 81.

33 Annemarieke Vermeer-Künzli, 'As If: The Legal Fiction in Diplomatic Protection', *European Journal of International Law*, 18(1): 2007, pp. 49–50.

34 Ibid, p. 49.

35 *Yearbook of the International Law Commission* (Vol. II) (United Nations, 1963), p. 228, para. 5; James Crawford, *The International Law Commission's Articles on State Responsibility: Introduction, Text and Commentaries* (Cambridge: Cambridge University Press, 2002), p. 74.

36 Crawford, ibid, pp. 1–2.

> framework – those rules denominated 'secondary', which indicate the consequences of a breach of an applicable primary obligation.[37]

Thus, while primary rules create and determine substantive obligations of states under international law including the exceptions to, and exemptions from, such obligations, secondary rules determine whether those obligations have been breached and the consequences of such breaches including the defenses available against such consequences. In the *Gabčíkovo-Nagymaros Project* case, the ICJ clarified the difference between primary and secondary rules of international law in the context of the relationship between the law of treaties and the law of responsibility.[38]

As such, therefore, the ARSIWA presents the secondary rules of international law of state responsibility, including necessity as contained in the final Article 25 thereof, as distinguished from the primary obligations that emanate from other sources of international law.[39] There are numerous objections to

---

37 Ibid, p. 16.

38 The Court stated: "Nor does the Court need to dwell upon the question of the relationship between the law of treaties and the law of State responsibility, to which the Parties devoted lengthy arguments, as those two branches of international law obviously have a scope that is distinct. A determination of whether a convention is or is not in force, and whether it has or has not been properly suspended or denounced, is to be made pursuant to the law of treaties [i.e., primary rules]. On the other hand, an evaluation of the extent to which the suspension or denunciation of a convention, seen as incompatible with the law of treaties, involves the responsibility of the State which proceeded to it, is to be made under the law of state responsibility [i.e., secondary rules]." *Case Concerning the Gabčíkovo-Nagymaros Project (Hungary v. Slovakia)*, Judgment, 25 September 1997, ICJ Rep. 1997, p. 38, para. 47.

39 Such distinction was early made by the ILC in 1970 as: "The Commission agreed on the need to concentrate its study on the determination of the principles which govern the responsibility of States for internationally wrongful acts, *maintaining a strict distinction between this task and the task of defining the rules that place obligations on States, the violation of which may generate responsibility*. Consideration of the various kinds of obligations placed on States in international law ... may have to be treated as a necessary element in assessing the gravity of an internationally wrongful act and as a criterion for determining the consequences it should have. But this must not obscure the essential fact that *it is one thing to define a rule and the content of the obligation it imposes, and another to determine whether that obligation has been violated and what should be the consequences of the violation. Only the second aspect of the matter comes within the sphere of responsibility proper* ... *Yearbook of the International Law Commission* (Vol. II) (United Nations, 1970), p. 306, para. 66(c). See also, A/CN.4/318 and Add.1 to 4, *Eighth Report on State Responsibility* by Mr. Roberto Ago, Special Rapporteur – the Internationally Wrongful Act of the State, Source of International Responsibility (Vol. II, Part I) (United Nations, 1979), p. 27, para. 50; *Yearbook of the International Law Commission* (Vol. II, Part II) (United

the 'indispensable'[40] classification of international law rules as primary or secondary.[41] Nevertheless, if a given concept is considered a primary rule in some fields of international law and a secondary rule in others, a comprehensive understanding of the nature of the rule in international law may become difficult especially if the elements of such concept in the different fields of international law share similarities. Necessity is probably the best example in this scenario; whereas the law state responsibility as codified in the ARSIWA presents necessity as a secondary rule, WTO law, for example, presents it as a primary rule.[42] In practice, such as in the *Caroline* case (1837), the 1960 *Belgian Dispatch of Parachutists to the Congo* incident (1960) and the Belgian defense before the ICJ of NATO's 1999 aerial campaign against Serbia, necessity defense was raised from the angle of the laws on the use of force, IHL and/or ARSIWA whereby the primary or secondary status of necessity can get entangled due to the distinction.[43] The conflation could have stemmed from the overlap between the law of treaties and the law on state responsibility.[44]

4.2.5 *Distinguishing Necessity from the Other Defenses*

With the conclusion of the drafting of the ARSIWA, the concept of necessity has been clearly distinguished from the other CPW. Some of the CPW require that another state be first engaged in some conduct before the state invoking the CPW can be considered as engaging in the wrongful act being defended. Consent, self-defense and countermeasure fall under this category. Necessity and distress on the contrary allow a state engage in the wrongful act without other states necessarily first giving any cause for the wrongful behavior.[45]

Nations, 2001), p. 31, para. 1; James Crawford, 'The International Court of Justice and the Law of State Responsibility', in Christian J. Tams and James Sloan (eds.), *The Development of International Law by the International Court of Justice* (Oxford: Oxford University Press, 2013), pp. 75–76.

40 Crawford, above note 35, p. 15.

41 Sloane presents three grounds for such criticism: (1) ambiguity of the rule either due to the nature of its application (for example, compensation for state expropriation) or the possibility of its invocation under different fields of international law (for example, self-defense under ARSIWA and *jus ad bellum*); (2) the difficulty at times of the simple dualistic distinction to capture the rich complexity of certain norms of international law such as diplomatic law; and (3) the possibility for problems to arise in practice (such as in investment arbitration) because the nature of primary/secondary rule interaction is complex and variable. Sloane, above note 2, pp. 491–492.

42 Ibid, p. 451.

43 Agius, above note 11, p. 112; ibid, pp. 494–495.

44 Agius, ibid.

45 Agius, above note 11, p. 101 referring to Christian Tomuschat, *International Law: Ensuring the Survival of Mankind on the Eve of a New Century: General Course on Public International*

Necessity also shares some definitional space with distress and *force majeure*. However, in contrast to *force majeure*, necessity implies an intentional failure to conform to the state's obligations and perfect awareness of deliberately acting act contrary to the obligations. *Force majeure* encompasses material impossibility to comply with the state's obligations. In contrast to distress, which focuses on averting a danger to a person, necessity is invoked to protect an essential interest of the state or other states or of the international community.[46]

4.2.6 *Current Status of the Concept of Necessity in International Law*

Sub-sections 4.2.1–4.2.5 showed that there is no consensus among scholars and state practices on the various issues that are raised in the process of discussing necessity in international law. This could be due to the various stages of development that different fields of international law have reached or how necessity is understood in comparison to other defenses in international law. Given the clarity of the respective texts and/or the density of consistent interpretations by respective tribunals, however, the WTO law and the CIL (ARSIWA) concepts of necessity (see Chapters 8 and 9 and Section 5.4) seem to be more refined than those in other fields of international law.

Nevertheless, despite the differences that may arise in the points of discussion mentioned in Sub-sections 4.2.1–4.2.5, necessity has been and will continue to be an indispensable rule of international law, so weaved to the complex net of international law that Ago stated:

> One last comment needs to be made. It may be that someone, taking an erroneous view of 'progressive development', will suggest that the concept of 'necessity' should be deleted entirely from among the possible circumstances precluding the wrongfulness of State conduct. We cannot agree. The application of the concept must, of course, be ruled out wherever it is actually dangerous, but not where it has been and continues to be useful as a 'safety-valve', to relieve the inevitably untoward

Law (1999), *Recueil des Cours/Collected Courses of The Hague Academy of International Law*, Vol. 281 (Cambridge, MA and The Hague: Kluwer Law International, 2001), p. 288.

46 Ole Spiermann, 'Humanitarian Intervention as a Necessity and the Threat or Use of *Jus Cogens*', *Nordic Journal of International Law*, 71(4): 2002, p. 527; Agius, ibid. The pioneering work on distinguishing state of necessity from the other CPW and self-preservation was done by Ago. Ago, above note 12, pp. 14–17, paras. 2–8. For an exhaustive analysis on such distinction, see, Federica I. Paddeu, 'A Genealogy of *Force Majeure* in International Law', *British Yearbook of International Law*, 82(1): 2012, pp. 461–467.

> consequences of a concern for adhering at all costs to the letter of the law ... Moreover, the concept of 'state of necessity' is far too deeply rooted in the consciousness of the members of the international community and of individuals within States. *If driven out of the door it would return through the window, if need be in other forms*; in that case, the only result would be the unhappy one of distorting and obscuring other concepts, the precise delimitation of which is no less essential (*emphasis added*).[47]

Chapter 5 will next present, in eight sections, the concept of necessity as contained in eight different fields of international law. As mentioned in the introduction to this book, these eight sections have been arranged from the perspective of the influence that the concept of necessity in some fields of PIL (Sections 5.1–5.3) had in developing the ARSIWA concept of necessity (Section 5.4, selected for comparison with the concept of necessity in WTO law) and, in turn, in the order of the influence that the ARSIWA concept of necessity has had in developing the concept of necessity in other fields of PIL (Sections 5.5–5.8).

47 *Yearbook of the International Law Commission* (Vol. II, Part I) (United Nations, 1980), p. 51, para. 80.

CHAPTER 5

The Concept of Necessity in Different Fields of International Law

Eight different fields of international law have been selected in this chapter because of the availability of treaty texts and case law on the concept of necessity in the respective fields. These are: the law of use of force; IHL; IEnL; the law of state responsibility as codified in the ARSIWA; IIL; IHRL; ICL; and the law of responsibility of international organizations as codified in the DARIO. Inquiry into such variety in the fields of international law can also give a more comprehensive view of the concept of necessity in international law. This chapter will show that the concept of necessity finds itself in different stages of development in text and practice across the different fields of international law. It is not plausible to claim that there is a uniform definition of the concept of necessity in international law despite the similarities that exist among the definitions and interpretations in some fields of international law. As shown in Chapters 2 and 3, WTO law has refined the concept of necessity mainly through the 'weighing and balancing' test that has been consistently applied in dozens of disputes brought under some WTO agreements with the likelihood of also being adopted by other WTO agreements.

For the purposes of this book, this chapter will give more emphasis to three of the eight fields of international law mentioned above: IEnL; the law of state responsibility as codified in the ARSIWA; and IIL. This is because – as this chapter aims to show – practice has shown that there is proximity between these three fields of international law and WTO law. And of these three fields of international law, the concept of necessity in the law of state responsibility (as codified in Article 25 of the ARSIWA) will be the focus of the analysis in Chapter 6 not only because of the detailed textual definition of necessity in Article 25, but also because, held to be the concept of necessity in CIL, the ARSIWA's concept of necessity has influenced the interpretation of the concept of necessity in other fields of international law (such as IEnL and IIL) and can inspire the interpretation of necessity concepts in other fields of international law.

 | DOI:10.1163/9789004700000_007

5.1 The Law of Use of Force

One of the fields of PIL where necessity has been frequently invoked for legitimacy of certain state actions has been the law of use of force. The fundamental doctrine in international law in this regard – at least since the establishment of the UN – is that contained in Article 2(4) of the UN Charter reading: "All Members shall *refrain* in their international relations from the threat or use of force against the territorial integrity or political independence of any state, or in any other manner *inconsistent with* the Purposes of the United Nations (*emphasis added*)." Thus, except for very limited exceptions consistent with the Charter, threat or use of force is prohibited. The one exception to the prohibition is the rule of self-defense contained in Article 51 of the UN Charter which reads: "Nothing in the present Charter shall impair the *inherent right* of individual or collective self-defense if an *armed attack* occurs against a Member of the United Nations, *until* the Security Council has taken the measures necessary to maintain international peace and security (*emphasis added*)."

A number of issues have been raised in conjunction with the use of force/ self-defense rules of the UN Charter. The introduction of the concept of necessity through the work of the ILC has furthered discussion on the said issues, i.e., whether, and how, exceptions to the prohibition of the use of force can be exercised by states in situations other than self-defense as enumerated in Article 51 of the UN Charter. These issues include preventive self-defense, preemptive self-defense, protection of nationals abroad, humanitarian intervention and rescuing of nationals abroad. Necessity becomes relevant in these areas through a number of angles such as whether: (a) necessity takes a different form in the UN Charter and the law of state responsibility as contained in the ARSIWA; (b) necessity constitutes an element of self-defense in the UN Charter; and (c) necessity, either as it applies in the ARSIWA or otherwise, can be invoked as an exception to the prohibition of the use of force to legitimize the issues listed earlier in this paragraph.

Moreover, the works of the ILC progressively identified necessity as a separate, secondary rule of international law under the rules of state responsibility. A number of incidents that happened in the years after the end of the Second World War (such as the rise in terrorist attacks, genocide and other forms of grave violations of human rights, abduction of nationals abroad, threat of war or the use of disastrous weapons etc.), however, necessitated discussions on whether necessity can, separately (in its customary form as contained in the ARSIWA) or within the UN Charter, be invoked to justify state measures taken to thwart the said incidents. These discussions also involved the issue of whether necessity – if sought within the text UN Charter – has an independent root or is part of self-defense (Article 51).

To discuss the above-mentioned points, it is important to first discuss whether it has attained the status of peremptory norm of international law (*jus cogens*). The contemporary essence of self-defense as contained in the UN Charter will then be mentioned.[1]

5.1.1 *Peremptory Status of the Prohibition of the Use of Force*

One of the questions that is relevant to the discussion on the possibility of invoking necessity as an exception to the prohibition of the use of force (Article 2(4) of the UN Charter) is whether the prohibition has attained the status of a peremptory norm of international law (*jus cogens*). Article 26 of the current ARSIWA provides: "Nothing in this chapter [containing CPW] precludes the wrongfulness of any act of a State which is not in conformity with an obligation arising under a peremptory norm of general international law." On 'peremptory norm of general international law', Article 53 of the VCLT provides:

> A treaty[2] is void if, at the time of its conclusion, it conflicts with a peremptory norm of general international law. For the purposes of the present Convention, a peremptory norm of general international law is a norm accepted and recognized by the international community of States as a whole as a norm from which no derogation is permitted and which can be modified only by a subsequent norm of general international law having the same character.

Thus, necessity can be invoked as a ground to use force within the UN Charter system only if the prohibition against the use of force (Article 2(4) of the UN Charter) has not attained the status of a peremptory norm of GIL. There seems to be no debate on whether all degrees of use of force are prohibited under Article 2(4) of the UN Charter. The debate is on whether the provision has a peremptory status in international law. International law recognizes a gradation of forms of use of force; some uses of force are less grave than others while

1 For a deeper reading on the issues discussed in this subject, see, Judith Gardam, *Necessity, Proportionality and the Use of Force by States* (Cambridge: Cambridge University Press, 2004), pp. 138–187.

2 Although the ARSIWA has not been (and the ILC did not advise that it has to be) elevated into a treaty, its contents may be discussed under the VCLT.

others, such as aggression or armed attack,[3] have been identified as the gravest forms of use of force such.[4] It is acknowledged that the prohibition in Article 2(4) of the UN Charter applies to all gradations; that is, even uses of force that are "circumscribed in magnitude and duration" and carried out for "limited purposes" and "without true aggressive intentions" are prohibited.[5] The question, for the purpose of discussing the possibility of invoking necessity as an exception to the use of force, is whether the prohibition of *all* grades of the use of force is a *jus cogens*.

That the prohibition against aggression is a *jus cogens* rule (and therefore the non-applicability of the necessity defense) is not debated.[6] Ago, however, doubts: (1) the liberty of extending the *jus cogens* status to less grave uses of force; and (b) the conclusion that the provision of Article 51 of the UN Charter should mean that *only* self-defense is the allowed exception to the prohibition of the use of force; i.e., that the drafters of the UN Charter did not leave any room for other defenses such as necessity to be raised against the prohibition in Article 2(4).[7] He, however, left the validation of his bifurcation of uses of force – into those which have attained the level of peremptory rule and those which have not – to the organs entrusted with the interpretation of the UN Charter.[8] Ago's belief had a following in scholars such as Ronzitti,[9] Raby[10] and Schachter.[11] Others, however, seem to favor a wholesome *jus cogens*

3 Article I of *UN General Assembly Resolution 3314 (XXIX) – Definition of Aggression* (14 December 1974), defines aggression as "the use of armed force by a State against the sovereignty, territorial integrity or political independence of another State, or in any other manner inconsistent with the Charter of the United Nations, as set out in this Definition". Article III provides six forms of aggression.

4 *Case Concerning Military and Paramilitary Activities in and against Nicaragua (Nicaragua v. United States of America)*, Judgment, 27 June 1986, ICJ Rep. 1986, p. 101, para. 191; Roberto Ago, 'The Internationally Wrongful Act of the State, Source of International Responsibility', *Eighth Report on State Responsibility*, Addendum (1980), ILC, 32nd sess., UN Doc. A/CN.4/318/Add.5–7, pp. 40–41, para. 58.

5 Ago, ibid.

6 Ibid, p. 41, para. 59.

7 Ibid.

8 Andreas Laursen, 'The Use of Force and (the State of) Necessity', *Vanderbilt Journal of Transnational Law*, 37(2): 2004, p. 509.

9 Natalino Ronzitti, 'Use of Force, Jus Cogens and State Consent', in Antonio Cassese (ed.), *The Current Legal Regulation of the Use of Force* (Dordrecht: Martinus Nijhoff Publishers, 1986), p. 150.

10 Jean Raby, 'The State of Necessity and the Use of Force to Protect Nationals', *Canadian Yearbook of International Law*, 26 (1988), p. 268.

11 Oscar Schachter, *International Law in Theory and Practice* (Dordrecht: Martinus Nijhoff Publishers, 1991), p. 171.

status for the prohibition of all forms of use of force. In its 1966 report, the ILC pointed out that "the law of the Charter concerning the prohibition of the use of force in itself constitutes a conspicuous example of a rule in international law having the character of *jus cogens*."[12] The ICJ added weight to this view by referring to the 1966 ILC statement in the *Military and Paramilitary Activities* case and the parties (Nicaragua and the US) agreed.[13] Albrecht Randelzhofer dismissed Raby's argument that concept of necessity can provide valid basis for protective measures involving use of force.[14] Crawford, in his second report on state responsibility,[15] and the ILC [16] reconfirmed the stand that Article 2(4) covers all forms of use of force and does "certainly rank" as a peremptory norm. The ILC was accordingly ready to disallow the use of necessity in the ARSIWA as an exception to Article 2(4) to be applied to some uses of force. However, Crawford's team – given Ago's widely accepted bifurcation of the use of force – was not ready to fully address whether necessity as contained in the ARSIWA may be invoked as an exception to the prohibition in Article 2(4) of the UN Charter in cases of humanitarian intervention. The team stated that necessity, as contained in the ARSIWA, should not be invoked as an exception to Article 2(4) of the UN Charter because it has been presented as a secondary rule in the ARSIWA.[17]

With the debate on whether Article 2(4) of the UN Charter is a peremptory norm of GIL not yet settled, it is therefore difficult to conclude whether necessity can, in limited circumstances, be considered an exception to Article 2(4). Assuming necessity can, like self-defense, be invoked as an exception to Article 2(4) (presented in more details in Sub-section 5.1.3), however, there is an important issue that needs to be addressed. The issue is the fact that in the realm of the UN Charter necessity has been identified *as an element of self-defense*. Does this mean, therefore, that necessity can be invoked as an exception to the Article 2(4) prohibition only as part of self-defense? Or is there a

12 *Yearbook of the International Law Commission* (Vol. II) (United Nations, 1966), p. 247, para. 1.

13 *Case Concerning Military and Paramilitary Activities in and against Nicaragua*, above note 4, p. 100, para. 190.

14 Albrecht Randelzhofer, 'Article 2(4)', in Bruno Simma (ed.), *The Charter of the United Nations: A Commentary* (Oxford: Clarendon Press, 1994), p. 125 (para. 55).

15 James Crawford, 'Second Report on State Responsibility' (1999), ILC, 51st sess., UN Doc. A/CN.4/498 and Add 1–4, p. 72, para. 288.

16 *Yearbook of the International Law Commission* (Vol. II, Part II) (United Nations, 1999), p. 82, para. 375.

17 See, Crawford's report on this matter at Crawford, above note 15, p. 72, paras. 288–289. See also, ibid.

difference between the invocation of necessity as an independent exception and its invocation as an element of self-defense under Article 51 of the UN Charter? Sub-section 5.1.3 addresses the debate.

5.1.2 *Self-Defense under Article 51 of the UN Charter*

The right of self-defense has been part of the general body of international law since the early 19th century. Until 1945, this right was broadly construed and armed force could be used to repel not only armed attacks to the territory of a state but also to repel attacks against what a state considered to be its vital interests.[18] Dinstein, who believes that "[t]he essence of self-defense is self-help"[19] defines self-defense as "a lawful use of force ... under conditions prescribed by international law, in response to a previous unlawful use (or, at least, a threat) of force".[20] Article 51 of the UN Charter brought about strict pre-conditions to the taking of self-defense measures. Firstly, there should be a prior armed attack by a state(s) or non-state actors.[21] Secondly, the attacked state can exercise the right to self-defense only until the UN Security Council takes measures it deems necessary in order to maintain or restore international peace and security.[22] Thirdly, the state engaged in taking self-defense measures must immediately report its actions to the Security Council.

As stated above, under the UN Charter self-defense is the only explicitly recognized exception to the prohibition of the use of force by states. It is also true that Article 21 of the ARSIWA recognizes self-defense as a CPW. Thus, whereas self-defense in Article 51 of the UN Charter operates, as a primary rule, within the *political* (owing mainly to the involvement of the Security Council) realm of the use of force, self-defense in Article 21 of the ARSIWA operates, as a secondary rule, within the *legal* realm of state responsibility. Despite this basic

18 Raby, above note 10, p. 254.

19 Yoram Dinstein, *War, Aggression and Self-Defense* (5th ed.) (Cambridge: Cambridge University Press, 2012), p. 187.

20 Yoram Dinstein, *War, Aggression and Self-Defense* (2nd ed.) (Cambridge: Cambridge University Press, 1994), p. 175.

21 *Case Concerning Military and Paramilitary Activities in and against Nicaragua*, above note 4, p. 103–104, para. 195; p. 122, para. 237.

22 Nicholas Tsagourias, 'Necessity and the Use of Force: A Special Regime', in Ige F. Dekker and E. Hey (eds.), *Netherlands Yearbook of International Law: Necessity across International Law*, Vol. 41 (The Hague: T.M.C. Asser Press, 2010), p. 18. Tsagourias observes that the extension of the first requirement to the concept of self-defense in CIL is controversial (f.n. 29). This could be partly because "customary international law has always recognized a broader right of self-defense, not only against actual but also against imminent attacks." (p. 19).

difference, however, there are some points of convergence where self-defense in these two realms merges.[23]

The *locus classicus* of the doctrine of self-defense is believed to have emerged out of the *Caroline* incident (1837)[24] mentioned in Sub-section 2.1.6. Through its Secretary of State, Daniel Webster, the US government stated that the British attack of the vessel could have been justified if the latter demonstrated the existence of "necessity of self-defense, instant, overwhelming, leaving no choice of means, and no moment for deliberation" as well as that the measures taken involved "nothing unreasonable or excessive, since the act justified by the necessity of self-defense, must be limited by that necessity, and kept clearly within it". Webster's definition of self-defense, widely accepted as the founding formula for the concept, has become a valuable tool in understanding self-defense in international law.[25]

Some argue that the term 'inherent' in Article 51 of the UN Charter refers to CIL (i.e., customary rule of self-defense) and is constituted by three[26] elements:

(a) Necessity. The principle of necessity means that no other peaceful alternative measures are available or effective. Use of force must be a measure of last resort.[27]
(b) Proportionality. Proportionality is considered to be "the essence of self-defense".[28] An inherently flexible criterion, it has been regarded as inserting a "standard of reasonableness" to the doctrine.[29]
(c) Immediacy. Immediacy requires that there will not be "an undue time-lag between the armed attack and the invocation of self-defense". This does not require, however, that the state being

23 Ibid, pp. 29–39.
24 Robert Y. Jennings, 'The *Caroline* and *McLeod* Cases', *American Journal of International Law*, 32(1): 1938, p. 92.
25 James Crawford, *Brownlie's Principles of Public International Law* (8th ed.) (Oxford: Oxford University Press, 2012), p. 43.
26 In the *Nicaragua* case, the ICJ highlighted two of these three elements (i.e., proportionality and necessity). *Case Concerning Military and Paramilitary Activities in and against Nicaragua*, above note 4, p. 94, para. 176. The ICJ did not discuss the third element (i.e., immediacy) because it was not made an issue in the case (p. 103, para. 194). See also, *Legality of the Threat or Use of Nuclear Weapons*, Advisory Opinion, 8 July 1996, ICJ Rep. 1996, p. 245, para. 41; *Case Concerning Oil Platforms* (*Iran v. USA*), Judgment, 6 November 2003, ICJ Rep. 2003, p. 198, para. 76; *Case Concerning Armed Activities on the Territory of the Congo* (*Congo v. Uganda*), Judgment, 19 December 2005, ICJ Rep. 2005, p. 53, para. 147. See also, Dinstein, above note 19, pp. 230–231.
27 For more elaboration, see, Dinstein, ibid, pp. 231–232.
28 Crawford, above note 25, p. 252.
29 For more elaboration, see, Dinstein, above note 19, pp. 232–233.

> attacked have "no moment for deliberation", i.e., self-defense must be exercised while the armed attack is still in progress.[30]

One can observe from the above that necessity, a full-fledged concept with its own elements in the ARSIWA, WTO law and other fields of international law, is also considered *an element of* self-defense in Article 51 of the UN Charter. For instance, the *Construction of a Wall* case before the ICJ which needed analyzing necessity under the UN Charter (Article 51), CIL as contained in ARSIWA (Article 25) and IHL (military necessity) is testament to the fact that "there is *still* a *conflation* between necessity elements under the self-defense doctrine, the circumstances precluding wrongfulness and the international humanitarian law (*emphasis added*)."[31] This should not, however, be a point of confusion because of the different purposes that necessity serves in the different fields of international law (as primary or secondary rule etc.) and the varying elements that constitute necessity in the different fields of international law.

Thus, within the UN Charter, there is a possibility for necessity to be invoked as a primary rule (right) in the form of: (a) an *independent exception* to the Article 2(4) prohibition; and (b) an element of the primary rule of self-defense under Article 51 of the UN Charter. This two-typed primary rule invocation of necessity under the UN Charter must be considered without conflating it with the secondary rule invocation of necessity under CIL (as contained in the ARSIWA). For the distinction between primary and secondary rules, see Sub-section 4.2.4. But what are the different circumstances under which necessity may be invoked as an independent exception to the Article 2(4) prohibition? Sub-section 5.1.3 briefly discusses three of these circumstances.

5.1.3 *Necessity as a Ground for Possible Exceptions to the Prohibition of the Use of Force*

The term 'inherent' in Article 51 of the UN Charter has been frequently relied upon to refer to CIL rules that allow use of force beyond the strict limitations put in Article 51. These rules include pre-emptive and preventive self-defense, humanitarian intervention and the rescuing of nationals in other territories which are discussed below.

Pre-emptive (anticipatory) or preventive forms of self-defense are raised, as requirements of Article 51 of the UN Charter, in the process of justifying circumstances where states use force before they are actually attacked. The

30 For more elaboration, see, ibid, pp. 233–234.

31 Maria Agius, 'The Invocation of Necessity in International Law', *Netherlands International Law Review*, 56(2): 2009, p. 122.

easiest distinction between the two is that whereas pre-emptive self-defense is use of force to thwart imminent attacks, preventive self-defense is use of force to thwart remote attacks.[32]

Pre-emptive self-defense has taken the form of pre-emptive attack of another state or pre-emptive attack to prevent terrorism. Examples of such attacks against other states include the *Caroline* case,[33] the declaration of war by the Netherlands on Japan on 8 December 1941 prior to the Japanese attack on the Dutch East Indies[34] and the Israeli attack of its neighbors in the 1967 Six-Days War.[35] While some agree that there is such right in CIL and in the 'inherent' right in Article 51 of the UN Charter,[36] others stick to the wording of Article 51 to argue that nothing other than an actual armed attack against a state triggers the use of the rights in that article.[37] The ICJ has been shying away from deciding on this issue.[38] Regarding pre-emptive attack to prevent terrorism (which became a controversial issue following the September 2002 Bush Doctrine,[39] adopted to justify[40] the subsequent invasion of Iraq),[41] there is still a debate whether there is such right under Article 51 of the UN Charter. Scholars, including Romano,[42] Shaw,[43]

32 Michael Walzer, *Just and Unjust Wars: A Moral Argument with Historical Illustrations* (4th ed.) (New York: Basic Books, 1977), pp. 74–85. Dinstein, however, notes that "[t]he difference in terminology between 'preemptive', 'anticipatory' and 'preventive' – expressions employed long before 9/11 – is not always transparent". Dinstein, above note 19, p. 195.

33 Jennings, above note 24, p. 92.

34 D. W. Greig, *International Law* (2nd ed.) (London: Butterworths, 1976), p. 894.

35 Dinstein, above note 19, pp. 206–207.

36 For example, Walzer, above note 32; Derek Bowett, 'Reprisals Involving Recourse to Armed Force', *The American Journal of International Law*, 66(1): 1972, pp. 1–36.

37 For example, Judge Schwebel's dissenting opinion in *Case Concerning Military and Paramilitary Activities in and against Nicaragua*, above note 4, pp. 347–348, paras. 172–173; Dinstein, above note 19, pp. 196–198.

38 *Case Concerning Military and Paramilitary Activities in and against Nicaragua*, ibid, p. 103, para. 194; *Case Concerning Armed Activities on the Territory of the Congo*, above note 26, p. 222, para. 147.

39 The White House, *The National Security Strategy of the United States of America*, September 2002, available at, https://2009-2017.state.gov/documents/organization/63562.pdf.

40 Ibid, p. 15.

41 Andru E. Wall, 'International Law and the Bush Doctrine', *Israel Yearbook of Human Rights*, 34 (2004), pp. 196–197, 212 (2004).

42 John-Alex Romano, 'Combating Terrorism and Weapons of Mass Destruction: Reviving the Doctrine of a State of Necessity', *Georgetown Law Journal*, 87(4): 1999, pp. 1023–1025.

43 Agius, above note 31, f.n. 127, referring to Malcolm N. Shaw, *International Law* (4th ed.) (Cambridge: Cambridge University Press, 1997), p. 806.

Johnstone[44] and Tsagourias[45] have made different opinions on the subject. Dwelling on the issue of necessity, Agius, stated that that "[l]ooking only to the technical criteria [of necessity], it is not unfeasible that terrorist threats would fit under the necessity plea in principle." She, however, admits that to a certain extent necessity, in the context of the use of force, has the same defects as the doctrine of self-preservation from which it has emanated and that even as it stands in the ARSIWA, necessity may not be fully successful as a defense.[46] Specifically she states that:

> it would thus appear that interventions against terrorist networks outside of the state's own territory, and other similar incursions and forceful practices, may in some extreme circumstances point legal interpreters towards the necessity doctrine, even *ex officio*. However, it is unlikely to be successfully invoked, for a number of more technical reasons.[47]

Whether preventive self-defense is fully recognized under CIL, especially under the just-war theory, is not as certain as the case with pre-emotive self-defense.[48] Owing mainly to the lack of immediacy of the threats suppressed by a preventive self-defense, this kind of use of force has not been generally welcomed.[49] Post-9/11 US did, however, justify its invasion of Afghanistan in terms echoing preventive self-defense both in its statement to the UN[50] and in its 2006 US National Security Strategy[51] which echoed the earlier 2002 National

44 Ian Johnstone, 'The Plea of Necessity in International Legal Discourse: Humanitarian Intervention and Counter-Terrorism', *Columbia Journal of Transnational Law*, 43(2): 2002, pp. 366–379.

45 Tsagourias, above note 22, p. 20.

46 Agius, above note 31, pp. 120–121.

47 Ibid, pp. 123–124.

48 Gregory M. Reichberg, 'Preventive War in Classical Just War Theory', *Journal of the History of International Law*, 9(1): 2007, pp. 5–6.

49 See, for instance, the advice of former British Attorney General Lord Goldsmith to the House of Lords (21 Paril 2004), available at, http://www.publications.parliament.uk/pa/ld200304/ldhansrd/vo040421/text/40421-07.htm#40421-07_head0.

50 See, *Letter dated 7 October 2001 from the Permanent Representative of the United States of America to the United Nations addressed to the President of the Security Council*, S/2001/946, p. 1, available at, http://www.hamamoto.law.kyoto-u.ac.jp/kogi/2005kiko/s-2001-946e.pdf.

51 The White House, *The National Security Strategy of the United States of America*, March 2006, available at, https://www.comw.org/qdr/fulltext/nss2006.pdf, p. 23. Please note that the paragraph uses the term 'pre-emption', but its essence reflects preventive self-defense.

Security Strategy.[52] The UN seems to have very slowly, yet only implicitly, recognized the use of preventive self-defense, but it has not expressly prohibited it either.[53] The possibility of invoking necessity in taking preventive self-defense measures apparently seems a narrow pathway. The requirement of immediacy in necessity, for instance in Article 25 of the ARSIWA or even as understood as an element of self-defense in Article 51 of the UN Charter, will prove to be incompatible with the temporal remoteness of a threat against which preventive force is intended to be used.

Thus, while state practice and scholars seem to have generally tolerated the invocation of necessity in the context of taking pre-emptive measures against terrorist attacks – hence an exception to UN Charter Article 2(4) – the invocation of necessity to take preventive measures, even to thwart future terrorist attacks, appears to have a weaker ground under the interpretation and practice of the UN Charter.

Humanitarian intervention (aka intervention for humanity) is, under international law, an instance of intervention for the purpose of vindicating the law of nations against outrage.[54] Massacres, acts of genocide and related humanitarian catastrophes have historically attracted intervention, singular or collective, from neighboring or other countries.[55] Although it is doubtful whether the interventions were purely based on humanitarian reasons or if the intervening states invoked other reasons for such interventions, there are records of

52 The White House was aware in issuing the 2002 Strategy that it was probably going against a view held by many when it stated that: "For centuries, *international law recognized that nations need not suffer an attack before they can lawfully take action* to defend themselves against forces that present an imminent danger of attack. Legal scholars and international jurists *often conditioned the legitimacy of preemption on the existence of an imminent threat* – most often a visible mobilization of armies, navies, and air forces preparing to attack … The United States has long maintained the option of preemptive actions to counter a sufficient threat to our national security. The greater the threat, the greater is the risk of inaction – and *the more compelling the case for taking anticipatory action* to defend ourselves, even if uncertainty remains as to the time and place of the enemy's attack. To forestall or prevent such hostile acts by our adversaries, *the United States will, if necessary, act preemptively* (*emphasis added*)". The White House, above note 39, p. 15. Please note that the statement uses the term 'pre-emption', but its essence reflects preventive self-defense.

53 Tsagourias, above note 22, p. 21. See also, *Report of the High-level Panel on Threats, Challenges and Change: A More Secure World: Our Shared Responsibility*, A/59/565, available at, https://www.un.org/ruleoflaw/files/gaA.59.565_En.pdf, paras. 188–191.

54 Ellery C. Stowell, *Intervention in International Law* (Washington, D.C.: John Byrne & Co., 1921), p. 51.

55 Tsagourias, above note 22, p. 23.

them since at least the beginning of the 19th century.[56] With the coming of the UN Charter, the issue of humanitarian intervention became difficult to discern within the text of the Charter. Self-defense (Article 51) could not plausibly be claimed as a ground because of the mere fact that in case of humanitarian intervention the intervening state is not the subject of an armed attack.[57] Thus, most of the discussion on humanitarian intervention has revolved around the scope of use of force under Article 2(4).[58] State practice also supports the use of force-humanitarian intervention link. A recurrently cited example is the defense statement by Rusen Ergec, counsel for Belgium, made during the oral proceedings in *Legality of Use of Force* before the ICJ, by citing Article 33 of the Draft State Responsibility Articles (necessity), in the alternative, that NATO's humanitarian intervention was a balancing[59] act of necessity which "justifies the violation of a binding rule in order to safeguard, in face of grave and imminent peril, values which are higher than those protected by the rule which has been breached."[60] On the contrary, Article 2(4) has been read to conclude that humanitarian intervention is a prohibited use of force.[61] Nevertheless, it may be argued that there is still a room, albeit contentious,[62] in Article 2(4) that allows humanitarian interventions if they are carried out in a manner that is neither against the territorial integrity or political independence of a state nor the purposes of the UN.[63]

The ILC came across the issue of justifying humanitarian intervention and necessity became the subject of the discussions. During the ILC's fifty-third session, The Netherlands requested the ILC to include in the Draft ARSIWA a new provision on humanitarian intervention as an exceptional circumstance excluding wrongfulness. Crawford's response was that:

56 See, Crawford, above note 25, pp. 339–340 and Stowell, above note 54, p. 481 for a list of some examples.

57 Johnstone, above note 44, p. 360.

58 Tsagourias, above note 22, p. 23.

59 Agius, above note 31, p. 125.

60 *Legality of Use of Force* (*Yugoslavia v. Belgium*) (Provisional Measures), Uncorrected Translation of Oral Pleadings of Belgium, ICJ Rep. 1999, record of 10 May 1999, 3 p. m., available at, http://www.icj-cij.org/icjwww/idocket/iybe/iybeframe.htm.

61 See, *Case Concerning Military and Paramilitary Activities in and against Nicaragua*, above note 4, p. 135, para. 268.

62 Johnstone, above note 44, pp. 360–361.

63 Tsagourias, above note 22, p. 23. See also, Johnstone, above note 44, pp. 360–361; *Secretary-General presents his annual report to General Assembly, Press Release SG/SM/7136, GA/9596*, available at, https://www.un.org/press/en/1999/19990920.sgsm7136.html; Robert D. Sloane, 'On the Use and Abuse of Necessity in the Law of State Responsibility', *American Journal of International Law*, 106(3): 2012, pp. 495–496.

> Chapter V [dealing with CPW] does not deal with the substantive primary rules relating to the use of force, or indeed generally with the international law of humanitarian assistance. *Cases not otherwise provided for may be dealt with in accordance with the criteria in article 26* (necessity) (*emphasis added*).[64]

Crawford's statement has been read by some scholars (Johnstone and Laursen, for example) as meaning that the ILC did not want to make a statement decisively on the topic of humanitarian intervention, but that if the criteria were met in a specific case, it was not impossible to subsume a particular action under necessity.[65] In practice, though, Crawford had observed that in modern cases of humanitarian intervention, the excuse of necessity has hardly ever been relied on and that by 1980 (Ago's report) the only such only example was the Belgian rescue operation in the Congo in 1960 for which no position was taken by the Security Council on the plea.[66] In spite of the ILC's statement that necessity, as contained in the ARSIWA, may be used to justify humanitarian intervention *in cases not otherwise provided for by primary rules*, the support for necessity to justify humanitarian intervention has been very small.[67] There are of course some writers such as Johnstone,[68] Harhoff,[69] Rytter[70] and Spiermann,[71] who reason that in absolutely extraordinary circumstances, necessity may still serve to justify humanitarian intervention. As far as the UN is concerned, the organization made its stand clear on humanitarian intervention (aka Responsibility to Protect) along the lines of the abovementioned view:

64 James Crawford, 'Fourth Report on State Responsibility, Addendum' (2001), ILC, 53rd sess., UN Doc. A/CN.4/517/Add.1, p. 4.

65 Agius, above note 31, pp. 124–125.

66 Crawford, above note 15, p. 68, para. 281 and f.n. 537.

67 See, Report of the International Law Commission (2001), ILC, 53rd sess., Supp. No. 10 (A/56/10), p. 205, para. [21] (Note: original text types paragraph number '20' twice, hence the liberty to change the cited paragraph's number to '21'). Crawford has also changed it to paragraph 21. See, Crawford, above note 35, p. 185. See also, Sloane, above note 63, p. 495; Agius, above note 31, p. 125–126.

68 Johnstone, above note 44, p. 364.

69 Frederik Harhoff, 'Unauthorized Humanitarian Interventions – Armed Violence in the Name of Humanity?', *Nordic Journal of International Law*, 70(1): 2001, pp. 65–119.

70 Jens Elo Rytter, 'Humanitarian Intervention without the Security Council: From San Francisco to Kosovo – and Beyond', *Nordic Journal of International Law*, 70(1): 2001, pp. 121–160.

71 Ole Spiermann, 'Humanitarian Intervention as a Necessity and the Threat or Use of *Jus Cogens*', *Nordic Journal of International Law*, 71(4): 2002, p. 543.

> We endorse the emerging norm that there is a *collective* international responsibility to protect, exercisable by the *Security Council authorizing military intervention as a last resort*, in the event of genocide and other largescale killing, ethnic cleansing or serious violations of international humanitarian law which sovereign Governments have proved powerless or unwilling to prevent.[72]

By way of concluding, therefore, it may be stated that there is a universal recognition of the need to engage in humanitarian intervention missions should situations on the ground call for that. The non-availability of self-defense, or the difficulty of invoking necessity, to justify singular or collective humanitarian use of force outside the UN system, however, leaves us with the mechanism of the UN Security Council authorization as the only way to carry out humanitarian intervention to maintain international peace and security.[73]

Regarding rescuing nationals abroad, there is enough state practice in this area. Bowett, for instance, notes that between 1813 and 1899 US military forces were deployed on at least 46 occasions to protect US citizens abroad and on 24 occasions between 1900 and 1927.[74] Prior to the establishment of the UN, the authority to rescue nationals abroad was found in a number of grounds such as self-preservation, self-protection, self-defense, as well as necessity.[75] Self-defense,[76] state of emergency[77] and necessity[78] have also been cited as defenses in rescues conducted after the Second World War. As to the entitlement to use force to rescue nationals, some authors maintain that an intervention to protect nationals is a legitimate use force recognized by CIL and not prohibited by the UN Charter. Others are of the opinion that the broad character of the prohibition of the use of force in Article 2(4) of the Charter disallows a unilateral use of force even for the alleged purpose of rescuing nationals

72 *Report of the High-level Panel*, above note 53, para. 203.

73 Tsagourias, above note 22, p. 25.

74 Derek W. Bowett, *Self-Defense in International Law* (Manchester: Manchester University Press, 1958), p. 97.

75 Johnstone, above note 44, p. 357.

76 Invoked to justify the rescue of its nationals from Entebbe, Uganda in 1976. Agius, above note 31, p. 127. The British government also claimed self-defense in its efforts to rescue its nationals who were at risk during the 1956 Suez Canal crisis. Johnstone, ibid, p. 359.

77 The understanding of the Dutch government on the reason for Israel's rescuing of nationals from Entebbe. Raby, above note 10, p. 270.

78 Invoked by Belgium to justify rescue of its nationals from Congo in 1960 and by the US in its attempt in 1980 to rescue its nationals held hostage in Tehran. Agius, above note 31, p. 127.

facing extreme danger.[79] The debate on rescue operations is not only on the legality of the operation as a use of force, but also on the grounds that may be invoked to justify the same. Necessity is one of such grounds, the other being self-defense.[80] Most writers who do not accept self-defense as a justification for rescue operations have examined the less discussed[81] possibility of invoking necessity. Raby, for example, examines each of the elements of necessity as contained in the draft ARSIWA and concludes that:

> The time has come to relieve an otherwise overburdened theory of self-defense and to rely on another concept, one that is better suited to respond to the different situations in which an intervention to protect nationals becomes necessary, that will be adoptable to the ever-changing international society, that will take into account what Professor Bowett has called 'the principle of the relativity of rights', according to which one state's right to territorial sovereignty must be weighed against the other state's right to protection of its nationals. It is the concept of 'necessity'.[82]

He adds:

> an intervention to protect nationals, if it stays within certain well-defined parameters, can be justified by the existence of a state of necessity. Nor in this case do any of the conditions apply which, under the Commission's draft Article 33(2) [of ARSIWA, now Article 25], would exclude the possibility of involving the defense of necessity.[83]

Agius, while similarly convinced that the elements of necessity are met by a rescue operation, has doubts on the issue of securing the consent of the state on whose territory the operation would be conducted. The said consent, which is part of the UN Charter requirement of the respect of territorial integrity of states, Agius admits, can be mentioned as an alternative to the otherwise forceful rescue operation – hence vitiating the requirement in the necessity rule

79 Raby, above note 10, p. 253.

80 On the use of self-defense to justify rescue operations, see, Johnstone, above note 44, pp. 357–358; Case Concerning *Military and Paramilitary Activities in and against Nicaragua*, above note 4, p. 103–104, para. 195; p. 122, para. 237; Raby, ibid, pp. 254–257; Agius, above note 31, p. 126; Oscar Schachter, 'The Right of States to Use Armed Force', *Michigan Law Review*, 82 (5&6): 1984, pp. 1629–1633; Johnstone, above note 44, pp. 357–359.

81 Raby, ibid, p. 259.

82 Ibid, p. 257.

83 Ibid, p. 267.

that the disputed measure be the *only* available measure. Only in the case of a failed state would, therefore, such a consent be not required.[84] She still is convinced, however, that:

> it is preferable to states to justify the right to rescue by invocation of 'sheer necessity of instant action' rather than self-defense. In light of the opposition against further stretching the doctrine of self-defense [as also stated by Raby] and the evermore frequent general attention given to the plea of necessity in international tribunals, such a notion seems credible. The plea of necessity seems well-fitted for the very temporary state of affairs that a hostage situation or similar rescue action is.[85]

As far as rescue operations are concerned, therefore, the tendency thus far has been resisting an expansive interpretation of self-defense under Article 51 of the UN Charter as a justification mainly because of the requirement of prior attack on the territory of the rescuing state. Scholars have begun to read the elements and circumstances of application of necessity as defined in the ARSIWA as allowing the invocation of necessity as a defense to rescue operations.

To conclude Section 5.1, therefore, prohibition of the use of force under international law is mainly analyzed within the limits of Article 2(4) of the UN Charter and only self-defense has been explicitly recognized by the Charter as an exception to the prohibition. Debates continue as to whether Article 51 can be interpreted to apply to situations that are beyond the ordinary limit of self-defense (i.e., that self-defense measures are taken after an attack has been made to the territory of a state). These situations include pre-emptive and preventive self-defense, humanitarian intervention and rescuing nationals abroad. Necessity – given that it is now accepted as a distinct defense – has, as defined by CIL (ARSIWA), is slowly being accepted as a defense that can, if appropriately interpreted within the UN Charter, provide justifications for such state actions.

5.2 International Humanitarian Law

Section 5.2 examines the evolution of the concept of necessity in IHL, i.e., military necessity. The peculiar nature of IHL which, unlike other fields of

84 Agius, above note 31, p. 128.

85 Ibid.

international law, applies in times of military conflict, varies military necessity from the concepts of necessity in WTO law and CIL, the latter as codified in the ARSIWA, by requiring that militarily necessary actions always consider the factor of humanity. Military necessity has not yet been clearly defined in IHL, but this section will show that the elements so far identified in practice and by IHL commentators to define it are similar to concepts of necessity in WTO law or CIL.

5.2.1 *General Remarks*

International law is designed to operate by default in times of peaceful international relations. Hence war is treated by international law as an exception to the normal operation of international law.[86] International law has developed rules for the conduct of war, also known as IHL. In the realm of IHL, military necessity, as in other fields of PIL, operates as an exception to the *normal* laws of war in that it allows the taking of measures not allowable under the said laws. McCoubrey asserts that military necessity "clearly functions as a principle of exception or suspension in the operation of the *jus in bello* and as such admits the variation or suspension of a *prima facie* applicable norm in given circumstances."[87]

The law of armed conflict is traditionally[88] divided into two phases: *jus ad bellum*[89] and *jus in bello* (essentially IHL).[90] There is a move to recognizing a third phase, *jus post bellum*, which involves rules and principles governing peace-making after conflict.[91] In its broadest sense necessity applies both in

86 Luís Paulo Bogliolo, *Rethinking Military Necessity in the Law of Armed Conflict* (unpublished LL.M. Thesis, London School of Economics), available at, http://ssrn.com/abstract=2201129, p. 4, *referring to*, Brian J. Bill, 'The Rendulic "Rule": Military Necessity, Commander's Knowledge, and Methods of Warfare', *Yearbook of International Humanitarian Law*, 12: 2009, pp. 119, 128.

87 Hilaire McCoubrey, 'The Nature of the Modern Doctrine of Military Necessity', *Military Law and the Law of War Review*, 30(215): 1991, p. 220.

88 Carsten Stahn, '"*Jus ad bellum*", "*jus in bello*" ... "*jus post bellum*"? – Rethinking the Conception of the Law of Armed Force', *European Journal of International Law*, 17(5): 2007, p. 921.

89 Described as the "conditions under which States may resort to war or to the use of armed force in general". ICRC, *What are* jus ad bellum *and* jus in bello? available at, https://www.icrc.org/en/document/what-are-jus-ad-bellum-and-jus-bello-0.

90 Described as the "conduct of parties engaged in an armed conflict. [IHL] is synonymous with *jus in bello*." Ibid. For a more detailed analysis and how *jus ad bellum* and *jus in bello* are related to the notion of military necessity, see, Craig J. S. Forrest, 'The Doctrine of Military Necessity and the Protection of Cultural Property During Armed Conflicts', *California Western International Law Journal*, 37(2): 2007, pp. 179–182.

91 Stahn, above note 88, pp. 921–923.

the initial resort to force and to its subsequent application in actual conflict, i.e., to both the *jus ad bellum* and *jus in bello*.[92] To achieve the goal of minimizing human suffering by regulating the conduct of conflicts, IHL has introduced fundamental principles the most important of which include the principles of: distinction between civilians and combatants (precaution); prohibition of attacks against those *hors de combat*; prohibition on the infliction of unnecessary suffering; proportionality; necessity; and humanity.[93] Although IHL operates by interweaving these principles, it particularly maintains its essence by maintaining the balance between the principles of military necessity and humanity.[94]

5.2.2 *History of the Principle of Military Necessity in Brief*

Let us start with a quote from Downey (1953):

> *One of the most important concepts in the law of war is that of military necessity, but there is no concept more elusive.* From the idea expressed by the German writers that military necessity (*kriegsraison*) overrode all law, to the recent holdings of the [Nuremberg] International Military Tribunals that military necessity is governed by positive international law, *the question [of necessity] has vexed both international lawyers and army officers.*[95]

As a sub-set of the broader concept of necessity in international law, military necessity shares the story of the evolution of the concept of necessity in international law in general. As such, the idea of military necessity "evolved from a vague pre-legal discourse to a legal doctrine".[96] The history of military

---

92 Bogliolo, above note 86, p. 11, *referring to*, Burleigh Cushing Rodick, *The Doctrine of Necessity in International Law* (New York: Columbia University Press, 1928), pp. 59–60; McCoubrey, above note 87, p. 217.

93 Nils Melzer, *Interpretive Guidance on the Notion of Direct Participation in Hostilities under International Humanitarian Law* (Geneva: ICRC, 2009), pp. 77–78; Nicholas Tsagourias and Alasdair Morrison, *International Humanitarian Law: Cases, Materials and Commentary* (Cambridge: Cambridge University Press, 2018), pp. 39–54. For a detailed discussion, see, Jonathan Crowe and Kylie Weston-Scheuber, *Principles of International Humanitarian Law* (Edward Elgar: Cheltenham (UK) and Northampton, MA (USA), 2013).

94 G. I. A. D. Draper, 'Military Necessity and Humanitarian Imperatives', *Military Law and the Law of War Review*, 27(2): 1973, pp. 129–142; Yoram Dinstein, *The Conduct of Hostilities under the Law of International Armed Conflict* (1st ed.) (Cambridge: Cambridge University Press, 2004), p. 5.

95 William G. Downey, 'The Law of War and Military Necessity', *American Journal of International Law*, 47(2): 1953, p. 252.

96 Bogliolo, above note 86, p. 13.

necessity shows how the concept has developed: (a) from a balancing factor in the war operations; (b) toward a justification for any, and unbridled, use of force; and finally (c) toward a more tamed principle balanced by the principle of humanity.[97] In fact, some writers have observed that the three stages through which military necessity developed correspond with the respective names given to the moniker of the law that governs the conduct of war: i.e., from the 'law of war' to the 'law of armed conflict' to 'IHL'.[98] The following paragraphs will briefly present a short history of the principle of military necessity in the following order: the Lieber Code; the St. Petersburg Declaration of 1868; the Hague Conventions of 1899 and 1907; the doctrine of *Kriegsräson* (necessity as justification for all acts of war); and the return to the *Kriegsräson* via the Nuremberg Trials.

On 24 April 1863, US Secretary of War Edwin M. Stanton, with the approval of President Abraham Lincoln, issued a document titled *Instructions for the Government of Armies of the United States in the Field, U.S. War Dep't General Orders No. 100* to address many questions hitherto asked by Union soldiers and to dictate how the soldiers should conduct themselves in wartime. The document, popularly known as the Lieber Code or Lieber Instructions,[99] was prepared by a committee appointed to revise the 1806 Articles of War. Its main drafter was Francis (Franz) Lieber (1798/1800–1872), a German jurist who fought in the Napoleonic Wars.[100] Regarding military necessity, Articles 14–16 of the Code have been hailed as laying the foundation for the concept of military necessity in international law:

> Article 14
>
> Military necessity, as understood by modern civilized nations, consists in the necessity of those measures which are indispensable for securing

97 For a more detailed reading on the concept, history and basics of military necessity, see, Sigrid Redse Johansen, *The Military Commander's Necessity: The Law of Armed Conflict and its Limits* (Cambridge: Cambridge University Press, 2019).

98 Michael N. Schmitt, 'Military Necessity and Humanity in International Humanitarian Law: Preserving the Delicate Balance', *Virginia Journal of International Law*, 50(4): 2010, pp. 805–806.

99 Text of the Lieber Code is available at, http://avalon.law.yale.edu/19th_century/lieber.asp.

100 Jordan J. Paust, 'Dr. Francis Lieber and the Lieber Code', *Proceedings of the Annual Meeting (American Society of International Law)*, 95: 2001, pp. 112–115; Matthew J. Mancini, 'Francis Lieber, Slavery, and the "Genesis" of the Laws of War', *The Journal of Southern History*, 77(2): 2011, pp. 325–348. See also, Rick Beard, 'The Lieber Codes', Opinionator, New York Times (24 April 2013), available at, https://opinionator.blogs.nytimes.com/2013/04/24/the-lieber-codes/.

> the ends of the war, and which are lawful according to the modern law and usages of war.
>
> Article 15
>
> Military necessity admits of all direct destruction of life or limb of armed enemies, and of other persons whose destruction is incidentally unavoidable in the armed contests of the war ... it allows of all destruction of property, and obstruction of the ways and channels of traffic, travel, or communication, and of all withholding of sustenance or means of life from the enemy.
>
> Article 16
>
> Military necessity does not admit of cruelty ... It does not admit of the use of poison in any way, nor of the wanton devastation of a district ... in general, military necessity does not include any act of hostility which makes the return to peace unnecessarily difficult.

Thus, from early on, military necessity, central to the Code,[101] has not only been crafted as authorizing a *specified* list of measures but also that the measure must be taken – witnessing an apparent influence of natural law in Lieber[102] – in tandem with humanity.[103]

Another crucial event in the development of the international regulation of war in general and the concept of military necessity in particular was the St. Petersburg Declaration of 1868, also known as the *Declaration Renouncing the Use, in Time of War, of Explosive Projectiles under 400 Grammes Weight*.[104] The last paragraph of the Declaration is often quoted by a number of authors[105] as

101 Jens David Ohlin and Larry May, *Necessity in International Law* (New York: Oxford University Press, 2016), p. 95.

102 Ibid.

103 Schmitt, above note 98, p. 802. Ohlin and May provide a more detailed analysis of how Lieber's military necessity operates within the bounds of the Code itself. Ohlin and May, above note 101, pp. 95–106.

104 Text of the St. Petersburg Declaration of 1868 is available at, 'The Declaration of St. Petersburg, 1868', *American Journal of International Law*, 1(2): 1907, pp. 95–96. A full analysis of the Declaration is available at, Hans-Peter Gasser, 'A Look at the Declaration of St Petersburg of 1868', *International Review of the Red Cross*, 33 (297): 1993, pp. 511–516.

105 Some of these works include: Nils Melzer, 'Keeping the Balance between Military Necessity and Humanity: A Response to Four Critiques of the ICRC's Interpretive Guidance on the Notion of Direct Participation in Hostilities', *New York University Journal of International Law and Politics*, 42(3): 2010, pp. 831–916; Draper, above note 94; Schmitt, above note 98, pp. 796–839; Nobuo Hayashi, 'Requirements of Military Necessity in International Humanitarian Law and International Criminal Law', *Boston University International Law Journal*, 28(1): 2010, pp. 46–47. See also, Schmitt, above note 103, p. 799.

one that established the continuing IHL principle of balancing necessity with humanity:

> The contracting or acceding parties reserve to themselves the right to come to an understanding, hereafter, whenever a precise proposition shall be drawn up, in view of future improvements which may be effected in the armament of troops, *in order to maintain the principles which they have established, and to reconcile the necessities of war with the laws of humanity* (*emphasis added*).

Then comes the story of the Hague Conventions of 1899 and 1907. Following the first[106] *Geneva Convention for the Amelioration of the Condition of the Wounded in Armies in the Field* of 1864 – considered to be the founding text of contemporary IHL[107] – the Hague Conventions of 1899 and 1907 stand high in their function as the complete textual basis for modern IHL. The conventions covered multiple facets of the conduct of hostilities on land, sea and even air (the use of balloons).[108] Regarding necessity, it has been observed that necessity found its way at least through three avenues to the Hague Conventions: (a) by specific references allowing necessity-driven deviations from regulated usage;[109] (b) by implicit references in such expressions as 'so far as possible'; and (c) by understandings between the military delegates in the *travaux préparatoires* that certain provisions were to be understood as conditional on military capacity.[110] The dominant visibility of military necessity in the Hague Conventions is, however, balanced by the principle of humanity. For example, the preamble to the fourth 1907 Convention Respecting the Laws and Customs of War on Land, reads:

---

106 For the evolution of the so-called Geneva Conventions, see, Dinstein, above note 94, pp. 10–11.

107 *The 1864 Geneva Convention*, available at, https://www.icrc.org/eng/resources/documents/treaty/geneva-convention-1864.htm.

108 Dinstein, above note 106.

109 For example, Article 23 (g) of Hague Convention 1907 (IV) reads that: "In addition to the prohibitions provided by special Conventions, it is especially forbidden … [t]o destroy or seize the enemy's property, *unless such destruction or seizure be imperatively demanded by the necessities of war* (*emphasis added*)."

110 Bogliolo, above note 86, pp. 11–12, *referring to*, Geoffrey Best, *Humanity in Warfare: the Modern History of the International Law of Armed Conflicts* (London: Methuen, 1983), p. 177.

> According to the views of the High Contracting Parties, these provisions, the wording of which has been inspired by the *desire to diminish the evils of war, as far as military requirements permit*, are intended to serve as a general rule of conduct for the belligerents in their mutual relations and in their relations with the inhabitants (*emphasis added*).

The two italicized phrases have been read together to refer to the necessity-humanity balance in IHL.[111] Another notable provision of the Hague Conventions was the preambular principle that "[t]he right of belligerents to adopt means of injuring the enemy is not unlimited."[112] Some have read this provision and similar provisions in the Hague Convention as representatives of "a carefully thought-out balance between the principles of military necessity and humanity. Every one of its rules constitutes a dialectical compromise between these two opposing forces".[113]

We now move to the conception of the doctrine of *Kriegsräson* (necessity as justification for all acts of war). In 1870, Prussia accepted the Lieber Code which had limited necessity to specified acts in specified circumstances and to a specified scope. When, however, Germany invaded Belgian territory in August 1914, German Chancellor Theobald von Bethmann-Hollweg stood before the Reichstag and said: "Gentlemen, *we are now [acting] in self-defense; and necessity knows no law! ... Gentlemen, this is against the rules of international law* ... France would wait but we could not! (*emphasis added*)."[114] The Chancellor's statement has been cited as the launching event for the concept of *Kriegsräson*, contained in the expression *Kriegsräson geht vor Kriegsmanier* (military expediency overrules the manner of warfare), a concept in IHL which advocates that military necessity outweighs *any* rule of the laws and customs of war.[115] The doctrine was heavily influenced by German philosophy which allowed disregard of the binding nature of laws of war in times of extreme necessity especially "when the sole means of avoiding severe danger was to violate the law or when compliance with the law might jeopardize the conflict's ultimate objectives."[116] The general application of necessity to any and

111 Bogliolo, ibid, pp. 4, 12–13.

112 See the preambles to the Convention with Respect to the Laws and Customs of War on Land (Convention II, 1899); and the Convention Respecting the Laws and Customs of War on Land (Convention IV, 1907).

113 Schmitt, above note 98, p. 798.

114 As cited in Michael Greenfield Partem, 'The Buffer System in International Relations', *The Journal of Conflict Resolution*, 27(1): 1983, p. 11.

115 Bogliolo, above note 86, pp. 10–11.

116 Schmitt, above note 98, pp. 796–797. See also, Bogliolo, ibid, p. 11.

all laws and customs of war – *jus ad bellum* and *jus in bello*[117] – was strongly rejected elsewhere to the point of pushing Elihu Root, then President of the American Society of International Law, to remark: "[e]ither the doctrine of *kriegsraison* must be abandoned definitely and finally, or there is an end of international law, and in its place will be left a world without law in which alliances of some nations to the extent of their power enforce their ideals of suitable conduct upon other nations."[118]

Finally, we mention the return to the *Kriegsräson* during the Nuremberg Trials. Although the Nuremberg International Military Tribunal established after the end of the Second World War was mainly remembered, *inter alia*, for its rulings on superior order,[119] it also rejected the concept of *kriegsräson*. In the *Hostages* case, the Tribunal stated that:

> It is apparent from the evidence of these defendants that *they considered military necessity, a matter to be determined by them, a complete justification of their acts. We do not concur* in the view that the rules of warfare are anything less than they purport to be. Military necessity or expediency do not justify a violation of positive rules. International law is prohibitive law … (*emphasis added*).[120]

A basis for the Tribunal's rejection of *kriegsräson* was its preference for the rules of the 1907 Hague Convention which "undoubtedly represented an advance over existing international law at the time of their adoption … but by 1939 these rules laid down in the Convention were recognized by all civilized nations, and were regarded as being declaratory of the laws and customs of war."[121] Such declaration, therefore, took back military necessity to its application only when allowed by specific positive rules. According to the Tribunal, "military necessity was not a justification independent of underlying rules; rather, it was applicable *only if the rule contemplated its applicability*, and then only *to the extent that the rule permitted* (*emphasis added*)."[122]

117 Schmitt, ibid.

118 Elihu Root, Opening Address, President, President of the American Society of International Law, 'Opening Address at the Fifteenth Annual Meeting of the American Society of International Law' (27 April 1921), *Proceedings of the American Society of International Law*, 15 (1921), Proc. 1, p. 3.

119 N. C. H. Dunbar, 'Military Necessity in War Crimes Trials', *British Year Book of International Law*, 29: 1952, p. 442.

120 As quoted in Downey, above note 95, p. 253.

121 As quoted in Dinstein, above note 94, p. 10.

122 As quoted in Bogliolo, above note 86, p. 15.

By way of summarizing this sub-section, therefore, one can observe that necessity as applied to the law of warfare (i.e., military necessity) has been recognized for application with the proviso that acts taken under military necessity are balanced with the principle of humanity. As far as the scope of military necessity is concerned, the concept began as a limited exception authorized only when specific provisions of the laws of war allow it. The Germans, through the concept of *kriegsräson*, tried to expand it as applicable against all laws of war. However, the experience of the Second World War led to the understanding that military necessity should, as originally regulated by the Lieber Code, apply only in circumstances specifically allowed by the rules governing military conduct.

5.2.3 *Military Necessity: A Rule of Exception, Justification or Excuse?*

The rule since the 'taming' of *kriegsräson* by the Nuremberg Tribunal has been to limit the application of military necessity to specific cases. Hayashi begins his analysis of the modern notion of military necessity by referring to the traditional distinction among exception, justification and excuse (see, Sub-section 4.2.2 above on the distinction between these three notions).[123] He then argues that whereas the way the relevant IHL instruments have been prepared so far strongly supports an *exception* form of military necessity, there is still a doubt if military necessity, like self-preservation/self-defense, can, under certain circumstances, go beyond express exceptional clauses.[124] Reference is made in this regard to the ICJ's statement in *Legality of the Threat or Use of Nuclear Weapons* that it "cannot lose sight of the fundamental right of every State to survival, and thus its right to resort to self-defense ... *when its survival is at stake* (*emphasis added*)"[125] and that it "cannot conclude definitively whether the threat or use of nuclear weapons would be lawful or unlawful in an extreme circumstance of self-defense, in which the very survival of a State would be at stake".[126] There seems, therefore, an undecided issue whether in situations of war calling for extreme self-defense there is a possibility for invoking military necessity against all laws of war.[127]

123 Hayashi, above note 105, pp. 49–50.

124 Ibid, p. 52.

125 *Legality of the Threat or Use of Nuclear Weapons*, above note 26, p. 263, para. 96.

126 Ibid, p. 266, para. E; p. 263, para. 97.

127 Ibid. Nevertheless, Hayashi cites a number of references to conclude that "[t]o most commentators, military necessity has no place in international humanitarian law outside the confines of specific exceptional clauses." Hayashi, above note 105, p. 55.

The concept of necessity in IHL is different from the concept of necessity in CIL codified in the ARSIWA. Whereas military necessity in IHL applies only if allowed by a provision of the relevant treaty and to the extent allowed by that provision, necessity in the ARSIWA applies to all provisions of a treaty unless there is a general provision in the treaty, or in some of the articles of the treaty, providing that the defense of necessity does not apply to the treaty, or to some of the articles of the treaty (Article 25(2)(a) of the ARSIWA). Hayashi also refers to another difference between them. In the ARSIWA, necessity may be invoked only where the act in question 'is the only means available' to safeguard an essential interest (Article 25(1)(a)). Military necessity does not contain this requirement.[128] But what are the contemporary elements of military necessity? Sub-section 5.2.4 addresses this question.

5.2.4 *The Elements of Military Necessity*

One of the issues with the notion of military necessity is that there is, except for the broad description in Lieber Code Article 14, no textual definition of military necessity.[129] The absence of textual definition has been compounded by the absence – unlike in the case of the concept of necessity in WTO law – of interpretation by IHL tribunals (for instance the ICTY)[130] identifying the elements of military necessity. Even the ICRC presents military necessity in general as permitting "only that degree and kind of force, not otherwise prohibited by the law of armed conflict" that is required in order to achieve the legitimate purpose of the conflict.[131] This scenario may have led to Downey's statement that military necessity is the most elusive concept in the law of war.[132] As a result, different authors have been presenting their own definitions of military necessity. For example, Downey defines military necessity as:

> an urgent need, admitting of no delay, for the taking by a commander of measures which are indispensable for forcing as quickly as possible the complete surrender of the enemy by means of regulated violence, and which are not forbidden by the laws and customs of war,

128 Ibid, p. 58.

129 Ibid, p. 59.

130 Regarding the ICTY, Hayashi observed that "the [ICTY] has not defined military necessity. Nor has it discussed the requirements of military necessity at any length. Yet the tribunal's various chambers have not shied away from making factual determinations about the existence or absence of military necessity in the context of specific incidents." Ibid, p. 101.

131 Melzer, above note 93, p. 79.

132 Downey, above note 95.

and then discusses four elements in his definition.[133]

Hayashi has, based on the relevant texts as well as national (for example, Israeli) and international cases (for example, ICJ, Nuremberg and ICTY) cases, come close to what may be presented as a definition of military necessity by identifying and discussing in detail four requirements, some of which resemble the WTO law notion of 'weighing and balancing' test:

1. that the measure was taken primarily for some specific military purpose;
2. that the measure was required for the attainment of the military purpose, further divided into three sub-elements;
   a. the measure was materially relevant to the attainment of the military purpose;
   b. of those materially relevant measures that were reasonably available, the measure taken was the least injurious;
   c. the injury that the measure would cause was not disproportionate to the gain that it would achieve;
3. that the military purpose for which the measure was taken was in conformity with IHL; and
4. that the measure itself was otherwise in conformity with IHL.[134]

He then adds miscellaneous requirements over and above those mentioned above: knowledge of the belligerent's purposes; urgency of the measure; degrees of gravity of the situation; and competence of the military personnel taking the measures.[135]

To conclude Section 5.2, therefore, at least since the release of the Lieber Code, necessity has generally been recognized as applicable to the laws of war. There seems to be no debate at least on one issue: that the carrying out of actions under military necessity must be balanced with the principle of humanity, the ubiquitous rule of IHL. Except during the short period when it was considered an exception to all laws of war (*kriegsräson*), military necessity has been accepted only as an exception to specific provisions of the laws of war which allow for the taking of actions under military necessity. As far as

133 Ibid, p. 254. The four elements of his definition of military necessity are: (1) an urgent need admitting of no delay for the taking by an army commander of; (2) measures which are indispensable for forcing as quickly as possible the complete surrender of the enemy; (3) by means of regulated violence, and (4) which are not forbidden by the laws and customs of war.

134 Hayashi, above note 105, pp. 62–93.

135 Ibid, pp. 94–101.

the relationship of military necessity with the other rules of IHL, there seems to be a consensus that military necessity takes the form of an exception to the specific rules it is tied to, and not the form of a justification or an excuse. Although military necessity is yet to be clearly defined and its elements articulated either by IHL treaties or state/tribunal practices, scholars have identified some elements for the concept of necessity in IHL which resemble the Concepts of necessity in WTO law and the ARSIWA.

5.3 International Environmental Law

Section 5.3 aims to show that IEnL has become a field of PIL where the WTO law and the ARSIWA concepts of necessity – which vary in their contents – have been adopted and therefore a challenge arises as to which one to select in which cases. The influence of the concept of necessity in WTO law on IEnL has been through provisions within the legal texts of the WTO Agreement which are understood to be relevant to IEnL. These provisions can take the form of substantive obligations (such as those in the TBT Agreement or the SPS Agreement) or the form of affirmative defense (such as Article XX(b) of the GATT 1994 or Article XIV(b) of the GATS). The influence of the CIL (ARSIWA) concept of necessity in IEnL has been recognized in environmental, or predominantly environmental, disputes outside of the WTO (for example, before the ICJ).

It is true that WTO law and IEnL are two different fields of PIL. However, a number of provisions of the WTO Agreement have been included in this Section, which discusses IEnL, for two reasons. Firstly, some leading publications on IEnL consider these provisions of the WTO Agreement as part of (relevant to) the study of IEnL.[136] These provisions and the case law on them

136 See, for instance, Philippe Sands, *Principles of International Environmental Law* (2nd ed.) (Cambridge: Cambridge University Press, 2003), pp. 940–1019; Alexandre Kiss and Dinah Shelton, *A Guide to International Environmental Law* (Leiden: Martinus Nijhoff Publishers, 2007), pp. 242–250; Malgosia Fitzmaurice, *Contemporary Issues in International Environmental Law* (Cheltenham (UK) and Northampton, MA (USA): Edward Elgar, 2009), pp. 22–26; Joanna Gomula, 'Environmental disputes in the WTO', in Malgosia Fitzmaurice, David M. Ong and Panos Merkouris (eds.), *Research Handbook on International Environmental Law* (Cheltenham (UK) and Northampton, MA (USA): Edward Elgar, 2010), pp. 401–425; Edith Brown Weiss, John H. Jackson and Nathalie Bernasconi-Osterwalder (eds.), *Reconciling Environment and Trade* (2nd ed.) (Leiden: Martinus Nijhoff, 2008); Elli Louka, *International Environmental Law: Fairness, Effectiveness, and World Order* (Cambridge: Cambridge University Press, 2006), pp. 383–423; Ernst-Ulrich Petersmann, 'International Trade Law and International Environmental

include the concept of necessity (i.e., environmental necessity). Secondly, this book aims to discuss the interoperability between the concepts of necessity in WTO law and other fields of international law. One of the fields of international law where the concepts of necessity in WTO law and CIL have both been used to defend measures taken as necessary to protect the environment has been IEnL. This experience in IEnL of reference to the concepts of necessity in WTO law and CIL will be important in giving context to the discussion in Chapter 6 on the interoperability between the concepts of necessity in WTO law and other fields of international law.

5.3.1 *General Remarks*

Necessity in IEnL is best discussed in the context of the preservation, protection and conservation[137] of the environment. The University of Oregon maintains an updatable database of IEAs. As at December 2023, the university identified over 3,700 environmental agreements, either multilateral, bilateral or of other nature.[138] Scattered within these agreements are provisions dealing with key principles of IEnL, common legal requirements and implementing measures such as assessment methods, regulatory measures, economic measures, domestic measures as well as national and inter-state measures.[139] The guiding principles of IEAs include: sovereignty over natural resources and the responsibility not to cause damage to the environment of other states or to areas beyond national jurisdiction; taking preventive action (prevention of harm); co-operation; sustainable development; precaution; the polluter-pays principle; common but differentiated responsibility; the duty to know; the duty to inform and consult; public participation; intergenerational equity; and equitable utilization of shared resources.[140]

One of the issues raised in the practice of taking measures for the protection of the environment is the necessity of taking the measures. In other words, it is possible that some IEAs or related international instruments (including

Law: Prevention and Settlement of International Environmental Disputes in GATT', *Journal of World Trade*, 21(1): 1993, pp. 43–81.

137 The terms 'preservation', 'protection' and 'conservation' may have, not only in the IEAs but also in other legal documents, different meanings. In this Section, unless there is a direct reference to a term specifically used by a given international legal instrument (for example the Preamble to the WTO Agreement), the term 'protect' or 'protection' has been used, for the purpose of convenience, to represent the cumulative idea, as the case may be, of these three and related terms.

138 Available at, https://iea.uoregon.edu.

139 As contained in detail in Kiss and Shelton, above note 136, pp. 111–154.

140 Sands, above note 136, pp. 231–289; ibid, pp. 89–109.

the legal texts of the WTO Agreement) may contain provisions that generally or specifically oblige or allow states to take 'necessary' measures for the protection of the environment. These authorizations may be presented in two forms. First, they may be presented as substantive rights/obligations, i.e., they entitle/oblige state parties to take measures that are necessary for the protection of the environment or to prevent an environmental hazard.[141] The focus of this section, however, is in the second form of authorization – necessity as a defense – i.e., allowing states to defend measures[142] otherwise inconsistent with their international obligations if the measures are necessary to protect the environment. It remains to be seen if both forms of environmental necessity have the same scope in the context of the concept of necessity. Sub-section 5.3.2 briefly refers to examples of the first form of necessity in IEnL and Sub-section 5.3.3 will discuss the second form of necessity in IEnL. Provisions of the WTO Agreement relevant to both forms of necessity will be discussed respectively under these two sub-sections.

5.3.2 *Substantive Rights/Obligations to Take Necessary Environmental Measures*

Substantive rights/obligations to take necessary environmental measures can be found in the IEAs themselves or related international legal instruments. The WTO's legal texts will be referred to as an example for the latter category of instruments.

The following four conventions may be cited as pertinent examples in the category of substantive necessary measures in IEAs. The Fourth recital of the preamble to the Basel Convention on the Control of Transboundary Movements of Hazardous Wastes and their Disposal provides: "[c]onvinced that *States should take necessary measures* to ensure that the management of hazardous wastes and other wastes… (*emphasis added*)". Article 4(2)(c) allows each Party to take measures to "ensure that persons involved in the management of hazardous wastes or other wastes within it *take such steps as are necessary* to prevent pollution due to hazardous wastes and other wastes… (*emphasis added*)".

---

141 See, for example, the fourth recital of the preamble to, as well as Articles 4(2)(c) [Article 4 is titled *General Obligations*], 9(2)(a) and 9(3) of the Basel Convention on the Control of Transboundary Movements of Hazardous Wastes and their Disposal and Articles 16(2), 17(4) and 18(1) of the Cartagena Protocol on Biosafety to the Convention on Biological Diversity.

142 For example, Article 25 of the ARSIWA or Article XX(b)/(g) of the GATT 1994 and Article XIV(b) of the GATS.

Article 16(2) of the Cartagena Protocol on Biosafety to the Convention on Biological Diversity provides that "[m]easures based on risk assessment shall be imposed *to the extent necessary* to prevent adverse effects of the living modified organism on the conservation and sustainable use of biological diversity (*emphasis added*)." Article 17(4) provides that "[i]n order to minimize any significant adverse effects on the conservation and sustainable use of biological diversity ... each Party ... shall immediately consult the affected or potentially affected State to ... and *initiate necessary action*, including emergency measures (*emphasis added*)." Moreover, Article 18(4) provides: "[i]n order to avoid adverse effects on the conservation and sustainable use of biological diversity ... each Party shall *take necessary measures* (*emphasis added*)."

There are also a number of provisions in the UNCLOS[143] referring to necessity (necessary measures). Article 117, for instance, obliges states to "take, or to cooperate with other States in taking, such measures for their respective nationals *as may be necessary* for the conservation of the living resources of the high seas (*emphasis added*)." Article 118 obliges states whose nationals exploit identical living resources, or different living resources in the same area to "enter into negotiations with a view to *taking the measures necessary* for the conservation of the living resources concerned (*emphasis added*). Article 145 mandates that "[*n*]*ecessary measures shall be taken* ... with respect to activities in the [seabed and ocean floor and subsoil thereof, beyond the limits of national jurisdiction] to ensure effective protection for the marine environment (*emphasis added*)." Article 146 provides that "[w]ith respect to activities in the [seabed and ocean floor and subsoil thereof, beyond the limits of national jurisdiction], *necessary measures shall be taken* to ensure effective protection of human life (*emphasis added*)." Finally, Article 194(5) provides that "[t]he measures taken in accordance with [Part XII of the Convention] shall include those *necessary to protect and preserve*[144] rare or fragile ecosystems as well as the habitat of depleted, threatened or endangered species and other forms of marine life (*emphasis added*)".

The Bamako Convention on the Ban of the Import into Africa and the Control of Transboundary Movement and Management of Hazardous Wastes within Africa, in paragraph 15 of its preamble, states: "[r]ecognizing also that *where necessary* hazardous wastes should be transported in accordance with

143 The term 'necessary' appears 115 times in different forms in this Convention. Only five have been selected.

144 The title of Article 194 is *Measures to prevent, reduce and control pollution of the marine environment.* Does the wording of paragraph (5) look like GATT 1994 Article XX(b) and GATS Article XIV(b) and, hence, call for a similar interpretation?

relevant international conventions and recommendations (*emphasis added*)." Article 4(3)(e) of the Convention obliges each party to "ensure that persons involved in the management of hazardous wastes within its jurisdiction *take such steps as are necessary* to prevent pollution arising from such wastes and 2 (*emphasis added*)."

There are also provisions in WTO law which allow (oblige) Members to take measures necessary to protect the environment. The first paragraph of the preamble to WTO Agreement refers to the recognition by the Members of their obligation to allow "for the optimal use of the world's resources in accordance with the objective of sustainable development, seeking both to protect and preserve the environment." This clause has been interpreted as imposing on the Members the obligation to take trade measures as allowed by the WTO Agreement while simultaneously taking measures necessary to protect the environment.[145]

The Decision on Trade and Environment issued by the WTO ministerial Council established the Committee on Trade and Environment[146] to address the question of balancing trade and environmental measures. This Decision has been understood as showing the intent of WTO Members to allow the implementation, in their trade relations, of WTO-consistent measures they deem necessary to protect and prevent the environment.[147]

Article 2.2 of the TBT Agreement specifically identifies the taking of measures necessary for the protection of the environment as one of its legitimate objectives. Under Article 2.2 of the TBT Agreement Members shall ensure that technical regulations, standards and conformity assessment procedures do not create unnecessary obstacles to international trade.

One of the principles of the SPS Agreement is that SPS measures must be applied only to the extent necessary to protect human, animal or plant life or health (Article 2.2) and that the measures must not be "more trade-restrictive than required to achieve their appropriate level of sanitary or phytosanitary

---

145 Appellate Body Report, *US – Gasoline* (*1996*), p. 30; Appellate Body Report, *US – Shrimp* (*1998*), para. 185. A detailed analysis on the works of the Appellate Body to balance trade and environment measures is available at, Gabrielle Marceau and Julian Wyatt, 'The WTO's Efforts to Balance Economic Development and Environmental Protection: A Short Review of Appellate Body Jurisprudence', *Latin American Journal of International Trade Law*, 1(1): 2013, pp. 291–314. See also, Sands, above note 136, p. 948.

146 For more on the CTE and its works see, WTO, *The Committee on Trade and Environment* (*'regular' CTE*), available at, https://www.wto.org/english/tratop_e/envir_e/wrk_committee_e.htm.

147 P. K. Rao, *The World Trade Organization and the Environment* (London: Macmillan Press Ltd., 2000), pp. 103–110.

protection." (Article 5.6). Article 5.7 of the SPS Agreement also lays out the precautionary principle, one of the main principles in IEnL, which has attracted a lot of scholarly attention. Discussing the precautionary principle is beyond the scope of this book, but its link to necessity can be investigated.[148]

5.3.3 *Environmental Necessity as a Defense*

International law allows, and IEnL discusses in much detail, the legitimization of measures taken to protect the environment in situations where the measures breach a substantive obligation under international law. Such legitimization usually comes from two main sources: (1) the CIL defense of necessity as codified in Article 25 of the ARSIWA and invoked mostly to defend 'environmentally necessary' measures taken in breach of obligations arising out of treaties, the law of the sea and IHRL; and (2) the environment-related paragraphs in the General Exceptions of WTO agreements such as the GATT 1994 and the GATS invoked to defend 'environmentally necessary' measures taken in breach of obligations arising out of the relevant WTO agreement. The CIL and the WTO law environmental necessity defenses are briefly presented below.

Let us begin with the environmental necessity defense under CIL. The practice of invoking environmental necessity under the CIL developed out of a series of incidents and disputes and finally the works of the ILC on state responsibility.[149] Since the details of some of the four cases discussed in this sub-section have been presented elsewhere in this book, they are briefly mentioned here for the purpose of showing that they contributed to the recognition of the environmental necessity defense under CIL.

In the *Russian Fur Seals Controversy* (1893) (the facts of this incident were presented in more detail in Section 2.1.7), the Russian Foreign Minister wrote to the British Ambassador that the disputed Russian measure was taken because of "'an 'absolute need' for 'an immediate provisional measure' in view of the 'imminence' of the hunting season".[150] While preparing ILC's Draft Articles on necessity, Professor Roberto Ago observed that the Russian Foreign Minister's communication presented a typical case of necessity defense in international law.[151]

---

148 See, for example, Daniel Dobos, 'The Necessity of Precaution: The Future of Ecological Necessity and the Precautionary Principle', *Fordham Environmental Law Review*, 13(2): 2002, pp. 375–408. See also, discussion in different sections of Malgosia Fitzmaurice, 'Necessity in International Environmental Law' in Dekker and Hey, above note 22, pp. 159–192.

149 Ibid, p. 159.

150 Fitzmaurice, above note 148, p. 164. See also, Ago, above note 4, p. 27, para. 33; Agius, above note 31, pp. 99–100.

151 Ago, ibid.

In the *Bering Fur Seals Fisheries Jurisdiction* arbitration (1893) (the facts of this incident were presented in more detail in Sub-ection 2.2.2), the US agent, in defending his government's seizure of British fishing ships, stated that "*the right of self-defense on the part of a nation is a perfect and paramount right to which all others are subordinate, and which upon no admitted theory of international law has ever been surrendered; that it extends to all the material interests of a nation important to be defended...*" and that a nation is "entitled to protect itself against the injury, *by whatever force may be reasonably necessary, according to the usages established in analogous cases* (*emphasis added*)."[152] Professor Ago argued that the US defense, though it made use of the term 'necessity' could not be considered a necessity defense but an act of self-protection,[153] while Professor Fitzmaurice argues on the contrary that although not all core elements of the concept of necessity defense were present in the US defense (such as the 'only means' element), "the most fundamental elements of this concept were included in the US approach, i.e., the protection of the 'essential interest' of the community of states and the 'imminent peril' to the conservation of seals."[154]

The Torrey *Canyon* incident (1967) where the British Government decided the bomb the vessel to avoid further oil spill,[155] is interesting to raise as a typical case of environmental necessity defense under CIL. Ago is convinced that "the action taken by the British Government outside the areas subject to its jurisdiction would have had to be recognized as internationally lawful, since the conditions for a 'state of necessity' were clearly fulfilled"[156] and Fitzmaurice is convinced that the incident meets all the elements of the defence of necessity under international law.[157] Ago used his discussion of the *Torrey Canyon* incident to underline the importance of proportionality in necessity defenses: "Any measures taken must, of course, be proportionate to the actual or threatened damage"[158] and the ILC based its illustration of the concept of proportionality on this incident.[159] The *Torrey Canyon* incident led to the 1969 International Maritime Organization Convention Relating to Intervention on the High Seas in cases of Oil Pollution Casualties. Article 1(1) of the Convention, reflecting,

152 Ibid, p. 27, para. 34.
153 Ibid, p. 28, para. 34.
154 Fitzmaurice, above note 148, p. 166.
155 A short summary of the incident is available at, Ago, above note 4, p. 28, para. 35.
156 Ibid.
157 Fitzmaurice, above note 148, p. 167.
158 Ago, above note 4, p. 29, para. 36.
159 As cited in Fitzmaurice, above note 148, pp. 167–168.

in part, the necessity defense, states that the Parties to the Convention may take "such measures on the high seas *as may be necessary to prevent, mitigate or eliminate grave and imminent danger* to their coastline or related interests from the pollution or threat of pollution of the sea by oil (*emphasis added*)."

Finally, in the *Gabčíkovo-Nagymaros Project* (Hungary *v.* Slovakia) (1997) (the facts in this incident will be briefly presented in Sub-section 6.4.2) the ICJ made a comprehensive analysis of the environmental necessity defense under CIL. Before the ICJ, Hungary defended its measure under the then Article 33 of the Draft ARSIWA stating a 'state of ecological necessity'. In the first case of its kind where draft Article 33 was invoked as a defense, the ICJ accepted the principles of Article 33 as defense and, in what has been hailed as a landmark ruling, declared that the contents of Article 33 reflect a rule of CIL and that the defense would be accepted only on an exceptional basis. The Court, after accepting 'ecological necessity' as a valid ground for defense in breach of a primary rule of international law, dissected Article 33 into its elements, applied them to Hungary's measures.[160] In examining whether Hungary could benefit from the defense, the Court addressed the following questions: (a) How should one understand necessity? (b) Under what conditions can necessity be invoked? (c) What are the legal consequences of a state of necessity? (d) To what extent can a state of necessity be regarded as part and parcel of existing international law? (e) To what extent can (transboundary) detrimental interference with the environment or the utilization of natural resources give rise to a state of necessity? (f) To what extent could Hungary validly invoke a state of necessity in order to justify an otherwise unlawful suspension and abandonment of works that it was committed to perform under the 1977 Treaty? (g) To what extent would a state of necessity free a state invoking such a state from a duty to pay compensation for damage caused to another state? (h) Who can authoritatively make such a factual assessment:[161] the state claiming necessity

160 *Case Concerning the Gabčíkovo-Nagymaros Project (Hungary v. Slovakia)*, Judgment, 25 September 1997, ICJ Rep. 1997, p. 40–41, paras. 51–52, as also confirmed in *Legal Consequences of the Construction of a Wall in the Occupied Palestinian Territory*, Advisory Opinion, 9 July 2004, ICJ Rep. 2004, p. 195, para. 140.

161 In *Gabčíkovo-Nagymaros Project*, the ICJ made it clear that "the State concerned is not the sole judge of whether those conditions [of state of necessity] have been met." *Case Concerning the Gabčíkovo-Nagymaros Project*, ibid, p. 40, para. 51. Agius' belief, based on her reading of this statement of the ICJ, is that: "the current position is that the assessment of whether a factual necessity is at hand must indeed be determined by the State, but that such an assessment may be scrutinized by affected parties, the international community as a whole and, as seen from case law, international legal bodies to which the case may be rendered". Maria Agius, *The Invocation of Necessity in International Law*,

or a third party such as the ICJ or a tribunal? In other words, is the determination of a state of necessity and the taking of necessary measures up to the state or it is reviewable?[162]

We not discuss environmental necessity defense under WTO law. There are provisions in some of the legal texts of the WTO Agreement, particularly the General Exceptions in the GATT 1994, the GATS and the TRIPS Agreement, that allow Members to take measures which, while in breach of the provisions of the said agreements, are necessary to protect the environment. These provisions show how the defense of environmental necessity in these WTO agreements can affect the understanding of necessity in IEnL.

Some paragraphs of the General Exceptions of the GATT 1994 have been recognized as embodying environmental defense. Particular reference is made to paragraphs (b) and (g) of Article XX[163] which respectively provide:

> Subject to the requirement that … nothing in this Agreement shall be construed to prevent the adoption or enforcement by any Member of measures:
> (b) necessary to protect human, animal or plant life or health;[164]
> (g) relating to the conservation of exhaustible natural resources if such measures are made effective in conjunction with restrictions on domestic production or consumption.

Article 27(2) of the TRIPS Agreement allows a WTO Member to defend the exclusion from patentability of some inventions for, *inter alia*, environmental reasons. The provision reads:

> Members may exclude from patentability inventions, the prevention within their territory of the commercial exploitation of which is *necessary* to protect *ordre public* or morality, including *to protect human, animal or plant life or health* or *to avoid serious prejudice to the environment*,

---

available at, https://www.uppsalajuristernasalumnistiftelse.se/wp-content/uploads/2014/11/Maria-Agius.pdf, p. 16.

162 Fitzmaurice, above note 148, pp. 175–176, 178.

163 Steve Charnovitz, 'Exploring the Environmental Exceptions in GATT Article XX', *Journal of World Trade*, 25(5): 1991, pp. 37–55; Indira Carr, 'International Trade Rules and Environmental Effects', in Shawkat Alam *et al.* (eds.), *Routledge Handbook of International Environmental Law* (London and New York: Routledge, 2013), pp. 547–560.

164 Also found in Article XIV(b) of the GATS.

provided that such exclusion is not made merely because the exploitation is prohibited by their law (*emphasis added*).

5.3.4 *Preference between Environmental Necessity Defenses*

Sub-section 5.3.3 showed that there are at least two types of environmental necessity defenses: necessity defense under CIL and necessity defenses under WTO law. As will be shown in further detail in Sub-section 11.3.1, there are some fundamental differences between these two types of defenses. For example:

(a) while the CIL defense of necessity requires that the disputed measure be the *only* reasonably available measure, the WTO law of necessity defense envisages the possibility of the disputed measure still being accepted despite the reasonable availability of *alternative* measures if the alternative measures are more trade-restrictive and/or cannot make the same level of contribution to attain the objectives; and

(b) the CIL defense of necessity requires that the measure protect a 'grave and imminent peril' to the environment, but WTO law of necessity defense does not have such a requirement regarding the protection of the environment.

As will also be shown in Chapter 11, given the requirements mentioned above and the additional requirements in Article 25 of the ARSIWA (more details are provided in Section 5.4), defending a measure under the CIL defense of necessity appears to be more difficult than under WTO law. As will be detailed in Chapter 11, it is possible that a state may find itself in a situation of choosing between the two sources of necessity. As in the Argentine financial measure disputes at the ICSID, discussed in detail in Section 5.5, a state may take measures inconsistent with its obligations under an investment treaty and defend them as measures necessary to protect the environment. The adjudicating organ may then examine the defense by relying either on the 'weighing and balancing' test developed within the WTO or the CIL necessity defense as elaborated by the ICJ.

Whether the defending state's plea of necessity is to be analyzed under the CIL or the concept of necessity in WTO law could depend on a number of points: (a) Are the states WTO Members, parties to a regional economic community or tied only by a bilateral treaty? (b) Is the treaty partly or substantially trade/investment-centered? (c) Are there provisions in the treaty embodying exceptions? (d) How were those exceptions drafted? (e) Do the exception provisions resemble Article 25 of the ARSIWA or the General Exceptions of the relevant WTO agreement? (f) What was the nature of the circumstances that gave rise to the non-performance of treaty obligations?

The necessity defenses both in WTO law and CIL have been found to be able to fully address *all* environment-protecting, yet treaty violating, measures deemed necessary by the state. Surely the ICJ has accepted Article 25 of the ARSIWA as a legitimate ground to defend environmental necessity measures, but the ICJ appears to have accepted the defense because the defending party invoked the ARSIWA defense and more conveniently because the ICJ found that Article 25 of the ARSIWA embodies CIL. The ICJ did not explicitly rule that environmental necessity defense under international law is available *only* through Article 25 of the ARSIWA. It is possible, therefore, that tribunals, learning from the ICSID tribunals' experience of referring to the General Exceptions of the GATT 1994 (see Section 5.5), may rely on the WTO law environmental necessity rules to resolve disputes. Even if such tribunals resort to the ARSIWA necessity defense, they may import some elements of the concept of necessity in WTO law in the process of their analysis. For instance, they may refer to the 'weighing and balancing' test to measure the level of necessity of the disputed measure. They may also loosely borrow the concepts of good faith implementation and preventing abuse of the necessary measure from the interpretation of the *chapeau* of the General Exceptions of the relevant WTO agreement. Such cross-fertilization between these two concepts of necessity (in the ARSIWA and WTO law) will be discussed in detail in Chapter 12.

To conclude Section 5.3, therefore, IEnL has benefitted from substantial practice of the consideration and interpretation of 'environmental' necessity. Like IIL (see Section 5.5), IEnL has become a field of PIL where the concept of necessity in WTO law or the concept of necessity in CIL can, depending on the circumstances, be applicable. The concept of necessity in WTO law is applied in the context of international trade, i.e., measures taken to protect the environment in violation of international trade commitments whereas the concept of necessity in CIL is not limited to trade-related treaty commitments. The practice of applying the concepts of necessity in WTO law and the CIL (ARSIWA) in IEnL, as in some of the fields of international law considered in this chapter, invites us to consider coherence, as much as is possible, between these two concepts of necessity towards a more coherent understanding of necessity in international law.

5.4 The Law of State Responsibility as Codified in the ARSIWA

Some of the sections and sub-sections above (4.2.1, 4.2.2, 4.2.4, 4.2.5, 5.1.3 and 5.3.3) showed that the CIL concept of necessity as codified in the ARSIWA has taken different natures and forms and that there is a widespread use of the concept in international law. Section 5.4 discusses in brief the evolution, scope and elements of the concept of necessity in CIL as now contained in Article 25 of the ARSIWA. The discussions in this section will be used as the ground for the comparative analysis with the concept of necessity in WTO law in Chapter 11. The history of the works of the ILC's working group on state responsibility, not within the scope of this book, is well-documented.[165] Of relevance, however, is the evolution of the provisions that contained the defense of necessity. This section will heavily rely on the works of Ago and Crawford who have left us extensive reports on their respective drafts of the ARSIWA provisions on necessity. The narration begins with the works of Amador. It needs to be noted, however, that in this section and elsewhere in this book identifying the different works of the ILC by the respective rapporteurs is only for the purpose of convenience; the labors of their colleagues are duly recognized.

5.4.1 *Amador's Text: Mingling Necessity with Other CPW*

Although Amador's work was focused on the substantive rules of the international law of diplomatic protection, it contained an elementary provision on necessity. Article 13 of the draft combined necessity with *force majeure* and the alien's fault as circumstances that enable exoneration of the state from responsibility:[166]

> 1. the State shall not be responsible for injuries caused to an alien if the measures taken are the consequence of *force majeure* or of a *state of necessity* due to a grave and imminent peril threatening some vital interest of the State, provided that the State did not provoke the peril and was unable to counteract it by other means.

165 James Crawford, *The International Law Commission's Articles on State Responsibility: Introduction, Text and Commentaries* (Cambridge: Cambridge University Press, 2002), pp. 1–60; see also *Yearbook of the International Law Commission* (Vol. II) (United Nations, 1969), pp. 229–233, paras. 64–83.

166 To see the reasons why Amador, who admitted that state of necessity closely resembled self-defense (pp. 52–53), did not in his draft include self-defense as a circumstance exonerating a State from responsibility see *Yearbook of the International Law Commission* (Vol. II) (United Nations, 1958), pp. 52–53.

2. Similarly, the State shall not be responsible for the injuries caused if the injurious act was provoked by some fault on the part of the alien himself.
3. *Force majeure,* state of necessity and the fault imputable to the alien shall, if not admissible as grounds for exoneration from responsibility, constitute extenuating circumstances in the determination of the quantum of reparation aggravating circumstances.[167]

Amador, while admitting that the existence of the state of necessity was denied in some circles and that there was uncertainty that surrounds it, expressed his intention for including the defense. He explained that it is for the very reason of the uncertainty that surrounds the subject of necessity that he decided to include it in his draft with the recommendation that is needs a proper definition.[168] His concept of necessity, therefore, consisted three elements: (a) the peril must be one which threatens some vital interest of the State; (b) the peril must be 'grave and imminent', and not a simple threat (and here he refers to the *Neptune* case (1797) where the tribunal held that "the necessity which can be admitted to supersede all laws and to dissolve the distinctions of property and rights must be absolute and irresistible"); and (c) the State must have been unable to counteract [the peril] by other means.[169]

5.4.2 *Ago's Text: Identifying State of Necessity as a Separate* CPW

Ago's group can take the credit for preparing the now customary form of the defense of necessity in PIL. The addendum for Ago's eighth report to the ILC contains: a lengthy analysis of the philosophical history of the defense of necessity; its similarity and difference with the other CPW; a summary of international cases where the defense was invoked explicitly or implicitly; its application to circumstances where the state had an obligation to do or to refrain from doing a certain act in various fields of international law; whether it can be used in situations of use of force and humanitarian intervention; and the constituent elements of his version of state of necessity.[170] Ago greatly expanded the scope of the mandate of his work (see Sub-section 4.2.4), separated necessity from *force majeure* and presented it in his draft Article 33 as:

167 Ibid, p. 50.
168 Ibid, p. 53.
169 Ibid.
170 Ago, above note 4, pp. 14–51, paras. 1–51.

1. A state of necessity may not be invoked by a State as a ground for precluding the wrongfulness of an act of that State not in conformity with an international obligation of the State unless:
   (a) the act was the only means of safeguarding an essential interest of the State against a grave and imminent peril; and
   (b) the act did not seriously impair an essential interest of the State towards which the obligation existed.
2. In any case, a state of necessity may not be invoked by a State as a ground for precluding wrongfulness:
   (a) if the international obligation with which the act of the State is not in conformity arises out of a peremptory norm of GIL; or
   (b) if the international obligation with which the act of the State is not in conformity is laid down by a treaty which, explicitly or implicitly, excludes the possibility of invoking the state of necessity with respect to that obligation; or
   (c) if the State in question has contributed to the occurrence of the state of necessity.[171]

Like Amador, Ago was aware of the 'special' nature of necessity in international law and the opposition on its existence and substance. Thus, in the process of maintaining it in his text, Ago cautioned that:

> A number of *particularly strict conditions* would therefore have to be met. We shall attempt to enumerate them, assisted by the results of a long and careful study of the subject by the most authoritative writers, largely on the basis of the principles accepted in this connection by national legal systems.
>
> The 'excuse of necessity' may conceivably be accepted in international law *only on condition that it is absolutely of an exceptional nature*. It follows that the interest of a State in defeating, if need be, any subjective right of another State must in turn be one of those interests which are of *exceptional importance* to the State seeking to assert it. We are not, however, suggesting that the interests to be taken into account be limited to the 'existence' of the State (*emphasis added*).[172]

171 Available at, *Yearbook of the International Law Commission* (Vol. II, Part II) (United Nations, 1980), p. 34.

172 Ago, above note 4, p. 19, paras. 11–12.

This 'special' nature of the state of necessity, in comparison with the other CPW, has been reflected in the drafting of Article 33 in the sense that it was crafted in a "negative formula" and therefore "invocation of a state of necessity as a justification must be considered as *really constituting an exception* – and one *even more rarely admissible than* is the case with the other circumstances precluding wrongfulness (*emphasis added*)."[173] Ago's report then dissects this definition of necessity into six elements and discusses each of them as follows.

a. The peril, grave and imminent, must threaten an essential interest of the State

Ago explained the nature of 'essential interest', partly, as follows:

> The 'necessity' then invoked is a 'necessity of State'. The alleged situation of extreme peril does not take the form of a threat to the life of individuals whose conduct is attributed to the State, but represents a grave danger to the existence of the State itself, its political or economic survival, the continued functioning of its essential services, the maintenance of internal peace, the survival of a sector of its population, the preservation of the environment of its territory or a part thereof, etc. The situation may or may not be due to a sudden unforeseen external event; it may also be the foreseeable but unavoidable consequence of factors which have long been present.[174]

For Ago, "[t]he threat to such an essential interest of the State must be *extremely grave*,[175] representing *a present danger* to the threatened interest, and its occurrence must be *entirely beyond the control of the State* whose interest is threatened (*emphasis added*)."[176] Nevertheless, the Commission decided not to spell out the 'essential interests' of a State and that determination of what

173 *Yearbook of the International Law Commission*, above note 171, p. 51, para. 40. The ICJ, pointing at the *negative formulation* of Article 33 (the only CPW negatively formulated) similarly affirmed the exceptional nature of the state of necessity and its strict requirements. *Case Concerning the Gabčíkovo-Nagymaros Project*, above note 160 p. 40, para. 51. See also, *Legal Consequences of the Construction of a Wall in the Occupied Palestinian Territory*, above note 160, p. 195, para. 140.

174 Ago, above note 4, p. 14, para. 2.

175 Although Ago identifies the Article 33 peril as 'extremely grave', neither the ILC Commentary nor Ago's Report specify criteria for measuring 'gravity' to determine whether the 'peril' falls within the meaning of Article 33. Roman Boed, 'State of Necessity as a Justification for Internationally Wrongful Conduct', *Yale Human Rights and Development Law Journal*, 3(1): 2000, p. 16.

176 Ago, above note 4, pp. 19–20, para. 13; *Yearbook of the International Law Commission* (Vol. II, Part II), above note 171, p. 49, para. 33.

is 'essential' "depends on all the circumstances in which the State is placed in different specific situations".[177]

b. The act must be the only measure available to the state

It is in nature of governments to seek alternative measures in initiating or maintaining certain courses of action. However, Ago's state of necessity, exceptional in its nature, gives states no room for alternative measures, even more onerous ones:

> The [measure taken] ... *must truly be the only means available to it* for averting the extremely grave and imminent peril which it fears; in other words, it must be impossible for the peril to be averted by any other means, *even one which is much more onerous* but which can be adopted without a breach of international obligations. In addition, the conduct in question must be *clearly indispensable in its totality*, and not only in part, in order to preserve the essential interest which is threatened (*emphasis added*).[178]

Some authors have interpreted, although in relation to self-preservation, this requirement to mean that all other alternatives must be exhausted before a state can invoke necessity to justify an internationally unlawful conduct.[179] The ARSIWA text is not clear on this and Ago did not make any indication if the 'only measure' element had an exhaustion requirement in it.

c. The interest protected must be superior to the interest sacrificed

Necessity allows a state to sacrifice the interest of another state(s). In a statement that echoes a test of proportionality[180] or balance of interests[181] within the Article 33 necessity, Ago stated that:

> the interest of the State towards which the obligation existed – the interest sacrificed to the need of assuring the otherwise impossible defense of an 'essential' interest of the State – must itself be a less essential interest of the State in question ... The Commission considered this point particularly important in view of its having barred the possibility of the state

177 *Yearbook*, ibid, para. 32.

178 Ago, above note 4, p. 20, para. 14; ibid, para. 33.

179 Bin Cheng, *General Principles of Law as Applied by International Courts and Tribunals* (Cambridge: Cambridge University Press, 2006 edn.), p. 74, also referred to in, Boed, above note 175, f.n. 86.

180 James Crawford, 'The International Court of Justice and the Law of State Responsibility', in Christian J. Tams and James Sloan (eds.), *The Development of International Law by the International Court of Justice* (Oxford: Oxford University Press, 2013), , p. 80.

181 Boed, above note 175, pp. 18–19.

of necessity being invocable to safeguard the State's interest in its own 'existence' and nothing else.[182]

d. Necessity cannot be invoked against a peremptory norm of GIL
Understandably Ago and his colleagues "exclude the possibility that state of necessity operates as a circumstance precluding the wrongfulness of conduct not in keeping with an obligation stemming from one of the rules of *jus cogens* or certain rules of humanitarian international law."[183]

e. Necessity cannot be invoked if its applicability is prohibited by the relevant rule of obligation

Ago elaborates this rule as:

> Even if the conditions thus far mentioned were all fulfilled in a particular case, the fact that a State invoked a state of necessity as an excuse could not have the effect of precluding the wrongfulness of conduct ... if the obligation in question had been specially designed to operate also, or in particular, in abnormal situations of peril to the obligated State or to its essential interests, or with the manifest intention of precluding the wrongfulness of a breach of that obligation on the ground of necessity.[184]

f. The state must not contribute to the state of necessity
On this, Ago and his colleagues commented that "the State claiming the benefit of the existence of a state of necessity must not itself have provoked, either deliberately or by negligence, the occurrence of the state of necessity."[185]

5.4.3 *Crawford's Final Text*

Crawford continued to crystallize Ago's works on the defense of necessity and expounded the commentary. Although he did not make radical changes to Ago's draft Article 33, Crawford's Article 25 made some noticeable changes.

Crawford's Article 25 reads:

> 1. Necessity may not be invoked by a State as a ground for precluding the wrongfulness of an act not in conformity with an international obligation of that State unless the act:

182 *Yearbook of the International Law Commission* (Vol. II, Part II), above note 171, p. 50, para. 35; Ago, above note 4, p. 20, para. 15; Cheng, above note 179.

183 Ago, ibid, pp. 20–21, para. 16; *Yearbook of the International Law Commission*, ibid, para. 37.

184 Ago, ibid, p. 20, para. 16; *Yearbook*, ibid, pp. 50–51, para. 38.

185 *Yearbook*, ibid, p. 50, para. 34.

(a) is the only way for the State to safeguard an essential interest against a grave and imminent peril; and
(b) does not seriously impair an essential interest of the State or States towards which the obligation exists, or of the international community as a whole.

2. In any case, necessity may not be invoked by a State as a ground for precluding wrongfulness if:
(a) the international obligation in question excludes the possibility of invoking necessity; or
(b) the State has contributed to the situation of necessity.

Article 25 made some key changes to Ago's Article 33:

i. Crawford's paragraph 1(a) changed Ago's "an essential interest[186] of the State" to "an essential interest" meaning that a state can safeguard not only its interest but also that of other states or the international community. Crawford's comment on this was that "[t]he extent to which a given interest is essential depends on all the circumstances, and cannot be prejudged. It extends to particular interests of the State and its people, as well as of the international community as a whole."[187]
ii. Crawford's paragraph 1(b) changed Ago's "an essential interest of the state towards which the obligation existed" to "an essential interest of the state or states towards which the obligation exists, or of the international community as a whole" thereby expanding the scope beyond the state which took the allegedly necessary action. Crawford's elaboration of the phrase was that "[i]n other words, the interest relied on must outweigh all other considerations, not merely from the point of view of the acting State but on a reasonable assessment of the competing interests [of other states], whether these are individual or collective."[188] By these 'expansions of scope' Crawford seems to have carefully maintained the balance that Ago tried to keep between paragraphs (a) and (b) of paragraph (1). In other words, whereas Ago balanced the essential interest of the state *only* with that of the other state towards which the obligation exists,

186 As distinguished from a 'fundamental interest' or 'collective interest'. See, ICJ Judge Simma's note on this at Bruno Simma, 'The Work of the International Law Commission at its Fifty-Third Session (2001)', *Nordic Journal of International Law*, 71(1): 2002, p. 129.
187 Crawford, above note 165, p. 184.
188 Ibid.

Crawford balanced the essential interests of the state, other states and/or the international community with that of another other state(s) towards which the obligation exists and/or that of the international community.

iii. Moreover, the limitation due to peremptory norm of GIL (Ago's Article 33) which was limited only to the defense of necessity has been expanded to apply to the other five CPW in Crawford's version (Article 26).

Crawford shares Ago's, and the ICJ's, observation that the way the defense of necessity has been drafted in the ARSIWA invites a *strict interpretation.* i.e., necessity can be invoked only "*under certain very limited conditions, and … stringent conditions are imposed before any such plea is allowed* … [T]o emphasize the exceptional nature of necessity and concerns about its possible abuse, article 25 is cast in negative language."[189]

Otherwise, Crawford's dissection of the other elements of Article 25 is similar to that of Ago's. Crawford dissects his draft Article 25 into four elements which are briefly presented below.

a. The action taken must be the only way to safeguard an essential interest from grave and imminent peril

Crawford states that sub-paragraph (1)(a) has two conditions:

> The first condition, set out in subparagraph (1) (a), is that necessity may only be invoked to safeguard an essential interest from a grave and imminent peril. The extent to which a given interest is 'essential' depends on all the circumstances, and cannot be prejudged … Whatever the interest may be, however, it is only when it is threatened by a grave and imminent peril that this condition is satisfied. The peril has to be objectively established and not merely apprehended as possible. In addition to being grave, the peril has to be imminent in the sense of proximate [but also in an ascertainable future[190]].[191]

This first element highlights the underlying notion that to invoke the necessity defense there must exist "an irreconcilable conflict between an essential interest on the one hand and an obligation of the State invoking necessity on the

189 Ibid, p. 183.

190 Crawford refers here (ibid, p. 183) to the ICJ's statement in *Case Concerning the Gabčíkovo-Nagymaros Project*, above note 160, p. 42, para. 54. See also, Crawford, ibid, p. 184.

191 Crawford, ibid, pp. 183–184.

other".[192] In expressions echoing Ago and the ICJ,[193] Crawford describes the second requirement (i.e., the measure must be the only measure available) in sub-paragraph 1(a) as:

> Moreover the course of action taken must be the 'only way' available to safeguard that interest. The plea is excluded if there are other (otherwise lawful) means available, even if they may be more costly or less convenient … The word 'way' in subparagraph (1)(a) is not limited to unilateral action but may also comprise other forms of conduct available through cooperative action with other States or through international organizations (for example, conservation measures for a fishery taken through the competent regional fisheries agency). Moreover the requirement of necessity is inherent in the plea: any conduct going beyond what is strictly necessary for the purpose will not be covered.[194]

The ICJ made it clear that a state of necessity does not terminate the obligation of the state; it merely suspends it until the end of the situation that gave rise to the necessity.[195]

b. The action must not impair essential interests of states which are owed the obligation or the international community as a whole

This requirement echoes proportionality in that necessity cannot be validly invoked if resort to the necessary action impairs essential interests of states which are owed the obligation or the international community at large, a notion which Crawford elaborates as: "[i]n other words, the interest relied on must outweigh all other considerations, not merely from the point of view of the acting State but on a reasonable assessment of the competing interests [of other states], whether these are individual or collective."[196]

c. The international obligation in question must not exclude the possibility of invoking necessity

---

192 *Yearbook of the International Law Commission* (Vol. II, Part II) (United Nations, 2001), p. 80, para. 2.

193 Ago, above note 178; *Case Concerning the Gabčíkovo-Nagymaros Project*, above note 160, pp. 40–41, para. 52.

194 Crawford, above note 165, p. 184.

195 *Case Concerning the Gabčíkovo-Nagymaros Project*, above note 160, p. 63, para. 101. See also, the statement by the ICSID tribunal in *CMS Gas Transmission Company v. Argentina* (ICSID Case No. ARB/01/8) (Award), 12 May 2005, para. 382: "even if the plea of necessity were accepted, compliance with the obligation would re-emerge as soon as the circumstances precluding wrongfulness no longer existed."

196 Crawford, above note 165, p. 184.

The phrase 'in any case' at the beginning of paragraph (2) of Article 25(2) of Crawford's draft is an indication that even if the action in question passes the test of paragraph (1), it may still be disallowed under paragraph (2)[197] which provides that necessity defense is not acceptable if the international obligation in question explicitly or implicitly excludes the possibility of invoking necessity. Ago's comment on this is:

> Thus certain humanitarian conventions applicable to armed conflict *expressly* exclude reliance on military necessity. Others while not explicitly excluding necessity are *intended to apply* in abnormal situations of peril for the responsible State and plainly engage its essential interests. In such a case the *non-availability of the plea of necessity emerges clearly from the object and the purpose of the rule* (*emphasis added*).[198]

d. Necessity cannot be invoked if the state has contributed to the situation of necessity

Crawford's comment on this requirement in sub-paragraph 2(b) is:

> For a plea of necessity to be precluded under subparagraph (2)(b), the contribution to the situation of necessity must be *sufficiently substantial and not merely incidental or peripheral.* Subparagraph (2)(b) is phrased in more categorical terms than articles 23(2)(a) and 24(2)(a), because necessity needs to be more narrowly confined (*emphasis added*).[199]

By way of concluding Section 5.4, therefore, it has been shown that through decades-long drafting process accompanied by extensive commentary and analyses, and case law of the ICJ, the present-day Article 25 of the ARSIWA has been accepted as reflecting the concept of necessity in CIL. The definition intends to balance the long-recognized sovereign right of states to take otherwise unlawful measures when their essential interests or, as expanded by Article 25, those of other states or the international community, are in grave and imminent danger with the obligation to consider the interest of states

197 Ibid, p. 185.

198 Ibid.

199 Ibid. Article 23(2)(a) states that *force majeure* cannot be invoked as a CPW if "[t]he situation of *force majeure* is due, either alone or in combination with other factors, to the conduct of the State invoking it". Similarly, Article 24(2)(a) states that distress cannot be invoked as a CPW if "[t]he situation of distress is due, either alone or in combination with other factors, to the conduct of the State invoking it".

which might be affected by the necessary measure and the interest of the international community.

In contrast with the concept of necessity in the General Exceptions of the GATT 1994/GATS, the ARSIWA presents necessity defense more as an excuse and does not, as will be discussed in Chapter 11, preclude the payment of compensation to states whose essential interests are affected by the measure taken as necessity (Article 27(b) of the ARSIWA). Moreover, the ARSIWA expects a *rare* application of the defense of necessity in times of exceptional difficulty while, as will be discussed in Chapters 8 and 9, the concept of necessity in WTO law – either as a secondary rule of defense in the General Exceptions or as a 'primary rule' of necessity in the WTO agreements such as the TBT and SPS agreements – has been invoked *frequently* in WTO disputes.

As stated at the end of Section 5.3, the ARSIWA defense of necessity does not limit itself to any field of international law whereas the WTO defense of necessity has been applied mainly in international trade disputes under the relevant texts of the WTO Agreement. It is, therefore, possible for these two concepts of necessity to be presented as alternative choices in some fields of PIL which are linked to, but not exclusively limited to, international trade. Sub-section 5.3.3, for example, discussed the concept of environmental defense of necessity in the context of IEnL where the concepts of necessity in the ARSIWA and WTO law may be invoked to defend otherwise unlawful measures taken to protect the environment. One field of PIL which needed to develop its definition of the necessity defense and where the concepts of necessity in the ARSIWA and WTO law have been referred to with respectively equivalent justifications, is IIL. Section 5.5 discusses this scenario.

5.5 International Investment Law

Section 5.3 discussed how the respective environmental necessity defenses under CIL (ARSIWA) and the GATT 1994 (Article XX) found spaces of choice in IEnL. What happened in IEnL appears to have been straightforward. With regards to disputes involving the 'environmental exceptions' within the WTO, there are texts to rely on such as paragraphs (b) and (g) in Article XX of the GATT 1994. In the other instances mentioned in Sub-section 5.3.3, the tribunals relied on the environmental necessity defense under CIL (later on codified under the ARSIWA). In IIL, however, the practice of referring to the concepts of necessity in CIL (as codified in the ARSIWA) or WTO law to interpret necessity provisions in investment treaties has created debate on the reasons for selecting either of these two different concepts of necessity.

Sub-section 5.5.1 will first briefly present the common contents of BITs. Sub-section 5.5.2 will introduce the regime of necessity defense in IIL. Section 5.5.3 will, by way of example, discuss in some detail the Argentine financial crisis disputes before the ICSID tribunals wherein the choice between the CIL and WTO law defenses of necessity has been strongly debated.

5.5.1 *Common Contents of BITs and International Investment Agreements*

A number of writings have summarized the frequently appearing common contents of BITs or IIAs.[200] According to Muchlinski, the common contents of IIAs (which by definition include BITs), include: (a) a preamble;[201] (b) scope and application of the treaty by reference to subject matter (*materiae*),[202] covered persons and entities (*personae*),[203] territory (*loci*)[204] and temporal effect (*temporis*);[205] (c) standards of treatment presented as general standards[206] and, in some IIAs, specific treatments;[207] and (d) dispute settlement.[208]

---

200 For instance, Chapters 6–11 in Marc Bungenberg *et al.*, *International Investment Law* (1st ed.) (Baden-Baden, München and Oxford: Nomos, C. H. Beck and Hart, 2015); Peter Muchlinski, 'The Framework of Investment Protection: The Content of BITs', in Karl P. Sauvant and Lisa E. Sachs (eds.), *The Effect of Treaties on Foreign Direct Investment: Bilateral Investment Treaties, Double Taxation Treaties, and Investment Flows* (Oxford: Oxford University Press, 2009), pp. 37–71; Chapters 3–10 in Rudolf Dolzer and Christoph Schreuer, *Principles of International Investment Law* (2nd ed.) (Oxford: Oxford University Press, 2012); Chapters 2–4, 7–12, 19–31 in Peter Muchlinski, Federico Ortino and Christoph Schreuer (eds.), *The Oxford Handbook of International Investment Law* (Oxford: Oxford University Press, 2008); UNCTAD, *Bilateral Investment Treaties (1995–2006): Trends in Investment Rulemaking*, available at, http://unctad.org/en/docs/iteiia20065_en.pdf.

201 Muchlinski, ibid, p. 38; UNCTAD, ibid, pp. 3–4.

202 Muchlinski, ibid, pp. 39–42.

203 Ibid, pp. 42–45.

204 Ibid, p. 45.

205 Ibid, pp. 45–46.

206 Ibid, pp. 46–59; UNCTAD, above note 200, pp. 28–43; Bungenberg *et al.*, above note 200, pp. 700–958; OCED, *Fair and Equitable Treatment Standard in International Investment Law*, OECD Working Papers on International Investment, 2004/03 (OECD Publishing, 2004), available at, https://www.oecd.org/daf/inv/investment-policy/WP-2004_3.pdf; Martins Paparinskis, *The International Minimum Standard and Fair and Equitable Treatment* (Oxford: Oxford University Press, 2013), pp. 154–180. See also, *L. F. H. Neer and Pauline Neer (United States of America) v. United Mexican States*, available at, http://legal.un.org/riaa/cases/vol_IV/60-66.pdf.; *Harry Roberts (United States of America) v. United Mexican States*, available at, http://legal.un.org/riaa/cases/vol_IV/77-81.pdf.

207 Muchlinski, above note 200, pp. 59–65; UNCTAD, above note 200, pp. 44–80.

208 Muchlinski, ibid, pp. 65–70; UNCTAD, ibid, pp. 99–130; Dolzer and Schreuer, above note 200, pp. 232–312.

5.5.2 *Necessity as Defense in BITs*

Like most treaties, BITs provide for exceptions or NPMs. BIT NPMs are usually contained either in the text of the treaty or in a binding protocol to the treaty.[209] Like other treaty exception clauses, BIT NPMs contain the three elements of exceptions.[210] Firstly, they specify the 'scope' of the exception, i.e., whether the exceptions apply to the entire treaty or to specific parts or provisions of the treaty. Secondly, each NPM is linked to permissible objectives such as: protection of essential security interests and/or public order; protection of public health, morality, safety or the environment; fulfilment of obligations with respect to the maintenance of international peace and security; control of circumstances of extreme emergency; maintaining prudential measures with respect to financial services; and the continued application of the contracting states' tax laws.[211] Thirdly, a specific 'nexus' term ties the NPM to the permissible objective. Such terms include 'necessary', 'required' and 'directed to'. This chapter focuses on the term 'necessary' in the NPMs, i.e., necessity defense in BITs.

In most BITs the defense of necessity is linked to the protection of essential security interests and/or public order. By way of an example, Article XI of the 1991 *Treaty between United States of America and the Argentine Republic Concerning the Reciprocal Encouragement and Protection of Investment* (hereinafter the "US-Argentina BIT") provided:

> This Treaty shall not preclude the application by either Party of measures necessary for the maintenance of public order, the fulfilment of its obligations with respect to the maintenance or restoration of international peace or security, or the protection of its own essential security interests.

A point of contention in the interpretation of the necessity defense in BITs has been whether the defense is historically linked to other defenses such as *force majeure*. Accordingly, the strictness of the interpretation of the necessity defense in BITs will depend on the other defense(s) with which necessity in BITs gets linked to. Four different views have emerged regarding the said link between necessity and the other defenses. The first view asserts that necessity defense in BITs is historically linked to *force majeure*, distress and especially

---

209 William W. Burke-White and Andreas von Staden, 'Investment Protection in Extraordinary Times: The Interpretation and Application of Non-Precluded Measures Provisions in Bilateral Investment Treaties', *Virginia Journal of International Law*, 48(2): 2008, p. 325.

210 Ibid, p. 329.

211 UNCTAD, above note 200, pp. 80–92; ibid, pp. 332–335.

the CIL defense of necessity as identified by the ILC.[212] The second view links defense of necessity in BITs and other fields of international law to self-defense and the use of force.[213] The third view, deriving its inspiration from the reading of Article XI of the US-Argentina BIT (hereinafter "Article XI") by the ICSID tribunal in the *Continental Casualty* dispute discussed below, believes that through the many FCN treaties, necessity defense in BITs is closely linked to the necessity defense in GATT 1994 and the GATS.[214] The fourth view maintains that necessity in BITs is, and has been designed to be, independent from any one of the other defenses (including concept of necessity in CIL) and must be interpreted within its own limits.[215] But how has the necessity defense in BITs been interpreted in practice? The most frequently cited experience is that of the many ICSID tribunals which interpreted the similarly worded necessity clauses in the BITs that Argentina signed before its financial crisis of 2001. Subsection 5.5.3 will discuss the experience in some detail.

---

212 José E. Alvarez and Kathryn Khamsi, 'The Argentine Crisis and Foreign Investors: A Glimpse into the Heart of the Investment Regime', in Karl P. Sauvant (ed.), *Yearbook on International Investment Law and Policy, 2008–2009* (Oxford: Oxford University Press, 2009), pp. 427–435; José E. Alvarez and Tegan Brink, 'Revisiting the Necessity Defense: *Continental Casualty v. Argentina*', in Karl P. Sauvant (ed.), *Yearbook on International Investment Law and Policy, 2010–2011* (Oxford: Oxford University Press, 2011), p. 336.

213 Paul Weidenbaum, 'Necessity in International Law', *Transactions of the Grotius Society*, Vol. 24, Problems of Peace and War, Papers Read before the Society in the Year 1938, pp. 105–132; Michael Waibel, 'Two Worlds of Necessity in ICSID Arbitration: CMS and LG&E', *Leiden Journal of International Law*, 20(3): 2007, p. 641, f.n. 28, referring to one of the best and earliest works on necessity defense in international law, Burleigh Cushing Rodick, *The Doctrine of Necessity in International Law* (New York: Columbia University Press, 1928).

214 Giorgio Sacerdoti, 'BIT Protections and Economic Crises: Limits to Their Coverage, the Impact of Multilateral Financial Regulation and the Defense of Necessity', *ICSID Review – Foreign Investment Law Journal*, 28(2): 2013, p. 382; Jürgen Kurtz, *The World Trade Organization and International Investment Law: Converging Systems* (Cambridge: Cambridge University Press, 2016), pp. 168–228; Luke Engan, 'In Search of Necessity: Congruence, Proportionality, and the Least-Restrictive Means in Investor-State Dispute Settlement', *Georgetown Journal of International Law*, 43(2): 2012, pp. 495–521; Andrew D. Mitchell and Caroline Henkels, 'Variations on A Theme: Comparing the Concept of "Necessity" in International Investment Law and WTO Law', *Chicago Journal of International Law*, 14(1): 2013, pp. 93–164 (in part).

215 Alberto Alvarez-Jiménez, 'The Interpretation of Necessity Clauses in Bilateral Investment Treaties after the Recent ICSID Annulment Decisions', in Sauvant, above note 212 (2011), pp. 419–450; Diane A. Desierto, 'Necessity and "Supplementary Means of Interpretation" for Non-Precluded Measures in Bilateral Investment Treaties', *University of Pennsylvania Journal of International Law*, 31(3): 2014, pp. 827–934; Burke-White and von Staden, above note 209, pp. 320–322.

5.5.3 *The Experience of the ICSID Tribunals on the Argentine Financial Crisis*

To address longstanding economic stagnation in its economy, particularly the accumulation of debt since the 1960s, Argentina took a number of international and domestic measures. Internationally, the country increased the number of BITs to 33 by 2000.[216] Domestically, it took a three-stage economic reform between 1977 and 2001.[217] With the support of international financial institutions, the country embarked upon a rigorous privatization program and introduced an investor-friendly regime in the utility sectors such as water, gas, electricity and communication.[218] Furthermore, the government issued the Currency Convertibility Law which established a currency board to oversee the fixing of the Argentine peso on a par with the US dollar, scheduled semi-annual adjustments and decreed that there would be no price freeze applicable to the tariff system unless compensation was paid to investors.[219] The reform area relevant to this book is that which Argentina introduced in the gas transportation and distribution sector where Argentina, under the 1992 Gas Law, privatized Gas del Estado S.E., the country's natural gas transportation and distribution monopoly, and divided it into two transportation companies and eight distribution companies. Large percentage of the shares of these new entities were sold to consortia of private investors among whom were the claimants in the ICSID disputes. The investors were allowed to calculate tariffs in US dollars and then convert them to Argentine pesos at the time of billing. The Argentine Government could not also rescind or modify the licenses without the consent of the licensees. The system worked well in the 1990s.[220]

The economic growth and stability were, however, met with a crisis in the late 1990s caused by a mix of internal and external causes. The crisis reached its

216 Antoine Martin, 'Investment Disputes after Argentina's Economic Crisis: Interpreting BIT Non-precluded Measures and the Doctrine of Necessity under Customary International Law', *Journal of International Arbitration*, 29(1): 2012, p. 49; UNCTAD, *Bilateral Investment Treaties (1959–1999)*, (2000), p. 7, available at, http://unctad.org/en/Docs/poiteiiad2.en.pdf.

217 Mario Damill, Roberto Frenkel and Martin Rapetti, *The Argentinian Debt: History, Default and Restructuring*, Initiative for Policy, Columbia University, Working Paper Series, available at, http://policydialogue.org/files/publications/Argentinian_Debt_History_Default_Damill_Frenkel_Rapetti.pdf, pp. 6–20.

218 Alvarez and Khamsi, above note 212, p. 388; S. R. Subramanian, 'Too Similar or Too Different: State of Necessity as a Defense under Customary International Law and the Bilateral Investment Treaty and their Relationship', *Manchester Journal of International Economic Law*, 9(1): 2012, p. 74.

219 Martin, above note 216, p. 50; Alzarez and Khamsi, ibid.

220 Alvarez and Khamsi, ibid, pp. 389–90; Martin, ibid, p. 50.

economic, social and political zenith towards the end of 2001[221] and Argentina took a number of responsive measures. A series of decrees and measures taken in December 2001, collectively known as *Corralito*, froze all accounts, restricted bank withdrawals and prohibited international currency transfers.[222] Then on 6 January 2002, the government issued an emergency law which declared a state of public emergency in the social, economic, administrative, financial and exchange areas. This emergency law, *inter alia*: abolished the currency board; eliminated the right to calculate tariffs in U.S. dollars; devalued the peso, redenominated tariffs in pesos at the rate of one peso to the US dollar; and required renegotiation of public utility contracts. In March 2002, the government ordered the gas regulating agency to discontinue all tariff reviews and to refrain from adjusting tariffs in any respect.[223] Although Argentina's economy stabilized after Dr. Néstor Kirchner took office as President in May 2003,[224] a lot of claims were instituted against Argentina by foreign investors before tribunals outside the country. As at 23 January 2024, the ICSID website showed 59 cases (51 concluded and 8 pending) brought against Argentina under the BITs it signed with the Austria, Belgium, Luxembourg, Chile, France, Germany, Spain, The Netherlands, UK and US.[225] Three cases[226] were also brought before UNCITRAL arbitration Tribunals. In the initial wave of cases, the claimants asked for compensation greater than USD 8 billion, more than the entire financial services of the Argentine government in 2002. Some have estimated the total value of potential claims against Argentina to reach as high as USD 80 billion.[227] We now discuss the cases before the ICSID tribunals and Annulment Committees in some detail.

It is true that the analysis of the cases brought before the ICSID tribunals should, instead of being discussed in this sub-section, have been kept in Chapter 6 where the contribution of international tribunals to the development of the concept of necessity is discussed. The main reason why the discussion on the ICSID disputes has been kept in this Chapter is that the author believed that the best way to discuss the concept of necessity in IIL is through

221 Burke-White and von Staden, above note 209, p. 309; see also, Alvarez and Khamsi, ibid.

222 Burke-White and von Staden, ibid, pp. 309–310; Alvarez and Khamsi, ibid.

223 Alvarez and Khmasi, ibid, pp. 389–90; Martin, above note 216, p. 50.

224 Alvarez and Khamsi, ibid, p. 390.

225 The list is available at, https://icsid.worldbank.org/cases/case-database.

226 These are: *BG Group Plc. v. The Argentine Republic*; *AWG Group Ltd. v. The Argentine Republic*; and *National Grid Plc. v. The Argentine Republic*. Lucy Reed, *Scorecard of Investment Treaty Cases Against Argentina Since 2001*, available at, http://kluwerarbitrationblog.com/2009/03/02/scorecard-of-investment-treaty-cases-against-argentina-since-2001/.

227 Burke-White and von Staden, above note 209, p. 311.

case law. However, instead of repeating the discussions of this sub-section in Chapter 6, cross-reference has been made in Sub-section 6.6.4 to Sub-section 5.5.3 to ensure that the experience of the ICSID tribunals is mentioned in Chapter 6. We now proceed to discussing the cases brought before the ICSID tribunals and Annulment Committees.

Scholarly attention has been attracted to the early cases based on US-Argentina BIT where US investors brought the Argentine government before ICSID tribunals, some of whose awards were brought before the ICSID Annulment Committees which review errors of law. The most discussed of these cases are (the first five being the most prominent): (1) *CMS Gas Transmission Company v. Argentine Republic (ICSID Case No. ARB/01/8)*, Award, 12 May 2005 ("*CMS*"); (2) *Enron Creditors Recovery Corporation (formerly Enron Corporation) and Ponderosa Assets, L.P. v. Argentine Republic* (ICSID Case No. ARB/01/3), Award, 22 May 2007 ("*Enron*"); (3) *LG&E Energy Corp., LG&E Capital Corp. and LG&E International Inc. v. Argentine Republic* (ICSID Case No. ARB/02/1), Award, 25 July 2007 ("*LG&E*"); (4) *Sempra Energy International v. Argentine Republic* (ICSID Case No. ARB/02/16), Award, 28 September 2007 ("*Sempra*"); (5) *Continental Casualty Company v. Argentine Republic* (ICSID Case No. ARB/03/9), Award, 5 September 2008 ("*Continental Casualty*"); (6) *Impregilo S.p.A. v. Argentine Republic* (ICSID Case No. ARB/08/14), Award, 21 June 2011 ("*Impreglio*"); (7) *El Paso Energy International Company v. Argentine Republic* (ICSID Case No. ARB/03/15), Award, 31 October 2011 ("*El Paso*"); and (8) *Suez, Sociedad General de Aguas de Barcelona S.A. and Vivendi Universal S.A v. Argentine Republic* (ICSID Case No. ARB/03/19), Award, 9 April 2015 ("*Suez*"). Crucial in the analyses that have developed in the Argentine cases are also the decisions of the *CMS, Enron, Sempra* and *Continental Casualty* Annulment Committees as well as the three UNCITRAL cases: *BG Group Plc. v. The Argentine Republic*, UNCITRAL, Final Award, 24 December 2007 ("*BG Group*"); *National Grid Plc. v. The Argentine Republic*, UNCITRAL, Final Award, 3 November 2008 ("*National Grid*"); and *AWG Group Ltd. v. The Argentine Republic*, UNCITRAL, Final Award, 9 April 2005.

In the first few, yet crucial,[228] cases before the ICSID tribunals, the Argentine government argued, *inter alia*, that: (a) it was using treaty-granted NPMs to protect its essential security interest and/or public order; or (b) the measures could be excused under Article 25 of the ARSIWA. The tribunals, rejecting Argentina's argument to the contrary, asserted jurisdiction in the cases and

228 'Crucial' in the sense, as we will see in the subsequent sub-sections, of laying the ground in interpreting the defense of necessity in BITs.

held that Argentina breached its obligations. So, the arguments before the tribunals mainly focused on whether Argentina could defend the emergency measures under the treaty-provided NPM rules or the plea of necessity under Article 25 of ARSIWA.

Writers have made at least nine observations regarding interpretation of the necessity defense by the tribunals: (1) the decisions were "not unanimous",[229] were "divergent"/"divergent and partly conflicting",[230] "diverged sharply",[231] were "fundamentally different [and] diverged crucially in their material finding [on necessity]";[232] (2) "[d]espite the largely similar factual situations, the tribunals have diverged crucially in their material findings [on necessity]";[233] (3) many of the panels "inconsistently interpreted and applied Argentina's necessity defense, by stirring much debate";[234] (4) the rulings "engage fundamentally different and at times conflicting methods of interpreting the relationship between the operative treaty exception and relevant customary law";[235] (5) the divergent results will "add to the current debate on inconsistent decisions in investment arbitration and their potentially damaging effect on investment arbitration in general if conflicting outcomes lead to a loss of predictability and stability of the system";[236] (6) the tribunals "[u]nfortunately ... have addressed NPM clauses to date [and] failed to engage in the kind of rigorous treaty interpretation mandated by the [VCLT] and instead have taken interpretive short-cuts that threaten the very legitimacy of the investor-state

229 Martin, above note 216, p. 50.

230 Subramanian, above note 218, p. 75; August Reinisch, 'Necessity in Investment Arbitration', in Dekker and Hey, above note 22, pp. 137, 147.

231 Waibel, above note 213, p. 638.

232 Christina Binder, 'Circumstances Precluding Wrongfulness', in Bungenberg *et al.*, above note 200, p. 450. Vasiljević and Jovanović call the conclusions "diametrically different". Mirko Vasiljević and Marko Jovanović, 'Necessity as a Ground for Precluding Wrongfulness in International Investment Law', *Belgrade Law Review*, Year LXIV, No. 3: 2016, p. 15.

233 Christina Binder and August Reinisch, 'Economic Emergency Powers: A Comparative Law Perspective', in Stephan W. Schill (ed.), *International Investment Law and Comparative Public Law* (Oxford: Oxford University Press, 2010), p. 510.

234 Kelley Chubb, 'The "State of Necessity" Defense: A Burden, Not A Blessing to the International Investment Arbitration System', *Cardozo Journal of Conflict Resolution*, 43(2): 2013, p. 532.

235 Jürgen Kurtz, 'Adjudging the Exceptional at International Investment Law: Security, Public Order and Financial Crisis', *International and Comparative Law Quarterly*, 59(2): 2010, p. 334.

236 August Reinisch, 'Necessity in International Investment Arbitration: An Unnecessary Split of Opinions in Recent ICSID Cases – Comments on *CMS v. Argentina* and *LG&E v. Argentina*', *Journal of World Investment & Trade*, 8(2): 2007, p. 212.

arbitration system";[237] (7) "resulting jurisprudence of the ICSID tribunals ... is deeply problematic, due in part to poor legal reasoning and questionable treaty interpretation and, in part, to the contradictory holdings in the awards" and the awards reached "contradictory and, at times, legally questionable conclusions";[238] (8) "despite similar factual backgrounds, the ... ICSID rulings reached inconsistent determinations on whether Argentina's actions in the early 2000s were necessary" and that they showed "conflicting attitudes towards necessity in ICSID proceedings";[239] and (9) "the reasoning of the tribunals is deeply problematic from an interpretive perspective ... None of the tribunals offer a coherent analysis of the 'necessary for' nexus ... the tribunals take interpretive shortcuts that push toward uniform interpretation of treaty terms, but fail to do justice to the interpretive rules of the VCLT."[240]

What makes the inconsistency of the findings of the tribunals concerning is that some of the tribunals which rendered inconsistent decisions heard the same expert testimonies on the same issues. For example, the *CMS* and *LG&E* tribunals heard similar testimonies on the issue of necessity from Dean Ann-Marie Slaughter and Professor José Alvarez. Moreover, some of the arbitrators sat not only in multiple tribunals/Annulment Committees, but also in tribunals/Annulment Committees that rendered the contradicting decisions.[241] This trend is better understood by identifying the points of convergence and points of divergence among the disputes.

Despite their widely criticized analyses of the necessity defense, the early ICSID cases on Argentina agreed on five points.

Firstly, the tribunals, in tandem with the ICJ's ruling, decided that Article 25 of the ARSIWA reflects CIL.[242]

237 Burke-White and von Staden, above note 209, p. 316.

238 William W. Burke-White, 'The Argentine Financial Crisis: State Liability Under BITs and the Legitimacy of The ICSID System', *Asian Journal of WTO and International Health Law and Policy*, 3(1): 2008, pp. 201, 209–210.

239 Cynthia C. Galvez, 'Necessity, Investor Rights, and State Sovereignty for NAFTA Investment Arbitration', *Cornell International Law Journal*, 46(1): 2013, p. 151; Thjoernelund concluded that even among those disputes which used the ARSIWA concept of necessity to interpret Article XI, the application was "contradictory". Marie Christine Hoelck Thjoernelund, 'State of Necessity as an Exemption from State Responsibility for Investments', in Armin von Bogdandy and Rüdiger Wolfrum (eds.), *Max Planck Yearbook of United Nations Law*, Vol. 13 (Leiden: Koninklijke Brill N.V., 2009), p. 474.

240 Burke-White and von Staden, above note 209, p. 337.

241 For more on this, see, Alvarez and Khamsi, above note 212, p. 380, f.n. 7.

242 Andrea K. Bjorklund, 'Economic Security Defenses in International Investment Law', in Muchlinski, Ortino and Schreuer, above note 200, p. 479.

Secondly, the tribunals interpreted the 'essential security' and 'public order' NPMs in the US – Argentina BIT broadly enough to include economic emergencies, i.e., they endorsed the concept of *economic/financial necessity* within CIL,[243] although they differed in their assessment of the gravity of the situation in Argentina in assessing it for economic necessity purposes.[244]

Thirdly, all the tribunals were in agreement that Article XI was not self-judging in that it was drafted, and should be interpreted, not to leave it to the state to determine whether the state found itself in a state of necessity and thereby leaving the tribunals only to objectively assess whether the decision was done in good faith and whether the measures were taken without abuse.[245]

Fourthly, none of them, at least the *CMS, Enron, Sempra* and *LG&E* tribunals, addressed Argentina's arguments that if its defense under the BIT had been accepted, any arguments under the ARSIWA would have become moot.[246]

Finally, all the tribunals agreed that a separate necessity defense benefiting Argentina could not be read into Article IV(3) of the BIT[247] which guaranteed equal treatment to national or companies of either party as a result of war or other armed conflict, revolution, state of national emergency, insurrection, civil disturbance or other similar events.

The tribunals diverged on a number of points. For purpose of convenience, we will divide the points of divergence into two broad categories. The first one is the tribunals' divergence on the relationship between NPMs and ARSIWA's state of necessity. The second one briefly looks into other points of divergence in relation to the necessity defense.

Regarding the first point of divergence – divergence on the relationship between NPMs and ARSIWA's state of necessity – it has been observed that the main ground for the inconsistencies or divergences in the analyses of the tribunals lay in their understanding of the relationship between Article XI and Article 25 of the ARSIWA. Binder classified the interpretations into three categories of tribunals.[248]

The first category of tribunals conflated Article XI and Article 25 of the ARSIWA. In response to Argentina's argument that Article XI should stand

---

243 Burke-White, above note 238, p. 212; ibid.

244 Chubb, above note 234, p. 549. See the views of the various tribunals in *CMS*, paras. 354, 319–320; *Enron*, para. 306; *Sempra*, para. 348; *LG&E*, paras. 251 and 257 (and Waibel, above note 213, p. 645).

245 *CMS*, para. 373; *Enron*, para. 337; *Sempra*, para. 388; *LG&E*, paras. 212–213; *Continental Casualty*, paras. 187–188.

246 Bjorklund, above note 242, p. 851.

247 Alvarez and Khamsi, above note 212, p. 395.

248 Binder, above note 232, pp. 452–455.

alone, separated from Article 25 and that a separate interpretation is owed Article XI,[249] this group of tribunals "effectively read the requirements of the CIL defense of necessity into the NPM clause of the Treaty, testing Argentina's invocation of the NPM clause against the basic requirements of the necessity defense in CIL".[250] The *CMS*,[251] *Enron*,[252] *Sempra*,[253] *Impreglio*,[254] *Suez*[255] and *National Grid*[256] tribunals and the *Enron* Annulment Committee,[257] fall under this category. In short, these panels "essentially equated Article XI with the customary international law defense of necessity."[258] Binder observed that none of the tribunals which used Article 25 to examine necessity discussed the mandatory requirement in that provision that the state which wants to benefit from Article 25 should not "seriously impair an essential interest of the State or States towards which the obligation exists, or of the international community as a whole."[259]

The first category of tribunals legitimized their interpretation of Article XI with Article 25 without still not fully separating them. The *LG&E* tribunal fits into this category. The tribunal held that although Article XI constituted a separate sphere of necessity worthy of an independent examination, a supportive, yet separate, examination of necessity was needed under Article 25 and other relevant laws (for example, Argentine domestic laws).[260]

The third category of tribunals separated Article XI from Article 25 and sought an independent interpretation for Article XI. The *CMS* and *Sempra* annulment decisions as well as the *Continental Casualty* and *El Paso* awards fall under this category whereby Article XI analysis comes first and stands alone without the need for supportive analysis under Article 25. It was the *CMS*

249 Bjorklund, above note 242, p. 849.

250 Burke-White, above note 238, p. 210; Binder, above note 232, p. 452.

251 See, *CMS*, paras. 308, 315–333, *CMS Annulment*, para. 135; Bjorklund, above note 242, p. 850.

252 *Enron*, paras. 303–342.

253 *Sempra*, paras. 376, 378.

254 *Impreglio*, paras. 336–359.

255 *Suez*, paras. 236–243.

256 *National Grid*, paras. 254–262. In para. 255, the tribunal stated that the emergency powers in Article XI "in the context of the state of necessity defense ... are best analyzed by turning to the conditions under which such defense is recognized under Article 25 of the [ARSIWA]".

257 *Enron Creditors Recovery Corp. Ponderosa Assets, L.P. v. The Argentine Republic* (ICSID Case No. ARB/01/3) (Annulment Proceeding), 30 July 2010 ("*Enron Annulment*"), paras. 355–395.

258 Alvarez and Khamsi, above note 212, p. 396.

259 Binder, above note 232, pp. 451.

260 *LG&E*, paras. 205–206, 245–258.

Annulment Committee, with James Crawford as a Member, that started the heavy criticism of the practice of mingling of Articles XI and Article 25 mainly because the two pleas operate in different norms of international law: Article XI as a primary norm and Article 25 as a secondary norm.[261] Similarly, the *Sempra* Annulment Committee reviewed the *Sempra* award which was entirely based on analysis under Article 25 and, in line with the logic of the CMS Annulment Committee – and *Continental Casualty* award below – held, *inter alia*, that: Article XI and Article 25 have fundamental differences; Article XI is autonomous enough for operation under the Treaty and that invocation of a state of necessity under the Treaty need not be legitimated by CIL concept of necessity; and that Article XI is *lex specialis* and must, therefore, be addressed first.[262] Because of its relevance to the main theme of this book, the way the *Continental Casualty* tribunal viewed and interpreted Article XI will be discussed in more detail as follows.

The *Continental Casualty* tribunal followed the CMS Annulment Committee's suit in first acknowledging that Articles XI and Article 25 are different,[263] although not completely irrelevant to each other in the sense that Article 25 may be employed in interpreting Article XI.[264] The tribunal was clear from the beginning of its analysis that it would start its analysis with, and seek meaning for, Article XI.[265] After finding that the Argentine financial crisis was a situation affecting Argentine public order or the country's essential security interests, the tribunal asked whether the measures taken by Argentina were 'necessary' under Article XI. Continental and Argentina submitted their own interpretations of necessity calling for a stricter and softer interpretation respectively with Continental relying on the strict definition under Article 25 and Argentina requiring the tribunal to see the situation with the highest deference towards it.[266]

It was mentioned earlier that the relevant tribunals which conflated Article XI and Article 25, in view of the absence of any definition of necessity in Article XI, referred to, and incorporated into Article XI, the interpretation of Article 25. It was, therefore, obvious that the *Continental Casualty* tribunal which decided to interpret Article XI with no reference to, or support from,

---

261 *CMS Annulment*, para. 124–125, 129–134.

262 *Sempra Energy International v. Argentine Republic* (ICSID Case No. ARB/02/16) (Annulment Proceeding), 29 June 2010, paras. 159–223.

263 *Continental Casualty*, paras. 163–167.

264 Ibid, para. 168.

265 Ibid, para. 162.

266 Ibid.

Article 25 (except for some assistive reasons) would nevertheless be confronted with the same lack of support from Article XI for which a separate interpretation had been developed. The solution that the tribunal came up with, reasoned in one paragraph, a solution which would go on to become one of the most hotly debated statements in the process of interpreting necessity in IIL, was to refer to the concept of necessity defense in WTO law. The tribunal stated:

> The Tribunal is thus faced with the task of determining the content of the concept of necessity in Art. XI, in order to decide whether the various Measures challenged by the Claimant were indeed necessary, as a matter of causation. With regard to the necessity test required for the application of the BIT, for the reasons stated above relating to the different role of Art. XI and of the defense of necessity in customary international law, the Tribunal does not share the opinion that 'the treaty thus becomes inseparable from the customary law standard insofar as to the conditions for the operation of the state of necessity are concerned', as stated in the *Enron Case* and submitted also by the Claimant. *Since the text of Art. XI derives from the parallel model clause of the U.S. FCN treaties and these treaties in turn reflect the formulation of Art. XX of GATT 1947, the Tribunal finds it more appropriate to refer to the GATT and WTO case law which has extensively dealt with the concept and requirements of necessity in the context of economic measures derogating to the obligations contained in GATT, rather than to refer to the requirement of necessity under customary international law (emphasis added).*[267]

Some authors hinted that the reference to the concept of necessity in WTO law might have been influenced by the chairman of the tribunal, Prof. Giorgio Sacerdoti, who was a former WTO Appellate Body Member and its Chairman.[268] Nevertheless, this bold step was recognized as "the first decision in relation to a NPM clause to engage in this form of cross-fertilization, demonstrating the increasing willingness of investment tribunals to acknowledge the interconnectedness of IEL's different strands."[269]

The tribunal then made a detailed examination of the different measures that Argentina took under the interpretation of the necessity defense developed for the General Exceptions of the GATT 1994/GATS and found in favor

267 Ibid, para. 192.
268 Mitchell and Henkels, above note 214, pp. 113–114.
269 Ibid, p. 114; Reinisch, above note 236, p. 152.

of Argentina in all but one of its measures.[270] Curiously, the tribunal, in an examination not part of the concept of necessity in WTO law defense, analyzed whether Argentina, by not adopting measures before the crisis, contributed to the creation of the circumstances that led to the crisis.[271]

Continental Casualty's use of the WTO law interpretation invited intense debate. Alzarez and Brink, for instance, published a lengthy criticism of *Continental Casualty's* resort to the WTO law interpretation of necessity by arguing that the tribunal: (a) failed to properly explain the reason for its reliance on the GATT 1994 Article XX interpretation of necessity; (b) made a wrong reference to the 'historical' link between GATT 1947 Article XX, FCN treaties and BIT NPMs; (c) failed to properly refer to the text of Article XX which, unlike in the case of most FCN Treaties and BITs, has a *chapeau* and not analogizing the defense of 'essential security interests' in Article XI to Article XXI of the GATT 1994 (Security Exceptions); (d) failed to properly consider the different purposes of BITs and the GATT; and (e) failed to consider the structural differences between investor-state and the WTO dispute settlement.[272] Desierto also found the tribunal's borrowing, and completely relying on, the WTO law interpretation of necessity defense unwarranted and improper under Article 32 of the VCLT (supplementary means of interpretation).[273] Others, such as Kurtz, Sacerdoti, Reinisch, Engan, Mitchell and Henkels have supported – some of them in a rebuttal to Alvarez and Brink – the reference to WTO law as the most logical measure to give a proper meaning to necessity in BITs and its contribution to the cross-fertilization of different disciplines of PIL.[274]

Whereas the *Continental Casualty* tribunal referred to the WTO Appellate Body's 'weighing and balancing' interpretation of necessity in interpreting Article XI, the *El Paso* tribunal, while adopting the *Continental Casualty* tribunal's rule of separately interpreting Article XI, did not fully adopt the 'weighing and balancing' test; it referred to the 'contribution' element only. For the *El Paso* tribunal, Article XI should be interpreted by asking if Argentina substantially contributed to the crisis by giving Argentina, the party with burden,[275] the benefit of the doubt. The tribunal found support to its 'substantial contribution' interpretation in, *inter alia*, *Continental Casualty*,[276]

270 *Continental Casualty*, paras. 193–222.
271 Ibid, paras. 223–230.
272 Alvarez and Brink, above note 212, pp. 315–358.
273 Desierto, above note 215.
274 Above note 214. See also, Engan, above note 214, p. 496.
275 *El Paso*, paras. 625–626.
276 *Continental Casualty*, para. 234.

LG&E[277] as well as Article 25 of the ARSIWA.[278]

Regarding the second point of divergence – other points of divergence in relation to the necessity defense – it has been observed that the fundamental differences of opinion among the tribunals and Annulment Committees in linking/delinking Article XI and Article 25 of the ARSIWA reflected themselves in concomitant matters resulting out of the respective interpretations of necessity in the Argentine crisis. Four such matters may be raised in this regard:[279] finding of wrongfulness/liability; views on 'the only way' requirement; the issue of contribution; and compensation.

Regarding finding of wrongfulness (liability), the findings in the cases largely depended on whether the tribunals tested the measures under the strict conditions of Article 25 of the ARSIWA or the less strict, even undefined, conditions of Article XI. Thus, the *CMS*, *Enron*, *Sempra*, *Impreglio*, *Suez* and *National Grid* tribunals which basically resorted to the Article 25 test, found Argentina's measures not to be necessary under Article XI, while the *LG&E* and *Continental Casualty* tribunals found Argentina's measures to be necessary under Article XI. The *El Paso* tribunal, which followed the *LG&E* and *Continental Casualty* pattern of not resorting to Article 25, nevertheless, found Argentina's measures not to be necessary under Article XI mainly because it heavily relied on Article 25 interpretation of 'contribution'. The *BG Group* tribunal did not believe that Article 25 would apply in the case because: (a) Article 25 applies to cases between states; and (b) the UK-Argentina BIT implies the exclusion of the use of Article 25. The tribunal, nevertheless, tested Argentina's measures under Article 25 and found them not to be compliant therewith.[280]

Regarding the requirement that the measure adopted should be 'the only way' possible, one observes a difference in finding whether Argentina had alternatives and the findings depended on whether Article 25 of the ARSIWA was

---

277 *LG&E*, para. 256.

278 *El Paso*, paras. 613, 616–617, 619, 624, 649–665. For a more expanded analysis on how in Argentina's case, and in similar cases in the future, regulatory failures should appropriately be considered as contributors to a situation of necessity under CIL, see, Alberto Alvarez-Jiménez, 'Foreign Investment Protection and Regulatory Failures as State's Contribution to the State of Necessity under Customary International Law: A New Approach Based on the Complexity of Argentina's 2001 Crisis', *Journal of International Arbitration*, 27(2): 2010, pp. 141–177.

279 There are other divergences as well. One of them was the divergence among the tribunals as to the beginning and the end of the situation of emergency (i.e., temporality). Whereas the *CMS* tribunal determined the duration of the crisis to be between 17 August 2000 and toward the end of 2004 or the beginning of 2005 (*CMS*, para. 250), the *LG&E* tribunal set the duration to be between 1 December 2001 and 26 April 2003 (*LG&E*, para. 226).

280 *BG Group*, paras. 407–412.

used to examine the state of necessity. Thus, *most* (for example, the *Impreglio* tribunal finding is to the contrary)[281] tribunals which referred to the strict conditions of Article 25[282] (for example, *CMS*,[283] *Enron*,[284] *Sempra* and[285] *Suez*[286]) found it easy to identify alternatives. The *LG&E*[287] and *Continental Casualty* tribunals,[288] not primarily relying on Article 25, however, concluded that Argentina had no reasonably available alternatives. Scholars who discussed the 'only way' requirement in Article 25 of the ARSIWA insist that in situations of financial necessity, where governments will almost always have alternative measures to select from, a strict application of this requirement will inevitably lead to a finding against the defending state. Sacerdoti, for example, finds this test to be "an almost impossible requirement to meet: usually authorities have the option, at least on paper, to choose among different economic measures".[289] Reinisch also argues that "[o]ne may be tempted to say that under such a standard any measure adopted would fail the test of Article 25 because there will always be an alternative."[290]

Regarding contribution of the state to the situation of necessity, the tribunals which based their analyses under Article 25 mandatorily referred to the element. Those which did not resort to Article 25 as the key reference used the 'contribution test' either as: (a) part of Article 25 analysis when they referred to Article 25 for confirmation (legitimization) (*LG&E*); (b) an independent test on top of a necessity test based on the WTO Appellate Body's interpretation of necessity (*Continental Casualty*); or (c) the sole element of the necessity test in Article XI (*El Paso*). The level of strictness on the contribution test, therefore, varies on which choice the tribunals selected. Accordingly, while the *CMS*,[291] *Enron*,[292] *Sempra*,[293] *Impreglio*,[294] *El Paso*[295] and *National Grid*[296] tribunals

281 *Impreglio*, para. 353.
282 Where even costlier or less convenient, yet treaty-compliant, alternatives are accepted.
283 *CMS*, para. 323.
284 *Enron*, para. 309.
285 *Sempra*, para. 350.
286 *Suez*, para. 238.
287 *LG&E*, para. 257.
288 *Continental Casualty*, para. 230.
289 Sacerdoti, above note 214, p. 374.
290 Reinisch, above note 236, p. 153. See also, Waibel, above note 213, p. 646.
291 *CMS*, para. 329, *Suez*, para. 238.
292 *Enron*, paras. 311–312.
293 *Sempra*, paras. 353–354.
294 *Impreglio*, para. 358.
295 *El Paso*, para. 665.
296 *National Grid*, para. 262.

easily found that Argentina contributed to the financial crisis, the *LG&E*[297] and *Continental Casualty*[298] tribunals easily decided otherwise. Like the 'only way' requirement, examining the 'contribution' requirement in instances of financial necessity has also been criticized, for instance by Sacerdoti, as one that is not practical.[299] Binder also identified the 'contribution' test as one of the limitations in Article 25(2) of the ARSIWA that "pose difficulties in times of economic emergencies"[300] while Reinisch argued it is "[a]nother highly problematic aspect of the law of necessity"[301] especially so in times of necessity.

Regarding compensation, it must be noted first that one of the fundamental differences between Article XI and Article 25 of the ARSIWA is that while Article XI operates against the entire BIT (including any provisions on compensation), Article 25, being a CPW, does not remove the duty to pay compensation. Adopting the plea of necessity under Article 25 of the ARSIWA to the defense of necessity under Article XI, thus, raised the question whether Argentina should compensate the investors affected by its emergency measures. The *CMS* tribunal, referring, in part, to Article 27(b) of the ARSIWA (compensation), stated, as did the *Enron*[302] and *Sepmra*[303] tribunals, that "the principle of necessity [in Article XI] may preclude the wrongfulness of an act, but it does not exclude the duty to compensate the owner of the right which had to be sacrificed."[304] On the contrary, the *LG&E* tribunal stated that "Article 27 of ILC's Draft Articles, as well as Article XI of the Treaty, does not specify if any compensation is payable to the party affected by losses during the state of necessity"[305] and added that "Article XI establishes the state of necessity as a ground for exclusion from wrongfulness of an act of the State, and therefore, the State is exempted from liability."[306] Similarly, the *Continental Casualty* tribunal awarded compensation only for the one measure that it found to be not necessary.[307]

What solutions can, therefore, be proposed?

---

297 *LG&E*, para. 257.
298 *Continental Casualty*, paras. 234–236.
299 For instance, Sacerdoti, above note 214, p. 374.
300 Binder, above note 232, p. 451.
301 Reinisch, above note 236, p. 154.
302 *Enron*, para. 345.
303 *Sempra*, para. 394.
304 *CMS*, paras. 388.
305 *LG&E*, para. 264.
306 Ibid, para. 261.
307 *Continental Casualty*, paras. 304–305.

Some authors who analyzed the Argentine cases before the ICSID tribunals proposed solutions to avoid the inconsistencies of the tribunals in interpreting necessity defense in BITs. Some of the proposed solutions include: (1) codification of a hierarchy of the legal authorities to interpret a BIT, especially the necessity defense;[308] (2) clarifying the elements of necessity in BITs through a multilateral agreement that defines the defense;[309] (3) [although this sounds radical] "completely eliminating use of the state of necessity defense under customary international law" in BIT disputes involving the defense of necessity;[310] (4) interpreting necessity along the 'least-restrictive alternative' approach developed by the WTO adjudicators;[311] (5) interpreting 'necessity' through a margin of appreciation to give deference to states;[312] (6) augment[313] the practice of precedent in investment tribunals (the Argentina BIT tribunals – although there is no *stare decicis* system in the ICSID – latently avoided referring to previous decisions on what were similar sets of facts and issues);[314] (7) introduce an appellate system, like in the WTO, for the international investment dispute settlement mechanism in ICSID, UNCITRAL etc.;[315] (8) "consolidation of proceedings and/or the appointment of identical arbitrators to formally separate arbitral procedures";[316] and (9) rigorous

---

308 Chubb, above note 234, pp. 552–553.

309 Ibid, p. 553.

310 Ibid, p. 555.

311 Burke-White and von Staden, above note 209, pp. 343–349. See also, Engan, above note 214, pp. 513–521.

312 Burke-White and von Staden, ibid, pp. 370–386, 409.

313 For discussion on the nature, practice and quantitative analysis of reference to precedents in select investment tribunals during the years 1972–2006, see, Jeffery P. Commission, 'Precedent in Investment Treaty Arbitration: A Citation Analysis of a Developing Jurisprudence', *Journal of International Arbitration*, 24(2): 2007, pp. 129–158.

314 August Reinisch, 'Investment Arbitration – The Role of Precedent in ICSID Arbitration', in Gerold Zeiler *et al.* (eds.), *Austrian Arbitration Yearbook 2008* (Wien: Manz'sche Verlags- und Universitätsbuchhandlung, 2008), pp. 495–510; Judith Gill, 'Is There a Special Role for Precedent in Investment Arbitration?', *ICSID Review – Foreign Investment Law Journal*, 25(1): 2010, pp. 87–94.

315 Asif H. Qureshi, 'An Appellate System in International Investment Arbitration?', in Muchlinski, Ortino and Schreuer, above note 200, pp. 1935–1950; Susan D. Franck, 'The Legitimacy Crisis in Investment Treaty Arbitration: Privatizing Public International Law through Inconsistent Decisions', *Fordham Law Review*, 73(4): 2005, pp. 1617–1625; Christian J. Tams, 'An Appealing Option? The Debate about an ICSID Appellate Structure', *Essays in Transnational Economic Law*, Working Paper No. 57, Martin-Luther-Universiät Halle-Wittenberg (2006), available at, http://tietje.jura.uni-halle.de/sites/default/files/altbestand/Heft57.pdf; Reinisch, above note 236, p. 214; Chubb, above note 234, pp. 553–555.

316 Reinisch, ibid.

academic elaboration of the fundamental principles in BITs for reference by tribunals.[317]

By way of concluding Section 5.5, therefore, the Argentine financial crisis disputes before the ICSID tribunals and Annulment Committees showed, for the first time, that the concept of necessity defense in WTO law can be successfully adopted in another, related field of PIL: IIL. Despite the choice by most of the tribunals to refer to the ARSIWA concept of necessity, the *CMS* Annulment Committee's caution not to confuse primary with secondary necessity defenses can lead to the conclusion that the WTO law defense of necessity, as selected by the *Continental Casualty* tribunal, may – since it is a primary norm as the defenses of necessity inserted in BITs – be more appropriate to interpret BIT provisions of necessity than the CIL defense of necessity. The experience of these tribunals and Annulment Committees to choose either of three options for interpreting necessity (i.e., the text of the treaty, Article 25 of the ARSIWA and the concept of necessity in WTO law), separately or in combination with one another (for example, the experience of the *Continental Casualty* tribunal, which, while employing the WTO concept of necessity, used the ARSIWA test to examine whether the respondent contributed to the situation of necessity), confirms the possibility for these different concepts of necessity to learn from each other towards, *mutatis mutandis*, a more coherent understanding, interpretation and application of the concept of necessity across different fields of international law. The varying (or opposite) results obtained in the Argentina ICSID cases as a result of the choice of different necessity concepts are a reminder to scholars and practitioners of international law to work towards seeking coherence between the concepts of necessity in various fields of international law. This exercise is the purpose of this book and Chapter 12 tries to examine the possibility for the concept of necessity in WTO law and the concept of necessity in CIL (Article 25 of the ARSIWA) to interact with each other and influence the concepts of necessity in other fields of international law.

5.6 International Human Rights Law

Section 5.6 discusses the concept of necessity in the field of IHRL. In IHRL treaties, necessity is contained in provisions that allow the taking of otherwise unlawful measures either in normal times (the so-called 'clawback' provisions) and/or in times of war or other emergencies (the so-called

317 Franck, above note 315, pp. 1613–1615.

'derogation' provisions). Whereas the term 'necessary'/'necessity' is found in most 'clawback' provisions, the element of 'necessity' has been identified in the derogation clauses through interpretation of the context of the right to take derogation measures. A concept of necessity is yet to be fully developed in IHRL and this section examines the suitability of making use of the concepts of necessity in WTO law and CIL in the context of necessity in IHRL.

5.6.1 *Balancing Individual and Community Rights*

It is the duty of all governments to maintain at all times – even though such task becomes difficult in times of crisis[318] – the balance between private rights and public interest. In other words, it is necessary for "human rights to be matched by accommodations in favor of the reasonable needs of the State to perform its public duties for the common good".[319] The notion that the rights of individuals are not unlimited, but that they must be exercised in consideration of the relevant community, has been at the core of the fundamental human rights conventions.[320] However, some abnormal situations may call for the limitation, suspension or derogation of treaty-based human rights and this can be done in different ways including: (a) denunciation of a treaty; (b) reservations as to terms of a treaty; (c) inserting treaty provisions which state that individual rights can only be exercised in conformity with the rights of others; (d) insertion of clauses in treaty texts interpreting the scope of rights guaranteed; (e) through 'clawback' or 'accommodation' clauses (i.e., clauses that allow breach of treaty obligations in normal circumstances for a specified number of reasons such as public morality, public health, public welfare, the rights of others, national security and *ordre public*) usually applicable to specific rights; and (f) through derogation clauses *stricto sensu* (i.e., clauses that allow the suspension or breach of certain treaty obligations in circumstances of war or public emergency) usually applicable to all but a few non-derogable rights (the so-called *notstandsfeste Rechte*).[321]

Sub-section 5.6.3 will briefly mention 'clawback' provisions in some IHRL treaties that contain the concept of necessity defense. Despite their closer relevance to this book than derogation provisions, however, 'clawback' provisions

318 Christoph Schreuer, 'Derogation of Human Rights in Situations of Public Emergency: The Experience of the European Convention on Human Rights', *Yale Journal of World Public Order*, 9(1): 1982, p. 113.

319 Rosalyn Higgins, 'Derogations under Human Rights Treaties', *British Yearbook of International Law*, 48(1): 1976–1977, p. 281.

320 Ibid, p. 283.

321 Ibid, pp. 281–282; Schreuer, above note 318, pp. 113–115.

will not be discussed in detail for lack of substantial literature on the defense of necessity in these provisions. The main focus of this section will, therefore, be on the concept of necessity derogation clauses (Sub-section 5.6.2) which has attracted in-depth examination.

For purpose of derogation clauses, emergency situations include armed conflicts, civil wars, insurrections, severe economic shocks, natural disasters and similar threats.[322] Two important considerations must be kept in mind while discussing the long-accepted national and international laws and practices of limiting human rights in explicitly identified abnormal situations. Firstly, there is an inherent need to balance the fear of abuse of human rights by governments in abnormal situations with the right and responsibility of governments to attend to the public interest in such times.[323] In other words a time of war or emergency is not an opportunity for states "to ignore the law but, a legitimate cause to decrease the level of legal protection".[324] Secondly, with respect to the different types of human rights, it must be remembered that not all human rights are *jus cogens*; therefore, in times of emergency[325] some of these rights may be suspended, limited or derogated under specified circumstances and with limitations, safeguards, notifications and review procedures.[326]

5.6.2 *Necessity as an Element of Derogation in Key* IHRL *Treaties*

Derogation provisions, samples of which are copied below, are not necessarily found in all IHRL treaties. For example, the Universal Declaration of Human Rights, the International Covenant on Economic, Social and Cultural Rights and the International Convention on the Rights of the Child do not have derogation provisions. Other IHRL treaties, however, explicitly provide for derogation. The three most frequently discussed IHRL instruments in which the concept of necessity defense is heavily represented have been Article 4 of the, Article 15 of the ECHR and Article 27 of the IACHR. Since their contents are, *mutatis mutandis*, essentially similar, only Article 4 of the ICCPR is cited below.

322 Emilie M. Hafner-Burton, Laurence R. Helfer and Christopher J. Fariss, 'Emergency and Escape: Explaining Derogations from Human Rights Treaties', *International Organization*, 65(4): 2011, p. 673.

323 Ibid, p. 676; Schreuer, above note 318.

324 Laurent Sermet, 'The Absence of a Derogation Clause from the African Charter on Human and Peoples' Rights: A Critical Discussion', *African Human Rights Law Journal*, 7(1): 2007, p. 143.

325 Cedric Ryngaert, 'State Responsibility, Necessity and Human Rights', in Dekker and Hey, above note 22, pp. 82–83.

326 Hafner-Burton, Helfer and Fariss, above note 322, p. 674.

Article 4 of the ICCPR

1. In time of public emergency which threatens the life of the nation and the existence of which is officially proclaimed, the States Parties to the present Covenant may take measures derogating from their obligations under the present Covenant to the extent strictly required by the exigencies of the situation, provided that such measures are not inconsistent with their other obligations under international law and do not involve discrimination solely on the ground of race, color, sex, language, religion or social origin.
2. No derogation from articles 6, 7, 8 (paragraphs 1 and 2), 11, 15, 16 and 18[327] may be made under this provision.
3. Any State Party to the present Covenant availing itself of the right of derogation shall immediately inform the other States Parties to the present Covenant, through the intermediary of the Secretary-General of the UN, of the provisions from which it has derogated and of the reasons by which it was actuated. A further communication shall be made, through the same intermediary, on the date on which it terminates such derogation.

Despite their minor differences,[328] the three instruments have been read together by writers as embodiments of the doctrine of derogation in IHRL.[329] The common elements[330] of the resort to derogation in these IHRL instruments

327 Respectively: (a) the right to life; (b) the right against exposure to torture or to cruel, inhuman or degrading treatment or punishment; (c) protection from slavery and servitude; (d) protection from imprisonment merely on the ground of inability to fulfill a contractual obligation; (e) protection from *ex-post facto* criminal laws; (f) the right to be recognized everywhere as a person before the law; and (g) the right to freedom of thought, conscience and religion.

328 Schreuer, above note 318, p. 117.

329 For example, Joan F. Hartman, 'Derogation from Human Rights Treaties in Public Emergencies – A Critique of Implementation by the European Commission and Court of Human Rights and the Human Rights Committee of the United Nations', *Harvard International Law Journal*, 22(1): 1981, pp. 1–52; Emanuele Sommario, 'Derogation from Human Rights Treaties in Situations of Natural or Man-Made Disasters', in Andrea de Guttry, Marco Gestri and Gabriella Venturini (eds.), *International Disaster Response Law* (The Hague: T.M.C. Asser Press, 2010), pp. 331–342; Sermet, above note 324, p. 150; Higgins, above note 319, pp. 286–289; ibid.

330 The common elements have been selected based on the text of the treaties and from the common elements identified by many authors. The elements identified may slightly differ. See, for instance, Aly Mokhtar, 'Human Rights Obligations *v.* Derogations: Article 15 of the European Convention on Human Rights', *International Journal of Human Rights*,

are the following: (1) the existence of war, public danger or public emergency; (2) maintaining the derogation the extent (time, scope and magnitude) strictly required by the exigencies of the situation; (3) taking derogation measures in a manner not inconsistent with the state's other obligations under international law; (4) notifying the derogation measure to the appropriate organ including the time of its beginning and end; and (5) review.

Necessity has been found by many writers to be part of the concept of the second criterion of derogation: *to the extent strictly required by the exigencies of the situation*. The concept of necessity is represented by the phrase *'strictly required'*. The other elements of derogation are proportionality, represented by the word *'to the extent'*, and the doctrine of margin of appreciation[331] (the margin of latitude or deference that the reviewer is willing to give the derogating state in taking the contested measures or that the reviewer will only intervene if the state has manifestly exceeded its discretion).[332] There have been different opinions on the exact meaning of the phrase *'to the extent strictly required'*. Some of the opinions are that the phrase refers to: (a) proportionality;[333] (b) necessity;[334] (c) proportionality, but necessity is contained within this principle of proportionality;[335] (d) necessity, but proportionality is contained within this principle of necessity;[336] and (e) both necessity and proportionality, but that they must be treated separately.[337] In all these opinions, however, necessity has been given similar meanings and has been found to lie at the heart of the practice and review of derogation clauses in the major human rights treaties.[338]

8(1): 2004, pp. 65–87; Schreuer, above note 318, p. 116; Hartman, ibid, pp. 15–31; Sermet, above note 329; Higgins, above note 319, pp. 290–307.

331 Mokhtar, ibid, pp. 70–74; Ryngaert, above note 325, pp. 88–90.

332 Margin of appreciation is a creation of the European Court of Human Rights in *The Cyprus Case* (*Greece v. the United Kingdom*) (1958–59). For more on the doctrine, see, Thomas A. O'Donnell, 'The Margin of Appreciation Doctrine: Standards in the Jurisprudence of the European Court of Human Rights', *Human Rights Quarterly*, 4(4): 1982, pp. 474–496; Michael R. Hutchinson, 'The Margin of Appreciation Doctrine in the European Court of Human Rights', *International and Comparative Law Quarterly*, 48(3): 1999, pp. 638–650; George Letsas, 'Two Concepts of the Margin of Appreciation', *Oxford Journal of Legal Studies*, 26(4): 2006, pp. 705–732.

333 Schreuer, above note 318, p. 126.

334 Sommario, above note 329, p. 335.

335 Schreuer, above note 318; ibid, p. 326.

336 Ryngaert, above note 325, p. 88.

337 For example, Sermet, above note 324, p. 150; Mokhtar, above note 330, pp. 70–72; Higgins, above note 319, pp. 282–283.

338 Lawrence Hill-Cawthorne, 'The Role of Necessity in International Humanitarian and Human Rights Law', *Israel Law Review*, 47(2): 2014, p. 235–236.

Although, as in IHL, a specific definition has not been given to the concept of necessity as it applies to derogations in IHRL, the following, extracted from decisions of the European Court of Human Rights and scholarly observations, can be listed as the elements of necessity in IHRL: (1) the derogation must be the only way to cope with the emergency; there should not be less drastic alternatives; (2) the derogation must be strictly related to the emergency or war situation; i.e., there must be a clear link between the facts of the emergency and the specific derogation measures chosen; (3) there must be clear and stringently applied checks and safeguards against abuse (i.e., excessive or unnecessary use of the derogation); and (4) the derogation measures must cease as soon as the situations that gave rise to the emergency no longer exist.[339] These elements (particularly elements 1 and 4) are more inclined toward the ARSIWA concept of necessity than the concept of necessity in WTO law. The inclination appears to be rational because given the history of its development, the ARSIWA concept of necessity appears more suited to explain necessity measures at times of emergency than the concept of necessity in WTO law that applies to measures at normal times.

5.6.3 *Interpreting Necessity in IHRL 'Clawback' Provisions*

A number of 'clawback' clauses in IHRL instruments contain the concept of necessity in the form of a defense if a state takes, in time of peace, some human-right violating measures to protect public safety, order, health, morals or the fundamental rights and freedoms of others. For example:

> Article 12(3) of the ICCPR
>
> The above-mentioned rights [of movement, residence and emigration] shall not be subject to any restrictions except those which are provided by law, are *necessary* to protect national security, public order (*ordre public*), public health or morals or the rights and freedoms of others, and are consistent with the other rights recognized in the present Covenant (*emphasis added*).
>
> Article 18(3) of the ICCPR
>
> Freedom to manifest one's religion or beliefs may be subject only to such limitations as are prescribed by law and are *necessary* to protect public safety, order, health, or morals … (*emphasis added*).
>
> Article 19(3) of the ICCPR

339 Schreuer, above note 318, pp. 126–129; Higgins, above note 319, pp. 302–305; Mokhtar, above note 330, pp. 71–72.

> The exercise of the rights provided for in paragraph 2 of this article carries with it special duties and responsibilities. It may therefore be subject to certain restrictions, but these shall only be such as are provided by law and are *necessary*: (a) for respect of the rights or reputations of others; (b) for the protection of national security or of public order (*ordre public*), or of public health or morals (*emphasis added*).

Similar provisions are also contained in: Articles 14(1), 21 and 22(2) of the ICCPR; Articles 2(2), 6(1), 8(2), 9(2), 10(2) and 11(2) of the ECHR; Articles 12(3), 13(2), 15, 16(2) and 22(3) of the IACHR; Article 8(1)(a) and (c) of the International Covenant on Economic, Social and Cultural Rights etc.

The UN Human Rights Committee noted, regarding the difference between derogation and the 'clawback' limitations, that "[d]erogation from some Covenant obligations in emergency situations is clearly distinct from restrictions or limitations allowed even in normal times under several provisions of the Covenant".[340] How must, therefore, the term 'necessary' be interpreted in the two groups of provisions (derogation vs 'clawback') which represent circumstances different from each other? For example, Article 2(2) of the ECHR provides that "[d]eprivation of life shall not be regarded as inflicted in contravention of this Article when it results from the use of force which is no more than *absolutely necessary* ... (*emphasis added*)." In interpreting the term 'absolutely necessary' the European Court of Human Rights stated that:

> In this respect the use of the term 'absolutely necessary' in Article [2(2)] indicates that *a stricter and more compelling test of necessity must be employed from that normally applicable when determining whether State action is 'necessary in a democratic society'* under [Articles 8(2), 9(2), 10(2) and 11(2)] of the Convention. In particular, the force used must be strictly proportionate to the achievement of the aims set out in [Article 2(2)(a),(b) and (c)]. In keeping with the importance of this provision (art. 2) in a democratic society, the Court must, in making its assessment, subject deprivations of life to the most careful scrutiny ... (*emphasis added*)[341]

---

340 Human Rights Committee, General Comment 29, States of Emergency (article 4), UN Doc. CCPR/C/21/Rev.1/Add.11 (2001), available at, http://hrlibrary.umn.edu/gencomm/hrc29.html.

341 *Case of McCann and Others v. the United Kingdom* (App. No. 18984/91), Judgment (27 September 1995), paras. 149–150.

With the Court determining that this level of necessity was the strictest form of necessity imposing a higher burden than the necessity requirement in, say, political rights,[342] there is at least an indication here that the ECHR recognizes different degrees of necessity. But what do these degrees of necessity have as common elements? With the ARSIWA concept of necessity unlikely to be available for adoption (see Sub-section 5.6.4), one may refer, as a basis, to the definition used for necessity in the derogation provisions. The Court's analysis may be read to support this because, for example, the Court indicated that the expression 'absolutely necessary' involves the use of force "strictly proportionate to the achievement of the aims set out in Article 2(2)(a),(b) and (c)", an element required in interpreting necessity in the derogation provisions.

A better suggestion, however, would be to adopt the concept of necessity in WTO law for the 'clawback' element of necessity. The experience of the *Continental Casualty* tribunal (see, Sub-section 5.5.3) could be relevant in this regard. Firstly, there is a strong textual similarity between the General Exceptions of the relevant WTO agreements and the clawback provisions in the ECHR. Secondly, both exceptions, unlike the derogation clauses, apply in 'normal' times. Thirdly, there is caution, in the introductory paragraphs of the General Exceptions and in the text of some 'clawback' provisions, that the 'necessary' measures must not be applied to abuse the rights of others. Thus, a treaty interpreter may adopt the concept of necessity in WTO law to the 'clawback' provisions by taking into consideration, as the *Continental Casualty* tribunal did, the context within which IHRL operates (for example by examining, as the European Court of Human Rights did, whether the contested measure is necessary in a democratic society).

5.6.4 *Non-applicability of the Concept of Necessity in CIL*

Applying the concept of necessity in Article 25 of the ARSIWA to interpret necessity in IHRL treaties appears to be not possible mainly because of the primary-secondary rule dichotomy that the ARSIWA commentaries highlight. For instance, when asked by The Netherlands if there should be a new provision on humanitarian intervention as an exceptional circumstance excluding wrongfulness, Special Rapporteur Crawford had commented: "Chapter V (CPW) does not deal with the substantive primary rules relating to the use of force, or indeed generally with the international law of humanitarian assistance. *Cases*

342 Ohlin and May, above note 101, p. 125.

not otherwise provided for may be dealt with in accordance with the criteria in article 26 [finally article 25] (Necessity) (emphasis added)."[343]

Human rights treaties have a number of provisions referring to necessity both in derogation and 'clawback' situations.[344] This may lead to the conclusion that, despite some similarities in the substances of the ARSIWA and IHRL concepts of necessity (mainly the derogation clauses):

> [IHRL treaties] should at the same time be seen as constituting a self-contained *régime*: the fact that necessity is so exhaustively regulated by the primary norms of [IHRL] suggests that, at least in relation to the human rights norms set out in the relevant treaties, necessity should, and can only, be invoked on the basis of primary human rights norms rather than on the basis of Article 25 of the ILC Articles. Put differently, the international human rights obligations in question arguably exclude the possibility of invoking necessity beyond the restrictions/justifications/excuses/derogations provided with respect to the primary norms containing the obligations.[345]

The substantive and procedural rules regulating 'necessity' set out in the relevant human rights treaties are more detailed and specific than the vague language of Article 25 of the ARSIWA. The level of specificity in human rights treaties is designed to more strictly circumscribe the invocation of necessity by states. If the human rights treaties did not include necessity clauses, the general provision in Article 25 of the ARSIWA would have been the only necessity defense available to states and there could be the danger of abuse in making use of Article 25. Therefore, an interpretation that takes into consideration the factor of abuse must be developed for the concept of necessity in the human rights conventions (particularly the derogation clauses) because of the need for a stronger protection of human rights.[346] The concept of necessity in WTO law is, in a number of provisions of the WTO agreements (such as the *chapeau* of the General Exceptions of the GATT 1994 and the GATS), linked to provisions that require the avoidance of abuse while taking necessary measures. It can thus be used as a start to develop a concept of necessity for IHRL.

343 James Crawford, 'Fourth Report on State Responsibility' (2001), ILC, 53rd sess., UN Doc. A/CN.4/517 and Add.1, p. 21.
344 Ryngaert, above note 325, p. 86.
345 Ibid, p. 88.
346 Ibid.

By way of concluding Section 5.6, therefore, it can be observed that necessity finds itself in two spheres in IHRL treaties, i.e., in 'clawback' provisions and in 'derogation'. Whereas the term 'necessary'/ 'necessity' is found in most 'clawback' provisions, the element of 'necessity' has been identified in the derogation clauses through interpretation of the context of taking derogation measures. A concept of necessity is yet to be fully developed in IHRL and this section has examined the suitability of adopting the concepts of necessity in WTO law and the CIL into the context of necessity in IHRL. A possibility has been identified for the adoption of the WTO law 'weighing and balancing' elements of necessity into the context of necessity in IHRL treaties, particularly the 'clawback' provisions which share similarities in text, context and/or purpose with the WTO agreements which provide for necessity (See Chapters 8 and 9). With the unlikeliness of adopting the concept of necessity in CIL to the derogation provisions of IHRL treaties, some elements of the concepts of necessity both in WTO law and CIL, as fitting IHRL, may be taken into consideration in developing a general concept of necessity for IHRL.

5.7 International Criminal Law

ICL, which has been in progress since the trials by the NIMT and the post-Cold War tribunals such as the ICTY (established in 1993), the ICTR (established in 1994), the Special Court for Sierra Leone (established in 2002) and the ECCC (established in 2005),[347] took a definite international shape with the signing of the Rome Statute of the ICC.[348] In comparison with the other fields of PIL discussed in this chapter, there is no substantial practice on, and interpretation of, the concept of necessity in ICL. Nevertheless, one of the crimes brought before the ICL tribunals – war crimes – has, when prosecuted in the NIMT, ICTY and ICC chambers, benefitted from the works on, and interpretations of, military necessity mainly because it emanates from the rules, and criminalizes a narrower subset, of IHL.[349] Section 5.7 mainly focuses on war crimes.

347 The ECCC is a national court established by an agreement between the Cambodian government and the UN; thus, it is considered a hybrid court. It judges are local and foreign.

348 On the experience of the main tribunals up to and including the ICC, see, Roberto Bellelli (ed.), *International Criminal Justice: Law and Practice from the Rome Statute to it Review* (Surrey (UK) and Burlington (US): Ashgate, 2010); William A. Schabas and Nadia Bernaz (eds.), *Routledge Handbook of International Criminal Law* (London and New York: Routledge, 2011), pp. 5–105.

349 For the relationship between war crimes and IHL, see, Robert Cryer *et al.*, *An Introduction to International Criminal Law and Procedure* (2nd ed.) (Cambridge: Cambridge University Press, 2010), pp. 271–273.

Similar to what has been stated in Sub-section 5.5.3 regarding the case law of the ICSID tribunals in the Argentine financial crisis disputes, it is true that the analysis of the cases brought before the various war crimes tribunals should, instead of being discussed in this Section, have been kept in Chapter 6 where the contribution of international tribunals to the development of the concept of necessity is discussed. The main reason why the discussion of the disputes brought before the various war crimes tribunals has been kept in this Chapter is that the author believes that the concept of necessity in ICL is best discussed through case law. To avoid repeating the discussion in this Section in Chapter 6, Sub-section 6.6.1 refers to this section to ensure that the experience of the various war crimes tribunals is mentioned in Chapter 6.

5.7.1 *The Nuremberg International Military Tribunal*

Article 6(b) of the Charter of the NIMT (Nuremberg Charter)[350] defined war crimes as:

> namely violations of the laws or customs of war. Such violations shall include, but not be limited to, murder, ill-treatment or deportation to slave labour or for any other purpose of civilian population of or in occupied territory, murder or ill-treatment of prisoners of war or persons on the seas, killing of hostages, plunder of public or private property, wanton destruction of cities, towns or villages, or devastation *not justified by military necessity* (*emphasis added*).

Under this provision, the defense of military necessity applied to *all* types of war crimes. The NIMT decided that the defense of military necessity is fully applicable if a provision of the Charter contemplated that the defense applies and to the extent the rule permitted.[351] In practice, Dunbar, writing in 1952, observed that the military necessity was considered by the war crimes tribunals established after the Second World War largely in connection with two categories of cases: (a) treatment of prisoners of war and unarmed enemy persons; and (b) deportation of civilian inhabitants from and devastation of property in occupied enemy territory.[352]

350 Available at, http://avalon.law.yale.edu/imt/imtconst.asp.

351 As quoted in Bogliolo, above note 86, p. 15.

352 Dunbar, above note 119, pp. 446–452.

5.7.2 *The ICTY*

The ICTY Charter[353] provided for the prosecution of grave breaches of the Geneva Conventions of 1949 (Article 2), violations of the laws or customs of war (Article 3), genocide (Article 4) and crimes against humanity (Article 5).[354] In a significant deviation from the Nuremberg Charter, the ICTY Charter limited the defense of necessity to *only one* of the eight acts listed in Article 2 (para. (d)), i.e., to the extensive destruction and appropriation of property, *not justified by military necessity and carried out unlawfully and wantonly* as well as to only one of the five acts listed in Article 3 (para. (b)), i.e., wanton destruction of cities, towns or villages, or devastation *not justified by military necessity.* Thus, by way of example, in *Galic*, the ICTY held that the prohibition against wilful and direct targeting of civilians is absolute and not subject to the defense of military necessity[355] and in *Strugar*, the Tribunal considered devastation not justified by military necessity because the ICTY statute did not provide for necessity defense for the acts.[356]

5.7.3 *The ICTR*

The ICTR Statute[357] prosecuted genocide (Article 2), crimes against humanity (Article 3) and violations of Article 3 Common to the Geneva Conventions and of Additional Protocol II (Article 3). It did not provide for necessity as a defense to these crimes for which traditionally the defense of necessity was not available. Regarding genocide, for example, the December 1948 Convention on the Prevention and Punishment of the Crime of Genocide, from which the definitions of genocide in the ICTY, ICTR and ICC Statutes were copied, does not provide for any defense to the crime of genocide. Regarding crimes against humanity, Article 6(c) of the Nuremberg Charter (which Article 5 of the ICTY

353 Available at, http://www.icty.org/x/file/Legal%20Library/Statute/statute_sept09_en.pdf.

354 Similar provisions are available in the Law on the Establishment of the Extraordinary Chambers of Cambodia which authorized the Chambers to preside over, *inter alia*, the crimes of genocide (Article 4), crimes against humanity (Article 5) and grave breaches of the Geneva Conventions of 12 August 1949 (Article 6). Only Article 6 allows an exception for one of the eight acts listed therein – destruction and serious damage to property, *not justified by military necessity* and carried out unlawfully and wantonly. Text of the law that established the ECCC is available at, https://www.eccc.gov.kh/sites/default/files/legal-documents/KR_Law_as_amended_27_Oct_2004_Eng.pdf.

355 *Prosecutor v. Galic*, Case No. IT-98-29-A, Appeals Chamber Judgment, 30 November 2006, paras. 90, 103–04.

356 *Prosecutor v. Strugar*, Case No. IT-01-42-T, Judgment, 31 January 2005, paras. 293–94.

357 Available at, http://legal.un.org/avl/pdf/ha/ictr_EF.pdf.

Charter closely followed and Article 3 of the ICTR Statutes does not deviate from) similarly did not provide for necessity defense for that crime.

5.7.4 *The Rome Statute of the ICC*

Article 5 of the Rome Statute provides the ICC with the jurisdiction over four types of international crimes: genocide, crimes against humanity, war crimes and aggression. The Statute provides for necessity in two forms: military necessity defense available to *specific* offenses; and necessity defense applicable to *all* crimes. Along the lines of the ICTY Charter, the Statute provides for military necessity defense for select acts considered war crimes:

> Article 8(2) – War crimes
>
> For the purpose of this Statute, 'war crimes' means:
>
> (a) grave breaches of the Geneva Conventions of 12 August 1949, namely, any of the following acts against persons or property protected under the provisions of the relevant Geneva Convention:
>
> (iv) extensive destruction and appropriation of property, *not justified by military necessity* and carried out unlawfully and wantonly (*emphasis added*);[358]
>
> (b) other serious violations of the laws and customs applicable in international armed conflict, within the established framework of international law, namely, any of the following acts:
>
> (xiii) destroying or seizing the enemy's property unless such destruction or seizure be *imperatively demanded by the necessities of war* (*emphasis added*);[359]
>
> (e) other serious violations of the laws and customs applicable in armed conflicts not of an international character ... namely, any of the following acts:
>
> (viii) ordering the displacement of the civilian population for reasons related to the conflict, *unless the security of the civilians involved or imperative military reasons so demand*;[360]

---

358 Bassiouni dissects this type of war crime as having seven elements, one of them being the destruction or appropriation was *not justified by military necessity*. Cherif M. Bassiouni, *Introduction to International Criminal Law: Second Revised Edition*, Vol. 1 (Leiden: Martinus Nijhoff Publishers, 2013), p. 171.

359 Bassiouni dissects this type of war crime as having seven elements, one of them being the destruction or seizure was *not justified by military necessity*. Ibid, p. 180.

360 Even though the term 'necessity' is not included in this paragraph, Bassiouni comments that there is a requirement here that the order should be one that is not justified by the security of the civilians involved or by military necessity. Ibid, p. 195.

(xii) destroying or seizing the property of an adversary unless such destruction or seizure be *imperatively demanded by the necessities of the conflict* (*emphasis added*);[361]

The Statute also makes necessity defense (not military defense) available as a ground for excluding criminal responsibility from *all* crimes listed in the Statute. The first codification at the international level of necessity [and duress] as defense in ICL,[362] Article 31(1)(d) of the Rome Statute provides:

Article 31- Grounds for excluding criminal responsibility

1. In addition to other grounds for excluding criminal responsibility provided for in this Statute, a person shall not be criminally responsible if, at the time of that person's conduct:
   (d) The conduct which is alleged to constitute a crime within the jurisdiction of the Court has been caused by duress resulting from a threat of imminent death or of continuing or imminent serious bodily harm against that person or another person, *and* the person acts *necessarily*[363] and reasonably to avoid this threat (*emphasis added*).

The defenses of necessity and duress were invoked before the NIMT.[364] Cases such as *Krauch*,[365] *Krupp*,[366] *Flick*[367] and *von Leeb*[368] may be cited as examples.

---

361 Bassiouni dissects the elements of this type of war crime as having seven elements, one of them being the destruction or seizure was *not required by military necessity*. Ibid, p. 197.

362 Cryer *et al.*, above note 349, p. 411.

363 That this adverb 'necessarily' means a defense of necessity and that it can be used as a defense against war crimes and crimes against humanity is asserted by Paola Gaeta, 'May Necessity Be Available as a Defense for Torture in the Interrogation of Suspected Terrorists?', *Journal of International Criminal Justice*, 2(3): 2004, pp. 789–792.

364 United Nations War Crimes Commission, *Law Reports of Trials of War Criminals*, Vol. XV (*Digest of Laws and Cases*) (1949), available at, https://www.loc.gov/rr/frd/Military_Law/pdf/Law-Reports_Vol-15.pdf, pp. 155–156, 170–176.

365 United Nations War Crimes Commission, *Law Reports of Trials of War Criminals*, Vol. X (1949), available at, https://www.loc.gov/rr/frd/Military_Law/pdf/Law-Reports_Vol-10.pdf, pp. 1–63.

366 Ibid, pp. 69–158.

367 United Nations War Crimes Commission, *Law Reports of Trials of War Criminals*, Vol. IX (1949), available at, https://www.loc.gov/rr/frd/Military_Law/pdf/Law-Reports_Vol-9.pdf, pp. 1–30.

368 United Nations War Crimes Commission, *Law Reports of Trials of War Criminals*, Vol. XII (*The German High Command Trial*) (1949), available at, https://www.loc.gov/rr/frd/Military_Law/pdf/Law-Reports_Vol-12.pdf, pp. 1–95.

It was observed that distinguishing among the three key defenses – duress, necessity and superior order – was not always easy and that an argument put forward in court may contain elements of more than one defense.[369] Nevertheless, Knoops notes that all pre-Rome Statute proposals and drafts made clear the distinctions between the defenses of necessity and duress. In the drafting process of the Rome Statute, the defenses of necessity and duress were separately drafted, but were unnecessarily put together in one provision, Article 31(1)(d). Knoops stated that "the mixture of these two defenses is not only unnecessary, juridical and inaccurate, *but accounts also for an underestimation of the defense of necessity in ICL* ... [I] will show why this defense deserves an independent place in ICL".[370] Knoops is keen to show that despite the 'mingling' of necessity and duress, necessity can still be separately explained. The practice, however, points to the contrary. For example, in *Erdemović*,[371] the ICTY's Trial Chamber, without disentangling the two defenses, proceeded to hear the defendant's case as that of "extreme necessity",[372] "moral duress and/ or a state of necessity",[373] "duress or the state of necessity",[374] "the extreme necessity in which Drazen Erdemovic allegedly found himself when placed under duress by the order",[375] the "[e]xtreme necessity arising from duress"[376] According to Knoops, there are three thresholds or prerequisites for the admissibility of the 'separate' defense of necessity in war crimes charges: (1) the act charged must have been done to prevent a significantly greater evil than inflicted; (2) there must have been no adequate alternative; and (3) the harm inflicted must not have been disproportionate to the harm avoided.[377] It has also been observed by other writers that international criminal courts and tribunals interpret the defense of necessity, as well as duress and superior order, particularly strictly.[378]

---

369 United Nations War Crimes Commission, above note 364, p. 156. Observe also that the commentary on duress (pp. 170–175) contains many references to necessity.

370 Geert-Jan Alexander Knoops, *Defenses in Contemporary International Criminal Law* (2nd ed.) (Leiden: Martinus Nijhoff Publishers, 2008), p. 82.

371 *Prosecutor v. Erdemović*, Case No. IT-96-22-T, Judgment, 29 November 1996, paras. 293–94.

372 Ibid, paras. 16, 91.

373 Ibid, para. 19.

374 Ibid.

375 Ibid, para. 86.

376 Ibid, para. 88(b).

377 Knoops, above note 370, p. 86.

378 Fabián O. Raimondo, *General Principles of Law in the Decisions of International Criminal Courts and Tribunals* (Leiden and Boston: Martinus Nijhoff Publishers, 2008), pp. 95, 176, 185.

By way of concluding Section 5.7, therefore, ICL is yet to develop a discernible interpretation of the defense of necessity in charges of international crimes. Until the coming of the Rome Statute, necessity had been limited to military necessity defense applicable only against war crimes. The Rome Statute, while continuing that tradition, has also provided for a necessity defense applicable to all crimes under the Statute. The elements of the defense are, however, yet to be clearly defined. Given that the crimes contained in ICL treaties are those committed mostly in times of war, emergencies or other abnormal times, reference to the concept of necessity in WTO law may not be suitable. Elements of the concept of necessity in CIL may, despite their being applicable as secondary norms, however, be adopted in ICL disputes keeping the context of international crimes in consideration.

5.8 The Law of Responsibility of International Organizations as Codified in the DARIO

In August 2011, the ILC completed its work on the responsibility of international organizations by submitting, in part, the DARIO. Article 25 of the DARIO deals with the invocation of necessity defense and reads:

> 1. Necessity may not be invoked by an international organization as a ground for precluding the wrongfulness of an act not in conformity with an international obligation of that organization unless the act:
>   (a) is the only means for the organization to safeguard against a grave and imminent peril an essential interest of *its member States or of the international community as a whole, when the organization has, in accordance with international law, the function to protect the interest in question* (*emphasis added*); and
>   (b) does not seriously impair an essential interest of the State or States towards which the international obligation exists, or of the international community as a whole.
> 2. In any case, necessity may not be invoked by an international organization as a ground for precluding wrongfulness if:
>   (a) the international obligation in question excludes the possibility of invoking necessity; or
>   (b) the organization has contributed to the situation of necessity.

Article 25 of the DARIO is almost a verbatim copy of the ARSIWA except that it does not allow the international organization, unlike in the case of ARSIWA, to invoke necessity to protect its own essential interest. The ILC admitted that there is a paucity of practice on the invocation of necessity regarding international organizations. The only case it cited was Judgment No. 2183 of the Administrative Tribunal of the ILO in the *T.O.R.N. v. CERN* case which involved accessing the electronic account of an employee who was on leave. The Tribunal stated that:

> in the event that access to an e-mail account *becomes necessary for reasons of urgency* or because of *the prolonged absence of the account holder*, it must be possible for organizations to open the account using appropriate technical safeguards. *That state of necessity, justifying access to data which may be confidential, must be assessed with the utmost care* (*emphasis added*).[379]

The ILC cited paucity of practice and considerable risk as reasons for not allowing the invocation of necessity by the interregional organization in protecting its essential interests:

> While the conditions set by article 25 on the responsibility of States for internationally wrongful acts would be applicable also with regard to international organizations, the scarcity of practice and the considerable risk that invocability of necessity entails for compliance with international obligations suggest that, as a matter of policy, necessity should not be invocable by international organizations as widely as by States. This may be achieved by limiting the essential interests which may be protected by the invocation of necessity to those of the member States and of the international community as a whole, to the extent that the organization has, in accordance with international law, the function to protect them. Thus, when an international organization has been given powers over certain matters, it may, in the use of these powers, invoke the need to safeguard an essential interest of the international community or of its member States, provided that this is consistent with the principle of speciality. On the other hand, an international organization may invoke one of its own essential interests only if it coincides with an essential

379 *T.O.R.N. v. European Organization for Nuclear Research* (CERN), International Labour Organization, Administrative Tribunal, 94th sess., 3 February 2003, para. 19, available at, http://www.ilo.org/dyn/triblex/triblexmain.fullText?p_lang=en&p_judgment_no=2183&p_language_code=EN. The ILC's reference to the case is available at, Report of the International Law Commission (2001), ILC, 63rd sess., Supp. No. 10 (A/66/10), p. 119, para. 3.

interest of the international community or of its member States. This solution may be regarded as an attempt to reach a compromise between two opposite positions with regard to necessity: the view of those who favor placing international organizations on the same level as States and the opinion of those who would totally rule out the invocability of necessity by international organizations.[380]

5.9 Lessons Learned from the Experiences with the Concepts of Necessity in Different Fields of International Law

This chapter navigated the concept of necessity in eight different fields of international law by examining their respective treaty texts, interpretations and practices. At the end of this navigation, a spectrum emerges as, on the one end of the spectrum (such as in the case of the use of force under the UN Charter, IHRL, ICL or the law of responsibility of international organizations (as codified in the DARIO)), there is little or no practice on understanding or interpretation of the concept of necessity, while on the other end (such as in the case of the law of state responsibility (as codified in the ARSIWA), IIL or IEnL) there is a relatively advanced set of interpretations and practices of the concept of necessity. Moreover, while some fields of international law (such as IHL) strive to develop their own concepts of necessity, others (such as the use of force under the UN Charter, IEnL, IIL, IHRL or the law of responsibility of international organizations) have relied, or can rely, on the two most recognizable concepts of necessity to-date (the concepts of necessity in WTO law and CIL) separately or by adopting elements from both concepts.

The possibility, based on the existing practice, of the application of the concepts of necessity in CIL and WTO law, either in circumscribed spheres (for example, in the case of IEnL) or as mutually exclusive alternatives (for example, in the case of IIL), gives an indication that there is a possibility to cross-fertilize the elements of these two concepts of necessity either to apply to other fields of PIL (for instance, IHRL) or to develop a more coherent understanding

380 Report of the International Law Commission, ibid, pp. 119–120, para. 4. For a reflection on this change and how it developed in the drafting process, see, August Reinisch, 'How Necessary is Necessity for International Organizations?', *International Organizations Law Review*, 3(2): 2006, pp. 177–183; Mirka Möldner, 'Responsibility of International Organizations: Introducing the ILC's DARIO', in Armin von Bogdandy and Rüdiger Wolfrum (eds.), *Max Planck Yearbook of United Nations Law*, Vol. 16 (Leiden: Koninklijke Brill N.V., 2012), pp. 304–306.

and application of the concept of necessity in international law. The analysis for this exercise will be made in Chapter 12. Before moving on to that analysis, however, Chapter 6 will identify the lessons that can be learned from the interpretations that different international tribunals (other than the pre-PCIJ tribunals and the GATT/WTO organs, both covered under Chapters 2 and 8–9 respectively) provided for the defense of necessity.

CHAPTER 6

The Role of International Courts and Tribunals in Developing the Concept of Necessity in Customary International Law

6.1 General Notes

In Chapter 2, state and tribunal practices of the plea of necessity before the establishment of the PCIJ in 1922 were presented and four pre-PCIJ disputes – the case of *The Neptune* (*1797*), the *Bering Fur Seal Fisheries Jurisdiction* arbitration (*1893*), the *Company General of the Orinoco* case (*1905*) and the *French Company of Venezuelan Railroads* case (*1905*) – were mentioned. The establishment of the PCIJ can be considered as a turning point in the internationalization of disputes. This chapter will continue with the presentation of disputes before international courts/tribunals since the establishment of the PCIJ (except the *Russian Indemnity* case (1921))[1] where the state of necessity was explicitly or implicitly mentioned or invoked at any time during the proceedings. The following general observations can be made regarding the way the defense of necessity was presented during the proceedings:

(a) in some of the disputes, necessity was expressly raised as defense while in other disputes, other defenses, most notably *force majeure*, were raised, but their content fits more the modern definition of necessity defense;
(b) in some of the disputes, necessity was specifically invoked and debated whereas in other disputes it was merely mentioned as a sub-set of other, bigger arguments; and
(c) in some of the disputes, the defense of necessity was made part of the proceedings whereas in other disputes it was raised during oral proceedings or other communications.

---

1 The *Russian Indemnity* dispute (*Russia v. Turkey*) that was decided in 1912 has been included in this chapter (which covers post-1922 disputes), not in Chapter 2 (pre-1922 disputes), mainly because it was decided by the PCA, an international court. The purpose for this inclusion is to link this dispute to the 'internationalization' era of the defense of necessity in international disputes since the works of the PCIJ.

 | DOI:10.1163/9789004700000_008

This chapter presents cases brought before eight international courts or tribunals: the PCA; the PCIJ; the ICJ; the ITLOS; the international crimes tribunals; the *Rainbow Warrior* (1990) tribunal; the tribunal for the *Libyan Arab Foreign Investment Company v. the Republic of Burundi* dispute (1991); and the tribunals and Annulment Committees of the ICSID. The contribution of these courts/tribunals in developing the concept of necessity in international law in general, and CIL in particular, will be discussed. The focus of the contribution of these disputes is on the development of the concept of necessity in CIL as now codified in the ARSIWA not only because the interpretations of necessity in these disputes resemble the concept of necessity in the ARSIWA, but also because the focus of the comparison in Chapter 11 will be between the concept of necessity in WTO law and the concept of necessity in CIL. Some of the disputes identified in this Chapter have already been discussed in the previous chapters, especially Chapters 2 and 5. It will be observed regarding the disputes discussed in this chapter that:

1. most of the disputes were related to the settlement of debts[2] – hence related to the notion of financial (economic) necessity – or to the protection of the interests of the citizens/companies of one state in the territory of another state;[3]
2. in many of the disputes the defenses were raised as *force majeure*, self-preservation or others, but read today they resemble the defense of necessity more than any other defense; and
3. the state of necessity was litigated in detail only in a few, later cases mainly because the elements of the state of necessity, as clearly distinguished from other defenses such as self-reservation, *force majeure*, self-defense and distress, started to be refined at an international level in the 1980s mainly through the reports of the ILC's works on state responsibility.

There is disparity in the length of the coverage given to the disputes discussed for two reasons: (a) the degree of contribution that the respective disputes made to the development of the concept of necessity in CIL; and (b) the relevance of the statements of the parties (during the proceedings) or the tribunals (in their awards) to the subject of this chapter.

2 Roberto Ago, 'The Internationally Wrongful Act of the State, Source of International Responsibility', *Eighth Report on State Responsibility*, Addendum (1980), U.N. Doc. A/CN.4/318/Add.5–7, p. 22, para. 22.

3 Ibid, p. 29, para. 38.

The cases discussed in this chapter greatly influenced, and were in turn influenced by, the provisions and commentaries of the ARSIWA provisions on necessity. The ILC reports, particularly Roberto Ago's works,[4] made detailed analysis of the most notable state of necessity cases since the 18th century and drew lessons from them in developing the draft ARSIWA provisions on necessity. The necessity provisions in the ARSIWA and the ILC commentaries on them in turn impacted the interpretation of necessity defense in the disputes that were litigated during and after the draft ARSIWA.

The lessons to be gathered from the court/tribunal practices discussed in this chapter will, together with the lessons from the international courts/tribunal practices mentioned in Chapters 2 and 8–9, be utilized in Chapter 12 where the concept of necessity in WTO law will be compared with the concepts of necessity in other fields of international law particularly the concept of necessity in CIL.

Chapters 5 and 6 could have been merged into one chapter to discuss the different fields of PIL (Chapter 5) and the relevant case law (Chapter 6) together so that the disputes discussed in this chapter would be read as case law for Chapter 5. This was not possible mainly because if the two chapters were merged, some sections in Chapter 5 (for instance, the law of use of force and the law of responsibility of international organizations) would be left without enough case law on necessity, leaving only some of the disputes discussed in this chapter (for instance, the disputes before the PCA, PCIJ and ITLOS) fitting into the in Chapter 5. However, there are some disputes discussed in this chapter (for instance, the *Gabcíkovo-Nagymaros Project (1997)* dispute and the disputes brought before international crimes tribunals) already mentioned in the previous chapters. To avoid repetition of the narration of such disputes, only references will be made in this chapter to the chapters where the same disputes were discussed.

6.2 The PCA

6.2.1 *Russian Indemnity (1912)*

This dispute[5] arose when the Russian Government refused to receive delayed payment from the Imperial Ottoman Government because the interest from

---

4 Ibid, pp. 22–34, paras. 22–48; Report of the International Law Commission (2001), ILC, 53rd sess., Supp. No. 10 (A/56/10), pp. 195–206, paras. 4–20.

5 The facts that lead to the dispute and the key findings of the tribunal are summarized in, author unknown, 'The Case of Russia against Turkey at the Hague Court of Arbitration', *American Journal of International Law*, 7(1): 1913, pp. 147–148.

the payment had not been paid.[6] A five-person tribunal was established to resolve the dispute. The Ottoman empire, in its defense for not being able to pay the debts submitted, in part, that it faced severe financial difficulties between 1881 and 1902, a situation which it referred to as *force majeure*. The tribunal established to resolve the dispute decided that the Ottoman government was liable to pay interest and rejected the Ottoman defense. The Tribunal first noted that the exception of *force majeure* may be cited in public and private international law and "*that the obligation of a State to fulfil treaties may give way 'if the very existence of the State should be in danger, if the observance of the international duty is … 'self-destructive'* (*emphasis in original*)" and, after analyzing Turkey's situation during the period between 1881 and 1902, found that the defense of *force majeure* could not be accepted.[7] It has been mentioned in Chapters 2 and 5 that situations threatening the very existence of a state are generally classified under 'self-preservation' rather than *force majeure*. Ago also read the circumstances that the parties and the PCA in this dispute referred to are more of a state of necessity than *force majeure* or situations that threaten the very existence of a state.[8]

The *Russian Indemnity* dispute contributed to the development of the concept of necessity in CIL, and through that in international law, by identifying a strict element in making a plea of necessity, i.e., the defending state must face a situation that imperils its existence or a serious jeopardy to its internal situation. The spirit of this element would later be reflected, albeit in a softer form, in the notion of 'essential interest' in the ARSIWA's definition of necessity.

6.3 The PCIJ

6.3.1 *S.S. Wimbledon* (1923)

After failure of negotiations with Germany, the British, French, Italian and Japanese governments brought Germany before the PCIJ claiming that Germany breached its treaty obligation (Article 380 the Versailles Treaty which declared the neutrality of the Kiel Canal) by refusing access to the *S.S.*

6 PCA, *Russian Claim for Interest on Indemnities* (*Damages Claimed by Russia for Delay in Payment of Compensation Owed to Russians Injured during the War of 1877–1878*) (*Russia v. Turkey*), Award of the Tribunal, 11 November 1912, available at, https://pcacases.com/web/sendAttach/643, pp. 4–7.

7 Ibid, pp. 12–13.

8 Ago, above note 2, pp. 22–23.

Wimbledon to go through the canal.[9] The PCIJ, which found that Germany breached the treaty and ordered payment of compensation,[10] did not dwell on the question of German defense at all.

During the oral proceedings, however, the Agents of France, Italy and Germany made mention, in clear terms, of the plea of necessity. Basevant, the Agent of the French Government, mentioned that he heard no arguments "on the ground either of impossibility of compliance [i.e., *force majeure*] or of *the danger which compliance with the provision might have created for Germany*; the *plea of necessity* was not made at all (*emphasis in cited source*)."[11] Pilotti, the Agent of the Italian Government, made statements that distinguished between material impossibility, *force majeure* and the state of necessity: he referred to material impossibility as one that is quite excluded from obligations; he stated that *force majeure* is what the German Civil Code refers to as the *status necessitates* and, in a statement introducing the plea of necessity, stated that a state must find itself in and "immediate and imminent danger, against which she would have had no other means of protection".[12] Mr. Schiffer, the Agent for Germany, while acknowledging the principle of '*jus necessitatis*', also stated that in this case Germany was not invoking the defense because its argument was that the German acts were in line with the Versailles Treaty.[13]

In this dispute, the defense of necessity in international law was recognized as originating in, or inspired by its definition under, the private law of the civil law legal system, but as a defense clearly separated from *force majeure* or material impossibility. The most important elements of the later ARSIWA definition of the plea of necessity – existence of an 'immediate and imminent danger' and 'availability of no other means of protection except the measure that was taken' – were also mentioned in unison by the Agents for France, Italy and Germany. Ago, who appears to have been inspired by the discussions on necessity in this dispute, adopted these two key elements into his definition of necessity under the ARSIWA.[14]

---

9 United Nations, *Summaries of Judgments, Advisory Opinions and Orders of the Permanent Court of International Justice*, ST/LEG/SER.F/1/Add.4 (New York: 2012), p. 12.

10 Ibid, pp. 14–15.

11 Ago, above note 2, p. 32, para. 44.

12 Ibid, p. 33, para. 45.

13 Ibid, p. 33, para. 46.

14 Ibid.

6.3.2 *Payment of Various Serbian Loans Issued in France* (1929)

This is a case where the respondent relied on a *force majeure* defense, but, as in the *Russian Indemnity* dispute, the circumstances which the respondent cited have been read to resemble a state of necessity. A number of French banks which lent money to the Kingdom of the Serbs, Croats and Slovenes in the form of bonds claimed that they must be paid in gold francs whereas the Serbian government, by referring to the terms of the contracts and a 1914 French law that made it impossible to pay in gold francs, argued that it could only pay in paper francs. Failing diplomatic efforts to settle the dispute, the French government brought the Serbian government before the PCIJ on behalf of the French bondholders.[15] The Serbian government raised two defenses under the umbrella of *force majeure*. The first defense was that it should not be compelled to pay in gold francs because of the 1914 French law. The Court reacted to this defense of *material impossibility* by stating that nothing in the agreements precluded payment in amount equivalent to gold francs even if gold francs were expressly identified as the means of payment in the contracts.[16] The second defense was that the new Serbian government was facing severe economic situation caused by the war. The Court's reaction to this was that although severe economic circumstances are a valid reason for excuse, the nature of the facts in this case did not reach that level of impossibility.[17]

As noted by Ago, the contribution of this dispute in the history of the development of the concept of necessity is that severe economic circumstances can be invoked as a valid ground for taking measures of necessity.[18]

6.3.3 *Oscar Chinn* (1934)

The contribution of this dispute to the development of the concept of necessity comes not from the judgment of the PCIJ, but from a few paragraphs in the dissenting opinion of one of the judges made under an assumption that certain facts were proved. Following a commercial depression that hit The Congo, the Belgian Government decreed in June 1931 that in order to reduce the cost price of colonial products, the freight charges of Unatra, a river transport company founded in 1925, and some other businesses which the Belgian Government had control over would, as of 31 July 1931, be lowered for the main

15 United Nations, above note 9, pp. 168–169.

16 PCIJ, *Case Concerning the Payment of Various Serbian Loans Issued in France* (*France v. Kingdom of the Serbs, Croats and Slovenes*), Judgment No. 14, 12 July 1929, available at, http://www.worldcourts.com/pcij/eng/decisions/1929.07.12_payment1.htm, para. 82.

17 Ibid, para. 83.

18 Ago, above note 2, pp. 24–25, para. 27.

categories of products to purely nominal figures. This had the effect of creating Unatra as a *de facto* monopoly. Oscar Chinn, a British national who opened a transport business in Leopoldville, and other transporters found it commercially impossible to carry on their businesses and Mr. Chinn approached the British Government for assistance. When friendly negotiations between the British and Belgian Governments bore no fruit, the former took the case to the PCIJ.[19] The PCIJ by majority found that the Belgian Government did not breach the general principle of international law of respect for vested rights as well as Articles 1 and 5 of the September 1919 *Convention of Saint-Germain-En-Laye*[20] and, hence, no reparation was owed to Mr. Chinn.[21]

Judge Anzilotti, in the minority, stated that he was ready to accept the fact that "[t]he situation would have been entirely different *if the Belgian Government had been acting under the law of necessity, since necessity may excuse the non-observance of international obligations* (*emphasis added*)."[22] He then outlined his opinion of the plea of necessity as follows:

> The question whether the Belgian Government was acting … under the law of necessity [must be] proved by the Belgian Government. [The Belgian Government] merely represented that the measures were taken *for grave reasons of public interest in order to save the colony from the disastrous consequences of the collapse in prices* … It rested with the Belgian Government to say what were the measures best adopted to overcome the crisis: provided always that … the existence of that freedom is incompatible with *the plea of necessity which, by definition, implies the impossibility of proceeding by any other method than the one contrary to law* (emphasis added).[23]

---

19 United Nations, above note 9, pp. 340–341.

20 Text of the Convention, whose full title is the *Convention of Saint-German-en-Laye of September 10th, 1919, revising the General Act of Berlin of February 26th, 1885, and the General Act and Declaration of Brussels of July 2nd, 1890*, is available at, https://iea.uoregon.edu/treaty-text/1919-congoriverentxt. Articles 1 and 5 respectively guaranteed commercial equality in the territories under the authority of the Signatory Powers and freedom of transportation in the waters of the Niger.

21 United Nations, above note 9, p. 343.

22 PCIJ, *The Oscar Chinn Case* (*Britain v. Belgium*), Judgment No. 61, 12 December 1934, available at, http://www.worldcourts.com/pcij/eng/decisions/1934.12.12_oscar_chinn.htm, para. 187.

23 As cited in Ago, above note 2, p. 31, para. 41.

According to Ago, Judge Anzilotti's opinion on the plea of necessity "'although an *obiter dictum*, [its verbal clarity and lucid reasoning is] one of the most famous statements of position on the question of necessity".[24] From Anzilotti's statement, Ago read the notion that the plea of necessity is restrictive in the sense of its: (a) application only in a situation of serious jeopardy to an interest of essential importance to the state; and (b) accepting the chosen act if such act is the only means to safeguard the threatened interest.[25]

The *Oscar Chinn* dispute, mainly through Judge Anzilotti, contributed to the concept of necessity in CIL as follows. Firstly, it expanded the concept of 'essential interest' of the state to any grave situation that affects public interest. Secondly, it clearly identified the plea of necessity as an *excuse* to the non-observance of international obligations, i.e., the wrongful act is not punished, yet compensation is paid to the victim. Thirdly, it allowed the state to determine which measure to take but subject to subsequent review to examine if the measure is as much as possible consistent with the state's international obligation. Fourthly, it highlighted the requirement that the measure selected should be the only measure available to the state. All these lessons from *Oscar Chinn* would later find themselves reflected in the definition of necessity under ARSIWA as drafted by Ago's team and continued by their successors.

6.3.4 *Société Commerciale de Belgique* (1939)

The contribution of this case to the development of the plea of necessity lies not in any statement that the PCIJ made, but in the implication of the exchange between the parties to the dispute, particularly the points where the Agents of both Parties came to an understanding of the situation. On 25 August 1925, the Greek Government and a Belgian company, the *Société Commerciale de Belgique*, entered into an agreement for the construction of railway lines and supply of necessary equipment in Greece. In 1932, the Greek Government was obliged, as a result of general financial crisis, to abandon the gold standard and defaulted on the service of its debt to *Société Commerciale* and the company brought the Greek Government to arbitration wherein the Greek Government was ordered to pay debts due to the company. When the Belgian Government took the case to the PCIJ on behalf of the company, the Greek Government referred to the "financial position of the country and to the difficulties of obtaining foreign currency" as the reason for not honoring its obligations under the contract[26] and asked the Court to hold, *inter alia*, that "*by reason of its*

24 Ibid.

25 Ibid.

26 United Nations, above note 9, pp. 425–426.

budgetary and monetary situation, however, it is materially impossible for the Greek Government to execute them (*emphasis added*)."[27]

In the oral proceedings, Mr. Youpis, Counsel for the Greek Government, stated that "[i]n the case in which payment of its debt endangers economic life or jeopardizes the administration the Government is, in the opinion of authors, authorized to suspend or even to reduce the service of debt."[28] He called this 'doctrine' the notion of *'force majeure'* but added that "various schools and writers express the same idea in the term 'state of [necessity]". He then said that regargless of nomenclature "everyone considers that the debtor State does not incur responsibility if it is in such a situation".[29] To this, Mr. Sands, the Counsel for Belgium reacted that: "Mr. Youpis stated … that a State is not obliged to pay its debt if in order to pay it would have to jeopardize its essential public services."[30] The Court held that it "*could only make* [a declaration of the existence of *force majeure*] *after having itself verified that the alleged financial situation really exists and after having ascertained the effect which the execution of the awards in full would have on that situation* (*emphasis added*)."[31] Regarding this statement of the Court, Ago first argued that what the Court referred to as *force majeure* should, reading Greek's written submissions, be identified as a state of financial necessity.[32] He also read the Court's statement as implicit acceptance of "the basic principle [of necessity] on which the two parties were in agreement".[33] In agreement between the Parties was the fact that "the wrongfulness of the conduct of the debtor State not in conformity with its international obligation *would cease to be precluded once the situation of necessity no longer existed, at which time the obligation would again take effect in respect of the entire debt.*"[34]

The key contribution of this dispute lies in the common understanding between the parties where they identified an important element of the concept of necessity: that a measure taken as a result of a situation of necessity must be stopped once the situation that gave rise to the situation of necessity ceases to exist.

27 PCIJ, *The "Société Commerciale de Belgique" (Belgium v. Greece)*, Judgment No. 31, 15 June 1939, available at, http://www.worldcourts.com/pcij/eng/decisions/1939.06.15_societe_commerciale.htm, para. 15.

28 As cited in Ago, above note 2, p. 25, para. 29.

29 Ibid, p. 26, para. 29.

30 Ibid, pp. 25–26, para. 29.

31 PCIJ, above note 27, para. 73.

32 Ago, above note 2, p. 25, para. 28.

33 Ibid, p. 26, para. 31.

34 Ibid, p. 26, para. 31. See also, ibid., p. 26, para. 30, f.n. 59.

6.4 The ICJ

6.4.1 *Rights of Nationals of the United States of America in Morocco (1952)*

In 1948 the French authorities in Morocco imposed a license control system on imports not benefitting from an official allocation of currency. The US brought France before the ICJ arguing that France breached a 1906 treaty between the two countries which guaranteed equality to US investors in Morocco and that France could not impose the restrictions without prior US consent.[35] The ICJ, after analyzing the 1906 treaty and the US-Morocco Treaty of 1806, found against France for violating the non-discrimination rule in general and the most-favored-nation treatment extended to the US in particular.[36] In its defense, the French Government asserted, *inter alia*, that as a result of "a *situation which had been rendered critical* by the fluctuation of the franc" the restrictions it imposed were "*essential to safeguard the country's economic balance*".[37] France argued that "the removal of exchange controls would imperil France's 'fundamental economic balance'" and described the situation as *force majeure*.[38] Ago once again argued, in light of his comparison of the state of necessity with *force majeure* and other defenses, that France was, in modern terminology, referring more to a situation of necessity than *force majeure*.[39]

This case contributed to the development of the concept of necessity in CIL by highlighting the principle that measures in contradiction of treaty obligations can be allowed if a state faces grave and imminent or otherwise unavoidable danger to an essential interest of the state, economic or otherwise.[40]

6.4.2 *Gabčíkovo-Nagymaros Project (1997)*

In 1977, Hungary and Czechoslovakia entered into a treaty on the Construction and Operation of the *Gabčíkovo-Nagymaros* System of Locks between them for a joint investment intended to produce hydroelectricity, improve navigation on the Danube River and prevent against flooding. After the Velvet

35 Available at, http://www.icj-cij.org/en/case/11. See also, *Case Concerning Rights of Nationals of the United States of America in Morocco (France v. United States of America)*, Judgment, 27 August 1952, ICJ Rep. 1952, p. 184.

36 *Case Concerning Rights of Nationals of the United States of America in Morocco*, above note 35, pp. 185–186.

37 Ago, above note 2, p. 31, para. 42.

38 Oral Proceedings, Part II for the *Case Concerning Rights of Nationals of the United States of America in Morocco*, available at, http://www.icj-cij.org/files/case-related/11/011-19520715-ORA-01-00-BI.pdf, pp. 182–184; ibid, pp. 31–32, para. 43.

39 Ago, above note 2, p. 31, para. 43.

40 Ibid.

Revolution split Czechoslovakia into the Czech and Slovak republics, Hungary and Slovakia agreed to ensure that the Danube's quality of water would not be impaired as a result of the Project and that both countries would comply with the obligations to protect nature. As a result of economic and environmental criticisms directed at the Project, the Hungarian government suspended works at *Nagymaros* and then abandoned the works in October 1989. Slovakia then proceeded on its own trying to put the series of locks at *Gabčíkovo* into operation by creating a diversion of the Danube, in its 'Variant C'. Before the ICJ, Hungary defended its measure, i.e., the suspension of the project and non-performance of its Treaty obligations, under the then Article 33 (later Article 25) of the Draft ARSIWA stating a 'state of ecological necessity'.[41] In the most relevant paragraphs of the judgment, the ICJ stated that:

> The Court considers, first of all, that the state of necessity is a ground recognized by customary international law for precluding the wrongfulness of an act not in conformity with an international obligation. It observes moreover that such ground for precluding wrongfulness can only be accepted on an exceptional basis ...
>
> Thus ... the state of necessity can only be invoked under certain strictly defined conditions which must be cumulatively satisfied; and the State concerned is not the sole judge of whether those conditions have been met.
>
> In the present case, the following basic conditions set forth in Draft Article 33 are relevant: it must have been occasioned by an 'essential interest' of the State which is the author of the act conflicting with one of its international obligations; that interest must have been threatened by a 'grave and imminent peril'; the act being challenged must have been the 'only means' of safeguarding that interest; that act must not have 'seriously impair[ed] an essential interest' of the State towards which the obligation existed; and the State which is the author of that act must not have 'contributed to the occurrence of the state of necessity'. Those conditions reflect customary international law.[42]

41 Malgosia Fitzmaurice, 'Necessity in International Environmental Law', in Ige F. Dekker and E. Hey (eds.), *Netherlands Yearbook of International Law: Necessity across International Law*, Vol. 41 (The Hague: T.M.C. Asser Press, 2010), pp. 173–174; Tim Stephens, *International Courts and Environmental Protection* (Cambridge: Cambridge University Press, 2009), pp. 174–177.

42 *Case Concerning the Gabčíkovo-Nagymaros Project* (*Hungary v. Slovakia*), Judgment, 25 September 1997, ICJ Rep. 1997, pp. 40–41, paras. 51–52.

The ICJ, through these paragraphs identified the following five as the characteristic elements of the state of necessity as defined by the ARSIWA: (1) the situation must involve an 'essential interest' of the state which has acted contrary to its international obligations; (2) the said essential interest must have been threatened by a 'grave and imminent peril'; (3) the act being challenged must have been the 'only means' of safeguarding the essential interest; (4) that act must not have 'seriously impair[ed] an essential interest' of the state towards which the obligation existed; and (5) the state which is the author of that act must not have 'contributed to the occurrence of the state of necessity'. Moreover, the ICJ added that: (1) the defense of necessity, as defined in the then Article 33 of the draft ARSIWA, reflects CIL; (2) the defense of necessity must be accepted on an exceptional basis; (3) the elements of necessity must be strictly applied to a case at hand; (4) the elements of necessity must be cumulatively satisfied; and (5) the state invoking necessity is not the sole judge whether the conditions have been met. i.e., the invocation is subject to review.

This is the first case that not only endorsed the elements of the defense of necessity as contained in the ARSIWA (in the then Article 33 of the draft ARSIWA), but also declared the state of necessity as a principle recognized in CIL that must be applied only in exceptional circumstances. We attribute the most comprehensive interpretation of the concept of necessity in CIL to the ICJ's reflection on the concept in this dispute. Through its analysis of the defense of necessity in this dispute, the ICJ in effect recognized the work of Ago's efforts to reflect on previous disputes which dwelt on the plea of necessity and drew clear boundaries between the plea of necessity and other defenses, especially the defense of *force majeure*.

6.4.3 *Fisheries Jurisdiction: Spain v. Canada (1998)*

In 1994 Canada amended its Coastal Fisheries Protection Act to prohibit the fishing of straddling stock in the high seas area[43] and on 9 March 1995 Canadian vessels arrested a Spanish fishing boat, *Estai*, and its crew in the high seas 245 miles from the Canadian coast for violating the Coastal Fisheries Protection Act.[44] The Spanish Government condemned the arrest as a flagrant violation of international law, particularly the Northwest Atlantic Fisheries Organization convention to which Canada is a Party and Article 92 and articles to the same effect of the 1982 Convention on the Law of the Sea according to which ships on the high seas shall be subject to the exclusive jurisdiction of the

43 *Fisheries Jurisdiction case (Spain v. Canada)*, Jurisdiction of the Court, Judgment, 4 December 1998, ICJ Rep. 1998, pp. 439–440, para. 15.

44 Ibid, p. 443, para. 19.

flag state. The Canadian Government replied, on 15 March, that "the arrest of the *Estai* was *necessary* in order to put a stop to the overfishing of Greenland halibut by Spanish fishermen (*emphasis added*)." The European Community and its Member States also sent, on 15 March, a Note Verbale to the Canadian government in which they stated that "[t]he arrest of a vessel in international waters by a State other than [the flag state] is an illegal act under both the NAFO Convention and customary international law, and *cannot be justified by any means* (*emphasis added*)."[45] Spain took Canada to the ICJ for violating principles of international law applicable to the high seas. Canada contested the Court's jurisdiction because the case was related to conservation and management measures and their enforcement.[46] The Court finally decided that it did not have jurisdiction.[47]

The fact that Spain did not, in its Memorial, argue against Canada's defense of necessity cited in its communications with Spain has been taken as an implied admission before the Court of the application of the doctrine of necessity in the field of IEnL.[48] For Crawford, who stated that "[t]he plea of necessity was *apparently* in issue in the *Fisheries Jurisdiction* case (*emphasis added*)."[49] Spain's silence to Canadian invocation meant that "the plea of necessity was not rejected a priori."[50] The contribution of this case to development of the concept of necessity in CIL is that it apparently affirmed the application of the plea of necessity in the law of the seas and IEnL.

6.4.4 *Legal Consequences of the Construction of a Wall in the Occupied Palestinian Territory (2004)*

In 2002, Israel began constructing a 'wall' running across its own territory and the occupied territory of the West Bank. Palestine opposed the construction stating that the wall was a form of illegal annexation of territory in an Israeli attempt to undermine the right of the Palestinians to self-determination. In December 2003 the UN General Assembly asked the ICJ for an advisory opinion on the question: What are the legal consequences arising from the construction of the wall being built by Israel, considering the rules and principles

45 Ibid, pp. 443–444, para. 20.

46 Ibid, p. 446, para. 23.

47 Ibid, p. 467, para. 87.

48 Fitzmaurice, above note 41, pp. 171–172.

49 James Crawford, *The International Law Commission's Articles on State Responsibility: Introduction, Text and Commentaries* (Cambridge: Cambridge University Press, 2002), p. 182.

50 As cited in Fitzmaurice, above note 41, p. 171.

of international law, including the Fourth Geneva Convention of 1949, and relevant Security Council and General Assembly resolutions?[51]

After asserting jurisdiction and affirming that it is proper for it to give opinion on the case,[52] the Court identified a number of rules and principles of international law relevant to the process of assessing the legality of the Israeli measures[53] and found, *inter alia*, that Israel breached its obligation to respect the right of the Palestinian people to self-determination[54] and the construction of the wall and its associated régime was contrary to a number of the relevant rules and principles of international law the Court identified.[55] The court then ruled that Article 51 of the Charter (the right to self-defense), which Israel defended, in part, its actions under, has no relevance in this case mainly because Israel did not claim that the attacks against it were imputable to a foreign State and because the threat which Israel regarded as justifying the construction of the wall originated within, and not outside, of the Occupied Palestinian Territory.[56]

In the subsequent paragraph, the Court asked itself – Israel did not make such a defense – whether Israel could benefit from the customary defense of necessity as contained in the ARSIWA – which the Court stated has already been confirmed in *Gabčíkovo-Nagymaros Project* – and found, after reflecting on the primary-secondary rule bifurcation, that Israel would not benefit from the necessity defense because of inconsistency of the measure with the 'only means' requirement.[57] Israel, the Court found, could not rely on the right of self-defense or on a state of necessity to preclude the wrongfulness of the construction of the wall which, therefore, rendered Israel's actions contrary to international law.[58]

Through this advisory opinion, the ICJ endorsed its dissection of the elements of necessity (Article 25 of the ARSIWA), confirmed its earlier finding in *Gabčíkovo-Nagymaros Project* that the state of necessity in the ARSIWA is part of CIL and then expanded the application of the state of necessity defense

51 Christine Gray, 'The ICJ Advisory Opinion on Legal Consequences of the Construction of a Wall in the Occupied Palestinian Territory', *Cambridge Law Journal*, 63(3): 2004, pp. 527–528.

52 *Legal Consequences of the Construction of a Wall in the Occupied Palestinian Territory*, Advisory Opinion, 9 July 2004, ICJ Rep. 2004, pp. 144–164, paras. 14–65.

53 Ibid, pp. 171–181, paras. 86–113.

54 Ibid, pp. 181–184, paras. 115–122.

55 Ibid, pp. 184–188, paras. 123–127.

56 Ibid, p. 194, paras. 138–139.

57 Ibid, pp. 194–195, para. 140.

58 Ibid, p. 195, para. 142.

beyond IEnL (*Gabčíkovo-Nagymaros Project*) as a one-for-all defense against a web of international law fields, provided that the primary rules of necessity defense within the various treaties and instruments representing those international law fields are first exhausted.

6.5 The ITLOS

On 28 October 1997, the *M/V Saiga* which was at a point south of the southern limit of the exclusive economic zone Guinea awaiting the arrival of fishing vessels to which it was to supply gas oil was attacked by a Guinean patrol boat, officers of the patrol boat boarded the ship and arrested it, brought its crew to Conakry for detention and subsequently the cargo of gas oil aboard the vessel was discharged.[59] Saint Vincent and the Grenadines, whose flag the *Saiga* flew, brought Guinea before the ITLOS claiming, *inter alia*, that Guinea violated the vessel's freedom of navigation and/or other internationally lawful uses of the sea guaranteed by the UNCLOS. Guinea in turn requested the tribunal to dismiss the claims by arguing that it did not violate the respective UNCLOS provisions Saint Vincent and the Grenadines invoked.[60] Alternatively/additionally, Guinea argued that it exercised its "inherent right to protect itself against unwarranted economic activities in its exclusive economic zone that considerably affect its public interest", or [invoked] the "doctrine of necessity", or ... "the customary principle of self-protection in case of grave and imminent perils which endanger essential aspects of its public interest".[61] The tribunal understood this to be an invocation of two separate defenses: "The first is a broad notion of 'public interest' or 'self-protection' which Guinea invokes to expand the scope of its jurisdiction in the exclusive economic zone, and the second is 'state of necessity' which it relies on to justify measures that would otherwise be wrongful under the Convention."[62] After finding Guinea's 'public interest' argument to be contrary to Article 58(3) of the UNCLOS mainly for reason of fear of abuse,[63] the tribunal then examined the defense of necessity.

The tribunal stated that in *Gabčíkovo-Nagymaros Project*, the ICJ had identified "two elements with approval" [they were more than two actually] of the

59 The *M/V "Saiga"* (No. 2) *Case* (*Saint Vincent and The Grenadines v. Guinea*), International Tribunal for the Law of the Sea, Judgment, 1 July 1999, paras. 31–38.

60 Ibid, paras. 28–30.

61 Ibid, para. 129.

62 Ibid.

63 Ibid, paras. 130–131.

necessity provision in Article 33 of the ARSIWA viz.: (a) the act was the only means of safeguarding an essential interest of the state against a grave and imminent peril; and (b) the act did not seriously impair an essential interest of the state towards which the obligation existed.[64] The tribunal then found that Guinea did not show that its essential interests were in grave and imminent danger and also that the only means of safeguarding that interest, if essential, was to extend its customs laws to parts of the exclusive economic zone.[65]

The main contribution of the dispute is that it expressly extended the application of the concept of necessity in CIL to the very broad field of the law of the sea as codified in the UNCLOS.[66]

6.6 Other International Tribunals

6.6.1 *The International Crimes Tribunals*

The history of the concept of necessity in international criminal law as it evolved in the 20th century and the contribution of the various relevant tribunals has already been discussed in Section 5.7.

6.6.2 *Rainbow Warrior (1990)*

The *Rainbow Warrior* arbitration[67] is the first case where the application of the defense of necessity as then being drafted by the ILC was examined in an international dispute. On 10 July 1985, a civilian vessel, the *Rainbow Warrior* brought to Auckland Harbor to disrupt French nuclear tests on the islands of French Polynesia, was sunk at its moorings in that harbor as a result of extensive damage caused by two high-explosive devices. One person was killed. On 12 July 1985, two French intelligence agents, Alain Mafart and Dominique Prieur, were arrested and prosecuted for the offense. On 4 November 1985, they pleaded guilty to manslaughter and willful damage to the ship and were sentenced to a term of ten years of imprisonment. After negotiations failed, New

64 Ibid, para. 133.

65 Ibid, para. 136.

66 Ben Chigara, 'International Tribunal for the Law of the Sea and Customary International Law', *Loyola of Los Angeles International and Comparative Law Review*, 22(4): 2000, pp. 449–450.

67 *Case Concerning the Difference between New Zealand and France Concerning the Interpretation or Application of Two Agreements, Concluded on 9 July 1986 between the Two States and which Related to the Problems Arising from the Rainbow Warrior Affair*, 30 April 1990, available at, United Nations, Reports of international Arbitral awards, Vol. XX, 2006, http://legal.un.org/riaa/cases/vol_XX/215-284.pdf, pp. 215–284.

Zealand and France approached the then UN Secretary-General Javier Pérez de Cuéllar in June 1986 requesting him to address, through a binding ruling, all the problems between them arising from the *Rainbow Warrior* affair for.[68] In July 1986, de Cuéllar released a decision on a number of issues and requested both governments to conclude binding agreements incorporating all of his rulings which the governments did in the same month.[69] Thereafter, the two agents were transferred from New Zealand to a French military facility on the island of Hao.[70] In December 1987 and May 1988 Mafart and Prieur were, despite objections from New Zealand, released from Hao for health reasons and later assigned to other posts.[71] The non-return of the two agents to Hao triggered a series of diplomatic exchanges between the two countries. That failing, New Zealand brought a case before a tribunal as required by de Cuéllar's Ruling. New Zealand submitted that France committed six breaches of the 1986 Agreements (three for each agent). New Zealand's arguments were based on breach of the Agreement as interpreted by the VCLT.[72] On its part, France argued that if interpreted correctly, the 1986 Agreements would not deny the possibility of the agents leaving Hao, without New Zealand's prior consent, for reasons of a special situation such as illness or pregnancy,[73] a situation which "made the transfer to Paris necessary" and rendered "its action bore no stain of illegality under the 1986 Agreement and the rules and principles of international law" since "*circumstances of extreme urgency* were involved (*emphasis added*)".[74]

Article 2 of the Supplementary Agreement of 14 February 1989 read that decisions of the tribunal would be based on the Agreement and the applicable rules and principles of international law.[75] The two Parties disputed on the source for the "rules and principles of international law." New Zealand insisted on the application of the 1986 Agreement and the VCLT.[76] France argued that since there were "very special circumstances"/"legitimate reasons"/"circumstances

68 As summarized by UN Secretary-General de Cuéllar in ibid, p. 223, paras. 8–11.

69 Ibid, p. 224, Clause 2 and Clause 3, paras. (a) and (b); p. 225, Clauses 4 and 6; pp. 225–226, Clause 5; p. 226, para. 13.

70 Ibid, para. 14.

71 Ibid, pp. 226–240, paras. 15–45, pp. 240–242, paras. 47–56, p. 243, para. 60. as summarized in Quimbee.com, *Rainbow Warrior* (*New Zealand v. France*), available at, https://www.quimbee.com/cases/rainbow-warrior-new-zealand-v-france.

72 Ibid, pp. 243–245, paras. 57–65.

73 Ibid, pp. 246–248, paras. 66–71.

74 Ibid, paras. 66, 71.

75 Ibid, p. 248, para. 72.

76 Ibid, pp. 249–250, para. 73.

of extreme urgency" for releasing the agents and/or not returning them to Hao, its actions should be interpreted under the law of state responsibility which at time was being codified by the ILC.[77] The tribunal responded that both the customary Law of Treaties under the VCLT and the customary law of state responsibility are relevant and applicable.[78]

Since France did not dispute that it took the disputed measures without New Zealand's prior consent, the tribunal examined, although France's only used the *force majeure* defense, if three circumstances precluding wrongfulness (*force majeure*, distress and necessity, in that order) could be successfully invoked by France. Regarding *force majeure*, the tribunal examined the elements of the draft ARSIWA (Article 31(1)) and concluded that the defense could not be successfully invoked because the act of release was not taken due to an irresistible force or an unforeseen external event beyond France's control which made it materially impossible for France to honor its obligation under the 1986 Agreement.[79] Regarding distress, the tribunal first referred to the ILC's note on the difference between distress (draft ARSIWA (Article 32(1)) and *force majeure*[80] and then referred to the ILC's note on the difference between distress and necessity as well as one academic publication. The references convinced the tribunal to doubt the existence of necessity in international law (as drafted in the then ARSIWA Article 33) and, if it is held that it exists, dub it "controversial".[81] After applying the test of distress to the case of the two agents,[82] the tribunal found with respect to Major Mafart that while France did not breach its obligations in removing him from Hao, it breached its obligations in not ordering him to return to Hao.[83] With regards to Captain Prieur, the tribunal found that France breached its obligations by not endeavoring to obtain in good faith New Zealand's consent to remove her from Hao, by removing her from Hao and by not ordering her to return to Hao.[84]

The significance of this case lies in its contribution in the need to clarify the difference between the application/interpretation of a treaty or other international obligation (i.e., primary rule) and the examination of the consequences

77 Ibid, pp. 246, 248, 250–251, paras. 66, 71, 74.

78 Ibid, pp. 251–252, para. 75.

79 Ibid, pp. 252–253, paras. 76–77.

80 Ibid, pp. 253–254, para. 78.

81 Ibid, pp. 254–255, para. 78.

82 The way the tribunal framed the issues did not actually (literally) require examination of the fulfilment of the elements of distress as contained in the draft ARSIWA; the tribunal introduced its own elements. Ibid, p. 255, para. 79.

83 Ibid, pp. 255–259, paras. 79–88.

84 Ibid, pp. 259–264 paras. 89–101.

of breach of a treaty (secondary rule) and in distinguishing the state of necessity from *force majeure* and distress. The tribunal, owing to its doubt on the existence/application of a general principle allowing the defense of necessity, did not examine the compatibility of France's actions to the defense.[85] The tribunal's doubt is an important take-away in that it supports the argument that there could be differences in the concepts of necessity found in different fields of international law.

6.6.3 *Libyan Arab Foreign Investment Company v. The Republic of Burundi (1991)*

In 1973, the Libyan Arab Republic and the Republic of Burundi signed a treaty and in 1975 agreed to establish the HALB which would invest in companies operating within certain sectors of Burundi's economy. Article 15(1) of the Agreement provided that the assets of HALB would not be nationalized, confiscated, sequestered or be subjected to any measure capable of infringing the rights of the shareholders or limiting its ability to achieve its objectives. In 1981 (other sources mention 1983), Libya transferred its shares in HALB (60%) to another Libyan state-owned company, the LAFICO. In April 1989, Burundi, invoking security reasons, broke off its diplomatic relations with Libya and took a number of measures against Libyans. In a meeting held with LAFICO representatives in May 1989, Burundian officials decided to liquidate HALB. As a result, LAFICO and Burundi agreed to take their case to arbitration pursuant to the 1975 treaty.[86] LAFICO claimed that Burundi breached the 1975 treaty and violated international law and sought compensation. Burundi stated that the action was taken because Libyan diplomatic personnel in particular and all Libyan nationals in general had for some time "been participating in activities of destabilization putting the peace and internal and external security of the Republic of Burundi in danger".[87]

The tribunal first held that Burundi violated the 1975 treaty which prohibited nationalization, confiscation, sequestration etc.[88] and then examined the defense that Burundi submitted to justify the measures it took. Burundi's

85 Crawford, above note 49, p. 181.

86 As summarized in Takuhei Yamada, 'State of Necessity in International Law: A Study of International Judicial Cases', *Kobe-Gakuin Law and Politics Review*, 34(4): 2005, pp. 139–140; Patrick Dumberry, 'Satisfaction as a Form of Reparation for Moral Damages Suffered by Investors and Respondent States in Investor-State Arbitration Disputes', *Journal of International Dispute Settlement*, 3(1): (2012), p. 221.

87 Yamada, ibid, p. 140.

88 Yamada, ibid, pp. 139–141; Dumberry, above note 86, pp. 221–222.

defended that under the CIL it had the right "to expel an alien who represents a threat to its security, subject to certain conditions fulfilled". The tribunal interpreted Burundi's defense as referring either to *force majeure* or state of necessity. The tribunal, first examining the *force majeure* concept in the then Article 31 of ARSIWA, held that Burundi could not benefit from the provision because "the alleged impossibility [was] not the result of an irresistible force or an unforeseen external event beyond the control of Burundi. In fact, the impossibility is the result of a unilateral decision of that State."[89] As to the defense of necessity, the tribunal stated that the defense "has been a matter of debate in the doctrine" proposed by the ILC, but that even if the then Article 33 of the ILC's draft (necessity) were to apply, Burundi's measures "do not appear to the Tribunal to have been the only means of safeguarding an essential interest of Burundi against a grave and imminent peril".[90]

The tribunal in this case had a doubt whether state of necessity should be codified at an international level. This is different from the *Rainbow Warrior* tribunal which, deliberating a year earlier than the *LAFICO* tribunal, chose to discuss the then draft Article 33 despite considering the concept 'controversial'. Nevertheless, the *LAFICO* award, also cited by ILC's rapporteur Crawford in his ensemble of international cases contributing to the drafting of Article 25 of the ARSIWA,[91] is important in its: (a) applying the doctrine of necessity in at least two very broad fields of PIL: the law of diplomatic relations and IIL; (b) linking the defense of necessity to the sensitive international law province of state sovereignty and invocation of national security; and (c) applying the 'grave and imminent peril' and 'only means' elements of the doctrine.

6.6.4 *ICSID Tribunals*

Sub-section 5.5.3 discussed in detail the contribution of the ICSID tribunals and Annulment Committees in analyzing necessity defense in the Argentine financial crisis disputes. Eight awards and annulment orders – *CMS*, *Enron*, *LG&E*, *Sempra*, *Continental Casualty*, *Impreglio*, *El Paso* and *Suez* – were discussed.

89 Yamada, ibid, p. 142; United Nations, above note 67, p. 157.

90 Yamada, ibid.

91 Crawford, above note 49, p. 181, f.n. 413. See also, United Nations, above note 67, pp. 175–176.

6.7 Lessons Learned from the Contributions of Various International Courts/Tribunals on the Development of the Concept of Necessity in International Law

The analysis in this chapter of disputes mostly entertained after 1922 (establishment of the PCIJ) is a continuation of the analysis of state and tribunal experiences between the second half of the 19th century and 1922 (see, Chapter 2). In Chapter 2, it was observed that it was difficult to distinguish the various defenses that states invoked to justify or excuse their actions which violated treaty obligations. It was also observed that these defenses (necessity, self-defense, self-protection, self-preservation and *force majeure*) were: (a) used mainly to justify politico-military actions taken in times of war or public emergency; (b) often used interchangeably; (c) generally raised without providing an exhaustive list of the constituent elements of the respective defenses; and (d) raised without much clarity, on whether they provided justifications or excuses.

The defense of necessity began to be analyzed in the PCIJ and post-PCIJ era under these circumstances. The PCIJ laid the ground for the steady process of distinguishing the defense of necessity from other defenses (particularly *force majeure*) and identifying its elements. The hitherto overarching defense of *force majeure*, had to be distinguished from circumstances that constitute a situation of necessity. As a result of the interpretations of the PCIJ and the other tribunals mentioned in this chapter, not only were the elements of the defense of necessity slowly identified, but the scope of its application expanded into areas beyond the traditional situations of war or public emergency (i.e., finance, investment, environment, law of the sea, diplomacy and national security). This quantum of experience culminated in the drafting of the defense of necessity in the ARSIWA. This long experience of litigating, interpreting and applying the defense of necessity convinced the ICJ to declare the plea of necessity (as codified in the ARSIWA) part of CIL.

As will be discussed in Chapter 8, one field of PIL that, since the early 1980s, had been developing its own interpretation of necessity is GATT/WTO law. Examination of the respective elements of the concept of necessity as developed in the GATT/WTO system and through the law of state responsibility (as codified in the ARSIWA) will show that there are similarities and differences between them. Although international law provides enough space for these two different concepts of necessity to develop and operate in their own spheres, the differences can lead to a couple of observations. Firstly, in fields where there is a possibility for choosing between these two concepts (for example in the fields of IEnL and IIL, as highlighted in Chapter 5), the defenses may lead to different, or opposite, results for the defending state. Secondly, in light of the need to address avoidable fragmentation in international law, since WTO law is part of international law, it may be important to examine if, at best, some of the differences between these two concepts can be reconciled or, at least, if the two concepts can influence each other. This search for interoperability between the two concepts of necessity will be carried out in Chapter 12.

PART 3

The Concept of Necessity in WTO Law

CHAPTER 7

History of the Drafting of the Necessity Defense Provisions in the General and Security Exceptions of the GATT 1994/GATS

Part 3 discusses the concept of necessity in WTO law, particularly the General Exceptions (Article XX) of the GATT 1994 and Article XIV the GATS.[1] This part begins, in this chapter, by presenting the history of the drafting of the necessity provisions in the GATT 1994 and the GATS.

7.1 Pre-GATT 1947 Trade Agreements and Treaties Containing General Exceptions-Like Provisions

The origins of the GATT 1994/GATS provisions on necessity can, expressed in different terminologies, be traced back to some bilateral and multilateral instruments dating as far back as the mid-19th century as well as the various international agreements, conferences and fora of the 1920s and early 1930s. Included in this chain of history are: (1) the 1860 Cobden-Chevalier treaty,[2] known as the "mother of all spaghetti bowls" of bilateral trade agreements;[3] (2) the various bilateral trade agreements that the US entered into between the 18th and 20th centuries;[4] (3) the various bilateral agreements of the 1920s-1940s which the US

---

1 It will be admitted at this juncture that although the reference in this chapter and the subsequent Chapters to the 'General Exceptions' and 'Security Exceptions' generally is to the similar provisions of the GATT 1994 Article XX and the GATS Article XIV (General Exceptions) as well as GATT 1994 Article XXI and GATS Article XIV *bis* (Security Exceptions), the history of 'General Exceptions' and 'Security Exceptions' in the pre-WTO era is related to Articles XX and XXI of the GATT 1947 because GATS is the product of the WTO Agreement.

2 Dr. Markus Lampe, one of the leading authors on the Cobden-Chevalier treaty, who emailed the author a copy of the treaty, is duly acknowledged here.

3 Markus Lampe, 'Explaining nineteenth-century bilateralism: economic and political determinants of the Cobden-Chevalier network', *Economic History Review*, 64(2): 2011, p. 645.

4 The texts of these bilateral treaties are available at, http://avalon.law.yale.edu/subject_menus/18th.asp (for the 18th century bilateral), http://avalon.law.yale.edu/subject_menus/19th.asp (for the 19th century agreements) and https://catalog.hathitrust.org/Search/Home?lookfor=reciprocal%20trade.%20Agreement&searchtype=all&ft=&setft=false (for the 20th century agreements).

 | DOI:10.1163/9789004700000_009

was not a party to;[5] (3) the 1921 Barcelona Convention and Statute on Freedom of Transit (particularly Article 5 of the Statute);[6] (4) the 1922 Genoa Economic and Financial Conference, particularly Article 7 of the Recommendations of the Economic Commission established during the conference;[7] (5) Articles 17 and 18 of the 1923 International Convention Relating to the Simplification of Customs Formalities;[8] (6) the 1927 World Economic Conference held under the auspices of the League of Nations, particularly Articles 4 and 5 of the draft document[9] produced during the conference;[10] (7) Articles 4 and 5 of the 1927 Convention for the Abolition of Import and Export Prohibitions and Restrictions;[11] and (8) Article 3 of the 1932 Ouchy Convention for the Lowering of Economic Barriers.[12]

It must be noted here that the term 'necessary' for which a detailed interpretation would develop in the GATT/WTO era *does not appear in any one* of the exceptions paragraphs of the above-cited bilateral agreements and treaties.

5 Such as: Article V of the France-Czechoslovakia Trade Agreement (99 L.N.T.S. (1930), p. 111); Article 4 of the Economic Union of Belgium & Luxemburg-Switzerland trade agreement of 1928 (105 L.N.T.S. (1930), pp. 13, 15); Article 6 of the 1929 Persian Empire-Republic of Czechoslovakia Trade Agreement (110 L.N.T.S. (1930–31), pp. 361, 363); Article 10 of the 1929 Romania-Turkish Republic Trade Agreement (112 L.N.T.S. (1931), p. 147); Article XIX of the 1933 Bulgaria-Czechoslovak Republic Trade Agreement (148 L.N.T.S. (1934), p. 29); and Article 9 of the 1933 Latvia-Lithuania Trade Agreement and Article 9 of the 1934 Estonia-Lithuania Trade Agreement of 1934 (148 L.N.T.S. (1934), pp. 103, 105, 345).

6 Text of the Convention is available at, 7 L.N.T.S. (1921–1922), pp. 12–33.

7 For detailed presentation of the conference, see, J. Saxon Mills, *The Genoa Conference* (London: Hutchinson & Co., 1925). See also, Wilson Harris, 'The Genoa Conference', *Journal of the British Institute of International Affairs*, 1(5): 1922, pp. 150–158.

8 Text of the Convention is available at, 30 L.N.T.S. (1924–1925), pp. 371–412.

9 League of Nations Doc. C.E.1.22. 1927 11.13 (1927). The document was titled *Abolition of Import and Export Prohibitions and Restrictions, Commentary and Preliminary Draft International Agreement drawn up by the Economic Committee of the League of Nations to serve as a Basis for an International Diplomatic Conference.* Steve Charnovitz, 'The Moral Exception in Trade Policy', *Virginia Journal of International Law*, 38(4): 1998, p. 706.

10 For more on the conference and the draft document, see, W. Leslie Runciman, 'The World Economic Conference at Geneva', *The Economic Journal*, 37(147): 1927, pp. 465–472; Royal Institute of International Affairs, 'The First World Economic Conference', *Bulletin of International News*, 3(10): 1927, pp. 5–7; Royal Institute of International Affairs, 'The Geneva Conference on the Abolition of Trade Prohibitions and Restrictions', *Bulletin of International News*, 4(9): 1927, pp. 193–196; Douglas A. Irwin *et al.*, *The Genesis of the GATT* (Cambridge: Cambridge University Press, 2008), p. 5.

11 Text of the Convention is available at, https://www.loc.gov/law/help/us-treaties/bevans/m-ust000002-0651.pdf.

12 For more on the history of the Convention, see, B. S. K., 'Recent Moves to Reduce Trade Barriers', *Bulletin of International News*, 14(1): 1937, pp. 3–9.

In these agreements, the terms 'relating/relative to' and 'imposed on/for/by' dominate, whereas in the General and Security Exceptions the term 'necessary' is a dominant key term followed by the key term 'relating to'. Most of the paragraphs on exceptions in the above-cited agreements and treaties found their ways to the General and Security Exceptions. However, the key terms used in these documents were replaced by terms such as 'essential to', 'involving', 'undertaken in pursuance of' 'taken' in the General and Security Exceptions. The most notable replacement would be the key term 'necessary'.

Nevertheless, the drafters of the GATT 1947 acknowledged the impact of these 18th to 20th century trade agreements and treaties in preparing the text of the GATT 1947. John M. Leddy, the economist who was the main draftsman of the GATT 1947,[13] admitted later that:

> I was the guy who sort of pulled together ... the old multilateral convention on commercial policy ... including various provisions on MFN, national treatment, marks of origin, customs formalities, customs valuation, quotas, the whole lot ... We had in the U.S. Government worked on these provisions *drawing them from the old bilateral trade agreements, as well as various multilateral instruments that had existed,* like the Freedom of Transit Convention, the Convention on Abolition of Prohibitions and Restrictions etc. In other words, *we drew from both U.S. and international sources* (*emphasis added*).[14]

Sections 7.2 and 7.3 present the history of the drafting of the necessity provisions in the General/Security Exceptions of the GATT 1947.

7.2 The US-UK Discussions for Post-Second World War International Trade Rules

After witnessing the continued economic effects of First World War and the negative impacts of the protectionist trade policies that followed it, some senior diplomats started to advocate for the positive impact that freer, non-discriminatory global trade could have in ensuing peace and avoiding another

13 Petros C. Mavroidis, *The Regulation of International Trade* (*Vol. 1: GATT*) (Cambridge, MA: MIT Press, 2015), p. 20.

14 Irwin *et al.*, above note 10, p. 80, f.n. 106. See also, Charnovitz, above note 9, pp. 703–710; Steve Charnovitz, 'Exploring the Environmental Exceptions in GATT Article XX', *Journal of World Trade*, 25(5): 1991, pp. 41–47.

world war. Cordell Hull who, since 1933, served as US Secretary of State for 11 years takes the credit for pushing this effort.[15] The failure of the trade agreement that was entered into between the US and the UK in 1938 and the outbreak of Second World War in September 1939 proved Hull right.[16]

Sub-sections 7.2.1 and 7.2.2, summarizing the very detailed narration by Irwin *et al.*,[17] will briefly present the US-UK negotiations that began in the middle of the Second World War and gave way to the multilateral negotiations that established the GATT 1947. It will be observed that the concept of necessity defense was included in these negotiations which provided context and laid the ground for the GATT negotiations during which the term 'necessary' would be inserted in the General/Security Exceptions of the GATT 1947. Details of the GATT 1947 negotiations relevant to the key term 'necessary' will be presented in Section 7.3.

7.2.1 *The Meade Proposal and the Proposed Multilateral Convention on Commercial Policy*

In July 1942, James Meade, a war-time staffer at the UK Economic Section wrote a short, 20-points memorandum entitled 'Proposal for an International Commercial Union', a precursor to what would eventually become the GATT. The UK War Cabinet considered Meade's proposal and included it in the meeting in September-October 1943 in Washington, D.C. between US and UK negotiators where post-war economic issues were discussed. to discuss two post-war issues: (a) monetary and financial arrangements; and (b) commercial and trade policy. Following this meeting these two issues took separate paths even at the Bretton Woods conference.[18] In May 1944, the Executive Committee on Economic Foreign Policy at the USSD headed by Dean Acheson, appointed a Committee on Trade Barriers to draft a possible convention as the basis for further discussions. In October 1944, a USSD-led interagency group completed the 'Proposed Multilateral Convention on Commercial Policy'.

---

15 Mavroidis, above note 13, pp. 7–9; Irwin *et al.*, above note 10, pp. 8–12.

16 Mavroidis, ibid, p. 10.

17 Irwin *et al.*, above note 10, pp. 12–77. See also, ibid, pp. 7–14.

18 John H. Jackson, *The World Trading System: Law and Policy of International Economic Relations* (2nd ed.) (Cambridge, Mass.: MIT Press, 1997), pp. 32, 37. See also, Irwin *et al.*, above note 10, pp. 22 (f.n. 21), 98–99; Mavroidis, above note 13, p. 7; John H. Jackson, *Sovereignty, the WTO and Changing Fundamentals of International Law* (Cambridge: Cambridge University Press, 2006), p. 92.

7.2.2 *The Term 'Necessary' Appears for the First Time in the USSD December 1945 Proposals*

By December 1945, the USSD released a document entitled 'Proposals for Expansion of World Trade and Employment' to the public. As mentioned in Section 7.1, the term 'necessary' did not appear, as it would later appear in three paragraphs of Article XX of the GATT 1947, in any one of the bilateral or multilateral trade instruments negotiated between the mid-19th century and the early 1930s. In the search conducted for this book, the first time the term appeared in the exceptions clauses of bilateral/multilateral trade documents was in the December 1945 Proposals prepared by the USSD.[19] In addition to calling for the convocation of an International Conference on Trade and Employment that, *inter alia*, would lead to the establishment of an ITO, the USSD Proposals contained an outline of principles to be incorporated into the convention that would establish the ITO. Section G of Chapter III of the draft ITO convention provided for the General Exceptions and it read:

> Section G. General Exceptions[20]
>
> The undertakings in this Chapter should not be construed, to prevent members from adopting or enforcing measures:
>
> 1. *necessary* to protect public morals;
> 2. *necessary* to protect human, animal or plant life or health …
> 5. *necessary* to induce compliance with laws or regulations, such as those relating to customs enforcement, deceptive practices, and the protection of patents, trademarks and copyrights, which are not inconsistent with the purposes of the Organization (*emphasis added*).

As we will see in more detail in Section 7.3, the September 1946 Suggested Charter for the ITO which modified the December 1945 USSD Proposals would be the base document used for the drafting of the GATT 1947 and the ITO Charter.[21] Article 32 of the Suggested Charter read:

---

19 Excerpts of the document are available as Annex A-5 in Irwin *et al.*, ibid.

20 Annex A, ibid, p. 260.

21 Irwin *et al.*, above note 10, p. 104. Mavroidis states that "75 of 89 provisions featured in the *Suggested Charter* found their way into the GATT 1947 text." Mavroidis, above note 13, p. 19. Irwin *et al.* state that 74 out of the 89 articles included in the *Suggested Charter* were accepted and included in the London Draft of the GATT. Ibid, p. 108.

Section I. General Exceptions[22]

Article 32. General Exceptions to Chapter IV [General Commercial Policy]

Nothing in Chapter IV of this Charter shall be construed to prevent the adoption or enforcement by any Member of measures:

(a) *necessary* to protect public morals;

(b) *necessary* to protect human, animal or plant life or health ...

(g) *necessary* to induce compliance with laws or regulations which are not inconsistent with the provisions of Chapter IV, such as those relating to customs enforcement, deceptive practices, and the protection of patents, trade-marks and copyrights (*emphasis added*).

One can observe that the contents of three paragraphs of the USSD Proposals in which the key term 'necessary' was first used remained unchanged in the Suggested Charter.

7.3 The Drafting of the General and Security Exceptions in the London-New York-Geneva-Havana Meetings (1946–1948)

The GATT 1947 is the offspring of the rounds of meetings of the UN Conference on Trade and Employment held between October 1946 and March 1948 under the auspices of the UN Economic and Social Council. By July 1945, the US had a rough conception of a two-track process for the post-war multilateral trade negotiations: i.e., one track for tariff negotiations and the other track for the formation of an ITO. Accordingly, the Economic and Social Council meetings were assigned to two groups: the first group was assigned to draft the GATT and negotiate tariff reductions; and the second group was assigned to prepare the ITO Charter. The works of the first group (the "GATT 1947 Group") are the interest of this book.[23] Sub-sections 7.3.1–7.3.4 will briefly summarize the process of the drafting of the General Exceptions (Article XX) of the GATT 1947 during the London-New York-Geneva-Havana meetings. Since one of the provisions of the GATT Security Exceptions (Article XXI) has a necessity element

22 *Suggested Charter for an International Trade Organization of the United Nations*, State Department Publication No. 2598, Commercial Policy Series 93 (September 1946), p. 24.

23 The GATT 1947 Group, which was organized in the form of a preparatory committee, met in London, New York, Geneva and Havana for 370 days and delivered a workable text – the GATT 1947 – on a very complicated issue. A total of 626 meetings were held by the GATT 1947 Group: 150 in London, 58 in Lake Success (New York) and 453 in Geneva. Irwin *et al.*, above note 10, p. 115.

in it, the process of drafting of GATT Article XXI will also be briefly mentioned. The credit in preparing these sub-sections goes mainly to Irwin *et al.*'s detailed narration of the meetings[24] as well as to John H. Jackson's seminal work, *World Trade and the Law of GATT* (1969). Substantial reference has also been made to negotiation documents of the Economic and Social Council available at Stanford's GATT Digital Library.[25]

Section 7.3 focuses on the drafting of the General/Security Exceptions of the GATT 1947 which were *one of the least debated provisions during the negotiations* that led to the drafting of the GATT 1947. Most of the discussions on the General/Security Exceptions focused on: (a) the scope of the exceptions (i.e., whether they would be exceptions to the entire ITO Charter or its chapter on general commercial policy (a chapter more or less similar to the GATT 1947);[26] and within the said chapter on general commercial policy, whether there should be exceptions only to import and export restrictions); (b) adding/not adding new paragraphs of exceptions to the list initially contained in the Suggested Charter; and (c) structuring the paragraphs of the General/Security Exceptions. Regarding substance, the *chapeau* and what would finally become paragraphs (b) and (g) of Article XX of the GATT 1947 invited more discussions than the other paragraphs of the draft General/Security Exceptions. Thus, it can be said that Article 32 of the US Suggested Charter, entitled General Exceptions to Chapter IV (General Commercial Policy), found itself in Articles XX and XXI of the GATT 1947 and Articles 45 and 99 of the Havana Charter for an ITO without substantial change in content.

Section 7.3 highlights the key discussions on the drafting of the General/Security Exceptions in the GATT 1947. However, given the limited number of cases that have interpreted the Security Exceptions, and more so the key term 'necessary' therein, the primary focus will be on the drafting of the General Exceptions with particular attention to the key term 'necessary' in the General Exceptions' paragraphs.

24 Ibid, pp. 77–133; 162–164.

25 Available at, http://gatt.stanford.edu/page/home. The documents are referenced in this book in the format given them by the UN Economic and Social Council such as E/PC/T/33, E/P/CT/C.II/50 etc. Page numbers in the documents have been used here whenever necessary.

26 This is a debate which echoes the often-raised question whether the General/Security Exceptions of the GATT 1994/GATS apply (should apply) only to the GATT 1994/GATS respectively or to the other WTO agreements as well.

7.3.1 *The London Meetings (October–November 1946)*

The UN Preparatory Committee for the International Conference on Trade and Employment began its meeting earlier in London. Between 5 October and 26 November 1946, the Preparatory Committee held its First Session.[27] The basis for the discussions was the Suggested Charter. It was generally recognized in the London discussions on General Exceptions (Article 32 of the Suggested Charter which, at the end of the London meetings, would become Article 37) that "there must be General Exceptions such as those usually included in commercial treaties, to protect public health, morals, etc."[28] It was, however, the concern of members of Committee II (committee on general commercial policy) that the General Exceptions may be abused, i.e., used for indirect protection, by Members which invoke them. To avoid the said abuse, a sentence similar to what is now the *chapeau* of the General Exceptions of the GATT 1994/GATS was proposed,[29] a sentence which was "generally accepted, subject to later review of its precise wording, particularly as to whether the scope of Article 32 should be limited to 'import and export restrictions'".[30]

No discussions or comments were made on the term 'necessary' as contained in the three paragraphs of Article 37. In one of the final meetings of Committee II, the issue of clarifying the meaning of some terms and phrases like 'like products', 'similar products', 'products of any Member country', 'country of origin' was discussed and it was proposed to include in the Charter "an Article to contain definitions of these and other terms *presenting any ambiguity or obscurity* (*emphasis added*)".[31] The Drafting Committee, which subsequently met in New York, did not provide definitions for such terms. It is the GATT and WTO dispute settlement organs that would later develop interpretations for such key terms as 'like products' and 'necessary'. Despite these discussions on the General Exceptions, however, the Technical sub-committee did not adopt Article 32/37 (as amended)[32] and the Preparatory Committee left the finalization of the drafting of the General Exceptions to the subsequent meetings.[33]

---

27 Full report of the Preparatory Committee on the London meetings is available at, E/PC/T/33.

28 E/PC/T/C.II/54, p. 26; E/PC/T/C.II/64, p. 7.

29 E/PC/T/C.II/50, pp. 6–7. Discussions among members of the committee and their opinions in approving the UK proposal are available at, E/PC/T/C.II/55, p. 4; E/PC/T/C.II/54/Rev.1, p. 36; E/PC/T/C.II/PRO/W/11, pp. 33–34.

30 E/PC/T/C.II/54, p. 33.

31 E/PC/T/C.II/64, p. 7.

32 E/PC/T/C.II/PRO/PV/14, p. 19.

33 E/PC/T/33, pp. 11, 33.

7.3.2 *The New York Meetings (January–February 1947)*

The group that met in Lake Success, New York between 20 January and 25 February 1947 was not the Preparatory Committee that sat and held its First Session in London but a Drafting Committee the establishment of which was agreed in London. In New York, the drafting of the GATT was disentangled from the drafting of the ITO Charter and the first full draft of the GATT 1947 containing 28 articles was produced by copying and developing it from the chapter in the draft ITO Charter on general commercial policy. Thus, General Exceptions (Article 37 in the draft ITO Charter) was made Article XX in the New York GATT draft; GATT Article XX was identified as "cf. Article 37 of the Charter".[34] Two relevant developments took place in New York with regards to Article 37. Firstly, the scope of Article 37 – unlike in the London draft limiting it to import and export restrictions – was brought back to its original scope to apply to the entire chapter on general commercial policy.[35] Secondly, the term 'necessary' in Article 37(b) was removed in New York[36] so that the term was left inserted in only two – unlike in the London draft where it was inserted in three – paragraphs of Article 37.[37] Once again, there were no specific discussions in New York regarding the meaning of the term 'necessary' in the General Exceptions paragraphs.

7.3.3 *The Geneva Meetings (April–October 1947)*

We owe the final substance and structure of the GATT 1947, the success of tariff negotiations as well as the preparation of the final ITO Charter to the Second Session of the Preparatory Committee that met at the Palais des Nations in Geneva between 10 April and 30 October 1947. The Geneva meetings had two objectives: (a) finalization of the ITO Charter; and (b) conclusion of tariff negotiations along with finalization of the draft of the GATT 1947, all to be ready for the final meeting set towards the end of the year in Havana. By mid-August 1947, the final texts of the GATT and the draft ITO Charter were finalized. Tariff negotiations, however, lingered for some time. The concluded tariff negotiations and the final draft of the GATT 1947 constituted the Geneva Final Act. Minor changes were made to the GATT 1947 and the ITO Charter during the final meeting in Havana. The GATT 1947, entered into force on 1 January 1948.[38]

---

34 E/PC/T/34, pp. 65–81 (esp. p. 77).
35 Ibid, p. 31; E/PC/T/C.6/41, p. 3.
36 E/PC/T/34, ibid.
37 Ibid, pp. 31–32; E/PC/T/C.6/85, p. 31.
38 Above note 34.

Some discussions were held on the substance and structure of the General Exceptions during the Geneva meetings.

On substance, the notable discussion was about the wording of paragraph (b) of Article 37 from which the term 'necessary' was removed during the New York meetings. On 7 May 1947, the delegates of France, Belgium, the Netherlands and Luxembourg, intending to introduce a better-wording, proposed an amendment to paragraph (b), an amendment that would return use of the term 'necessary'.[39] After much debate the delegates approved a US proposal to redraft paragraph (b) as "necessary to protect human, animal or plant life or health".[40] Outside of paragraph (b) discussions, there were proposals to add new paragraphs to the General Exceptions.[41]

On structure, on 24 July 1947, the structure of the New York drafts (of the GATT and the ITO Charter) were revised and it was concluded that a certain degree of rearrangement was needed to the structure of the articles and paragraphs of the draft instruments. Thus, the General Exceptions which were Article XX of the GATT in the New York draft were made Article XIX in Geneva. The structure of Geneva's GATT Article XIX was then divided into two paragraphs: paragraph (1) which looks like today's GATT 1994 Article XX and paragraph (2) which looks like today's GATT 1994 Article XXI.[42] During the discussion held on 13 September 1947, however, the two paragraphs of Article XIX were split in to two different paragraphs that: (a) paragraph (1) of Article XIX was modified and became Article XX which was given the title "General Exceptions" which contained two groups of exceptions (paragraphs (a)-(i) and paragraphs (a)-(c) respectively); and (b) paragraph (2) of Article XIX was modified and became Article XXI which was given the title "Security Exceptions".[43] Since the contents of the General Exceptions in the GATT and ITO Charter were duplicates of each other, the bifurcation of GATT Article XIX into Articles XX and XXI similarly occurred in Article 37 of the draft ITO Charter (made Article 43 in Geneva). Article 43 was first divided into two paragraphs[44] but subsequently divided into two separate articles as Article 43 (General Exceptions Chapter IV (general commercial policy) of ITO Charter), with contents similar to GATT Article XX[45] and Article 94 (General Exceptions to the entire ITO Charter),

39 E/PC/T/W.46. See also, E/PC/T/103, p. 44.

40 E/PC/T/W/245, p. 1; E/PC/T/A/PV/30, pp. 7–14.

41 E/PC/T/W/269; E/PC/T/W/281; E/PC/T/W/293.

42 E/PC/T/135, pp. 2, 11. See the text of Article XIX of the Geneva draft at pp. 54–55 of this document.

43 E/PC/T/196, pp. 51–53.

44 E/PC/T/180, pp. 97–99.

45 E/PC/T/186 and Corr. 1, pp. 36–37.

with contents similar to GATT Article XXI.[46] Thus, for the first time in Geneva, the exceptions were divided (in the GATT and the ITO Charter) into General Exceptions and Security Exceptions as we know them today.

7.3.4 *The Havana Meetings (November 1947–March 1948)*

It was in Havana, where representatives sat between 17 November 1947 and 24 March 1948, that the final versions of the GATT 1947 and the ITO Charter were endorsed. The Havana meetings, unfortunately, were held at a time when the focus of the US and Europe was geared towards realizing the dreams of the Marshall Plan and preparing for the Cold War. The fate of the ITO was finally sealed when President Truman, in reaction to many developments in the US that made it impossible to push for finalization of the Havana meetings, announced in December 1950 that his administration would not seek ratification of the ITO Charter by the US Senate, effectively rendering the Havana Charter, in the words of Prof. Petersmann, "stillborn".[47] Despite its "flawed constitutional beginnings", however, the GATT gradually turned into an institution, or a *de facto* ITO, where increasing numbers of problems of the Contracting Parties were handled.[48]

Since the text of the GATT was concluded during the Geneva meetings, Articles XX and XXI of the GATT 1947 did not go through noticeable change during the Havana meetings. Structurally, what was Article 43 in the Geneva ITO Charter draft became Article 45 in the final Havana Charter and Article 94 of the Geneva draft became Article 99 in Havana.

7.3.5 *Post-Havana Developments (1948–1994)*

The structure or substance of GATT 1947 Articles XX and XXI was left untouched during the 46 years between the end of the Geneva meetings and the conclusion

46 Ibid, p. 56.

47 Ernst-Ulrich Petersmann, 'How Should WTO Members React to Their WTO Crises?', *World Trade Review*, 18(3): 2019, p. 516; Richard Toye, 'Developing Multilateralism: The Havana Charter and the Fight for the International Trade Organization, 1947–1948', *The International History Review*, 25(2): 2003, pp. 282–305. See also, Autar Krishen Koul, *Guide to the WTO and GATT: Economics, Law and Politics* (New Delhi and Singapore: Satyam Law International and Springer, 2018), p. 6.

48 Jackson, *The World Trading System*, above note 18, pp. 92–98. Professor Lowenfeld, while narrating the genesis of the GATT, stated that the GATT was born "almost by accident". Andreas Lowenfeld, *International Economic Law* (2nd ed.) (Oxford: Oxford University Press, 2008), pp. 25–28. Koul also stated: "[t]he birth of GATT was essentially a historical accident." Koul, ibid, p. 7.

of the Uruguay Round.[49] One of the recurrent discussions regarding Article XX was extending the expiry date for the three sub-paragraphs of paragraph (2) of Article XX. Article XX of GATT 1947 had two paragraphs ((1) and (2)) which respectively contained sub-paragraphs (a)-(i) and (a)-(c). Sub-paragraphs (a)-(c) of paragraph (2) read:

> (a) essential to the acquisition or distribution of products in general or local short supply; provided that ... ;
> (b) essential to the control of prices by a contracting party undergoing shortages subsequent to the war;
> (c) essential to the orderly liquidation of temporary surpluses of stocks owned or controlled by the Government of any contracting party or of industries developed in the territory of any contracting party owing to the exigencies of the war which it would be uneconomic to maintain in normal conditions; provided that ...
>
> Measures instituted or maintained under [paragraph] II of this Article which are inconsistent with the other provisions of this Agreement shall be removed as soon as the conditions giving rise to them have ceased, and in any event not later than 1 January 1951.

In a series of meetings of the GATT Contracting Parties, the expiry date of 1 January 1951 was consecutively extended to 1 January 1952,[50] 1 January 1954[51] and 1 July 1955.[52] Following several requests, the Contracting Parties resolved that paragraphs (b) and (c) of Article XX(2) should be removed.[53] Accordingly, paragraph (a) was moved to paragraph (1) and became sub-paragraph (j) in paragraph (1). From that moment onwards, therefore, Article XX has maintained only a single list of exceptions. The deadline for paragraph (j) of Article XX was then consecutively extended to 30 June 1960,[54] 30 June 1965[55] and 1970.[56] No further amendment has hitherto been made to the structure or substance of GATT Article XX.

---

49 Stefan Zleptnig, *Non-Economic Objectives in WTO Law: Justification Provisions of GATT, GATS, SPS and TBT* (London and Boston: Martinus Nijhoff Publishers, 2010), p. 104.
50 GATT/CP. 5/17 (2 November 1950).
51 GATT/CP. 6/38 (20 October 1951).
52 L/135 (23 September 1953).
53 L/189 15 (12 April 1954); L/261/Add.1, 30 (12 November 1954); L/334 14 (1 March 1955).
54 BISD, Third Supplement (1960), p. 230.
55 SR.16/3 (May 1960).
56 W.22/7 (12 March 1965) and L/3361 (25 February 1970).

With no statements recorded on the intention of the drafters of GATT 1947 on the meaning of the key term 'necessary' in the General/Security Exceptions, therefore, interpretation of the concept of necessity was left to the GATT and WTO dispute settlement organs. Section 8.2 will cover the development of the interpretation of the term 'necessary' in the General Exceptions.

CHAPTER 8

Evolution of the Interpretation of the Concept of Necessity in the General and Security Exceptions of the GATT (1947 and 1994) and the GATS

8.1 General Observations on the Nature and Practice of the General Exceptions

Like most legal instruments, the legal texts of the WTO Agreement have rules and exceptions to the rules. These exceptions take many forms. Some exceptions are provided to give WTO Members some form of autonomy to pursue specific economic or non-economic objectives while others aim to provide developing or least-developed Members a chance to progressively achieve the level of commitment required by the obligatory rules. Section 8.1 provides observations on the General Exceptions-related disputes in the era of the GATT and the WTO where the term 'necessary' was interpreted. Section 8.2 will present the evolution of the interpretation of the concept of necessity in the General Exceptions during the GATT and WTO eras. Given the paucity of case law on it, notes on the concept of necessity in the Security Exceptions (to be discussed in Section 8.3) will not be covered in depth in Section 8.1.

8.1.1 *The Realm of Exceptions in the GATT (1947 and 1994)*

The observation on the realm of exceptions in general in the GATT (1947 and 1994) focuses on three points: purpose of the exceptions, the priority between the rules and the exceptions and the categories of the GATT exceptions.

Regarding purpose, the negotiators of the GATT, and the WTO, intended to create a global trading system fostering and protecting trade liberalization, market access and non-discrimination. Governments, however, do not engage in trade relations at the expense of other policy objectives they pursue such as the need to ensure public order and security, protect health and moral standard of their population, ensure environmental sustainability, preserve national heritage, protect consumers etc. The protection and promotion of these objectives may often conflict with the states' international commitments, inclusive of international trade commitments. In establishing international trade and other rules, governments do, and must, ensure, at least, that such potential conflicts are resolved or, at best, that the domestic interests and international

 | DOI:10.1163/9789004700000_010

commitments work in tandem with each other.[1] GATT and WTO negotiators were not unaware of the potential conflict between the protection of "important and legitimate" domestic policies[2] and GATT/WTO law obligations. They, thus, provided for exceptions which allow the Members to act inconsistently with their international trade commitments to protect and promote, and thereby give priority to, societal and related values.

Regarding priority between international trade rules and their exceptions, there are different opinions. Some, like Ortino, argued that the rules (such as the MFN, national treatment and other obligations) take the form of primary rules and the policy exceptions are relegated into, and take the form of, secondary rules.[3] Klabbers, without separating GATT rules and the General Exceptions as primary or secondary norms, argued that since the General Exceptions must be interpreted restrictively "any broad interpretation of Article XX would run counter to the object and purpose of GATT."[4] Others, like Trachtman, argue that neither trade values nor social values take precedence over the other.[5] The manner of interpreting the exceptions – for instance the General Exceptions of the GATT 1994 – that the Appellate Body developed seems to agree with the interpretation which Trachtman suggested. The Appellate Body made it clear from early on that trade rules and policy exceptions, specifically the General Exceptions, have been sewn together into the cloth of the GATT 1994 and must, therefore, be interpreted without one of them being prioritized over the other. In *US – Gasoline (1996)*, the Appellate Body, underlined:

> [GATT] Article XX(g) and its phrase, 'relating to the conservation of exhaustible natural resources', need to be read in context and in such a manner as to give effect to the purposes and objects of the *General*

1 Peter Van den Bossche and Werner Zdouc, *The Law and Policy of the World Trade Organization* (4th ed.) (Cambridge: Cambridge University Press, 2017), pp. 544–546. Prof. John Jackson stated that GATT Article XX "recognizes the importance of a sovereign nation being able to act to promote the purposes on this list, even when such action otherwise conflicts with various obligations relating to international trade." John H. Jackson, *The World Trading System: Law and Policy of International Economic Relations* (Cambridge, Mass.: MIT Press. 1989), p. 206.

2 The Appellate Body used the term "important and legitimate" domestic policies to identify the values listed in paragraphs (a)-(j) of Article XX of the GATT 1994. Appellate Body Report, *US – Shrimp (1998)*, para. 121.

3 Federico Ortino, 'From "non-discrimination" to "reasonableness": a paradigm shift in international economic law?', *Jean Monnet Working Paper 01/05* (2005), p. 54.

4 Jan Klabbers, 'Jurisprudence in International Trade Law: Article XX of GATT', *Journal of World Trade*, 26(2): 1992, p. 88.

5 Joel Trachtman, 'Trade and ... Problems, Cost-Benefit Analysis and Subsidiarity', *European Journal of International Law*, 9(1): 1998, p. 33.

> *Agreement*. The context of Article XX(g) includes the provisions of the rest of the *General Agreement*, including in particular Articles I, III and XI; conversely, the context of Articles I and III and XI includes Article XX. Accordingly, the phrase 'relating to the conservation of exhaustible natural resources' may not be read so expansively as seriously to subvert the purpose and object of Article III:4. Nor may Article III:4 be given so broad a reach as effectively to emasculate Article XX(g) and the policies and interests it embodies. The relationship between the affirmative commitments set out in, *e.g.*, Articles I, III and XI, and the policies and interests embodied in the 'General Exceptions' listed in Article XX, can be given meaning within the framework of the *General Agreement* and its object and purpose by a treaty interpreter only on a case-to-case basis, by careful scrutiny of the factual and legal context in a given dispute, without disregarding the words actually used by the WTO Members themselves to express their intent and purpose.[6]

The equal treatment of the substantive obligations and the General Exceptions has led to the understanding by GATT/WTO dispute settlement organs that the General Exceptions, though *limited* and *conditional*[7] by their very crafting,[8] should not be read narrowly in comparison with substantive GATT 1994 obligations such as MFN and national treatment.[9] In other words, a 'line of equilibrium'[10] must be maintained between the two sets of provisions.[11]

Regarding the categories of the GATT exceptions, it is noted at the outset that the GATT was designed to formulate general principles that would govern

---

6 Appellate Body Report, *US – Gasoline* (*1996*), p. 18. See also, WTO Panel Report, *EC – Tariff Preferences* (*2004*), para. 7.52 where the Appellate Body re-endorsed the interpretation of the panel (Appellate Body Report, *EC – Tariff Preferences* (*2004*), para. 94).

7 See, GATT Panel Report, *US – Section 337* (*1989*), para. 5.9; Appellate Body Report, *Brazil – Retreaded Tyres* (*2007*), para. 139; Petros C. Mavroidis, *The Regulation of International Trade* (Vol. 1: GATT) (Cambridge, MA: MIT Press, 2015), p. 417; Van den Bossche and Zdouc, above note 1, p. 547; Panagiotis Delimatsis, 'The Principle of Necessity in the WTO – Lessons for the GATS Negotiations on Domestic Regulation', *Tilburg Law School Legal Studies Research Paper Series No. 04/2014*, p. 6 (where he calls the necessity defense a "breathing space" for regulators).

8 See, Appellate Body Report, *US – Shrimp* (*1998*), para. 157.

9 Appellate Body Report, *US – Gasoline* (*1996*), p. 18.

10 This term was first used by the Appellate Body in the *US – Shrimp* dispute. Appellate Body Report, *US – Shrimp* (*1998*), para. 159.

11 Appellate Body Report, *Thailand – Cigarettes* (*Philippines*) (*2011*), para. 173. See also, Van den Bossche and Zdouc, above note 1, pp. 547–548.

the complex and highly politicized subject of ITL.[12] The GATT 1947 had to balance the myriad of obligations it demanded with the sovereign independence of nations to structure their international trade relations in conditions that suit their respective wishes and realities. To this end, the GATT was "riddled with exceptions" that relax the obligations of the GATT members in a number of situations.[13] Different scholars categorize GATT exceptions (the General Exceptions and others) into different groups. Mavroidis, for instance, divides them into three: (a) business exceptions such as anti-dumping and countervailing duties, safeguards, infant industry protection and renegotiation of bound duties; (b) non-business exceptions such as non-economic excuses such as the General Exceptions (Article XX) and Security Exceptions (Article XXI); and (c) institutional exceptions such as regional integration, special and differential treatment for developing countries, balance of payments, exchange restrictions, waivers and withdrawal of concessions.[14] Hoeckman and Kostecki distinguish between exceptions that lead to temporary suspension of obligations and those that lead to permanent suspension of obligations.[15] Zleptnig distinguishes between exceptions for economic reasons and exceptions for non-economic reasons.[16] John H. Jackson divided GATT exceptions into two major groups: universal exceptions (i.e., those that apply to all the obligations enumerated in the GATT 1994) and particular exceptions (i.e., those that apply only to specific obligations of the GATT 1994).[17]

None of these categorizations divide the GATT exceptions based on the key terms or concepts (such as 'necessary', 'relating to' etc.) used in the exceptions.

12 John H. Jackson, *World Trade and the Law of GATT* (Indianapolis: Bobbs-Merill, 1969), p. 536.

13 Ibid, p. 535. While Nichols stated that "exceptions are sprinkled throughout the General Agreement" (Philip M. Nichols, 'GATT Doctrine', *Virginia Journal of International Law*, 36(2): 1996, p. 430), Ehrenhaft also mentioned that the GATT "is largely composed of exceptions". Peter D. Ehrenhaft, Book Review of *Trade Policies for a Better Future: The 'Leutwiler Report', the GATT and the Uruguay Round* (Dordrecht: Martinus Nijhoff Publishers, 1987), *American Journal of International Law*, 84(1): 1990, p. 335.

14 Petros Mavroidis, *The General Agreement on Tariffs and Trade: A Commentary* (Vol. 1) (Oxford: Oxford University Press, 2005), Ch. 3.

15 Bernard Hoeckman and Michael Kostecki, *The Political Economy of the World Trading System: WTO and Beyond* (2nd ed.) (Oxford: Oxford University Press, 2001), pp. 303ff.

16 Stefan Zleptnig, *Non-Economic Objectives in WTO Law: Justification Provisions of GATT, GATS, SPS and TBT* (London and Boston: Martinus Nijhoff Publishers, 2010), p. 101. Sykes calls them "non-trade international legal norms". Katie Sykes, 'Sealing Animal Welfare into the GATT Exceptions: The International Dimension of Animal Welfare in WTO Disputes', *World Trade Review*, 13(3): 2014, pp. 471–498.

17 Jackson, above note 12, pp. 535–539.

It is admittedly difficult to come up with a categorization based on such key terms. The concept of necessity can, therefore, be discussed only within the context of the General or Security Exceptions, not within the context of the categorization where the General or Security Exceptions may be placed. We, therefore, focus below on discussing the General Exceptions of the GATT 1994 (and by analogy the GATS) wherein the concept of necessity is embodied.

8.1.2 *The Structure and Two-Tier Interpretation of the General Exceptions*

Article XX of the GATT 1994 and Article XIV of the GATS have a list of ten and five exceptions, listed as paragraphs (a)-(j) and (a)-(e) respectively, which may be invoked individually or simultaneously.[18] Since these are exceptions, the respondent, which has an overall burden of proving consistency of its measures with the General Exceptions,[19] cannot resort to a justification under one or more of the paragraphs unless a contested measure has first been held to be inconsistent with a given GATT 1994/GATS obligation(s)

18 Often, the respondent may argue that its affirmative defense is based, separately or alternatively, under two or more paragraphs of the General Exceptions. See, for instance, WTO Panel Report, *US – Gasoline* (*1996*), paras. 6.20–6.29 (paragraph (b)), paras. 6.30–6.34 (paragraph (d)), paras. 6.35–6.40 (paragraph (g)) and para. 8.1 (a summary finding on the three defenses); GATT Panel Report, *US – Tuna I* (*Mexico*) (*1991*), paras. 3.6 (paragraph (b)), 5.23–5.34 (paragraphs (b) and (g)); Appellate Body Report, *US – Shrimp* (*1998*), paras. 10, 146 (paragraphs (b) and (g)); WTO Panel Report, *Indonesia – Raw Materials* (*2022*), para. 7.345; WTO Panel Report, *US – Tariff Measures* (*2020*), para. 7.242; WTO Panel Report, *Turkey – Pharmaceutical Products* (*EU*) (*2022*), para. 7.129. In the reverse, a single paragraph of Article XX may be invoked for justifying inconsistencies with two or more provisions of the GATT. See, *China – Auto Parts* (*2009*), paras. 7.276–7.278, GATT Panel Report, *EEC – Parts and Components* (*1990*), paras. 5.12–5.18 and 5.24; WTO Panel Report, *Mexico – Taxes on Soft Drinks* (*2006*), modified by Appellate Body Report, *Mexico – Taxes on Soft Drinks* (*2006*), para. 8.162.

19 GATT Panel Report, *Canada – FIRA* (*1984*), para. 5.20; GATT Panel Report, *US – Section 337* (*1989*), para. 5.27; Appellate Body Report, *US – Gasoline* (*1996*), pp. 22–23; Appellate Body Report, *Korea – Various Measures on Beef* (*2001*), para. 157; WTO Panel Report, *US – Shrimp* (*Article 21.5 – Malaysia*) (*2001*), paras. 5.17–5.32; Appellate Body Report, *Mexico – Taxes on Soft Drinks* (*2006*), para. 67; WTO Panel Report, *EC – Trademarks and Geographical Indications* (*Australia*) (*2005*), paras. 7.293, 7.442; Appellate Body Report, *Brazil – Retreaded Tyres* (*2007*), paras. 7.38, 7.222; Appellate Body Report, *US – Wool Shirts and Blouses* (*1997*), pp. 15–16; WTO Panel Reports, *China – Auto Parts* (*2009*), para. 7.92; WTO Panel Report, *US – Gambling* (*2005*), para. 6.450. It often happens that the complaining party presents a claim that if a violation of the GATT obligation has been found, the respondent's actions do not also fall under the Article XX Exceptions. For Example, GATT Panel Report, *Canada – Herring and Salmon* (*1988*), para. 3.1; GATT Panel Report, *US – Tuna II* (*1994*), para. 3.1 (a) and (b); GATT Panel Report, *US – Spring Assemblies* (*1983*), paras. 33–39.

such as national treatment and MFN.[20] Assuming the contested measure has been held to be inconsistent with the relevant GATT 1994/GATS obligation(s), the respondent, if it opts to defend under the General Exceptions, has to initially provide a provisional justification for the measure under one of the General Exceptions paragraphs. Following such provisional justification,[21] the respondent is then required to qualify the *manner of application* of its GATT 1994/GATS-inconsistent measure[22] under the introductory clause of the General Exceptions, called the *chapeau*.[23] The Appellate Body has, since

20 In *US – Spring Assemblies (1983)*, the panel, despite its finding that GATT 1994 Articles II:1(b), III:1, 2 and 4, XI:1 and XX were the bases for Canada's claim against the US, came to the conclusion, in a rather strange way of first discussing the affirmative defense (i.e., Article XX). GATT Panel Report, *US – Spring Assemblies (1983)*, paras. 49–50, 61. From the next case that discussed Article XX, *Canada – FIRA (1984)*, onwards, however, the dispute settlement organs have moved to analyze GATT Article XX defenses only after a finding of violation of other GATT obligations. However, the Appellate Body in its discretion has, in some cases, proceeded with analysis of Article XX despite finding that the relevant GATT provision has not been breached (for example, Appellate Body Report, *EC – Asbestos (2001)*, paras. 126, 141, 147–48, 155–175, 192 (b)-(f)) in order to build upon the interpretation being developed on Article XX and expand the Panel's analysis of the relevant paragraph in Article XX.

21 It is now the practice of the WTO dispute settlement organs that the analysis of the *chapeau* has to come *only after* a finding that the contested measure has met the requirements of one of the paragraphs of Article XX. In the first Article XX(d) dispute, the *US – Spring Assemblies (1983)*, the panel had first discussed the *chapeau* before it turned to discuss the provisions of paragraph (d). GATT Panel Report, *US – Spring Assemblies (1983)*, paras. 54–60. See also, Appellate Body Report, *Brazil – Retreaded Tyres (2007)*, para. 139; Appellate Body Reports, *EC – Seal Products (2014)*, para. 5.169; and Appellate Body Report, *Colombia – Textiles (2016)*, para. 6.20. However, the practice subsequent to *US – Spring Assemblies (1983)* has demonstrated that a dispute settlement organ has to first discuss the paragraph and then move to the *chapeau*. See, Appellate Body Report, *US – Shrimp (1998)*, paras. 117–122.

22 GATT Panel Report, *US – Spring Assemblies (1983)*, para. 56; Appellate Body Report, *US – Gasoline (1996)*, p. 22. The Appellate Body added that interpretation of the *chapeau* requires maintaining a careful balance between a Member's right to invoke the exceptions and the substantive rights of other Members under the GATT 1994. *See*, Appellate Body Report, *US – Shrimp (1998)*, paras. 156–159; Appellate Body Report, *Brazil – Retreaded Tyres (2007)*, paras. 224, 227; Appellate Body Report, *US – Gambling (2005)*, para. 339; WTO Panel Report, *Argentina – Hides and Leather (2001)*, para. 11.312.

23 The *chapeau* reads: "Subject to the requirement that such measures are not applied in a manner which would constitute a means of arbitrary or unjustifiable discrimination between countries where the same conditions prevail, or a disguised restriction on international trade, nothing in this Agreement shall be construed to prevent the adoption or enforcement by any contracting party of measures …" The Appellate Body summarized the substance of the *chapeau* as serving to "ensure that Members' rights to avail themselves of exceptions are exercised in good faith to protect interests considered legitimate

the *US – Gasoline (1996)* dispute, corrected the "convoluted Article XX jurisprudence of the past"[24] and accordingly laid the foundation for the procedure of analyzing the General Exception defenses as first requiring that the measure at issue come under the particular exceptions in the paragraphs and then further appraising the measure under the *chapeau* provisional finding under the paragraphs.[25] However, the Appellate Body, in the *Indonesia – Import Licensing Regimes (2017)* dispute indicated that a panel's decision to first address the measure under the *chapeau* may not, depending on the circumstances of the particular case, necessarily be a legal error.[26]

A dispute settlement organ need not proceed to analyze the *chapeau* if the contested measure fails to meet the requirements of the General Exceptions paragraph in dispute.[27] Three trends can be observed regarding the practice in this regard. The first trend is the practice of not moving to discuss the *chapeau* after finding inconsistencies with the paragraphs.[28] The second trend, as can be

under Article XX, not as a means to circumvent one Member's obligations towards other WTO Members". Appellate Body Report, *Brazil – Retreaded Tyres (2007)*, para. 215.

24 Steve Charnovitz, 'The WTO's Environmental Progress', *Journal of International Economic Law*, 10(3): 2007, p. 696. In *US – Spring Assemblies (1983)*, for instance, the panel first discussed the *chapeau* and then moved to discuss paragraph (d). GATT Panel Report, *US – Spring Assemblies (1983)*, paras. 51–61.

25 Appellate Body Report, *US – Gasoline (1996)*, p. 22; Appellate Body Report, *Brazil – Retreaded Tyres (2007)*, para. 139; Appellate Body Report, *Dominican Republic – Import and Sale of Cigarettes (2005)*, para. 64; WTO Panel Report, *Argentina – Hides and Leather (2001)*, para. 11.288. Note that the earliest of the GATT panels had, viewed in light of the current interpretation, 'wrongly' analyzed Article XX defenses in the order written in Article XX, i.e., they discussed conformity of the challenged measure first in light of the *chapeau* and then in light of the specific Article XX paragraph. GATT Panel Report, *US – Spring Assemblies (1983)*, paras. 51–61; see also, GATT Panel Report, *US – Canadian Tuna (1982)*, paras. 4.7–4.13.

26 Appellate Body Report, *Indonesia – Import Licensing Regimes (2017)*, para. 6.7. The analysis of the Appellate Body is found in paras. 5.86–5.101 of the report. See also, WTO Panel Report, *US – Tariff Measures on Certain Goods from China (2020)*, paras. 7.241–7.242.

27 Appellate Body Report, *US – Shrimp (1998)*, paras. 119–20; WTO Panel Report, *Brazil – Retreaded Tyres (2007)*, para. 7.107; WTO Panel Reports, *China – Auto Parts (2009)*, para. 7.469.

28 See, for instance, the consistent statements of the dispute settlement organs in: Appellate Body Report, *Korea – Various Measures on Beef (2001)*, para. 156; WTO Panel Report, *Canada – Wheat Exports and Grain Imports (2004)*, para. 5.38, *referring to*, Appellate Body Report, *US – Shrimp (1998)*, para. 149; Appellate Body Report, *Dominican Republic – Import and Sale of Cigarettes (2005)*, para. 74; WTO Panel Reports, *EC – Trademarks and Geographical Indications (Australia) (2005)*, paras. 7.306, 7.462; Appellate Body Report, *Mexico – Taxes on Soft Drinks (2006)*, para. 81; WTO Panel Report, *Brazil – Retreaded Tyres (2007)*, para. 7.37; WTO Panel Report, *US – Customs Bond Directive (2008)*, paras. 7.292–7.293; WTO Panel Report, *Indonesia – Raw Materials (2022)*, paras. 7.344–7.345; WTO Panel

observed from the reports of the panels in EC – *Tariff Preferences* (2004)[29] and *US – Gambling* (2005),[30] is the practice of 'completing' the General Exceptions analysis by discussing the contested measure in light of the *chapeau* despite the finding that the measure failed to meet the requirements of the relevant General Exceptions paragraph. The third trend is the practice of continuing to discuss the remaining requirements of the paragraphs if one (or some) of the requirements of the paragraphs are not met and then not proceeding to the *chapeau*.[31]

8.1.3 *Trends on the Practice of Interpreting the General Exceptions So Far*

Eight trends can be observed regarding the interpretation thus far developed on the General Exceptions.

(1) The General Exceptions are affirmative defenses that can only be raised after a violation(s) of one of the obligations of the GATT 1994/GATS have been found to exist.[32]

Report, *Turkey – Pharmaceutical Products (EU)* (2022), para. 7.213. The same trend can also be observed regarding examination of the Security Exceptions in Article XXI of the GATT 1994 in WTO Panel Report, *US – Origin Marking Requirement* (2022), para. 7.361.

29 WTO Panel Report, EC – *Tariff Preferences* (2004), paras. 7.210, 7.223–7.224.

30 WTO Panel Report, *US – Gambling* (2005), para. 6.566.

31 The EC – *Trademarks and Geographical Indications (Australia)* (2005) panel, for instance, initially had found that the two EC measures in dispute were applied to secure compliance with laws or regulations that the panel respectively found to be *inconsistent with* the GATT. WTO Panel Report, EC – *Trademarks and Geographical Indications (Australia)* (2005), paras. 7.293–7.297 and 7.442–7.448 respectively. Thus, the panel, like earlier panels, would have been expected to stop the Article XX(d) analysis there. However, the panel decided to proceed with discussing whether the said measures were 'necessary' (paras. 7.298–7.305 and 7.449–7.461 respectively) and found those measure not necessary. Thereafter, the panel found it not desirable to discuss the *chapeau* (WTO Panel Report, EC – *Trademarks and Geographical Indications (Australia)* (2005), paras. 7.306–7.307 and 7.462–7.463 respectively). See also, WTO Panel Reports, *China – Auto Parts* (2009), paras. 7.297–7.298, 7.314–7.315, 7.346–7.347, 7.347–7.364, 7.365; WTO Panel Report, *EU – Energy Package* (2018), paras. 7.1325–7.1382.

32 The possibility (non-possibility) of extending the application of the General Exceptions to a responding Member's Accession Protocol has been thoroughly analyzed in the case of China in *China – Publications and Audiovisual Products* (2010), *China – Raw Materials* (2012) and *China – Rare Earths* (2014). For a detailed discussion on the subject, see, Elisa Baroncini, 'The Applicability of GATT Article XX to China's WTO Accession Protocol in the Appellate Body Report of the *China-Raw Materials* Case: Suggestions for a Different Interpretative Approach', *China-EU Law Journal*, 1(3): 2013, pp. 1–34; Ilaria Espa, 'The Appellate Body Approach to the Applicability of Article XX GATT in the Light of *China – Raw Materials:* A Missed Opportunity?', *Journal of World Trade*, 46(6): 2012, pp. 1399–1424. For the possibility of the applicability of GATT 1994 Article XX defense to inconsistencies with the agreements in Annex 1A to the WTO Agreement (which are goods-related) and

(2) The General Exceptions defenses are not examined unless invoked by the respondent.[33]

(3) Even if set as exceptions to the GATT 1994/GATS obligations, the General Exceptions are on a par with the other GATT obligations in pursuing the general objectives of the WTO.[34]

(4) Regarding the substantive obligations violated and General Exception paragraphs invoked in GATT/WTO disputes the following observations can be made:

 (a) Although the General Exceptions are defenses to violations of any one of the GATT 1994/GATS obligations, the majority of disputes regarding the General Exceptions have dealt with violations of MFN, national treatment and/or quotas and other quantitative restrictions;[35]

 (b) Although the General Exceptions of the GATT 1994/GATS respectively contain a list of ten and five societal values or interests available for affirmative defense, the majority of the disputes involved measures: necessary to protect public morals (or to maintain public order)[36] (GATT 1994 Article XX(a)/GATS Article XIV(a)); necessary to protect human, animal or plant life or health (GATT 1994 Article XX(b)/GATS Article XIV(b));[37] necessary to secure compliance with laws or regulations which are not-inconsistent with the provisions of the GATT 1994/GATS … (GATT 1994 Article XX(d)/GATS Article XIV(c)); and relating to

---

even to WTO agreements other than those contained in Annex 1A, see, Yenkong Ngangjoh-Hodu 'Relationship of GATT Article XX Exceptions to Other WTO Agreements', *Nordic Journal of International Law*, 80(2): 2011, pp. 232–233. See also, Senai W. Andemariam, 'Can (Should) Article XX(b) GATT Be a Defense against Inconsistencies with the SPS and TBT Agreements?', *Journal of World Investment and Trade*, 7(4): 2006, pp. 519–544.

33 GATT Panel Report, *EEC – Parts and Components* (*1990*), para. 5.11, *referring to*, GATT Panel Report, *US – Manufacturing Clause* (*1984*), paras. 34, 42(i); GATT Panel Report, *US – Tuna I* (*Mexico*) (*1991*), para. 5.22.

34 See Sub-section 8.1.1.

35 In fact, the Appellate Body, whether intentionally or simply by way of illustration, made a special reference to GATT Articles I, III and XI in elaborating the contextual correlation in the analysis of the General Agreement and the General Exceptions. Appellate Body Report, *US – Gasoline* (*1996*), p. 18. See also, Appellate Body Report, *US – Shrimp* (*1998*), para. 150.

36 GATS Article XIV(a) which is similar to the GATT 1994 Article XX(a) has the additional phrase "public order" which Diebold calls a "surprising difference". Nicolas F. Diebold, 'The Morals and Order Exceptions in WTO Law: Balancing the Toothless Tiger and the Undermining Mole', *Journal of International Economic Law*, 11(1): 2007, p. 44.

37 No measure has yet been defended under GATS Article XIV(b).

the conservation of exhaustible natural resources ... (GATT 1994 Article XX(g))[38]; and

(c) In the majority of the disputes which discussed the General Exceptions, the respondents failed to pass the complex test of the General Exceptions (the paragraphs and the *chapeau*); only two defenses (one during the GATT era and the other during the WTO era) have succeeded (*US – Spring Assemblies* (*1983*) and *US – Shrimp* (*Article 21.5 – Malaysia*) (*2001*)).

(5) The increase[39] in disputes involving the General Exceptions has required dispute settlement organs to provide a workable construal of the key introductory words/phrases at the beginning of the paragraphs in the General Exceptions ('necessary', 'relating to', 'essential' etc.).[40] Thus, in the process of finding out whether the respondent has provisionally defended its measure under the General Exceptions paragraphs, the Appellate Body further dissected the examination of the paragraphs into two: (a) first, ensure that the disputed measure is *designed* to addresses the particular interest specified in in the respective paragraphs; and next, ensure that the required degree of connection (sufficient nexus) between the disputed measure and the relevant societal value or interest (which connection is identified by terms such as 'necessary', 'relating to', essential etc.) exists.[41]

---

38 In *EEC – Bananas II* (*1994*), the panel examined the application of Article XX(h) of the GATT 1947 and in *India – Solar Cells* (*2016*) the panel and Appellate Body examined the application of Article XX(j) of the GATT 1994.

39 The list of 55 GATT/WTO disputes where General Exceptions defenses were made shows that in some particular years (1994, 2001, 2005 and 2016) the defenses were invoked in at least three cases per year and in others (1988, 1990, 1992, 2004, 2008, 2009, 2010, 2014, 2015 and 2017) the defenses were invoked in at least two cases per year. A statistical summary of the rate on annual increase/decrease in the number of invocations has not been made in this book; however, it can be generally observed that the number and types of defenses under GATT 1994/GATS has not shown a decline over the years.

40 Appellate Body Report, *US – Gasoline* (*1996*), pp. 17–18.

41 Appellate Body Report, *US – Gambling* (*2005*), para. 292; Appellate Body Reports, *EC – Seal Products* (*2014*), para. 5.169; Appellate Body Report, *Colombia – Textiles* (*2016*), paras. 5.67–5.68; WTO Panel Report, *US – Tariff Measures on Certain Goods from China* (*2020*), paras. 7.109–7.112. The process of assessing whether the measure is designed to protect the relevant societal value or interest often requires a preliminary determination of what the policy objective pursued by the measure is and whether that policy objective is within the scope of the relevant paragraph in the General Exceptions. WTO Panel Report, *Brazil – Retreaded Tyres* (*2007*), paras. 7.40–7.43, 7.96; WTO Panel Report, *Brazil – Taxation* (*2017*), paras. 7.518–7.529, 7.551; *US – Tariff Measures on Certain Goods from China* (*2020*), para. 7.110.

(6) Of the key connecting terms, the term 'necessary' has been the most extensively analyzed term in the GATT/WTO General Exceptions disputes. The term 'relating to' has also been discussed in a number of disputes. The term 'essential' as it appears in the GATT 1994 Article XX(j) was interpreted for the first time in the *India – Solar Cells (2016)* dispute.[42]

(7) The WTO dispute settlement organs have found it fit to apply the interpretation developed for GATT 1994 Article XX to the similar provisions in GATS Article XIV and *vice versa*.[43]

(8) The interpretation once developed for the term 'necessary' has been applied similarly to the GATT 1994[44] and GATS[45] General Exceptions paragraphs which contain the term, regardless of the content of the policies embodied in those paragraphs.

8.1.4 *Rate of Success*

The statistic in this sub-section covers GATT/WTO disputes between February 1982 and December 2023. The General Exceptions have been invoked by respondents in a large number of disputes since the GATT years. In at least seven disputes (argued mainly under the TBT Agreement and the SPS Agreement), the defenses under Article XX of the GATT 1994 were held irrelevant mainly as a

---

42 WTO Panel Report, *India – Solar Cells (2016)*, paras. 7.334–7.382. In this dispute, the Appellate Body supported interpreting the term 'essential' in light of the term 'necessary'. Appellate Body Report, *India – Solar Cells (2016)*, para. 5.62. See also, WTO Panel Report, *EU – Energy Package (2018)*, paras. 7.1325–7.1381.

43 Appellate Body Report, *US – Gambling (2005)*, paras. 291–292; WTO Panel Report, *US – Gambling (2005)*, paras. 6.447–6.448. See also, WTO Panel Report, *Argentina – Financial Services (2015)*, paras. 7.585 and 7.590; WTO Panel Report, *China – Publications and Audiovisual Products (2010)*, para. 7.759; WTO Panel Reports, *EC – Seal Products (2014)*, para. 7.381.

44 The first Article XX cases involved paragraphs (d) and (g). When the first paragraph (b) dispute was brought to a GATT panel in the *Thailand-Cigarettes (1990)* case, the panel, confronted with the wisdom of applying the same interpretation provided for the word 'necessary' as earlier developed by the *US-Section 337 (1989)* panel, decided to apply the same interpretation for the term necessity in paragraph (b). GATT Panel Report, *Thailand – Cigarettes (1990)*, paras. 74–75. See also, Appellate Body Report, *EC – Asbestos (2001)*, paras. 171–172; WTO Panel Report, *US – Gambling (2005)*, paras. 6.475–6.478; Appellate Body Report, *US – Gambling (2005)*, paras. 291–292 (see, f.n. 349–351), 304–311; Appellate Body Report, *Brazil – Retreaded Tyres (2007)*, para. 141.

45 In justifying the wisdom of applying the same interpretation developed in Article XX disputes to the corresponding GATS Article XIV disputes, the Appellate Body referred to, *inter alia*, the similarity in structure, wording and purpose of the two provisions. Appellate Body Report, *US – Gambling (2005)*, paras. 291–292, 304–327.

result of the interpretative relationship between the GATT 1994 and the other two WTO agreements: (1) *EC – Hormones (US and Canada)* (*1998*); (2) *EC – Biotech* (*2006*); (3) *EC – Salmon (Norway)* (*2007*); (4) *US – COOL* (*2012*); (5) *US – Poultry (China)* (*2010*); (6) *US – Clove Cigarettes* (*2012*); and (7) *US – Animal Products (Argentina)* (*2015*).

In at least 55[46] other GATT/WTO disputes (14 GATT and 41 WTO disputes, three[47] of which included GATS General Exception arguments), the General Exception defense was raised and produced different results. The following may be considered an approximate summary of the results. The summary has been prepared cognizant of the fact that the Appellate Body has: (a) reversed the practices of the GATT/WTO panels on how to structurally read the General Exceptions; and (b) changed, or added to, the way the elements of the various paragraphs in the General Exceptions must be interpreted. The disputes are divided into two categories: GATT disputes and WTO disputes.

The 14 GATT era disputes are: (1) *US – Canadian Tuna* (*1982*); (2) *US – Spring Assemblies* (*1983*); (3) *Canada – FIRA* (*1984*); (4) *Japan – Agricultural Products I* (*1988*); (5) *Canada – Herring and Salmon* (*1988*); (6) *US – Section 337* (*1989*); (7) *EEC – Parts and Components* (*1990*); (8) *Thailand – Cigarettes* (*1990*); (9) *US – Tuna I (Mexico)* (*1991*); (10) *Canada – Provincial Liquor Boards (US)* (*1992*); (11) *US – Malt Beverages* (*1992*); (12) *EEC – Bananas II* (*1994*); (13) *US – Tuna II (EEC)* (*1994*); and (14) *US – Taxes on Automobiles* (*1994*). The 41 WTO era disputes are (1) *US – Gasoline* (*1996*); (2) *Canada – Periodicals* (*1997*); (3) *US – Shrimp* (*1998*); (4) *Korea – Various Measures on Beef* (*2001*); (5) *EC – Asbestos* (*2001*); (6) *Argentina – Hides and Leather* (*2001*); (7) *US – Shrimp (Article 21.5 – Malaysia)* (*2001*); (8) *Canada – Wheat Exports and Grain Imports* (*2004*); (9) *EC – Tariff Preferences* (*2004*); (10) *US – Gambling* (*2005*); (11) *Dominican Republic – Import and Sale of Cigarettes* (*2005*); (12) *EC – Trademarks and Geographical Indications (Australia)* (*2005*); (13) *EC – Trademarks and Geographical Indications (US)*

46 Some of the disputes counted as one may have had two or more Dispute Settlement (DS) numbers because of multiple complaints. For instance, *China – Raw Materials* (*2012*) had three complaints: WT/DS394 (complaint by the US); WT/DS395 (complaint by the European Union); and WT/DS398 (complaint by Mexico). If these individual complaints were numbered separately, the list of General Exception disputes *would have increased*. Moreover, please note that for the respective reasons mentioned in footnote numbers 48–50, the *Brazil – Taxation* (*2017*), *Indonesia – Import Licensing Regimes* (*2017*) and *EU – Energy Package* (*2018*) disputes have each been counted as two disputes (Nos. 31/32, 33/34 and 36/37 respectively in the WTO era disputes list); otherwise, the actual number of disputes discussed in this sub-section would have been slightly different.

47 *US – Gambling* (*2005*) (Article XIV(a) and (c)), *Argentina – Financial Services* (*2016*) (Article XIV(c)) and *EU – Energy Package* (*2018*).

(2005); (14) *Mexico – Taxes on Soft Drinks* (2006); (15) *Brazil – Retreaded Tyres* (2007); (16) *US – Customs Bond Directive* (2008); (17) *US – Shrimp (Thailand)* (2008); (18) *China – Auto Parts* (2009); (19) *Colombia – Ports of Entry* (2009); (20) *US – Poultry (China)* (2010); (21) *China – Publications and Audiovisual Products* (2010); (22) *Thailand – Cigarettes (Philippines)* (2011); (23) *China – Raw Materials* (2012); (24) *China – Rare Earths* (2014); (25) *EC – Seal Products* (2014); (26) *US – COOL (Article 21.5 – Canada and Mexico)* (2015); (27) *US – Tuna II (Mexico) (Article 21.5)* (2015); (28) *Argentina – Financial Services* (2016); (29) *Colombia – Textiles* (2016); (30) *India – Solar Cells* (2016); (31) *Brazil – Taxation* (2017); (32) *Brazil – Taxation* (2017);[48] (33) *Indonesia – Import Licensing Regimes* (2017); (34) *Indonesia – Import Licensing Regimes* (2017);[49] (35) *Indonesia – Chicken* (2017); (36) *EU – Energy Package* (2018); (37) *EU – Energy Package* (2018);[50] (38) *US – Tuna II (Mexico) (Article 21.5 II)* (2019); (39) *US – Tariff Measures on Certain Goods from China* (2020); (40) *Indonesia – Raw Materials* (2022); and (41) *Turkey – Pharmaceutical Products (EU)* (2022).

The rate of wins and losses in these General Exceptions disputes and the observations from the statistics are presented below.

Regarding the number of disputes won by the respondents, in only four of the above-listed disputes (i.e., 7.3% of the total number of disputes) has the respondent been fully successful under the General Exceptions defense. These are *US – Spring Assemblies* (1983) (GATT 1947 Article XX(d)), *EC – Asbestos* (2001), (GATT 1994 Article XX(b)), *US – Shrimp (Article 21.5 – Malaysia)* (2001) (GATT 1994 Article XX(g)) and *US – Tuna II (Mexico) (Article 21.5 II)* (2019) (GATT 1994 Article XX(g)).[51]

---

48 The *Brazil – Taxation* (2017) dispute has been listed twice because Brazil defended a couple of measures (known by their acronyms as the PATVD and INOVAR-AUTO) separately under Articles XX(a) and XX(d)/(g) respectively. Both defenses were lost at the 'connecting terms' level (i.e., the 'necessary' and 'relating to' levels, although the paragraph (g) defense also failed at the 'even-handedness level).

49 The *Indonesia – Import Licensing Regimes* (2017) dispute has been listed twice because, as mentioned in Sub-section 8.1.2 above, two groups of measures which were defended under paragraphs (a), (b) and (d) of Article XX failed at the 'necessity' test of the paragraphs and the third group defended under paragraph (b) failed at the *chapeau* level.

50 The *EU – Energy Package* (2018) dispute has been listed twice because the European Union made two separate defenses for two separate measures under Article XIV(a) of the GATS and Article XX(j) of the GATT 1994 respectively. Thus, if the *Brazil – Taxation* (2017), *Indonesia – Import Licensing Regimes* (2017) and *EU – Energy Package* (2018) had been counted as one dispute each, the actual number of disputes discussed in this sub-section would have been slightly different.

51 In *EC – Asbestos* (2001), the panel, after finding an inconsistency with GATT 1994 Article III:4, examined whether the European Communities could justify its measure under Article XX(b). The panel concluded that the contested measure met the requirements

In the other 51 instances of reliance on the General Exceptions (i.e., 92.7% of the total instances of reliance on the General Exceptions), the respondents were not successful. In other words, to use Van den Bossche and Zdouc's wording, the General Exceptions were "'unsuccessfully' or 'incorrectly'"[52] invoked in 92.7% of the instances of reliance on the General Exceptions at different levels. These 51 instances have been identified as 'lost disputes'. In tune with the three steps of examining the General Exceptions identified by the Appellate Body, one can categorize the stages at which the respondents' case was lost as follows: (1) *losses at the level of the design of the measures* (i.e., disputes where the respondents were unable to prove that the measures were designed to protect the relevant societal value or interest indicated in the paragraphs); (2) *losses due to failure to prove the connecting terms* (i.e., disputes where the respondents, despite proving that the measures were designed to protect the relevant societal value or interest indicated in the paragraphs, were unable to connect the measures with the value or interest by proving that the measures were 'necessary', 'relating to', 'essential', etc.); and (3) *losses due to failure to prove the requirements of the* chapeau (i.e., disputes where the respondents provisionally justified their measures at the level of the paragraphs, but failed the test of the *chapeau*). In some of the disputes, the defenses were made under more than one paragraph of the General Exceptions or defended both under the GATT 1994 and the GATS. If in a given dispute the respondent had invoked more than one paragraph of the General Exceptions and lost the defense, such loss has been counted as one.[53]

Let us begin with the *losses at the level of the design of the measures*. In 14 of the 51 lost disputes (i.e., 27.5% of the 51 lost disputes or 25.5% of all the 55 disputes where the General Exceptions were invoked), the respondents were

of paragraph (b) and the *chapeau*. On appeal, the Appellate Body reversed the panel on its finding on Article III:4 (i.e., the Appellate Body found no inconsistency with Article III:4), hence no need for the EC to justify its measure under Article XX(b). Nevertheless, the Appellate Body examined the panel's analysis of Article XX(b) defense and upheld the panel's findings. Thus, the *EC – Asbestos (2001)* has been included in the 'win' list.

52 Van den Bossche and Zdouc, above note 1, p. 556, f.n. 48.

53 The only exceptions where the disputes have been counted twice are *Brazil – Taxation (2017)*, *Indonesia – Import Licensing Regimes (2017)* and *EU – Energy Package (2018)* because the simultaneous defenses: (a) were lost at the level of two different connecting terms ('necessary' and 'relating to') (*Brazil – Taxation (2017)*); (b) despite being argued under paragraphs (a), (b) and (d) which carry the same connecting term 'necessary, were, however lost at different stages (at the connecting term level and at the *chapeau* level) (*Indonesia – Import Licensing Regimes (2017)*); or (c) were defended under the GATT and GATS (*EU – Energy Package (2018)*), hence the need to count them twice. See also, above notes 48–50.

unable to prove the justifications at the level of the design of the measures linked to the different paragraphs of the General Exceptions.[54]

Regarding the *losses due to failure to prove the connecting terms*, in 27 of the 51 lost disputes (i.e., 52.9% of the 51 lost disputes or 49.1% of all the 55 disputes where the General Exceptions were invoked), the respondents were unable to prove that their measures were 'necessary', 'relating to', 'essential', 'involving' etc. All of the respondents' losses at the level of the connecting terms+ involved either the term 'necessary' or 'relating to'. 24 of the 27 disputes lost due to failure to prove the connecting terms (i.e., 88.9% of the disputes lost due to failure to prove the connecting terms, or 47% of the 51 lost disputes or 43.6% of all the 55 disputes where the General Exceptions were invoked) were lost because the respondents were unable to prove that their measures were 'necessary' to achieve the value or social interest contained in one or more of the three General Exceptions paragraphs.[55] Three of the 27 disputes lost due to

---

54 The disputes are: (1) *Japan – Agricultural Products I* (*1988*); (2) EEC – *Parts and Components* (*1990*); (3) *Canada – Provincial Liquor Boards (US)* (*1992*); (4) *US – Taxes on Automobiles* (*1994*); (5) EEC – *Bananas II* (*1994*); (6) EC – *Tariff Preferences* (*2004*); (7) *US – Poultry (China)* (*2010*); (8) *Thailand – Cigarettes (Philippines)* (*2011*); (9) *China – Raw Materials* (*2012*); (10) *China – Rare Earths* (*2014*); (11) *US* – COOL (*Article 21.5 – Canada and Mexico*) (*2015*); (12) *India – Solar Cells* (*2016*); (13) *EU – Energy Package* (*2018*) [for the defense under Article XX(j) of the GATT]; and (14) *Turkey – Pharmaceutical Products (EU)* (*2022*). In *Canada – Provincial Liquor Boards (US)* (*1992*), Canada opted not to use Article XX(d), but made an alternative argument under Article XX(b). The panel, pursuant to Canada's choice, did not discuss Article XX(d), but for reasons that are not clear did not examine the defense under Article XX(b). GATT Panel Report, *Canada – Provincial Liquor Boards (US)* (*1992*), paras. 4.73, 5.15.

55 The disputes are: (1) *Canada* – FIRA (*1984*); (2) *US – Section 337* (*1989*); (3) *Thailand – Cigarettes* (*1990*); (4) *US – Tuna I (Mexico)* (*1991*); (5) *US – Malt Beverages* (*1992*); (6) *US – Tuna II* (*1994*); (7) *Canada – Periodicals* (*1997*); (8) *Korea – Various Measures on Beef* (*2001*); (9) *Canada – Wheat Exports and Grain Imports* (*2004*); (10) *Dominican Republic – Import and Sale of Cigarettes* (*2005*); (11) EC – *Trademarks and Geographical Indications (Australia)* (*2005*); (12) EC – *Trademarks and Geographical Indications (US)* (*2005*); (13) *Mexico – Taxes on Soft Drinks* (*2006*); (14) *US – Customs Bond Directive* (*2008*); (15) *US – Shrimp (Thailand)* (*2008*); (16) *China – Auto Parts* (*2009*); (17) *Colombia – Ports of Entry* (*2009*); (18) *China – Publications and Audiovisual Products* (*2010*); (19) *Colombia – Textiles* (*2016*); (20) *Brazil – Taxation* (*2017*) [for the GATT 1994 Article XX(a) and (d)]; (21) *Indonesia – Import Licensing Regimes* (*2017*) [for the two groups of measures which were defended under paragraphs (a), (b) and (d) of Article XX]; (22) *Indonesia – Chicken* (*2017*); (23) *US – Tariff Measures on Certain Goods from China* (*2020*); and (24) *Indonesia – Raw Materials* (*2022*). In *US – Tuna I (Mexico)* (*1991*) and *US – Tuna II* (*1994*), the US made defenses under paragraphs (b), (d) and (g) of the GATT 1947 Article XX, but failed the necessity test of paragraph (b) (hence including this case in this list), the test of the design of the measures under paragraph (d) and the 'relating to' test of paragraph (g). GATT Panel Report, *US – Tuna I (Mexico)* (*1991*), paras. 5.22–5.40; GATT Panel Report, *US – Tuna II* (*1994*), paras. 5.11–5.43.

failure to prove the connecting terms (i.e., 11.1% of the disputes lost due to failure to prove the connecting terms, or 5.9% of the 51 lost disputes or 5.5% of all the 55 disputes where the General Exceptions were invoked) were lost because the respondents were unable to prove that their measures were 'relating to' the value or social interest contained in the GATT Article XX(g).[56]

Regarding the *losses due to failure to prove the requirements of the* chapeau, in 10 of the 51 'lost' disputes (i.e., 19.6% of the 51 lost disputes or 18.2% of all the 55 disputes where the General Exceptions were invoked), the respondents were unable to meet the requirements of the *chapeau* after provisionally justifying their measures under the respective General Exceptions paragraphs. Seven out of these 10 losses (i.e., 70% of the cases lost at the *chapeau* level, 13.7% of the 51 lost disputes or 12.7% of all the 55 disputes where the General Exceptions were invoked) were occasioned after passing the test of the paragraphs with the connecting term 'necessary'.[57] Three out of these 10 losses (i.e., 30% of the cases lost at the *chapeau* level, 5.9% of the 51 lost disputes or 5.5% of all the 55 disputes where the General Exceptions were invoked) were occasioned after passing the test of the paragraph with the connecting term 'relating to'.[58]

A tabulated presentation of the win-loss rate in the General Exception disputes looks as indicated in the next page.

8.1.5 *Observations on the Win-Loss Rates under the General Exception Defenses*

This sub-section presents some general observations regarding the win-loss rates under the General Exception defenses in the GATT/WTO era and the necessity defense in particular.

The rate of losing the General Exceptions defense for more than 40 years (between February 1982 and December 2023) has been much higher (around

In *Colombia – Textiles (2016)*, Colombia made defenses under paragraphs (a) and (d) of the GATT 1947 Article XX, but lost its defense for lack of clarity of its 'necessity' defense which appears in both paragraphs. Appellate Body Report, *Colombia – Textiles (2016)*, paras. 6.4–6.10.

56 The disputes are: (1) *US – Canadian Tuna (1982)*; (2) *Canada – Herring and Salmon (1988)*; and (3) *Brazil – Taxation (2017)* [for the defense under Article XX(g) of the GATT 1994].

57 The disputes are: (1) *Argentina – Hides and Leather (2001)*; (2) *US – Gambling (2005)*; (3) *Brazil – Retreaded Tyres (2007)*; (4) *EC – Seal Products (2014)*; (5) *Argentina – Financial Services (2016)*; (6) *Indonesia – Import Licensing Regimes (2017)* [for the one measure which was defended under paragraph (b) of Article XX]; and (7) *EU – Energy Package (2018)* [for the defense under Article XIV(a) of the GATS].

58 The disputes are: (1) *US – Gasoline (1996)*; (2) *US – Shrimp (1998)*; and (3) *US – Tuna II (Mexico) (Article 21.5) (2015)*.

TABLE 1 Tabulated presentation of the win-loss rate of 55 GATT/WTO General Exception disputes (1982–2023)

<table>
<tr><th colspan="8">62 General Exception invocations</th></tr>
<tr><th>7 invocations rejected</th><th colspan="6">55 accepted invocations (100%)</th><th>Percentile</th></tr>
<tr><td></td><td>4 invocations won (7.3%)</td><td colspan="5">51 invocations lost (92.7%)</td><td>100%</td></tr>
<tr><td></td><td></td><td>14 lost at the level of the design of the measure (27.5%)</td><td colspan="2">27 lost due to failure to prove connecting term (52.9%)</td><td colspan="2">10 lost due to failure to prove the requirements of the chapeau (19.6%)</td><td>100%</td></tr>
<tr><td></td><td></td><td>14 lost at the level of the design of the measure (27.5%)</td><td>3 lost due to failure to prove that the measure was ‘relating to’ (5.9%)</td><td>24 lost due to failure to prove that the measure was ‘necessary’ (47%)</td><td>3 failed after passing the test of the paragraph with the connecting term ‘relating to’ (5.9%)</td><td>7 failed after passing the test of the paragraphs with the connecting term ‘necessary’ (13.7%)</td><td>100%</td></tr>
</table>

12.7 times) than that of winning (i.e., a win/loss ratio 92.7% and 7.3% respectively). This is despite the Appellate Body's instruction not to read the General Exceptions narrower than the other provisions in the GATT 1994 or the GATS. One report which made an arguably extreme conclusion about the record dubbed the win/loss ratio a "dismal record"[59] and called for drastic changes in the process of interpretation of the General Exceptions (such as placing all the burdens of proof on the complainant) if, for instance, General Exceptions-like provisions are inserted in investment treaties. Van den Bossche and Zdouc, on the other hand, while acknowledging the very low rate of successful reliance on the General Exceptions make two important observations:

> First, many of the otherwise GATT-inconsistent measures adopted to promote or protect societal values, which were initially found non-justifiable under Article XX, were subsequently modified (rather than withdrawn) in accordance with the DSB recommendations and rulings, and were *not* further challenged. Secondly, Members adopt or maintain very many otherwise GATT-inconsistent measures to promote or protect societal values, which clearly meet the requirements of Article XX. These measures seldom go to WTO dispute settlement. Therefore, the limited success Members have had in invoking Article XX does *not* indicate that Article XX plays only a marginal role in allowing WTO Members to adopt or maintain otherwise GATT-inconsistent measures to promote or protect societal values. Rather, the opposite is true.[60]

Regarding the experience with the necessity defense in the General Exceptions disputes, it was noted that 24 out of the 27 disputes lost due to failure to prove the connecting terms concerned failure to prove that the measure was 'necessary'.[61] Moreover, in 7 out of the 10 disputes lost due to failure to prove the requirements of the *chapeau* the respondent successfully invoked a paragraph with the connecting term 'necessary'.[62] Thus, the defense of 'necessity' occupied 60.1% (i.e., 31 out) of the 51 lost disputes or 56.4% (i.e., 30 out) of all the 55 disputes where the General Exceptions were invoked. It is admitted here

59 *Only One of 44 Attempts to Use the GATT Article XX/GATS Article XIV "General Exception" Has Ever Succeeded: Replicating the WTO Exception Construct Will Not Provide for an Effective TPP General Exception*, available at, https://www.citizen.org/documents/general-exception.pdf, p. 1.

60 Van den Bossche and Zdouc, above note 1, p. 556.

61 Above note 55.

62 Above note 57.

that the fact that the term 'necessary' is contained in three of the General Exceptions paragraphs may have contributed to the large number of defenses made under the paragraphs that contain the term. Nevertheless, this high proportion of reliance on the necessity defense is testament to the importance that necessity has occupied in the regime of defenses in WTO law specifically and, through that, in PIL generally. It is, thus, important to discuss, as shown in Chapter 12, the interplay between the concepts of necessity in WTO law and the other fields of international law.

8.2 Interpreting the Term 'Necessary' in the General Exceptions

This section presents the evolution of the interpretation of the term 'necessary' in the General Exceptions during the GATT and WTO eras respectively. Although the interpretation of the concept has been in a continuous development since the GATT era, the discussions have been split into the GATT and WTO eras to highlight the shift of the interpretation of the term from the GATT era to the WTO era.

Once the respondent has shown that the measure in dispute falls within the scope of the policy objectives under Article XX(a), (b) or (d) of the GATT 1994 or Article XIV (a), (b) or (c) of the GATS, the next challenge is to show that the disputed measure is *necessary* to implement the policy objectives contained in the paragraphs. The term 'necessary', like other terms inserted at the beginning of all General Exceptions paragraphs, is understood as showing the intent of the drafters on the various levels (degrees) of connections that exist between the disputed measures and the policies or state interests.[63] Hence, in Article XX of the GATT 1994, for example, the term 'necessary' (as listed in paragraphs (a), (b) and (d)) is different in its degree of connection to the state interests referred to in those paragraphs from the terms 'relating to' (as referred to in paragraphs (c), (e) and (g)), 'essential' (paragraph (j)) and 'involving' (paragraph (i)).[64] This section will show the GATT/WTO dispute settlement organs have developed a structured, although complex, interpretation for the term 'necessary' in the General Exceptions. In the words of Charnovitz:

63 Appellate Body Report, *US – Gasoline (1996)*, pp. 17–18; Appellate Body Report, *US – Gambling (2005)*, paras. 291–292.

64 GATT Panel Report, *Canada – Herring and Salmon (1988)*, para. 4.6; GATT Panel Report, *US – Taxes on Automobiles (1994)*, para. 5.63; WTO Panel Report, *US – Gasoline (1996)*, para. 6.39.

> The challenge ... has not been in identifying measures that actually fit within [the paragraphs]; rather, the challenge has been to show that a contested measure is 'necessary' ... The method to be used in determining whether the challenged measure is 'necessary' (to achieve its intended purpose) is *difficult* to outline succinctly because the jurisprudence is *confusing* (*emphasis added*).[65]

The development of the interpretation of the term 'necessary' started with the *US – Spring Assemblies* (*1983*) dispute and continues to develop. The development of the interpretation by the GATT panels is first presented in Subsection 8.2.1. At least six GATT panels (*US – Spring Assemblies* (*1983*), *Canada – FIRA* (*1984*), *US – Section 337* (*1989*), *Thailand – Cigarettes* (*1990*), *US – Tuna I* (*Mexico*) (*1991*) and *US – Malt Beverages* (*1992*)) explained their interpretation of the term 'necessary' in GATT Article XX. The first four of these disputes will be discussed. The last two of these disputes will not be discussed because the analysis of the panels on the term 'necessary' was focused mainly on the application of the interpretation developed earlier on by the previous panels.

8.2.1 *The GATT Era Interpretation of Necessity in the GATT 1947 General/ Security Exceptions Paragraphs*

The interpretation of the concept of necessity in the GATT 1947 General Exceptions paragraphs went to three stages.

The *US – Spring Assemblies* (*1983*) panel was the first panel that interpreted the concept of necessity. After finding that a measure taken under Section 337 of the 1930 US Tariff Act was inconsistent with Article III:4 of the GATT, the panel had to determine whether the measure could be defended under Article XX(d). The panel first found that the US Patent Law was consistent with the GATT 1947, and then examined whether the measure at issue was 'necessary' to secure compliance with the US Patent Law. In defining the word 'necessary' the panel "examined *whether a satisfactory and effective alternative existed* under civil court procedures which would have provided the patent holder ... a sufficiently effective remedy against the violation of its patent by foreign producers including the Canadian producer (*emphasis added*)".[66] Thus, for the panel a

65 Charnovitz, above note 24, p. 697. Such difficulty or confusion is in part due to the fact that the term 'necessary' is not textually defined in the GATT 1994 and the GATS. Cottier *et al.* rightly stated that "[t]he 'necessity' test in Article XX GATT and Article XIV GATS is not defined in the agreements itself and was mainly developed over time through jurisprudence." Thomas Cottier *et al.* 'The Principle of Proportionality in International Law: Foundations and Variations', *Journal of World Investment & Trade*, 18(4): 2017, p. 646.

66 GATT Panel Report, *US – Spring Assemblies* (*1983*), para. 58.

measure would be 'necessary' under Article XX only if there were no better alternatives to accomplish the desired objective. Such interpretation of the term 'necessary' by the *US – Spring Assemblies (1983)* panel would later become instrumental for the current WTO law interpretation of the term.[67]

The *Canada – FIRA (1984)* panel first found the disputed measure to be inconsistent with Article III:4 of the GATT 1947. In determining whether the measure could be defended under Article XX(d), it first found that the Canadian Foreign Investment Review Act was consistent with the GATT and the examined whether the measure was 'necessary' to secure compliance with that law. The panel did not provide sufficient reasoning why it concluded that the measures were not 'necessary'. In fact, the record shows that the panel jumped to the conclusion through a rather vague statement. The panel stated, in relevant part, that it:

> *was not clear to the Panel why a detailed review of investment proposals without purchasing requirements would not be sufficient to enable the Canadian government to determine whether the proposed investments were or were likely to be of significant benefit to Canada* within the meaning of Section 2 of the [FIRA]. (*emphasis added*).[68]

Here the panel used common sense in deciding whether the domestic purchase requirements were *essential to attainment of the goals* of the law. The panel made a loose conclusion by just stating that without the domestic purchase requirements the aims of the FIRA could still be attained.

The importance of setting the standard for the word 'necessary' did not get much attention until the 1989 case that revisited Section 337 of the 1930 US Tariff Act: the *US – Section 337 (1989)* dispute to which the credit for the first working interpretation of the term can be given.[69] The panel first found

67 For a good summary of the evolution of the concept of necessity, see, Deborah Akoth Osiro, 'GATT/WTO Necessity Analysis: Evolutionary Interpretation and its Impact on the Autonomy of Domestic Regulation', *Legal Issues of Economic Integration*, 29(2): 2002, pp. 123–141; Ingo Venzke, 'Making General Exceptions: The Spell of Precedents in Developing Article XX GATT into Standards for Domestic Regulatory Policy', *German Law Journal*, 12(5): 2011, pp. 1111–1140. A more comprehensive elaboration of necessity test in the GATT 1994, GATS and other WTO agreements (TRIPS, SPS, TBT) has been presented in Fei-Chen Hsiao's Master's Thesis, *Necessity Test in the Jurisprudence of the Appellate Body of the World Trade Organization*, World Trade Institute's MILE 5 Program, September 2005, pp. 6–71.

68 GATT Panel Report, *Canada – FIRA (1984)*, para. 5.20.

69 Gisele Kapterian, 'A Critique of the WTO Jurisprudence on "Necessity"', *International and Comparative Law Quarterly*, 59(1): 2010, p. 101.

that Section 337 of the 1930 US Tariff Act was inconsistent with Article III:4 and accepted the various interpretations presented by the parties regarding the interpretation of the defense under Article XX(d) in general and the term 'necessary' in particular. After noting the differences in these varying interpretations of the parties regarding the term 'necessary, the panel then outlined what may be called the working definition of the term 'necessary' for many years to come:

> It was clear to the Panel that a contacting party cannot justify a measure inconsistent with another GATT provision as 'necessary' in terms of Article XX(d) *if an alternative measure which it could reasonably be expected to employ and which is not inconsistent with other GATT provisions is available to it*. By the same token in cases *where a measure consistent with other GATT provisions is not reasonably available, a contracting party is bound to use, among the measures reasonably available to it, that which entails the least degree of inconsistency with other GATT provisions*. The Panel wished to make it clear that this does not mean that a contracting party could be asked to change its substantive patent law or its desired level of enforcement of that law, provided that such law and such level of enforcement are the same for imported and domestically-produced products. However, it does mean that, if a contracting party could reasonably secure that level of enforcement in a manner that is not inconsistent with other GATT provisions, it would be required to do so (*emphasis added*).[70]

In this dispute, unlike in *US – Spring Assemblies (1983)* where the measure at issue was held to be the exclusion order given under Section 337, the panel held that the measure at issue that had to be 'necessary' was Section 337 itself.[71] Using the above-cited interpretation, the panel found an alternative and held that Section 337 was not a 'necessary' measure under Article XX(d)

70 GATT Panel Report, *US – Section 337 (1989)*, para. 5.26.

71 Mavroidis states that in *US – Gasoline (1996)* (p. 16), the Appellate Body opted for a wider interpretation of the term 'measure' when it disagreed with the panel which had ruled that it was the 'less favorable treatment' that must be examined under the GATT 1994 Article XX. After stating that the Appellate Body used the same interpretation of the term 'measure' in the *Thailand – Cigarettes (Philippines) (2011)* dispute (para. 177), Mavroidis shares his doubts whether the Appellate Body used the same interpretation when examining the contested measure in the *EC – Seal Products (2014)* dispute (para[s]. [5.185 and] 5.190). Mavroidis, above note 7, pp. 425–426. See also, the Appellate Body's observation on the issue in *Argentina – Financial Services (2016)*, paras. 6.164–6.179.

of the GATT 1947. Para. 5.26 of the panel's report cited above may be identified as the foundation for the interpretation developed for the term 'necessary' in the General Exceptions. As we shall later discuss in Sub-section 8.2.2 below, the WTO Appellate Body referred to this paragraph when laying out its 'weighing and balancing' test. However, the panel in *US – Section 337 (1989)* did not explain how (or why) it came up with the test they introduced through para. 5.26 of the report. The context of the paragraph does not explain the origin of the test either. Sub-section 8.2.3 will discuss the likely origin of the test.

The three GATT disputes discussed above where the term 'necessary' was interpreted were related to paragraph (d) of Article XX. In *Thailand – Cigarettes (1990)* an issue arose whether a measure was found to be inconsistent with GATT Article XI and the respondent justified the disputed measure under, *inter alia*, Article XX(b). in examining the measure under Article XX(b), the first acknowledged that an earlier panel (the *US – Section 337 (1989)*) "had discussed the meaning of the term 'necessary' in the context of Article XX(d)"[72] and stated that since the objective of both paragraphs is "to allow contracting parties to impose trade restrictive measures inconsistent with the General Agreement to pursue overriding public policy goals to the extent that such inconsistencies were unavoidable", it "could see no reason why under Article XX the meaning of the term 'necessary' under paragraph (d) should not be the same as in paragraph (b)" and that the difference in the objectives pursued by both paragraphs "did not justify a different interpretation of the term 'necessary'".[73]

The two key notions of the interpretation of the term as developed by the *US – Section 337 (1989)* and *Thailand – Cigarettes (1990)* panels and followed by the subsequent GATT panels that dwelt on the term (such as the *US – Tuna I (Mexico) (1991)* and *US – Malt Beverages (1992)* panels) may be summarized as follows. Firstly, the panels required that for a measure to be 'necessary' there should not be any reasonably available GATT-consistent or less GATT-inconsistent measures. It must be noted here that the panels did not state that for measure to be 'necessary' under the General Exceptions, it should be the only measure (as Article 25 of the ARSIWA would require for necessity [see Section 5.4]). Secondly, the phrase 'an alternative measure which [the respondent] could reasonably be expected to employ' meant that the burden is on the respondent to show that there were no reasonably available GATT-consistent or less GATT-inconsistent measures.[74] It will be shown in Sub-section 8.2.2 that

72 GATT Panel Report, *Thailand – Cigarettes (1990)*, para. 74.

73 Ibid.

74 Klabbers, above note 4, p. 89.

under the existing interpretation, it is for the complaining party to point at the alternatives and for the respondent to show that they are not reasonably available.[75]

8.2.2 *The WTO Era Interpretation of Necessity in the GATT 1994/GATS General Exceptions Paragraphs*

In *Korea – Various Measures on Beef (2001)*, the first WTO dispute that involved a GATT 1994 Article XX paragraph that contains the term 'necessary', the Appellate Body embarked on an interpretation of the term that 'has evolved considerably over the years'.[76] After finding, by reversing the panel, that the Dual Retail System introduced under the Korean Unfair Competition Act breached Article III:4 of the GATT by leading to a *de facto* discrimination to the detriment of imported beef 1994,[77] the Appellate Body proceeded to examine if the measure could be justified under Article XX(d). In providing meaning to the term 'necessary', the Appellate Body first referred, with caution, to the dictionary meaning of the term 'necessary', a term which "normally denotes something 'that cannot be dispensed with or done without, requisite, essential, needful'".[78] The 'caution' that the Appellate Body referred to was that the term 'necessary':

> must be considered in the connection in which it is used, as it is a word susceptible of various meanings. It may import absolute physical necessity or inevitability, or it may import that which is only convenient, useful, appropriate, suitable, proper, or conducive to the end sought. It is an adjective expressing degrees, and may express mere convenience or that which is indispensable or an absolute physical necessity.[79]

The Appellate Body's statements in the subsequent paragraph, repeatedly referred to thereafter,[80] would lay the foundation for the WTO-era

75 Appellate Body Report, *US – Gambling* (*2005*), paras. 309–311. See also, Appellate Body Report, *Brazil – Retreaded Tyres* (*2007*), para. 156; Appellate Body Reports, *EC – Seal Products* (*2014*), para. 5.261.

76 Van den Bossche and Zdouc, above note 1, p. 559.

77 Appellate Body Report, *Korea – Various Measures on Beef* (*2001*), paras. 134–136, 142–144.

78 Ibid, para. 160.

79 Ibid.

80 For instance, see, WTO Panel Report, *US – Gambling* (*2005*), para. 6.475; Appellate Body Report, *US – Gambling* (*2005*), para. 310; WTO Panel Report, *EC – Trademarks and Geographical Indications* (*US*) (*2005*), para. 7.298; Appellate Body Report, *Brazil – Retreaded Tyres* (*2007*), para. 141; WTO Panel Report, *Colombia – Ports of Entry* (*2009*), para.

understanding of the term 'necessary' and some other related phrases in Article XX (such as the term 'essential'):[81]

> We believe that, as used in the context of Article XX(d) [and as would later be applied to paragraphs (a) and (b)], the reach of the word 'necessary' is not limited to that which is 'indispensable' or 'of absolute necessity' or 'inevitable'. *Measures which are indispensable or of absolute necessity or inevitable to secure compliance certainly fulfil the [necessity] requirements of Article XX(d)*. But other measures, too, may fall within the ambit of this exception. As used in Article XX(d), the term 'necessary' refers, in our view, to a range of degrees of necessity. At one end of this continuum lies 'necessary' understood as 'indispensable'; at the other end, is 'necessary' taken to mean as 'making a contribution to'. We consider that *a 'necessary' measure is, in this continuum, located significantly closer to the pole of 'indispensable' than to the opposite pole of simply 'making a contribution to'* (*emphasis added*).[82]

Immediately after introducing its 'continuum' concept for generally placing the necessity of a measure significantly to the pole of 'indispensability' than the other pole of 'making contribution to', the Appellate Body laid out the so-called 'weighing and balancing' test which has hitherto been repeatedly recited[83] as the standard for the preliminary[84] conclusion of whether the contested measure is necessary or not:

7.546; WTO Panel Reports, *China – Raw Materials* (*2012*), para. 7.480; and Appellate Body Reports, *EC – Seal Products* (*2014*), f.n. 1300.

81 On application of the *Korea-Beef* 'continuum' interpretation to the term 'essential' in the GATT 1994 Article XX(j), see, Appellate Body Report, *India – Solar Cells* (*2016*), para. 5.62.

82 Appellate Body Report, *Korea – Various Measures on Beef* (*2001*), para. 161.

83 See, Appellate Body Report, *EC – Asbestos* (*2001*), para. 172; WTO Panel Report, *US – Gambling* (*2005*), paras. 6.476–6.477; Appellate Body Report, *US – Gambling* (*2005*), paras. 305–306; WTO Panel Report, *EC – Trademarks and Geographical Indications* (*US*) (*2005*), para. 7.449; Appellate Body Report, *Brazil – Retreaded Tyres* (*2007*), paras. 142–143; WTO Panel Report, *Colombia – Ports of Entry* (*2009*), para. 7.547; WTO Panel Report, *China – Publications and Audiovisual Products* (*2010*), paras. 7.782–7.786; WTO Panel Reports, *China – Raw Materials* (*2012*), para. 7.480; Appellate Body Reports, *EC – Seal Products* (*2014*), paras. 5.169, 5.214–5.215; WTO Panel Report, *Colombia – Textiles* (*2016*), para. 7.403; Appellate Body Report, *Colombia – Textiles* (*2016*), para. 5.102; and Appellate Body Report, *India – Solar Cells* (*2016*), para. 5.59; WTO Panel Reports, *Brazil – Taxation* (*2017*), para. 7.524; WTO Panel Report, *Indonesia – Chicken* (*2017*), paras. 7.136, 7.224, 7.420; *EU – Energy Package* (*2018*), paras. 7.1209, 7.1359.

84 At the 'weighing and balancing' test level, a measure which has passed the test is only preliminarily necessary because its trade-restrictiveness and contribution to achieve the

> In sum, determination of whether a measure, which is not 'indispensable',[85] may nevertheless be 'necessary' within the contemplation of Article XX(d), involves in every case a process of weighing and balancing a series of factors which prominently include the contribution made by the compliance measure to the enforcement of the law or regulation at issue, the importance of the common interests or values protected by that law or regulation, and the accompanying impact of the law or regulation on imports or exports.[86]

The Appellate Body, in introducing the 'weighing and balancing' test, made it clear that it was not deviating from, or replacing, the long-held *US – Section 337 (1989)* interpretation of necessity which focused on finding WTO-consistent/least inconsistent alternatives.[87] Like the *US – Section 337 (1989)* panel, however, the Appellate Body did not, except for a dictionary meaning of the term 'necessary' as well as for references to its interpretation in *US – Shrimp (1998)* of the term 'relating to' in Article XX(g) and the Preamble to the GATT 1994,[88] explain how or why it came up with the 'weighing and balancing' test through

objective has to be compared with the trade-restrictiveness and contribution of WTO-consistent alternatives that the complaining party identifies. In recent cases, however, panels have begun to combine the three elements of the 'weighing and balancing' test with the additional requirement of comparing the measure with alternatives so that there are 'four' elements and, hence, no need for a 'preliminary' passing of necessity test. See, for example, WTO Panel Reports, *Brazil – Taxation (2017)*, paras. 7.524–7.531; WTO Panel Report, *Indonesia – Chicken (2017)*, paras. 7.136, 7.224, 7.420.

85 Obviously, the 'weighing and balancing' test applies mainly to measures that are *not* 'indispensable', 'absolutely necessary' or 'inevitable' as the Appellate Body (in para. 161) stated, "Measures which are indispensable or of absolute necessity or inevitable to secure compliance certainly fulfil the [necessity] requirements of Article XX(d). But other measures, too, may fall within the ambit of this exception."

86 Appellate Body Report, *Korea – Various Measures on Beef (2001)*, para. 164.

87 The Appellate Body stated: "The standard described by the panel in *United States – Section 337* encapsulates the general considerations we have adverted to above [in para. 164]. In our view, the weighing and balancing process we have outlined is *comprehended in* the determination of whether a WTO-consistent alternative measure which the Member concerned could 'reasonably be expected to employ' is available, or whether a less WTO-inconsistent measure is 'reasonably available'". Ibid, para. 166. Neumann and Türk, who examined the WTO necessity rules in light of proportionality principle, called the Appellate Body's requirement for the search of a 'WTO-consistent alternative measure' an "abstract criterion". Jan Neumann and Elisabeth Türk, 'Necessity Revisited: Proportionality in World Trade Organization Law after *Korea – Beef, EC – Asbestos* and *EC – Sardines*', *Journal of World Trade*, 37(1): 2003, p. 214.

88 Appellate Body Report, *Korea – Various Measures on Beef (2001)*, paras. 160–163 (f.n. 102–105).

paragraph 164. The context of the paragraph does not explain the origin of the test either. Sub-section 8.2.3 will discuss the likely origin of the test contained in this paragraph.

Building on the interpretation it developed in *Korea – Various Measures on Beef* (*2001*), the Appellate Body, in *US – Gambling* (*2005*), held that the 'weighing and balancing' test *begins* with the assessment of the relative importance of the values furthered by the contested measure and then "[h]aving ascertained the importance of the particular interests at stake, a panel should then turn to the [at least two] other factors that are to be 'weighed and balanced'", i.e., "the contribution of the measure to the realization of the ends pursued by it… [and] the restrictive impact of the measure on international commerce".[89] Thus, the three 'weighing and balancing' factors thus far identified are: (a) the relative importance of the values furthered by the contested measure; (b) the contribution of the measure to the realization of the ends pursued by it; and (c) the restrictive impact of the measure on international commerce.[90] In listing the 'weighing and balancing' test factors, the Appellate Body, in *Korea – Various Measures on Beef* (*2001*), made it clear that the test is not limited to the three factors because the test is about "a series of factors which prominently include…"[91] Let us briefly present the understanding thus far developed regarding the three factors.

Regarding the first factor (i.e., relative importance of the values furthered by the contested measure), the Appellate Body consistently held that "the more vital or important the interests or values that are reflected in the objective of the measure, the easier it would be to accept a measure as 'necessary'".[92] Since the first WTO dispute, *US – Gasoline* (*1996*), it has been consistently made clear that WTO Members are at liberty to identify the nature, and level of protection of, the values that they choose to pursue and the panels and the Appellate Body have consistently respected the nature and level of protection (including zero-risk) of the policy goals that the respondents adopted.[93] In no case

89 Appellate Body Report, *US – Gambling* (*2005*), para. 306.

90 In *India – Solar Cells* (*2016*), the Appellate Body has decided that the 'weighing and balancing' test must also be applied to the GATT 1994 Article XX(j) when examining the term 'essential'. Appellate Body Report, *India – Solar Cells* (*2016*), para. 5.63.

91 Appellate Body Report, *Korea – Various Measures on Beef* (*2001*), para. 164.

92 Appellate Body Report, *Korea – Various Measures on Beef* (*2001*), para. 162; Appellate Body Report, *EC – Asbestos* (*2001*), para. 172; WTO Panel Reports, *China – Raw Materials* (*2012*), para. 7.482; Appellate Body Reports, *EC – Seal Products* (*2014*), para. 5.203; Appellate Body Report, *Colombia – Textiles* (*2016*), paras. 5.71, 5.103.

93 Appellate Body Report, *EC – Asbestos* (*2001*), para. 168; WTO Panel Report, *US – Gambling* (*2005*), para. 6.461; Appellate Body Report, *US – Gambling* (*2005*), para. 308; WTO Panel Report, *Brazil – Retreaded Tyres* (*2007*), para. 7.108; Appellate Body Report,

have the WTO dispute settlement organs yet found the value or interest at hand to be of less or no importance. Moreover, despite the differences in the degree of importance of the interests in each of the cases above, the panels/Appellate Body gave the respondents a similar, unreserved 'pass' on the first of the three 'weighing and balancing' test. Although the panels and the Appellate Body have not yet embarked upon identifying criteria for prioritizing among the vital interests that WTO Members may adopt, they have not restrained themselves, by using different expressions, from stating that the value of some interests is important or of the highest importance.[94] These expressions include referring to the measure as "vital and important in the highest degree", "[one that] should also be considered important", "an important interest to WTO Members", "among the most important values or interests" and "a vital and important interest". It may, thus, be argued whether the panels/Appellate Body have some *mental ranking* among the myriad of policy objectives in the General Exceptions paragraphs which contain the term 'necessary'/'essential'. The *China – Publications and Audiovisual Products* (*2010*) panel *gave an indication*, in a statement neither appealed against nor disturbed by the Appellate Body, that the alphabetical placement of the term 'necessary' in three paragraphs of the GATT-1994 Article XX (i.e., paragraphs (a), (b) and (d) respectively) may mean that the interest in paragraph (a) (protection of public morals) is of the highest ranking:

> In our view, it is undoubtedly the case that the protection of public morals ranks among the most important values or interests pursued by Members as a matter of public policy. *We do not consider it simply accident that the exception relating to 'public morals' is the first exception identified in the ten sub-paragraphs of Article XX* (*emphasis added*).[95]

Brazil – Retreaded Tyres (*2007*), para. 140; Appellate Body Reports, EC – *Seal Products* (*2014*), para. 5.200; Appellate Body Report, *Colombia – Textiles* (*2016*), para. 5.115.

94 Appellate Body Report, EC – *Asbestos* (*2001*), para. 172; WTO Panel Report, *US – Gambling* (*2005*), para. 6.558; WTO Panel Report, *Brazil – Retreaded Tyres* (*2007*), paras. 7.109, 7.112; WTO Panel Reports, *China – Auto Parts* (*2009*), para. 7.360; WTO Panel Report, *China – Publications and Audiovisual Products* (*2010*), para. 7.817; WTO Panel Reports, EC – *Seal Products* (*2014*), para. 7.632; WTO Panel Report, *Colombia – Textiles* (*2016*), para. 7.408.

95 WTO Panel Report, *China – Publications and Audiovisual Products* (*2010*), para. 7.817. The Appellate Body made no comment regarding this paragraph in the panel's report. Appellate Body Report, *China – Publications and Audiovisual Products* (*2010*), para. 243 and f.n. 462 refers to para. 7.817 of the panel's report with no comment thereon.

Professor Regan has noted that the fact that in *Korea – Various Measures on Beef* (*2001*) the Appellate Body, as part of defining the first 'weighing and balancing' test, allowed Members to choose their own level of protection *contradicts* in essence with the remaining 'objective' examination process of applying the other two 'weighing and balancing' factors and the search for WTO-consistent alternative measures. The latter processes, according to Regan, are in principle cost-benefit analyzes and he finds it hard to see how these 'objective' analyzes match with the 'subjective' right of the defending Member to choose a level of protection of its choice. Although there is no clear textual indication in the General Exceptions paragraphs (such as 'which the Member deems') that the degree of the importance to be given to the societal value or interest in issue should be the degree of importance given to the value or interest given by the respondent Member, the practice shows that the panels and the Appellate Body recognize (give deference) to the degree of importance that the respondent Member gives to that value or interest.[96]

Regarding the second factor (i.e., contribution of the measure to the realization of the ends pursued by it), the Appellate Body, in *Brazil – Retreaded Tyres* (*2007*), held that "a panel must be satisfied that [the measure] *brings about a material contribution* to the achievement of its objective." and the panel "might conclude that [the measure] is necessary on the basis of a demonstration that the [measure] at issue is *apt to produce a material contribution* to the achievement of its objective (*emphasis added*)".[97] In *Brazil – Retreaded Tyres* (*2007*) the Appellate Body echoed the *Korea – Various Measures on Beef* (*2001*) interpretation of continuum of necessity in general and in *EC – Seal Products* (*2014*), the Appellate Body had to clarify whether *material contribution* of the measure was mandatory in determining its necessity. The Appellate Body stated that it did *not* (in *Brazil – Retreaded Tyres* (*2007*)) "set out a generally applicable standard requiring the use of a pre-determined threshold of 'material' contribution in analyzing the necessity of a measure under Article XX of the GATT 1994"[98] and rejected the contention that "the Panel was required to apply a standard

96 Donald H. Regan, 'The Meaning of "necessary" in GATT Article XX and GATS Article XIV: The Myth of Cost-Benefit Balancing', *World Trade Review*, 6(3): 2007, pp. 347–369. WTO Panel Report, *Colombia – Ports of Entry* (*2009*), para. 7.551–7.566 (especially paras. 7.562–7.566); WTO Panel Report, *Colombia – Textiles* (*2016*), paras. 7.522–7.524; WTO Panel Report, *Indonesia – Chicken* (*2017*), paras. 7.138–7.139; WTO Panel Report, *US – Tariff Measures on Certain Goods from China* (*2020*), paras. 7.167–7.169.

97 Appellate Body Report, *Brazil – Retreaded Tyres* (*2007*), para. 151. See also, Appellate Body Report, *China – Publications and Audiovisual Products* (*2010*), para. 253; WTO Panel Reports, *China – Rare Earths* (*2014*), para. 7.146.

98 Appellate Body Reports, *EC – Seal Products* (*2014*), para. 5.213.

of 'materiality' as a generally applicable pre-determined threshold in its contribution analysis."[99] After a long discussion on whether a Panel is required to ascertain the *actual* contribution in contrast to its *capability* or *possibility* to make contribution,[100] the Appellate Body upheld the Panel's finding that a measure can be 'necessary' if it "is capable of making and does make '*some* contribution' to its objective, or that it makes a contribution '*to a certain extent*' (*emphasis added*)".[101]

A question that could be raised at this juncture is whether, by allowing the possibility of a measure to make *some* contribution or its contributing *to a certain extent*, the Appellate Body slightly moved the overall continuum needle of necessity from the point which, as originally set out in *Korea – Various Measures on Beef* (*2001*), is significantly closer to the pole of *indispensability* towards the opposite pole of *making contribution to.* It must be emphasized that this question focuses on only *one* of the elements of the 'weighing and balancing' interpretation of necessity[102] within the full definition of necessity in the 'weighing and balancing' test.[103] The question therefore, is: if, according to the Appellate Body, the measure has to make some contribution to achieve the objective, does this standard affect the overall requirement that in order to be necessary the measure must be found out to be closer to being 'indispensable' than simply 'making a contribution' to achieving its objective? How can a measure which, as one of the three tests of necessity, is required only to make 'some contribution' to achieve its objective, be expected, after the other two tests of necessity have been conducted, to be 'indispensable' to achieve its objectives?

Now that the Appellate Body stated its openness to accepting an *EC – Seal Products* (*2014*) 'making some contribution/ contributing to a certain extent' part-definition of necessity and due to the fact that a severely trade-restrictive measure can still be necessary if it can 'make some contribution/contribute

99 Ibid, para. 5.215.

100 Ibid, paras. 5.218–5.227.

101 Ibid, para. 5.228.

102 The Appellate Body has made it clear that the contribution of the measure is only one of the elements of the 'weighing and balancing' test for the disputed measure on top of the search for a WTO-consistent alternative. Ibid, para. 5.215. See also, Appellate Body Reports, *China – Rare Earths* (*2014*), para. 5.116.

103 In other words, while the Appellate Body's reference to the pole of 'indispensability' in *Korea – Various Measures on Beef* (*2001*) was about *the necessity of the measure in general* (as one holistic package of its three elements), the Appellate Body's references to 'material contribution' and 'some contribution' in *Brazil – Retreaded Tyres* (*2007*) and *EC – Seal Products* (*2014*) were only about *one of the three elements of necessity* as set out *Korea – Various Measures on Beef* (*2001*) (the element of the contribution of the measure).

to a certain extent',[104] does this mean that, as far as the overall definition of necessity is concerned, getting closer to the pole of indispensability is not as strictly required as it was in the first few years after *Korea – Various Measures on Beef* (2001)?[105] It can be argued that the Appellate Body's statements in *Korea – Various Measures on Beef* (2001) that the measure has to generally be nearly indispensable, its statement in *Brazil – Retreaded Tyres* (2007) that the measure must make 'material contribution' of the measure and its statement in EC – *Seal Products* (2014) that the measure has to make 'some contribution' are not as contradictory as they appear. Firstly, in EC – *Seal Products* (2014) the Appellate Body only stated that the measure must *at least* make some contribution to achieve its objectives. A measure that makes *no* contribution at all to achieve its objectives cannot be considered a necessary measure (even if the requirements of the other elements of necessity are met). In other words, the Appellate Body simply stated in EC – *Seal Products* (2014) that there should not be a minimum threshold of contribution. A measure that makes *material* contribution is also necessary (provided the requirements of the other elements of necessity are met). Secondly, the Appellate Body's statement in EC – *Seal Products* (2014) on the test of contribution must be viewed in light of the standard set out by the Appellate Body whereby the determination of necessity is, as noted below, a *holistic* exercise in which all three elements must, as first identified by the Appellate Body in *Korea – Various Measures on Beef* (2001), be considered and none of the elements must stand out as a determinative element of the concept of necessity.

Regarding the third factor (i.e., restrictive impact of the measure on international commerce), the Appellate Body revealed in *Korea – Various Measures on Beef* (2001) that "[a] measure with a relatively slight impact upon imported products [international trade] might more easily be considered as 'necessary' than a measure with intense or broader restrictive effects."[106] As observed by Van den Bossche and Zdouc,[107] the trade-restrictiveness factor, unveiled in *Korea – Various Measures on Beef* (2001), was not "explicitly [referred to]" in the subsequent case that applied the 'weighing and balancing' test, EC – *Asbestos*

104 See Appellate Body Report, *Brazil – Retreaded Tyres* (2007), para. 150; Appellate Body Report, *China – Publications and Audiovisual Products* (2010), para. 310.

105 For a detailed observation on the apparently different standards of contribution required by the Appellate Body in *Brazil – Retreaded Tyres* (2007) and EC – *Seal Products* (2014), see, Mavroidis, above note 7, pp. 438–440.

106 Appellate Body Report, *Korea – Various Measures on Beef* (2001), para. 163. Also cited in WTO Panel Report, *US – Gambling* (2005), para. 6.477(c); WTO Panel Reports, *China – Raw Materials* (2012), para. 7.487.

107 Van den Bossche and Zdouc, above note 1, p. 560.

(*2001*).[108] But since[109] the *Canada – Wheat Exports and Grain Imports* (*2004*) panel report,[110] it has regularly[111] become part of the 'weighing and balancing' exercise. The WTO dispute settlement reports show that the trade-restrictiveness of the disputed measure is examined in view of its restrictive effect on 'international commerce',[112] 'imported goods/products',[113] 'imports or exports'[114] and 'actual or potential imports'[115] terms which the Appellate Body held can be represented in the term 'international trade' as contained in the *chapeau*.[116]

Following the separate notes on the three 'weighing and balancing' factors above, the following three points may be made as to the common application of these three factors as applies to all cases where a General Exception defense of 'necessity' arises. Firstly, regarding the sequence of the examination of the three factors, despite the varying experience on which of the three

108 Appellate Body Report, *EC – Asbestos* (*2001*), para. 172.

109 See, for instance, WTO Panel Report, *US – Gambling* (*2005*), paras. 6.476–6.477; Appellate Body Report, *US – Gambling* (*2005*), para. 306; WTO Panel Report, *Brazil – Retreaded Tyres* (*2007*), para. 7.104; Appellate Body Report, *Brazil – Retreaded Tyres* (*2007*), para. 150; WTO Panel Report, *Colombia – Ports of Entry* (*2009*), paras. 7.547–7.550; WTO Panel Reports, *China – Auto Parts* (*2009*), paras. 7.347–7.349; WTO Panel Report, *China – Publications and Audiovisual Products* (*2010*), paras. 7.782–7.783; Appellate Body Report, *China – Publications and Audiovisual Products* (*2010*), paras. 300–311; WTO Panel Reports, *China – Raw Materials* (*2012*), para. 7.487; WTO Panel Reports, *EC – Seal Products* (*2014*), paras. 7.630, 7.636–7.638; Appellate Body Reports, *EC – Seal Products* (*2014*), paras. 5.169, 5.205 (panel's finding on trade-restrictiveness was not appealed); WTO Panel Report, *Colombia – Textiles* (*2016*), paras. 7.403, 7.438–7.444; Appellate Body Report, *Colombia – Textiles* (*2016*), paras. 5.70, 5.73, 5.77, 5.111–5.116; WTO Panel Report, *India – Solar Cells* (*2016*), paras. 7.349, 7.351, 7.355–7.360;Appellate Body Report, *India – Solar Cells* (*2016*), paras. 5.59, 5.63; WTO Panel Report, *Brazil – Taxation* (*2017*), paras. 7.603–7.607; WTO Panel Report, *Indonesia – Chicken* (*2017*), paras. 7.143–7.147, 7.227; WTO Panel Report, *EU – Energy Package* (*2018*), paras. 7.1225–7.1228; WTO Panel Report, *US – Tariff Measures on Certain Goods from China* (*2020*), paras. 7.170–7.171; and WTO Panel Report, *Indonesia – Raw Materials* (*2022*), paras. 7.255–7.259.

110 WTO Panel Report, *Canada – Wheat Exports and Grain Imports* (*2004*), paras. 6.222–6.227.

111 There are some reports that did not fully discuss this and the other two elements of the 'weighing and balancing' test. The *EC – Trademarks and Geographical Indications* (*2005*) panel, for instance, in discussing necessity under the GATT 1994 Article XX(d), focused mainly on the search of WTO-consistent alternatives. WTO Panel Report, *EC – Trademarks and Geographical Indications* (*US*) (*2005*), paras. 7.449–7.463.

112 Appellate Body Report, *Korea – Various Measures on Beef* (*2001*), para. 163.

113 Ibid.

114 Ibid, para. 164.

115 Appellate Body Report, *China – Publications and Audiovisual Products* (*2010*), paras. 303–306.

116 Ibid, para. 303.

factors is examined first,[117] a dispute settlement organ may begin with any one of them, although the experience shows that the trade-restrictiveness factor almost always comes last. Secondly, a strong reason why sequencing of the three 'weighing and balancing' test factors may not matter is the statement of the Appellate Body in *Brazil – Retreaded Tyres* (2007) that the test "is a holistic operation that involves putting all the variables of the equation together and evaluating them in relation to each other after having examined them individually, in order to reach an overall judgement".[118] Thirdly, even if it seems settled that there is no need to sequence the three factors, one may ask if there is a difference in the significance or weight among the three factors. In different disputes, for instance in *Korea – Various Measures on Beef* (2001),[119] *Brazil – Retreaded Tyres* (2007) and[120] in *China – Publications and Audiovisual Products* (2010),[121] the Appellate made statements which may narrowly be read as indicating that one of the three factors could be more significant (generally or in that particular dispute) than the other factors. The trend set by the Appellate Body in examining necessity in the General Exceptions, however, leads to the opposite conclusion: that the Appellate Body made these varying statements not to compare the significance of one factor with that of the others but to highlight that the weighing and balancing process requires not only the individual assessment of each factor but also a holistic examination where the overall result of the process leads to the conclusion whether the measure is necessary or not.

---

117 See, for instance, Appellate Body Report, EC – *Asbestos* (2001), para. 172; Appellate Body Report, *Korea – Various Measures on Beef* (2001), para. 164; Appellate Body Report, *US – Gambling* (2005), para. 306; Appellate Body Report, *Dominican Republic – Import and Sale of Cigarettes* (2005), para. 70; Appellate Body Report, *Brazil – Retreaded Tyres* (2007), paras. 156, 178, 182; Appellate Body Report, *China – Publications and Audiovisual Products* (2010), paras. 237–238, 239–241; WTO Panel Reports, EC – *Seal Products* (2014), paras. 7.349, 7.630.

118 Appellate Body Report, *Brazil – Retreaded Tyres* (2007), para. 182. See also, WTO Panel Reports, *China – Raw Materials* (2012), paras. 7.488, 7.563; Appellate Body Reports, EC – *Seal Products* (2014), para. 5.214; WTO Panel Report, *India – Solar Cells* (2016), para. 7.349; WTO Panel Report, *Colombia – Textiles* (2016), paras. 5.102, 7.309; WTO Panel Reports, *China – Raw Materials* (2012), paras. 7.488, 7.563; Appellate Body Reports, EC – *Seal Products* (2014), para. 5.215; WTO Panel Report, *Indonesia – Chicken* (2017), paras. 7.134–7.137; WTO Panel Reports, *Brazil – Taxation* (2017), paras. 7.523–7.125, 7.134–7.135, 7.584, 7.599, 7.622, 7.961; WTO Panel Report, *US – Tariff Measures on Certain Goods from China* (2020), paras. 7.111, 7.139, 7.152–7.159.

119 Appellate Body Report, *Korea – Various Measures on Beef* (2001), para. 163.

120 Appellate Body Report, *Brazil – Retreaded Tyres* (2007), para. 150.

121 Appellate Body Report, *China – Publications and Audiovisual Products* (2010), para. 310. Cited in WTO Panel Reports, *China – Raw Materials* (2012), para. 7.487.

The test that the Appellate Body introduced for examining the necessity of a measure does not stop at examining the disputed measure in light of the three factors discussed above. There is an additional examination that has to be conducted: ascertaining whether there are reasonably available alternatives which are less trade restrictive and provide an equivalent contribution to the achievement of the objective pursued. In *Korea – Various Measures on Beef* (*2001*), the Appellate Body stated that its 'weighing and balancing' test is comprehended in the *US – Section 337* (*1989*) 'GATT-consistent alternative measure' test.[122] In practice, however, the Appellate Body introduced a new, more complex, two-step necessity test from *Korea – Various Measures on Beef* (*2001*) onwards. The Appellate Body's reference to *US – Section 337* (*1989*) appears to be more an attempt not to divert from GATT case law than abiding by the GATT necessity test. The only GATT necessity test element that the Appellate Body adopted was the requirement of examining alternative measures when it stated:

> The [weighing and balancing] process begins with an assessment of the 'relative importance' of the interests or values furthered by the challenged measure ... [A] panel should then turn to the other factors that are to be 'weighed and balanced' ...
>
> A comparison between the challenged measure and possible alternatives should then be undertaken, and the results of such comparison should be considered in the light of the importance of the interests at issue. It is on the basis of this 'weighing and balancing' and comparison of measures, taking into account the interests or values at stake, that a panel determines whether a measure is 'necessary' or, alternatively, whether another, WTO-consistent measure is 'reasonably available' (*emphasis added*).[123]

At this stage, the Appellate Body explained that the challenged measure and the proposed alternative must be compared in light of the interests or values at stake (i.e., the first of the three 'weighing and balancing' factors). In the subsequent paragraphs[124] the Appellate Body stated that the panel must, as part of this comparison process, also consider the capacity of the proposed

122 Appellate Body Report, *Korea – Various Measures on Beef* (*2001*), para. 166. Cottier *et al.* note that "[i]n the early GATT cases, necessity was merely tested on the basis of the availability of an alternative, less intrusive measure which a WTO Member could reasonably be expected to employ." Cottier *et al.*, above note 65.

123 Appellate Body Report, *US – Gambling* (*2005*), paras. 306–307.

124 Ibid, paras. 308–311.

alternative measure to achieve the already identified objectives. It was, however, in *Brazil – Retreaded Tyres* (2007) that the Appellate Body introduced a clear process whereby the panels should consider not only the respective contributions of the challenged and proposed alternative measures to achieving the objective, but also the respective trade-restrictiveness of the challenged and proposed alternative measures:

> In order to determine whether a measure is 'necessary' ..., a panel must assess all the relevant factors, particularly the extent of the contribution to the achievement of a measure's objective and its trade restrictiveness, in the light of the importance of the interests or values at stake. If this analysis yields a preliminary conclusion that the measure is necessary, this result must be confirmed by comparing the measure with its possible alternatives, which may be *less trade restrictive* while *providing an equivalent contribution to the achievement of the objective pursued* ... We recall that, in order to qualify as an alternative, a measure proposed by the complaining Member must be *not only less trade restrictive than the measure at issue*, but should also 'preserve for the responding Member its right to achieve its desired level of protection with respect to the objective pursued (*emphasis added*)'.[125]

In *US – Gambling* (2005) the Appellate Body made it clear that it is for the complaining party to point at the alternatives and for the respondent to show that the said alternatives are not reasonably available.[126] From *Brazil – Retreaded Tyres* (2007) onwards, it became clear that once the contested measure has been examined and the measure has been preliminarily found to be necessary, the proposed alternative measure is then examined in light of its contribution

---

125 Appellate Body Report, *Brazil – Retreaded Tyres* (2007), para. 156; Appellate Body Report, *China – Publications and Audiovisual Products* (2010), paras. 241–242 (and f.n. 442); WTO Panel Reports, *EC – Seal Products* (2014), para. 7.630; WTO Panel Report, *Colombia – Textiles* (2016), para. 7.325; WTO Panel Reports, *Brazil – Taxation* (2017), f.n., 902; WTO Panel Report, *US – Tariff Measures on Certain Goods from China* (2020), para. 7.232. In the *EC – Seal Products* (2014) report, the Appellate Body indicated that there are circumstances when the preliminary examination of the necessity of the disputed measure may not be confirmed by examining the alternative measures. Appellate Body Reports, *EC – Seal Products* (2014), f.n. 1299, referred to by WTO Panel Report, *Indonesia – Chicken* (2017), paras. 7.148 (f.n. 252); WTO Panel Report, *US – Tariff Measures on Certain Goods from China* (2020), para. 40 (f.n. 13).

126 Appellate Body Report, *US – Gambling* (2005), paras. 309–311. See also, Appellate Body Report, *Brazil – Retreaded Tyres* (2007), para. 156; Appellate Body Reports, *EC – Seal Products* (2014), para. 5.261.

to achieving the objective and its trade-restrictiveness. The *Canada – Wheat Exports and Grain Imports (2004)* panel, referring to the Appellate Body reports in *EC – Asbestos (2001)* and *Korea – Various Measures on Beef (2001)*, held that the relevant factors to determine whether an alternative measure is reasonably available are the extent to which the alternative measure contributes to the achievement of the policy objective, the difficulty of implementing the alternative measure; and the impact of the alternative measure on international trade.[127] In summary, currently a reasonably available, WTO-consistent alternative is understood as one that: (1) is not merely theoretical (i.e., one that is capable to be taken, or one that does not impose undue burden such as prohibitive cost or substantial technical difficulties);[128] (2) is less trade restrictive than the measure at issue; and (3) would preserve for the responding Member its right to achieve its desired level of protection with respect to the objective pursued.[129]

8.2.3 *Proportionality Test as the Likely Origin of the 'Weighing and Balancing' Test: The Pescatore-Ehlermann Influence*

Sweet and Mathews have published what could be taken as some of the most detailed accounts on the origins and gradual internationalization of the proportionality analysis, i.e., the series of tests that domestic and international courts have developed in examining the legality of otherwise unlawful measures to curb, for some definite reasons, the exercise of rights.[130] They trace the origin

---

127 WTO Panel Report, *Canada – Wheat Exports and Grain Imports (2004)*, para. 6.226. for a clearer presentation of this view, see, Appellate Body Report, *China – Publications and Audiovisual Products (2010)*, paras. 239 and 242.

128 Appellate Body Report, *Dominican Republic – Import and Sale of Cigarettes (2005)* paras. 68, 70; Appellate Body Report, *US – Gambling (2005)*, para. 308; Appellate Body Report, *Brazil – Retreaded Tyres (2007)*, para. 156; WTO Panel Reports, *China – Raw Materials (2012)*, para. 7.490; WTO Panel Reports, *EC – Seal Products (2014)*, para. 7.493; WTO Panel Report, *Argentina – Financial Services (2015)*, para. 7.729; Appellate Body Report, *Colombia – Textiles (2016)*, para. 5.74.

129 Appellate Body Report, *US – Gambling (2005)*, para. 308; Appellate Body Report, *Brazil – Retreaded Tyres (2007)*, paras. 156, 178; Appellate Body Reports, *EC – Seal Products (2014)*, para. 5.261; WTO Panel Report, *Colombia – Textiles (2016)*, para. 7.327; WTO Panel Reports, *Brazil – Taxation (2017)*, para. 7.532.

130 Alec Stone Sweet and Jud Mathews, 'Proportionality Balancing and Global Constitutionalism', *Columbia Journal of Transnational Law*, 47(1): 2008, pp. 72–164. They have published a book on the subject as well: Alec Stone Sweet and Jud Mathews, *Proportionality Balancing and Constitutional Governance: A Comparative and Global Approach* (Oxford: Oxford University Press, 2019). See also, Mads Andenas and Stefan Zleptnig, 'Proportionality: WTO Law in Comparative Perspective', *Texas International Law Journal*, 42(3): 2007, pp. 371–427.

of the proportionality analysis back to the *Polizeirecht* (law applicable to the police force) in the late 18th century which allowed the police to take measures designed to promote and protect public welfare, morality and safety. Jurists such as Carl Gotllieb Svarez (1746–1798) and Gunther Heinrich von Berg (1765–1843) who reflected on such police authority argued that although the natural rights of individuals generally prevail over the actions of the state, individuals give up some of their freedom in order to realize collective goals through the state. However, in exercising this power to limit the rights of individuals, the police or the state may not abridge the natural freedoms of individuals beyond the requirements of the goal that necessitated the action. This delicate act of balancing individual and state rights was first exercised in the 1880s by German administrative courts in reviewing the proportionality of administrative police actions which limited individual rights in order to preserve public interest, morality, safety etc. The key element in this review process was to examine if less restrictive measures were available to the police. Scholars continued to recommend additional ingredients to this review process such as the 'proportionality (balancing) in *stricto sensu*' test where the benefits of the state act are weighed against the costs incurred by infringement of the right. Finally, the German Federal Constitutional Court gave the proportionality analysis test its complete form in the landmark *Apothekenurteil* case (1958) and in 1965 the court declared that the proportionality test possesses constitutional status.[131] This complete form of the proportionality analysis has four elements: (1) ensuring that the actor, i.e., the state, is constitutionally legitimate to take the action (the legitimacy test); (2) ensuring that the means adopted by the actor are rationally and carefully designed to achieve the stated policy objective (the suitability test); (3) ensuring that the measure does not curtail the right any more than is necessary to achieve the stated objective by, if possible, searching for less restrictive means (the necessity test); and (4) ensuring that the effects of the contested act are balanced against the costs for infringing the right in light of the objectives sought to be attained by the contested act (the proportionality (balancing) in the strict sense (*stricto sensu*) test).[132]

---

131 Sweet and Mathews (2008), ibid, pp. 98–110.

132 Ibid, pp. 76–77; Neumann and Türk, above note 87, p. 203; Mads Andenas and Stefan Zleptnig. 'The Rule of Law and Proportionality in WTO Law', in Wenhua Shan *et al.* (eds.), *Redefining Sovereignty in International Economic Law* (Oxford and Portland: Hart Publishing, 2008), p. 174. Jans drops the legitimacy test and lists suitability, necessity and proportionality *stricto sensu* as the three elements of proportionality which must be assessed cumulatively. Jan H. Jans, 'Proportionality Revisited', *Legal Issues of Economic Integration*, 27(27): 2000, pp. 240–241. Cottier *et al.* also identify the three as the 'subprinciples' of the principle of proportionality. Cottier *et al.*, above note 65, p. 630.

Sweet and Mathews then narrate how the wave of 'New Constitutionalism',[133] which necessitates massive delegation of authority to the courts, enabled the 'viral' internationalization (diffusion) of the 'pervasive' German practice of proportionality analysis.[134] They state that from its German origins proportionality analysis spread across Europe including post-Communist states in Europe, to the Commonwealth systems as well as Central and South America and that by the end of the 1990s every constitutional system in the world adopted the analysis with the partial exception of the US.[135] They then add:

> *Strikingly, proportionality has also migrated to the three treaty-based regimes* that have serious claims to be considered 'constitutional' in some meaningful sense: the European Union (EU), the European Convention on Human Rights (ECHR), *and the World Trade Organization (WTO) (emphasis added).*[136]

As mentioned in Sub-sections 8.2.1 and 8.2.2, in the two key disputes that laid the foundation for the concept of necessity in GATT/WTO law (*US – Section 337 (1989)* and *Korea – Various Measures on Beef (2001)*), the GATT panel and the Appellate Body, in the respective paragraphs (5.26 and 164) where they laid out their interpretation of necessity in GATT Article XX, did not explain *how* or *why* they brought up their tests for necessity. It can be observed, however, that while the two elements of the German proportionality analysis (suitability [i.e., design] test and the necessity test) have been adopted, in the broader sense, into the current interpretation of necessity in the General Exceptions, the proportionality *stricto sensu* element may have been reflected in the interpretation of the *chapeau* of the General Exceptions. Sweet and Mathews

---

133 For characteristics of New Constitutionalism, see, Sweet and Mathews, ibid, pp. 85–86.

134 Ibid, pp. 112–160.

135 Ibid, p. 75.

136 Ibid. on the contrary, Desmedt concluded that "there is not one single overarching (unwritten) proportionality principle in WTO law." Axel Desmedt, 'Proportionality in WTO Law', *Journal of International Economic Law*, 4(3): 2001, p. 441. Hilf, on the other hand argues that "the principle of proportionality is one of the more basic principles underlying the multilateral trading system". Meinhard Hilf, 'Power, Rules and Principles: Which Orientation for WTO/GATT Law?', *Journal of International Economic Law*, 4(1): 2001, p. 120.

While admitting that proportionality, despite finding its way into international law, is not generally recognized as part of the general principles of CIL, Cottier *et al.* make respective arguments to trace the notion of proportionality in a number of fields of PIL viz. IHRL, the law of countermeasures (particularly the law on the use of force), law of the sea (maritime boundary delimitation), WTO law and IIL. Cottier *et al.*, above note 65, pp. 630–665.

speculate how these two paragraphs in *US – Section 337 (1989)* and *Korea – Various Measures on Beef (2001)* could, without contradicting each other, have ended up defining the concept of necessity in WTO law: the presence of Prof. Pierre Pescatore and Prof. Claus-Dieter Ehlermann:

> First, the emergence and early consolidation of [proportionality analysis] depended heavily on the influence of legal scholars on judging, in Germany, and then on the influence of Germany on European law. Second, *specific identifiable agents (judges and law professors-turned-judges) were instrumental in bringing [proportionality analysis] to treaty-based regimes,* including Hans Kutscher and Pierre Pescatore (to the ECJ), Jochen Frowein (to the ECHR), *Pescatore and Claus-Dieter Ehlermann (to the WTO) (emphasis added).*[137]

The authors link the backgrounds of Pescatore and Ehlermann to the crafting of the two paragraphs in *US – Section 337 (1989)* and *Korea – Various Measures on Beef (2001)*. As an academic, Prof. Pescatore strongly advocated use of the proportionality analysis in interpreting the relationship between Articles 28 and 30 of the Treaty of Rome. In 1967 Pescatore left his professorship to join the ECJ – which had by then developed a refined interpretation of proportionality along the German lines[138] – and served there until 1985.[139] While in the ECJ he identified the proportionality analysis as a general principle of law.[140] Pescatore had this background in adjudication of pan-European trade disputes when he sat as one of the three panelists in the *US – Section 337 (1989)* dispute.[141] The author of this book conducted an interview with Prof. Ernst-Ulrich Petersmann, former Counsellor at the Legal Affairs Division of the GATT Secretariat (1981–89), about his recollections of *US – Section 337 (1989)*.[142] Petersmann said that

137 Sweet and Mathews, ibid, p. 162.

138 Ibid, pp. 139–144.

139 Ibid, p. 144.

140 Pierre Pescatore, 'Fundamental Rights and Freedoms in the System of the European Communities', *American Journal of Comparative* Law, 18(2): 1970, p. 350.

141 The other two panelists were Mr. Graham Fortune (New Zealand's Permanent Representative in Geneva, 1987–1990) and Professor Andreas Lowenfeld (from New York University School of Law).

142 Personal interview, 28 September 2017 (during the annual WTO Public Forum, Geneva). The quoted transcription of his statements was confirmed by him following an email communication on 2 September 2021. The purpose of including this interview is not to precisely identify the drafter of para. 5.26 or to identify Pescatore as its drafter but to embolden the well-founded speculation by Sweet and Mathews that Pescatore, given his

Stone and Mathews speculated that *US – Section 337 (1989)* was drafted by Pescatore. On Pescatore, Petersmann mentioned that it was him (Petersmann) who brought Pescatore into the GATT, but that the latter, though delighted by the invitation, made it clear that he (Pescatore) was not going to allow anyone draft his panel reports. Thus, concluded, Petersmann:

> you can be reasonably sure that [para. 5.26] was drafted by him and it was drafted in the light of his experience as a judge of the European Court of Justice. You know that Article XX GATT corresponds to what was Article 30 of the European Union Treaty, the sovereign right to restrict trade. I knew Pescatore very well and his insistence on drafting himself his legal findings as a GATT panel member. We must assume that he drafted this paragraph himself influenced by his judicial experiences with Article 30 of the EEC Treaty. I also recall that Pescatore told me how – when he represented Luxembourg in the negotiations on the drafting of the EEC Treaty in 1956 – the drafters of the customs union provisions (including Article 30 EEC Treaty) used the relevant GATT obligations of all EEC member states (i.e., also Article XX GATT) as commonly shared drafting inspirations. Even if the context of the EEC Treaty is different from the context of GATT, there are good reasons for arguing that the underlying principles for *bona fide* reconciliation of rights and obligations in customs unions are equally valid in the context of Article XX GATT.[143]

If we believe that Pescatore had drafted (had a strong influence in drafting) paragraph 5.26 of *US – Section 337 (1989)* along his ECJ practice, we can see that the paragraph introduced only the third of the four elements of the proportionality analysis tests listed above: the 'necessity test', which focuses on the availability of alternatives.[144] It needed another dispute litigated 12 years

background, may have strongly influenced the introduction of the concept represented in that paragraph.

143 Ibid. Also confirmed by Dr. Werner Zdouc, former Director of the WTO Appellate Body Secretariat, in a personal interview, 28 June 2017 (at the Faculty of Law of Maastricht University). Dr. Zdouc stated that "Judge Pescatore was probably inspired by the ECJ's proportionality test when he was a panelist in the *Section 337* panel (obviously the other panelists also had a say, but I would believe that he had a strong influence)." Email communication on 3 September 2021.

144 Van den Bossche noted that the interpretation of 'necessity' in GATT Article XX(b) by the *Thailand – Cigarettes (1990)* panel, which adopted the interpretation of 'necessity' earlier on introduced by the *US – Section 337 (1989)* panel for GATT Article XX(d), bears close resemblance to the necessity test in the proportionality test. Peter Van den Bossche,

later, *Korea – Various Measures on Beef* (*2001*), to present the necessity test in Article XX in a manner that may also have reflected another element of the proportionality analysis (the suitability [design]test),[145] although the Appellate Body's necessity test is more comprehensive and flexible in its form. Once again, we can assume the contribution (at least) of another strong proponent of the ECJ's proportionality analysis in *Korea – Various Measures on Beef* (*2001*): Prof. Ehlermann.

Ehlermann was the presiding member of the Appellate Body in *Korea – Various Measures on Beef* (*2001*).[146] He came to the Appellate Body following, among others, his job as the Director-General of the Legal Service of the European Commission (1977–1987). In the words of Petersmann, "[Ehlermann] came exactly from the same epistemic community as Pescatore". Sweet and Mathews recognize Ehlermann as "a leading proponent of [proportionality analysis] in trade law".[147] Speculating, like Sweet and Mathews, that Ehlermann, given his background, "likely wrote the [*Korea – Beef*] decision"[148] may be too much an assumption, but it can be stated that he definitely had contribution in preparation of the paragraphs on the necessity test (particularly in drafting of paragraph 164).[149] The finding in *Korea – Various Measures on Beef* (*2001*), through the 'weighing and balancing' test, reflected, in part, the 'German/ECJ' proportionality analysis in the WTO law analysis of the General Exceptions by adopting the suitability and necessity tests.[150] It may be observed, although not

'Looking for Proportionality in WTO Law', *Legal Issues of Economic Integration*, 35(3): 2008, p. 287.

145 Ibid.

146 Of course, the individual and combined experience and caliber of the other two Appellate Body Members (Prof. Georges Abi-Saab and Justice Florentino Feliciano) in giving the 'weighing and balancing' test its final form in *Korea – Various Measures on Beef* (*2001*) cannot be underestimated.

147 Sweet and Mathews (2008), above note 130, p. 160.

148 Ibid.

149 Prof. Petersmann also seemed confident that Ehlermann introduced the 'weighing and balancing' test in *Korea – Various Measures on Beef* (*2001*) which has some similarities with the ECJ concept of proportionality analysis developed for trade law. Above note 142.

150 Van den Bossche stated that the definition of proportionality "borrowed from the EC legal order, is the most widely applied definition of proportionality in WTO law as well". Van den Bossche, above note 144, p. 285. See also, Neumann and Türk, above note 87, pp. 201–202. Cottier *et al.* also observed that:

> The need to strike a balance between divergent trade interests of [WTO] Members and also between the trade interest and other legitimate policy goals is implicit to the WTO framework. Proportionality therefore is of inherent importance to international trade regulation in balancing divergent interests at stake. *While there is no explicit reference to the principle of proportionality in WTO law, there are several references to notions that either form a part of proportionality test or fulfil an analogous function.* WTO law often resorts to the terms 'necessary', 'less trade restrictive', 'appropriate', which allow the

within the scope of this book, that the third element of the German/ECJ' proportionality (i.e., proportionality *stricto sensu*), which appears not embodied in the interpretation of necessity in the paragraphs of the General Exceptions, may have been reflected in part in the Appellate Body's interpretation of the *chapeau* of the General Exceptions as reflecting 'equilibrium'.[151] Thus, it may be asked – or argued, as did Cottier *et al.* – whether the three key elements of the proportionality analysis (suitability, necessity and proportionality *stricto sensu*) have been reflected into the *combined* meanings of the 'weighing and balancing' test and the *chapeau* of the General Exceptions as follows: (a) the 'suitability' element in the proportionality analysis may be equated to the two elements ('importance of the objective' and 'contribution of the measure to achieve the objective') of the 'weighing and balancing' test; (b) the 'necessity' element in the proportionality analysis may be equated to the two elements ('trade-restrictiveness' and 'search for alternatives') of the 'weighing and balancing' test; and (c) the 'balancing in the strict sense' element in the proportionality analysis may be equated to the balancing exercise in the *chapeau* of the General Exceptions. Cottier *et al.* make a similar comparison:

> The first step [In WTO law of examining whether the objective pursued is found in the General Exceptions paragraphs] arguably amounts to the first element of standard proportionality test, namely the suitability of the measure. The second step and third step [in WTO law, respectively, of the necessity test and the examination under the chapeau], as explained below, correspondingly reflect the elements [in the proportionality test] of the necessity and appropriateness requirements.[152]

> WTO adjudicating bodies to perform the balancing exercise on a case-by-case basis … *An implied reflection of the principle of proportionality can be found both in Article XX GATT and Article XIV GATS (emphasis added).*

Cottier *et al.*, above note 65, pp. 644–645.

151 Van den Bossche, ibid, pp. 288–293. Van den Bossche asks, although with doubt as to an affirmative reply, whether the statement in Appellate Body Report, *Brazil – Retreaded Tyres* (2007), para. 210 that "the contribution of the measure has to be weighed against its trade restrictiveness, taking into account the importance of the interests or the values underlying the objective pursued by it" may be read to reflect the element of proportionality *stricto sensu* assessment and therefore lead to the conclusion that the application of the 'weighing and balancing' test entails the three steps of the full proportionality test. Van den Bossche, above note 144, p. 294. On whether the *chapeau* of the General Exceptions embodies the element of proportionality *stricto sensu*, Cottier *et al.* stated: "The Appellate Body in *US-Shrimp* suggested that the terms 'unjustifiable', 'arbitrary' or 'necessary' define 'a line of equilibrium' and thus require weighing and balancing *along the lines of the proportionality principle* (*emphasis added*)." Cottier *et al.*, ibid, p. 648.

152 Cottier *et al.*, ibid, pp. 646.

However, they caution that:

> [t]he precise status and function of proportionality in assessing exceptions in pursuit of legitimate policy goals is difficult to assess. Neither the WTO covered agreements, nor the WTO jurisprudence give an explicit answer to the question whether the principle of proportionality as a general principle of law forms part of WTO law.[153]

and since "[t]he case law of WTO does not follow the trias of fitness and suitability, necessity and proportionality *stricto sensu* but is rather informed by an overall process of weighing and balancing interests in assessing [necessity of the measures] ...",[154]

> [i]t is conceivable to structure the operation of interpretation of necessity in line with the three-tier test set out above. Measures could be assessed whether they are suitable, necessary and only then engaging in an overall balancing of interests at stake. Yet, whatever approach is chosen, the heart of the matter lies with the perception of deference of WTO law towards its Members and their sovereign right to regulate.[155]

Their careful conclusion is, therefore:

> it is submitted that the general principle of proportionality is implicitly recognized in WTO law and has been tailored to the special needs of the international trade environment, taking into consideration the nature of WTO law as a *sui generis*, but not self-contained regime. Proportionality in WTO law can be seen as a guiding principle and flexible tool to guide judicial inquiry into the lawfulness of domestic measures. Essentially, it is a guarantee against the abuse of rights, which in turn – and again – is founded in equity.[156]

8.2.4 *The GATT/WTO Concept of Necessity in Context of the CIL Concept of Necessity*

At the time the GATT was developing a workable interpretation for the concept of necessity (the 1980s), the ILC had, based mainly on the pre-Second World

153 Ibid, p. 653.
154 Ibid.
155 Ibid, p. 654.
156 Ibid.

War understanding of necessity, already developed a well-articulated definition for the concept of necessity as distinguished from other defenses such as *force majeure*, distress and self-defense. As will be detailed in Chapter 10, ITL was long considered not to be part of PIL and this understanding may have been partly reflected in the 'separate' interpretation developed for the concept of necessity in GATT Article XX as compared to the concept of necessity being refined at that time by the ILC. For instance, whereas the ILC required that there should be *no alternative* to the measure taken under necessity, i.e., the contested measure has to be the 'only' available measure, the GATT insisted on comparing the contested measure with alternative measures and would consider the contested measure *not* necessary only when a less GATT-inconsistent alternative measure was reasonably available. Moreover, whereas the ILC developed, in part, its definition along the principle of compensating the parties whose interests have been affected by the contested measure (excuse), the GATT General/Security Exceptions do not require the payment of compensation if the measure is successfully defended as necessary (justification). The similarities and differences between these two views is discussed in detail in Chapter 11.

It is not clear why the GATT/WTO dispute settlement organs developed a concept of necessity different from the concept of necessity being developed by the ILC. The difference may have to do with the context within which the two concepts of necessity operate: the ILC-type of necessity usually operates in circumstances of grave and imminent threats to the interests or the survival of a state (hence the measure to be taken has to be the 'only' available measure), necessity in the General Exceptions operates within the context of international trade and protecting a non-trade objective (hence, the possibility for the contested measure not to be the only measure available). Nevertheless, the three key elements of the 'weighing and balancing' test developed by the Appellate Body appear to be rational choices and are working well.

8.3 The Concept of Necessity in the Security Exceptions

Section 8.3 picks up from the end of Sub-section 7.3.5 and discusses the different path that the Security Exceptions took contrasted to the General Exceptions. In WTO agreements, the Security Exceptions are found in Article XXI of the GATT 1994, Article XIV *bis* of the GATS, Article 73 of the TRIPS Agreement, Article 3 of the TRIMS Agreement (by reference to Article XXI of the GATT 1994), Article XXIII:1 of the Agreement on Government Procurement and Article 24(7) of the Agreement on Trade Facilitation (by reference to Article XXI of the GATT

1994). The Design of International Trade Agreements Database reveals that 291 regional and preferential trade agreements incorporate a national security exception.[157] The Security Exceptions in the WTO agreements contain the concept of necessity in them. Section 8.3, after briefly presenting the history of the drafting of the Security Exceptions in the GATT 1947, discusses the experience of the invocation of Security Exceptions in the GATT and WTO eras. Suggestions will then be made on how the concept of necessity in the Security Exceptions may be interpreted.

8.3.1 *Drafting History of the Security Exceptions in the GATT 1947*

It was mentioned in Sub-section 7.3.3 that the General Exceptions in the draft GATT 1947 and the ITO Charter (Articles XIX and 43 respectively) were divided into two articles each (Articles XX/XXI and 43/94 respectively) to be called the General Exceptions and Security Exceptions respectively. In Havana, Article 43 became Article 45 and was made an exception only to Chapter IV of the Draft Charter (commercial policy), but that Article 94, which became Article 99, was made an exception to the entire ITO Charter. The failure of the establishment of the ITO left only Articles XX and XXI of the GATT 1947 as exceptions to the GATT 1947. Under the WTO Agreement, Security Exceptions, similar to Article XXI of the GATT 1994, were found in the GATS (Article XIV *bis*) and the TRIPS Agreement (Article 73) as exceptions to the respective WTO agreements and not to the entire WTO Agreement.

Article XXI of the GATT 1994 reads:

Nothing in this Agreement shall be construed:

1. to require any contracting party to furnish any information the disclosure of which it considers contrary to its essential security interests; or
2. to prevent any contracting party from taking any action which it considers necessary for the protection of its essential security interests
   (i) relating to fissionable materials or the materials from which they are derived;
   (ii) relating to the traffic in arms, ammunition and implements of war and to such traffic in other goods and materials as is

157 Peter Van den Bossche, 'The National Security Exception in International Trade Law Today: Can We Avoid Abuse?', in *Vereeniging 'Handelsrecht' Preadviezen 2020: Toetsing van buitenlandse investeringen in geopolitiek en juridisch perspectief* (Zutphen: Uitgeverij Paris bv, 2020), p. 112.

carried on directly or indirectly for the purpose of supplying a military establishment;

(iii) taken in time of war or other emergency in international relations; or

3. to prevent any contracting party from taking any action in pursuance of its obligations under the UN Charter for the maintenance of international peace and security.

Pre-GATT bilateral and multilateral conventions, conferences and fora had referred to security exceptions in general terms. The most recurrent form used to refer to security exceptions was that nothing in those agreements shall extend to prohibitions or restrictions "relative to public security". The General Exceptions part of the December 1945 USSD Proposals (Sub-section 7.2.2) referred to security exceptions only in general terms (see paragraphs 7 and 8 of the Proposals). Article 32 of the September 1946 Suggested Charter (Section 7.3) also contained four paragraphs which finally found themselves in what are now known as Security Exceptions in the GATT 1994, the GATS and the TRIPS Agreement. These four security-related paragraphs did not have the phrase 'which it considers necessary' which, as now contained in these WTO agreements, has been largely interpreted as giving the invoking state a broader autonomy in determining the actions that it can take when the situations contained in the paragraphs arise.

The current shape of the Security Exceptions with the phrase 'which it considers necessary' (as also contained in the GATT 1947 and the ITO Charter) was first prepared during the Geneva meeting of the Preparatory Committee of the UN Conference on Trade and Employment.[158] Except for a few comments that the US delegation made regarding the scope of, and the perspective for understanding, the security exceptions in its Suggested Charter (which became the basis for the GATT 1947 discussions), there is little drafting history in respect of the provisions of Article XXI of the GATT 1947, particularly paragraphs (a) and (b)(i)/(ii).[159] The *Russia – Traffic in Transit (2019)* panel noted that the US delegation was itself divided regarding the phrase 'which it considers necessary' between a group that favored freedom of action in relation to security interests and those who believed that such unilateral action may be abused by some countries and that finally the position of the latter group prevailed and:

158 E/PC/T/196, p. 52; E/PC/T/180, p. 178.

159 MTN.GNG/NG7/W/16, *GATT Negotiating Group on GATT Articles* (Article XXI, Note by the Secretariat, 18 August 1987), p. 4.

> [t]heir position, that *the scope of unilateral action accorded to a Member invoking the security exceptions would be limited to the necessity of the measure and would not extend to the determination of the other elements of the provision*, was reflected in the United States' proposal [for Article 94 of the draft ITO Charter] of 4 July 1947[160] (*emphasis added*).[161]

During the Geneva discussions the US delegation was asked by the delegate for The Netherlands about the meaning of the terms 'essential security interests' and 'emergency in international relations' in response to which the US delegate made known the earlier understanding among members of his delegation on the limits of invoking the security exceptions. In other words, it was the opinion of the US delegation that a "proper balance" needs to be maintained between allowing the taking of measured "needed purely for security reasons" and the need to ensure that countries will not "under the guise of security" will not put on measured which have a commercial purpose.[162] Such an understanding of the security measures echoes the majority view of the 17th and 18th century philosophers who agreed that the powers of the Westphalian sovereign to take necessary actions for reason of state must be limited (see Subsection 1.3.1). Given the US' interpretation of the Security Exceptions during the Geneva session, it is quite strange[163] that in *Russia – Traffic in Transit* (2019), out of the ten third parties which submitted arguments in the dispute,[164] only the US initially insisted that Article XXI(b)(iii) – and in subsequent disputes[165] the US would argue that the entire Article XXI – is self-judging and that a panel

160 The final version of Article 94 that looks exactly like the one in GATT Article XXI today is the draft prepared on 22 August 1947 in Geneva. WTO Panel Report, *Russia – Measures Concerning Traffic in Transit* (2019), para. 7.96. For an exhaustive presentation of the drafting of Article XXI of the GATT, particularly the input of the US Delegation in the process of drafting that article, see, Mona Pinchis-Paulse, 'Trade Multilateralism and U.S. National Security: The Making of the GATT Security Exceptions', *Michigan Journal of International Law*, 41(1): 2019, pp. 109–194.

161 WTO Panel Report, *Russia – Measures Concerning Traffic in Transit* (2019), paras. 7.89–7.91.

162 Ibid, paras. 7.92–7.93.

163 Or not strange, looking at the Trump administration's view of the WTO or the not-much-changed attitude of the Biden administration.

164 WTO Panel Report, *Russia – Traffic in Transit* (2019), paras. 7.35–7.51.

165 For instance, WTO Panel Report, *US – Origin Marking Requirement* (2022), para. 7.29, WTO Panel Report, *US – Certain Measures on Steel and Aluminum Products* (*Norway*) (2022), paras. 7.93, 7.1116 etc.; WTO Panel Report, *US – Certain Measures on Steel and Aluminum Products* (*Switzerland*) (2022), paras. 7.2, 7.123 etc.; WTO Panel Report, *US – Certain Measures on Steel and Aluminum Products* (*Türkiye*) (2022), paras. 7.120–7.121; WTO Panel Report, *US – Certain Measures on Steel and Aluminum Products* (*China*) (2022), paras. 7.2, 7.105 etc.

cannot determine whether Article XXI(b) was correctly invoked.[166] The US argued, in part, that "every WTO Member retains the authority to determine for itself those matters that it considers necessary for the protection of its essential security interests, as 'reflected' in the text of Article XXI" and that "this is an 'inherent right' that has been repeatedly recognized by GATT contracting parties and WTO Members."[167] The US also submitted that "the dispute is 'non-justiciable' because there are no legal criteria by which the issue of a Member's consideration of its essential security interests can be judged."[168] The panel noted that the US "bases its position on its interpretation of the text of Article XXI, specifically, the 'self-judging' language of the chapeau in Article XXI(b) '*which it considers necessary* for the protection of its essential security interests'".[169] In Article XXI of the GATT 1994, the term 'necessary' is found only in the introductory clause to (*chapeau* of) paragraph (b): "to prevent any Member from taking any action which it considers necessary for the protection of its essential security interests". This is the same with the GATS (Article XIV *bis* (1)(b)) and the TRIPS Agreement (Article 73(b)). The main focus of Section 8.3 will, therefore, be on how the term 'necessity' has been, or must be, interpreted in the realm of WTO Security Exceptions.

8.3.2 *Invocation of the Security Exceptions during the GATT and WTO Eras*

This sub-section briefly presents the practice of invoking the Security Exceptions during the GATT and WTO eras. The records show, compared to the General Exceptions, a very low use (self-restraint in the use) of the Security Exceptions. The publications on the subject and the GATT/WTO records state that the main reason for this trend is the concern that the Security Exceptions may be abused by the states which invoke them.[170] Another reason could be that most of the facts involved in Security Exception defenses constitute sensitive matters[171] (such as military or political matters) that are usually addressed in venues other than a trade dispute organ. Nevertheless, this sub-section will discuss the history of Security Exceptions disputes in the GATT/WTO era with special focus on the 'necessity' element in the Security Exceptions and

166 WTO Panel Report, *Russia – Traffic in Transit* (2019), para. 7.52.
167 Ibid, para. 7.51.
168 Ibid, para. 7.52.
169 Ibid.
170 Van den Bossche, above note 157, p. 115.
171 Tania Voon, 'The Security Exception in WTO Law: Entering a New Era', *American Journal of International Law*, 113: 2019, p. 45.

will suggest alternatives on how necessity should be defined in the Security Exceptions.

In the history of the GATT, only one measure taken under Article XXI(b)(ii) was brought before a GATT panel,[172] at least nine measures taken under Article XXI(b)(iii) were discussed[173] by the Contracting Parties[174] and one measure taken under Article XXI(c) was raised in a Contracting Party's notification.[175] The cases or discussions on Article XXI(b) – related to this book – almost entirely focused on the issue of whether the taking of Article XXI measures is 'self-judging', i.e., whether a panel could review the validity or justification of invoking Article XXI. In other words, the thrust of the debates, including those in the numerous academic publications on the subject,[176] was whether Article XXI measures are 'justiciable' and, if so, up to which level in the paragraphs. In reaction to the *EC, Australia and Canada – Trade Measures against Argentina (1982)*, the Contracting Parties issued a Ministerial Declaration which decided that: (1) subject to the exception in Article XXI:a, contracting parties should be informed to the fullest extent possible of trade measures taken under Article XXI (b) when action is taken under Article XXI, all contracting parties affected by such action retain their full rights under the General Agreement; and (c) the Council may be requested to give further consideration to this matter in due course.[177] The tendency in the GATT disputes and discussions was, therefore, that the Contracting Parties were not ready to seriously consider the claim that, as Ghana stated for example, "under [Article XXI(b)] each contracting

172 *US – Embargo on Strategic Goods (1949)* at MTN.GNG/NG7/W/16, above note 159, p. 5.

173 In *US – Trade Measures Affecting Nicaragua (1986)*, a panel was established but its terms of reference prohibited it from examining the justification of the US' invocation of Article XXI. Ibid, p. 7.

174 *US – Suspension of Obligations between the US and Czechoslovakia (1951)*; *Prohibition of Czechoslovakian Imports by Peru (1954)*; *Ghana – Ban on Imports of Portuguese Goods (1961)*; *US – Embargo on Trade with Cuba (1962)*; *Egypt – Boycott against Israel and Secondary Boycott (1970)*; *EC, Australia and Canada – Trade Measures against Argentina (1982)*; *US – Imports of Sugar from Nicaragua (1982)*; *US – Trade Measures Affecting Nicaragua (1986)*; *Sweden – Import Quota System for Footwear (1975)*; and *EC – Trade Measures against Yugoslavia (1991)*. See also, ibid, pp. 5–7; GATT, *Analytical Index: Guide to GATT Law and Practice* (updated 6th ed., 1995), pp. 600–605.

175 India's notification of GATT Article XX(c) measures against Iraq, Fiji, Serbia and Montenegro. GATT, ibid, p. 605. The EC's measure against Yugoslavia also had raised an issue under Article XX(c). GATT, ibid, p. 604.

176 A good summary of these debates is available at, Jaemin Lee, 'Commercializing National Security? National Security Exceptions' Outer Parameter under GATT Article XXI', *Asian Journal of WTO & International Health Law and Policy*, 13(2): 2018, pp. 290–292.

177 GATT, above note 174, p. 606.

party was the sole judge of what was necessary in its essential security interests."[178] Finally, the *US – Embargo on Trade with Nicaragua (1985)* panel, which was prohibited by the terms of reference from making a finding on Article XXI made an interesting note on the invocation of Security Exceptions that "the GATT could not achieve its basic aims unless each contracting party, whenever it made use of its rights under Article XXI, carefully weighed its security needs against the need to maintain stable trade relations."[179]

In the WTO era, the trend of not making frequent use (invocation) of Security Exceptions continued until the last few years. The first dispute where an Article XXI defense was invoked was the *US – Cuban Liberty and Democracy Solidarity Act (Helms – Burton Act) (1996)* where the US, in response to an EU complaint that the US Cuban Liberty and Democratic Solidarity Act of 1996 violated GATT 1994 Articles I, III and XI, argued that the measures against Cuba were justified by national security concerns (Article XXI) and cannot, therefore, be reviewed by a WTO panel.[180] In 1999, in a response to a complaint by Colombia and Honduras that its sanctions against them violated the GATT 1994 (*Nicaragua – Measures Affecting Imports from Honduras and Colombia (1999)*, DS188 and DS201), Nicaragua invoked Article XXI of the GATT 1994 and GATS Article XIV *bis* to claim that its actions were non-justiciable. The panel was never established.[181] Peng also claims that in *China – Raw Materials (2012)* and *China – Rare Earths (2014)* China considered, but eventually decided against, invoking the Security Exceptions.[182]

Since 2016, however, invocations of Security Exceptions have proliferated. Following failure of consultations, Ukraine applied for the establishment of a panel to resolve its dispute with Russia regarding alleged restrictions on traffic in transit from Ukraine, through Russia, to Kazakhstan and other countries. The *ad hoc Russia – Traffic in Transit (2019)* panel issued its report and interpreted Article XXI(b) of the GATT 1994.[183] The interpretation of the *Russia – Traffic in Transit (2019)* panel is discussed below.

178 MTN.GNG/NG7/W/16, above note 159, p. 6.

179 GATT Panel Report, *US – Trade Measures Affecting Nicaragua (1986)*, para. 5.16.

180 Request for Consultations, *United States – The Cuban Liberty and Democratic Solidarity Act (Helms – Burton Act)*, WT/DS38/1.

181 Shin-yi Peng, 'Cybersecurity Threats and the WTO National Security Exceptions', *Journal of International Economic Law*, 18(2): 2015, p. 461.

182 Ibid.

183 *Russia – Measures Concerning Traffic in Transit (2019)*, available at, https://www.wto.org/english/tratop_e/dispu_e/cases_e/ds512_e.htm.

In its August 2017 request for consultations with the UAE,[184] Qatar raised a number of claims against the UAE for using coercive measures against it in violation of the GATT 1994, the GATS and the TRIPS Agreement and the UAE, *inter alia*, invoked the Security Exceptions in those WTO agreements and argued that the matter is not justiciable. The panel was composed in September 2018. In January 2021, the Chair of the panel informed the Dispute Settlement Body that it had granted Qatar's request, to which the UAE agreed, that the panel suspend its proceedings until further notice.[185]

Between April and July 2018, nine WTO Members (China, India, Canada, the EU, Mexico, Norway, Russia, Switzerland and Turkey) complained before the WTO that the impositions by the US of duties of 25% on imports of steel and 10% on imports of aluminum products, respectively, are inconsistent with provisions of the GATT 1994 and the Agreement on Safeguards.[186] The US responded that it took the measures under Section 232 of its Trade Expansion Act of 1962, which authorizes the President of the US to impose import restrictions to protect US national security. The US persisted in arguing that Article XXI is self-judging, i.e., whenever a respondent invokes Article XXI of the GATT 1994 the disputes are non-justiciable and, therefore, the panel should limit its findings only to recognizing the invocation of Article XXI. In December 2022, the panel issued its report on the complaints made by China, Norway, Switzerland and Türkiye which have been appealed. Mutually agreed solutions were notified regarding the complaints from Canada, EU, India and Mexico. The panel on the Russian complaint is yet to issue its report.

---

184 Request for Consultations by Qatar, *UAE – Measures Relating to Trade in Goods, Services and Trade Related Aspects of Intellectual Property Rights*, WTO Doc. WT/DS/526/1.

185 *UAE – Measures Relating to Trade in Goods, Services and Trade Related Aspects of Intellectual Property Rights*, available at, https://www.wto.org/english/tratop_e/dispu_e/cases_e/ds526_e.htm.

186 Request for Consultations by China, *United States – Certain Measures on Steel and Aluminum Products*, WTO Doc. WT/DS/544/1; Request for Consultations by Canada, *United States – Certain Measures on Steel and Aluminum Products*, WTO Doc. WT/DS/550/1; Request for Consultations by the European Union, *United States – Certain Measures on Steel and Aluminum Products*, WTO Doc. WT/DS/548/1; Request for Consultations by India, *United States – Certain Measures on Steel and Aluminum Products*, WTO Doc. WT/DS/547/1; Request for Consultations by Mexico, *United States – Certain Measures on Steel and Aluminum Products*, WTO Doc. WT/DS/551/1; Request for Consultations by Norway, *United States – Certain Measures on Steel and Aluminum Products*, WTO Doc. WT/DS/552/1; Request for Consultations by the Russian Federation, *United States – Certain Measures on Steel and Aluminum Products*, WTO Doc. WT/DS/554/1; Request for Consultations by Switzerland, *United States – Certain Measures on Steel and Aluminum Products*, WTO Doc. WT/DS/556/1; and Request for Consultations by Turkey, *United States – Certain Measures on Steel and Aluminum Products*, WTO Doc. WT/DS/556/1.

In November 2018, Qatar requested the establishment of a panel to resolve its dispute with Saudi Arabia and the panel issued its report (currently under appeal) in June 2020.[187] Qatar complained that Saudi Arabia violated its obligations under the TRIPS Agreement and Saudi Arabia defended its measures under Article 73(b)(iii) of the TRIPS Agreement (Security Exceptions). The panel interpreted Article 73(b)(iii) along the same lines as the interpretation developed by the *Russia – Traffic in Transit (2019)* panel which interpreted the similarly worded Article XXI(b)(iii) of the GATT 1994. The interpretation of the *Saudi Arabia – Measures Concerning IP Rights (2020)* panel is discussed below.

In its September 2019 request for consultations with Japan, South Korea complained about Japan's imposition of restrictions through export licensing policies and procedures imposing certain licensing requirements on exports of some materials as well as their related technologies destined for Korea.[188] When consultations failed, Korea requested the establishment of a panel. At a Dispute Settlement Body meeting held in June 2020, Japan stated that Article XXI of the GATT 1994 "fully recognizes the rights of WTO Members to adopt export control policies and implement an export control system in order to prevent unintended export of goods that can be potentially diverted for use in weapons and for other military uses, and the right of members to decide on the enforcement of such restrictions."[189] The complaint was withdrawn in March 2023.

8.3.3 *Interpreting Necessity in the Security Exceptions*

The first, and surely landmark, WTO dispute where a panel decided on the substance of the Security Exceptions, including the controversial issue of justiciability of their invocation, is the *Russia – Traffic in Transit (2019)* dispute. As mentioned in Sub-section 8.3.2, the panel had to decide first whether Article XXI(b)(iii) of the GATT 1994 is non-justiciable. In a nutshell, the panel, chaired by Professor Georges Abi-Saab, after asserting jurisdiction over Russia's argument,[190] interpreted the provision to mean that while the responding Member determines the necessity of its measure to protect its essential security interests, the panel would review whether the situations giving rise to the emergency measures exist. The panel, by referring to the negotiating history of

187 WTO Panel Report, *Saudi Arabia – Measures Concerning IP Rights (2020)*.

188 Request for Consultations by the Republic of Korea, *Japan – Measures Related to the Exportation of Products and Technology to Korea*, WTO Doc. WT/DS/590/1.

189 WTO, *DS590: Japan – Measures Related to the Exportation of Products and Technology to Korea*, available at, www.wto.org/english/news_e/news20_e/dsb29jun20_e.htm.

190 WTO Panel Report, *Russia – Traffic in Transit (2019)*, paras. 7.53–7.58.

Article XXI, stated that its interpretation meant that "*the scope of unilateral action accorded to a Member invoking the security exceptions would be limited to the necessity of the measure* [i.e., to the introductory clause to paragraph (b)] *and would not extend to the determination of the other elements of the provision* [i.e., sub-paragraphs (i)-(iii)]."[191] In other words, the panel split Article XXI(b)(iii) into two parts – justiciable (sub-paragraphs (i)-(iii)) and non-justiciable (the introductory clause) – or, as Boklan and Bahri stated, respectively into 'objective' and 'subjective' determinations which reflect the need to balance protection of national security interests with the obligation to promote international commerce.[192] The panel found that the elements of sub-paragraph (iii) were met and, true to its reading of the introductory clause in paragraph (b), left the determination and application of the necessary measures to Russia's decision provided that Russia convinces the panel that it: (a) sufficiently articulated the essential security interests;[193] (b) identified and took the measures in good faith;[194] and (c) determined the connection between the essential security interests and those measures in good faith.[195]

Of particular interest to this book is the panel's reading of the phrase 'which it considers'. The panel stated – as the *US – Origin Marking Requirement* (*2022*) later did very elaborately[196] – that 'which it considers' must mean of one of the following: (a) the respondent's right to determine the necessity of the measures for the protection of 'its essential security interests'; or (b) the respondent's right to determine what its essential security interests are as well as the necessity of the measures for protecting those essential security interests; or (c) finally and maximally, on top of determining the elements of

191 Ibid, para. 7.91.

192 Daria Boklan and Amrita Bahri, 'The First WTO's Ruling on National Security Exception: Balancing Interests or Opening Pandora's Box?', *World Trade Review*, 19(1): 2020, pp. 126–136. Prazeres appreciated such reading of Article XXI(b)(iii) by the panel as "... well balanced [and] addressed the challenge of respecting Members' sovereignty in matters of national security while also defining parameters for a legal review of a provision which is integral to the WTO's legal framework". Tatiana Lacerda Prazeres, 'Trade and National Security: Rising Risks for the WTO', *World Trade Review*, 19(1): 2020, p. 141. See also, Alan S. Alexandroff and Rajeev Sharma, 'The National Security Provision-GATT Article XXI', in Patrick F. J. Macrory, Arthur E. Appleton and Michael G. Plummer (eds.), *The World Trade Organization: Legal, Economic and Political Analysis* (Vol. I) (New York: Springer Science+ Business Media, Inc., 2005), p. 1572. See also, Lee's support to the 'subjective' and 'objective' bifurcation of paragraph (b) of Article XXI in Lee, above note 176, p. 289.

193 WTO Panel Report, *Russia – Traffic in Transit* (*2019*), paras. 7.134–135.

194 Ibid, paras. 7.59–7.149, especially paras. 7.132–133.

195 Ibid, para. 7.138.

196 WTO Panel Report, *US – Origin Marking Requirement* (*2022*), para. 7.22–7.190.

the introductory clause (i.e., elements (a) and (b)), the respondent's right to determine the elements of sub-paragraphs (i)-(iii). The panel first split paragraph (b) into justiciable (sub-paragraphs (i)-(iii)) and non-justiciable (the introductory clause) parts. The panel then held that while it is for the responding Member to determine its essential security interests[197] and the necessity of the measures for protecting those interests,[198] the Member must articulate its essential security interests and show that it took the measures and determined the connection between the interests and the measures in good faith.[199] A number of scholars have also advocated such balance between the respondent's discretion and the caution to prevent abuse by the respondent (i.e., good faith requirement).[200]

However, as far as determining the necessity of the measures, the panel, and the subsequent panels which examined Security Exception disputes,[201] left us

---

197 The panel's stated that 'essential security interests' is evidently a narrower concept than 'security interests' and could refer to "the quintessential functions of the state, namely, the protection of its territory and its population from external threats, and the maintenance of law and public order internally" and that the situation varies with changing circumstances and is therefore "left, in general, to every Member to define what it considers to be its essential security interests". WTO Panel Report, *Russia – Traffic in Transit* (2019), paras. 7.130–131.

198 On this issue the panel stated that "[t]his conclusion follows by logical necessity if the adjectival clause 'which it considers' is to be given legal effect." Ibid, para. 7.146. In footnote 222, the panel also added that its conclusion in para. 7.146 "is also confirmed by the negotiating history of Article XXI" which it discussed at length in para. 7.92 of the report.

199 Ibid, paras. 7.63, 7.128–7.138. The *Saudi Arabia – Measures Concerning IP Rights* (2020) panel, by reference to the *Russia – Traffic in Transit* (2019) report, made similar conclusions regarding which issues are 'justiciable' or 'reviewable' in a dispute involving the Security Exceptions under Article XXI(b) of the GATT 1994 and Article 73(b) of the TRIPS agreement. WTO Panel Report, *Saudi Arabia – Measures Concerning IP Rights* (2020), para. 7.242.

200 Van den Bossche and Zdouc, above note 1, p. 620; Van den Bossche, above note 157, pp. 118, 139–140; Voon, above note 171, pp. 47–50; Ji Yeong Yoo and Dukgeun Ahn, 'Security Exceptions in the WTO System: Bridge or Bottle-neck for Trade and Security?', *Journal of International Economic Law*, 19(2): (2016); pp. 417–444; Roger Alford, 'The Self-Judging WTO Security Exception' *Utah Law Review*, 3: 2011, p. 758; R. V. Anuradha, 'Petrificus Totalus: The Spell of National Security', *Asian Journal of WTO & International Health Law and Policy*, 13(2): 2018, pp. 311–328 (look at f.n. 1 for related references of other publications sharing the view).

201 The subsequent panels (see the list in above note 165) could not be expected to provide definition for the term 'necessary', because they already found – before they could discuss the phrase 'which it considers necessary' in the introductory clause in paragraph (b) of Article XXI – that the respondent failed to meet the requirements of sub-paragraph (iii) of paragraph (b). The only subsequent panel which dwelt on the concept of necessity in a line similar to that of the panel in *Russia – Traffic in Transit* (2019) is the *Saudi*

with no guide on the elements of necessity in the Security Exceptions except with the finding that determining necessity is discretion of the responding Member provided it takes the action in good faith. The *Russia – Traffic in Transit (2019)* panel briefly stated: "it is for Russia to determine the 'necessity' of the actions for the protection of its essential security interests. This conclusion follows by logical necessity if the adjectival clause 'which it considers' is to be given legal effect."[202] The panel's opinion is limited to stating that the respondent has the discretion to determine whether a given action is necessary to protect its essential security interests. Surely the panel did not leave it wholly up to the respondent to determine the necessity of the measures as it stated that the respondent must show, to the satisfaction of the panel, that it determined the necessity of the measures and their connection with the essential security interests in good faith and applied the measures in good faith.

Saudi Arabia – Measures Concerning IP Rights (2020) is the next WTO era dispute that involved Security Exceptions claims. In June 2017, Saudi Arabia, the UAE, Egypt and Bahrain severed all relations with Qatar and issued a list of preconditions on Qatar if they are to resume relations with it.[203] Relevant to this WTO dispute, the Saudi government took a series of measures against, or affecting, the Qatar-based global sports and entertainment company, beIN Media Group LLC.[204] In August 2017 a broadcasting entity known as beoutQ emerged and began, with Saudi Arabia's support, the unauthorized distribution, streaming and rebroadcasting of media content that is created by or licensed to beIN.[205] Qatar's complaint against Saudi Arabia's identified six measures that harmed beIN's interests which resulted in multiple violations of Saudi Arabia's obligations under TRIPS Agreement only three of which were accepted by the panel (the so-called 'anti-sympathy' measures examined under Articles 41 and 42 of the TRIPS Agreement and the non-application of criminal procedures and penalties to beoutQ examined under Article 61 of the TRIPS Agreement).[206] Saudi Arabia's main response was that its measures were justifiable as Security Exceptions under Article 73(b)(iii) of the TRIPS Agreement.

Arabia – Measures Concerning IP Rights (2020). See, WTO Panel Report, *Saudi Arabia – Measures Concerning IP Rights (2020)*, paras. 7.271–7.293.

202 WTO Panel Report, *Russia – Traffic in Transit (2019)*, para. 7.146 and f.n. 222.

203 WTO Panel Report, *Saudi Arabia – Measures Concerning IP Rights (2020)*, paras. 2.16, 2.29.

204 Ibid, paras. 2.36–2.38, 7.79.

205 Ibid, paras. 2.30–2.45, 7.157–7.163.

206 Ibid, paras. 2.46–2.48, 3.1, paras. 7.37–7.164.

On order of analysis, panel took a path opposite to that taken by the panel in *Russia – Traffic in Transit* (*2019*)[207] and decided to first examine whether Saudi Arabia acted inconsistently with its obligations under the relevant provisions in the TRIPS Agreement and, if the finding is in the affirmative, examine if Saudi Arabia could justify its actions under Article 73(b)(iii) of the TRIPS Agreement.[208] Accordingly the panel concluded that the disputed measures were inconsistent with Saudi Arabia's obligation under Articles 41.1, 42 and 61 of the TRIPS Agreement.[209] The panel then began its analysis of Article 73(b)(iii) by noting that this provision is identical to Article XXI(b)(iii) of the GATT 1994 which was considered by the *Russia – Traffic in Transit* (*2019*)[210] and that the parties interpreted Article 73(b)(iii) "by reference to, and consistently with, the interpretation of Article XXI(b)(iii) of the GATT 1994 developed by the panel in *Russia – Traffic in Transit*".[211] Thus the panel, closely following the interpretation developed by the *Russia – Traffic in Transit* (*2019*) panel and finally concluded that Saudi Arabia's defense under Article 73(b)(iii) was successful in relation to its anti-sympathy measures, but not in relation to its non-application of criminal procedures and penalties to beoutQ.[212]

Regarding the concept of necessity in Article 73(b), the panel followed the analysis[213] of the *Russia – Traffic in Transit* (*2019*) panel that, while it is for the responding Member to determine the 'necessity' of the measures for the protection of its essential security interests, the responding Member must show: (a) good faith in articulating its essential security interests; (b) good faith in the process of identifying and applying the measures it considered necessary; and (c) that the measures are not so remote from, or unrelated to, the emergency that it becomes implausible that the Member implemented the measures for the protection of its essential security interests arising out of the emergency.[214]

---

207 The panel had decided, and provided reasons for its decision, to first examine whether Russia's measures could be justified under Article XXI(b) and, if it found in the negative, then examine consistency of Russia's measures under Articles V and X of the GATT 1994. WTO Panel Report, *Russia – Traffic in Transit* (*2019*), paras. 7.109–7.109.

208 WTO Panel Report, *Saudi Arabia – Measures Concerning IP Rights* (*2020*), paras. 7.3–7.6.

209 Ibid, paras. 7.24–7.221.

210 Ibid, paras. 7.231, 7.241, and f.n. 752 to para. 7.241.

211 Ibid, paras. 7.232, 7.243.

212 Ibid, para. 7.294.

213 Ibid, paras. 7.271–7.293.

214 Ibid, paras. 7.128–7.138.

8.3.4 *Three Possible Interpretations of the Term 'Necessary' in the Security Exceptions*

Except for the three tests in ascertaining whether the responding Member properly identified and applied the measure selected as necessary (articulation of essential security interests, good faith in identifying and applying the measures deemed necessary and the closeness/remoteness of the measures from the emergency situation), the *Russia – Traffic in Transit* (2019) and *Saudi Arabia – Measures Concerning IP Rights* (2020) panels left open the answer to the question: what is meant by 'necessary' in the Security Exceptions of the GATT 1994 and the TRIPS Agreement (and arguably also in GATS Article XIV *bis*)? Three possible interpretations may be suggested:

1. The panels did not state that it is left up to the respondent to *define* 'necessity' but to *decide*, that a given measure is necessary or not (provided that there is a common understanding of what constitutes 'necessity'). In other words, and to use the General Exceptions for clarification, one can argue that 'necessity' may have an objective meaning both in the General Exceptions and Security Exceptions.[215] In this case, we can make use of the 'objective' elements developed for interpreting necessity in the General Exceptions disputes. The only difference will then be that while in the General Exceptions the necessity of a given measure is reviewed by the dispute settlement organ, in the Security Exceptions the determination is made, without review, by the respondent provided it can show that it identified and took the measure in good faith. Peng, for example, proposes that we use the test of the non-availability of less trade-restrictive alternatives as a tool to examine the fairness of the determination of necessity by the respondent in an Article XXI(b) case.[216] If, however, we read the *Russia – Traffic in Transit* (2019) panel's finding to mean that the Member *defines* necessity *and* then *decides* whether its measure is accordingly necessary, it may be difficult for a panel to detect whether there was good faith on the part of the respondent in determining necessity.
2. The interpretation in the previous paragraph may sound too intrusive to the discretion provided to the respondent under the *Russia – Traffic in Transit* (2019) and *Saudi Arabia – Measures Concerning IP*

215 Peter Lindsay, 'The Ambiguity of GATT Article XXI: Subtle Success or Rampant Failure?', *Duke Law Journal*, 52(6): 2003, p. 1282.

216 Peng, above note 181, p. 474.

Rights (2020) panels' reading of paragraphs (b) and (b) respectively of Article XXI of the GATT 1994 and Article 73 of the TRIPS Agreement. It may be argued, in fact, that the proper way to balance the 'objective' (the three sub-paragraphs under these two paragraphs) and 'subjective' (the *chapeau*) parts of these paragraphs is to allow the respondent to *define* 'necessary' on a case-by-case basis. Bhala,[217] Akande and Williams[218] and others[219] seem to agree with this interpretation of necessity in these two paragraphs. The absence in the Security Exceptions of a *chapeau* like that of the General Exceptions (i.e., the strict balancing requirement) may also favor this line of interpretation.

3. There is at least one writer who tries to link the nature of the Security Exceptions to the history of necessity defense under customary international law. It was shown in Section 5.4 that the definition of necessity in Article 25 of the ARSIWA heavily drew from the philosophical discussions on the limitations of Westphalian sovereign acts taken for reasons of state (most of which are taken to protect national security). Thus, the term 'necessary' can be understood along the lines of the definition of necessity in Article 25 of the ARSIWA:

> *Since the security exceptions in Article XXI can trace its roots back to the 'necessity defense' under customary international law, this understanding of Article 25 of the ILC Draft Articles should offer an important guideline for the interpretation of Article XXI*. In particular, a claimed 'emergency' situation under subparagraph (iii) of paragraph (b) should be understood and interpreted in connection with 'essential interest', [in Article 25 of the ARSIWA] now 'essential security interest' as phrased in the *chapeau* of paragraph (b). If anything, this analysis could be regarded as an instance of 'contextual' interpretation, a prong under Article 31 of the VCLT. Likewise, the concept of 'essentiality' can be also

217 Raj Bhala, 'National Security and International Trade Law: What the GATT Says, and What the United States Does', *University of Pennsylvania Journal of International Economic Law*, 19(2): 1998, pp. 264–269.

218 Dapo Akande and Sope Williams, 'International Adjudication on National Security Issues: What Role for the WTO?' *Virginia Journal of International Law*, 43(2): 2003, p. 387.

219 For example, Regis Bonnan, 'The GATT Security Exception in a Dispute Resolution Context: Necessity or Incompatibility?', *Currents: International Trade Law Journal*, 19(1): 2010, p. 5.

> reflected from the WTO case law as well as the illustrated investment disputes … (*emphasis added*).[220]

8.3.5 *Have the GATT 1994/GATS General/Security Exception Disputes Laid the Foundation for Defining the Concept of Necessity in WTO Law?*

The paucity of guidance by the drafters of the GATT/ITO on their understanding of the concept of necessity in the General Exceptions and the historical nebulousness of its meaning (see Chapter 1) left the GATT/WTO dispute settlement organs with the task of developing a workable definition for the concept in GATT/WTO law. As we will discuss in Chapter 9, this task further required WTO panels and the Appellate Body to provide working definitions for the concept of necessity contained in WTO agreements other than the GATT 1994 and the GATS. This further task, as we will also discuss in Chapter 9, required answering the question whether the concept of necessity in these other WTO agreements should be defined along the lines of the definition developed for necessity in the General Exceptions.

Since the General Exceptions and the Security Exceptions were split in the Geneva meetings of 1947, their respective interpretations have followed different paths. Whereas the General Exceptions have been argued in 55 GATT/WTO disputes (as at December 2023) and a consistent interpretation has been developed for them, the Security Exceptions have not been thoroughly analyzed until the findings of the *Russia – Traffic in Transit* (*2019*) and the *Saudi Arabia – Measures Concerning IP Rights* (*2020*) panels. Whereas the concept of necessity in the General Exceptions has been well-defined in more than 40-year long practice in the GATT/WTO, the concept of necessity in the Security Exceptions has only begun to be interpreted in 2019. Despite the difference in perspective of the interpretations of the General Exceptions and the Security Exceptions, it is likely that the definition of necessity in both types of exceptions should be considered similar, the only difference being who determines whether the measure is necessary. It may, therefore, be concluded – and if one also discerns how necessity has been understood in WTO agreements other than the GATT 1994/GATS, as we will see in Chapter 9 – that a definition of the concept of necessity has emerged in WTO law albeit with different implications in different contexts (for instance, between the General and Security Exceptions). Given that the meaning of 'necessary' is yet to be defined in the context of the Security Exceptions, the well-developed interpretation of necessity in the General Exceptions of the GATT 1994/GATS (given also its influence

220 Lee, above note 176, p. 299.

on the interpretations for necessity in the other WTO agreements, as we will see in Chapter 9) may, for now, be referred to as the interpretation of necessity in WTO law and that is the reason why this book, as will be detailed in Chapters 11 and 12, has chosen the General Exceptions interpretation of necessity for comparison with the other fields of international law.

One of the most notable contributions of the GATT/WTO interpretation of necessity is that the GATT/WTO dispute settlement organs not only contributed in distinguishing necessity from the other defenses in international law (self-defense, *force majeure* and distress)[221] but also in distinguishing it from the definition given to it in the ARSIWA.

This book aims to relate the 'concept of necessity in WTO law' with the concepts of necessity contained in other fields of international law and discuss what the concept of necessity in WTO law can learn from the concepts of necessity in different fields of international law and *vice versa*. Before that interoperability can be examined though, a couple of discussions need to take place. Firstly, the concept of necessity as contained and interpreted in WTO agreements other than the GATT 1994 and the GATS has to be examined. This is covered in Chapter 9 at the end of which we can have a clearer picture of the 'concept of necessity in WTO law'. With that covered, the next step will be to examine the interoperability between the concepts of necessity in WTO law and other fields of international law (to culminate in Chapter 12). For now, though, the focus will be in completing the picture of the concept of necessity in WTO law by analyzing, in Chapter 9, how WTO panels and the Appellate Body have defined necessity in WTO agreements other than the GATT 1994 and the GATS.

---

221 Although this was mainly done by the ILC in producing the ARSIWA.

CHAPTER 9

The Concept of Necessity in Other WTO Agreements, the TBT, SPS and TRIPS Agreements in Particular

Chapter 8 discussed how the concept of necessity has been interpreted in the General Exceptions of the GATT 1994 and the GATS. It also made suggestions on how the concept should be understood or interpreted in the Security Exceptions of the legal texts of the WTO Agreement. Since necessity is contained in WTO agreements other than the GATT 1994 and the GATS, it was stated at the end of Chapter 8 that one can refer to a 'concept of necessity in WTO law' if the interpretation developed for necessity in the General Exceptions is (can be) adopted in the necessity provisions in other WTO agreements. Chapter 9 will show that the term 'necessity' has now been well-defined in at least two other WTO agreements: the TBT Agreement and the SPS Agreement. WTO panels and the Appellate Body have concluded that the concept of necessity in these two agreements has to be generally interpreted, *mutatis mutandis*,[1] along the lines of the interpretation developed for the concept in the General Exceptions of the GATT 1994/GATS. Almost all of the disputes that have interpreted necessity in WTO agreements other than the GATT 1994 and the GATS are related to the TBT and SPS agreements. Although the TRIPS Agreement contains General Exceptions-like provisions, the WTO dispute settlement organs are yet to decide if the term 'necessary' therein should, as with the case of the TBT and SPS agreements, follow the interpretation already developed for the term 'necessary' in the General Exceptions of the GATT 1994/GATS. Thus, the focus of this chapter will be on the TBT, SPS and TRIPS agreements.

Section 9.1 presents the topography of the term 'necessary'/'necessity' in the WTO agreements other than the GATT 1994 and the GATS with special emphasis on the TBT, SPS and TRIPS agreements. Section 9.2 will first, as context, present short background information on the TBT and SPS agreements and their objectives as well as the relationship which exists not only between them but also between them and the GATT 1994 regarding the concept of necessity. Section 9.3 then discusses the interpretation so far developed for the concept

1 For example, as we will see in Section 9.3, whereas 'necessity' in the General Exceptions is an affirmative defense that the respondent must raise, in the TBT and SPS agreements necessity is a substantive obligation the violation of which the complainant must prove.

 | DOI:10.1163/9789004700000_011

of necessity in the TBT and SPS agreements. Section 9.4 will interrelate the interpretations respectively developed for the concept of necessity in the GATT 1994/GATS, the TBT and the SPS agreements and draw some conclusions. Section 9.5 will briefly discuss how the concept of necessity is likely to (should) be interpreted in the TRIPS Agreement. Section 9.6 will respond to the question whether a WTO law concept of necessary has emerged.

To date, necessity, as found in several WTO agreements, has been similarly interpreted in at least four WTO agreements (the GATT 1994, the GATS, the TBT Agreement and the SPS Agreement). As mentioned in Section 8.3, the two disputes that involved the Security Exceptions in the GATT 1994 and the TRIPS Agreement (*Russia – Traffic in Transit* (*2019*) and *Saudi Arabia – Measures Concerning IP Rights* (*2020*) respectively) discussed necessity as found in the Security Exceptions, although what is 'necessary' in the realm of Security Exceptions is yet to be clarified. This chapter will argue that the interpretation developed for the concept of necessity in the General Exceptions in the GATT 1994, the GATS and similarly worded provisions in other WTO agreements may also be applied for the concepts of necessity in similarly worded provisions in other WTO agreements (for example, the TRIPS Agreement, the TRIMS Agreement, the Safeguards Agreement and the GP Agreement). Accordingly, this chapter will conclude that the General Exceptions-TBT Agreement-SPS Agreement interpretation of necessity may be held to represent the 'concept of necessity in WTO law' for the purpose of interrelating it, as will be done in Chapter 6, with the concepts of necessity contained in other fields of international law.

9.1 Textual Presence of the Term (Concept of) Necessity

Regardless of the context within which it operates, the word 'necessary' has a visible presence in the legal texts of the WTO Agreement. A search of these legal texts[2] revealed that the word 'necessary' appears 249 times throughout these documents. The term takes many forms such as: 'necessary'; 'necessary to'; 'necessary for'; 'any necessary'; 'to the extent necessary'; '(as) may be necessary'; 'as deemed necessary'; 'as often as necessary'; 'where (it is) necessary'; 'if necessary'; or 'unnecessary'. By way of example, the term appears, including in footnotes and respective annexes: 37 times in the GATT 1994; 25 times in

2 As available at, https://www.wto.org/english/docs_e/legal_e/final_e.htm. The Microsoft Word search was also done on 21 October 2023.

the SCM Agreement; 24 times in the GATS; 23 times in the TBT Agreement; 18 times in the Customs Valuation Agreement; 17 times in the SPS Agreement; 16 times in the GP Agreement; 11 times in the Agreement on Textiles and Clothing; 11 times in the Anti-dumping Agreement; nine times in the Agreement on Rules of Origin; seven times in the TRIPS Agreement; seven times in the WTO Agreement (not including its annexes); seven times in the Agreement on Agriculture; five times in the Safeguards Agreement; four times in the DSU; four times in the TRIMS Agreement; and once in the Trade Policy Review Mechanism.

Three general observations can be made regarding the term 'necessary' as it appears in the legal texts of the WTO Agreement. Firstly, the term has, in practice, been initially given its dictionary meaning and defined, *inter alia*, as: "something 'that cannot be dispensed with or done without, requisite, essential, needful'",[3] or one that ranges in a continuum of meanings between 'indispensable' and '(capable of) making a contribution to'[4] or other meanings.[5] Secondly, in light of the focus of the enquiry of this book, the term 'necessary' has been placed either in the form of a substantive obligation or an affirmative defense in the legal texts of the WTO Agreement. Thirdly, this chapter will show that the WTO panels/Appellate Body have adopted the interpretation they developed for the concept of necessity in the GATT 1994/GATS General Exceptions to the concept of necessity in similarly worded provisions in the TBT and SPS agreements. We are yet to see if that interpretation will also be adopted for the concept of necessity found in similarly worded provisions in other agreements such as Article XXIII:1 and 2 of the GP Agreement and Article 5.1 of the Safeguards Agreement.[6] However, the case with the TRIMS Agreement which makes explicit reference, in part, to the General and Security Exceptions of the GATT 1994 appears to be straightforward. Article 3

3 Appellate Body Report, *Korea – Various Measures on Beef* (*2001*), para. 160.

4 Ibid, para. 161; Appellate Body Reports, *EC – Seal Products* (*2014*), para. 5.228.

5 For example, the *US – Wheat Gluten* (*2001*) panel picked the meaning "requiring to be done, achieved, requisite, essential" for the term 'necessary' as it appears in Article 5.1 of the Safeguards Agreement. WTO Panel Report, *US – Wheat Gluten* (*2001*), paras. 108–111.

6 Article XXIII:1 of the GP Agreement is equivalent in wording to the Security Exceptions of the GATT 1994/GATS/TRIPS Agreement and Article XXIII:2 of the GP Agreement is equivalent in wording to the General Exceptions of the GATT 1994/GATS. The necessity provisions in the GP Agreement may, therefore, be interpreted along the lines of the interpretation developed (to be developed) for the necessity provisions in the GATT 1994/GATS General and Security Exceptions. Article 5.1 of the Safeguards Agreement was identified for comparison not because it is equivalent in wording to the General Exceptions, but because its wording is similar to Article 2.2 of the SPS Agreement whose term 'necessary' has been interpreted like the term 'necessary' in the General Exceptions.

of the TRIMS Agreement states: "All exceptions under GATT 1994 shall apply, as appropriate, to the provisions of this agreement." It can be argued that the interpretation developed for Article XX of the GATT 1994, inclusive of the term 'necessary' therein, will be applied to the exceptions regime in Article 3 of the TRIMS Agreement.[7] The same can also be argued for Article 24(7) of the Agreement on Trade Facilitation which, like Article 3 of the TRIMS Agreement, makes reference to 'all exceptions' of the GATT 1994.

Of all the legal texts of the WTO agreements, the TBT, SPS and TRIPS agreements have provisions containing the term 'necessary' in a General Exceptions-like context. The term 'necessary' appears, in different forms, 23 times in the TBT Agreement. These are: the fifth, sixth and seventh recitals of the preamble;[8] Articles 2.2, 2.5, 2.10, 5.1.2, 5.2.2, 5.2.3, 5.2.6, 5.2.7, 5.7, 6.1, 12.3, 12.7, 13.1, 13.3, 15.4; Annex 2 (paragraph 4); and Annex 3 (paragraphs E and N). Of these, the provisions so far raised in the TBT Agreement disputes, or may in the future be raised, as related to the concept of necessity in the GATT 1994/GATS General Exceptions (in text, context and/or purpose) are: the fifth, sixth and seventh recitals of the preamble, Article 2.2, Article 2.5, Article 5.1.2 and Annex 3(E). The term 'necessary' appears, in different forms, 17 times in the SPS Agreement. These are: the first and eighth recitals of the preamble;[9] Articles 2.1, 2.2, 3.2, 5.7, 6.3, 9.1, 12.1, 12.3, 12.5; Annex A(1); Annex B(6); Annex C(1)(b), (c), (e) and (h); and Annex C(2). Of these, the provisions so far raised in the SPS Agreement disputes, or may in the future be raised, as related to the concept of necessity in the GATT 1994/GATS General Exceptions (in text, context and/or purpose) are: the first and eighth recitals of the preamble, Article 2.1, Article 2.2, Article 2.4, Article 3.2 and Article 5.6. The term 'necessary' appears, in different forms, seven times in the TRIPS Agreement.[10] These are the second recital of the

---

7 The *Indonesia – Autos (1998)* and *India – Solar Cells (2016)* panels, for instance, briefly noted the obligation-exception relationship between Articles 2.1 and 3 of the TRIMS Agreement. WTO Panel Report, *Indonesia – Autos (1998)*, paras. 6.84, 14.61, 14.92; WTO Panel Report, *India – Solar Cells (2016)*, para. 7.188 (f.n. 480).

8 The TBT Agreement does not have the titular term 'Preamble' for the recital paragraphs. Nevertheless, the panels/Appellate Body have used the term since their early reports. See, WTO Panel Report, EC *– Asbestos (2001)*, para. 8.22; WTO Panel Report, EC *– Sardines (2002)*, para. 7.119; Appellate Body Report, EC *– Sardines (2002)*, para. 215; Appellate Body Report, *US – Clove Cigarettes (2012)*, para. 88.

9 The SPS Agreement does not have the titular term 'Preamble' for the recital paragraphs. Nevertheless, the panels/Appellate Body have used the term since their early reports. See, WTO Panel Report, EC *– Hormones (Canada) (1998)*, para. 8.89; WTO Panel Report, EC *– Hormones (US) (1998)*, para. 8.86; Appellate Body Report, EC *– Hormones (1998)*, para. 124; Appellate Body Report, *Australia – Salmon (1998)*, para. 251.

10 Articles 3.1, 3.2, 8.1, 27.2, 39.3, 43.2, 50.5 and 73(b).

preamble[11] and Articles 3.1, 3.2, 8.1, 27.2, 39.3, 43.2, 50.5 and 73(b). Of these, the provisions so far raised in the TRIPS Agreement disputes, or may the future be raised, as related to the concept of necessity in the GATT 1994/GATS General Exceptions (in text, context and/or purpose)[12] are the second recital of the preamble, Article 3.2, Article 8.1, Article 27.2, Article 39.3 and Article 73(b).

9.2 General Background on the TBT and the SPS Agreements

9.2.1 *Drafting History in Brief*

The discussions of the GATT Contracting Parties during the first two decades following the creation of the GATT mainly focused on the elimination of discriminatory practices and tariff reduction. With the increasing GATT success in these areas, the focus of the 1970s was turned to non-tariff trade barriers.[13] Following the Kennedy Round of GATT negotiations (1963–1967), the Contracting Parties realized that the use of varying national technical regulations and standards was becoming a potential trade barrier and, owing to the insufficiency of GATT rules to discipline the said national regulatory measures,[14] they needed intervention through harmonization of standards at an international level. Such intervention was expected to ensure that national standards are not used "so as to afford protection to the domestic production".[15] Technical regulations

11 The TRIPS Agreement does not have the titular term 'Preamble' for the recital paragraphs. Nevertheless, the panels/Appellate Body used the term since their early reports. For example, WTO Panel Report, *India – Patents (US) (1998)*, para. 7.21; WTO Panel Report, *Canada – Pharmaceutical Patents (2000)*, para. 7.14; Appellate Body Report, *India – Patents (1998)*, f.n. 38; Appellate Body Report, *Canada – Patent Term (2000)*, para. 59.

12 The *EC – Trademarks and Geographical Indications (Australia) (2005)* and the *Canada – Pharmaceutical Patents (2000)* panels, for instance, entertained arguments on the relationship between some provisions of the TRIPS Agreement and Article XX of the GATT 1994.

13 Robert Howse and Elizabeth Türk, 'The WTO Impact Upon Internal Regulations: A Case Study of the *Canada – EC Asbestos* Dispute', in George Bermann and Petros Mavroidis (eds.), *Trade and Human Health and Safety* (Cambridge: Cambridge University Press, 2006), pp. 78–79; Michael Ming Du, 'Domestic Regulatory Autonomy under the TBT Agreement: From Non-discrimination to Harmonization', *Chinese Journal of International Law*, 6(2): 2007, pp. 269–270; Lukasz Gruszczynski, *Regulating Health and Environmental Risks under WTO Law: A Critical Analysis of the SPS Agreement* (Oxford: Oxford University Press, 2010), p. 35.

14 Gruszczynski, ibid.

15 Gabrielle Marceau and Joel P. Trachtman, 'A Map of the World Trade Organization Law of Domestic Regulation of Goods: The Technical Barriers to Trade Agreement, the Sanitary and Phytosanitary Measures Agreement, and the General Agreement on Tariffs and Trade', *Journal of World Trade*, 48 (2): 2014, pp. 354–355.

could restrict trade by raising the cost of business for producers who likely had to modify their products to satisfy the requirements imposed by different countries and this had to be dealt with.[16] The said concern of the Contracting Parties led to the preparation of a Draft Code for Preventing Technical Barriers to Trade that was finalized during the next GATT Round – the Tokyo Round (1973–1979). During the Tokyo Round the task of detailing the draft Code was entrusted to a Sub-Group on Technical Barriers which prepared an extensive work by the end of mid-1977.[17] 43[18] of the Contracting Parties signed the Tokyo Round's Agreement on Technical Barriers to Trade, otherwise known as the Standards Code,[19] which entered into force on 1 January 1980 with expectations to address the "much more serious and complex problem of non-tariff distortions of trade".[20]

Before the adoption of the Standards Code, the only provision that addressed food safety as well as animal and plant life and health was GATT Article XX(b) which was designed to serve as a defense against violations of other GATT provisions. The Standards Code had only three references related to human, animal or plant life or health.[21] In the decade following the adoption of the Standards Code, it became clear that the Standards Code could not,

16 Jonathan Carlone, 'An Added Exception to the TBT Agreement after *Clove, Tuna II,* and COOL', *Boston College International & Comparative Law Review*, 37(1): 2014, p. 106.

17 Edmond L. M. Völker, 'The Agreement on Technical Barriers to Trade', in Jacques H. J. Bourgeois, Frédérique Berrod and Eric Gippini Fournier (eds.), *The Uruguay Round Results: A European Lawyer's Perspective* (Brussels: Intereuropean University Press, 1995), p. 282.

18 Marceau and Trachtman, above note 15, p. 355. Prévost and Van den Bossche refer to 32 signatories. Denise Prévost and Peter Van den Bossche, 'The Agreement on the Application of Sanitary and Phytosanitary Measures', in Patrick F. J. Macrory, Arthur E. Appleton and Michael G. Plummer (eds.), *The World Trade Organization: Legal, Economic and Political Analysis* (Vol. I) (New York: Springer, 2005), p. 237.

19 Available at, https://www.wto.org/english/docs_e/legal_e/tokyo_tbt_e.pdf. The full title of the Standards Code is the Agreement on Technical Barriers to Trade, 12 April 1979, 1186 UNTS 276, GATT, BISD, 26th Supp 8 (1980).

20 R. W. Middleton, 'The GATT Standards Code', *Journal of World Trade Law*, 14(3): 1980, p. 201. For a summary of the substance of the Standard Code see, Marceau and Trachtman, above note 15, p. 355. For a brief summary of the history of the TBT Agreement from the late 1960s till the Uruguay Round, see, Simon Lester and William Stemberg, 'The GATT Origins of TBT Agreement Articles 2.1 and 2.2', *Journal of International Economic Law,* 17(1): 2014, pp. 215–232; Simon Lester, 'Finding the Boundaries of International Economic Law', *Journal of International Economic Law,* 17(1): 2014, pp. 4–7.

21 Standards Code, above note 19, sixth recital of the preamble, Article 2.2 and Article 14.9. Gruszczynski, referring to David A Wirth, claims that the Standards Code "was specifically designed for technical regulations, *including a sub-category of measures that relate to food safety, and animal and plant life and health* (*emphasis added*)." Gruszczynski, above note

as it was, specifically tackle the increasingly proliferating SPS measures which were being used to restrict trade in agricultural and food products.[22] The negotiators of the Uruguay Round (1986–1994) were, thus, already aware of the need to prepare a separate agreement to address SPS measures and, in 1988,[23] they formed a separate Working Party to draft an SPS Agreement.[24] With the conclusion of the Uruguay Round, the TBT and SPS agreements as well as the GATT 1947 and the other negotiated agreements, except the plurilateral agreements, became part of the 'single package'[25] WTO Agreement. However, given the close textual and historical relationship between the TBT and SPS agreements, it may sometimes be difficult to categorize whether a certain life or health-related measure falls within the realm of the TBT or SPS Agreement.[26]

13, p. 36, f.n. 5. Looking at the Standards Code, however, it is not clear which sub-category he (or Wirth) could have referred to.

22 For a detailed description of the numerous weaknesses of the GATT 1947 and the Standards Code in stemming the threat from increases in SPS measures on trade in agricultural and food products, see, Prévost and Van den Bossche, above note 18, pp. 238–239. See also, Donna Roberts, 'Preliminary Assessment of the Effects of the WTO Agreement on Sanitary and Phytosanitary Trade Regulations', *Journal of International Trade Law*, 1(2): 1998, p. 380; Peter Van den Bossche and Werner Zdouc, *The Law and Policy of the World Trade Organization* (4th ed. Cambridge: Cambridge University Press, 2017), pp. 935–936; Senai W. Andemariam, 'Can (Should) Article XX(b) GATT Be a Defense against Inconsistencies with the SPS and TBT Agreements?', *The Journal of World Investment and Trade*, 7(4): 2006, pp. 522–523.

23 Prévost and Van den Bossche, as part of a longer narration on the SPS Agreement drafting process, state that the Working Group, called the Working Group on Sanitary and Phytosanitary Regulations and Barriers, was formed in 1989 to work under the Negotiating Group on Agriculture. Prévost and Van den Bossche, above note 18, p. 239. For the longer narration, see pp. 239–242.

24 Marceau and Trachtman, above note 15, p. 356.

25 Compared to the GATT *á la carte* where the separate agreements negotiated during the Tokyo Round bound only the Contracting Parties that accepted them. Gruszczynski, above note 13, p. 36; Marceau and Trachtman, above note 15, pp. 355–356; Carlone, above note 16, pp. 107. The Appellate Body and WTO panels repeatedly stated that 'single package' means that: (a) all WTO obligations are generally cumulative; (b) Members must comply with the cumulative obligations simultaneously; and (c) all WTO agreements must be given harmonious meaning. Appellate Body Report, *Korea – Dairy* (*2000*), paras. 74–81. See also, Appellate Body Report, *Canada – Periodicals* (*1997*), p. 19; Appellate Body Report, *EC – Bananas III* (*1997*), paras. 221–222; WTO Panel Report, *Indonesia – Autos* (*1998*), paras. 14.47–14.56; WTO Panel Report, *US – Line Pipe* (*2002*), paras. 7.25–7.50; Appellate Body Report, *US – Upland Cotton* (*2005*), paras. 529–550; Appellate Body Reports, *EC – Seal Products* (*2014*), para. 5.123 etc. See also, Marceau and Trachtman, ibid, pp. 418–420.

26 Van den Bossche and Zdouc, above note 22, pp. 861–862; Roberts, above note 22, p. 383; Marceau and Trachtman, ibid, pp. 420–421. It cannot be denied that "to a great extent, the TBT and SPS Agreements can be seen as an evolution of GATT provisions." Marceau and Trachtman, ibid, p. 358.

9.2.2 *Main Objectives of the TBT and SPS Agreements*

In 15 articles and three annexes, the TBT Agreement embodies the core objective of avoiding unnecessary obstacles to international trade that may ensue as Members exercise their right to prepare, adopt and apply technical specifications to achieve goals at levels the Members deem appropriate.[27] Maintaining this crucial balance, the Appellate Body has held,[28] must be the fulcrum for interpreting the TBT Agreement. The focus of the TBT Agreement is on three types of technical specifications whose preparation, adoption and application must not create unnecessary obstacles to international trade: technical regulations, standards and conformity assessment procedures.

The key objective of the SPS Agreement is not different from that of the TBT Agreement, in that it tries to balance the right of Members to take SPS measures in their territories against risks from imported products with the objective of trade liberalization in agricultural and food products.[29] In 14 articles and three annexes, the SPS Agreement tries to achieve these "twin [yet, in the words of the Appellate Body,[30] balanced] objectives"[31] through a number of concepts and principles. In comparison to the TBT Agreement, the SPS Agreement is more specific in that its application is limited only to all SPS measures which may, directly or indirectly, affect international trade.[32] For this reason of specificity, regulatory measures, even if they meet the definition of technical regulations, standards and conformity assessment procedures under the TBT Agreement, will fall under the SPS Agreement if they are aimed at protecting the life or health of humans, animals or plants against risks specified in

27 Preamble to the TBT Agreement, paras. 5–6.

28 Appellate Body Report, *US – Shrimp* (*1998*), paras. 156–157; Appellate Body Report, *US – Clove Cigarettes* (*2012*), paras. 89–102; Appellate Body Report, *US – Tuna II* (*Mexico*) (*2012*), para. 316; Appellate Body Reports, *EC – Seal Products* (*2014*), paras. 5.121–5.129. See also, Benn McGrady, 'Necessity Exceptions in WTO Law: Retreaded Tyres, Regulatory Purpose and Cumulative Regulatory Measures', *Journal of International Economic Law*, 12(1): 2008, p. 154.

29 Prévost and Van den Bossche, above note 18, pp. 242–243. See also, Gruszczynski, above note 13, p. 38.

30 In *EC – Hormones* (*1998*), the Appellate Body made note of the "the delicate and carefully negotiated balance in the *SPS Agreement* between the shared, but sometimes competing, interests of promoting international trade and of protecting the life and health of human beings". Appellate Body Report, *EC – Hormones* (*1998*), para. 177.

31 Wagner states that the stated aim of the SPS Agreement is: "the twin goals of curbing protectionism while providing protecting from genuine risk". Markus Wagner, 'Interpreting the SPS Agreement: Navigating Risk, Scientific Evidence and Regulatory Autonomy', available at, https://ssrn.com/abstract=2887361 or http://dx.doi.org/10.2139/ssrn.2887361, p. 4.

32 Article 1 of the SPS Agreement.

the SPS Agreement.[33] Thus, Article 1.5 of the TBT Agreement provides that its provisions "do not apply to [SPS] measures as defined in Annex A of the [SPS Agreement]".

9.2.3 *Relationships among the GATT 1994, the TBT Agreement and the SPS Agreement*

The evolution from the GATT 1947 – especially Article XX(b) – to the TBT and SPS agreements shows that the three agreements have relationships in text, context and/or purpose. For example, some provisions of the GATT 1994, particularly Articles I, III and XX, are similarly worded as the fundamental provisions of the TBT and SPS agreements. Moreover, there is some textual similarity between the TBT and SPS agreements. The following three similarities may be cited as relevant to the necessity requirements in the TBT and SPS agreements: (a) recitals of both agreements make it clear that the respective agreements intend to respect the right of Members to set their TBT/SPS measures at levels the Members consider appropriate;[34] (b) both agreements allow Members to take measures 'necessary' to achieve legitimate objectives; and (c) TBT or SPS measures which have been prepared in accordance with international standards are presumed *at least* not to create unnecessary obstacles to international trade.[35]

Furthermore, it was mentioned in Sub-section 9.2.2 that the core objective of the TBT and SPS agreements is to maintain balance between promoting international trade and accommodating the protection of legitimate national concerns through domestic regulations. The GATT 1994 shares, as the Appellate Body has repeatedly found, this objective in that through its rule-exception structure it maintains balance between the obligations of Members and their regulatory autonomy.[36] The balance between trade obligations and regulatory autonomy is not only at the heart of interpreting the GATT 1994 as well as the TBT and SPS agreements, but must also be utilized in all WTO agreements because, as the Appellate Body ascertained, it is the sense that one gets after reading the introductory paragraphs of the WTO Agreement.[37]

33 The risks are specified in paragraphs (a)-(d) of Annex A(1) of the SPS Agreement.

34 See, the sixth recital of the preamble to the TBT Agreement and the sixth recital of the preamble to the SPS Agreement.

35 Article 2.5 of the TBT Agreement and Article 3.2 of the SPS Agreement.

36 Above note 28.

37 In the words of the Appellate Body: "[W]e understand the *WTO Agreement, as a whole*, to reflect the balance struck by WTO Members between trade and non-trade-related concerns." Appellate Body Reports, *China – Raw Materials* (2012), para. 355.

9.3 The Concepts of Necessity in the TBT and the SPS Agreements

9.3.1 *General Remarks*

Section 9.3 discusses the interpretation that the WTO panels and the Appellate Body have developed for the concept of necessity in the TBT and SPS agreements. Sub-section 9.3.1 begins with some general remarks based on the texts of the two agreements as well as the analyses of the WTO panels and the Appellate Body regarding the concept of necessity in the two agreements. Sub-sections 9.3.2 and 9.3.3 go into the details of the interpretations developed for the concept of necessity in the TBT and SPS agreements respectively.

The general remarks focus on three points. The first point is on the interoperability between the interpretation of necessity in the General Exceptions of the GATT 1994/GATS and the necessity provisions in the TBT and SPS agreements. The second point is on whether the necessity provisions in the TBT and SPS agreements are substantive obligations or, like the General Exceptions of the GATT 1994/GATS, affirmative defenses. The third point is on the allocation of burden of proof between the parties in a TBT or an SPS dispute.

Regarding the first point, i.e., interoperability, it is to be remembered that Section 9.1 identified provisions of the TBT Agreement (Articles 2.2 and 2.5 and Annex 3(E)) and the SPS Agreement (2.1, 2.2, 3.2 and 5.6) that embody a concept of necessity contained in a context similar to the concept of necessity in the GATT 1994/GATS General Exceptions. These provisions describe, or have been held to describe,[38] the concept of necessity in the following terms: (a) '*more trade-restrictive* than *necessary* to fulfill a legitimate objective, taking account of the risks non-fulfilment would create' (TBT Agreement Article 2.2); (b) *unnecessary* obstacle to international trade (TBT Agreement Article 2.5); (c) *necessary for* the protection of human, animal or plant life or health (SPS Agreement Article 2.1); (d) *only to the extent necessary to* protect human, animal or plant life or health (SPS Agreement Article 2.2); (e) *deemed to be necessary to* protect human, animal or plant life or health (SPS Agreement Article 3.2); (f) *not more trade-restrictive than required to achieve* their appropriate

38 For example, Article 5.6 of the SPS Agreement does not contain the term 'necessary', but it has been held to embody the principle of necessity owing mainly to its similarity to the interpretation of necessity developed for Article 2.2 of the SPS Agreement which heavily drew its interpretation from the interpretation developed for the term 'necessary' in the General Exceptions of the GATT 1994/GATS (see Sub-section 9.3.3 below). WTO Panel Report, *Australia – Salmon (1998)*, para. 8.165; Appellate Body Report, *Australia – Salmon (1998)*, para. 213 (f.n. 166); Appellate Body Report, *Australia – Apples (2010)*, paras. 338–340; Appellate Body Report, *India – Agricultural Products (2015)*, para. 5.208.

level of SPS protection … (SPS Agreement Article 5.6); and (g) a measure is *not more trade-restrictive than required* unless there is another measure, reasonably available taking into account technical and economic feasibility, that achieves the appropriate level of sanitary or phytosanitary protection and *is significantly less restrictive to trade* (SPS Agreement Article 5.6 and its footnote 3).

It can be observed that the drafting of the above-listed texts of the TBT and SPS agreements may have been influenced by the GATT era interpretation of the necessity provision in the General Exceptions. It is also likely that the interpretation developed for the concept of necessity in the General Exceptions in the WTO era may in turn have been influenced by the relevant texts of the TBT and SPS agreements. Desmedt asserts that the key concept of 'less trade-restrictiveness' in the TBT and SPS agreements (found, at least in text, in Articles 2.2 and 5.6 respectively)[39] "is derived from earlier GATT panel reports[40] on the interpretation of the word 'necessary' in Article XX(b) and XX(d)".[41] Surely, the Standards Code (Article 2.1) only required that the Contracting Parties avoid 'unnecessary obstacles to international trade'; it did not contain the 'trade-restrictiveness' phrase in today's TBT Agreement Article 2.2 and SPS Agreement Article 5.6. Where could the 'trade-restrictiveness' element in the texts of the TBT and SPS agreements have originated from? The General Exceptions of the GATT 1947 and 1994 do not contain the term 'trade-restrictive/ness'. The sources for the 'trade-restrictiveness' phrases in the texts of the TBT and SPS agreements are likely the interpretations developed by the GATT panels for the term 'necessary' in GATT 1947 Article XX (the availability of a GATT-consistent/less GATT-inconsistent alternative measure, i.e., the availability of a less trade-restrictive alternative measure).

It is also possible that the texts of the TBT and SPS agreements may in turn have influenced the interpretation developed for the term 'necessary' in the General Exceptions of the GATT 1994 and the GATS. In *Korea – Various*

39 The *India – Agricultural Products* (*2015*) panel, for instance, by reference to the interpretation developed for the concept of necessity in the General Exceptions of the GATT 1994/GATS, Article 2.2 of the TBT Agreement and Article 5.6 of the SPS Agreement, read an element of 'trade-restrictiveness' in the term 'necessary' in SPS Agreement Article 2.2 even though the term 'trade-restrictive' is not textually present. WTO Panel Report, *India – Agricultural Products* (*2015*), paras. 7.606–7.613.

40 The reports Desmedt refers to are: GATT Panel Report, *US – Section 337* (*1989*) [para. 5.26]; GATT Panel Report, *Thailand – Cigarettes* (*1990*), para. 75; GATT Panel Report, *US – Malt Beverages* (*1992*), paras. 5.40–5.43, 5.52.

41 Axel Desmedt, 'Proportionality in WTO Law', *Journal of International Economic Law*, 4(3): 2001, p. 460.

Measures on Beef (*2001*), the Appellate Body introduced the 'weighing and balancing' test[42] and affirmed that its interpretation did not deviate from the *US – Section 337* (*1989*) interpretation.[43] According to the Appellate Body, one of the three basic elements of the 'weighing and balancing' test – restrictive impact of the measure on import or export – is likely to have been influenced by one of the objectives of the GATT 1994, i.e., elimination of discriminatory treatment in international commerce.[44] A point in consideration is whether the Appellate Body may also have found inspiration for the trade-restrictiveness element in the texts of the TBT[45] and SPS agreements which explicitly refer to trade-restrictiveness in weighing the legality, i.e., necessity, of the disputed measures. Admittedly, the Appellate Body's developing of the 'trade-restrictiveness' element in the 'weighing and balancing' test does not show any explicit reference to the 'trade-restrictiveness' provisions of the TBT and SPS agreements. Nevertheless, the fact that 'trade-restrictiveness' is an element considered in assessing the necessity of a measure under the GATT 1994/GATS General Exceptions and the TBT/SPS agreements may at least be read to show consistency in interpreting the defense of necessity in the relevant legal texts of the WTO Agreement.

Sub-sections 9.3.2 and 9.3.3 will show that the WTO-era interpretation of the concept of necessity in the General Exceptions has influenced the interpretation of the concept of necessity in the TBT and SPS agreements. In short, there has been *a circle of interoperability* between the texts and interpretations of necessity in the General Exceptions of the GATT 1994/GATS and the relevant provisions of the TBT/SPS agreements. The flow of influence has mainly been from the General Exceptions to the TBT/SPS agreements rather than the other way round understandably because of the historical relationship between the

42 Appellate Body Report, *Korea – Various Measures on Beef* (*2001*), paras. 162–164.

43 Ibid, para. 166.

44 Ibid, f.n. 105. This perception of link between discrimination and trade-restrictiveness was also found to exist in Article 2.1 of the TBT Agreement. WTO Panel Report, *US – Tuna II* (*Mexico*) (*2012*), para. 7.445; WTO Panel Reports, *US – COOL* (*2012*), paras. 7.574–7.575.

45 In the next dispute that consolidated the 'weighing and balancing' test, *EC – Asbestos* (*2001*), the parties argued, before the panel and the Appellate Body, on the meaning of the phrase 'more trade-restrictive than *necessary* to fulfill a legitimate objective' in Article 2.2 of the TBT Agreement. That the Appellate Body did not pursue examining the dispute under the TBT Agreement is true, but could the text of Article 2.2 of the TBT Agreement have had an influence on the Appellate Body's affirmation of the 'trade-restrictiveness' element (already developed in *Korea – Various Measures on Beef* (*2001*)) in using the 'weighing and balancing' test?

General Exceptions, particularly the GATT 1994 Article XX(b), and the TBT/SPS agreements.

Regarding the second point, i.e., whether the necessity provisions in the TBT/SPS agreements are substantive obligations or exceptions, the WTO panels and the Appellate Body made it clear since the early TBT/SPS disputes that the rule-exception relationship between substantive obligations and the General Exceptions of the GATT 1994/GATS, which contain the necessity defense in some of their paragraphs, does *not* generally exist in the TBT and SPS agreements.[46] This means, therefore, that the necessity and other provisions in the TBT/SPS agreements which are similar to the General Exceptions do not serve as exceptions to, or justifications against, inconsistencies with the substantive obligations of the agreements. The necessity provisions are, and have in practice been, separately argued and defended as substantive obligations.[47]

---

46 Regarding the SPS Agreement, the *EC – Hormones (1998)* panel made it clear that: "the general approach adopted in Article XX(b) of GATT is fundamentally different from the approach adopted in the SPS Agreement. Article XX(b)... provides for a general *exception* which can be invoked to justify any violation of another GATT provision. The SPS Agreement, on the other hand, provides for specific *obligations* to be met in order for a Member to enact or maintain specific types of measures, namely sanitary and phytosanitary measures." WTO Panel Report, *EC – Hormones (Canada) (1998)*, para. 8.42; WTO Panel Report, *EC – Hormones (US) (1998)*, para. 8.39. Regarding the TBT Agreement, the Appellate Body, in para. 101 of the *US – Clove Cigarettes (2012)* report, stated that "the TBT Agreement does not contain among its provisions a general exceptions clause. This may be contrasted with the GATT 1994, which contains a general exceptions clause in Article XX [of the GATT 1994]." Appellate Body Report, *US – Clove Cigarettes (2012)*, para. 101.

47 The order of analysis set by the panels in the following disputes shows that the respective necessity provisions in the TBT and SPS agreements were examined separately on their own, i.e., without: (a) first finding (in)consistencies with the other provisions selected to be examined before the necessity provisions; and (b) the results of the necessity examination in turn affecting the analyses of the other provisions examined after the necessity provisions. Regarding the TBT Agreement, see: WTO Panel Report, *EC – Sardines (2002)*, paras. 7.14–7.19; WTO Panel Report, *US – Clove Cigarettes (2012)*, para. 7.7–7.19; WTO Panel Report, *US – Tuna II (Mexico) (2012)*, paras. 7.35–7.46; WTO Panel Reports, *US – COOL (2012)*, paras. 7.68–7.74; WTO Panel Reports, *EC – Seal Products (2014)*, paras. 7.57–7.69. The Appellate Body followed the same order of analysis in these disputes: Appellate Body Report, *EC – Sardines (2012)*, paras. 134 (j), 312–314; Appellate Body Report, *US – Tuna II (Mexico) (2012)*, para. 406; Appellate Body Reports, *US – COOL (2012)*, paras. 235–236; and Appellate Body Reports, *EC – Seal Products (2014)*, paras. 5.70–5.71. Regarding the SPS Agreement, see: WTO Panel Report, *Australia – Salmon (1998)*, paras. 8.38–8.39; WTO Panel Report, *Japan – Apples (2003)*, para. 8.4; WTO Panel Report, *US – Animals (2015)*, paras. 7.1–7.20; WTO Panel Report, *India – Agricultural Products (2015)*, paras. 7.115–7.126; WTO Panel Report, *Costa Rica – Avocados (Mexico) (2022)*, paras. 7.14–7.28.

Regarding the third point, i.e., burden of proof, the different nature of the necessity provisions in the TBT/SPS agreements *vis-à-vis* the necessity defenses in the General Exceptions, as described in the previous paragraph, has an impact on allocating the burden of proof between the parties.[48] In a TBT or SPS Agreement dispute, the complainant has the burden to present a *prima facie* case of inconsistency of the disputed measures with *most* provisions of the agreements, including the necessity provisions.[49] Since the General Exceptions in the GATT 1994 and the GATS are affirmative defenses, the respondent has the ultimate[50] burden of proof to show that its measures qualify under the General Exceptions.[51]

---

48 The Appellate Body laid out the general rule on burden of proof in WTO dispute in Appellate Body Report, *US – Wool Shirts and Blouses* (*1997*), pp. 15–16. See also, WTO Panel Reports, *China – Auto Parts* (*2009*), para. 7.92.

49 On the TBT Agreement, see, for example, Appellate Body Report, *EC – Sardines* (*2002*), paras. 269–282; Appellate Body Report, *US – Tuna II* (*Mexico*) (*2012*), para. 216; Appellate Body Report, *US – Clove Cigarettes* (*2012*), paras. 182, 289. In para. 289 of the *US – Clove Cigarettes* (*2012*) report, the Appellate Body placed the initial burden on the respondent, under Article 2.12 of the TBT Agreement, to present "a *prima facie* case that an interval of not less than six months 'would be ineffective to fulfil the legitimate objectives pursued' by its technical regulation". On the SPS Agreement, see, for example, Appellate Body Report, *EC – Hormones* (*1998*), para. 98; Appellate Body Report, *Japan – Apples* (*2003*), para. 157; Appellate Body, *India – Agricultural Products* (*2015*), para. 5.220; Appellate Body Report, *Japan – Agricultural Products* (*1999*), para. 80. In para. 80 of the *Japan – Agricultural Products* (*1999*) report, the Appellate Body declared Article 5.7 of the SPS Agreement to be "a *qualified* exemption from the obligation under Article 2.2 not to maintain SPS measures without sufficient scientific evidence". This has made Article 5.7 of the SPS Argument "arguably an exception to be invoked by the defendant and for which the defendant bears the burden of proof [of the four elements of Article 5.7]". Joost Pauwelyn, 'The WTO Agreement on Sanitary and Phytosanitary (SPS) Measures as Applied in the First Three SPS Disputes: *EC – Hormones, Australia – Salmon* and *Japan – Varietals*', *Journal of International Economic Law*, 2(4): 1999, f.n. 107. See, WTO Panel Report, *US – Animals* (*2015*), para. 7.292; WTO Panel Report, *Russia – Pigs* (*EU*) (*2017*), para. 7.643.

50 The term 'ultimate' has been used because, in the multi-layered General Exceptions argument, the complaining Member bears the responsibility of identifying alternatives after which the responding Member must show why the said alternatives are not reasonably available and cannot attain the level of enforcement set by the responding Member. Appellate Body Report, *US – Gambling* (*2005*), paras. 309–311. See also, Appellate Body Report, *Brazil – Retreaded Tyres* (*2007*), para. 156; Appellate Body Reports, *EC – Seal Products* (*2014*), para. 5.261.

51 On burden of proof in some of the provisions of the TBT Agreement, see, Fay Valinaki, '"Repairing the Defects" of Article 2.1 of the WTO Technical Barriers to Trade Agreement: An Amendment Proposal', *Legal Issues of Economic Integration*, 43(1): 2016, pp. 75–76, 86, 90, 93–95. On burden of proof in some of the provisions of the SPS Agreement, see, Pauwelyn, above note 49, pp. 659–660. See also, Kamala Dawar and Eyal Ronen, 'How "Necessary"? A Comparison of Legal and Economic Assessments Under GATT Dispute

Sections 9.3.2 and 9.3.3 will discuss how the necessity provisions in the TBT and SPS agreements have been interpreted respectively. The discussions generally follow the presentation by Van den Bossche and Zdouc.[52]

9.3.2 *Necessity under the TBT Agreement*

Three points will be raised in discussing the concept of necessity in the TBT Agreement. First, four key sentenced in Article 2.2 of the TBT Agreement will be discussed as an introduction. Next, the steps for examining necessity in Article 2.2 will be explained. Finally, it will be presented how the necessity test in Article 2.2 has been ruled to apply to Article 5.1.2 and should also apply to Annex 3(E) as the substance of these three provisions in the TBT Agreement is similar.

We begin with the text of Article 2.2 and the four key sentences therein. Article 2.2 states:

> Members shall ensure that technical regulations are not prepared, adopted or applied with a view to or with the effect of creating *unnecessary* obstacles to international trade. For this purpose, technical regulations shall not be more trade-restrictive than *necessary* to fulfil a legitimate objective, taking account of the risks non-fulfilment would create. Such legitimate objectives are, *inter alia*: national security requirements; the prevention of deceptive practices; protection of human health or safety, animal or plant life or health, or the environment. In assessing such risks, relevant elements of consideration are, *inter alia*: available scientific and technical information, related processing technology or intended end-uses of products (*emphasis added*).

Article 2.2 has four sentences or elements. The first sentence underlines the obligation not to create unnecessary obstacles in international trade through the use of technical regulations. The second sentence clarifies the obligation in the first sentence by stating that technical regulations shall not be more trade-restrictive than *necessary* to fulfill a legitimate objective, taking account of the risks non-fulfilment would create. The third and fourth sentences clarify

Settlements, Article XX(b), TBT 2.2 and SPS 5.6', *Trade, Law and Development*, 8(1) (2016), p. 18; Appellate Body Report, *US – Tuna II (Mexico)* (2012), para. 323; Appellate Body Reports, *US – COOL (Article 21.5 – Canada and Mexico)* (2015), paras. 5.328–5.333; Appellate Body Report, *Russia – Railway Equipment* (2020), paras. 5.188–5.189.

52 Van den Bossche and Zdouc, above note 22, pp. 912–921 (for the TBT Agreement) and pp. 945–946, 964–967 (for the SPS Agreement).

the phrases 'legitimate objective' and 'the risks non-fulfilment would create' with an illustrative list. For the Appellate Body, the two key sentences are the first and second sentences "[both of] which refer to the concept of necessity"[53] as tied by the phrase "for this purpose" which, by creating a nexus between the two sentenced, "suggests that the second sentence qualifies the terms of the first sentence and elaborates on the scope and meaning of the obligation contained in that sentence".[54] Thus, in essence, the concept of necessity is enclosed in the phrase 'creating unnecessary obstacles to international trade' in the first sentence.[55] The following is the summary of the process of interpreting the term 'more trade-restrictive than necessary' which the Appellate Body laid out:

> In sum, we consider that an assessment of whether a technical regulation is 'more trade-restrictive than necessary' within the meaning of Article 2.2 of the *TBT Agreement* involves an evaluation of a number of factors. A panel should begin by considering factors that include: (i) the degree of contribution made by the measure to the legitimate objective at issue; (ii) the trade-restrictiveness of the measure; and (iii) the nature of the risks at issue and the gravity of consequences that would arise from non-fulfilment of the objective(s) pursued by the Member through the measure. In most cases, a comparison of the challenged measure and possible alternative measures should be undertaken. fn 647 In particular, it may be relevant for the purpose of this comparison to consider whether the proposed alternative is less trade-restrictive, whether it would make an equivalent contribution to the relevant legitimate objective, taking account of the risks non-fulfilment would create, and whether it is reasonably available.[56]
>
> fn 647 We can identify at least two instances where a comparison of the challenged measure and possible alternative measures may not be required. For example, it would seem to us that if a measure is not trade-restrictive, then it may not be inconsistent with Article 2.2. Conversely, if a measure is trade-restrictive and makes no contribution to the

53 Please note that the term 'necessary' appears in both sentences.

54 Appellate Body Reports, *US – COOL* (2012), para. 369; Appellate Body Report, *US – Tuna II (Mexico)* (2012), para. 318.

55 WTO Panel Report, *Australia – Plain Packaging* (2018), paras. 7.39–7.40.

56 Appellate Body Report, *US – Tuna II (Mexico)* (2012), para. 322 (and also para. 318). See also, WTO Panel Report, *Russia – Railway Equipment* (2020), para. 7.411.

achievement of the legitimate objective, then it may be inconsistent with Article 2.2.

The interpretation developed by the Appellate Body is largely imported from the interpretation developed for the concept of necessity in the General Exceptions of the GATT 1994/GATS.[57]

The second point of discussion is the steps adopted for examining necessity under Article 2.2 of the TBT Agreement. The way the Appellate Body interpreted, in *US – Tuna II (Mexico)* (*2012*), the phrase "more trade-restrictive than necessary" in Article 2.2 of the TBT Agreement has been dissected into a series of sub-steps.[58] The following six paragraphs present and comment on these sub-steps.

Firstly, the 'objective' of the disputed technical regulation needs to be ascertained by looking at "the texts of statutes, legislative history, and other evidence regarding the structure and operation of the measure" without being necessarily bound by "a Member's characterization of the objectives it pursues through the measure, but [by] independently and objectively assess[ing] them".[59]

Secondly, the panel must examine whether the said objective is 'legitimate' by searching whether it is one that can be: (a) found in the list in Article 2.2; (b) part of the several objectives listed in the sixth and sevenths recitals to the TBT Agreement most of which overlap with the list in Article 2.2; or

57 See, for example, in the *US – Tuna II (Mexico)* (*2012*), dispute, the Appellate Body Report's references in: (a) para. 317 (f.n. 641, referring to Appellate Body Report, *China – Publications and Audiovisual Products* (*2010*), para. 252); (b) para. 318 (f.n. 642, referring to Appellate Body Report, *Korea – Various Measures on Beef* (*2001*), para. 161 and f.n. 643 referring to Appellate Body Report, *US – Gambling* (*2005*), paras. 306–308 and Appellate Body Report, *Brazil – Retreaded Tyres* (*2007*), para. 178); (c) para. 319 (f.n. 644, referring to Appellate Body Reports, *China – Raw Materials* (*2012*), para. 319); and (d) para. 320 (f.n. 645, referring to Appellate Body Report, *Korea – Various Measures on Beef* (*2001*), para. 166). See also, Appellate Body Reports, *US – COOL* (*2012*), para. 374, f.n. 745.

58 In *US – COOL (Article 21.5 – Canada and Mexico)* (*2015*), the Appellate Body, by reference to the General Exceptions practice of interpreting necessity, stressed the need to follow "a certain sequence" in the order of analyzing Article 2.2. Appellate Body Reports, *US – COOL (Article 21.5 – Canada and Mexico)* (*2015*), paras. 5.227–5.229, 5.235. For a summarized presentation of these steps, see, Yoshimichi Ishikawa, 'Plain Packaging Requirements and Article 2.2 of the TBT Agreement', *Chinese (Taiwan) Yearbook of International Law and Affairs*, 30: 2012, pp. 84–110.

59 Appellate Body Report, *US – Tuna II (Mexico)* (*2012*), para. 314; Appellate Body Reports, *US – COOL* (*2012*), para. 371. Such an ascertainment first appeared in Appellate Body Report, *US – Gambling* (*2005*), para. 304.

(c) fall under any of the objectives under the covered agreements of the WTO Agreement.[60]

Thirdly, the measure has to be tested whether it 'fulfils' the legitimate objective. The TBT Agreement recognizes the right of Members to set the level to pursue the particular legitimate objective at hand. Accordingly, at this stage the panel examines *whether* the technical regulation makes contribution toward achievement of the legitimate objective at the level set by the Member. The *extent* of such contribution is not examined at this stage; it is examined at a later stage. To examine whether the measure makes contribution to achieve the legitimate objective, the panel can refer to "the design, structure, and operation of the technical regulation, as well as from evidence relating to the application of the measure". This can help to, later on, find out "to what degree, if at all" the measure makes a contribution.[61] No minimum threshold of degree of contribution is needed;[62] if the measure makes 'partial'[63] or 'some'[64] contribution, it fits the purpose of this test.

Fourthly, the panel has to analyze whether the measure is trade-restrictive. Trade-restrictiveness has been interpreted to mean "having a limiting effect on trade".[65] At this level, the only analysis needed is *whether* the measure is trade-restrictive, not the *extent* of its trade-restrictiveness. The Appellate Body observed that since the ultimate test is 'more trade-restrictive than necessary' some trade-restrictiveness is allowed under Article 2.2; thus, at this stage, the panel needs to only discern some impact of the measure on international trade.[66]

Fifthly, the panel must examine whether the measure is '*more* trade-restrictive than *necessary*'. To do so, the panel must identify the *extent* of the measure's trade-restrictiveness and assess whether the trade-restrictiveness was more than necessary. The Appellate Body referred to its previous analysis of the term 'necessary' in *US – Gambling* (2005)[67] and *Brazil – Retreaded Tyres*

60 Appellate Body Report, *US – Tuna II (Mexico)* (2012), para. 313; Appellate Body Reports, *US – COOL* (2012), para. 372.

61 Appellate Body Report, *US – Tuna II (Mexico)* (2012), paras. 315–317; Appellate Body Reports, *US – COOL* (2012), para. 373.

62 Appellate Body Reports, *US – COOL* (2012), para. 368.

63 Appellate Body Report, *US – Tuna II (Mexico)* (2012), para. 341.

64 Appellate Body Reports, *US – COOL* (2012), para. 379.

65 Appellate Body Report, *US – Tuna II (Mexico)* (2012), para. 319; WTO Panel Report, *Australia – Plain Packaging* (2018), para. 7.1072.

66 Appellate Body Report, *US – Tuna II (Mexico)* (2012), para. 319; Appellate Body Reports, *US – COOL* (2012), para. 375.

67 Appellate Body Report, *US – Gambling* (2005), paras. 306–308.

(*2007*)[68] to state that the elements of the 'weighing and balancing' test apply to examine the necessity of the trade-restrictiveness of the measure contested under Article 2.2 of the TBT Agreement. The three factors that the Appellate Body thus identified to examine the necessity of the trade-restrictiveness of the measure contested under Article 2.2 of the TBT Agreement are a *relational* analysis of: (a) the *extent* of the trade-restrictiveness of the technical regulation; (b) the *degree* of contribution that it makes to the achievement of a legitimate objective; (c) and the risks non-fulfilment of the objective would create.[69] In this 'relational analysis' test, the *extent* of the trade-restrictiveness and the contribution of the measure to achieve the objective are examined, not *whether* the measure is trade-restrictive or makes some contribution to achieving the legitimate objective (examinations which are done earlier). The third element of the relational analysis, i.e., the risks non-fulfilment of the objective pursued would create, it appears, has been taken from the fourth sentence of Article 2.2.[70] This element is not found in the interpretation developed for necessity in the General Exceptions of the GATT 1994/GATS. It may be argued that this element is similar to the 'importance of the societal value pursued' element in the 'weighing and balancing' test. However, there is a crucial difference between the two: whereas the 'importance of the societal value pursued' element focuses on the *importance* of the objective pursued, the 'risks non-fulfilment would create' element focuses on the *fulfilment* of the objective pursued. Still, it may be counter-argued that the two elements are linked in that the more important the societal value pursued is, the higher the risk of its non-fulfilment. Nevertheless, it is worth considering whether the 'risks non-fulfilment would create' element could be imported into the GATT 1994/GATS General Exceptions necessity test by considering it as an extension either of

68 Appellate Body Report, *Brazil – Retreaded Tyres* (*2007*), para. 178.

69 Appellate Body Report, *US – Tuna II* (*Mexico*) (*2012*), para. 318; Appellate Body Reports, *US – COOL* (*2012*), para. 376.

70 The Appellate Body was clear in its statement that it was adding: "*a further element of weighing and balancing in the determination of whether the trade-restrictiveness of a technical regulation is 'necessary'* or, alternatively, whether a possible alternative measure, which is less trade-restrictive, would make an equivalent contribution to the relevant legitimate objective, taking account of the risks non-fulfilment would create, and would be reasonably available (*emphasis added*)". Appellate Body Report, *US – Tuna II* (*Mexico*) (*2012*), para. 321. See also, Appellate Body Reports, *US – COOL* (*2012*), paras. 377, 461; WTO Panel Report, *Australia – Plain Packaging* (*2018*), para. 7.1259 (f.n. 3074) where the panel summarized the Appellate Body's statements in *US – COOL* (*2012*) as: "As the Appellate Body held in *US – COOL* [para. 461], the comparative analysis of the challenged measure and the proposed alternatives is distinct from the establishment of the risk non-fulfilment would create (*emphasis added*)."

the 'importance of the societal value pursued' element or the 'degree of contribution' element. It is to be remembered that the 'weighing and balancing' test focuses only on the importance of the objective pursued and the degree of contribution that the measure makes to achieving the objective. It does not examine the risks non-fulfilment of the objective would create. Including the element of examining risks non-fulfilment of the objective would create, it may be argued, could further refine the interpretation already developed for necessity under the General Exceptions of the GATT 1994/GATS.[71] If, as much as the interpretation developed for necessity under the General Exceptions of the GATT 1994/GATS has influenced the development of the interpretation of necessity in Article 2.2 of the TBT Agreement, the opposite is also done, this can help develop a more comprehensive interpretation of necessity in the various WTO agreements.

Finally, a panel should complete the Article 2.2 tests by conducting a 'comparative analysis', i.e., by examining proposed alternative measures to find out whether they are less trade-restrictive, whether they would make an equivalent contribution to the relevant legitimate objective, taking account of the risks non-fulfilment would create, and whether they are reasonably available.[72] The Appellate Body clarified that the obligation to consider the elements listed in the fourth sentence of Article 2.2 (available scientific and technical information, related processing technology or intended end-uses of products) suggests the requirement to compare the challenged measure and possible alternative measures "in the light of the nature of the risks at issue and the gravity of the consequences that would arise from non-fulfilment of the legitimate objective".[73]

---

71 It may be relevant to mention that while interpreting the 'risks non-fulfilment would create' test of Article 2.2 of the TBT the Appellate Body, in *US – COOL (Article 21.5 – Canada and Mexico) (2015)*, showed the willingness to refer to the interpretation of necessity developed for Article XX of the GATT 1994 (the reference being to Appellate Body Reports, *EC – Seal Products (2014)*, para. 5.198) even if such element is not found in the Article XX interpretation of necessity. Appellate Body Reports, *US – COOL (Article 21.5 – Canada and Mexico) (2015)*, para. 5.218. The question, therefore, is should the Appellate Body's linking the 'risks non-fulfilment would create' test to the Article XX necessity test be seized as an indication for the possibility of introducing the 'risks non-fulfilment would create' element – if not as a separate, fourth element of the 'weighing and balancing' test, but – at least as an extension of the contribution element in interpreting necessity under the General Exceptions?

72 Appellate Body Report, *US – Tuna II (Mexico) (2012)*, para. 322. See also, Appellate Body Reports, *US – COOL (2012)*, para. 378; WTO Panel Report, *Australia – Plain Packaging (2018)*, paras. 7.30, 7.45.

73 Appellate Body Report, *US – Tuna II (Mexico) (2012)*, para. 321; Appellate Body Reports, *US – COOL (2012)*, para. 377; Appellate Body Reports, *US – COOL (Article 21.5 – Canada and*

The third point of discussion is whether the necessity test in Article 2.2 *applies* to Article 5.1.2 (and *should also* apply to Annex 3(E)). Under the TBT Agreement, a number of provisions applicable to technical regulations also apply to standards and conformity assessment procedures.[74] It is logical, therefore, to expect the adoption of interpretations developed for the provisions related to technical regulations for similar provisions on standards and/or conformity assessment procedures and *vice versa*. Relevant to necessity, the contents of Articles 2.2 on technical regulations are *similar* to the contents of Article 5.1.2 on conformity assessment procedures and Annex 3(E) on standards. The *Russia – Railway Equipment* (*2018*) panel noted that there are similarities in the wordings of the first sentences of Articles 2.2 and 5.1.2 which call for the avoidance of *'unnecessary obstacles to international trade'* and in the wordings of the second sentences of Articles 2.2 and 5.1.2 which require that the measures not be *'more trade-restrictive than necessary'*. The panel also observed that there are also differences in the wordings of Article 2.2 and 5.1.2; however, it read both provisions as referring to the avoidance of unnecessary obstacles to international trade and decided to abide by the interpretation developed by the Appellate Body for Article 2.2 which was itself heavily influenced by the interpretation of the concept of necessity in the General Exceptions of the GATT 1994/GATS.[75] Along the same line of thinking, given the similarity between Articles 2.2, Article 5.1.2 and Annex 3(E) of the TBT Agreement, it may be argued that the similar interpretation developed for the concept of necessity in Articles 2.2 and Article 5.1.2 should also apply for the concept of necessity in Annex 3(E) of the TBT Agreement.

The conclusion on the interpretation of the concept of necessity in the TBT Agreement is, therefore, that the Appellate Body, after examining the textual and contextual similarities between the General Exceptions of the GATT 1994/

Mexico) (*2015*), para. 5.217; WTO Panel Report, *Australia – Plain Packaging* (*2018*), paras. 7.1256–7.1257.

74 For instance, see the parallels among Article 2.2, Annex 3(E) and Article 5.1.2 (regarding the obligation not to create unnecessary obstacles to international trade), Article 2.4, Annex 3(F) and Article 5.4 (regarding the obligation to use available international standards) and Articles 2.7 and 6.1 (regarding the obligation to consider as equivalent technical regulations or conformity assessment procedures adopted by other Members).

75 WTO Panel Report, *Russia – Railway Equipment* (*2020*), paras. 7.409–7.413 (regarding the first sentences of Articles 2.2 and 5.1.2) and paras. 7.417–7.420 (regarding the second sentences of Articles 2.2 and 5.1.2). The Appellate Body considered the relationship between Articles 2.2 and 5.1.2 of the TBT Agreement and agreed that the concept of necessity in Article 5.1.2 has to be, *mutatis mutandis*, interpreted along the way the concept of necessity has been interpreted in Article 2.2. Appellate Body Report, *Russia – Railway Equipment* (*2020*), paras. 5.181–5.197.

GATS and the relevant provisions of the TBT Agreement and considering the key objective in these agreements, and the WTO Agreement in general, of maintaining balance between treaty obligations and regulatory autonomy, rightly chose to adopt the interpretation it developed for the concept of necessity in the General Exceptions to the necessity test in the TBT Agreement. The minor differences between the texts of the General Exceptions and Articles 2.2, 5.1.2 as well as Annex 3(E) of the TBT Agreement as well as those among these three provisions of the TBT Agreement, have not affected (should not affect) the adoption of a similar interpretation for the concept of necessity in the General Exception and the TBT Agreement.

9.3.3 *Necessity under the SPS Agreement*

Three points will be raised in discussing the concept of necessity in the SPS Agreement. First, the relationship between the two key provisions of the SPS Agreement on necessity (Articles 2.2 and 5.6) will be discussed. Next, the three-tier test for interpreting Article 5.6 will be presented. Finally, the link between the necessity tests in Articles 2.2 and 5.6 will be analyzed.

We begin with the relationship between Articles 2.2 and 5.6 of the SPS Agreement which respectively read:

> Article 2.2
>
> Members shall ensure that any sanitary or phytosanitary measure is *applied only to the extent necessary to* protect human, animal or plant life or health, is based on scientific principles and is not maintained without sufficient scientific evidence, except as provided for in paragraph 7 of Article 5 (*emphasis added*).
>
> Article 5.6
>
> Without prejudice to paragraph 2 of Article 3, when establishing or maintaining sanitary or phytosanitary measures to achieve the appropriate level of sanitary or phytosanitary protection, Members shall ensure that such measures are *not more trade-restrictive than required to achieve their appropriate level of sanitary or phytosanitary protection*, taking into account technical and economic feasibility.[3]
>
> [3] For purposes of paragraph 6 of Article 5, a measure is *not more trade-restrictive than required* unless there is another measure, *reasonably available taking into account technical and economic feasibility, that achieves the appropriate level of sanitary or phytosanitary protection* and *is significantly less restrictive to trade* (*emphasis added*).

It is to be observed that Article 2.2 of contains the term 'necessary' while Article 5.6 does not have the term 'necessary', but the term 'not more-restrictive than required to achieve [the] appropriate level of [SPS] protection'. as well as the definition in footnote 3 thereof are descriptions familiar to the interpretation developed for the concept of necessity in the General Exceptions of the GATT 1994/GATS as well as Article 2.2 of the TBT Agreement.[76] Article 2 of the SPS Agreement (titled *Basic Rights and Obligations*) is more general than the provisions of Article 5 (titled *Assessment of Risk and Determination of the Appropriate Level of Sanitary or Phytosanitary Protection*).[77] In *Australia – Apples (2010)*, the Appellate Body observed that the phrases 'only to the extent necessary to protect' in Article 2.2 and the requirement in Article 5.6 that SPS measures be 'no more trade-restrictive than required to achieve' create a direct link between the two provisions:

> Article 2.2 'informs',[78] 'impart[s] meaning to',[79] and 'is made operative in',[80] other provisions of the *SPS Agreement*, including certain of the more specific obligations set out in Article 5 … Thus, in *EC – Hormones*, the Appellate Body stated that 'Articles 2.2 and 5.1 should constantly be read together. Article 2.2 informs Article 5.1: the elements that define the basic obligation set out in Article 2.2 impart meaning to Article 5.1'.[81] The same type of relationship exists between Articles 2.2 and 5.2 and *between Articles 2.2 and 5.6*. In this connection, *we take particular note of the similarities* between the requirement in Article 2.2 that Members apply their SPS measures 'only to the extent necessary to protect', and the requirement in Article 5.6 that SPS measures be 'no more trade-restrictive than required to achieve' the relevant objectives (*emphasis added*).[82]

Accordingly, it has been the *general* practice to examine Article 5.6 first[83]

76 WTO Panel Report, *India – Agricultural Products (2015)*, paras. 7.606–7.613.

77 Ibid, para. 7.613.

78 Referring to Appellate Body Report, *EC – Hormones (1998)*, para. 180.

79 Referring to ibid.

80 Referring to Appellate Body Reports, *US/Canada – Continued Suspension (2008)*, para. 674.

81 Referring to Appellate Body Report, *EC – Hormones (1998)*, paras. 180, 212.

82 Appellate Body Report, *Australia – Apples (2010)*, para. 339. See also, Appellate Body Report, *India – Agricultural Products (2015)*, para. 5.208.

83 In WTO Panel Report, *Costa Rica – Avocados (Mexico) (2022)*, the panel presented some justifications to first examine consistency of the measures under Article 2.2 before examining their consistency under Article 5.6 (see paras. 7.24–7.28). However, it must be noted – within the context of this sub-section, where it has been stated that the

"in context and, in particular, in light of Article 2.2".[84] Until the findings of the *India – Agricultural Products (2015)* panel,[85] neither the Appellate Body nor the panels had decided, regarding the relationship between Articles 5.1/5.2 and Article 2.2 of the SPS Agreement, that inconsistency with Article 5.6 may lead to a presumption of inconsistency with the necessity requirement in Article 2.2.[86] This presumption, as has been the practice, means that the panel will exercise judicial economy unless the respondent wants to prove necessity of the measure under Article 2.2 of the SPS Agreement.[87]

The second point of discussion is the three-tier test for interpreting Article 5.6. In *Australia – Salmon (1998)*, the Appellate Body took note that the phrase 'not more trade-restrictive than required' in Article 5.6 has to be interpreted by reference to footnote 3 thereof and confirmed the panel's identification of a three-pronged test under footnote 3 to examine consistency with Article

---

practice regarding the concepts of necessity in Articles 2.2 and 5.6 has been to first begin examining necessity of the disputed measure under Article 5.6 – the focus of the panel's examination in *Costa Rica – Avocados (Mexico) (2022)*, which began its examination with Article 2.2, was on the issue of whether Costa Rica's measures were "based on scientific principles and are not maintained without sufficient scientific evidence" (paras. 7.1724–7.1735), not whether they were "applied only to the extent necessary" under Article 2.2.

84 Appellate Body Report, *Australia – Salmon (1998)*, para. 180, referring to WTO Panel Report, *Australia – Salmon (1998)*, para. 8.165. The panel in *India – Agricultural Products (2015)* also added that: "In our view, the crux of the ... relationship between Articles 5.6 and 2.2, relates to the extent to which 'necessity' in Article 2.2 may be understood in light of the substance of the more specific obligation in Article 5.6." WTO Panel Report, *India – Agricultural Products (2015)*, para. 7.605.

85 See, WTO Panel Report, *India – Agricultural Products (2015)*, para. 7.61; WTO Panel Report, *Russia – Pigs (EU) (2017)*, paras. 7.840–7.841. In para. 5.208, f.n. 616 of Appellate Body Report, *India – Agricultural Products (2015)*, the Appellate Body referred to Appellate Body Report, *Australia – Apples (2010)*, para. 340 where it had stated that the presumptive relationship between Articles 2.2 and 5.6 was not clear. After thoroughly examining the appeal on Article 5.6, however, the Appellate Body confirmed in this dispute that a panel's finding that a measure is in consistent with Article 5.6 because it is significantly more trade restrictive than required to achieve the respondent's appropriate level of protection makes it unnecessary, for reasons of judicial economy, to address whether the respondent's measures are inconsistent with Article 2.2. Appellate Body Report, *India – Agricultural Products (2015)*, para. 5.244. The panel's presumption of Article 2.2 inconsistency, therefore, remains undisturbed. For a scholarly support of this presumption, see, Gruszczynski, above note 13, p. 250.

86 Appellate Body Report, *Australia – Salmon (1998)*, para. 213; Appellate Body Report, *Australia – Apples (2010)*, para. 340; WTO Panel Report, *India – Agricultural Products (2015)*, paras. 7.600–7.604.

87 See, for instance, WTO Panel Report, *India – Agricultural Products (2015)*, para. 7.615; Appellate Body Report, *India – Agricultural Products (2015)*, para. 5.244; WTO Panel Report, *Russia – Pigs (EU) (2017)*, paras. 7.844–7.846.

5.6. The test involves examining whether the alternative measure proposed by the complainant: (1) is reasonably available taking into account technical and economic feasibility; (2) achieves the Member's appropriate level of SPS protection; and (3) is significantly less restrictive to trade than the SPS measure contested.[88] The Appellate Body asserted that "[t]hese three elements are cumulative in the sense that, to establish inconsistency with Article 5.6, all of them have to be met. If any of these elements is not fulfilled, the measure in dispute would be consistent with Article 5.6."[89] In *Australia – Apples (2010)* the Appellate Body stated that the main purpose of Article 5.6 is "to ensure that SPS measures are not more trade-restrictive than necessary to achieve a Member's appropriate level of protection ... through a comparison of the measure at issue to possible alternative measures".[90] But, which aspects of the disputed and the alternative measure are compared? In *Australia – Apples (2010)*, the Appellate Body stated that, whereas the elements of the reasonable availability of the alternative measure and its ability to achieve the Member's appropriate level of protection focus on assessing the alterative measure, "[o]nly in examining whether the third condition is fulfilled [i.e., whether the alternative measure is significantly less restrictive to trade than the disputed measure] will a panel need to compare the proposed alternative measure with the contested SPS measure."[91] Let us briefly see how the three elements of footnote 3 of Article 5.6 have been interpreted. There has not been consistency, as observed by the *India – Agricultural Products (2015)* panel, on the order of examination of these three elements.[92]

88 Appellate Body Report, *Australia – Salmon (1998)*, para. 194. See also, WTO Panel Report, *Japan – Agricultural Products (1999)*, para. 8.72; Appellate Body Report, *Australia – Apples (2010)*, para. 337; WTO Panel Report, *India – Agricultural Products (2015)*, paras. 7.521–7.522.

89 Appellate Body Report, *Australia – Apples (2010)*, para. 337; Appellate Body Report, *Australia – Salmon (1998)*, para. 194; Appellate Body Report, *India – Agricultural Products (2015)*, para. 5.203. In *Costa Rica – Avocados (Mexico) (2022)*, the panel, after finding that the alternatives proposed by the claimant failed to achieve the respondent's appropriate level of protection (para. 7.1892), stated that it need not continue to examine the other two elements (para. 7.1893), but nevertheless continued to examine them "in order to be exhaustive in its analysis" (para. 7.1894). Despite finding in the affirmative for the complainant on these two elements (paras. 7.1894–7.1934), the panel, stating that the three criteria in footnote 3 of Article 5.6 are "cumulative", found for the respondent (paras. 7.1935–7.1938).

90 Appellate Body Report, *Australia – Apples (2010)*, para. 363.

91 Ibid, paras. 337, 344. See also, Appellate Body Report, *India – Agricultural Products (2015)*, para. 206.

92 WTO Panel Report, *India – Agricultural Products (2015)*, para. 7.523, f.n. 983.

Regarding the reasonable availability of the alternative measure taking into account technical and economic feasibility, the *Australia – Salmon* (*1998*) and *Australia – Salmon* (*Article 21.5 – Canada*) (*2000*) panels determined that they would look at the facts of the dispute, the characteristics of the contested measure and the alternative measures considered during risk assessment in order to determine which one of the proposed alternative measures is a feasible choice.[93] The phrase 'taking into account technical and economic feasibility' is understood to require determination of "whether the alternative measure would constitute an option reasonably available taking into account technical and economic feasibility in the real world".[94] Regarding the alternative measure's ability to achieve the Member's appropriate level of SPS protection, the Appellate Body has identified a three-tier test: (a) identifying the level of protection that the respondent has set as its appropriate level;[95] (b) determining what level of protection would be achieved by the complainant's alternative measure; and (c) determining whether the level of protection that would be achieved by the alternative measure would satisfy the respondent's appropriate level of protection.[96] Regarding whether the test of the alternative measure is significantly less restrictive to trade than the SPS measure contested, it has been observed that the panel should examine whether the adoption of the alternative measure would substantially increase market access.[97]

The third point of discussion is on the link that exists between the necessity tests in Articles 2.2 and 5.6.

---

93 Van den Bossche and Zdouc, above note 22, p. 965, referring to WTO Panel Report, *Australia – Salmon* (*1998*), para. 8.171 and WTO Panel Report, *Australia – Salmon* (*Article 21.5 – Canada*) [*2000*], paras. 7.146–7.149. WTO Panel Report, *India – Agricultural Products* (*2015*), paras. 7.526–7.534 may be added.

94 WTO Panel Report, *Japan – Apples* (*Article 21.5 – US*) (*2005*), para. 8.171. See also, WTO Panel Report, *Australia – Apples* (*2010*), para. 7.1334; WTO Panel Report, *India – Agricultural Products* (*2015*), para. 7.540.

95 Although Members enjoy the prerogative of setting their levels of SPS protection, they have, however, an obligation to set them as clearly as possible. Otherwise, panels are "free to establish the level based on the level of protection reflected in the SPS measure actually applied." Appellate Body Report, *Australia – Salmon* (*1998*), para. 207. Panels are cautioned not to infer, from the measure at hand, the member's clear appropriate level of protection if the latter has been set in a relatively clearer way. Appellate Body Report, *Australia – Salmon* (*1998*), paras. 199–201.

96 Appellate Body Report, *Australia – Apples* (*2010*), para. 368. See also, an analysis of the three-tier test in para. 344.

97 WTO Panel Report, *Australia – Salmon* (*Article 21.5 – Canada*) (*2000*), paras. 7.150–7.152; WTO Panel Report, *Japan – Agricultural Products* (*Article 21.5 – US*) (*2005*), paras. 8.186–8.188; WTO Panel Report, *India – Agricultural Products* (*2015*), paras. 7.595–7.596.

It has been stated above that there is a link of presumption between the necessity requirements in Articles 2.2 and 5.6 of the SPS Agreement in that inconsistency with Article 5.6 may lead to a presumption of inconsistency with the necessity requirement in Article 2.2. It was the *India – Agricultural Products (2015)* panel that provided the justification for such link of presumption. After lengthy examination of the consistency of the contested measure under Article 5.6 by applying the three elements of footnote 3 to the alternative measure proposed by the complainant,[98] the panel stated:

> the Panel is particularly mindful of the resonance of these common elements of 'necessity' in Article XX of the GATT 1994, Article XIV of the GATS, and Article 2.2 of the TBT Agreement, with the elements that must be demonstrated under Article 5.6 of the SPS Agreement.
>
> *The Appellate Body's interpretation of each of these provisions is probative of the relationship between Article 2.2 and Article 5.6 of the SPS Agreement.* The Appellate Body's interpretation of 'necessity' in the respective contexts discussed above accords to a substantial degree with the requirements of Article 5.6 of the SPS Agreement …
>
> based on this finding, and considering the fact that Article 2.2 is 'made operative in' the specific obligations in Article 5, and that Article 2.2 and Article 5.6 should be constantly read together, we consider that a finding that a measure is inconsistent with Article 5.6 may lead to a presumption that the same measure is inconsistent with the obligation in Article 2.2 to ensure that an SPS measure is applied only to the extent necessary to protect human, animal or plant life or health (*emphasis added*).[99]

Four points must be considered in examining the link of presumption of necessity between Articles 5.6 and 2.2.

Firstly, the focus of the necessity in the two provisions is different. Article 2.2 aims to ensure that 'SPS measures *are applied* only to the extent necessary to protect'. whereas Article 5.6 aims to ensure that 'SPS measures *are* not more trade-restrictive than required'. Thus, while the focus of Article 5.6 is on the necessity of the SPS measures, the focus of Article 5.2 is on the necessity of the application of the SPS measures.[100]

98 WTO Panel Report, *India – Agricultural Products (2015)*, paras. 7.514–7.597.

99 Ibid, paras. 7.611–7.614.

100 See Gruszczynski, above note 13, p. 244. Marceau and Trachtman, however, argue that Article 5.6 of the SPS Agreement covers the contested measure and its application as well and that the distinction between the measure and its application is unclear. Marceau and Trachtman, above note 15, pp. 382–383.

Secondly, Article 5.6 is limited in its scope in the sense that it does not apply to the necessity of the SPS measure as a whole but only to the *necessity of its trade-restrictiveness*. It is the trade-restrictiveness of the disputed measure that is compared with the trade-restrictiveness of the alternative measure in order to determine the necessity of the trade-restrictiveness of the disputed measure under Article 5.6.[101] The examination under Article 5.6 does not include, nor has it been interpreted to include, the full application of the 'weighing and balancing' test which compares not only the trade-restrictiveness of the disputed and the alternative measures but also the respective degrees of their contribution to achieve the objective.[102]

Thirdly, whereas the requirement of necessity in Article 5.6 and its footnote 3 has been *textually* defined and also interpreted by few panels and the Appellate Body, the requirement of necessity in Article 2.2 has not yet (as of the writing of this book) been interpreted by these organs. Prévost and Van den Bossche,[103] Gruszczynski,[104] Purba,[105] Scott[106] suggest that the interpretation developed for necessity under Article XX(b) of the GATT 1994 (which uses a very similar concept of necessity to that contained in Article 2.2 of the SPS Agreement) may provide guidance to interpret necessity under Article 2.2. One may read the statement of the *India – Agricultural Products (2015)* panel[107] as having indicated that the 'weighing and balancing' test would be applied to examine necessity under Article 2.2 of the SPS Agreement.[108]

Fourthly, the presumption between Article 5.6 and Article 2.2 works only the case of inconsistency of the measure with Article 5.6. A measure consistent

101 Above note 91.

102 Dawar and Ronen, above note 51, p. 14; Marceau and Trachtman, above note 15, pp. 422–423. In fact, Schebesta and Sinopoli argue that Article 5.6 is not a "regular" or "straightforward" necessity test but an "excessivity" test. Hanna Schebesta and Dominique Sinopoli, 'The Potency of the SPS Agreement's Excessivity Test: The Impact of Article 5.6 on Trade Liberalization and the Regulatory Power of WTO Members to take Sanitary and Phytosanitary Measures', *Journal of International Economic Law*, 21(1): 2018, pp. 124–126.

103 Prévost and Van den Bossche, above note 18, pp. 255–256.

104 Lukasz Gruszczynski, 'Risk Management Policies under the WTO Agreement on the Application of Sanitary and Phytosanitary Measures', *Asian Journal of WTO and International Health Law and Policy*, 3(1): 2008, p. 292.

105 Elbinsar Purba, 'Necessary Measure under the SPS Agreement', *Asian Journal of WTO & International Health Law and Policy*, 13(1): 2018, pp. 205–227.

106 Joanne Scott, *The WTO Agreement on Sanitary and Phytosanitary Measures: A Commentary* (New York: Oxford University Press, 2007), p. 160.

107 Above note 99.

108 Purba, above note 105, p. 212.

with Article 5.6 cannot be presumed to be consistent with Article 2.2; such measure may still be inconsistent with Article 2.2.[109]

Therefore, the presumption of link between Article 5.6 and 2.2 means that if a measure is found to be inconsistent under Article 5.6 (because it is more trade-restrictive than necessary), its *application* will be presumed to be not necessary under Article 2.2 unless the respondent rebuts such presumption. But how does the respondent rebut such presumption? The answer to this question is difficult at the moment because the concept of necessity of the application of the SPS measure in Article 2.2 has not been clearly interpreted yet. Should it be interpreted along the lines of the 'weighing and balancing' test? If the 'weighing and balancing' test will be applied to interpret the necessity under Article 2.2 of the SPS Agreement, however, the way the respondent can rebut the presumption becomes clearer. It was stated above that the necessity requirement in Article 5.6 is different from that in Article 2.2. Thus, as a result of the presumption carried from Article 5.6, the *application* of the measure will be presumed to be inconsistent with Article 2.2, i.e., not necessary to protect human, animal or plant life or health. In other words, assuming the 'weighing and balancing' test is applied to Article 2.2, it will be presumed that the *application* of the contested measure: (a) does not contribute to achieve the objectives set by the Member or contributes less than the application of the alternative measure; or (b) is more restrictive than the application of the alternative measure.[110] The respondent will, therefore, rebut the presumption under Article 2.2 by showing that the application of the contested measure: (a) contributes more to achieving the objectives set by the Member than the application of the alternative measure; and (b) is less trade-restrictive than the application of the alternative measure.[111]

The conclusion on the interpretation of the concept of necessity in the SPS Agreement is, therefore, that the Appellate Body and the panels have, as with the TBT Agreement, recognized the textual and/or contextual proximities

109 Gruszczynski, above note 13, pp. 250–251.

110 The third element of the 'weighing and balancing' test, i.e., relative importance of the values furthered by the contested measure, will not be difficult to examine because of the recognized importance of the objective of protecting of human, animal or plant life or health. Purba, above note 105, p. 223.

111 Due to the fact that under Article 5.6 the alternative measure needs to be *significantly less* trade-restrictive than the disputed SPS measure, Gruszczynski argues that what needs to be presumed under Article 2.2 is that the application of the alternative measure is *significantly* less trade-restrictive than the application disputed SPS measure and not, as the 'weighing and balancing' test would require, simply that it is *less* trade-restrictive than the application disputed SPS measure. Gruszczynski, above note 13, pp. 250–251.

among the necessity provisions of the SPS Agreement, the TBT Agreement and the General Exceptions of the GATT 1994/GATS. The concept of necessity under Article 2.2 of the SPS Agreement has not yet been interpreted, but an argument has been made to show that it will likely be interpreted using the 'weighing and balancing' test. The concept of necessity as contained in the text of Article 5.6 and the case law thereon reflects the elements of the 'weighing and balancing test'.[112] It may, thus, be argued that the 'weighing and balancing' test of necessity is also contained in the relevant provisions of the SPS Agreement. Moreover, the link of presumption of inconsistency between Article 5.6 and 2.2 can work easily if the interpretation to be developed for Article 2.2 of the SPS Agreement follows the interpretation already developed for the concept of necessity in the General Exceptions of the GATT 1994/GATS and Article 2.2 of the TBT Agreement.

To conclude the discussion on the concept of necessity in the TBT and the SPS agreements, the necessity provisions of the General Exceptions, the TBT Agreement and the SPS Agreement are similar in text, context and/or purpose (the purpose being balancing trade obligations with regulatory autonomy). The practice of interpreting these provisions has shown that not only have the necessity provisions in the TBT and SPS agreements been interpreted along the lines of the interpretation developed for necessity in the General Exceptions, but also that the concept of necessity in Article 2.2 of the SPS Agreement will likely adopt, like the interpretation developed for the concept of necessity in the TBT Agreement, the interpretation developed for necessity in the General Exceptions General Exceptions.

At this stage, a pattern of similar interpretation of the concept of necessity – whether presented as a substantive obligation (SPS and TBT agreements) or affirmative defense (General Exceptions) – is observed in the WTO Agreement especially if the texts of the respective agreements are similar in content. Delimatsis summarizes the GATT 1994-GATS-TBT-SPS line of uniform interpretation of the concept of necessity as: "the GATT/WTO interpretation of the concept of necessity has converged across the WTO Agreement."[113]

Despite the uniformity of interpretation of necessity in the General Exceptions of the GATT 1994/GATS and the TBT Agreement and the likelihood

112 Dawar and Ronen, above note 51, pp. 1, 14.

113 Panagiotis Delimatsis, 'Who's Afraid of Necessity? And Why it Matters?', in Aik Hoe Lim and Bart De Meester (eds.), *WTO Domestic Regulation and Services Trade: Putting Principles into Practice* (New York: Cambridge University Press, 2014), pp. 97–98. It must be noted that his analysis only considered the GATT 1994, the GATS, the TBT Agreement and the SPS Agreement.

of a similar interpretation for Article 2.2 of the SPS Agreement, however, there are some nuanced differences among them. Section 9.4 identifies nine factors that can compare the interpretations of necessity developed (to be developed) for the General Exceptions, the TBT Agreement and the SPS Agreement so that the similarities and differences are highlighted.

9.4 Comparing the Interpretations of Necessity in the General Exceptions of the GATT 1994/GATS, the TBT Agreement and the SPS Agreement

Section 9.4 will present nine points for comparing the interpretations developed (to be developed) for the concept of necessity in the General Exceptions, the TBT Agreement and the SPS Agreement. Paragraphs (i), (ii) and (iii) in all nine points of comparison will respectively discuss the General Exceptions, the TBT Agreement and the SPS Agreement respectively. The expression "to be developed" refers to the concept of necessity to be developed for Article 2.2 of the SPS Agreement which, as argued above, will likely follow the 'weighing and balancing' test used for the General Exceptions and Article 2.2 of the TBT Agreement.

9.4.1 *Should Inconsistencies with Other Substantive Obligations Be Ascertained before Examining Necessity of the Disputed Measure?*

(i) Since the General Exceptions are affirmative defenses, finding inconsistencies with other GATT 1994 obligations is a prerequisite.

(ii) Article 2.2 of the TBT Agreement (necessity) is not an affirmative defense. There is no requirement to first find inconsistences with other obligations such as the non-discrimination obligation in Article 2.1.

(iii) Articles 2.2 and 5.6 of the SPS Agreement (necessity) are not affirmative defenses even against each other; there is no need to first find inconsistences with other obligations such as risk assessment (Articles 2.2, 5.1, 5.2 and 5.7), risk management (Articles 2.3, 5.3–5.5) or non-discrimination (Article 2.1).

9.4.2 *Textual Presentation of the Term 'Necessary'*

(i) In the General Exceptions, necessity is represented by the term 'necessary' in the respective paragraphs.

(ii) In the TBT Agreement necessity is represented by the terms/expressions: (a) '(un)necessary' in the fifth and seventh recitals of the preamble; (b) 'unnecessary obstacles to international trade' in Article 2.2

(first sentence); and (c) 'more trade-restrictive than necessary to fulfill a legitimate objective' in Article 2.2 (second sentence).

(iii) In the SPS Agreement necessity is represented by the terms/expressions: (a)'necessary to protect human, animal or plant life or health' in the first recital of the preamble; (b) 'necessary for the protection of human, animal or plant life or health' in Article 2.1; (c) 'only to the extent necessary to protect human, animal or plant life or health' in Article 2.2; (d) 'deemed to be necessary to protect human, animal or plant life or health' in Article 3.2; (e) 'not more trade-restrictive than required to achieve their appropriate level of sanitary or phytosanitary protection' in Article 5.6 (although the term used here is 'required' and not 'necessary', the phrase has been understood to be similar to the interpretation developed for the concept of necessity in Article 2.2 of the TBT Agreement and the General Exceptions of the GATT 1994/GATS); and (f) the entire footnote 3 of Article 5.6.

9.4.3 *What Is It That Must Be Necessary?*

(i) In the General Exceptions, the Appellate Body has, since *US – Gasoline* (*1996*), held that it is the totality of the measure in dispute, not the part of the measure that violates the GATT 1994 that must be examined for necessity under Article XX.[114] That had been the standard for a number of years.[115] In *Thailand – Cigarettes* (*Philippines*) (*2011*), however, the Appellate Body stated that it is the part of the measure that is found to be inconsistent that must be held to be necessary.[116]

---

114 Appellate Body Report, *US – Gasoline* (*1996*), pp. 13–14. The Appellate Body stated, in part, that "[E]arlier panels had not interpreted 'measures' more broadly under Article XX to include provisions not themselves found inconsistent with Article III:4."

115 Appellate Body Report, *Korea – Various Measures on Beef* (*2001*), para. 164; Appellate Body Report, Appellate Body Report, *US – Gambling* (*2005*), paras. 304–308. Appellate Body Report, *Brazil – Retreaded Tyres* (*2007*), para. 156.

116 Appellate Body Report, *Thailand – Cigarettes* (*Philippines*) (*2011*), para. 177. Marceau identifies this shift from focus on the measure toward a focus on the part of the measure that is found to be inconsistent an *evolution* of the case law in this regard. Marceau noted that the Appellate Body, after stating that "what must be shown to be 'necessary' is the treatment giving rise to the finding of less favorable treatment", "then cites [GATT Panel Report, *US – Section 337* (*1989*), para. 5.27] in the footnote [270] to that sentence, but not *Gasoline*." Gabrielle Marceau, 'The New TBT Jurisprudence in *US – Clove Cigarettes, WTO US – Tuna II*, and *US – COOL*', *Asian Journal of WTO & International Health Law and Policy*, 8(1): 2013, p. 18 (f.n. 71). Para. 5.27 of GATT Panel Report, *US – Section 337* (*1989*) read: "...in the view of the Panel, *what has to be justified as 'necessary' under Article XX(d) is each of the inconsistencies with another GATT Article found to exist ... (emphasis added).*"

(ii) In the TBT Agreement, owing to the phrase 'more trade-restrictive than necessary' in the second sentence of Article 2.2, it is the level of trade-restrictiveness of the measure/technical regulation, not the measure/technical regulation itself, which must be examined for necessity.[117] Some authors, by reading the Appellate Body's analysis of Article 2.2 of the TBT Agreement in *US – Tuna II (Mexico) (2012)*, believe that it is the technical regulation as a whole that must be examined for necessity.[118]

(iii) Article 2.2 of the SPS Agreement requires that SPS measures be 'applied to the extent necessary' and Article 5.6 requires that the SPS measure be 'not more trade-restrictive than required to achieve the Member's appropriate level of [SPS] protection'. Thus, while it is the necessity of the application of the SPS measure that is examined under Article 2.2, it is the necessity of the trade-restrictiveness of the measure that is examined under Article 5.6.[119]

9.4.4 Burden to Prove Necessity (*Prima Facie*)

The difference in the burden of proof in arguing necessity in the General Exceptions of the GATT 1994/GATS *vis-à-vis* the TBT and SPS agreements has been discussed in Sub-section 9.3.1.

9.4.5 *Existence of Grounds to Presume Necessity*

(i) There exists no link of presumption of necessity between the various provisions of the GATT 1994/GATS and their General Exceptions. After the complainant proves inconsistency with one of the other provisions of the GATT 1994/GATS, there is no presumption that the measure is, or is not, necessary under the relevant paragraphs of the General Exceptions. The test of necessity under the General Exceptions is independent of the result of inconsistency under the other provisions of the GATT 1994/GATS. One possibility for presumption is when an SPS measure meets the requirements of the SPS Agreement (Article 2.4) or conforms to international standards, guidelines or recommendations

---

117 Appellate Body Report, *US – Tuna II (Mexico) (2012)*, para. 319, where the Appellate Body confirmed that "[w]hat has to be assessed for 'necessity' is the trade-restrictiveness of the measure at issue." See also, Ishikawa, above note 58, p. 13; Marceau and Trachtman, above note 15, p. 374.

118 Benn McGrady and Alexandra Jones, 'Tobacco Control and Beyond: The Broader Implications of *United States – Clove Cigarettes* for Non-Communicable Diseases', *American Journal of Law & Medicine*, 39 (2 & 3): 2013, pp. 283–284.

119 Above note 91; Marceau and Trachtman, above note 117.

(Article 3.2), in which cases the measure is presumed to be consistent with the SPS-relevant provisions of GATT 1994 including the General Exceptions. In case of Article 2.4 of the SPS Agreement, there is a particular presumption of consistency with Article XX(b) of the GATT 1994. Thus, a respondent which meets the requirements of the SPS Agreement has the benefit of presumption of consistency with the relevant GATT 1994 provisions, especially Article XX(b) which contains the concept of necessity.

(ii) Article 2.5 of the TBT Agreement allows a rebuttable presumption of necessity of the measure under Article 2.2 if the technical regulation is prepared, adopted or applied for one of the legitimate objectives explicitly mentioned in Article 2.2 and is in accordance with relevant international standards.

(iii) Article 3.2 of the SPS Agreement provides that measures that conform to international standards, guidelines or recommendations shall be deemed necessary to protect human, animal or plant life or health (i.e., consistent with Articles 2.1 and 2.2).

9.4.6 *Textual/Conceptual Presence of 'Legitimate Objective' in Relation to the Concept of Necessity*

(i) The policy objectives in the list of the General Exceptions of the GATT 1994/GATS are 'legitimate'. Pursuit of these objectives provides the respondent with a legal ground, if it also meets the tests of the 'connecting terms' and the *chapeau*, to justify the application of the disputed measures. As part of the necessity test, the Appellate Body required the examination of 'the relative value' of these policies, but not questioning whether they are legitimate at all. Their mere inclusion in the General Exceptions renders them legitimate enough. Moreover, the objectives of the paragraphs of the General Exceptions have been used as references for ascertaining legitimacy of some objectives which are not clearly listed in either of the TBT or SPS agreements.[120]

(ii) The phrase 'legitimate objective(s)' is found in Articles 2.2, 2.4 and 2.5 of the TBT Agreement. The term 'legitimate commercial interests' is also found in Article 5.2.4.

(iii) The phrase 'legitimate objective(s)' is not found as such in the SPS Agreement. With the *India – Agricultural Products* (2015) panel

120 For instance, the Appellate Body ascertained the legitimacy of the objective sought in the COOL dispute (informing consumers) by reference to the GATT 1994 Article XX(d). Appellate Body Reports, *US – COOL* (2012), para. 445.

indicating the willingness to apply the 'weighing and balancing' test for the necessity principle in Article 2.2 of the SPS Agreement, however, the concept of legitimacy of the objective sought by the contested SPS measure will be important. In that case, it will become obvious that the objective of the SPS measure (i.e., protection of the life or health of human, animals or plants) is a legitimate objective.[121] The list of objectives contained in Annex A(1) of the SPS Agreement can also be identified as legitimate objectives for purposes of the necessity argument under the SPS Agreement. The term 'legitimate commercial interests' is also contained in Annex B(11) of the SPS Agreement.

9.4.7 *The Need to Assess the Degree of Contribution That a Measure Makes towards Fulfilling the Objective*

(i) Assessing the degree of contribution of the contested measure towards achieving the objective is one of the elements in conducting the 'weighing and balancing' test developed for the General Exceptions. A measure is 'necessary' if it is capable of making or does make some contribution to its objective or if it makes a contribution to a certain extent. There is no pre-determined threshold of contribution.[122]

(ii) The Appellate Body has made it clear that as part of analyzing the second sentence of Article 2.2 of the TBT Agreement, the 'weighing and balancing' test it developed for the General Exceptions (which includes identifying the degree of contribution of the contested measure) must be conducted.[123] The Appellate Body also stated that there is no need for minimum threshold of contribution[124] and that the measure passes muster even if it makes 'partial'[125] or 'some'[126] contribution.

(iii) Scholars have argued that the second of the three-tier test in footnote 3 of Article 5.6 of the SPS Agreement – i.e., ascertaining whether

121 Gruszczynski states that as far as the first element of the 'weighing and balancing' test (i.e., relative importance of the values furthered by the challenged measure) the protection of human life or health is recognized in the WTO case law as vital and important in the highest degree. Gruszczynski, above note 13, p. 245. See also, Appellate Body Report, *EC – Asbestos (2001)*, para. 172, WTO Panel Report, *Brazil – Retreaded Tyres (2007)*, para. 7.112.

122 Appellate Body Reports, *EC – Seal Products (2014)*, paras. 5.213, 5.215–5.216, 5.228.

123 Appellate Body Report, *US – Tuna II (Mexico) (2012)*, para. 318; Appellate Body Reports, *US – COOL (2012)*, para. 376.

124 Appellate Body Reports, *US – COOL (2012)*, para. 461.

125 Appellate Body Report, *US – Tuna II (Mexico) (2012)*, para. 341.

126 Appellate Body Reports, *US – COOL (2012)*, para. 476.

the alternative measure is one that 'achieves the appropriate level of sanitary or phytosanitary protection' – is short of the requirement to assess the *degree* of contribution of the alternative measure.[127] What is required is for the panel to only find that the alternative measure would achieve the respondent's appropriate level of SPS protection. Dawar and Ronen note that "[s]ince Article 5.6 ignores balancing the contribution to a legitimate objective, the tribunal need not reject the use of a measure [under Article 5.6] merely because it did not *adequately contribute* to its objective and is highly trade-restrictive."[128] Under Article 2.2 of the SPS Agreement, however, examination of necessity would involve determining the contribution of the *application* of the disputed and alternative measures to the end pursued because examination of the term 'necessary' in Article 2.2 is likely[129] to be conducted under the 'weighing and balancing' test which involves considering the element of contribution to the end pursued. Accordingly, if the disputed measure is found to be inconsistent with Article 5.6 of the SPS Agreement, its application could still be found to be consistent (or inconsistent) with Article 2.2 of the SPS Agreement because of the contribution factor.

9.4.8 *Textual Definition of the Requirements of an Alternative Measure*

(i) There is no textual definition of an alternative measure in the General Exceptions. The concept was developed in the process of interpreting necessity in the General Exceptions.

(ii) There is no textual definition of an alternative measure in the TBT Agreement. The concept was developed in the process of interpreting necessity in Article 2.2.

(iii) footnote 3 of Article 5.6 of the SPS Agreement defines the elements that the proposed alternative measures must have.

127 Gabrielle Marceau and Joel P. Trachtman, 'The Technical Barriers to Trade Agreement, the Sanitary and Phytosanitary Measures Agreement, and the General Agreement on Tariffs and Trade: A Map of the World Trade Organization Law of Domestic Regulation of Goods', *Journal of World Trade*, 36(5): 2002, pp. 856, 871; Marceau and Trachtman, above note 15, pp. 410, 423; Dawar and Ronen, above note 51, p. 14.

128 Dawar and Ronen, ibid. See also, Marceau and Trachtman, ibid, pp. 422–423.

129 See discussion in Sub-section 9.3.3 regarding the link that exists between the necessity tests in Articles 2.2 and 5.6.

9.4.9 *Odds of Winning the Necessity Argument for the Complainant*

The following may be observed regarding the respective rates of success for the complainants under the General Exceptions, the TBT Agreement and the SPS Agreement from the point of view of the allocation of burden of proof to show necessity.

(i) Table 1 in Sub-section 8.1.4 showed a very high rate of the respondents' losing of defenses based on the General Exceptions of the GATT 1994/GATS and a very low rate of success of necessity defenses under the relevant paragraphs of the General Exceptions. The fact that the respondent has the burden of proof under the 'weighing and balancing' test may have contributed to such a low rate of success.

(ii) In the TBT Agreement – at least by comparison with the results of the analyses of Articles 2.1 and 2.2 in *US – Clove Cigarettes* (*2012*), *US – Tuna II* (*Mexico*) (*2012*) and *US – COOL* (*2012*) – it has been observed that the complainants found it more difficult to show that the measure is not necessary (Article 2.2) than to show that the measure is discriminatory (Article 2.1).[130] Carlone tries to make sense of this trend by referring to the balance that the Appellate Body wants to maintain between free trade and regulatory autonomy:

> In *U.S. – Clove Cigarettes, U.S. – Tuna II,* and *U.S. – COOL*, the Appellate Body showed its preference for finding violations under Article 2.1 as opposed to Article 2.2 ...
>
> By finding *all* of the disputed measures consistent with Article 2.2, the Appellate Body indicated that *it would be difficult for a complainant to prove a measure violates that provision.* The Appellate Body presumably made this claim difficult to prove *because it is more comfortable finding a violation using non-discrimination, which is widely recognized as the WTO's core function, rather than necessity.* Additionally, because the TBT Agreement does not have exception provisions like GATT Article XX, if interpreted differently by the Appellate Body, Article 2.2 could greatly constrain the regulatory authority of WTO members. Thus, the Appellate Body's unwillingness to find violations under the necessity provision reflects appropriate deference toward WTO members' regulatory authority (*emphasis added*).[131]

The high rate of loss for the respondents to prove, under the General Exceptions, that the measure is necessary and the high rate of loss for

130 Marceau, above note 116, p. 22.

131 Carlone, above note 16, pp. 127–128. Carlone's statements on the *chapeau* are based on his reference to Appellate Body Report, *US – Clove Cigarettes* (*2012*), paras. 96, 109.

the complainants to prove, under Article 2.2 of the TBT Agreement, that the measure is not necessary leads to one conclusion: the difficulty of presenting proof under the 'weighing and balancing' test makes it hard for the party with burden, regardless of whether the burden is to prove the existence of necessity (i.e., for the respondent to show in the General Exceptions) or to prove the non-existence of necessity (i.e., for the complainant to show in Article 2.2 of TBT Agreement).

(iii) The necessity provisions in the TBT and SPS agreements (i.e., Articles 2.2 and 2.2/5.6 respectively) have been interpreted similar to the way the necessity defense has been interpreted in the General Provisions of the GATT 1994/GATS. Paragraphs (i) and (ii) above shown that it has been difficult for the respondents and the complainants to prevail respectively in the necessity arguments under the General Exceptions and the TBT Agreement. Given the fact that the complainant, as in the TBT Agreement, bears the burden of proof in Article 5.6 of the SPS Agreement to show that the disputed measure is not necessary, a rate of success similar to that in the TBT Agreement is likely to be expected. The trend so far, however, has been the opposite with the findings of the panels regarding the necessity argument in Article 5.6 and the Appellate Body's trend is not fully clear to discern whether it wants Article 5.6 findings to follow in the direction of Article 2.2 of the TBT Agreement.

Table 2 below presents a preliminary review of the results for the complainant under Article 5.6 in 11 SPS Agreement disputes. The disputes have been arranged chronologically.

The table shows that in seven of the eight disputes where they made definitive findings (*Australia – Salmon* (*1998*), *Japan – Agricultural Products* (*1999*), *Australia – Apples* (*2010*), *India – Agricultural Products* (*2015*), *US – Animals* (*2015*), *Russia – Pigs* (*2017*) and *Korea – Radionuclides* (*2019*)), the panels found inconsistencies with Article 5.6. In *Japan – Agricultural Products* (*1999*) and *Australia – Apples* (*2010*), a few (not all) of the multiple measures in dispute were held to be inconsistent with Article 5.6. Only in *Costa Rica – Avocados* (*Mexico*) (*2022*) was the complainant unable to prove inconsistency of the measure with Article 5.6.

In the four disputes where it made definitive findings (*Japan – Agricultural Products* (*1999*), *Australia – Apples* (*2010*), *India – Agricultural Products* (*2015*) and *Korea – Radionuclides* (*2019*)), the Appellate Body reversed the respective panels in two disputes (*Japan – Agricultural Products* (*1999*), *Australia – Apples* (*2010*) and *Korea – Radionuclides* (*2019*)) after finding most or all of the

TABLE 2 Results for the complainant on the necessity requirement in select SPS Agreement disputes

Dispute	Result for the complainant at the panel level	Result for the complainant at the appellate body level
EC – *Hormones (Canada) (1998)*	Panel refrained from making findings on Article 5.6 after it found inconsistency under Article 5.5 (para. 8.250)	Even if it reversed the panel on Article 5.5, the Appellate Body refrained from examining Article 5.6 for lack of facts in the panel report (paras. 251–252)
EC – *Hormones (US) (1998)*	Panel refrained from making findings on Article 5.6 after it found inconsistency under Article 5.5 (para. 8.247)	Even if it reversed the panel on Article 5.5, the Appellate Body refrained from examining Article 5.6 for lack of facts in the panel report (paras. 251–252)
Australia – Salmon (1998)	Complainant proved inconsistency of the measure with Article 5.6 (para. 8.183)	The Appellate Body could not make a conclusion because it reversed the panel on the SPS measure that had to be examined (paras. 241–242)
Japan–Agricultural Products (1999)	– On the first alternative called 'testing by product', the complainant did not prove inconsistency of the measure with Article 5.6 because this alternative would not achieve the respondent's appropriate level of SPS protection (para. 8.84) – On the second alterative called 'determining sorption level', complainant proved inconsistency of the measure with Article 5.6 (paras. 8.102–8.104)	The Appellate Body reversed the panel after ascertaining that the 'determining sorption level' alternative (para. 143(d)) could achieve the respondent's appropriate level of SPS protection

TABLE 2 Results for the complainant on the necessity requirement in select SPS Agreement disputes (*cont.*)

Dispute	Result for the complainant at the panel level	Result for the complainant at the appellate body level
Japan – Apples (2003)	The panel, having found that the measure breached Articles 2.2, 5.7 and 5.1, exercised judicial economy because it believed its analysis under Article 5.6 would not add anything in terms of legal implications (paras. 8.299–8.304)	Finding not made an issue in appeal
Australia – Apples (2010)	Complainant proved inconsistency of the measure with Article 5.6 in 13 out of 17 measures examined (para. 7.1403)	The Appellate Body reversed panel mainly because the panel did not properly analyze evidence of risk of the alterative measure proposed by the complainant under the second condition of footnote 3 of Article 5.6 (para. 407)
India–Agricultural Products (2015)	Complainant proved inconsistency of the measure with Article 5.6 (para. 7.597)	The Appellate Body upheld the panel (para. 5.244)
US – Animals (2015)	Complainant proved inconsistency of the measure with Article 5.6 (para. 8.1(g))	Panel report not appealed against
Russia – Pigs (2017)	Complainant proved inconsistency of the measure with Article 5.6 in the two categories of products in four countries (plus the EU), except that the measure was not found to be consistent with Article 5.6 in one category of the products in	Finding not made an issue in appeal

TABLE 2 Results for the complainant on the necessity requirement in select SPS Agreement disputes (*cont.*)

Dispute	Result for the complainant at the panel level	Result for the complainant at the appellate body level
	one country. In essence, only one out of ten combinations of products by category and place of export was found to be consistent (paras. 7.834, 7.1245–7.1246)	
Korea – Radionuclides (*2019*)	Complainant proved inconsistency of the measure with Article 5.6 (para. 8.2)	The Appellate Body reversed panel's finding of inconsistency with respect to most of the measures mainly because the panel did not examine whether the alternative measure proposed by the complainant satisfied all of the elements of the respondent's appropriate level of protection that the panel had identified (para. 6.1)
Costa Rica – Avocados (*Mexico*) (*2022*)	Complainant failed to prove inconsistency of the measure with Article 5.6 because this alternative would not achieve the respondent's appropriate level of SPS protection (paras. 7.1892, 7.1935–7.1938)	Currently under appeal

measures to be consistent with Article 5.6, while it upheld the panel's finding of inconsistency in *India – Agricultural Products* (*2015*).

Table 3 below is a tabulated presentation of Section 4 of this chapter, i.e., the nine points of comparison of the concepts of necessity as developed (to

TABLE 3 Tabulated presentation of the nine points of comparison of the concepts of necessity in the GATT 1994 (General Exceptions), the TBT Agreement and the SPS Agreement

	Point of comparison	General exceptions	TBT Agreement	SPS Agreement
1	Should inconsistencies with other substantive obligations be ascertained before examining necessity of the disputed measure?	yes	no	no
2	Textual presentation of the term 'necessary'	'necessary'	– '(un)necessary' – 'unnecessary obstacles to international trade' – 'more trade-restrictive than necessary to fulfill a legitimate objective'	– 'necessary to protect'. – 'necessary for the protection of human, animal or plant life or health' – 'only to the extent necessary to protect'. – 'deemed to be necessary to protect'. – 'not more trade-restrictive than required to achieve their appropriate level of SPS protection'

TABLE 3 Tabulated presentation of the nine points of comparison of the concepts of necessity in the GATT 1994 (General Exceptions), the TBT Agreement and the SPS Agreement (*cont.*)

	Point of comparison	General exceptions	TBT Agreement	SPS Agreement
3	What is it that must be necessary?	the treatment giving rise to the inconsistency with the relevant GATT 1994 obligation	level of trade-restrictiveness of the measure/technical regulation	trade-restrictiveness (application) of the SPS measure
4	Burden to prove necessity (*prima facie*)	It is generally on the respondent; complainant to identify alternative measures	complainant to prove that the disputed measure is not necessary	complainant to prove that the disputed measure is not necessary
5	Existence of grounds to presume necessity	There are grounds (via the SPS Agreement only)	There are grounds	There are grounds
6	Textual/conceptual presence of 'legitimate objective' in relation to the concept of necessity	yes	yes	yes

TABLE 3 Tabulated presentation of the nine points of comparison of the concepts of necessity in the GATT 1994 (General Exceptions), the TBT Agreement and the SPS Agreement (*cont.*)

	Point of comparison	**General exceptions**	**TBT Agreement**	**SPS Agreement**
7	The need to assess the degree of contribution a measure makes towards fulfilling the objective	must be done	must be done	not required under Article 5.6; may be introduced in Article 2.2
8	Textual definition of an alternative measure	no	no	yes
9	Odds of winning the necessity argument for the complainant	very high	low	not clear so far

be developed) for the General Exceptions, the TBT Agreement and the SPS Agreement.

9.5 Necessity under the TRIPS Agreement

9.5.1 *The Texts*

Articles 3.2, 8.1, 27.2, 39.3 and 73(b) of the TRIPS Agreement embody the defense of necessity. Of these, Articles 3.2, 8.1, 27.2, 39.3 have similarities with the General Exceptions of the GATT 1994/GATS while Article 73(b) is similar to the Security Exceptions of the GATT 1994/GATS.

> Article 3.2
>
> Members may avail themselves of the exceptions permitted under paragraph 1 … only where such exceptions are *necessary to* secure compliance with laws and regulations which are not inconsistent with the provisions of this Agreement and where such practices are not applied in a manner which would constitute a disguised restriction on trade.
>
> Article 8.1
>
> Members may, in formulating or amending their laws and regulations, adopt measures *necessary to* protect public health and nutrition, and to promote the public interest in sectors of vital importance to their socio-economic and technological development, provided that such measures are consistent with the provisions of this Agreement.
>
> Article 27.2
>
> Members may exclude from patentability inventions, the prevention within their territory of the commercial exploitation of which is *necessary to* protect *ordre public* or morality, including to protect human, animal or plant life or health or to avoid serious prejudice to the environment, provided that such exclusion is not made merely because the exploitation is prohibited by their law.
>
> Article 39.3
>
> Members, when requiring, as a condition of approving the marketing of pharmaceutical or of agricultural chemical products which utilize new chemical entities, the submission of undisclosed test or other data, the origination of which involves a considerable effort, shall protect such data against unfair commercial use. In addition, Members shall protect such data against disclosure, *except where necessary to* protect the public, or unless steps are taken to ensure that the data are protected against unfair commercial use.

Article 73(b)

Nothing in this Agreement shall be construed:

(b) ... to prevent a Member from taking any action which it considers *necessary for* the protection of its essential security interests.

9.5.2 *The Context for Interpreting the TRIPS Agreement 'Exceptions'*

TRIPS Agreement provisions such as those cited above and others (such as Articles 3.1, 13, 17, 26(2), 30 and [the amendment to Article] 31) have generally been called 'general exceptions',[132] whether they apply to the entire TRIPS Agreement (such as Articles 3, 8.1 or 73) or to specific intellectual property rights (such as Articles 13, 17, 26(2), 30 and 31). Each of these exceptions has its own specifications and limitations. It is these specifications and limitations that are often cited to show the differences between the TRIPS Agreement exceptions and the General Exceptions of the GATT 1994/GATS. For example, Article 8.1 of the TRIPS Agreement is often compared with the General Exceptions in the GATT 1994/GATS which are invoked as affirmative defenses against violations of any provision in the GATT 1994/GATS; i.e., in invoking the General Exceptions there is no requirement to meet the requirements of any one of the other provisions of the GATT 1994/GATS. In the case of Article 8.1 of the TRIPS, however, the necessity exception is qualified by the requirement that "such [necessary] measures are consistent with the provisions of this Agreement."[133] For this reason, Brand calls Article 8.1 of the TRIPS Agreement 'not a proper exception'[134] in comparison to the General Exceptions in the GATT 1994/GATS which are "proper exceptions, [because unlike Article 8.1 they] lack a corresponding compatibility clause. Exceptions to the protection granted by [the TRIPS Agreement] are permissible only if they are recognized by a particular provision of the agreement itself."[135]

132 Rodrigues has, for instance, dedicated an entire book to the "General Exceptions Clauses of the TRIPS Agreement". Edson Beas Rodrigues, Jr., *The General Exceptions Clauses of the TRIPS Agreement: Promoting Sustainable Development* (Cambridge: Cambridge University Press, 2012).

133 Slade cautions that "it would be wrong to jump to the conclusion that Article 8.1 is an exceptions provision like Article XX of the GATT and Article XIV GATS" because of the requirement in Article 8.1 for measures taken as necessary to be consistent with the TRIPS Agreement. Alison Slade, 'The Objectives and Principles of the WTO TRIPS Agreement: A Detailed Anatomy', *Osgoode Hall Law Journal*, 53(3): 2016, p. 981.

134 Oliver Brand, Commentary on Article 8 of the TRIPS Agreement, in Peter-Tobias Stoll, Jan Busche and Katrin Arend (eds.), *WTO – Trade-Related Aspects of Intellectual Property Rights (Max Planck Commentaries on World Trade Law, Vol. 7)* (Leiden and Boston: Martinus Nijhoff Publishers, 2009), pp. 189.

135 Brand, ibid, pp. 197–198. See also, Van den Bossche and Zdouc, above note 22, p. 997.

The EC – *Trademarks and Geographical Indications* (*Australia*) (2005) panel explained the reason for the absence of a General Exception-like provision in the TRIPS Agreement as follows:

> These principles [of Article 8.1] reflect the fact that the TRIPS Agreement does not generally provide for the grant of positive rights to exploit or use certain subject matter, but rather provides for the grant of negative rights to prevent certain acts. This fundamental feature of intellectual property protection inherently grants Members freedom to pursue legitimate public policy objectives since many measures to attain those public policy objectives lie outside the scope of intellectual property rights and do not require an exception under the TRIPS Agreement.[136]

Regardless of the differences in wording and scope between them, the 'exceptions' provisions of the TRIPS Agreement are interpreted within the context of the objective that the TRIPS Agreement seeks to attain: maintaining equilibrium between rewarding creators of intellectual property and protecting the public interest (Article 7).[137] Thus, the exceptions provisions of the TRIPS Agreement, including the term 'necessary' in some of them, must be interpreted to attain the objective of maintaining balance of 'rights and obligations' (Article 7), i.e., balance between treaty obligations and regulatory autonomy. As discussed in Chapter 8 and Sections 9.2–9.4, this same objective of maintaining balance is also sought in the exercise of interpreting necessity in the General Exceptions of the GATT 1994/GATS, the TBT Agreement and SPS Agreement.

9.5.3 *Interpreting the Concept of Necessity in the TRIPS Agreement Based on the Interpretation of the Concept of Necessity in the General Exceptions of the GATT 1994/GATS*

If the texts and the objectives of interpreting the 'necessity exceptions' of the TRIPS Agreement are similar to those of the necessity provisions in the General Exceptions of the GATT 1994/GATS, the TBT Agreement and SPS Agreement, it may be argued that the necessity exceptions of the TRIPS argument should, *mutatis mutandis*, be interpreted along the lines of the *similar* interpretation

136 WTO Panel Report, EC – *Trademarks and Geographical Indications* (*Australia*) (2005), paras. 7.209–7.210. See also, WTO Panel Report, EC – *Trademarks and Geographical Indications* (*US*) (2005), paras. 7.245–7.246.

137 Van den Bossche and Zdouc, above note 135 (regarding Article 8.1). See also, WTO Panel Report, *Canada – Pharmaceutical Patents* (2000), para. 7.26 (regarding Article 30).

thus far developed for the necessity provisions in the General Exceptions of the GATT 1994/GATS, the TBT Agreement and SPS Agreement. Similarity of texts between provisions of the TRIPS Agreement and other covered agreements has encouraged, and should encourage, dispute settlement organs to adopt interpretations already developed for some provisions in the covered agreements to interpret similarly-worded provisions of the TRIPS and other agreements.[138] In *US – Section 211 Appropriations Act* (*2002*), for example, the panel held that the interpretation of Article III:4 of the GATT 1994 may be useful in interpreting Article 3.1 of the TRIPS Agreement due to the similarity of their language.[139] In *EC – Trademarks and Geographical Indications* (*US*) (*2005*), the panel similarly stated that the interpretation developed foe the term 'no less favorable' in other covered agreements (like Article III:4 of the GATT 1994) may, *mutatis mutandis*, be "relevant in interpreting Article 3.1 of the TRIPS Agreement".[140] Similarly, the *Saudi Arabia – Measures Concerning IP Rights* (*2020*) panel decided that Article 73(b) of the TRIPS Agreement (Security Exceptions), which contains the concept of necessity, has to be interpreted along the same line as the interpretation developed by the *Russia – Traffic in Transit* (*2019*) for the similarly worded Article XXI(b) of the GATT 1994. Based on this trend of adopting, to the TRIPS Agreement, previous interpretations developed for similarly-worded provisions in other covered agreements, Rodrigues argues that since both the GATT 1994 and the TRIPS Agreement are integral parts of the WTO Agreement, the interpretation developed for the term 'necessary' in the GATT 1994 must be considered in the process of interpreting the term 'necessary' in Article 8.1 the TRIPS Agreement. He adds:

> In keeping with this understanding … *it may be argued that when the wording of a TRIPS provision is similar to the wording of a provision from*

138 Haugen argues "The WTO Agreement represents a 'single undertaking'. Therefore, all agreements that were annexed to the WTO Agreement must be understood in light of the other agreements" and refers to the GATT 1994 as an example: "GATT 1994 is particularly relevant as interpretative material which can be applied in order to interpret TRIPS provisions. First, GATT 1994 is based upon GATT 1947, which is the 'original' agreement. Second, GATT 1994 is the WTO agreement which has the most explicit provisions on exceptions, related to the taking of measures." Hans Morten Haugen, *The Right to Food and the TRIPS Agreement: With a Particular Emphasis on Developing Countries Measures for Food Production and Distribution* (Leiden and Boston: Martinus Nijhoff Publishers, 2007), p. 75 (and f.n. 108).

139 WTO Panel Report, *US – Section 211 Appropriations Act* (*2002*), para. 8.129; Appellate Body Report, *US – Section 211 Appropriations Act* (*2002*), para. 242.

140 *EC – Trademarks and Geographical Indications* (*US*) (*2005*), para. 7.135.

another WTO agreement, it is possible to resort to the case law regarding the latter to clarify the meaning of the former, provided the interpreter takes note of the relevant differences.

That said, to clarify the meaning of the necessity standard embedded in art. 8 of the TRIPS Agreement, it is useful to have recourse to the reports, adopted under the GATT and the WTO systems, dedicated to clarify its meaning in the context of art. XX of the GATT (1947 and 1994) (*emphasis added*).[141]

By focusing on the specific, 'public health' nature of the necessity element in Article 8.1 of the TRIPS Agreement, Slade cautions us, though, against 'directly transposing' the GATT 1994/GATS General Exceptions necessity interpretation to the necessity element in Article 8.1.[142] In her detailed analysis of the applicability of GATT 1994 jurisprudence to the interpretation of the TRIPS Agreement, Frankel points at the difference in flexibilities that exists (should exist) between the exceptions clauses of the TRIPS Agreement and the General Exceptions and suggests that the absence of a *chapeau* in the former should lead towards a *less strict interpretation* of the necessity exceptions in the TRIPS Agreement.[143]

The difference in the various recommendations above for adopting the General Exceptions interpretation of necessity to the necessity exceptions of TRIPS Agreement lies mainly on how strict the necessity element should be interpreted in the TRIPS Agreement. There is, however, no doubt among the commentators on the need to interpret the TRIPS Agreement necessity provisions – including the necessity element in the Security Exceptions in Article 73[144] – along the lines of the interpretation already developed (or to be developed) for necessity provisions in the GATT 1994/GATS, the TBT Agreement and the SPS Agreement.

---

141 Rodrigues, above note 132, pp. 46–47. Brand also recommends that in interpreting the 'necessity' requirement of Article 8.1 of the TRIPS Agreement "[o]f particular importance in this context are the reports of the WTO adjudicating bodies on [Article XX(b) and (d) of the] GATT 1994". Brand, above note 134, p. 197.

142 Slade, above note 133.

143 Susy Frankel, 'The Applicability of GATT Jurisprudence to the Interpretation of the TRIPS Agreement', in Carlos M. Correa (ed.), *Research Handbook on the Interpretation and Enforcement of Intellectual Property under WTO Rules: Intellectual Property in the WTO* (Vol. II) (Cheltenham: Edward Elgar, 2010), pp. 21–22.

144 This aligns with the suggestion made in Sub-section 8.3.4 to interpret the concept of necessity in Article 73 of the TRIPS Agreement along the line of the interpretation developed for the concept of necessity in the Security Exceptions of the GATT 1994/GATS.

What can, therefore, be concluded regarding the concept of necessity in the TRIPS Agreement? The necessity provisions in the General and Security Exceptions of the TRIPS Agreement are to some extent similar to the necessity requirement in the General Exceptions of the GATT 1994/GATS. These similarities may lend support for adopting the necessity interpretation developed (or to be developed) in the contexts of the GATT 1994/GATS, the TBT Agreement and the SPS Agreement to the corresponding provisions of the TRIPS Agreement. As discussed in Section 8.3 the *Saudi Arabia – Measures Concerning IP Rights (2020)* panel decided that Article 73(b) of the TRIPS Agreement (Security Exceptions), which contains the concept of necessity, has to adopt the interpretation used by the panel in *Russia – Traffic in Transit (2019)* for the similarly worded Article XXI(b) of the GATT 1994. This supports the argument that the concept of necessity in TRIPS Agreement provisions similar to those in the GATT 1994/GATS should be interpreted like the way the concept of necessity has been interpreted in the GATT 1994/GATS General Exceptions disputes.

9.6 Has a 'WTO Law Concept of Necessity' Emerged?

This chapter sought to inquire whether a 'concept of necessity in WTO law' molded by the most settled interpretation of necessity in WTO law – the interpretation of necessity in the General Exceptions of the GATT 1994/GATS – could be traced in the interpretations developed for the necessity provisions contained in the other WTO agreements. Although, at text level, the concept of necessity is scattered throughout the agreements other than the General Exceptions in the GATT 1994 and the GATS, it has been well interpreted only in two agreements, the TBT and SPS agreements. The way the concepts of necessity in the TBT and SPS agreements have been interpreted can give an indication of how the WTO dispute settlement organs will likely interpret the concept of necessity in other WTO agreements. Of the other WTO agreements, the TRIPS Agreement has been examined in this chapter because of the similarity, *mutatis mutandis*, of its necessity provisions with the necessity provisions in the General Exceptions of the GATT 1994/GATS, the TBT Agreement and the SPS Agreement. There are differences in the interpretations of necessity developed (or to be developed) for the GATT 1994, the GATS, the TBT Agreement, the SPS Agreement and the TRIPS Agreement. These differences include presentation of the plea of necessity as an affirmative defense or substantive obligation (affecting burden of proof), whether there are additional elements to be considered in establishing necessity and how strict the necessity of the disputed measures should be interpreted.

What has finally emerged as a trend in the various interpretations developed in more than 70 GATT/WTO disputes referred to in Chapters 8 and 9 for the necessity provisions in the various WTO agreements is that the 'weighing and balancing' test, initially developed for the necessity provision in the General Exceptions of the GATT 1994/GATS, serves (can serve) the objective of balancing treaty obligations with regulatory autonomy, an objective which is found not only in most of these agreements but also is a key objective of the WTO Agreement. Therefore, this test can be adopted to other WTO agreements which contain necessity provisions similar in text, context and/or purpose to the General Exceptions of the GATT 1994 and the GATS. The result of the inquiry in Chapters 8 and 9 is that there is evidence to claim that the 'weighing and balancing' test – with its minimally differing application in the different WTO agreements – may, *mutatis mutandis*, be identified as the 'concept of necessity in WTO law'.

Chapter 5 ended with the reminder that this book intends to interrelate the concept of necessity in other fields of international law (particularly the concept of necessity in customary international law as codified in Article 25 of the ARSIWA) with the concept of necessity in WTO law. Now that this chapter has given us an idea of what the concept of necessity in WTO law means, the next exercise will be to examine if the concepts of necessity in customary international law and WTO law can learn from (i.e., interact with) each other so we have a more coherent concept of necessity in international law. Part 4 dwells on this issue of interoperability.

PART 4

The Interaction between the Concepts of Necessity in Customary International Law and WTO Law

CHAPTER 10

The Interface between Customary International Law and WTO Law

10.1 Contextualizing the Relationship

Parts 2 and 3 navigated through the respective concepts of necessity as contained, interpreted and/or applied in different fields of international law and observed that the concepts of necessity in WTO law and in CIL (as codified in the ARSIWA) have come out as the two notable and refined concepts of necessity in international law. Parts 2 and 3 argued that these two concepts of necessity have also been 'competing' for influence in some fields of international law particularly IIL and IEnL. It remains to be seen whether the other fields of international law discussed in this book such as IHL, IHRL and ICL will develop their own versions of the concept of necessity or adopt the concepts under WTO law or CIL.

Two observations can be made from the discussions in Parts 2 and 3 by way preparing the ground for the analysis in Part 4. Firstly, in fields where there is a possibility for choosing between these two concepts (for example IEnL and IIL, as highlighted in Chapter 5), defenses made under either of the two concepts may lead to different, and even opposite, results for the defending state as observed in the Argentine financial crisis cases before ICSID tribunals and Annulment Committees. Secondly, in light of the need to address unnecessary fragmentation in international law – since WTO law is part of international law – it may be important to examine if, at best, coherence can be achieved between these two concepts or, at least, if the two concepts can influence each other. This second concern is addressed in Part 4. It will be discussed whether the interoperability exercise can lead to the conclusion that the GATT 1994 and, by extension, the WTO Agreement, as declared by the WTO's Appellate Body in *US – Gasoline* (*1996*), has not been read in clinical isolation from PIL.

Analyzing the potential for interoperability between the two well-developed and applied concepts of necessity in international law (i.e., the concepts of necessity in WTO law and CIL), after identifying the key similarities and differences between them, is the key exercise in this book. The exercise is timely especially if seen in light of the debates on the fragmentation of international law. Do the similarities between the two concepts of necessity warrant the conclusion that the concept of necessity has now been crystalized into

 | DOI:10.1163/9789004700000_012

one concept for purposes of international law (inclusive of PIL) and GIL?[1] Or do the differences warrant the conclusion that there is a 'conflict' in the concepts of necessity at the level international law? Can the differences be reconciled? Are the two fields of comparison where these two concepts of necessity operate (i.e., WTO law and the fields of PIL which have adopted the concept of necessity in WTO law on one hand, and the CIL and the fields of PIL which have adopted the concept of necessity in CIL on the other) 'closed' to any lessons that can be learned from each other? More specifically, is the WTO-regime a 'self-contained regime'? If one accepts that the two concepts of necessity can, or have to, continue to develop in their respective spheres of influence, is there room for interoperability between the two concepts, i.e., can the concept of necessity in WTO law benefit from some of the elements of the concept of necessity in CIL and *vice versa*? What are the grounds for such 'interoperability'?

It was observed at the introduction to the 41st volume of the *Netherlands Yearbook of International Law* (2010) which was published to analyze the doctrine and practices of necessity across international law that:

> Necessity is as a basic legal concept in all the covered areas – conflict and security law, humanitarian law, human rights law, economic law, investment law, environmental law, and European law. Its main function is that it regulates claims that a situation is beyond the boundaries of the normal operation of the legal regime concerned. In the areas of law of collective security and the law of armed conflict, this function is the

1 In Part 4, the terms 'other fields of international law', PIL, GIL and CIL are to be understood in accordance with the definition given to them in the 'key terminologies' section of the introduction to this book and the so. In Part 4, reference will be made to GIL because: (1) GIL includes CIL (a key subject of discussion in Part 4); (2) some general principles of law (which are part of GIL) such as good faith and avoidance of abuse have already been included in defining the elements of necessity in international law (for instance in interpreting necessity under the Security Exceptions in some WTO Agreements as discussed in Section 8.3); and (3) key publications on 'self-contained regimes' and the *lex specialis* rule which are discussed in relative detail in this chapter are mainly based on the relationship between the secondary rules of self-contained regimes and GIL. For the definition of PIL, see, Donald McRae, 'International Economic Law and Public International Law: The Past and the Future', *Journal of International Economic Law*, 17(3): 2014, pp. 627–638. For the definition of GIL, see, Joost Pauwelyn, 'The Role of Public International law in the WTO: How Far Can We Go?' *American Journal of International Law*, 95(3): 2001, p. 536. See also, Malcolm N. Shaw, *International Law* (8th ed.) (Cambridge: Cambridge University Press, 2017), pp. 1–2; Sir Robert Y. Jennings, 'International Law', in Rudolf Burnhardt (ed.), *Encyclopedia of Public International Law* (Vol. 7) (Amsterdam, New York and Oxford: Elsevier Science Publishers, 1984), pp. 278–297.

> rational – or at least one of the main sources – of the legal sub-regime as such. In other words, the regulation of the use of armed force, whether in the context of the *jus ad bellum* or the *jus in bello*, is fundamentally governed by the concept of (military) necessity and by that giving these regimes their very special character. In *all other areas* necessity only functions as a possible ground for the justification of measures that are normally unlawful within the legal sub-regime. The concept of necessity, furthermore, differs in those branches in some important respects. *Each sub-regime has evolved its own principles, norms and rules and developed its own management and enforcement mechanisms. The general picture is thus one of fragmentation in the sense of a varied set of legal regimes of necessity that are connected by the fact that they are all part of the international legal system but are different regarding their substantive and institutional content as well as their operation in practice.*
>
> However, it seems that in some instances judicial bodies are willing to mitigate these differences in that *they are broadening their interpretive guidelines by looking at the interpretation of the requirements of necessity given in the case law of other areas of international law* (*emphasis added*).[2]

This book aims to contribute to this process of looking for potential interface between different concepts of necessity in international law by focusing on the two notable concepts of necessity thus far refined (i.e., the concept of necessity in WTO law and the concept of necessity in CIL as codified in the ARSIWA). The analysis will begin in Chapter 10 by discussing the relationship between WTO law and international law in general. The rules and practices of interoperability between WTO law and international law will then be presented in Chapter 11 to lay a ground for the discussion on interoperability between the concepts of necessity in WTO law and CIL. The questions listed in the previous paragraph related to these 'two concepts'[3] of necessity will then be addressed in further detail in Chapter 12.

---

2 Tarcisio Gazzini, Wouter G. Werner and Ige F. Dekker, 'Necessity across International Law: An Introduction', in Ige F. Dekker and E. Hey (eds.), *Netherlands Yearbook of International Law: Necessity across International Law*, Vol. 41 (The Hague: T.M.C. Asser Press, 2010), pp. 8–9.

3 That there are at least these 'two concepts' of necessity was highlighted in the Argentine cases before the ICSID tribunals as shown in detail in Section 5.5. For example, Sacerdoti wrote an article where he reviewed "as to the defense of necessity ... the evolution of the case law concerning the Argentine Republic, especially as to necessity precluding wrongfulness under customary law, or rather as a balancing criterion of interpretation in light of the WTO law *concept* (*emphasis added*)". Giorgio Sacerdoti, 'BIT Protections and Economic

10.2 WTO Law in the Universe of International Law

10.2.1 *WTO Law as Integral Part of International Law*

In 1996, Professor Donald McRae was invited to lecture at The Hague Academy of International Law. In a contribution regarded as one of the best discussions on the relationship between IEL, ITL and international law,[4] McRae tried to convince his audience that ITL, long considered *not* part of international law, should, following the post-Cold War events related to globalization, be considered part and parcel of international law and have its contribution to international law acknowledged.[5] McRae[6] is not the only ITL scholar to grapple with, or question, the unenthusiastic acceptance into the universe of international law of the fields of IEL, especially ITL, by the academics and practitioners of international law. Professors John Jackson,[7] E. U. Petersmann[8] and Steve Charnovitz[9] submitted excellent contributions in defense of IEL/ITL's rightful place in the field of international law, regardless of ITL's status as a self-contained regime in many of its aspects. These scholars attributed the said reluctance of the academics and practitioners of international law to: (a) the traditional understanding of the nature of international law as being

Crises: Limits to Their Coverage, the Impact of Multilateral Financial Regulation and the Defense of Necessity', *ICSID Review – Foreign Investment Law Journal*, 28(2): 2013, p. 351.

4 On the relationship between IEL, ITL and international law, see, Steve Charnovitz, 'What is International Economic Law?', *Journal of International Economic Law*, 14(1): 2011, p. 20; Steve Charnovitz, 'The Field of International Economic Law', *Journal of International Economic Law*, 17(3): 2014, p. 624.

5 Donald M. McRae, 'The Contribution of International Trade Law to the Development of International Law', *Recueil des Cours*, 260(1): 1996, pp. 109–232.

6 He followed up on his Hague Academy contribution with another article. McRae, above note 1.

7 John H. Jackson, *Sovereignty, the WTO, and Changing Fundamentals of International Law* (Cambridge: Cambridge University Press, 2006), pp. 46–49, 164–168.

8 In 2002, Professor Petersmann was engaged in a 'celebrated exchange' with Professor Phillip Alston with the latter arguing that IEL does not have, unlike human rights law, the 'human dignity' foundation to be part of PIL. McRae, above note 1, p. 633. The exchange came in the form of three articles published in 2002: Ernst-Ulrich Petersmann, 'Time for a United Nations "Global Compact" for Integrating Human Rights into the Law of Worldwide Organizations: Lessons from European Integration', *European Journal of International Law*, 13(3): 2002, pp. 621–650; Phillip Alston, 'Resisting the Merger and Acquisition of Human Rights by Trade Law: A Reply to Petersmann', *European Journal of International Law*, 13(4): 2002, pp. 815–844; and Ernst-Ulrich Petersmann, 'Taking Human Dignity, Poverty and Empowerment of Individuals More Seriously, Rejoinder to Alston', *European Journal of International Law*, 13(4): 2002, pp. 845–851.

9 Charnovitz, above note 4 (2011), pp. 3–22; Charnovitz, above note 4 (2014), pp. 607–626.

essentially created to maintain peace, security and human dignity and not to regulate the international economy; and (b) to the 'misguided' understanding that IEL has a lot of 'private' – as opposed to 'public' – elements to govern.[10] McRae, for instance, voices his concern:

> At a certain level, the reaction of public international lawyers grows out of the narrow perception of public international law held by the fathers of the discipline, who saw international law in purely state-to-state terms focusing on sovereignty and peace and security. Such a model was inadequate when it came to dealing with the actions of private actors – from diplomatic protection to human rights – and this had important implications for trade, which was perceived as private and not as state behavior. It also reflects a preoccupation of international lawyers with customary international law as the starting point in any field of international law, an approach that marginalizes treaty-based regimes that are not grounded in a core of customary international law.[11]

It is now settled, however, that the reluctant acceptance remains mainly in the minds of few (mainly the less IEL/ITL-initiated) practitioners of other fields of international law and that IEL/ITL has rightfully earned its status,[12] albeit a *lex specialis* status in many aspects, in international law. Professor Jackson's verdict on the matter, through an argument relevant to the examination of interface between the concepts of necessity in WTO law and CIL conducted in this chapter, is that:

> [IEL] has now become a standard 'sub-subject' of international law, like many other subjects ...
>
> A very important question ... is whether [IEL], or particular parts of [IEL], *such as WTO law,* are part of international law generally, as opposed to being 'separate regimes' walled off from general [international law]. This author's view on this question strongly supports the position of [IEL] (and the WTO ...) as part of international law, *and thus general [international law] norms not expressly embraced in the IEL (or WTO) treaty structure can have an impact on the application of [IEL] norms. Of course ... there are serious and complicated issues about how great such an*

10 McRae, above note 5, pp. 111–119.

11 McRae, above note 1, p. 636.

12 Above note 1.

> *impact can appropriately be.* ***Reciprocally****, the practice of* [IEL] *activity can be highly relevant to general international law and its norm application.*
>
> The general relationship of [IEL] to [international law] arises in a variety of situations when it is argued that the [IEL] rule is interpreted in the light of the [international law] rule (e.g. a customary international law rule [of treaty interpretation] about 'estoppel', or 'fairness' or 'good faith'). Even more complex can be the hierarchy of norms when there appears to be a 'conflict' between a general [international law] norm and a particular (usually treaty-based) [IEL] norm. Absent an assertion of *jus cogens* for the international norm (an assertion that often is challenged by the party opposing the norm application), it could be the case that the IEL treaty norm is sufficiently detailed and specific to give rise to a claim of '*lex specialis derogat legi generali*', so that the [IEL] treaty norm will trump the general international law ... (*emphasis added*).[13]

Jackson's stand seems to emanate from the overwhelming presence that IEL (inclusive of WTO law), owing to the many sub-fields it embraces,[14] has in the sphere of international law and the concomitant interaction or interface between the two:

> Indeed, it is plausible to suggest that ninety percent of international law work is in reality [IEL] in some form or another ... [IEL] cannot be separated or compartmentalized from general or 'public' international law. The activities and cases relating to [IEL] contain much practice which is relevant to general principles of international law, especially concerning treaty law and practice.[15]

Trachtman also pointed at the interrelation that IEL has with PIL, private international law and international business law, and hailed the IEL 'revolution' that collapsed the distinctions between public and private international law and changed the underlying assumptions in international law regarding

---

13 Jackson, above note 7, pp. 46–49.

14 Charnovitz, for example, lists nearly 45 sub-fields of IEL to conclude that IEL is "[i]ndeed too broad" and that "the intersection of international + economic + law yields a very broad body of law." Charnovitz, above note 4 (2011), pp. 5–6. Similarly, Jackson stated that IEL has a 'very broad scope' in that it "covers virtually every economic activity which has a relationship that crosses national boundaries" and then lists around 15 fields of study that "it can easily embrace". Ibid, p. 46.

15 John H. Jackson, 'Reflections on International Economic Law', *University of Pennsylvania Journal of International Economic Law*, 17(1): 1996, p. 18.

the domain reserved to the state.[16] The analyses in Chapters 10–12 are, therefore, based on the idea above that WTO law is an integral part of international law and that there is a potential for interoperability between the two.

10.2.2 *WTO Law as a Special Regime in International Law*

The exercise of examining the possibility for interoperability between the concepts of necessity in WTO law and CIL should begin with a discussion of the concept of fragmentation of international law. The concept of fragmentation also includes the notion of 'self-contained' or special regimes within international law which are allowed to develop their own concepts at variance with principles in international law, i.e., the rules within these special regimes become *lex specialis*. This subsection addresses three points. First, it introduces the concept of fragmentation in international law in general. Next, the notion of SCR will be discussed. Finally, WTO law is examined within this context of fragmentation/SCR and the issue of whether WTO law is (could be) 'closed' to international law will be analyzed.

We begin with the introduction of the notion of fragmentation of international law.

In 1953, the international lawyer and later Director-General of the International Labour Organization, Clarence Wilfred Jenks, published an article, *The Conflict of Law-Making Treaties*, where he laid the foundation for an international debate on the subject of fragmentation of international law. He argued that in the absence of a world legislature with a general law-making mandate, treaties tend to develop in different ways and groupings that they "inevitably react upon each other and their co-existence accordingly gives rise to problems which can be conveniently described, on the analogy of the conflict of laws, as the conflict of law-making treaties".[17] Not only did Jenks perceive increasing conflict among the different fields of international law, but he also saw a potential conflict within each treaty as it gets modified or updated:

> One of the most serious sources of conflict between law-making treaties is the imperfect development of the law governing the revision of multipartite instruments and defining the legal effect of such revision. Whenever, for instance, a revised international instrument, certain of the provisions

---

16 Joel Trachtman, 'The International Economic Law Revolution', *University of Pennsylvania Journal of International Economic Law*, 17(1): 1996, pp. 33–34. See also, McRae, above note 1, p. 629; Charnovitz, above note 4 (2011), p. 19.

17 Clarence Wilfred Jenks, 'The Conflict of Law-Making Treaties', *British Yearbook of International Law*, 30: 1953, p. 403.

> of which are incompatible with those of the original instrument, comes into force for some but not all of the parties to the original instrument, and the original and revised instruments remain in force simultaneously for the parties to both of them in respect of their relations with different groups of co-contractants, a conflict arises.[18]

For Jenks, "[a] conflict in the strict sense of direct incompatibility arises only where a party to the two treaties cannot simultaneously comply with its obligations under both treaties."[19] Jenks, who admitted that such conflict and fragmentation "must be accepted as being in certain circumstances an inevitable incident of growth", advised that "it becomes an essential part of the duty of international lawyers, while encouraging the adoption of procedures which will minimize the occurrence of such conflict, also to formulate principles for resolving such conflict when it arises."[20]

71 years after Jenks' call (in 2024, that is), we find ourselves with thousands of treaties. Koskenniemi, for instance, stated that as at 2006 over 50,000 treaties were registered in the UN system and that in the 20th century about 6,000 multilateral treaties were concluded of which around 30 per cent were general treaties open for all states to participate in.[21] Jenks' wish was fulfilled when the ILC decided in 2000 to include the topic 'risks ensuing from the fragmentation of international law' into its long-term program of work. In 2003, the ILC appointed Professor Martti Koskenniemi as chairman of a group to study the subject and produce a report. In April 2006, Koskenniemi's group submitted a 256-page report entitled *Fragmentation of International Law: Difficulties arising From the Diversification and Expansion of International Law* where fragmentation of international law was discussed from many angles.

The report, after first outlining the nature and scope of fragmentation in PIL, identified four areas where fragmentation can occur: (a) conflicts between general law and special law as reflected in special provisions within or across treaties, self-contained regimes and/or regionalism; (b) conflicts between successive norms either as conflicts between earlier and latter treaties or *inter se* agreements with variations of party memberships; (c) hierarchy of norms such

18 Ibid.

19 Ibid, p. 426.

20 Ibid, p. 405.

21 Martti Koskenniemi, 'Fragmentation of International Law: Difficulties arising From the Diversification and Expansion of International Law', *Report of the Study Group of the International Law Commission* (2006), ILC, 58th sess., U.N. Doc. A/CN.4/L. 682, p. 10, f.n. 10.

as Article 103 of the UN Charter, *jus cogens* rules and obligations *erga omnes*; and (d) systemic integration through Article 31(3)(c) of the VCLT and the case law of many institutions such as the Iran-US Claims Tribunal, the European Court of Human Rights, the WTO and the ICJ.[22] The study did not intend to set up definite relationships of priority between the different rules or rule-systems of international law. Since it accepted fragmentation as a natural consequence of the complexity of the world we live in, the report did not address fragmentation as an ill to be cured for the end of coherence; it softly suggested techniques or considerations that may be employed to solve 'real' conflicts within the different fields of international law.[23]

We next discuss the universe of SCR. The narration of the development of the notion of SCR shows that the term was first coined by international courts and later on explained further by scholars and the ILC.

The PCIJ coined the term 'self-contained' in 1923 in the *SS Wimbledon* dispute, discussed in Sub-section 6.3.1. One of the issues the PCIJ addressed was the status of the legal regime applicable to the Kiel Canal – which, under the Treaty of Versailles, had to be left free and open to the vessels of commerce and of war of all nations at peace with Germany – compared to the legal regime applicable to German waters, including internal waters. The PCIJ noted that dedication of a separate article in the Treaty of Versailles made the Kiel Canal a special waterway and thus the legal regime applicable to the Canal was *special* in contrast to the general law applicable to all German waters:

> The provisions relating to the Kiel Canal in the Treaty of Versailles are therefore *self-contained*; if they had to be supplemented and interpreted by the aid of those referring to the inland navigable waterways of Germany in the previous Sections of Part XII, they would lose their 'raison d'être' ... The idea which underlies Article 380 and the following articles of the Treaty is not to be sought by drawing an analogy from these provisions but rather by arguing *a contrario*, a method of argument which excludes them (*emphasis added*).[24]

46 years after the *SS Wimbledon* decision, in 1979, the US government brought Iran before the ICJ in respect of the seizure and holding as hostages of members

22 Ibid, pp. 30–243.

23 Ibid, pp. 245–254.

24 PCIJ, *Case of the S.S. 'Wimbledon' (United Kingdom, France, Italy & Japan v. Germany)*, Judgment, 17 August 1923, available at, http://www.worldcourts.com/pcij/eng/decisions/1923.08.17_wimbledon.htm, paras. 32–33.

of the US diplomatic and consular staff and certain other US nationals. Iran requested the Court to look at the broader context in which the dispute arose and therefore reject the claim of the US. In particular, Iran pointed at "more than 25 years of continual interference by the US in the internal affairs of Iran, the shameless exploitation of our country, and numerous crimes perpetrated against the Iranian people, contrary to and in conflict with all international and humanitarian norms" as well as the Central Intelligence Agency's role in the 1953 *coup d'état* and restoration of the Shah.[25] In its memorial, the US responded that even if these facts occurred, Iran could not resort to the measures it took and that as a matter of CIL, as reflected in Article 9 of the VCDR, the sole remedy available to Iran was to declare the US diplomatic and consular *persona no grata* and require their recall to the US.[26] The ICJ agreed with the US' view and held that conduct of the US personnel did not warrant, under the VCDR, the actions taken by Iran:[27]

> In any case, even if the alleged criminal activities of the United States in Iran could be considered as having been established, the question would remain *whether they could be regarded by the Court as constituting a justification of Iran's conduct and thus a defense to the United States' claims in the present case*. The Court, however, is unable to accept that they can be so regarded. This is because *diplomatic law itself provides the necessary means of defense against, and sanction for, illicit activities by members of diplomatic or consular missions* (*emphasis added*).[28]

The essence of the Court's judgment was that the VCDR is complete enough to govern, on primary rule basis, diplomatic relations between countries and that in instances of violations of the primary rules of the Convention, no reference need, or must, be made to a rule of international law other than to the secondary rules for remedy provided for in the Convention. In short, the VCDR is a SCR:

25 *Case Concerning United States Diplomatic and Consular Staff in Tehran* (*United States of America v. Iran*), Judgment, 24 May 1980, ICJ Rep. 1980, p. 5, para. 1; p. 8, para. 10; p. 19, para. 35.

26 ICJ Pleadings, *Case Concerning United States Diplomatic and Consular Staff in Tehran*, Memorial of the United States of America, pp. 184–185.

27 *Case Concerning United States Diplomatic and Consular Staff in Tehran*, above note 25, pp. 38–41, paras. 80–88.

28 Ibid, p. 39, para. 83.

> *The rules of diplomatic law, in short, constitute a self-contained régime* which, on the one hand, lays down the receiving State's obligations regarding the facilities, privileges and immunities to be accorded to diplomatic missions and, on the other, foresees their possible abuse by members of the mission and specifies the means at the disposal of the receiving State to counter any such abuse [secondary norms]. These means are, by their nature, entirely efficacious (*emphasis added*).[29]

Since the *Tehran Hostages* dispute, scholarly attention has been drawn to elaborating the concept of SCR in international law, especially as the concept is related to the notion of fragmentation of international law. One of the earliest contributions in this regard is Judge Bruno Simma's 1985 Article, *Self-Contained Regimes* with the *Netherlands Yearbook of International Law*.[30] Simma begins his analysis with a summary of the *Tehran Hostages* dispute and comments on the ideas that ILC special rapporteur on state responsibility, Willem Riphagen (1980–1986) had developed for SCR or 'sub-systems of international law', as Riphagen called them. Riphagen stated that international law is composed of interrelated, yet a variety of, 'sub-systems' which have their own primary and secondary rules that are intertwined and inseparable.[31] Simma, however, argued that the notion of SCR should be linked to how exclusive, full and definite the secondary rules of the treaty-based regimes are. In other words, a SCR is one "which is intended to exclude more or less totally the application of the general consequences of wrongful acts, in particular the application of the countermeasures normally at the disposal of an injured party".[32] Simma then applies his definition of SCR to examine whether diplomatic immunities law, the European Community Treaty and human rights treaties can be identified

29 Ibid, p. 40, para. 86.

30 Bruno Simma, 'Self-contained regimes', *Netherlands Yearbook of International Law*, 16: 1985, pp. 111–136. See also, Davorin Lapaš, 'Some Remarks on Fragmentation of International Law: Disintegration or Transformation?', *Comparative and International Law Journal of Southern Africa*, 40(1): 2007, pp. 1–29; Math Noortmann, *Enforcing International Law: From Self-help to Self-contained Regimes* (London and New York: Routledge, 2016); Anja Lindroos and Michael Mehling, 'Dispelling the Chimera of 'Self-Contained Regimes': International Law and the WTO', *European Journal of International Law*, 16(5): 2005, pp. 857–877; Liana Andreea Ioniță, 'Is European Union Law a Fully Self-Contained Regime? A Theoretical Inquiry of the Functional Legal Regimes in the Context of Fragmentation of International Law', *Studia Politica: Romanian Political Science Review*, 15(1): 2015, pp. 39–59.

31 Willem Riphagen, 'Third Report on the Content, Forms and Degrees of International Responsibility' (1982), U.N. Doc. A/CN.4/354 and Corr.1 and Add.1 & 2 (United Nations: 1982), p. 28, para. 35.

32 Simma, above note 30, p. 117.

as SCR. His conclusions, on top of the limitations he identifies for each of the three SCRs,[33] are that: (a) there is no such scenario as a completely closed SCR; (b) a state which claims that the secondary rules in a treaty are self-contained (i.e., not allowing the application of the 'normal' or 'general' secondary rules) bears the burden of proof of showing so; (c) exclusion of the normal or general secondary rules must not be presumed; (d) a SCR must serve to ensure effectiveness of the primary rules; and (e) if the SCR, by which states contract out of the general rules of consequences of treaty violations, do not work for mutual benefit, the principles of *inadimplenti non est adimplendum* (one side of a contract does not have to be complied with if the other side has not been complied with) and *clausula rebus sic stantibus* (a party to a treaty may invoke fundamental change of circumstances from those which existed at the time of the conclusion of a treaty as a ground for terminating or suspending the operation of the treaty) allow states to 'fall-back' to the general regime.[34]

The two cluster reports of the ILC – on state responsibility and on fragmentation – also extensively dwelt on the subject of SCR.

A summary of the works of the successive rapporteurs on state responsibility shows that the rapporteurs chose to discuss SCR in light of the possibility of the limitation, through treaties, of the consequences of treaty violations.[35] Ago, for instance, believed that a single, generally applicable set of rules about wrongfulness that could cover the breach of any primary rules could be set up, hence avoiding the recognition of SCR containing secondary rules.[36] Riphagen was open to the idea of special treaties (subsystems) providing for an exclusive list of secondary rules applicable for violations of the primary rules within treaties[37] and tried to classify the consequences of treaty violations by the

33 For example, he states that the secondary rules of diplomatic law must be limited by proportionality, *jus cogens* and UN Charter and even accepts the temporary detention of a diplomat in case of a *flagrate delicto* as well as taking countermeasures (including self-defense) in case of very serious offenses (such as terrorism) by the diplomatic personnel. Ibid, pp. 120–122. In case of the EEC Treaty, he is of the opinion that the Treaty does have a room for a residual application of GIL-based secondary measures. For instance, he argues, the Treaty allows the taking of countermeasures against persistent violation of EEC law. Ibid, p. 127.

34 Ibid, pp. 135–136.

35 The summary is partly taken from that which Koskenniemi provided for the ILC's fragmentation report. Koskenniemi, above note 21, pp. 74–81.

36 Roberto Ago, 'Fifth Report on State Responsibility', U.N. Doc. A/CN.4/291 and Add.1 and 2, p. 6, paras. 12–15, in *Yearbook of the International Law Commission* (Vol. II, part I) (United Nations: 1976).

37 Willem Riphagen, 'Fourth Report on State Responsibility', U.N. Doc. A/CN.4/366 and Add.1, pp. 8–24, paras. 31–130, in *Yearbook of the International Law Commission* (Vol. II, part I) (United Nations: 1983).

sources or contents of those obligations.[38] Riphagen's successor Arangio-Ruiz accepted his predecessor's argument that it is possible to have treaty-based subsystems within international law which considerably govern the relationships among the state parties (i.e., through primary rules) and particular rules equally governing the consequences of any breaches of the obligations of the state parties under the system (i.e., secondary rules).[39] He responded with an emphatic 'no' to the question of whether the remedial measures in the SCR bar the possibility of resort (i.e., 'fall-back') to remedies included in GIL.[40] He concluded that fall-back to GIL should be allowed in extreme cases, such as when the injured state does not receive effective reparation or where the unlawful act persisted while the procedures in the special regime are in progress.[41] Crawford's opinion on SCR was included in his comments on Article 55 of the ARSIWA (*lex specialis*) which allows treaty-based deviations from the state responsibility rules of the ARSIWA. Crawford's response to the question whether these treaty deviations are exclusive (i.e., whether they allow a fall-back to ARSIWA) was that this was a question of interpretation in each case.[42] Crawford indicated that not all Article 55 deviations are SCR and distinguished between 'normatively strong' and 'normatively weak' forms of *lex specialis* depending on whether the deviation is limited only to secondary rules (weak) or contains primary and secondary rules (strong).[43]

Working on fragmentation, Koskenniemi targeted SCR as one sources of fragmentation of international law. He identified three forms of SCR based on the breadth of their scope, although the three are interrelated:

1. The first, narrowest category refers to a special system of secondary rules – envisaged by Article 55 of the ARSIWA, *lex specialis* – usually created by a single treaty or very closely related set of treaties. These are special sets of secondary rules which, under the law of state responsibility, claim primacy over the general rules concerning consequences of a violation. One example is the 'non-compliance system' under the 1985 Vienna Convention on the Protection of the

38 Riphagen, above note 31, pp. 40–44, paras. 106–128.

39 Gaetano Arangio-Ruiz, 'Third Report on State Responsibility', U.N. Doc. A/CN.4/440 and Add.1, p. 25, para. 84, in *Yearbook of the International Law Commission* (Vol. II, part I) (United Nations: 1991).

40 Ibid, p. 26, paras. 85–86; p. 40, para. 112.

41 Ibid, p. 40, paras. 112 and 114; pp. 40–41, para. 115.

42 James Crawford, 'Third Report on State Responsibility', UN document A/CN.4/507/Add.4 (2001), p. 27, para. 420.

43 *Yearbook of the International Law Commission* (Vol. II, part II) (United Nations: 2001), pp. 140–141, para. 5.

Ozone Layer and related 1987 Montreal Protocol that has priority over the standard dispute settlement clause in the Vienna Convention.

2. The second, broader category refers to SCR as interrelated wholes of primary and secondary rules, also referred to as 'systems' or 'subsystems' of rules, which cover some particular problem differently from the way general law covers it. Here the reference is to a special regime on some problem area which may cover several instruments and practices united by their orientation towards a single problem. The establishment of a free trade area or a universal trade regime such as the one administered under the WTO [which may, for other reasons, also be included in the third category] is a good example. A treaty-regime may be both special in the first and the second categories, that is as a SCR of remedies (state responsibility) and a set of special rules on adoption, modification, administration or termination of the relevant obligations.
3. The third, widest category refers to a whole area of functional specialization or teleological orientation at a universal scale. Examples include the laws of armed conflict which have been identified as *leges speciales* by the ICJ in the *Legality of the Threat or Use of Nuclear Weapons* dispute or environmental law, often thought to be accompanied with special principles (such as the principles of precaution, 'polluter pays' and 'sustainable development') that administer environmental matters. Under this category, fields such as 'human rights law', 'WTO law', 'European law/EU law', 'humanitarian law', 'space law', among others, are often identified as 'special' in the sense that rules of GIL are assumed to be modified or even excluded in their administration.[44]

After an extensive study of the relationship between SCRs and GIL and examining SCRs such as human rights treaties and the WTO, Koskenniemi concluded:

> [GIL continues to apply as long as it has not been specifically excluded by a treaty] Where the application of the general law concerning reactions to breaches (especially countermeasures) might be inappropriate or counterproductive, a [SCR] such as, for instance, the system of *persona non grata* under diplomatic law, may be better suited to deal with such breaches. However, … it is equally clear that if the general law has

44 Koskenniemi, above note 21, p. 68, paras. 128–129; pp. 72–73, paras. 135–136.

> the character of *jus cogens*, then no derogation is permitted. In fact, the assumption seems to be that in order to justify derogation, the special rules [must] 'have at least the same legal status as those expressed in this article [i.e., Article 55 of the ARSIWA]'.
>
> But no regime is self-contained. Even in the case of well-developed regimes, general law has at least two types of function. *First, it provides the normative background that comes in to fulfil aspects of its operation not specifically provided by it ... Second, the rules of general law also come to operate if the special regime fails to function properly ...*
>
> Third, the term 'self-contained regime' is a misnomer. No legal regime is isolated from [GIL]. It is doubtful whether such isolation is even possible: a regime can receive (or fail to receive) legally binding force ('validity') only by reference to (valid and binding) rules or principles *outside* it. In previous debates within the Commission over [SCR], 'regimes' and 'subsystems, there never was any assumption that they would be hermetically isolated from [GIL] (*emphasis added*).[45]

More from the academia, one of the best and frequently cited contributions to the concept and practice of SCRs as *lex specialis* to GIL is Judge Bruno Simma's and Prof. Dirk Pulkowski's 2006 article[46] which also occurred as a book chapter with a small variation.[47] They begin their discussion with the note that the principle of *lex specialis derogat legi generali*, well-recognized in PIL,[48] best

45 Ibid, pp. 99–100, paras. 191–193.

46 Bruno Simma and Dirk Pulkowski, 'Of Planets and the Universe: Self-contained Regimes in International Law', *European Journal of International Law*, 17(3): 2006, pp. 483–529.

47 Bruno Simma and Dirk Pulkowski, '*Leges Speciales* and Self-Contained Regimes', in James Crawford, Alain Pellet and Simon Olleson (eds.), *The Law of International Responsibility* (Oxford: Oxford University Press, 2010), pp. 139–163.

48 Joost Pauwelyn, *Conflict of Norms in Public International Law: How WTO Law Relates to Other Rules of International Law* (Cambridge: Cambridge University Press, 2003), pp. 387–388. Judge Hsu Mo, in his dissenting opinion in *Ambatielos Case* (*Greece v. United Kingdom*), Preliminary Objection, Judgment (1 July 1952), p. 88 stated that "[i]t is a well-recognized principle of interpretation that a specific provision prevails over a general provision." In the *Nicaragua Paramilitary Activities* case, the ICJ also stated that "[i]n general, treaty rules being *lex specialis,* it would not be appropriate that a State should bring a claim based on a customary-law rule if it has by treaty already provided means for settlement of such a claim." *Case Concerning Military and Paramilitary Activities in and against Nicaragua* (*Nicaragua v. United States of America*), Judgment, 27 June 1986, ICJ Rep. 1986, p. 137, para. 274. See also, *Case Concerning the Gabčíkovo-Nagymaros Project* (*Hungary v. Slovakia*), Judgment, 25 September 1997, ICJ Rep. 1997, p. 76, para. 132; *INA Corporation v. Iran*, Iran-US Claims Tribunal, Award No. 184-161-1, 12 August 1985, para.

fits in harmonizing the relationship between GIL and the increasingly specializing fields of PIL and the relationships among these fields of PIL, especially regarding the secondary rules governing consequences of treaty violations. The embodiment of *lex specialis* regime in secondary rules of PIL is Article 55 of the ARSIWA which reads:

> These articles do not apply where and to the extent that the conditions for the existence of an internationally wrongful act or the content or implementation of the international responsibility of a state are governed by special rules of international law.

Simma and Pulkowski argue that owing to the seriousness that states assuredly maintain as they engage in the process of designing treaties, secondary rules selectively kept in treaties indicate strong commitment by the state parties to enforce the primary rules through the secondary rules.[49] As to practice of applying secondary rules in treaties, the authors point at an important variation. One group of tribunals, such as the ICJ (in *Gabčíkovo-Nagymaros Project* and *Nicaragua*) and the Iran-US Claims tribunal (in *INA Corporation*) "in a first step, [examine] the content of the rule of general international law and [then consider], in a second step, whether states in the particular case had derogated from this standard by creating a more special set of rules". Another group of tribunals "established under a special legal subsystem – such as WTO panels or the ECJ – generally follow the reverse order of examination. They are primarily concerned with the content of 'their' special law. Only in a second step, if this special regime proves insufficient to resolve a case, is resort had to general international rules." In short, "[w]hile tribunals working on the basis of general international law [the first group] resort to the *lex specialis* principle to justify the non-application of general international law, special tribunals [the second group] are not required to provide a comparable justification for applying the special rules under which they were created."[50]

The authors' subsequent discussion is focused on the second group of tribunals mentioned in the previous paragraph and they begin their discussion thereon by identifying three problems[51] with *lex specialis*. The first problem is related to the process of identification of 'specialness' of a given rule. How

[24], available at, https://jusmundi.com/en/document/decision/en-ina-corporation-v-the-government-of-the-islamic-republic-of-iran-award-award-no-184-161-1-tuesday-13th-august-1985#decision_4872.

49 Simma and Pulkowski, above note 46, pp. 485, 487.

50 Ibid, p. 488.

51 Ibid, pp. 488–490.

can we determine that the two sets of laws cover the same subject matter at the beginning? When can it be exactly said that one rule is more special than another? How do we determine the extent of the 'specialness' of the specific rule?[52] The second problem is determining exactly that the makers of the treaty wanted the rule to be special in comparison to a general rule. The third problem is how and when to apply the special rule.

Simma and Pulkowski, who focus their article on secondary rule *lex specialis*,[53] observe that the scale of 'specialness' in Article 55 of the ARSIWA vacillates between two extremes, i.e., between 'weak' and 'strong' forms of secondary rule *lex specialis*. On one side are special rules that are only designed to replace a single or a few provisions of the rules on state responsibility, while leaving the other rules of state responsibility untouched. Thus, a given treaty may explicitly provide for a variation, modification or non-application, of one or more of the remedies to the violation of the primary rules of the treaty. On the other side are 'strong' forms of *lex specialis* which explicitly or implicitly exclude the application of the general regime of state responsibility altogether by establishing a treaty regime's particular structure, its object and/or purpose. SCRs belong to this 'strong' form of *lex specialis*.[54]

The authors then discuss the two dominant views on the relationship between SCRs and GIL. The view of the 'universalists' group, which accepts a 'system-oriented model', begins the approach at the level of GIL and the applicability of GIL rules to any treaty regime. Believing in the 'unity' of GIL, this view puts the burden on states to show that their 'special' treaties have contracted out of GIL. The view of the 'particularists' group tries to avoid an inaccurate homogenization that may flow from the focus on GIL and accepts a 'regime-oriented model'. This group begins the approach at the level of special

52 The authors later on provide answers to these questions in 'two simple steps': "First, the rules of the special regime, ordinarily codified in a treaty instrument, must be interpreted according to Article 31 of the Vienna Convention on the Law of Treaties in order to establish whether the states parties intended the regime's secondary rules to be exhaustive and complete. Second, resort must be had to general international law to verify whether the latter permits such derogation." Ibid, pp. 500–501.

53 It must be noted, however, that the notion of *lex specialis* or a SCR is not, in practice, limited to secondary rules only. For instance, the PCIJ's declaration of Article 380 of the Treaty of Versailles in the *S.S. Wimbledon* case as a self-contained rule was related to the relationship between two sets of primary international obligations (Article 380 *vis-à-vis* the law generally applicable to German waters). On the contrary, the ICJ's declaration of the VCDR as a SCR in the *Tehran Hostages* case was related to the relationship between two sets of secondary obligations (the *persona non grata* rule *vis-à-vis* the remedies under the law of State responsibility). Ibid, p. 491.

54 Ibid, pp. 490–491.

regimes and then moves to the concomitant exclusion of the rules of GIL. This view, which presumes completeness of the special regimes, holds that the special regimes evolve into auto-constitutionality and remain, in principle, autonomous. This view is sceptical towards the 'smuggling' of alien elements into a special regime because of its near-acceptance of the *expressio unius est exclusio alterius* rule. Making use of norms outside the regime is "more of an 'emergency operation' than a desirable practice" and any resort to state responsibility rules, which are considered not generally a fall-back field to fill gaps, requires a special justification.[55]

According to Summa and Pulkowski, the two views suffer defects because of the level of analysis they have chosen. The universalist view, which beings its analysis at the level of GIL, tends to lead the observer into a position that exaggerates the impact of the GIL upon the particular regimes and accordingly discounts the impact of the latter on the former. The particularist view, which begins analysis at the special regimes, can similarly lead into a distortion opposite to that of the universalists, i.e., towards a marked exaggeration of the differences among sub-systems and a certain blindness to their common systemic construction.[56] For solution, the authors recommend the operationalization of the principle of effectiveness in the SCR-GIL relationship.[57] The way effectiveness can operate in the SCR-GIL relationship is to first give deference to the rules of the special regime and apply GIL should the need arise to enhance the effectiveness, the *effet utile* of the rules of the obligations contained in the SCR.[58] The authors then list three scenarios for a 'fall-back' to the application of GIL over a SCR: (a) in the case of continuous violation of an obligation under a special system, despite a decision to the contrary by the system's competent dispute settlement body; (b) in the case of an injured state's failure to obtain reparation, despite a respective decision by the system's competent dispute settlement body; and (c) if unilateral action is necessary as a defensive measure.[59]

Next, they test their proposals in the secondary rules regimes in diplomatic law, WTO law, the European Communities legal system and human rights protection treaties. Regarding WTO law, they first observe that the WTO Agreement

---

55 Ibid, pp. 493–494. See also, Georges Abi-Saab, 'Fragmentation or Unification: Some Concluding Remarks', *New York University Journal of International Law and Politics*, 31(4): 1999, p. 926.

56 Simma and Pulkowski, ibid, pp. 495–506.

57 Ibid, pp. 508–509.

58 Ibid, p. 510.

59 Ibid, p. 509.

appears to be more independent and 'closed' towards GIL than the GATT 1947, but that simultaneously the WTO Agreement has increasingly 'opened' to a common culture of international lawyers.[60] Since their focus is on examining the 'specialty' or 'closedness' of secondary rules in SCR, they focus on Article 23 of Annex 2 of the WTO Agreement, the DSU, which reads, "When Members seek the redress of a violation ... they shall have recourse to, and abide by, the rules and procedures of this Understanding." Two contrary views have been made on the 'openness' of Article 23 to other enforcement rules available under GIL (i.e., on whether Article 23 is an express derogation from the rules of state responsibility). The ILC states that it is an express derogation, but other authors [the Simma and Pulkowski refer here to Mariano Garcia-Rubio[61]] argue that it is not or at least that its wording "neither specifically permits nor prohibits recourse to additional remedies under general international law beyond those provided by WTO law".[62] The question, therefore, remains if there are remedies under the law of state responsibility that WTO law does not contain and hence the possibility for WTO law (DSU) to refer to, or make use of, the remedies under the law of state responsibility. Simma and Pulkowski readily admit that the DSU contains *lex specialis* rules (Article 19) on the remedies of cessation of the breach and continued performance of the obligation. They then examine if, and find in the affirmative that, the DSU (Article 22) mechanisms of 'compensation' and 'suspension of concessions' respectively echo the GIL remedies of reparation and countermeasures.[63] Their conclusion on the question is that "[c]onsequently, strong grounds exist for regarding the WTO rules on retaliation as *leges speciales vis-à-vis* countermeasures under general international law. Recourse to reprisals parallel to or in lieu of WTO-authorized sanctions is thus precluded (*emphasis added*)."[64]

The authors then pose one crucial question regarding the nature of the DSU as secondary rule SCR: can WTO Members resort to state responsibility rules of reprisal if the suspension of concessions under the DSU proves ineffective? The

60 Ibid, p. 519.

61 Mariano Garcia-Rubio, *Unilateral Measures as a Means of Enforcement of WTO Recommendations and Decisions* (The Hague: Academy of International Law, 2001) and Petros Mavroidis, 'Remedies in the WTO Legal System: Between a Rock and a Hard Place', *European Journal of International Law*, 11(4): 2000, pp. 763–813.

62 Simma and Pulkowski, above note 46, p. 520. See also, Sahib Singh, 'Non-proliferation law and countermeasures', in Marco Roscini and Daniel Joyner (eds.), *Non-Proliferation Law as a Special Regime: A Contribution to Fragmentation Theory in International Law* (Cambridge: Cambridge University Press, 2012), p. 232.

63 Simma and Pulkowski, ibid, pp. 520–521.

64 Ibid, pp. 521.

authors read the DSU and the relevant ILC commentary on the DSU's enforcement mechanism to allow a room for an affirmative reply.[65] After arguing that there is no fall-back for a retrospective monetary compensation from the DSU system, the authors conclude, regarding the fall-back relationship between the DSU and GIL, that whereas generally the WTO system, being a SCR, does not allow a Member to have recourse to a parallel recourse for compensation under the rules of state responsibility, in cases of continuous non-compliance, however, countermeasures outside the WTO system remain an option. Thus, "arguably, not even the WTO is completely decoupled from the secondary rules governing the consequences of breaches under general international law."[66]

What is the takeaway from the reflections of the ILC and scholars on the SCR nature of the WTO Agreement *vis-à-vis* international law? The writings do not hesitate to consider the WTO Agreement a well-developed regime containing primary rules enforced by secondary rules some of which derogate from (are exclusive of) the secondary rules in GIL: the WTO system is a SCR. However, the authors have found some grounds for the possibility, at the least, of reference to, or, at best, fall-back to GIL from the secondary rules of WTO law mostly contained in the DSU. The concept of necessity in the WTO Agreement, when raised as a defense, is a secondary rule contained in the WTO Agreement. It is also a well-recognized secondary rule contained in other fields of international law. There is, therefore, a possibility not only for interoperability between these two concepts of necessity (that in WTO law and those in other fields of international law) within the broader context of avoiding unnecessary fragmentation of international law in the area of necessity defense.

The third point in this sub-section is to examine the relationship between WTO law, as a SCR, and other fields of international law by asking whether WTO Agreement is 'closed' to other fields of international law and, if so, at which level it is closed. The responses to the questions will lay the ground for the analyses in Chapters 11 and 12 which examine the interoperability between the concepts of necessity in WTO law and CIL.

In an article he wrote in 1994,[67] Prof. Pieter Jan Kuijper, asked: 'Is the GATT a self-contained system?' After approaching the question from many angles of the GATT practice and the possibility for a Contracting Party which won a dispute to seek retaliation outside the GATT system (i.e., in case of inability

65 Ibid, p. 522.

66 Ibid, p. 523.

67 Pieter. J. Kuyper, 'The Law of GATT as a Special Field of International Law: Ignorance, Further Refinement or Self-Contained System of International Law', *Netherlands Yearbook of International Law*, 25: 1994, pp. 227–257.

to obtain compliance by the losing Party), he concluded, despite an opposite stance by other scholars,[68] that:

> [t]he final question whether GATT is or is about to become a self-contained system of international law, *cannot yet be answered affirmatively. Certainly in the recent past it has not functioned as such,* mainly because of US insistence that in certain situations of blockage of the dispute settlement system the normal remedy of unilateral reprisal could be applied ... *The intention to move further towards a self-contained system certainly underlies the WTO Agreement and its Dispute Settlement Understanding, but it remains to be seen how the WTO Members will make it function* (*emphasis added*).[69]

Simma and Pulkowski picked up from this point to clear Kuijper's uncertainties about the WTO, an uncertainty made obvious by his writing the article during the launch of the WTO, and stated:

> In an article for the *Netherlands Yearbook of International Law,* Pieter Kuyper contrasted the GATT, 'which was a self-contained regime of international law only in aspiration but not in reality', with the (then) newly created WTO, which 'has moved decisively in the direction of such a self-contained regime'. From a legal point of view, the WTO appears to be more independent of and 'closed' towards general international law than the GATT. At the same time, however, the WTO has increasingly 'opened' to a common culture of international lawyers.[70]

But, as a recognized SCR, how 'closed' is WTO law to other fields of international law? Or at which level is WTO law closed to other fields of international law? According to Simma and Pulkowski, the 'specialty' or 'closedness' of a special regime can be 'weak' or 'strong'; i.e., the treaty may either replace a single or a few of the rules of state responsibility (weak) or may explicitly or implicitly exclude the application of the general regime of state responsibility altogether (strong).[71] Sir Robert Jennings and Sir Arthur Watts had also indicated that the

---

68 He referred to a conclusion by Prof. Laurence Boisson de Chazournes who characterized the GATT as a self-contained system purely on the basis of its legal provisions. Ibid, p. 252, f.n. 76.

69 Ibid, p. 257.

70 Simma and Pulkowski, above note 46, p. 519.

71 Ibid, pp. 490–491.

specialis-generali comparison is not limited to the relationship between treaties but that the principle of *lex specialis* (connected to SCR) "has sometimes been applied to resolve apparent conflicts between two differing and potentially applicable rules [within treaties, or between the rules of a treaty and other fields of international law]".[72] Thus, the 'closedness' of a treaty to other fields of international law can be at the level of the treaty itself or at the level of some of the provisions or rules of the treaty. We can accordingly compare the *specialis-generali* or related relationship between the concepts of necessity in WTO law and other fields of international law in general or between the concepts of necessity in WTO law and CIL (as codified in the ARSIWA) in particular. One can envisage at least three levels in the structure of the WTO Agreement where it can be viewed as 'closed' to other fields of international law: at the gate (i.e., the entire WTO Agreement); at the level of the legal texts; or within and across WTO legal texts.

The view that the WTO Agreement is closed at the gate means that the WTO Agreement, the principles contained in it and the administrative works and practices emanating out of the WTO Agreement (the works of the Councils, Committees etc.) are totally 'closed' to other fields of international law. On the contrary, if the WTO Agreement is totally open to other fields of international law, it would mean that the WTO Agreement is allows all-out interoperability of interpretations and applications from the other fields of international law. In the words of Koskenniemi, it is difficult to envisage a system of international law that is totally closed to other fields of international law.[73] On a relevant note, Palmeter's and Mavroidis' concluded:

> The WTO is the product of an international agreement, and that agreement and the agreements annexed to it constitute the basic source of WTO law. The reports of panels and the Appellate Body, however, add a growingly important gloss to those texts. Most WTO disputes will be resolved primarily, if not solely, with reference to the texts and to prior reports, and in this sense the WTO legal system may be thought of as largely self-contained.
>
> But if the WTO legal system is largely self-contained, it is *not entirely* self-contained. To the contrary, it is an important part of the larger system of public international law, as reflected not only by the interpretive principles that are brought to bear on its texts, which are explicitly those

72 Sir Robert Jennings and Sir Arthur Watts (eds.), *Oppenheim's International Law* (9th ed.) Vol. 1 (London: Longman, 1992), pp. 1270–1280.

73 Koskenniemi, above note 21, p. 91, para. 172; p. 92, para. 174.

> of public international law, but also by its increasing recourse to the other traditional sources of public international law: custom, the teachings of publicists, general principles of law, and other international instruments, particularly those incorporated by reference into the WTO and its agreements (*emphasis added*).[74]

Thus, since the WTO Agreement is not totally closed to other fields of international law, the rules and principles of other fields of international law can be used in the interpretation or practice of the WTO Agreement and *vice versa*. Specifically, Article 3.2 of the DSU states that the dispute settlement system of the WTO serves to "to clarify the existing provisions of those agreements in accordance with customary rules of interpretation of public international law". Article 17.6(ii) of the Anti-Dumping Agreement also requires panels presiding over anti-dumping to "interpret the relevant provisions of the Agreement in accordance with customary rules of interpretation of public international law". However, despite the WTO Agreement being generally 'open' to influence, as needed, by the other fields of international law, is there a limitation to such influence at the level of the legal texts of the WTO Agreement as a system of law? In other words, is there a level deeper than the 'gate' of the WTO Agreement closed to other fields of international law? In other words, is there is 'closedness' at the level of some or all of the legal texts of the WTO Agreement. This issue requires an extensive discussion as in below.

It has been underlined above that WTO law is not totally closed to other fields of international law. However, a division starts to be discerned on the question of how far WTO law is open, or closed, to other fields of international law when one examines how the panels/Appellate Body have made recourse to other fields of international law in interpreting the covered agreements under the DSU. Two polar views have been aired in this regard and Professor Marceau, who examined the extent to which WTO panels and the Appellate Body may use outside sources of law to resolve tension that may be created during a possibly simultaneous application of a WTO covered agreement and

74 David Palmeter and Petros C. Mavroidis, 'The WTO Legal System: Sources of Law', *American Journal of International Law*, 92(3): 1998, p. 413. In 2004, they followed up with a book where they expounded their discussion on the sources for WTO law. David Palmeter and Petros C. Mavroidis, *Dispute Settlement in the World Trade Organization: Practice and Procedure* (Cambridge: Cambridge University Press, 2004), pp. 49–84. Mavroidis also followed up with a critical assessment of the corpus of law that the WTO panels and the Appellate Body used in their adjudicatory roles. Petros C. Mavroidis, 'No Outsourcing of Law? WTO Law as Practiced by WTO Courts', *American Journal of International Law*, 102(3): 2008, pp. 421–474.

other laws to the same set of facts (she focused on studying such likely tension between Article XX of the GATT 1994 and IEnL), explained the two views as follows:

> The starting point in this analysis is to note that there exists a spectrum of views about the extent to which the WTO system is, and should be, integrated into the broader body of international law. At one end of this spectrum is the view that *the WTO and its dispute settlement system is essentially a closed system that is independent of public international law rules and principles*. This view is critical of the Appellate Body's use of outside legal rules and obligations to interpret the WTO texts. At the other end of the spectrum is the view that *the WTO dispute settlement system is essentially a court of 'general jurisdiction' that may enforce a variety of legal rights and obligations in addition to those specifically set out in the WTO agreements*.
>
> Here, we will make a distinction between three types of WTO situations. First, are the WTO 'covered agreements', which must be applied and enforced by WTO adjudicating bodies. Second, are legal rights and obligations that are formed outside the WTO system, but that are *explicitly referenced* within the WTO texts. Depending on the wording of the reference, these may be either enforced as part of the covered agreements or used as a necessary tool of interpretation by WTO adjudicating bodes. Third, are all other international rules that, according to customary rules of interpretation, *may, and in certain cases must*, be used to interpret WTO provisions (*emphasis added*).[75]

75 Gabrielle Marceau, 'A Call for Coherence in International Law: Praises for the Prohibition against "Clinical Isolation" in WTO Dispute Settlement', *Journal of World Trade*, 33(5): 1999, p. 107. See a similar observation and opinion by Thomas Cottier *et al.*, 'Introduction: Fragmentation and Coherence in International Trade Regulation: Analysis and Conceptual Foundations', in Thomas Cottier and Panagiotis Delimatsis (eds.), *The Prospects of International Trade Regulation: From Fragmentation to Coherence* (Cambridge: Cambridge University Press, 2011), pp. 15–19. For a more exhaustive discussion on the use of sources other than the WTO Agreement to settle WTO disputes, see, Peter Van den Bossche and Werner Zdouc, *The Law and Policy of the World Trade Organization* (4th ed.) (Cambridge: Cambridge University Press, 2017), pp. 54–64, where they refer to nine other sources, binding or otherwise, of WTO law including CIL and general principles of law.

These varying opinions on how 'closed' the WTO Agreement is (must be) to other fields of international law emanate mainly from the respective interpretations of the following provisions of the DSU:

i. Article 3.2:
The dispute settlement system of the WTO is a central element in providing security and predictability to the multilateral trading system. The Members recognize that it serves to preserve the rights and obligations of Members *under the covered agreements, and to clarify the existing provisions of those agreements in accordance with customary rules of interpretation of public international law.* Recommendations and rulings of the DSB *cannot add to or diminish the rights and obligations provided in the covered agreements* (*emphasis added*).

ii. Article 3.2 as repeated in Article 19.2: "in their findings and recommendations, the panel and Appellate Body cannot add to or diminish the rights and obligations provided in the covered agreements."

iii. Article 7.1 and 7.2:
(1) Panels shall have the following terms of reference unless the parties to the dispute agree otherwise within 20 days from the establishment of the panel:
'To examine, in the light of the relevant provisions in (name of the covered agreement(s) cited by the parties to the dispute), the matter referred to the DSB by (name of party) in document ... and to make such findings as will assist the DSB in making the recommendations or in giving the rulings provided for in that/those agreement(s)'.
(2) Panels shall address the relevant provisions in any covered agreement or agreements cited by the parties to the dispute.

iv. Article 11
The function of panels is to assist the DSB in discharging its responsibilities under this Understanding and the covered agreements. Accordingly, a panel should make an objective assessment of the matter before it, including an objective assessment of the facts of the case and the applicability of and conformity with the relevant covered agreements, and make such other findings as will assist the DSB in making the recommendations or in giving the rulings provided for in the covered agreements.

Professor Trachtman's interpretation of the DSU seems to fall on the first group identified by Marceau in that he argues, according to his reading of Article

3.2 of the DSU, that "[t]he mandate to WTO dispute resolution panels, to the Appellate Body, and to the Dispute Settlement Body is clear: apply (directly) only WTO law." He adds that the duty in Article 3.2 not to "add to or diminish the rights and obligations provided in the covered agreements" would be "absurd if rights and obligations arising from other international law could be applied by the DSB". He also reads Article 7 and 11 of the DSU, which have so many references to the WTO covered agreements, to means that "it would be odd if the members intended non-WTO law to be applicable".[76] He, however, accepts the application of non-WTO international law only in two situations: reference customary rules of interpretation of PIL as required by Article 3.2 of the DSU; and when substantive non-WTO is incorporated by explicit (such as in the TRIPS Agreement) or indirect reference (such as Article XX(b) of the GATT 1994) in the text of a WTO agreement or by the text of a waiver by the WTO (such as the Lomé waiver).[77]

Professors Palmeter, Mavroidis and Pauwelyn, among others, could belong to Marceau's second group as they have argued that there is a wider room for accepting non-WTO law in disputes brought under WTO law. Palmeter and Mavroidis take the stance further by stating that although the texts of the WTO covered agreements are the first sources for settling disputes, the other sources of identified in Article 38(1) of the ICJ Charter "all contribute to the rapidly growing and increasingly important body of law known as 'WTO law'" and that the way Articles 3.2 and 7 of the DSU are prepared do not prohibit the use of the other sources listed in Article 38(1) of the ICJ Charter.[78]

Pauwelyn, another 'universalist' according to Simma and Pulkowski,[79] took it even further than Palmeter and Mavroidis. After examining, in detail, the interaction that exists (must exist) between WTO law and international law, he identified five sets of rules which "portray the universe of international law relevant to WTO", the last two of which refer to non-WTO rules which influence WTO law:

1. WTO rules that add previously non-existent rights or obligations to the corpus of international law (such as non-discrimination principles in trade in services);
2. WTO rules that contract out of [GIL] (such as rules in the DSU on the 'suspension of concessions', *which contract out of general international*

76 Joel P. Trachtman, 'The Domain of WTO Dispute Resolution', *Harvard Journal of International Law*, 40(2): 1999, p. 342.

77 Ibid, p. 343.

78 Palmeter and Mavroidis, above note 74, pp. 398–399.

79 Simma and Pulkowski, above note 46, p. 501.

law rules on countermeasures [as noted above, Simma and Pulkowski disagree on this point]) or deviate from, or even replace, other pre-existing rules of international law (such as bilateral quota or tariff arrangements and the Tokyo Round codes);

3. WTO rules that confirm pre-existing rules of international law, be they of [GIL] (such as DSU Article 3.2 confirming that WTO covered agreements are to be interpreted 'in accordance with customary rules of interpretation of PIL') or pre-existing treaty law (such as GATT 1994 incorporating GATT 1947 and the TRIPS Agreement incorporating parts of certain WIPO conventions);
4. non-WTO rules that already existed when the WTO treaty was concluded (on 15 April 1994) and that are: (a) *relevant to and may have an impact on WTO rules* [for instance the concept of necessity]; and (b) *have not been contracted out of, deviated from, or replaced by the WTO treaty.*

   These non-WTO rules consist mainly of [GIL], in particular rules on the law of treaties, state responsibility [which includes the plea of necessity], and settlement of disputes, but also of other treaty rules that regulate or have an impact on the trade relations between states (such as certain rules in environmental or human rights conventions and customs unions or free trade arrangements); and
5. non-WTO rules [including treaties] that are created subsequently to the WTO treaty (post-April 1994) and: (a) are relevant to and may have an impact on WTO rules; (b) either add to or confirm existing WTO rules or contract out of, deviate from, or replace aspects of existing WTO rules; and (c) if the latter is the case, do so in a manner consistent with interplay and conflict rules in the WTO treaty and general international law.[80]

After further examining the limit of the jurisdiction of WTO panels and the laws they can apply, Pauwelyn made the following conclusions:

> First, both the WTO treaty and WTO dispute settlement are integral parts of public international law. *They are not 'closed' or 'self-contained' regimes; they were created in the wider context of general international law, as well as other treaties.* This other international law continues to apply in the WTO unless the WTO treaty has contracted out of it. Depending on the

80 Pauwelyn, above note 1, pp. 540–541, 547.

relevant conflict rules, pre-1994 non-WTO rules may prevail over the WTO treaty.

Second, the WTO treaty, WTO panels, and the Appellate Body were not only created in the wider context of public international law; they continue to exist in that context. The WTO treaty is not static. It is inherently dynamic. Depending on the relevant conflict rules, post-1994 non-WTO rules may prevail over the WTO treaty.

Third, although the substantive jurisdiction of WTO panels is limited to claims under WTO covered agreements (combined with elements of implied jurisdiction), *the international law they may apply in resolving these claims is not limited. It potentially includes all rules of international law. In practice, this inclusiveness means that a defendant should be allowed to invoke non-WTO rules as a justification for breach of WTO rules, even if the WTO treaty itself does not offer such justification* (say, with respect to human rights). However, such a justification should be recognized only when both disputing parties are bound by the non-WTO rule and that rule prevails over the WTO rule pursuant to conflict rules of international law. *Hence, public international law fills gaps left open by the WTO treaty and the WTO treaty must be interpreted in the light of other rules of international law.* But this is not the only window of opportunity for public international law. *More important, non-WTO rules may actually apply before a WTO panel and overrule WTO rules.*[81]

Fourth, interpretation may result in 'interpreting away' apparent conflicts, but it does not resolve genuine conflicts between WTO rules and other rules of international law. Moreover, any interpretation of the WTO treaty must be based on the common intentions of all WTO members, not merely those of the disputing parties.

---

81 Pauwelyn's argument that non-WTO rules can generally apply is supported by Schoenbaum who argued that Article 19 of the DSU contains an "implied powers clause which should be interpreted broadly so that the Panels and Appellate Body can decide all aspects of a case". Thomas J. Schoenbaum, 'WTO Dispute Settlement: Praises and Suggestions for Reform', *International & Comparative Law Quarterly*, 47(3): 1998, p. 647. As far as limiting the use of non-WTO law to a justification (defense) – and not a claim – by a Member, James Bacchus similarly held that this notion was part of the Appellate Body's 'not in clinical isolation' statement in *US – Gasoline (1996)*. James Bacchus, 'Not in Clinical Isolation', in Gabrielle Marceau (ed.), *A History of Law and Lawyers in the GATT/WTO: The Development of the Rule of Law in the Multilateral Trading System* (Cambridge: Cambridge University Press, 2015), p. 514. In a subsequent publication, Pauwelyn put the emphasis mainly on the possibility of the application of non-WTO rules of international law as a justification for breach of WTO rules. Pauwelyn, above note 48, pp. 456–472.

It is crucial to distinguish between (1) panel jurisdiction, (2) applicable law, and (3) the process of interpreting the WTO treaty. Equally important is the distinction between amending the WTO treaty and accepting inter se modifications to it. The limited *jurisdiction* of panels has led to unjustified restrictions on the distinct matter of *applicable law* before a panel. In turn, the realization by some that a panel should be allowed to consider more than WTO covered agreements (a matter of *applicable law*) has led commentators wrongly to accept even non-WTO rules that do not reflect the common intentions of all WTO members as reference material in *interpreting* WTO treaty terms. Moreover, those authors correctly accepting that potentially all international law may be *applicable law* before a panel have erroneously restricted the impact of these non-WTO rules (in the sense that, in their view, WTO rules always prevail) with reference to restrictions on treaty *interpretation* (e.g., DSU Art. 3.2). Finally, the strict requirements imposed to *amend* the WTO treaty have been wrongly invoked as an obstacle to allowing inter se *modifications* to the treaty. Within this framework more work is needed to clearly define those rules of general international law from which the WTO treaty did not contract out (and hence should also apply in the WTO), and point out those non-WTO rules that conflict with the WTO treaty and must prevail over it. The latter necessitates application of the broad definition of conflict defended here and consideration of the WTO treaty as a 'continuing treaty' with *lex generalis* features *vis-a-vis* many other nontrade agreements, and setting out reciprocal rights and obligations that allow for a variety of inter se modifications in a context of regulatory diversity.

Fifth, *the interaction between WTO law and public international law is not one-sided. It is a continuing process of cross-fertilization. Just as public international law enriches WTO law, so WTO law should further develop international law. General international law, in particular its 'secondary' rules on the law of treaties, state responsibility* [*such as necessity*], *and judicial settlement of disputes, is the dynamic engine of treaty-based regimes such as the WTO. These rules are also essential to ensuring the coherence and integrity of public international law as the legal system encompassing the WTO. Hence, if the WTO neglected other rules of international law, it would not only impoverish the WTO legal system and risk reducing it to a uniform one-rule-fits-all framework implemented as a trade-only 'safe*

> *haven'. In addition, it would threaten the unity of international law* (*emphasis added*).[82]

A third, more central view may be that represented by Marceau herself, Bartels, Koskenniemi as well as Simma and Pulkowski. Marceau, who referred to the two 'poles' above, holds a stand that lies in between:

> Between these poles, lies the approach suggested in this article. While *non-WTO legal rules may be used when interpreting and applying WTO provisions*, the specific and circumscribed mandate and jurisdiction of WTO adjudicating bodies *does not extend so far as to permit them to enforce independent rights and obligations embodied in public international law* (*emphasis added*).[83]

For Marceau, like most others, "[i]t is clear from the provisions of the DSU and from existing WTO jurisprudence that the WTO is not a closed system that is impervious to other sources of international law" and she provides four factors that support this observation.[84] Marceau's reading of Articles 7 and 11 of the DSU is that under the DSU not all sources of law may be applied or enforced by WTO adjudicating bodies.[85] She suggests that "with regard to the use of non-WTO obligations, an important distinction is to be made between the 'application' (and enforcement) of WTO provisions and their 'interpretation'":[86]

> Therefore, as a general rule, only WTO rights and obligations can constitute the applicable law and be enforced before WTO adjudicating bodies and these WTO provisions are those identified in the covered agreements. However, even if not *applied or enforced*, and therefore not strictly a source of WTO obligation, non-WTO treaties, practices, customs and general principles of law may be relevant in the *interpretation* of WTO provisions and, therefore, can become fairly influential in defining the parameters and the content of WTO obligations.[87]

She further adds:

---

82 Pauwelyn, above note 1, pp. 577–578.

83 Marceau, above note 75, p. 107.

84 Ibid, pp. 107–108.

85 Ibid, pp. 110–112.

86 Ibid, p. 113.

87 Ibid, p. 114.

> Panels and the Appellate Body will be required to examine outside sources of law where they are expressly used to define or delimit a WTO obligation.[88]
>
> It is yet not clear which other provisions of the Vienna Convention [on the Law of Treaties] could be considered public international law customary rules of interpretation. Strictly speaking, in the Vienna Convention, the provisions on the interpretation of treaties are mentioned in Articles 31, 32 and 33. The other provisions of the Vienna Convention refer to other aspects of the performance of treaties … *Panels and the Appellate Body are obliged (Article 31.3(c) of the Vienna Convention) to take into account all other rules of international law. This would include many customs, general principles of laws and treaties, including provisions of the Vienna convention in certain circumstances.*[89]
>
> [despite the many examples where the panels and the Appellate Body made use of other interpretative rules of GIL as well as provisions in the VCLT other than Articles 31–33] *the full extent to which Panels and the Appellate Body are required to use non-WTO rules to interpret the WTO agreements remains somewhat unclear*. The identification of these rules and their parameters, to the extent not agreed by Members, will have to be determined by Panels and the Appellate Body on a case-by-case basis, by reference to doctrine, other tribunals and expert assessments and the facts of each case.[90]
>
> It can be argued that when interpreting WTO provisions, Panels and the Appellate Body are obliged to 'take into account' a broad range of relevant rules of international law, including treaties, customary rules and general principles of international law, in fact, all sources of international law obligations as defined by Article 38 of the Statute of the ICJ (*emphasis added*).[91]

Bartels, with a stand that appears to point away from Marceau's stand toward the Pauwelyn-Palmeter/Mavroidis pole, reads Articles 3.2 and 19 of the DSU as welcoming doors to international law rules and their use as conflict rules in case of discrepancy between the WTO covered agreements and non-WTO international law.[92] While he agrees that Article 1.1 of the DSU limits the jurisdiction of

88 Ibid, p. 115.
89 Ibid, p. 116.
90 Ibid, p. 122.
91 Ibid, p. 123.
92 Lorand Bartels, 'Applicable Law in WTO Dispute Settlement Proceedings', *Journal of World Trade*, 35(3): 2001, pp. 506–508.

the panels only to cases arising out of the WTO covered agreements,[93] Bartels, as does Koskenniemi, reads the phrase "in the light of" in Article 7.1 as not limiting the sources of law that might be relevant in examining the case.[94] After detailing[95] the inconsistent[96] practice of the panels and the Appellate Body in making use of 'other' international law, Bartels identifies three different ways in which, mainly based on the practice of WTO law, international law can be used in deciding a WTO dispute: (1) as an aid to the interpretation of a given provision of an agreement; (2) as evidence of a Member's compliance with its obligations; and (3) as law in the chain of legal reasoning.[97] Some of his conclusions are:

1. The DSU clearly recognizes Panels and the Appellate Body as tribunals of limited jurisdiction to settle disputes only based on the dispute settlement provisions of the covered agreements. The DSU does not exclude *a priori* application of any source of international law in disputes, i.e., *all sources of international law should be accepted as potentially applicable in WTO dispute settlement proceedings*.
2. Importantly, though, this broad statement is subject to the qualification that where there is a genuine conflict between the rights and obligations contained in the covered agreements and other norms, the conflicts rule in Articles 3.2 and 19.2 of the DSU will ensure that these rights and obligations prevail to the extent of any inconsistency.
3. The codified nature and special subject matter of the WTO agreements means that *in most cases 'other' international law will be used, if at all, in the interpretation of provisions in the covered agreements,*

93 Ibid, pp. 502–503.

94 Ibid, p. 505. See also, Koskenniemi similarly noted that "[w]hile the WTO [DSU] limits the jurisdiction to claims which arise under the WTO covered agreements only, there is no explicit provision identifying the scope of applicable law." Koskenniemi, above note 21, p. 29, para. 45. Lindroos' and Mehling also stated: "no provision in the rules on world trade identifies or limits the law that ultimately should apply to disputes. While jurisdiction is mostly limited to the covered agreements, no similarly explicit statement can be found with regard to the sources of applicable law." Lindroos and Mehling, above note 30, p. 861.

95 He refers to instances in *EC – Hormones (1998)*, *Guatemala – Cement I (1998)*, *Argentina – Footwear (2000)*, *EC – Hormones (Article 22.6 – EC) (1999)* and *EC – Poultry (1998)*. Bartels, above note 92, p. 508.

96 He deduced from the examples, ibid, that: (1) in some cases, the rules of the VCLT are used to exclude a non-WTO international law; (2) in others it is claimed that the non-WTO international law does not apply because it is not contained in a WTO covered agreement; and (3) in other cases again, the WTO covered agreements are simply assumed to "override" the other law. Ibid, p. 509.

97 Ibid, pp. 510–518.

or as evidence of a party's compliance with its obligations under these agreements.

4. However, this model attempts to account for 'hard' cases *in which the rules in the covered agreements are insufficient to resolve a dispute*, and for those cases in which it is necessary to ensure that rights under the covered agreements are being used fairly. In these cases – which include many instances involving secondary WTO law and WTO-related agreements – Panels and the Appellate Body are entitled to *apply* the 'definitions, principles or rules' of PIL not contained in the covered agreements. It would be wrong to see this as going beyond their role. On the contrary, it is necessary precisely in order to maintain the security and predictability of the multilateral trading system.[98]

Moving towards the Trachtman pole from Marceau's middle position is Koskenniemi's view. He used WTO law as an example in examining the relationship between SCRs and GIL. He observed, within the perspective of his group's study on fragmentation of international law, that even the Appellate Body rejected the notion that the WTO system is closed when it noted that WTO agreements should not be read "in clinical isolation from public international law". He then summarized the two views on the issue in away similar to that observed by Marceau and concluded that:

> In practice, however, the two positions may not be altogether difficult to reconcile with almost any practice under the WTO. The latter view [which limits dispute settlement only to the use of WTO covered agreements] may accept even a wide use of [CIL] and other treaties by viewing them as incorporated into the WTO either specifically (through article 3(2) DSU) or implicitly by reference to the context in which the WTO agreements were made. In any case, both positions can accommodate a very wide-ranging practice (somewhat like the 'monist' and 'dualist' positions within domestic law) … There seems, thus, little reason of principle to depart from the view that *general international law supplements WTO law unless it has been specifically excluded and that so do other treaties which should, preferably, be read in harmony with the WTO covered treaties (emphasis added).*[99]

98 Ibid, pp. 518–519. See also, Van den Bossche and Zdouc, above note 75.

99 Koskenniemi, above note 21, p. 87, para. 165; p. 90, para. 169.

Most scholars who welcome application of non-WTO law justify their argument not only from their reading of the DSU, but also from statements made by WTO panels/Appellate Body which indicate the progressive linking of WTO law and other fields of international law. The most notable of these is the Appellate Body's now-famous 'not in clinical isolation' statement in the first case under the DSU, *US – Gasoline (1996)*:

> As such, [Article 31(1) of the VCLT] forms part of the 'customary rules of interpretation of public international law' which the Appellate Body has been directed, by Article 3(2) of the *DSU*, to apply in seeking to clarify the provisions of the *General Agreement* and the other 'covered agreements' of the [WTO Agreement] ... That direction reflects a measure of recognition that *the General Agreement is not to be read in clinical isolation from public international law (emphasis added)*.[100]

In his contribution to Prof. Marceau's book, *A History of Law and Lawyers in the GATT/WTO*, James Bacchus, a former Member and Chairperson of the Appellate Body, strongly defends the place of WTO law in PIL. Bacchus narrates how he and two of his Appellate Body colleagues, sitting for lunch in a café in the outskirts of Geneva, debated with a veteran of the GATT 1947 who strongly argued, like most practitioners and trade negotiators of the GATT 1947, that the GATT was 'closed' to other fields of international law and how the debate led to the conclusion that Article 3.2 of the DSU meant that WTO law, as first reflected in *US – Gasoline (1996)*, is not closed to PIL.[101]

---

100 Appellate Body Report, *US – Gasoline (1996)*, p. 17.

101 Bacchus' reminiscence is worth quoting here:

> The notion that some trade advocates might think WTO law should not be seen as a part of public international law had never occurred to me until one sunny day in the Swiss village of Grand-Saconnex in early 1996. Newly appointed among the seven founding members of the Appellate Body of the WTO, Florentino Feliciano, Claus-Dieter Ehlermann and I were enjoying a relaxing lunch on the shaded veranda of a charming I in that village on the outskirts of Geneva with one of the longtime luminaries of the institutional predecessor of the WTO, the General Agreement on Tariffs and Trade (GATT). Over coffee, Judge Feliciano – 'Toy' as he taught us all to call him – happened to mention during a wide-ranging discussion about our exciting new endeavor on behalf of the members of the WTO: 'well, of course, WTO law is a part of overall public international law'. Claus and I simply nodded and continued sipping our coffee, but our lunch companion suddenly found himself sputtering in disagreement. Old GATT hand that he was, he had always assumed that the GATT was not only a place in Geneva separate and apart from all other international institutions, but a unique legal enterprise separate and apart from the rest of the making and upholding of international law. In his mind, based on his long decades of GATT experience, there was something outside the unique realm of trade called 'international law', and there was also something entirely

Another crucial statement was made by the *Korea – Government Procurement* (*2000*) panel which dwelt on the issue of referring to non-WTO international law, particularly CIL. Article 3.2 of the DSU obliges the panels and the Appellate Body to apply customary *rules of interpretation* of PIL. The panel addressed the issue of whether this provision allows the treaty interpreters to also apply other customary rules of PIL:

> We take note that Article 3.2 of the DSU requires that we seek within the context of a particular dispute to clarify the existing provisions of the WTO agreements in accordance with customary rules of interpretation

---

> distinct within the realm of trade called 'GATT law'. And never the twain should meet. From my own previous involvement with trade negotiations, I did not doubt then that the vast majority of trade negotiators at the time shared this tacit assumption. To many of them, international law was something vague and messy and applicable somewhere else. By contrast, 'GATT law' was practical and workable and self-contained. Others, in their unworldly idealism, might pursue the elusive dream of creating international law in a world of squabbling states. Meanwhile, those who dealt with the GATT would labour together on the worldly business of easing trade in this or that product. Making international law might be a worthy goal; but the more modest commercial tasks of the GATT were eminently more doable. If this was the shared assumption of many who negotiated the WTO treaty, it was nowhere expressed in the treaty they negotiated. Indeed, the text of the treaty seems to imply instead that the WTO is but a part of public international law. As we seven founders of the Appellate Body looked for the first time in 1996 at the responsibility with which we had been entrusted by the members of the WTO, we saw a clear instruction from them in Article 3.2 of the Dispute Settlement Understanding (DSU) to clarify the provisions of the WTO treaty 'in accordance with customary rules of interpretation of public international law'. Back then, at the very beginning of our work together, we concluded that those customary rules find expression in the Vienna Convention on the Law of Treaties. In my recollection, the members of the WTO engaged in dispute settlement at the time readily agreed, and this has been the view and the practice in WTO dispute settlement ever since. In the report resulting from the very first appeal to the Appellate Body, *US – Gasoline*, we thought it appropriate, while musing on the meaning of Article 3.2 of the DSU, to state that this particular provision in the WTO treaty reflects 'a measure of recognition that the General Agreement is not to be read in clinical isolation from public international law'. Peter Van den Bossche, current member of the Appellate Body, and Werner Zdouc, current Director of the Appellate Body Secretariat, who are two of the leading WTO thinkers and scholars around, are of the view that this single statement on page 16 of the Appellate Body report in the *US – Gasoline* case in 1996 marks 'a genuine turning point in the relationship between international law and international trade law'. Nearly two decades and more than one hundred Appellate Body reports later, I see no reason to disagree with them ... But it is one thing not to read WTO law in clinical isolation from the rest of international law. It is quite another to define the lines where WTO law and the rest of international law overlap and where they do not.

Bacchus, above note 81, pp. 507–508, 510.

> of [PIL]. *However, the relationship of the WTO Agreements to customary international law is broader than this. Customary international law applies generally to the economic relations between the WTO Members. Such international law applies to the extent that the WTO treaty agreements do not 'contract out' from it.* To put it another way, *to the extent there is no conflict or inconsistency, or an expression in a covered WTO agreement that implies differently, we are of the view that the customary rules of international law apply to the WTO treaties and to the process of treaty formation under the WTO.*[102]
>
> We should also note that we can see no basis here for an *a contrario* implication that rules of international law other than rules of interpretation do not apply. The language of 3.2 in this regard applies to a specific problem that had arisen under the GATT to the effect that, among other things, reliance on negotiating history was being utilized in a manner arguably inconsistent with the requirements of the rules of treaty interpretation of customary international law.[103]

Pauwelyn lists some additional VCLT[104] and related GIL rules that may be referred to, under Article 3.2 of the DSU, on top of the customary rules of interpretation of PIL, as long as WTO law bot contracted out of them. These include "certain rules on the conclusion, invalidity, application, modification, suspension, or termination of treaties come to mind, but also rules on state responsibility, on judicial settlement of disputes, and on how to solve conflicts between norms must apply".[105]

The general consensus appears, therefore, to be that while WTO law is open to being influenced by rules and principles of other fields of international law, there are limitations to such influence including: (a) if WTO law expressly contracts out of non-WTO rules, the latter cannot be used in a WTO Agreement dispute; (b) (a) non-WTO law may not be used as a ground for claim in WTO dispute settlement; (c) non-WTO law, unless explicitly referred to in the WTO Agreement, cannot be enforced through WTO law; and (d) non-WTO law may

102 WTO Panel Report, *Korea – Government Procurement* (2000), para. 7.96.

103 Ibid, f.n. 753.

104 Mavroidis investigated the sources of law used, and the practice of utilization of the VCLT, by WTO panels and Appellate Body in and criticized the 'compartmentalized' use of the VCLT. Mavroidis, above note 74, pp. 421–474 (conclusions in p. 470).

105 Pauwelyn, above note 1, p. 543. Regarding reference to the rules of state responsibility, the practice in WTO has so far been limited mainly to attribution and countermeasures. See, f.n. 145 and 146 below.

be referred to for other purposes such as interpreting the WTO Agreement and ensuring compliance of the acts of Members with their obligations under the WTO Agreement.

By way of further refining the discussion, we may, given that use non-WTO law in WTO law is generally allowed to the level of the legal texts of the WTO Agreement, ask: (a) how deep such possibility goes within the legal texts (i.e., down to paragraphs, clauses, phrases, words as well as the structures and contexts of each covered agreement); and (b) if that is possible, whether the application of non-WTO rule in one covered agreement can be transported into another covered agreement which contains similar paragraphs, clauses, phrases, words and structures. The practice of interpreting the different legal texts of the WTO Agreement shows that the rules and principles of other fields of international law have been applied as far as individual paragraphs, clauses, phrases, words as well as the structures and contexts of each WTO covered agreement. Therefore, with the aid of the rules and principles of other fields of international law, similar interpretation may be developed, depending on their respective contexts, for similar terms, phrases, principles and concepts (such as the concept of necessity) of WTO law that are found in different covered agreements.[106]

It can be mentioned here that there are other sources for developing interpretation of the legal texts of the WTO Agreement including: WTO panel/ Appellate Body reports and Working Procedures; decisions of the WTO organs; subsequent agreements of WTO Members, determinations of the Chairpersons of WTO organs; 'WTO law-related' agreements and other instruments (e.g., regional trade agreements, decisions of dispute settlement mechanisms under regional trade agreements, mutually agreed solutions to disputes, related bilateral agreements on dispute settlement proceedings, and agreements to which the WTO is a party).[107]

106 For a general read on the practices of treaty interpretation by the WTO panels and the Appellate Body, see, Isabelle Van Damme, *Treaty Interpretation by the WTO Appellate Body* (Oxford: Oxford University Press, 2009); Georges Abi-Saab, 'The Appellate Body and Treaty Interpretation', in Malgosia Fitzmaurice, Olufemi Elias and Panos Merkouris (eds.), *Treaty Interpretation and the Vienna Convention on the Law of Treaties: 30 Years on*. Vol. 1 (Leiden & Boston: Martinus Nijhoff, 2010), pp. 99–109; Isabelle Van Damme, 'Treaty Interpretation by the WTO Appellate Body', *European Journal of International Law*, 21(3): 2010, pp. 605–648.

107 Bartels, above note 92, pp. 500–501. See also, Van den Bossche and Zdouc, above note 75.

10.3 The Two-Way Relationship between WTO Law and International Law

WTO law has earned its place in the universe of international law and has contributed to the development of international law. Bacchus argues that:

> Today, WTO law is seen worldwide as one of the main sources of international law. In fact, WTO dispute settlement may well have produced more new international law in the form of international jurisprudence in the past two decades [1995–2015] than all the other proliferating sources of international law combined.[108]

It is therefore important to ensure, as much as possible, that – to borrow Simma's and Pulkowski's analogy of planets and the universe – the WTO law 'planet' rotates and revolves harmoniously – i.e., avoids unnecessary fragmentation – with other 'planets' in the 'universe' of international law. Despite being a SCR, WTO law, like all fields of international law, has been read not to be completely closed to other fields of international law. The practice of the WTO panels and the Appellate Body as well as the opinions of scholars shows a rainbow of opinions as to the level or extent of 'openness' of the WTO Agreement to other fields of international law. The practices and opinions are mainly based on interpreting key provisions of the DSU such as Articles 3.2, 7.1, 7.2, 11 and 19.2. WTO Agreement is in principle open to the influence of the other fields of international law with some limitations mentioned above.

Moreover, as much as the legal texts of the WTO Agreement can be influenced by principles and concepts in other fields of international law, principles and concepts contained in the WTO Agreement and the interpretations developed for its many concepts can similarly influence other fields of international law. The history of the concept of necessity in GATT/WTO law and its practices – as discussed in Chapters 7–9 – and the other fields of international law and their practices – as discussed in Chapters 5–6 – is a good example. It was discussed in those chapters that the development of the concept of necessity in WTO law appears to have been partly influenced by the concept of proportionality developed within the ECJ and the interpretation of the concept of necessity under WTO law in turn influenced the interpretation of the concept of necessity in IIL and IEnL with the potential to also influence interpretation of the concept of necessity in other fields of international law. The concept

108 Bacchus, above note 81, p. 509.

of necessity in WTO can still learn from the concepts of necessity developed (which may develop) in other fields of international law. But how should such interoperability be processed? Are there (should there be) some rules to guide the process of interoperability between the concepts of necessity in WTO law and the other fields of international law? Chapters 11 and 12 aim to answer these questions.

CHAPTER 11

Rules for Interfacing the Concepts of Necessity in WTO Law and Other Fields of International Law

Chapter 11 aims to build on the foundation laid by Chapter 10 that WTO law is an active part of international law with the potential to influence and in turn be influenced by the rules and practices of the other fields of international law. How is this potential to be realized? This Chapter begins, in Section 11.1, to answer this question by presenting the rules and practices to carry out the exercise of interoperability between any two fields of international law or between one field of international law and international law in general. In Section 11.1, the exercise is between WTO law and the other fields of international law in general. In then goes to the specific subject of interoperability which is the subject matter of this book: the interface between the concepts of necessity in WTO law and CIL as now codified in Article 25 of the ARSIWA. Since the interoperability exercise between these two concepts of necessity will be conducted in details in Chapter 12, Section 11.2 transitions between this Chapter and Chapter 12 by focusing on a couple of initial issues in the exercise of interoperability between these two concepts of necessity: their similarities and differences and the potential for conflict between them.

11.1 Rules and Practices of Interoperability

Since *US – Gasoline (1996)*, WTO adjudicators, through the Appellate Body's statement that "the General Agreement is not to be read in clinical isolation from PIL", made clear their intention to make WTO law a legal regime that will grow with the respect of, and guidance from, international law in many aspects (i.e., interpretation and beyond) with the potential also to influence other fields of international law. The design, operation, structure, dispute settlement mechanism and enforcement rules of the WTO Agreement have rightfully enabled WTO law to be identified not only as a distinct and autonomous subsystem of international law, but also – and rather quickly – as an SCR. As Koskenniemi observed, "WTO covered treaties are creations of and constantly

 | DOI:10.1163/9789004700000_013

interact with other norms of international law."[1] Lindroos and Mehling describe the inherent nature of WTO law to be influenced by international law by stating that since WTO law "was born into the wider body of international law" it "continues to be governed by the precepts of public international law, at least to the extent that these have not been contracted out, deviated from, or otherwise replaced".[2]

The fragmentation and integration of international law necessitates that a SCR not only make use of the rules and concepts developed under of other fields of international law, but also contribute in the development of the other fields of international law by developing or expounding concepts that can be adopted by those other fields. Different authors have made different comments on the subject. Yearwood calls such relationship between WTO law and the other fields of international law an "intra-systemic interreaction" (i.e., the relation with GIL and PIL in general) and "inter-systemic interreaction" (i.e., the relation with other treaties).[3] WTO law finds itself in this scenario. Pauwelyn, who asked the questions "[h]ow does the [WTO law] relate to the wider corpus of public international law? What, in turn, is the role of public international law in WTO dispute settlement?" commented that:

> the interaction between WTO law and public international law *is not one-sided. It is a continuing process of cross-fertilization. Just as public international law enriches WTO law, so WTO law should further develop international law* ... Hence, if the WTO neglected other rules of international law, it would not only impoverish the WTO legal system and risk reducing it to a uniform one-rule-fits-all framework implemented as a trade-only 'safe haven'. In addition, it would threaten the unity of international law (*emphasis added*).[4]

---

1 Martti Koskenniemi, 'Fragmentation of International Law: Difficulties arising From the Diversification and Expansion of International Law', *Report of the Study Group of the International Law Commission* (2006), ILC, 58th sess., U.N. Doc. A/CN.4/L. 682, p. 29, para. 45.

2 Anja Lindroos and Michael Mehling, 'Dispelling the Chimera of 'Self-Contained Regimes': International Law and the WTO', *European Journal of International Law*, 16(5): 2005, p. 861.

3 Ronnie R. F. Yearwood, *The Interaction between World Trade Organisation (WTO) Law and External International Law: The Constrained Openness of WTO Law (A Prologue to a Theory)* (London and New York: Routledge, 2012), pp. 32–34.

4 Joost Pauwelyn, 'The Role of Public International law in the WTO: How Far Can We Go?' *American Journal of International Law*, 95(3): 2001, p. 578.

The point, however, is *how much* has the influence been from the direction of the other fields of international law to WTO law and *vice versa*. Understandably, WTO law, at least given its age and the high specificity of its legal texts, is expected to be more influenced by the other fields of international law than its contribution to other fields of international law and/or other international agreements. Writing in 1998, i.e., during the early years of the WTO, Palmeter and Mavroidis could only remain hopeful of the influence of WTO law on PIL:

> Public international law has clearly made an important contribution to WTO law. *It is not yet clear that the reverse will be true*, that other international tribunals will begin to see the WTO, as reflected in its adopted reports, as a source of law. Given the growing quantity and high overall quality of those reports, however, *it seems likely that it is only a matter of time before this recognition begins to take place* (*emphasis added*).[5]

Charnovitz, who examined 'normative influences to and from [IEL]', also wrote along the same lines as Palmeter and Mavroidis:

> [t]here are so many examples in WTO jurisprudence of the way in which general and specialized international law have influenced WTO law. *Less well appreciated, but equally important, is the way that trade law influences public international law.* A spotlight was shined on that area of study by Don McRae's excellent Hague Academy lecture in 1996 (*emphasis added*).[6]

McRae, in his 1996 lecture, pointed at the overall contribution that IEL/ITL had – although not an easy impact – in changing the focus of international law: "A final important implication of international trade law for international law may be that we are seeing a structural change from a 'peace and security' basis as the starting point for thinking about international law to an 'economic welfare' basis."[7] Let us now look at the practices thus far of the interoperability between WTO law and the other fields of international law.

5 David Palmeter and Petros C. Mavroidis, 'The WTO Legal System: Sources of Law', *American Journal of International Law*, 92(3): 1998, p. 413.

6 Steve Charnovitz, 'The Field of International Economic Law', *Journal of International Economic Law*, 17(3): 2014, p. 624.

7 Donald M. McRae, 'The Contribution of International Trade Law to the Development of International Law', *Recueil des Cours*, 260(1): 1996, p. 232. He also analyzed the interinfluence between ITL and other fields of PIL such as IEL, international labor law and international human rights regime.

11.1.1 *Other Fields of International Law Referring to and Applying WTO Law*

The influence of WTO law on other fields of international law can be observed from two perspectives: direct and indirect.

There are a few areas where WTO law has direct, outgoing influence. One such influence has been the application of the concept of necessity of in Article XX of the GATT 1994 in interpreting necessity provisions in bilateral investment treaties as discussed in Sub-section 5.5.3. There has also been some discussion on the influence that WTO law may have on EU law and domestic legal systems.[8]

Indirect influence of WTO law occurs when a 'trade and ...' dispute is brought before the WTO dispute settlement organs thereby subjecting non-WTO issues to a WTO dispute settlement process. In his Hague Academy lecture, McRae highlighted this scenario as the main tool for ITL to influence other fields of international law. He argued that 'trade and ...' cases are brought to the WTO dispute settlement system – hance making it an 'arbiter' in these cases – that the other way round because of the relative strength and efficiency of WTO law compared to other fields of international law (such as IEnL and IHRL):

> Why has the field of international trade law been able to assert this role as arbiter? Why are issues relating to the environment coming before trade dispute settlement mechanisms, but trade issues are not being ruled on in environmental or human rights fora? In part, *no doubt this is due to the fact that although such mechanisms have been developed in the trade law field, they are less well developed, or non-existent, in other areas* (*emphasis added*).[9]

8 A notable publication on this kind of WTO influence is Claudio Dordi's edited volume where the experiences of the effects of WTO law on the EU legal system, the case law of the ECJ and the domestic legal systems of five countries (Austria, the US, Canada, Japan and Switzerland) were discussed. Claudio Dordi (ed.), *The Absence of Direct Effect of WTO Law in the EC and in Other Countries* (Turin: Giappicchelli Editore, 2010). See also, Jiangyu Wang, 'The Rule of Law in China: A Realistic View of the Concept, the Impact of the WTO, and the Prospects for Future Development', *Singapore Journal of Legal Studies*, 2004, pp. 347–389; Bashar H. Malkawi, 'Anatomy of the Case of Arab Countries and the WTO', *Arab Law Quarterly*, 20(2): 2006, pp. 110–151; Luca Barani, 'Relationship of the EU legal order with WTO Law: Studying Judicial Activism', Garnet Working Paper No: 70/09 September 2009, available at, http://www2.warwick.ac.uk/fac/soc/pais/research/researchcentres/csgr/garnet/workingpapers/7009.pdf.

9 McRae, above note 7, p. 192.

Former WTO Director-General Pascal Lamy, in his May 2006 address before the European Society of International Law at the Sorbonne, entitled *The Place and Role of the WTO (WTO Law) in the International Legal Order*, also made similar observations about the relative advantage and strength of WTO law and its dispute settlement system. He reminded his audience of the need to seek 'equilibrium' between the "relative power" of the WTO with other systems (such as the IEnL system) in order to tackle the problem of "lack of coherence of our international legal system".[10]

The much discussed[11] 'environmental' decisions of the panels and the Appellate Body under, *inter alia*, Article XX (b) and (g) of the GATT 1994 as well as the TBT Agreement and the SPS Agreement which involve references to MEAs and principles of IEnL are examples of the 'indirect' influence that WTO law may have not only on the MEAs but also on GIL. The Appellate Body's analysis, in *EC – Hormones (1998)*, whereby it related the contribution of the SPS Agreement (Article 5.7) to the debate on whether the precautionary principle has crystallized into a general principle of customary IEnL or has even been accepted as a principle of GIL or CIL, is a good example.[12] In the *EC – Hormones (1998)* report (f.n. 93), the Appellate Body stated that the ICJ, in *Gabčíkovo-Nagymaros Project* (paras. 111–114), did not identify the precautionary principle as one of the new norms and standards recently developed in the field of environmental protection. The views of the Appellate Body regarding the precautionary principle are mentioned here since the Appellate Body's view on the CIL status of the precautionary principle, partly influenced by the ICJ's ruling, is related to IEnL and can in turn influence the understanding of

---

10 Pascal Lamy, 'The Place and Role of the WTO (WTO Law) in the International Legal Order', Address before the European Society of International Law, available at, https://www.wto.org/english/news_e/sppl_e/sppl26_e.htm, as published later in Pascal Lamy, 'The Place of the WTO and its Law in the International Legal Order', *European Journal of International Law*, 17(5): 2006, pp. 983–984.

11 A good example would be Gabrielle Marceau, 'Conflicts of Norms and Conflicts of Jurisdictions: The Relationship between the WTO Agreement and MEAs and other Treaties', *Journal of World Trade*, 35(6): 2001, pp. 1081–1131. Other publications include: P. K. Rao, *The World Trade Organization and the Environment* (London: Macmillan Press Ltd., 2000); Fiona MacMillan, *WTO and the Environment* (London: Sweet & Maxwell, 2001); Gary Sampson and John Whalley (eds.), *The WTO, Trade and the Environment: Critical Perspectives on the Global Trading System and the WTO* (Cheltenham (UK) and Northampton (MA, USA): Edward Elgar Publishing Ltd., 2005); Edith Brown Weiss, John H. Jackson and Nathalie Bernasconi-Osterwalder (eds.), *Reconciling Environment and Trade* (2nd ed.) (Leiden: Martinus Nijhoff, 2008).

12 Appellate Body Report, *EC – Hormones (1998)*, paras. 123–124. See also, Appellate Body Report, *Japan – Apples (2003)*, para. 233.

the precautionary principle when relevant to other fields of international law or international tribunals (including the ICJ itself in future disputes brought to it).

11.1.2 *WTO Law Referring to and Applying Rules of the Other Fields of International Law*

Non-WTO international law texts and concepts, including the decisions of international tribunals,[13] have been substantially utilized in litigations under WTO law. There are two ways through which these sources have been used in WTO jurisprudence: mandated and non-mandated.

Mandated reference occurs when a legal text of the WTO Agreement requires or makes explicit reference to such sources. The following nine instances can be mentioned: (1) the TRIPS Agreement requires compliance with the Paris Convention (1967), the Berne Convention, the Rome Convention and the Treaty on Intellectual Property in Respect of Integrated Circuits;[14] (2) the TBT Agreement requires the use of international standards;[15] (3) the SPS Agreement refers to international standards, guidelines and recommendations developed by, and requests WTO Members to contact and play a full part in, the Codex Alimentarius Commission, the International Office of Epizootics, and the international and regional organizations operating within the framework of the International Plant Protection Convention;[16] (4) the SPS Agreement recognizes certain dispute settlement mechanisms outside of the WTO;[17] (5) Annex I(k) of the SCM Agreement[18] has been interpreted not to consider as export subsidies government grants of export credits in conformity with the provisions of the Arrangement on Guidelines for Officially

13 Gomula has provided us with an extensive list of PCIJ (and some ICJ) decisions cited for many purposes (confirmation, guidance and application) by WTO panels and the Appellate Body. Joanna Gomula, 'The Heritage of the Permanent Court of International Justice in WTO Concept', in Christian J. Tams and Malgosia Fitzmaurice (eds.), *Legacies of the Permanent Court of International Justice* (Leiden & Boston: Martinus Nijhoff, 2013), pp. 175–200.

14 Article 2 of the TRIPS Agreement.

15 For example, Articles 1.1 and 2.4 of the TBT Agreement.

16 Sixth recital of the preamble as well as Articles 3.4 and 12.3 of the SPS Agreement.

17 Article 11.3 of the SPS Agreement.

18 Which reads: "if a Member is a party to an international undertaking on official export credits to which at least twelve original Members to this Agreement are parties as of 1 January 1979 (or a successor undertaking which has been adopted by those original Members), or if in practice a Member applies the interest rates provisions of the relevant undertaking, an export credit practice which is in conformity with those provisions shall not be considered an export subsidy prohibited by this Agreement."

Supported Export Credits (Arrangements on Guidelines) of the Organization for Economic Development;[19] (6) Article XX(h) of the GATT 1994 refers to obligations created under "any intergovernmental commodity agreement which conforms to criteria submitted to the Contracting Parties and not disapproved by them or which is itself so submitted and not so disapproved"; (7) Article XXI(c) of the GATT 1994 and Article XIV *bis* of the GATS refer to obligations under the UN Charter; (8) Article 3.2 of the DSU refers to customary rules of interpretation of PIL; and (9) an external source may be referenced in a WTO-sanctioned waiver.[20] It may be noted here that these non-WTO law sources are used only in respect of examining violation under, and enforcing,[21] the provisions of the WTO covered agreements refer to them. A WTO Member cannot bring another Member before a WTO panel claiming violations under these external sources.[22]

Non-mandated reference of non-WTO law in a WTO dispute settlement involves references by WTO dispute settlement organs to non-WTO sources for purposes of interpretation or application of WTO rules without the WTO Agreement explicitly obliging them to do so. External sources, especially GIL rules, have been profusely relied upon by the panels and the Appellate Body[23] for at least three purposes. These are: (a) for interpreting the covered agreements; (b) for evidence of compliance with a covered agreement; and (c) for application of rules, each of which will be mentioned below.[24]

---

19 Petros C. Mavroidis, 'No Outsourcing of Law? WTO Law as Practiced by WTO Courts', *American Journal of International Law*, 102(3): 2008, p. 427.

20 A good example would be the way the *EC – Bananas III (US) (1997)* panel and the Appellate Body accepted the Lomé Convention and the need to interpret it in order to resolve the dispute brought under the DSU. WTO Panel Report, *EC – Bananas III (US) (1997)*, para. 7.98; Appellate Body Report, *EC – Bananas III (US) (1997)*, para. 167.

21 Gabrielle Marceau, 'A Call for Coherence in International Law: Praises for the Prohibition against "Clinical Isolation" in WTO Dispute Settlement', *Journal of World Trade*, 33(5): 1999, p. 112.

22 Pauwelyn, above note 4, p. 555; Mavroidis, above note 19, pp. 428–429; Lorand Bartels, 'Applicable Law in WTO Dispute Settlement Proceedings', *Journal of World Trade*, 35(3): 2001, p. 510; ibid, p. 113.

23 Treves states that due to the relative 'closedness' of the DSU to GIL/PIL, it was "painful" for the panes and the Appellate Body to regularize the reference to GIL in the WTO dispute settlement process. Tullio Treves, 'Fragmentation of International Law: The Judicial Perspective', *Agenda Internacional*, Año XVI (N° 27): 2009, p. 240.

24 These three purposes have been extracted mainly from: (1) Pauwelyn, above note 4, p. 555; (2) Lorand Bartels, 'Applicable Law in WTO Dispute Settlement Proceedings', *Journal of World Trade*, 35(3): 2001, pp. 510–512; and (3) Repertory of Appellate Body Reports (*Principles and Concepts of General Public International Law*, available at, https://www.wto.org/english/tratop_e/dispu_e/repertory_e/p3_e.htm#P. 3.1 and *Interpretation*, available at, https://www.wto.org/english/tratop_e/dispu_e/repertory_e/i3_e.htm#I.3.13).

Examples of reliance on non-WTO rules for the purpose of interpreting WTO covered agreements include: (1) the meaning of 'exhaustible natural resources' in Article XX(g) of the GATT 1994;[25] (2) the principle of presumption against the retroactive effect of treaties;[26] (3) good faith;[27] (4) abuse of rights;[28] (5) estoppel and acquiescence;[29] (6) *in dubio mitius*;[30] (7) *ejusdem generis*;[31]

A more exhaustive read on this regard is Andrew D. Mitchell's *Legal Principles in WTO Disputes* (Cambridge: Cambridge University Press, 2008) which examines such principles as good faith, proportionality, due process as well as special and differential treatment as they have been adopted to the WTO jurisprudence. See also, Joost Pauwelyn, 'Sources of International Trade Law: Mantras and Controversies at the World Trade Organization', in Samantha Besson and Jean d'Aspremont (eds.), *The Oxford Handbook of the Sources of International Law* (Oxford: Oxford University Press, 2018), pp. 1027–1047; Sonia E. Rolland, *Development at the WTO* (Oxford: Oxford University Press, 2012), p. 120; Thomas Cottier *et al.*, 'Introduction: Fragmentation and Coherence in International Trade Regulation: Analysis and Conceptual Foundations', in Thomas Cottier and Panagiotis Delimatsis (eds.), *The Prospects of International Trade Regulation: From Fragmentation to Coherence* (Cambridge: Cambridge University Press, 2011), pp. 1–26.

25 Where reference was made, in *US – Shrimp (1998)*, to a number of IEnL treaties and reports of the ICJ, in part, to define 'exhaustible natural resources' in Article XX(g) of the GATT 1994. Appellate Body Report, *US – Shrimp (1998)*, paras. 127–142.

26 Appellate Body Report, *Canada – Patent Term (2000)*, paras. 71–74. See also, Appellate Body Report, *Brazil – Desiccated Coconut (1997)*, p. 15; Appellate Body Report, *EC – Bananas III (US) (1997)*, paras. 235, 237; Appellate Body Report, *EC – Hormones (1998)*, para. 128; Appellate Body Report, *EC and certain member States – Large Civil Aircraft (2011)*, paras. 672, 675, 677–679, 685.

27 Appellate Body Report, *US – Shrimp (1998)*, para. 158; Appellate Body Report, *US – FSC (2000)*, para. 166; Appellate Body Report, *US – Cotton Yarn (2001)*, para. 81; Appellate Body Report, *US – Hot-Rolled Steel (2001)*, para. 101; Appellate Body Report, *Peru – Agricultural Products (2015)*, paras. 5.15–5.28; WTO Panel Report, *Russia – Traffic in Transit (2019)*, paras. 7.132–7.138.

28 Appellate Body Report, *US – Gasoline (1996)*, pp. 22–23; Appellate Body Report, *US – Shrimp (1998)*, paras. 116, 151, 158.

29 WTO Panel Report, *Guatemala – Cement II (2000)*, para. 8.24; WTO Panel Report, *EC – Asbestos (2000)*, para. 8.60; Appellate Body Reports, *EC – Export Subsidies on Sugar (2005)*, paras. 307–313.

30 Appellate Body Report, *EC – Hormones (1998)*, para. 165, f.n. 154. The term means that "… [i]f the meaning of a term is ambiguous, that meaning is to be preferred which is less onerous to the party assuming an obligation, or which interferes less with the territorial and personal supremacy of a party, or involves less general restrictions upon the parties." See also, Appellate Body Report, *China – Publications and Audiovisual Products (2010)*, para. 411.

31 Appellate Body Reports, *US – COOL (2012)*, paras. 443–444 and f.n. 897; Appellate Body Report, *US – Large Civil Aircraft (2nd complaint) (2012)*, para. 615, f.n. 1290. *Ejusdem generis* is a canon of construction which states that "when a general word or phrase follows a list of specifics, the general word or phrase will be interpreted to include only items of the

and (8) various aspects of the law treaties such as error in treaty formation,[32] termination (Articles 60 and 70 of the VCLT),[33] *inter se* agreements,[34] successive treaties (Articles 30[35] and 59[36] of the VCLT) and *lex specialis*.[37]

Examples of WTO disputes where non-WTO rules were relied on for use as evidence of compliance with a covered agreement include *US – Shrimp (1998)* (where the Appellate Body, in interpreting the *chapeau* of Article XX of the GATT 1994, referred to the Inter-American Convention for the Protection and Conservation of Sea Turtles to support its decision that the US had other reasonably available courses of action and hence the US measure constituted unjustifiable discrimination)[38] and *India – Patents (1997)* and *US – Anti-Dumping Act of 1916 (2000)* (where the Appellate Body and the panel respectively stated that municipal law can also constitute evidence of a party's compliance with its international obligations).[39]

Examples of non-WTO rules used to effectively interpret WTO covered agreements include: (1) state responsibility rules (countermeasures[40] and attribution)[41] by referring to the work of the ILC; (2) standing;[42] (3) representation by a private counsel;[43] (4) *la compétence de la compétence*;[44] (5) burden of proof;[45]

same type as those listed." Bryan A. Garner (ed.), *Black's Law Dictionary* (8th ed.) (St. Paul, MN: Thomson West, 2004), p. 1568.

32 WTO Panel Report, *Korea – Government Procurement (2000)*, paras. 7.123–7.126.

33 Decision by the Arbitrator, *Brazil – Aircraft (Article 22.6 – Brazil) (2000)*, para. 3.10.

34 WTO Panel Report, *Turkey – Textiles (1999)*, para. 9.181.

35 Appellate Body Report, *EC – Poultry (1998)*, para. 79; Decision by the Arbitrator, *EC – Hormones (US) (Article 22.6 – EC) (1999)*, para. 51.

36 Appellate Body Report, *EC – Poultry (1998)*, ibid.

37 WTO Panel Report, *US – 1916 Act (2000)*, para. 6.269; WTO Panel Report, *Turkey – Textiles (1999)*, paras. 9.92–9.95, 9.186; WTO Panel Report, *India – Quantitative Restrictions (1999)*, para. 4.20; WTO Panel Report, *EC – Bananas III (US) (1997)*, para. 7.75; Appellate Body Report, *US – Softwood Lumber V (Article 21.5 – Canada) (2006)*, paras. 132, 135–136.

38 Appellate Body Report, *US – Shrimp (1998)*, paras. 169–176.

39 Appellate Body Report, *India – Patents (US) (1998)*, para. 65; WTO Panel Report, *US – 1916 Act (2000)*, para. 6.36.

40 WTO Panel Report, *Korea – Government Procurement (2000)*, paras. 7.123–7.126.

41 WTO Panel Report, *EC – Bananas III (US) (1997)*, para. 6.16.

42 Ibid, 7.49–7.50.

43 Appellate Body Report, *EC – Bananas III (US) (1997)*, para. 10; WTO Panel Report, *Indonesia – Autos (1998)*, para. 4.11; WTO Panel Report, *Korea – Alcoholic Beverages (1999)*, para. 10.31.

44 WTO Panel Report, *US – 1916 Act (2000)*, para. 54, f.n. 30.

45 WTO Panel Report, *US – Wool Shirts and Blouses (1997)*, p. 14.

(6) the acceptability of *amicus curiae* briefs;[46] (7) authority to draw adverse inferences;[47] and (8) judicial economy.[48]

11.2 Interoperability in the Context of the Current Crisis of the WTO Dispute Settlement System

The issue of influence of WTO law on other fields of international law and *vice versa* as well as the process of such influence cannot be discussed in isolation from the current crisis of the WTO dispute settlement system. Although reform and strengthening of the WTO dispute settlement system has been discussed for many years within the WTO (mainly through making reform of the system part of the Doha Development Agenda)[49] and in academic publications,[50] a real damage to the system – Simon Lester calls it "the Trump Administration's destruction of the Appellate Body"[51] – has been caused as a result of persistent US attack (since late 2018)[52] directed at the Appellate Body.[53] Members of the WTO continued to discuss the improvement of the dispute settlement system

46 Appellate Body Report, *US – Shrimp (1998)*, para. 107.

47 Appellate Body Report, *Canada – Aircraft (1999)*, para. 202.

48 Appellate Body Report, *US – Wool Shirts and Blouses (1997)*, pp. 22–24.

49 WT/MIN(01)/DEC/1 (20 November 2001), WTO Fourth Ministerial Declaration, adopted on 14 November 2021, available at, https://www.wto.org/english/thewto_e/minist_e/min01_e/mindecl_e.htm#dispute, para. 30.

50 For instance, Rufus Yerxa and Bruce Wilson (eds.), *Key Issues in WTO Dispute Settlement: The First Ten Years* (Cambridge: Cambridge University Press, 2005); Giorgio Sacerdoti 'The WTO Dispute Settlement System: Consolidating Success and Confronting New Challenges', in Manfred Elsig, Bernard Hoekman and Joost Pauwelyn (eds.), *Assessing the World Trade Organization: Fit for Purpose?* (Cambridge: Cambridge University Press, 2017), pp. 147–173; Thomas J. Schoenbaum, 'WTO Dispute Settlement: Praise and Suggestions for Reform', *International and Comparative Law Quarterly*, 47(3): 2008, pp. 647–658; Bernard M. Hoekman and Petros C. Mavroidis, 'To AB or Not to AB? Dispute Settlement in WTO Reform', *Journal of International Economic Law*, 23(3): 2020, pp. 703–722.

51 Simon Lester, 'Can Interim Appeal Arbitration Preserve the WTO Dispute System?', Free Trade Bulletin (1 September 2020), available at, https://www.cato.org/sites/cato.org/files/2020-08/FTB-77.pdf.

52 Professor Petersmann calls these actions the 'US attack on the WTO legal and dispute settlement system'. Ernst-Ulrich Petersmann, 'How Should WTO Members React to Their WTO Crises?', *World Trade Review*, 18(3): 2019, p. 505. Hoekman and Mavroidis call the US 'the instigator of the [Appellate Body] Crisis'. Hoekman and Mavroidis, above note 50, p. 704.

53 A consolidated version of US concerns about the WTO dispute settlement and the Appellate Body can be read at, United States Trade Representative, *The President's 2018 Trade Policy Agenda*, available at, https://ustr.gov/sites/default/files/files/Press/Reports/2018/AR/2018%20Annual%20Report%20I.pdf, pp. 22–28.

generally[54] and to respond to US concerns[55] on the Appellate Body specifically.[56] Academics have also continued to suggest solutions on how to reform the Appellate Body and its work.[57] The broader concerns of the US with the WTO dispute settlement system, and particularly with the approach of the Appellate Body, focused on numerous crosscutting issues presented in meetings of the

54 For a brief report of these efforts, see, WTO, *Negotiations to Improve Dispute Settlement Procedures*, available at, https://www.wto.org/english/tratop_e/dispu_e/dispu_negs_e.htm.

55 The evolution of persistent US criticism of the Appellate Body and its final actions that led to the current demise of the Appellate Body, efforts of other WTO Members to address concerns of the US directed at the Appellate Body as well as suggested solutions can be read at: Robert McDougall, 'The Crisis in WTO Dispute Settlement: Fixing Birth Defects to Restore Balance', *Journal of World Trade*, 52(6): 2018, pp. 867–896; Pieter J. Kuijper, 'From the Board: The US Attack on the WTO Appellate Body', *Legal Issues of Economic Integration*, 45(1): 2018, pp. 1–12; Petersmann, above note 52, pp. 505–512; Cosette D. Creamer, 'Can International Law Recover? From the WTO's Crown Jewel to Its Crown of Thorns', *AJIL Unbound*, 113: 2019, pp. 51–55. Some of the authors, such as Kuijper (p. 1) and McDougal (pp. 878–879), state that the US was overly optimistic about the WTO's dispute settlement process at the beginning, but started to be critical of the system later.

56 See WT/GC/W/752, *Communication from the European Union, China, Canada, India, Norway, New Zealand, Switzerland, Australia, Republic of Korea, Iceland, Singapore and Mexico to the General Council*, dated 23 November 2018 and WT/GC/W/753, *Communication from the European Union, China and India to the General Council*, dated 23 November 2018.

57 A notable read in this regard is Chang-fa Lo, Junji Nakagawa and Tsai-fang Chen (eds.), *The Appellate Body of the WTO and Its Reform* (Singapore: Springer, 2020). The Journal of World Investment & Trade also published a special issue containing four relevant articles: Giorgio Sacerdoti, 'Solving the WTO Dispute Settlement System Crisis: An Introduction', *Journal of World Investment & Trade*, 29(6): 2020, pp. 785–791; Yuka Fukunaga, 'The Appellate Body's Power to Interpret the WTO Agreements and WTO Members' Power to Disagree with the Appellate Body', *Journal of World Investment & Trade*, 29(6): 2020, pp. 792–819; Geraldo Vidigal, 'Living Without the Appellate Body: Multilateral, Bilateral and Plurilateral Solutions to the WTO Dispute Settlement Crisis', *Journal of World Investment &Trade*, 29(6): 2020, pp. 862–890; Joshua Paine, 'The WTO's Dispute Settlement Body as a Voice Mechanism', *Journal of World Investment & Trade*, 29(6): 2020, pp. 820–861. See also, Tomohiko Kobayashi and Yuka Fukunaga, 'Like a Rolling Stone: Exploring Viable Options for the WTO Dispute Settlement Mechanism to Evolve Forward in the Post-WTO Era', in Meredith Kolsky Lewis *et al.*, *A Post-WTO International Legal Order: Utopian, Dystopian and Other Scenarios* (Cham: Springer, 2020), pp. 133–147; Jennifer Hillman, 'Three Approaches to Fixing the World Trade Organization's Appellate Body: The Good, the Bad and the Ugly?' (*Institute of International Economic Law, Georgetown University Law Center, December 2018*), available at, https://georgetown.app.box.com/s/966hfvosmran4m31biblgfszj42za40b; Kuijper, above note 55. For a criticism of US opposition to the Appellate Body, see, James Bacchus, 'Might Unmakes Right: The American Assault on the Rule of Law in World Trade', Centre for International Governance Innovation' CIGI Papers No. 173 (May 2018), available at, https://www.cigionline.org/sites/default/files/documents/Paper%20no.173.pdf.

WTO Dispute Settlement Body, all of which resulted in a situation where the "dispute-settlement process over the years has really diminished what we bargained for or imposed obligations that we do not believe we agreed to."[58]

The issue of the interaction (interoperability) between WTO law and the other fields of international law, the subject of this book, has been made an express issue neither of the specific US objections directed at the now-defunct Appellate Body nor any one of the general discussions concerning the strengthening of the WTO dispute settlement system. However, there is a possibility for the concept of interoperability to be impacted by the results of these discussions and actions concerning the WTO dispute settlement system. Three of the specific criticisms of the US directed at the Appellate Body are related to the latter's practice of interpreting the legal texts of the WTO Agreement.[59] The US claims that rights and obligations under the WTO Agreement are being added to or diminished as a result of the Appellate Body's interpretation of key terms in the legal texts of the WTO Agreement. For instance, the US objects to the Appellate Body's interpretation of the term 'public body'.[60] Moreover, the US expressed its concern on what it called 'non-text-based interpretation' of some legal texts of the WTO Agreement (the US refers, by way of example, to Article XIX of the GATT 1994 and the Safeguards Agreement), a practice that the US said "has seriously undermined the ability of Members to use safeguards measures [as the] Appellate Body has disregarded the agreed WTO text and read text into the Agreement, applying standards of its own devising".[61]

The other Members of the WTO have not yet specifically responded to – or may even have disregarded – the US concern on the Appellate Body's way of interpreting the WTO Agreement.[62] It is possible, however, that the Appellate Body, should it be reconstituted, or the arbitrators of the MPIA[63] may, as a result

58 Markus Wagner, 'The Impending Demise of the WTO Appellate Body: From Centrepiece to Historical Relic?', in Lo, Nakagawa and Chen, ibid, p. 80; Petersmann, above note 52, pp. 507–508.

59 These are: the Appellate Body's misapplication of the standard of review (review of facts and review of a Member's domestic law *de novo*); the Appellate Body's claim that its reports are entitled to be treated as precedent; and adding to or diminishing the rights and obligations of Members in various disputes.

60 United States Trade Representative, above note 53, p. 23 (f.n. 17).

61 Ibid, p. 24.

62 See recommendations by the respective WTO Members in WT/GC/W/752 and WT/GC/W/753, above note 56.

63 The MPIA is an EU-led arrangement established on 27 March 2020 and in effect since 30 April 2020. Its purpose is to function under Article 25 of the DSU as an *ex ante* appeal system to preserve the two-tier dispute settlement system of the DSU until the Appellate Body is once again able to function. The MPIA has now begun to release reports. For more

of the limitations of the MPIA or to accommodate US concerns, be more cautious in following the Appellate Body's trend of actively encouraging the use of non-WTO rules and principles in interpreting or refining the meanings of the legal texts of the WTO Agreement.[64] This can in turn affect the ability of the interpretations to be developed (or refined) for the provisions of the legal texts of the WTO Agreement to influence interpretation and practice in other fields of international law. The interpretation developed for the concept of necessity in WTO law and its future refinement as well as its potential interoperability with the concepts of necessity in other fields of international law should be looked at in the context of the developments discussed in this Sub-section 11.2.

By way of summarizing the result of the discussions in Sections 11.1 and 11.2, therefore, there is substantial experience whereby, on top of instances where WTO law must make reference to other fields of international law/other treaties, the dispute settlement organs on both sides have made references to, and adopted, principles and interpretations developed in the other regime, although between WTO law and the other fields of international law, the flow has been more towards the WTO law than otherwise. The impact of the current crisis of the WTO dispute settlement process on this trend of interoperability is yet to be seen.

Given this trend, it is possible also that the two regimes (WTO law and the other fields of international law) may each other learn from interpretations respectively developed for concepts or rules that are contained in both regimes. One of these concepts is necessity which, as shown in Chapters 5–9, has had respective interpretations developed for it within the WTO Agreement and the other fields of international law, particularly CIL as codified in Article 25 of the ARSIWA. This book aims to show that there is a potential for interaction between these respective concepts of necessity and will, in Chapter 12, argue that the influence could flow more from the concept in WTO law to the

detailed information on the rationale and process of forming the Multi-Party Interim Appeal Arbitration Arrangement, see, Elisa Baroncini, 'The EU Approach to Overcome the WTO Dispute Settlement Vacuum: Article 25 DSU Interim Appeal Arbitration as a Bridge Between Renovation and Innovation', in Lewis *et al.*, above note 57, pp. 115–131. See also, strong support of such an arrangement in Elisa Baroncini, 'Preserving the Appellate State in the WTO Dispute Settlement Mechanism: The EU and the Multi-Party Interim Appeal Arbitration Arrangement', *The Italian Yearbook of International Law*, 29(1): 2020, pp. 33–52; Vidigal, above note 57, pp. 881–889; Xiaoling Li, 'DSU Article 25 Appeal Arbitration: A Viable Interim Alternative to the WTO Appellate Body?', *Global Trade and Customs Journal*, 15(10): 2020, pp. 461–478.

64 For observations regarding limitations of the MPIA and potential issues regarding its practice of interpreting the legal texts of WTO Agreement, see, Lester, above note 51.

concept in CIL than the other way round. Section 11.3 will lay the ground for the exercise of interoperability by first discussing, in Sub-section 11.3.1, the similarities and differences between the concepts of necessity in WTO law and CIL. Sub-section 11.3.2 will then discuss if there is a conflict between the two concepts as the final step before conducting the exercise of interoperability in Chapter 12.

11.3 Contrasting the Concepts of Necessity in WTO Law and CIL

This section will compare and contrast the concepts of necessity developed under WTO law and the other fields of international law, especially the concept of necessity in CIL as codified in Article 25 of the ARSIWA, to find out if there is a conflict between them as they apply to trade relations between states.

11.3.1 *Similarities and Differences between the Concepts of Necessity in WTO Law and CIL*

Chapters 5–9 showed that of the nine fields of international law examined (i.e., WTO law, the law of state responsibility as codified in the ARSIWA, IEnL, IIL, IHL, the law of use of force, the law of responsibility of international organizations as codified in the DARIO, IHRL and ICL), WTO law and ARSIWA have well-developed concepts of necessity not only because of the substantial case law on the concepts of necessity, but also the increasing influence of their respective concepts of necessity on, or adoption by, the other fields of international law. The following is a summary of how the concept of necessity is perceived in the other seven fields of international law.

1. Regarding IEnL, it was observed that both WTO law (for example, in *US – Shrimp (1998)*) and ARSIWA (for example, the *Gabčíkovo-Nagymaros Project* case) have been applied to examine environmental justifications depending mainly on where the parties took their cases to. In Sub-section 5.3.4, a few considerations that could be employed in choosing either the WTO law or the concept of necessity in CIL in disputes involving environmental necessity defenses were also identified.
2. Regarding IIL, it was discussed in Section 5.5 that the necessity defense in the term 'necessary for the maintenance of public order' usually inserted in bilateral investment treaties has been interpreted by tribunals either along the lines of Article 25 of the ARSIWA or the General Exceptions of the GATT 1994.

3. Regarding IHL, Sub-section 5.2.4 listed what could be identified as possible elements of necessity in IHL.[65]
4. Regarding the law of use of force under the UN Charter, Sub-section 5.1.3 discussed that necessity (either as part, or independent, of self-defense), as contained in the ARSIWA, may be used as a possible exception to the prohibition on the use of force and as an excuse to three contentious state actions viz. pre-emptive and preventive self-defense, humanitarian intervention and rescuing nationals abroad.
5. Regarding the DARIO, it was briefly stated in Section 5.8 that there is a dearth of practice on the subject but that the DARIO has adopted the ARSIWA concept of necessity and is therefore expected to adopt the interpretation developed for the ARSIWA concept of necessity.
6. Regarding IHRL, it was noted in Sub-section 5.6.2 that since necessity as contained in IHRL instruments reflects a primary norm, the ARSIWA concept of necessity has not been welcomed for use in interpreting IHRL provisions of necessity. Instead, a list of what could constitute necessity in IHRL was provided as extracted from the texts and case law of IHRL.[66]
7. Regarding ICL, it was stated in Sub-section 5.7.4 that the texts of most ICL treaties link the defense of necessity to the IHL concept of necessity and based on the texts and case law of ICL some elements of necessity can be extracted for ICL, especially for war crimes.[67]

As repeatedly mentioned in the previous chapters, given the limitations of the other seven fields of international law, the ARSIWA definition of necessity (which has codified the concept of necessity in CIL), given its influence on the other fields of international law, will be picked up for the purpose of comparison with the concept of necessity in WTO law.

As identified by Crawford, the elements of necessity in Article 25 of the ARSIWA are the following: (1) the action taken must be the only way to safeguard an essential interest from grave and imminent peril; (2) the action must

65 Nobuo Hayashi, 'Requirements of Military Necessity in International Humanitarian Law and International Criminal Law', *Boston University International Law Journal*, 28(1): 2010, pp. 62–93.

66 Christoph Schreuer, 'Derogation of Human Rights in Situations of Public Emergency: The Experience of the European Convention on Human Rights', *Yale Journal of World Public Order*, 9(1): 1982, pp. 126–129; Rosalyn Higgins, 'Derogations under Human Rights Treaties', *British Yearbook of International Law*, 48(1): 1976–1977, pp. 302–305; Aly Mokhtar, 'Human Rights Obligations *v.* Derogations: Article 15 of the European Convention on Human Rights', *International Journal of Human Rights*, 8(1): 2004, pp. 71–72.

67 Geert-Jan Alexander Knoops, *Defenses in Contemporary International Criminal Law* (2nd ed.) (Leiden: Martinus Nijhoff Publishers, 2008), p. 86.

not impair essential interests of states which are owed the obligation or the international community as a whole; (3) the international obligation in question must not exclude the possibility of invoking necessity; (4) necessity cannot be invoked if the state has contributed to the situation of necessity; moreover, (5) the upholding of the disputed measure as a necessary measure does not preclude the payment of compensation to the state(s) injured by the measure; and (6) the measure cannot be upheld against a peremptory norm of GIL.

The working definition for the concept of necessity in WTO law was laid out by the Appellate Body in *Brazil – Retreaded Tyres* (*2007*):

> In order to determine whether a measure is 'necessary' within the meaning of Article XX(b) of the GATT 1994, a panel must assess all the relevant factors, particularly the extent of the contribution to the achievement of a measure's objective and its trade restrictiveness, in the light of the importance of the interests or values at stake. If this analysis yields a preliminary conclusion that the measure is necessary, this result must be confirmed by comparing the measure with its possible alternatives, which may be less trade restrictive while providing an equivalent contribution to the achievement of the objective pursued. It rests upon the complaining Member to identify possible alternatives to the measure at issue that the responding Member could have taken. As the Appellate Body indicated in *US – Gambling*, while the responding Member must show that a measure is necessary, it does not have to 'show, in the first instance, that there are *no* reasonably available alternatives to achieve its objectives'. We recall that, in order to qualify as an alternative, a measure proposed by the complaining Member must be not only less trade restrictive than the measure at issue, but should also 'preserve for the responding Member its right to achieve its desired level of protection with respect to the objective pursued'. If the complaining Member has put forward a possible alternative measure, the responding Member may seek to show that the proposed measure does not allow it to achieve the level of protection it has chosen and, therefore, is not a genuine alternative. The responding Member may also seek to demonstrate that the proposed alternative is not, in fact, 'reasonably available'. As the Appellate Body indicated in *US – Gambling*, '[a]n alternative measure may be found not to be 'reasonably available' ... where it is merely theoretical in nature, for instance, where the responding Member is not capable of taking it, or where the measure imposes an undue burden on that Member, such as prohibitive costs or substantial technical difficulties'. If the responding Member demonstrates that the measure proposed by the complaining

> Member is not a genuine alternative or is not 'reasonably available', taking into account the interests or values being pursued and the responding Member's desired level of protection, it follows that the measure at issue is necessary.[68]

What are, therefore, the similarities and differences between these two concepts of necessity?

The two concepts share the following seven key similarities.

1. Both concepts apply within the context of *balancing* the duty of states to abide by their obligations under international law, whether created by treaties or under CIL, and the right to protect legitimate interests of individual states, other states or the international community as a whole.
2. Necessity gives states the right to act in a manner that would otherwise be inconsistent with their obligations under international law.[69]
3. The interest sought to be protected by the measure at issue must be a *recognizable* and *tangible* interest, not one that exists in the abstract.
4. Both concepts are not *fully* self-judging, i.e., it is not left to the states to define what is necessary. The dispute settlement organs ascertain whether the measures were necessary. The investigation to determine whether a state appropriately used its necessity defense is generally an *objective*[70] test.
5. The process of determining whether a state appropriately used its necessity defense involves examining whether there were alternatives for protecting the interest in issue.
6. The process of determining whether a state appropriately used its necessity defense requires, although more highlighted in CIL than in WTO law, examination of the negative impact of the acts of the defending state on

68 Appellate Body Report, *Brazil – Retreaded Tyres* (2007), para. 156.

69 Paul Weidenbaum, *Necessity in International Law*, Transactions of the Grotius Society, Vol. 24, Problems of Peace and War, Papers Read before the Society in the Year 1938 (1938), pp. 105–132; Appellate Body Report, *US – Gambling* (2005), para. 291; Appellate Body Report, *US – Shrimp* (1998), para. 158.

70 Appellate Body Report, *US – Gambling* (2005), para. 304 (regarding the concept of necessity in WTO law); Lawrence Hill-Cawthorne, 'The Role of Necessity in International Humanitarian and Human Rights Law', *Israel Law Review*, 47(2): 2014, p. 240; Mirko Vasiljević and Marko Jovanović, 'Necessity as a Ground for Precluding Wrongfulness in International Investment Law', *Belgrade Law Review*, Year LXIV, No. 3 (2016), p. 17 (regarding the concept in CIL). It needs to be mentioned that under WTO law determination of the necessity of measures to be taken for protecting national security is self-judging. See, Section 8.3.

the specific states affected by the act and the international community as a whole.

7. Article 25 of the ARSIWA presents necessity in a *negative form* ("Necessity may *not* be invoked by a state ... unless ...") "in order to show ... that the case of invocation of a state of necessity as a justification must be considered as really constituting an exception – and one even more rarely admissible than is the case with the other circumstances precluding wrongfulness".[71] The concept of necessity in WTO law has been presented in *positive form* ("Nothing in this Agreement shall be construed to prevent the adoption or enforcement by any contracting party of measures ... necessary to ..."). Despite such positive construction, however, the concept of necessity in the General Exceptions of the GATT 1994/GATS has been interpreted with limits and conditions (i.e., strictly)[72] like the ARSIWA's defense of necessity.[73]

The two concepts have the following 11 key differences.

---

71 Report of the International Law Commission (1980), ILC, 33rd sess., A/CN.4/SER.A/1980/Add.1 (Part 2), *Yearbook of the International Law Commission* (Vol. II, part II) (United Nations: 1980), p. 51, para. 40; Roberto Ago, 'The Internationally Wrongful Act of the State, Source of International Responsibility', *Eighth Report on State Responsibility*, Addendum (1980), ILC, 32nd sess., UN Doc. A/CN.4/318/Add.5–7, p. 19, para. 11–12. See also, *Case Concerning the Gabčíkovo-Nagymaros Project (Hungary v. Slovakia)*, Judgment, 25 September 1997, ICJ Rep. 1997, p. 40, para. 51 and *Legal Consequences of the Construction of a Wall in the Occupied Palestinian Territory*, Advisory Opinion, 9 July 2004, ICJ Rep. 2004, p. 195, para. 140.

72 In *EC – Hormones (1998)*, the Appellate Body stated that "merely characterizing a treaty provision as an 'exception' *does not by itself justify a 'stricter' or 'narrower' interpretation of that provision* than would be warranted by examination of the ordinary meaning of the actual treaty words, viewed in context and in the light of the treaty's object and purpose." Appellate Body Report, *EC – Hormones (1998)*, para. 124. The Appellate Body's statement did not preclude a narrower or stricter reading of some exceptions in the WTO Agreement if the text, context, object and purpose of the exceptions so allows. The General Exceptions of the GATT 1994/GATS are one of these exceptions and have for long been interpreted narrowly. See, GATT Panel Report, *US – Tuna I (Mexico) (1991)*, para. 5.22. See also, GATT Panel Report, *US – Section 337 (1989)*, para. 5.9; GATT Panel Report, *US – Malt Beverages (1992)*, para. 5.41; Appellate Body Report, *US – Shrimp (1998)*, para. 157. Yenkong Ngangjoh-Hodu 'Relationship of GATT Article XX Exceptions to Other WTO Agreements', *Nordic Journal of International Law*, 80(2): 2011, p. 223; Panagiotis Delimatsis, *International Trade in Services and Domestic Regulations – Necessity, Transparency, and Regulatory Diversity* (Oxford: Oxford University Press, 2007), p. 177.

73 James Crawford, *The International Law Commission's Articles on State Responsibility: Introduction, Text and Commentaries* (Cambridge: Cambridge University Press, 2002), pp. 183–184.

1. Whereas the ARSIWA concept of necessity is text-based, the concept of necessity in WTO law was developed mainly by case-law without textual definition (except in the case of footnote 3 of Article 5.6 of the SPS Agreement) or adequate *travaux préparatoires*.
2. The concept of necessity in WTO law is presented either as an affirmative defense (for instance, in the GATT 1994/GATS General/Security Exceptions) or as part of substantive obligations (for instance, in the SPS and TBT Agreements). In CIL, however, necessity is always invoked as an affirmative defense.
3. The drafting history and practice of the application of the necessity defense in the ARSIWA seems to show that the importance of the interest sought to be protected is determined on case-by-case basis[74] (i.e., the trier must adjust the definition of the term 'essential' to the particular case at hand), whereas in WTO law practice the dispute settlement organs tend to have generally examined whether the interest sought to be protected is *objectively* important, although with due deference given to the degree of importance that the respondent Member gives to that value or interest.
4. There is a difference regarding the examination of the availability of alternatives. In WTO law, necessity must be examined in light of the reasonable availability of alternatives which are less trade-restrictive than the measure in dispute. In WTO law, alternatives – even ones that are less trade-restrictive and have an equivalent capacity to achieve the objective – that are theoretical, impossible to be taken, prohibitively costly or have substantial technical difficulties are not acceptable.[75] In the ARSIWA, however, the measure being challenged must have been the 'only means' of safeguarding that interest. The plea of necessity is rejected "if there are other (otherwise lawful) means available, *even if they may be more costly or less convenient* (*emphasis added*)".[76]
5. In the ARSIWA, the necessity of the disputed measures is examined in light of the general relationship between the defending state and the

74 *Yearbook of the International Law Commission*, above note 71, p. 49, para. 32.

75 Appellate Body Report, *Dominican Republic – Import and Sale of Cigarettes* (2005) paras. 68, 70; Appellate Body Report, *US – Gambling* (2005), para. 308; Appellate Body Report, *Brazil – Retreaded Tyres* (2007), para. 156; WTO Panel Reports, *China – Raw Materials* (2012), para. 7.490; WTO Panel Reports, *EC – Seal Products* (2014), para. 7.493; WTO Panel Report, *Argentina – Financial Services* (2015), para. 7.729; Appellate Body Report, *Colombia – Textiles* (2016), para. 5.74.

76 *Yearbook of the International Law Commission* (Vol. II, Part II) (United Nations: 2001), p. 83, para. 15; Crawford, above note 73, p. 184; Ago, above note 71, p. 14, para. 2.

states whose interests are affected by the measure. Specifically, examination of the degree of contribution of the defending state to the occurrence of a state of necessity is needed. The trier must also examine if an essential interest of the state towards which the obligation existed was seriously impaired. No such requirements have yet been contemplated in WTO law.

6. In the ARSIWA, a measure can be taken only to safeguard an essential interest 'against a grave and imminent peril'. In WTO law, however, the only requirement is that the necessary measure must have been applied in relation to the various interests contained in the relevant WTO agreement; there is no requirement that these interests or the defending state face grave and imminent peril.
7. On Extraterritoriality.
What in earlier ARSIWA drafts read as 'to safeguard an essential interest *of that state* against a grave and imminent peril' was, in the 2001 ARSIWA, changed to 'to safeguard an essential interest against a grave and imminent peril' to indicate that currently the defending state's right to protect "extends to particular interests of the state and its people, as well as of the international community as a whole".[77] In GATT/WTO law, the trend of interpretation – from GATT *US – Tuna I* (*Mexico*) (*1991*)[78] to GATT *US – Tuna II* (*1994*)[79] to WTO *US – Shrimp* (*1998*)[80] and to WTO *US – Tuna II* (*Mexico*) (*2012*)[81] – has been to progressively recognize that the protection of interests can extend from a Member's territory to beyond its territory provided that efforts to protect the interest within domestic territory have *sufficient nexus* with the area beyond national territory for the latter area to be accepted as a target for protection.[82] Thus, while it seems clear that an ARSIWA necessity defense allows extraterritorial protection, even delinked from domestic protection, it is yet to be clear, although it appears less likely, whether the WTO law allows a Member to

77 *Yearbook of the International Law Commission*, ibid; Crawford, ibid, p. 183.
78 GATT Panel Report, *US – Tuna I* (*Mexico*) (*1991*), paras. 5.24–5.29.
79 GATT Panel Report, *US – Tuna II* (*1994*), paras. 5.28–5.32.
80 Appellate Body Report, *US – Shrimp* (*1998*), paras. 121, 133.
81 Appellate Body Report, *US – Tuna II* (*Mexico*) (*2012*), para. 166.
82 For a brief observation on the said trend of view on extraterritorial application of domestic measures, see, Gabrielle Marceau, 'The New TBT Jurisprudence in *US – Clove Cigarettes, WTO US – Tuna II,* and *US – COOL*', *Asian Journal of WTO & International Health Law and Policy*, 8(1): 2013, p. 13, especially f.n. 43.

protect an extraterritorial interest that has no link to a related domestic interest.

8. Under the ARSIWA, necessity may not be invoked if: (a) the measure is not in conformity with an obligation arising under a peremptory norm of general international law;[83] and/or (b)the relevant international instrument excludes the invocation of necessity.[84] There are no similar exceptions in the invocation of necessity in WTO law. In other words, there are no 'exceptions to the defense of necessity' in the texts of the WTO Agreement such as the General Exceptions of the GATT 1994/GATS.[85]
9. Winning a plea of necessity *defense* argument in the General Exceptions of the GATT 1994/GATS does not finally lead to a successful defense for the responding Member. The responding Member must also prevail in the respective *chapeaux*. There is no such 'second-tier' test in the ARSIWA. This difference is, however, only tangential because the focus of this comparison is on the concepts of necessity, not on additional requirements for a successful defense.
10. In the ARSIWA, resort to necessary measures is without prejudice to the state's "obligation to compensate for the damage caused thereby, insofar as such damage is not made good by restitution"[86] whereas in WTO law there is no such obligation if the measure is accepted as necessary.
11. Based on the discussions in Chapter 1 on the difference between justification and excuse – at least based on the requirement to compensating the state whose interests have been affected by the 'necessary' measure and the obligation to continue to respect the essential interests of the other state even during times of necessity – it can be argued that the concept of necessity is presented in WTO law as a justification (i.e., as precluding wrongfulness) whereas the concept of necessity is presented in the ARSIWA as an excuse (i.e., precluding responsibility, but still giving rise to a duty to compensate).[87]

---

83 Article 26 of the ARSIWA.

84 Article 25(2)(a) of the ARSIWA.

85 Unless, of course, the *chapeau* in the General Exceptions of the GATT 1994/GATS is taken as an *exception* to the right to take necessary measures. The *chapeau* could be better taken as a *limitation* to the right to take necessary measures.

86 Article 27(b) of the ARSIWA.

87 The ILC rapporteurs had different opinions on the status of the ARSIWA defenses: Francisco V. Garcià Amador recognized the defenses only as excuses; Roberto Ago recognized them only as justifications and James Crawford was open to distinction between the two and, regarding necessity, he maintained that it better be viewed as an excuse. Federica Paddeu, *Justification and Excuse in International Law: Concept and Theory of*

11.3.2 *Is There a Conflict between the Concepts of Necessity in WTO Law and CIL?*

A question that follows the identification of the similarities and differences between the concepts of necessity in WTO law and CIL (as codified in the ARSIWA), and before trying to see if they can influence each other, is whether there is a *conflict* between them, as conflict is understood in the realm of fragmentation of international law or "conflict of norms" (to borrow the term from Pauwelyn). Some of the questions that will be addressed in this regard are: (a) What is conflict between provisions in treaties or between norms in different fields of international law? (b) Is there a conflict between the concepts of necessity in WTO law and CIL? (c) Has the concept of necessity in WTO law made it difficult to presume that there is no conflict between the concepts of necessity in WTO law and CIL (in applying the international law principle of presumption against conflicts)?[88] (d) As asked by Ohlin and May,[89] does the *lex specialis* rule apply only between *treaties as a whole* or does it even extend *to concepts (such as necessity) contained within* treaties or other fields of international law? In other words, does the *lex specialis* rule in Article 55 of the ARSIWA apply to the concept of necessity in WTO law *vis-à-vis* the concept of necessity in CIL in Article 25 of the ARSIWA? (e) If there is no conflict between

---

General Defenses (Cambridge: Cambridge University Press, 2018), pp. 37–49, 396; James Crawford, 'Second Report on State Responsibility', U.N. Doc. A/CN.4/498 and Add.1–4 (1999), pp. 59–60, paras. 225–231, especially para. 231. Roberto Ago, 'Fifth Report on State Responsibility', U.N. Doc. A/CN.4/291 and Add.1 and 2, p. 6, paras. 12–15, in *Yearbook of the International Law Commission* (Vol. II, part I) (United Nations: 1976). An ICSID tribunal, where Crawford sat as a member, also held that "Article 25 [of the ARSIWA, necessity,] is an excuse which is only relevant once it has been decided that there has otherwise been a breach of those substantive obligations." *CMS Gas Transmission Company v. Argentina* (ICSID Case No ARB/01/8) (Annulment Proceeding), 25 September 2007, para. 129. Sloane concludes that, despite the ARSIWA's characterization of the defenses as circumstances precluding *wrongfulness* (hence, justifications), the ILC's commentary gives a mixed signal as to whether they are justifications or excuses. Robert D. Sloane, 'On the Use and Abuse of Necessity in the Law of State Responsibility', *American Journal of International Law*, 106(3): 2012, pp. 482–486. Paddeu (pp. 414–429) presents detailed arguments for considering the plea of necessity under CIL an excuse because of such reasons as the duty to compare and balance the two interests (the protected interest and the harmed interest – hence the focus is on the state) and the duty of compensation. These exercises are absent in the concept of necessity in WTO law which lead to the conclusion that it appears to be a justification.

88 Clarence Wilfred Jenks, 'The Conflict of Law-Making Treaties', *British Yearbook of International Law*, 30: 1953, pp. 427 *et seq*.

89 Jens David Ohlin and Larry May, *Necessity in International Law* (New York: Oxford University Press, 2016), pp. 126–127.

the two concepts of necessity, has the WTO's concept on necessity, therefore, not been developing in clinical isolation from international law?

The discussion begins by defining conflict. Jenks, who first highlighted the issue of conflict of treaties in international law, defined conflict, as distinguished from divergence, as:

> A divergence between treaty provisions dealing with the same subject or related subjects does not in itself constitute a conflict. Two law-making treaties with a number of common parties may deal with the same subject from different points of view or be applicable in different circumstances, or one of the treaties may embody obligations more far-reaching than, but not inconsistent with, those of the other. *A conflict in the strict sense of direct incompatibility arises only where a party to the two treaties cannot simultaneously comply with its obligations under both treaties* (*emphasis added*).[90]

Karl also states:

> [T]echnically speaking, there is a conflict when two (or more) treaty instruments contain obligations which cannot be complied with simultaneously. This may be the case when treaties on the same subject-matter (*in pari materia*) diverge from each other. *Not every such divergence constitutes a conflict, however*. For *treaties may deal with the same subject from different points of view*; *they may be applicable under different circumstances* (i.e., in times of peace or war); they may simply offer a choice (e.g. between different ways towards the peaceful settlement of disputes); or *they may be supplementary to each other*. Sometimes a 'conflict' is merely factual or political: for example, a tariff agreement may lose its attractiveness for a State whose competitor is granted the same concessions, yet there is no legal conflict between the treaties involved.
>
> Incompatibility of contents is an essential condition of conflict; for treaties to conflict in actual fact, however, they must have at least one party in common, although the question may also arise in the abstract … In a way, conflicts which can be solved by resorting to interpretation or

90 Jenks, above note 88, pp. 425–426.

> legal principle are not real so much as only prima facie conflicts (*emphasis added*).[91]

In a more detailed application of the concept of conflicts, the *Indonesia – Autos (1998)* panel, asked to examine if there is a conflict between certain provisions of the SCM Agreement and Article III of the GATT 1994, and consequently if the SCM Agreement, by the conflicts rule in Annex 1A to the WTO Agreement, would be the only applicable law in the case, stated: "we recall first that in public international law there is a presumption against conflict" and explained its understanding of the concept of conflict as follows:

> In international law for a conflict to exist between two treaties, *three conditions* have to be satisfied. First, the treaties concerned must have the same parties. Second, the treaties must cover the same substantive subject matter. Were it otherwise, there would be no possibility for conflict. Third, *the provisions must conflict, in the sense that the provisions must impose mutually exclusive obligations*. '[T]echnically speaking, there is a conflict when two (or more) treaty instruments contain obligations which cannot be complied with simultaneously ... Not every such divergence constitutes a conflict, however ... Incompatibility of contents is an essential condition of conflict' ... The *lex specialis derogat legi generali* principle 'which [is] inseparably linked with the question of conflict' ... *between two treaties or between two provisions* (one arguably being more specific than the other), does not apply if the two treaties 'deal with the same subject from different point of view or [are] applicable in different circumstances, or one provision is more far-reaching than but not inconsistent with, those of the other' ... For in such a case it is possible for a state which is a signatory of both treaties to comply with both treaties at the same time. The presumption against conflict is especially reinforced in cases where separate agreements are concluded between the same parties, since it can be presumed that they are meant to be consistent with themselves, failing any evidence to the contrary (*emphasis added*).[92]

Marceau's working definition in her work on the conflict of norms between WTO law and MEAs is similar:

---

91 Wolfram Karl, 'Treaties, Conflict Between', in Rudolf Burnhardt (ed.), *Encyclopedia of Public International Law* (Vol. 7) (Amsterdam, New York and Oxford: Elsevier Science Publishers, 1984), p. 468.

92 WTO Panel Report, *Indonesia – Autos (1998)*, para. 14.28 and f.n. 649.

> A conflict may be defined narrowly or broadly. Generally, in international law, for a conflict to exist three conditions must be satisfied. First, two States must be bound by *two different treaties,* or *two different obligations*. Second, the treaties (or the obligations) must cover the same substantive subject-matter. Third, the provisions must conflict, in the sense that the provisions must impose mutually exclusive obligations (*emphasis added*).[93]

Conflict in norms under international law is usually discussed as it exists between treaties. Marceau's definition is important to this book as it opens the possibility for comparing *two different obligations* under international law (i.e., treaty *v.* treaty; treaty *v.* non-treaty, non-treaty *v.* non-treaty). The *Indonesia – Autos (1998)* panel also mentioned that conflict may arise between *two provisions in* two sources of international obligation. In this, Marceau joins Akehurst, Bos and Pauwelyn in recognizing non-treaty sources of international law for studying hierarchy and conflict in international law.[94] Thus, the discussion below proceeds with the possibility that conflict can arise between a treaty norm (for instance, the WTO law of necessity) and a non-treaty norm (for instance, the concept of necessity in CIL as codified in the ARSIWA). Let us go through the three conditions of conflict identified by Marceau to find out if there is a conflict between the concepts of necessity in WTO law and CIL. For the purpose of the discussion, the term 'obligation' which is at the heart of Marceau's three conditions has been interpreted to refer to the actions that the defending state must carry out under the WTO law and CIL regimes.

The first element for conflict is that the two states must be bound by two different obligations. We can begin with the *Korea – Government Procurement (2000)* panel's statement that:

> We take note that Article 3.2 of the DSU requires that we seek within the context of a particular dispute to clarify the existing provisions of the WTO agreements in accordance with customary rules of interpretation of public international law. *However, the relationship of the WTO Agreements*

93 Marceau, above note 11, p. 1084.

94 Michael Akehurst, 'The Hierarchy of the Sources of International Law' *British Yearbook of International Law*, 47(1): 1976, p. 273; Maarten Bos, 'The Hierarchy among the Recognized Manifestations ("Sources") of International Law', *Netherlands International Law Review*, 25(3): 1978, p. 334; Joost Pauwelyn, *Conflict of Norms in Public International Law: How WTO Law Relates to Other Rules of International Law* (Cambridge: Cambridge University Press, 2003), pp. 11, 89–157.

> *to customary international law is broader than this.* ***Customary international law applies generally to the economic relations between the WTO Members.*** *Such international law applies to the extent that the WTO treaty agreements do not 'contract out' from it.* To put it another way, *to the extent there is no conflict or inconsistency, or an expression in a covered WTO agreement that implies differently, we are of the view that the customary rules of international law apply to the WTO treaties and to the process of treaty formation under the WTO* (*emphasis added*).[95]

Surely between two WTO Members the concept of necessity in WTO law applies. The concept of necessity codified in Article 25 of the ARSIWA, as the *Korea – Government Procurement* (*2000*) panel observed, also applies as a norm because of its CIL status. The concept of necessity in CIL may theoretically apply if the disputing Members choose to settle their dispute by mediation, conciliation or use of good offices under the DSU and opt to apply the concept of necessity in CIL to examine the defense of necessity invoked by the defending Member.[96] If the case is, however, brought before a WTO panel, the question remains whether and how far the concept of necessity in WTO law – which will be applied to the dispute brought before the panel – was historically developed by intentionally 'contracting out' of the concept of necessity in CIL to, therefore, block the applicability of the concept of necessity in CIL in any way by the panel.

As discussed in Chapter 8, the history of the development of the concept of necessity in WTO law does not show that it was developed in conscious *contracting out* of the concept of necessity in CIL. What can be observed from the consistent application of the concept of necessity in WTO law is only that the GATT/WTO dispute settlement organs developed an interpretation of necessity *different* from that designed for the ARSIWA. In other words, since the two

95 WTO Panel Report, *Korea – Government Procurement* (*2000*), para. 7.96.

96 This idea of the possibility of WTO Members – if they decide to settle their dispute by mediation, conciliation or use of good offices under the DSU – opting to apply the CIL defense of necessity is based on the argument that the DSU does not oblige WTO Members to apply interpretations developed by the WTO dispute settlement organs. Peter Van den Bossche and Werner Zdouc, *The Law and Policy of the World Trade Organization* (4th ed.) (Cambridge: Cambridge University Press, 2017), pp. 168–169. It is also assumed here that in case the parties take their dispute to a WTO panel, the panel would most likely apply the 'weighing and balancing' test. It is known that mediation, conciliation or use of good offices give the parties more flexibility in mutually arranging the process of dispute settlement, including selecting the interpretation that should apply to the concept in dispute (necessity in this case).

concepts of necessity have not, in express terms, mutually excluded each other, there is a possibility, in principle, to accommodate some elements of the CIL (ARSIWA) concept of necessity in the concept of necessity in WTO law as the WTO panel resolves the matter. It appears, however, that there is one particular reason why the GATT/WTO adjudicators could have developed a concept of necessity for GATT/WTO law 'different' from that contained in the ARSIWA. In the ARSIWA, the plea of necessity is *residual* to the primary norm of obligations,[97] i.e., the plea does not apply if "the international obligation in question [primary norm] excludes the possibility of invoking necessity" (Article 25(2)(a) of the ARSIWA). In WTO law, however, the possibility to take necessary measures (whether as an obligation or affirmative defense) is a primary right of WTO Members.

The second element for conflict is that the obligations must cover the same substantive subject-matter. Both WTO and CIL concepts of necessity cover the subject matter of justifying an otherwise unlawful measure and, as explained in Sub-section 11.3.1., share many similarities in their definition.

The third element for conflict is that the provisions must *conflict* in the sense that the provisions must impose mutually exclusive obligations were they to apply to the same case. Sub-section 11.3.1 listed at least 11 key differences between the two concepts, some of which are fundamental (for example, the duty not to harm an essential interest of the injured state and the duty to compensate the injured state) as to indicate the existence of conflict between the two concepts. There are two points to consider in discussing this third element of conflict.

1. The first point is the possibility for simultaneous application of the two concepts of necessity in a dispute between two states in three different scenarios.
   (a) In a dispute between two WTO Members brought before a WTO panel (assuming other options have not succeeded), WTO case law has shown that the concept of necessity in WTO law will apply absent cogent reasons to make use of the concept of necessity in CIL. However, does this mean that the concept of necessity in CIL is automatically excluded in its entirety? Is the case law on the concept of necessity in WTO law authoritative enough to prevent the use of any element of the concept of necessity in CIL? Since, as it stands now, the concept of

97 Sarah Heathcote, *State of Necessity and International Law*, Thesis no. 772, submitted to the University of Geneva for PhD in Law (Geneva: 2005), p. 6.

necessity in WTO law has not explicitly contracted itself out of the concept of necessity in CIL, should, in the line of the *Korea – Government Procurement* (2000) statement on the co-existence of WTO law and CIL quoted above, some space be given for a coherent application of the concepts of necessity in WTO law and CIL?

At an abstract, and probably impractical, level though, it may be stated that the case of the two concepts is *more a matter of choice between them than their simultaneous application* (*a potential conflict*). This could be because the concept of necessity in WTO law is only a body of case law with a *de facto* value of precedence[98] and not an intentional, text-based exclusion of the concept of necessity in CIL. Thus, may the WTO dispute settlement organs choose from either of the two concepts in a dispute before them? It may even be asked if these organs can incorporate some elements of the concept of necessity in CIL into the concept of necessity in WTO law. The subsequent discussions in this Chapter and in Chapter 12 address these questions.

(b) In a dispute between two WTO Members which, under the DSU, agree to settle their dispute by mediation, conciliation, use of good offices or to special terms of reference for a panel (Article 7 of the DSU) and mutually agree to apply the concept of necessity in CIL to examine the plea of necessity raised in that dispute, the concept of necessity in CIL is more likely to be applied. Moreover, in the case of a trade dispute between two WTO Members arising out of a regime outside of WTO law (for example a free trade area or an investment treaty to which both WTO Members belong), the dispute will be brought to a non-WTO dispute settlement system and there is no obligation for the dispute settler to apply the concept of necessity in WTO law simply because the parties are WTO Members. However, as it happened in the Argentine financial crisis disputes (see, Sub-section 5.5.3), which were investment disputes between countries which also

98 Raj Bhala, 'The Myth About Stare Decisis and International Trade Law (Part One of a Trilogy)', *American University International Law Review*, 14(4): 1999, pp. 845–956; Raj Bhala, 'The Precedent Setters: *De Facto Stare Decisis* in WTO Adjudication (Part Two of a Trilogy)', *Florida State University Journal of Transnational Law* & Policy, 9(1): 1999, pp. 1–151; Raj Bhala, 'The Power of the Past: Towards *De Jure Stare Decisis* in WTO Adjudication (Part Three of a Trilogy)', *George Washington International Law Review*, 33(3&4): 2001, pp. 873–978.

happened to be WTO Members, either of the two concepts of necessity may be freely chosen. The case of the two concepts therefore becomes *a matter of choice between them, not their simultaneous application* (*a potential conflict*) in the scenarios presented in this paragraph.

(c) In a dispute between two non-WTO countries or a WTO Member and a non-Member, the dispute will be brought to a non-WTO dispute settlement system and the concept of necessity in CIL will likely apply, but this does not automatically prevent the application of the concept of necessity in WTO law simply because both parties, or one of them, are not WTO Members. The dispute settler can apply the concept of necessity in CIL and may incorporate some elements of the concept of necessity in WTO law or, if the parties agree, make use of the concept of necessity in WTO law. Nevertheless, this scenario once again creates *a matter of choice between them, not their simultaneous application* (*a potential conflict*).

2. The second point is how strictly must 'conflict' or 'mutual exclusivity' be interpreted between the two concepts of necessity? It was argued above that when two WTO Members bring their dispute before a WTO panel, there is a slim chance for the simultaneous application of (hence a *potential* conflict between) the concepts of necessity in WTO law and CIL. But, are the differences between the two concepts so fundamental as to warrant a conflict? The answer is in the affirmative. For instance, if the respondent wins the *justification* in the General Exceptions of the GATT 1994/GATS necessity defense, the defendant owes no duty of compensation or other care to the complaining party as far as the 'necessary' measure is concerned. However, the otherwise applicable *excuse* of the concept of necessity in CIL carries with it the duty not to harm the complaining party's essential interest and the duty to compensate. Thus, the two concepts of necessity which are likely co-applicable (without conflating their essential differences) in a dispute between two WTO Members have potentially conflicting characteristics within them. With this situation as a background,

With the situation described in paragraph (2) above as a background, let us now look how (or which one of) three WTO practices mentioned below on addressing 'conflict' or 'mutual exclusivity' between two norms applies to the concepts of necessity in WTO law and CIL. Reference has been made here to Pauwelyn who identified these three practices within the WTO Agreement.[99]

(i) The first is practice is a situation where, in case of mutual exclusivity, *the stricter of the two obligations prevails*. The panel, in *EC – Bananas III (1997)*, while explaining the interrelationship between the GATT 1994, on the one hand, and the Licensing Agreement and the TRIMS Agreement, on the other, used the relationship between Article XI:1 of the GATT 1994 and Article 2 of the Textiles and Clothing Agreement as a reference.[100] The Appellate Body, in *US – Upland Cotton (2005)* also allowed the same interpretation regarding the relationship between Article 3.1(b) of the SCM Agreement and the Agreement on Agriculture.[101]

(ii) The second practice is a situation where one seeks to *find ways for the simultaneous application of the two norms*. The *Indonesia – Autos (1998)* panel, in examining a possible conflict between Article III:2 of the GATT 1994 and Article 27.3 of the SCM Agreement, interpreted both provisions in such a way as to enable the simultaneous application of both provisions without mutual exclusivity because "Article 27.3 [of the SCM Agreement] is unrelated to, and cannot reasonably be considered to 'authorize', the imposition of discriminatory product taxes."[102]

(iii) The third practice is a situation where *conflict is strictly interpreted*. In *Guatemala – Cement I (1998)*, the Appellate Body, while examining the relationship between Article 17 of the Anti-Dumping Agreement and the rules and procedures of the DSU, stated that conflict between two norms of the WTO Agreement arises "in a situation where adherence to the one provision will lead to a violation of the other provision", i.e., when the two norms, owing to "an *inconsistency* or a *difference*" between them "*cannot* be read as *complementing* each other." Specifically, the Appellate Body added that

99 Pauwelyn, above note 94, pp. 188–197. After exploring potential conflicts among the GATT 1994, the GATS and the Agreement on Trade-Related Aspects of Intellectual Property Rights, Chase concludes that it is unlikely that a situation of conflict will arise within the WTO Agreement because of its nature, and the need to interpret it, as a 'single undertaking'. Claude Chase, 'Norm Conflict between WTO Covered Agreements – Real, Apparent or Avoided?', *International and Comparative Law Quarterly*, 61(4): 2012, pp. 791–821.

100 Panel Report, *EC – Bananas III (US) (1997)*, paras. 7.157–7.163, f.n. 403.

101 Appellate Body Report, *US – Upland Cotton (2005)*, paras. 537, 549–550.

102 WTO Panel Report, *Indonesia – Autos (1998)*, paras. 14.97–14.100.

"[a] special or additional provision [Article 17 of the Anti-Dumping Agreement in this case] should only be found to *prevail* over a provision of the DSU in a situation where adherence to the one provision will lead to a violation of the other provision, that is, in the case of a *conflict* between them." After analyzing the relationship between the relevant provisions of the DSU and Article 17 of the Anti-Dumping Agreement, the Appellate Body found no such inconsistency or conflict between them.[103]

How do these three practices relate to the two concepts of necessity being compared in this chapter? These practices were of course observed in light of possible conflict situations between legal texts of the WTO Agreement, not between a concept contained in the WTO Agreement and in a non-WTO law source of law. However, the extensive practice in WTO jurisprudence of referring to other fields of international law can be relied upon to also make reference to these three practices in examining whether there is a conflict between a concept in WTO law (necessity) and a concept in non-WTO, specifically CIL (necessity).

As far as the first practice mentioned in paragraph (i) is concerned, treaty interpreters of both concepts (the Appellate Body and the ICJ, for instance) have held that both forms of necessity must be *strictly* interpreted.[104] This does not, however, mean that both concepts of necessity are equally strict. It can be argued that the concept of necessity in CIL is stricter than the concept of necessity in WTO law because in the case of the former the measure must be 'the only way' to achieve the objective while in the case of the latter the existence of less restrictive and reasonably available alternatives that achieve the objective is examined.

As far as the second practice mentioned in paragraph (ii) above is concerned, the concepts of necessity in WTO law and CIL are the same in nature and essence[105] but with basic differences. Therefore, their simultaneous application seems impossible; one of them has to apply.

103 Appellate Body Report, *Guatemala – Cement I (1998)*, paras. 65–67. See also, Appellate Body Report, *US – Hot-Rolled Steel (2001)*, paras. 50–62 on the relationship between Article 17.6 of the Anti-Dumping Agreement and Article 11 of the DSU.

104 Tracey Epps and Michael J. Trebilcock (eds.), *Research Handbook on the WTO and Technical Barriers to Trade* (Cheltenham (UK) and Northampton (MA, USA): Edward Elgar Publishing Ltd., 2013), p. 44; WTO, *Principles of the Trading System*, available at, https://www.wto.org/english/thewto_e/whatis_e/tif_e/fact2_e.htm; *Case Concerning the Gabčíkovo-Nagymaros Project*, above note 71, p. 40, para. 51; *Legal Consequences of the Construction of a Wall in the Occupied Palestinian Territory*, above note 71, p. 195, para. 140.

105 Pauwelyn commented on the panel/Appellate Body views on conflict, *inter alia*, on whether the comparison was made between a *command* and a *prohibition*, or an *obligation*

As far as the third practice mentioned in paragraph (ii) above is concerned, there is, as indicated in paragraph 1(a) above, a possibility for a *potential conflict* between the two concepts of necessity arises if two WTO Members bring their dispute before a WTO panel. A WTO Member may in that scenario be bound by the concepts of necessity in WTO law and CIL simultaneously; thus, adherence to one can lead to potential conflict with the other (at least because of the CIL elements of not harming the essential interest of the injured party and compensating that party). But the WTO dispute settlement organs, seeing their role as primarily applying WTO law, and not CIL, will likely not apply the concept of necessity in CIL to the case at all, thereby avoiding any conflict. In other scenarios (paragraphs 1(b) and 1(c) above), there appears to be no problem of conflict because the situation becomes one of choosing between the two concepts of necessity, not their simultaneous application (and hence potential conflict).

The overall conclusion on the potential for conflict between the concepts of necessity in WTO law and CIL, therefore, is that although, owing to the similarities and differences between the two concepts of necessity, there is *a possibility for potential conflict between them* if two WTO Members bring their case before a WTO panel, the conflict can be avoided because the panel/Appellate Body will most likely, and the disputants would be expected to, resort to the concept of necessity in WTO law. What does this leave us with then?

One option is to cut the discussion short by resorting to the *lex specialis* rule under Article 55 of the ARSIWA to exclude the concept of necessity in CIL and apply the concept of necessity in WTO law in a dispute between two WTO Members arising out of the WTO Agreement. *Lex specialis* rule does not only apply between treaties as well as between treaties and non-treaties; it can also apply between rules or principles that are found in two treaties, two non-treaties as well as in a treaty and a non-treaty.[106] Article 55 of the ARSIWA

---

and a *right*. For instance, whereas Article XI:1 of the GATT 1994 is a rule of prohibition, Article 2 of the Textiles and Clothing Agreement is a rule of rights. The concepts of necessity in WTO law and CIL have the same nature as *rights* and/or *obligations*. Pauwelyn, above note 94, pp. 184.

106 Once again reference is made to Jennings and Watts who indicated that the principle of *lex specialis* "has sometimes been applied to resolve apparent conflicts between two differing and potentially applicable rules" and that the *specialis-generali* comparison is not limited only to between treaties.' Sir Robert Jennings and Sir Arthur Watts (eds.), *Oppenheim's International Law* (9th ed.) Vol. I (London: Longman, 1992), pp. 1270–1280. Koskenniemi's study of fragmentation of international law included a review of the case-law of *lex specialis*. He stated: "Also international case-law appears to accept the *lex specialis* maxim although again normally without great elaboration. Four different situations may be distinguished. The maxim may operate (a) within a single instrument;

states that "[t]hese *articles* do not apply where and to the extent that the conditions for the existence of an internationally wrongful act or the content or implementation of the international responsibility of a state are governed by *special rules* of international law (*emphasis added*)." Article 25 is one of the *articles* of the ARSIWA and can be made inapplicable before a WTO panel due to the *special rule* of the concept of necessity in WTO law.

The *lex specialis* rule may only settle the debate regarding 'conflict' between the two concepts of necessity in trade disputes between WTO Members brought before WTO dispute settlement organs. The other situations of 'choice' (paragraphs 1(b) and (c) above), where there is no conflict situation, however, can – and already have in practice (for instance, IEnL and IIL cases as discussed respectively in Sections 5.3 and 5.5) – create some *incoherence* (*not conflict*) in the understanding and practice of necessity. Given that the concept of necessity in CIL is, owing to its many elements, more difficult to meet – hence stricter – than the concept of necessity in WTO law, what would, for instance, happen if the parties to a 'environmental dispute' under Article XX of the GATT 1994 agree, under the DSU, to mediation, conciliation, use of good offices or to special terms of reference for a panel (Article 7 of the DSU), to apply the concept of necessity in CIL to examine the plea of necessity invoked by the defending Member? Moreover, as argued in Chapter 5, there are some fields of international law (IEnL and IIL, for instance) which, owing to their very nature, have 'selected' from the concepts of necessity in WTO law and CIL and completely different outcomes resulted in. In other words, what would have happened if the *Continental Casualty* tribunal had applied the concept of necessity in the concept of necessity in CIL, or if the other ICSID tribunals which applied the concept of necessity in the concept of necessity in CIL had applied the concept of necessity in WTO law? In PIL fields open to choosing between the concepts of necessity in WTO law and the CIL, a defending state would, it can be argued, want to resort to the concept in WTO law than otherwise, and the injured state would opt for the concept of necessity in CIL which is harder to meet. Avoiding forum shopping is one of the aims of coherence in any legal system, domestic or international and, therefore, better coherence between these two different concepts of necessity could at least reduce the risk of forum shopping.

(b) between two different instruments; (c) *between a treaty and a non-treaty standard* and (d) between two non-treaty standards (*emphasis added*)". Koskenniemi, above note 1, p. 40, para. 68; pp. 40–47, paras. 69–84.

Since some of the differences between the two concepts are basic, we must seek for ways to find coherence between the two concepts of necessity as they apply to international trade, investment, environment and related regimes. The need for coherence becomes more evident if one looks at the rise in the number of cases where necessity is, and will be, invoked as a defense before the WTO, investment tribunals, the ICJ, the ITLOS etc. Rolland observes that the growing spectrum of conflict between WTO law and other treaties or regimes will possibly push the WTO system to be "cognizant of external evolution" and be more adoptive of the rules developed elsewhere, including CIL, at a faster rate than it has been adopting.[107] The best tool to achieve this coherence, one advocated by this book, is to see if it is possible for the concept of necessity in WTO law to adopt some of the elements of the concept of necessity in CIL and *vice versa*. This possibility will be discussed in Chapter 12.

107 Rolland, above note 24.

CHAPTER 12

The Exercise of Interfacing the Concepts of Necessity in WTO Law and CIL

This chapter picks up from the conclusion in Chapter 11 that the similarities and differences between the concepts of necessity in WTO law and the other fields of international law, particularly CIL as now codified in Article 25 of the ARSIWA, as well as the potential for conflict between them necessitate the exercise of interoperability between them towards the higher purpose of ensuring coherence in international law. It will first layout the grounds/justifications for such interface (interoperability) and identify the possible interfaces. As noted above, such coherence has to be achieved between the concepts of necessity in WTO law and CIL.

12.1 Grounds for Considering Interoperability

12.1.1 *Grounds for the Influence of the Concept of Necessity in WTO Law on the Concept of Necessity in CIL*

The main reason why elements of the concept of necessity in WTO law can be utilized in interpreting or refining, as applies, the concepts of necessity in other fields of international law, particularly CIL, is that the concept of necessity in WTO law was not developed to exclusively apply to matters of international trade. In fact, it was developed within the context of accommodating non-trade objectives or interests (morality, public order, health/environment, law enforcement, national security etc.) in the General/Security Exceptions paragraphs of the GATT 1994 and the GATS and similar provisions in other legal texts of the WTO Agreement. In the concept of necessity in WTO law, concerns of international trade come only in the process of examining the trade-restrictiveness of the disputed/alternative measures and at the *chapeau* level (in the General Exceptions) where the measure already accepted as necessary is examined to determine if its application constitutes a means of arbitrary or unjustifiable discrimination between countries where the same conditions prevail, or a disguised restriction on international trade, i.e., to examine if the application of the measure constitutes a misuse or abuse of the exceptions listed in the General Exceptions paragraphs. Making use of this third element of the interpretation of necessity in WTO law (i.e., trade-restrictiveness) in

 | DOI:10.1163/9789004700000_014

interpreting or refining the concepts of necessity in the other fields of international law cannot be difficult since this element can be adopted by analogy (for example, in the field of IIL the 'trade-restrictiveness' element can be adopted as 'investment-restrictiveness' and in CIL as restrictiveness of whichever area (sector) the dispute is related to etc.). It can also be argued that the other two elements of the 'weighing and balancing' test (i.e., examining the relative importance of the values furthered by the contested measure and the contribution of the measure to realization of the ends pursued by it) may be adopted to the concepts of necessity in CIL and other fields of PIL.

12.1.2 *Grounds for the Influence of the Concept of Necessity in CIL on the Concept of Necessity in WTO Law*

Chapter 11 concluded that it is better to seek for coherence between the concepts of necessity in WTO law and CIL or to examine if they can influence each other than simply exclude these possibilities by considering the concept in WTO law *lex specialis* to the concept in CIL because of the possibility of conflict in the simultaneous application of both concepts before a WTO panel. Are there, therefore, grounds for adopting some elements of the concept of necessity in CIL into the concept of necessity in WTO law without adding to or diminishing the rights and obligations of WTO Members? There are at least six such grounds.

Firstly, effective interpretation, as noted by the *Korea – Government Procurement* (2000) panel, requires us to co-apply both concepts of necessity without adding to or diminishing the rights and obligations of WTO Members under WTO agreements. This should be understood, therefore, to mean that the panels can choose from the elements of the concept of necessity in CIL those that can bolster the existing interpretation developed for the concept of necessity in WTO law and avoid those elements that will contradict the provisions of the WTO agreements (for instance, the requirement in the concept of necessity in CIL that the disputed measure be the only available measure and the requirement of compensating the injured Member). Secondly, it needs to be highlighted that the Appellate Body, in introducing the 'weighing and balancing' test, did not state that the three elements of the test it identified and in use to-date are the only elements of the test. In *Korea – Various Measures on Beef* (2001), where the elements were first introduced, the Appellate Body left open the possibility for including other elements that may be recognized in the future by stating that the test required weighing and balancing "a series of factors which prominently include …"[1] In *US – Gambling* (2005), the Appellate Body reaffirmed that the fact that it referred to some elements of the test is

1 Appellate Body Report, *Korea – Various Measures on Beef* (2001), para. 164.

"not necessarily exhaustive of factors that might be considered".[2] In *Brazil – Retreaded Tyres* (*2007*), the Appellate Body again made it clear that the panel, in conducting the test "must assess all the relevant factors, particularly."[3] These statements can be referred to argue, as detailed in Sub-section 12.2.2, that some elements of the concept of necessity in CIL may be added to the three key elements so far used to interpret or clarify the concept of necessity in WTO law.

Thirdly, the non-trade objectives for which necessary measures are allowed under the various provisions of the WTO Agreement (health, environment, morality, public order, all of which are also parts of human rights regime[4] etc.) are inherently linked to other fields of international law. It has also been stated in Chapter 5 that the concept of necessity in CIL has been influential in defining the concepts of necessity in other fields of international law. Thus, in *'trade and …'* areas, the adjudicators must be cognizant of the differing interpretations of necessity developed in WTO law and the other fields of international law and see how these concepts can influence each other.

Fourthly, the practice of interpretation by the WTO dispute settlement organs encourages us to rely on relevant rules of CIL in interpreting concepts included in the WTO Agreement such as the concept of necessity. Since *US – Gasoline* (*1996*), the WTO panels and Appellate Body have, in accordance with Article 3.2 of the DSU, been interpreting WTO agreements by considering the rules of interpretation contained in Articles 31 and 32 of the VCLT as customary rules of interpretation of PIL. Article 31(1) requires that treaties be interpreted "in good faith in accordance with the ordinary meaning to be given to the terms of the treaty in their context and in the light of its object and purpose". Article 31(2) defines context as including the text of the treaty, the preamble to the treaty, its annexes and other considerations.[5] Article 31(3) further lists other elements in considering the context of a treaty one of which (paragraph (c)) is 'any relevant rules of international law applicable in the relations between the parties'. The term 'rules of international law' is understood to include GIL and other sources of international law listed in Article 38 of the Statute of the

2 Appellate Body Report, *US – Gambling* (*2005*), para. 306.

3 Appellate Body Report, *Brazil – Retreaded Tyres* (*2007*), para. 156.

4 On the inter-play between WTO law (inclusive of GATT 1994 Article XX) and human rights law, see, Gabrielle Marceau, 'WTO Dispute Settlement and Human Rights', *European Journal of International Law*, 13(4): 2002, pp. 753–814.

5 The additional considerations being: (a) any agreement relating to the treaty which was made between all the parties in connection with the conclusion of the treaty; and (b) any instrument which was made by one or more parties in connection with the conclusion of the treaty and accepted by the other parties as an instrument related to the treaty.

ICJ.[6] The term 'applicable in the relations between the parties' has, in relation to interpreting the WTO legal texts under the DSU, been generally understood either to refer treaties entered into by all WTO Members or, although this interpretation is disputed, to treaties that bind the parties to the particular dispute.[7] The former view has attracted criticisms mainly because of its potential to isolate other treaties as the number of WTO Members and number of members of the other treaties cannot be expected to be congruent.[8] Nevertheless, adopting the relevant parts of the concept of necessity in CIL to interpreting the concept

---

6 Appellate Body Report, *US – Anti-Dumping and Countervailing Duties* (*China*) (*2011*), para. 308; Marceau, above note 4, p. 780.

7 GATT Panel Report, *US – Tuna II* (*1994*), para. 5.19 and WTO Panel Reports, *EC – Biotech Products* (*2006*), paras. 7.67–7.75, 7.92–7.93; Appellate Body Report, *EC and certain member States – Large Civil Aircraft* (*2011*), paras. 845–846; Appellate Body Reports, *US – Anti-Dumping and Countervailing Duties* (*China*) (*2011*), para. 308; Appellate Body Report, *Peru – Agricultural Products* (*2015*), paras. 5.99–5.106. See also, Marceau, ibid, p. 781. Marceau argues that "[a]rguably, [Article 31(3)(c)] aims to promote 'coherence' in the interpretation of treaty obligations, so that the treaty and other relevant international law rules are interpreted in a way that is mutually supportive and avoids conflict, in compliance with the international law presumption against conflicts." Gabrielle Marceau, 'A Call for Coherence in International Law: Praises for the Prohibition against "Clinical Isolation" in WTO Dispute Settlement', *Journal of World Trade*, 33(5): 1999, p. 117. Regarding the highly disputed interpretation that rules contained in treaties signed only by some Members of the WTO can be considered as 'relevant rules of international law applicable in the relations between the parties' in a WTO dispute, see, Peter Van den Bossche and Werner Zdouc, *The Law and Policy of the World Trade Organization* (4th ed.) (Cambridge: Cambridge University Press, 2017), pp. 195–197.

8 Criticisms to the *EC – Biotech Products* (*2006*) panel's holding (ibid) (that only agreements to which all WTO members were parties could be taken into account under Article 31(3)(c) in the interpretation of WTO agreements) include those aired by the ILC's study group on fragmentation of international law. Martti Koskenniemi, 'Fragmentation of International Law: Difficulties arising From the Diversification and Expansion of International Law', *Report of the Study Group of the International Law Commission* (2006), ILC, 58th sess., U.N. Doc. A/CN.4/L. 682, p. 237, para. 471. For a similar line of observation, but focusing on the term 'parties' in Article 31(3)(c) of the VCLT, see, Marceau, above note 4, pp. 780–783. Van den Bossche and Zdouc correctly observed, referring to paras. 7.92–7.93 of the *EC – Biotech Products* (*2006*) panel report, that the panel "did not rule that a treaty interpreter may not take into account treaties to which not all WTO Members are a party, but that a treaty interpreter is not required to do so". They then take the reader through the rulings of the Appellate Body regarding the use, in WTO law disputes, of the rules referred to in Article 31(3)(c) of the VCLT. Van den Bossche and Zdouc, ibid, pp. 195–196. The relevant Appellate Body statement they referred to is Appellate Body Report, *EC and certain member States – Large Civil Aircraft* (*2011*), para. 845: "[i]n a multilateral context such as the WTO, when recourse is had to a non-WTO rule for the purposes of interpreting provisions of the WTO agreements, a delicate balance must be struck between, on the one hand, taking due account of an individual WTO Member's international obligations and, on the other hand, ensuring a consistent and harmonious approach to the interpretation of WTO law among all WTO Members."

of necessity in WTO law should not in principle be a problem because the concept of necessity, as part of CIL, applies to any Member of the WTO[9] and meets other relevant tests such as that it "must reflect the 'common intentions' of the WTO members"[10] or that of the relevant international communality.[11] Thus, elements of the concept of necessity in CIL as a "relevant rule of international law applicable in the relations between the parties" can be properly adopted to the concept of necessity in WTO law.

In *US – Anti-Dumping and Countervailing Duties (China) (2011)*, the Appellate Body was required to examine whether Articles 4, 5 and 8 of the ARSIWA can be referred to in interpreting Article 1.1(a)(1) of the Agreement on Subsidies and Countervailing Measures. The Appellate Body replied by reference to Article 31(1)(c) of the VCLT and regarding the term 'applicable in the relations between the parties' in that provision of the VLCT held that "the ILC Articles are not binding *by virtue of* being part of an international treaty. *However, insofar as they reflect customary international law or general principles of law, these Articles are applicable in the relations between the parties (emphasis added)*."[12] While reflecting on how the *Korea – Government Procurement (2000)* panel's statement on the interplay between WTO law and CIL[13] can actually be put into practice, Koskenniemi, who saw the interlay from the point of view of fragmentation and coherence of international law, also confirmed that the practice set by the Appellate Body would support non-WTO standards in international law which are relevant rules under Article 31(1)(c) of the VCLT.[14]

Fifthly, the substantial WTO law practice of reference to non-WTO laws and principles supports the argument that elements of the concept of necessity in CIL can be incorporated into the concept of necessity in WTO law. Scholars encourage the use of secondary norms of international law, particularly those in the ARSIWA, in the interpretative and enforcement exercises of treaties.[15]

9 Appellate Body Report, *US – Anti-Dumping and Countervailing Duties (China) (2011)*, para. 308.

10 Appellate Body Report, *EC – Computer Equipment (1998)*, para. 93; Appellate Body Report, *EC and certain member States – Large Civil Aircraft (2011)*, para. 845; Joost Pauwelyn, 'The Role of Public International law in the WTO: How Far Can We Go?' *American Journal of International Law*, 95(3): 2001, pp. 575–576.

11 Marceau, above note 4, p. 782.

12 Appellate Body Report, *US – Anti-Dumping and Countervailing Duties (China) (2011)*, paras. 307–308.

13 WTO Panel Report, *Korea – Government Procurement (2000)*, para. 7.96. See full citation in Sub-section 11.3.2.

14 Koskenniemi, above note 8, pp. 88–89.

15 Bruno Simma and Dirk Pulkowski, 'Of Planets and the Universe: Self-contained Regimes in International Law', *European Journal of International Law*, 17(3): 2006, pp. 492–493;

Simma and Pulkowski, for instance, state that "[i]n special systems [such as the WTO], the general international law on state responsibility may be relevant in various ways, including problems of attribution, *circumstances precluding wrongfulness* [such as necessity], or the irrelevance of internal law (*emphasis added*)."[16]

Sixthly, in light of the application (enforcement)-interpretation dichotomy,[17] it must be noted that the recommendation for adopting elements of the concept of necessity in CIL to the concept of necessity in WTO law vouched for in this chapter is not one for the more complicated exercise of application (enforcement), but for the less cumbersome tasks of: (a) interpretation; and/or (a) confirming an already existent interpretation in WTO law.[18] In this regard Marceau states that "the full extent to which Panels and the Appellate Body are required to use non-WTO rules *to interpret* the WTO agreements *remains somewhat unclear*" and that "the identification of these rules and their parameters, to the extent not agreed by Members, will have to be determined by Panels and the Appellate Body *on a case-by-case basis, by reference to doctrine*." She adds that when interpreting WTO provisions, a broad range of relevant rules of international law, including CIL and general principles of international law and those listed in Article 38 of the ICJ Statute must be taken into account.[19] She ends that analysis as follows:

> [W]hat must Panels and the Appellate Body do with these relevant rules of international law [under Article 31(3)(c) of the VCLT]? Article 31.3(c) requires Panels and the Appellate Body to "take into account" any relevant rules ... *This ensures that WTO obligations are clarified in a way that promotes coherence in international law. This proposal is compatible with the international law presumption against conflicts.* At the same time, any interpretation must respect the parameters embodied in Article 26 of the Vienna Convention, that a treaty is binding only on its contracting parties (*pacta sunt servanda*). The answer to this dilemma is that the purpose of this obligation to 'take into account' non-WTO rules is not to

---

Pauwelyn, above note 10, pp. 578; Koskenniemi, above note 8, p. 87, para. 165; p. 90, para. 169.

16 Simma and Pulkoswski, ibid, p. 507.

17 Where she stated: "Therefore, it is suggested that with regard to the use of non-WTO obligations, an important distinction seems to arise between the 'application' (and enforcement) of WTO provisions and their 'interpretation'." Marceau, above note 7, p. 113.

18 Lorand Bartels, 'Applicable Law in WTO Dispute Settlement Proceedings', *Journal of World Trade*, 35(3): 2001, pp. 510–518; Pauwelyn, above note 10, pp. 540–541.

19 Marceau, above note 7, pp. 122–123.

> impose, apply or enforce these non-WTO rights and obligations. *Instead, the purpose is to take them into account, where relevant, in interpreting the WTO rights and obligations in order to ensure that the WTO sub-system of international law develops coherently with other systems of law in light of the international principle of presumption against conflicts and for effective interpretation* (*emphasis added*).[20]

12.1.3 *Lessons Learned from the Two-Way Reasons of Interface and Limits*

What is, therefore, the lesson to be learned from the discussions in Sub-sections 12.1.1 and 12.1.2? In her seminal book on treaty interpretation by the Appellate Body, Isabelle Van Damme dedicates a whole chapter[21] on WTO treaty interpretation against the background of other international law. In that chapter, Van Damme argues that in interpreting the WTO Agreement the use of 'any relevant rules of international law' under VCLT Article 31(1)(c) has to be conducted in the context of the fragmentation and coherence of international law. Her argument also holds true when WTO law is used to interpret provisions in other fields of international law. Thus, with due care taken not to disturb the fundamental differences between the concepts of necessity in WTO law and CIL – with additional care to be taken not to add to or diminish the rights of WTO Members – there is ground for interoperability between both concepts. Such interoperability serves the purposes, *inter alia*, of: (a) enhancing coherence between both concepts of necessity; (b) enhancing, through coherence between the two concepts of necessity, the coherence between WTO law and the other fields of international law which are influenced by the concept of necessity in CIL; and (c) further consolidating the Appellate Body's assertion that the General Agreement [and by extension the WTO Agreement] "is not to be read in clinical isolation from public international law".[22] Section 12.2 will present the possible elements of interoperability.

12.2 Potential Interoperability

Some elements of the concept of necessity in WTO law can be used in introducing or further developing the concepts of necessity in other fields of international law. Sub-section 12.2.1 will discuss this exercise. Likewise, some elements

20 Ibid, p. 127.

21 Isabelle Van Damme, *Treaty Interpretation by the WTO Appellate Body* (Oxford: Oxford University Press, 2009), pp. 355–376 (Chapter 9).

22 Appellate Body Report, *US – Gasoline* (*1996*), p. 17.

of the concept of necessity in CIL can be used to further consolidate the concept of necessity in WTO law. Sub-section 12.2.2 will discuss this exercise.

12.2.1 *Contributions of the Concept of Necessity in WTO Law to the Concepts of Necessity in PIL/CIL*

The concept of necessity in WTO law can contribute to introducing or further developing the concepts of necessity in international law in the following manner. Its contribution to the concepts of necessity in other fields of PIL will be discussed first and then followed by its contribution to the concept of necessity in CIL.

Regarding contributions of the concept of necessity in WTO law to the concepts of necessity in PIL, it was noted in Sub-section 12.1.1 that two of the three elements of the 'weighing and balancing' test (the element of evaluating the importance of the objective sought to be attained by the measure and the element of examining the capacity of the disputed measure to contribute to attainment of the objective) can, owing to their 'subject-neutral' character, be adopted with relative ease to any field of PIL. The application of these two elements of the WTO law interpretation of necessity was clearly laid out by the Appellate Body in *Korea – Various Measures on Beef* (2001) in that "the more vital or important those common interests or values are, the easier it would be to accept as 'necessary' a measure" and "[t]he greater the contribution, the more easily a measure might be considered to be 'necessary'".[23] As far as the third element (i.e., the trade-restrictiveness of the measure), it was also argued that the essence of this element is 'restrictiveness' and that 'trade-restrictiveness' is examined because the 'weighing and balancing' test was developed for GATT/WTO law (trade regime). As this element gets transported to other fields of PIL, it was suggested, it can be analogized (individualized) into the field of PIL to where it is sought to be used. The resulting tests would, therefore, be 'investment-restrictiveness', 'human rights-restrictiveness' etc. Thus, the three elements of the 'weighing and balancing' interpretation of necessity in WTO law so far identified can be used in the other fields of international law in assessing the necessity of the measures disputed.

How about the further test of assessing the contribution and restrictiveness alternative measures including their technical and economic feasibility? The concept of necessity in WTO law examines the reasonable availability of alternatives (including their technical and economic feasibility) and whether they, while being less trade-restrictive, can achieve the same level of enforcement

23 Appellate Body Report, *Korea – Various Measures on Beef* (2001), paras. 162–163.

as the disputed measure. It then compares them with the disputed measure already examined. It may be argued that these rules developed for examining alternatives can also be adopted to other fields of PIL because of their subject-neutral' character.

Regarding contributions of the concept of necessity in WTO law to the concepts of necessity in CIL, the arguments made above in justifying the use of the three elements of the 'weighing and balancing' test to other fields of PIL also apply to CIL. Although the definition of necessity in CIL is now confined to the text of Article 25 of the ARSIWA, which must be narrowly and strictly read, there appears to be some room in introducing the 'weighing and balancing' test elements to the concept of necessity in CIL. In *Gabčíkovo-Nagymaros*, the ICJ, in interpreting the term 'essential interest' in Article 25 (then Article 33) of the ARSIWA, only explained how essential environmental protection is:

> The Court *has no difficulty in acknowledging* that the concerns expressed by Hungary for its natural environment in the region affected by the *Gabčíkovo-Nagymaros Project* related to an 'essential interest' of that State …
>
> The Commission, in its Commentary, indicated that *one should not, in that context, reduce an 'essential interest' to a matter only of the 'existence' of the State, and that the whole question was, ultimately, to be judged in the light of the particular case* … at the same time, it included among the situations that could occasion a state of necessity, 'a grave danger to … the ecological preservation of all or some of [the] territory [of a State]' …
>
> The Court recalls that it has recently had occasion to stress, in the following terms, the great significance that it attaches to respect for the environment, not only for States but also for the whole of mankind (*emphasis added*).[24]

The ICJ's statement can be read to mean that the Court is willing to look into the significance of the interest to the responding state, the environment in the *Gabčíkovo-Nagymaros* dispute. Introducing the WTO law's 'importance of the objective' test, it appears, would not be considered as introducing a new, non-textual test to Article 25 of ARSIWA, but a further reconsolidation of the Court's view of assessing 'essential interest'.

24 *Case Concerning the Gabčíkovo-Nagymaros Project* (*Hungary v. Slovakia*), Judgment, 25 September 1997, ICJ Rep. 1997, p. 41, para. 53.

An argument may also be made regarding the use, in the concept of necessity in CIL, of the 'contribution' element in the 'weighing and balancing' test. Article 25(1)(a) of the ARSIWA requires that the disputed measure be 'the only way for the state *to safeguard* an essential interest'. The 'weighing and balancing' test was first introduced in *Korea – Various Measures on Beef* (*2001*) while interpreting the phrase 'necessary *to secure compliance with*'. in paragraph (d) of the GATT Article XX. The test was later on adopted to paragraphs (a) and (b) in Article XX and the corresponding paragraphs in GATS Article XIV which contain the phrase 'necessary *to protect*'. Whether it be 'to safeguard', 'to ensure compliance' or 'to protect', the essence is that the disputed measure must be introduced to realize and enforce the objective. Thus, it can be concluded that the 'contribution' element in the 'weighing and balancing' test can be applied in interpreting the phrase 'to safeguard' in Article 25 of the ARSIWA.

Regarding the adaption of 'trade-restrictiveness', the argument made above about 'analogizing' this element to any field of PIL also applies to any field of international law about the violation of which the CIL defense of necessity is invoked. In other words, it is possible, in the process of examining the CIL plea of necessity, to assess the level of restrictiveness of the disputed measure on the field of international law in that case.

Adopting the requirement, under WTO law, of examining alternative measures to the concept of necessity in CIL is arguably difficult because Article 25 of the ARSIWA requires that the measure in dispute must be the *only way* for the state to safeguard an essential interest. The argument in the next paragraph, nevertheless, tries to find some space in Article 25 of the ARSIWA for examining alternatives. The concepts of necessity in WTO law and CIL welcome examining alternatives; they *only* differ in how far they are willing to accept more burdensome alternatives. The 'weighing and balancing' test in WTO law provides that if the proposed alternative measures impose an undue burden on a WTO Member, such as *prohibitive costs or substantial technical difficulties*,[25] or if the alternative measure is not technically and economically feasible,[26] the disputed measure is necessary because the alternative measure is not 'reasonably available'. On the contrary, the CIL definition of necessity provides that if there are alternative measures, even if they *may be more*

25 Appellate Body Report, *US – Gambling* (*2005*), para. 308; Appellate Body Report, *Brazil – Retreaded Tyres* (*2007*), para. 156.

26 Appellate Body Report, *Australia – Salmon* (*1998*), para. 194; WTO Panel Report, *Japan – Agricultural Products* (*1999*), paras. 8.72, 8.171; WTO Panel Report, *Australia – Apples* (*2010*), para. 7.1334; Appellate Body Report, *Australia – Apples* (*2010*), para. 337; WTO Panel Report, *India – Agricultural Products* (*2015*), paras. 7.521–7.522, 7.540.

costly or less convenient,[27] the disputed measure is not necessary. The question, therefore, is whether the body that examines the necessity of a measure defended under CIL, *in order to further crystalize the CIL requirement* that the disputed measure be 'the only measure', should, learning from the WTO law test of examining alternative measures, inquire if the alternatives, regardless of their being costlier or less convenient: (a) are more (or less) restrictive[28] than the disputed measure; *and* (b) can achieve the desired level of protection with respect to the objective pursued.

12.2.2 *Contributions of the Concept of Necessity in CIL to the Concept of Necessity in WTO Law*

Given the fact that the concepts of necessity in some fields of international law are, as discussed in Chapter 5, not as well-defined and developed as the concept of necessity in CIL, the following paragraphs will focus on the contributions that the concept of necessity in CIL can have in further developing and strengthening the concept of necessity in WTO law. Three such contributions are identified: (a) the notion of respecting peremptory norms of GIL as an interpretative aid; (b) the possibility for the concept of necessity in CIL to confirm the concept of necessity in WTO law; and (c) the element of examining the contribution of the respondent to creating the state of necessity.

Regarding the notion of respecting peremptory norms of GIL as an interpretative aid, Article 26 of the ARSIWA, which applies to all CPW, reads that "[n]othing in this chapter precludes the wrongfulness of any act of a State which is not in conformity with an obligation arising under a peremptory norm of general international law." Article 26 is understood to prohibit the use of CPW, including the plea of necessity, as an excuse to violate obligations arising out peremptory norms of GIL.[29] Peremptory norms of GIL (*jus cogens*) as well as obligations *erga omnes*[30] find themselves at a higher level in the hierarchy of international law and are justifiably used as instruments for

27 *Yearbook of the International Law Commission* (Vol. II, Part II) (United Nations: 2001), p. 83, para. 15.

28 See discussions in Chapter 8 (Sub-section 8.2.2) and Chapter 9 (Sub-section 9.3.3) on the concept of restrictiveness.

29 Ibid, p. 85, para. 4.

30 Article 53 of the VCLT defines a peremptory norm of GIL as "a norm accepted and recognized by the international community of States as a whole as a norm from which no derogation is permitted and which can be modified only by a subsequent norm of general international law having the same character". An obligation *erga omnes* is one that is owed to the 'international community as a whole'. Koskenniemi, above note 8, p. 193.

harmonizing treaties.[31] No primary or secondary rule is allowed to operate in contradiction with them.[32] As far as peremptory norms are concerned, Article 53 of the VCLT provides that "[a] treaty is void if, at the time of its conclusion, it conflicts with a peremptory norm of general international law." Article 64 of the VCLT adds: "[i]f a new peremptory norm of general international law emerges, any existing treaty which is in conflict with that norm becomes void and terminates."

The Appellate Body has read Articles 31 and 32 of the VCLT as the 'customary rules of interpretation of PIL' indicated in Article 3.2 of the DSU. As to the application of the other provisions of the VCLT, the *Korea – Government Procurement (2000)* panel's statement in that regard[33] indicates that there is a possibility to apply such crucial VCLT provisions as Article 53 as well as, by the same logic, Article 26 of the ARSIWA which make it mandatory to comply with norms that are above all treaties, the WTO treaty inclusive.[34] Moreover, there is some indication that the Appellate Body may have implicitly accepted the provisions of the VCLT which have attained the status of CIL as interpretative tools. Cameron and Gray argue:

> What constitutes customary international law in the interpretation of treaties is generally taken to be expressed in Articles 31 and 32 of the VCLT. The Appellate Body noted that there was a need to achieve clarification of the WTO agreements by reference to the fundamental rule of treaty interpretation in Article 31(1) of the VCLT. *The universal application of the provisions of the VCLT to international trade law is problematic*, as some WTO Members, including the United States, are not parties. However, the Appellate Body in *Japan-Taxes*[35] *implicitly resolved any uncertainty about its application to non-parties by declaring that the VCLT represents a*

31 Koskenniemi, ibid, pp. 166–206, paras. 324–409.

32 *Yearbook of the International Law Commission*, above note 27, p. 84, paras. 2–6.

33 WTO Panel Report, *Korea – Government Procurement (2000)*, para. 7.96. See full citation in Sub-section 11.3.2.

34 See, Petros C. Mavroidis, 'No Outsourcing of Law? WTO Law as Practiced by WTO Courts', *American Journal of International Law*, 102(3): 2008, p. 436.

35 The authors here refer to Appellate Body Report, *Japan – Alcoholic Beverages II (1996)*, p. 10, where the Appellate Body stated that Article 32 of the VCLT which deals with the role of supplementary means of interpretation has attained the status of 'customary or general international law' as Article 31(1) was similarly declared by the Appellate Body in *US – Gasoline (1996)*.

> *codification of customary international law and is therefore binding on all States (emphasis added).*[36]

Debatable as this may be, the panels and the Appellate Body cannot be expected to interpret the covered agreements in a manner that is absurd, illogical or unreasonable[37] in the sense of endorsing measures that are contrary to peremptory norms of GIL (*jus cogens*). By upholding the rule of not endorsing measures that are contrary to peremptory norms, the panels and the Appellate Body further endorse the Appellate Body's statement that the covered agreements must not be interpreted in clinical isolation from PIL. It is true that the obligation not to contradict peremptory norms has been specifically provided for in Article 26 of the ARSIWA whereas there is no such express textual obligation in the WTO Agreement. Nevertheless, this should not mean that the WTO Agreement has a loophole allowing the taking of enforcement measures that are contrary to peremptory norms of GIL. Therefore, the concept of necessity in WTO law, in light of the declared rule of not interpreting the covered agreements in clinical isolation from PIL, should abide by the principles in Article 26 of the ARSIWA and Article 53 of the VCLT that measures taken as necessary to protect the respective objectives should be validated if they are contrary to a peremptory norm of GIL.

Regarding the possibility for the concept of necessity in CIL to confirm the concept of necessity in WTO law, it was mentioned in Sub-section 10.2.2 that non-WTO rules which have been created subsequent to the WTO treaty may be used to confirm an already existing interpretation in WTO law.[38] It must be asked whether the concept of necessity in CIL came before or after the concept of necessity in WTO law. The doctrine of necessity in CIL has been traced to have started developing long before the GATT 1947 and took a definite form through codification in the late 1970s and early 1980s by the works of the ILC, but was declared a CIL rule in 1997 by the ICJ in the *Gabčíkovo-Nagymaros Project* dispute. Although the term 'necessary' was initially put into text in the GATT in 1947, the concept of necessity in WTO law, started to develop through interpretation in the early 1980s (see Sub-section 8.2.1) and took its current shape after the *Korea – Various Measures on Beef* dispute in 2001 (around the time when the ARSIWA was adopted by the UN General Assembly). There are

---

36 James Cameron and Kevin R. Gray, 'Principles of International Law in the WTO Dispute Settlement Body', *International and Comparative Law Quarterly*, 50(2): 2001, p. 254.

37 Appellate Body Report, *US – Zeroing (Japan) (2007)*, para. 125; Appellate Body Report, *US – Cotton Yarn (2001)*, para. 120; Van Damme, above note 21, pp. 279–280.

38 Pauwelyn, above note 10, pp. 540–541, p. 547.

parallels in the developments of the two concepts of necessity. Thus, it is possible for one of the concepts to be used for confirmation of the interpretation developed for the other concept. We can refer to the element of looking for reasonably available alternatives as an example of such interoperability.

The test of looking for reasonably available alternative measures as part of determining the necessity of the disputed measure is not a text-based requirement either in the legal texts of the WTO Agreement (except in footnote 3 of Article 5.6 of the SPS Agreement)[39] or in Article 25 of the ARSIWA. In GATT/WTO law, the interpretation of necessity (which examines the reasonable availability of alternative measures) was developed by case law. In CIL, the issue of examining the necessity of the disputed measure in light of the reasonable availability of alternative measures is widely discussed in the ILC commentaries for Article 25 of the ARSIWA. Although the search for alternatives is not a text-based requirement in the WTO Agreement (except in footnote 3 of Article 5.6 of the SPS Agreement) for critics who may question the wisdom of comparing the disputed measure with alternatives in WTO legal texts other than Article 5.6 of the SPS Agreement, the history of drafting of the Article 25 of the ARSIWA can be used as confirmation of the GATT/WTO law interpretation of necessity which requires examination of reasonably available alternatives.

Regarding the possibility of introducing, to the concept of necessary in WTO law, the element of examining the contribution of the respondent to creating the state of necessity, the best start is Article 25(2)(b) of the ARSIWA which provides that "necessity may not be invoked by a State as a ground for precluding wrongfulness if ... the State has contributed to the situation of necessity." Crawford explains this provision as "[f]or a plea of necessity to be precluded under subparagraph (2)(b), the contribution to the situation of necessity must be *sufficiently substantial and not merely incidental or peripheral (emphasis added)*."[40] This provision requires that the situation that triggered the taking of the allegedly necessary measures not be caused by the defending state. One can also read a requirement of good faith in this provision, as commented upon by Crawford, in the sense that the situation of necessity must have come

39 Which provides that "[f]or purposes of paragraph 6 of Article 5, a measure is not more trade-restrictive than required unless there is another measure, reasonably available taking into account technical and economic feasibility, that achieves the appropriate level of sanitary or phytosanitary protection and is significantly less restrictive to trade."

40 James Crawford, *The International Law Commission's Articles on State Responsibility: Introduction, Text and Commentaries* (Cambridge: Cambridge University Press, 2002), p. 185.

on its own and that the state should not be given the advantage of defending a situation of necessity that it partly or substantially caused.

The WTO law's 'weighing and balancing' test focuses on the *nature of the measure* not on the *situation that led to the taking of the measure*. Moreover, under some legal texts of WTO law (i.e., the General Exceptions in the GATT 1994 and the GATS), good faith of the defending Member is examined not at the level of examining the necessity of the measure, but at the level of examining the *manner of its application* (i.e., the *chapeau*). It may be asked whether the necessity test under WTO law should also include examining whether the defending Member substantially contributed to the situation of necessity. Reference may be made here to the *Continental Casualty* ICSID tribunal which, after examining the necessity of Argentina's measures by using the 'weighing and balancing' test, further examined whether Argentina, by not adopting preventive measures before the crisis, contributed to the creation of the circumstances that led to the crisis.[41] More specifically, in paragraph 227 of its award, the tribunal stated that its examination of Argentina's contribution to the situation of necessity was conducted *"in conformity with the concept of 'necessity' discussed above"*, a concept the panel adopted from the concept of necessity in WTO law. The 'weighing and balancing' test does not contain an element of examining the contribution of the respondent to creating the state of necessity. The question that follows is whether the *Continental Casualty* panel's reading of this element of contribution in the WTO law 'weighing and balancing' test can be *further confirmed* by the CIL requirement (under Article 25(2)(b) of the ARSIWA) to examine such contribution. It may, however, be counter-argued whether adopting this element of contribution (used in IIL and CIL) to the concept of necessity in WTO law would greatly diminish the chances of successful justification of measures under the necessity test in WTO law.

By way of concluding this Chapter, therefore, possibilities for interoperability between the concepts of necessity in WTO law and CIL has been explored and both concepts can influence each other to achieve better coherence and avoid the fragmentation and dissonance that has occurred (for example, in the Argentine financial crisis disputes) and may occur in the future. Coherence in the concept of necessity can encourage coherence in other concepts not only between WTO law and CIL, but also across different fields of international law. As to the potential for interoperability in general between WTO law and the other fields of international law, scholars had doubted if WTO law could

41 *Continental Casualty Company v. Argentine Republic* (ICSID Case No. ARB/03/9), Award, 5 September 2008, paras. 223–230.

make an important contribution to other fields of international law. In 1998, i.e., during the early years of the WTO, Palmeter and Mavroidis noted:

> PIL has clearly made an important contribution to WTO law. *It is not yet clear that the reverse will be true*, that other international tribunals will begin to see the WTO, as reflected in its adopted reports, as a source of law. Given the growing quantity and high overall quality of those reports, however, *it seems likely that it is only a matter of time before this recognition begins to take place*, particularly with regard to evidentiary and procedural issues that could have wider application.[42]

Partly responding to Palmeter and Mavroidis, this chapter has shown that regarding necessity, other fields of international law have more to be influenced by WTO law than the other way round. This chapter found some space for interoperability between the concepts of necessity in WTO law and CIL. It has also been mentioned that the *lex specialis* rule cannot fully address the issues around the simultaneous application of these two different concepts of necessity. It has been shown that the concepts of necessity in WTO law and CIL can, while maintaining their respective uniqueness, further enhance and crystallize their respective substance by the process of interoperability examined in this chapter. The possibility of such interoperability discussed in this chapter has tried to address an issue raised by John Jackson:

> A very important question … is whether IEL, or particular parts of IEL, *such as WTO law*, are part of international law generally, as opposed to being 'separate regimes' walled off from general [international law]. This author's view on this question strongly supports the position of IEL (and the WTO …) as part of international law, *and thus general [international law] norms not expressly embraced in the IEL (or WTO) treaty structure can have an impact on the application of IEL norms. Of course … there are serious and complicated issues about how great such an impact can appropriately be. Reciprocally, the practice of IEL activity can be highly relevant to general international law and its norm application (emphasis added)*.[43]

42 David Palmeter and Petros C. Mavroidis, 'The WTO Legal System: Sources of Law', *American Journal of International Law*, 92(3): 1998, p. 413. Also, Steve Charnovitz, 'The Field of International Economic Law', *Journal of International Economic Law*, 17(3): 2014, pp. 624 *et seq.* where he discusses "normative influences *to* [IEL from other fields of international law] and *from* [IEL to other fields of international law] (*emphasis added*)".

43 John H. Jackson, *Sovereignty, the WTO, and Changing Fundamentals of International Law* (Cambridge: Cambridge University Press, 2006), pp. 46–49.

In the context of fragmentation and coherence of international law, further study is recommended here to examine if the possibility for interoperability between the concepts of necessity in WTO law and CIL conducted in this chapter can also be applied to examine the possibility of interoperability between other rules or concepts in WTO law and other fields of international law, or between rules or concepts similarly found in fields of international law other than WTO law.

Conclusion and Final Remarks

This book aims, among others, to contribute to the discussion on the fragmentation and coherence of international law. In its 2006 report on fragmentation of international law the ILC observed that it is still possible to maintain coherence in international law despite the increase in its fragmentation. Different fields of international law and, as shown in this book, similar concepts which have different definitions in different fields of international law can, while respectively maintaining their unique definitions, learn and borrow elements of definition from each other and achieve more coherence through the process.

This book focused on the concept of necessity as it is defined in different fields of international law to test that possibility of coherence. It has been shown that despite basic differences in the substance and scope of the concepts of necessity in different fields of international law – hence fragmentation – there is a possibility to minimize those differences – hence achieve more coherence – by identifying elements of the concept of necessity in one field of international law which can be adopted by another field of international law and *vice versa*. However, any effort to achieve coherence by examining possibilities for interoperability between different definitions of a similar concept in different fields of international law or between different fields of international law needs to recognize the inevitability of fragmentation which is the result of the expanding universe of international law.

The exercise, as this book has shown, to find room for coherence between different definitions of similar concepts in different fields of international law (i.e., interoperability) can be conducted if:

(a) there are some basic similarities (or common characteristics) between the concepts found in the different fields of international law;
(b) the relationship between these same concepts found in different fields of international law (such as a *lex specialis* relationship or a rule-exception relationship) is carefully examined to ascertain the possibility for interoperability;
(c) there is a possibility for the same concepts found in different fields of international law to be alternatively applied to solve a given international dispute or influence the development of the interpretation of a similar concept in another field of international law; and
(d) the exercise of interoperability is conducted with the aim of avoiding conflict between the same concepts or the different fields of international law where these concepts operate.

 | DOI:10.1163/9789004700000_015

Analysis of the contribution of the WTO law to the scholarship on the fragmentation and coherence of international law must begin with the now common understanding that WTO law is part of PIL. What three of the first seven members of the WTO Appellate Body (James Bacchus, Florentino Feliciano and Claus-Dieter Ehlermann) aspired for the WTO law over lunch in Grand-Saconnex in early 1996 was not in vain. Their aspiration was to ensure that WTO law, the then 'new' field in international law in whose development they would play a pioneering role through their mandate as members of the newly established Appellate Body, "is a part of overall public international law".[1] The statement of the Appellate Body in *US – Gasoline (1996)* that the "the General Agreement is not to be read in clinical isolation from public international law"[2] followed a few months later. 28 years (as at January 2024) and 621 disputes later,[3] WTO law has not only asserted itself as a very actively developing field of PIL but also one that has reached a level where it can also influence concepts in other fields of international law. This book has shown that that the interpretations developed for the concept of necessity in WTO law and the other fields of international law and the potential for interoperability between the concepts of necessity in WTO law and the other fields of international law are testament to the fact that the WTO Agreement is not to be read in clinical isolation from international law.

This book considers the narration and analysis in Chapters 1–9 as a novel contribution to the scholarship on the concept of necessity in international law through its focus on comparing the concepts of necessity in WTO law and CIL. The discussions in this book were kept parallel with the development of international law from its early origins to the recent efforts to maintain a balance between fragmentation and coherence of international law.

An underlined truth throughout the latter history of the development of the concept of necessity in international law (from the Peace of Westphalia up to the present time) has always been that, although the exercise of absolute state sovereignty (manifested more brightly in exercising such rights as necessity and national security measures) was slowly reduced – not eroded – as a result of the constant growth of the system of international law, a balance has always

1 James Bacchus, 'Not in Clinical Isolation', in Gabrielle Marceau (ed.), *A History of Law and Lawyers in the GATT/WTO: The Development of the Rule of Law in the Multilateral Trading System* (Cambridge: Cambridge University Press, 2015), pp. 507, 509.

2 Appellate Body Report, *US – Gasoline (1996)*, p. 17.

3 As at 23 January 2024, the dispute settlement process page at the WTO website indicated a list of 621 disputes at all levels of the dispute settlement process. WTO, *Current Status of Disputes*, available at, https://www.wto.org/english/tratop_e/dispu_e/dispu_current_status_e.htm.

been kept between state sovereignty and international law obligations through the consent of states which are the fundamental actors of international law.

The narration in Chapters 1–3 and the practice of international tribunals as discussed in Chapters 2 and 6 showed that the concept of necessity was initially understood as having the same meaning, although often conflated with the meanings of other defenses such as *force majeure*, in any field of international law which recognized the use of necessary measures by the responding states. The second half of the 20th century has, however, shown that with the proliferation of many fields of PIL, hence the fragmentation of international law, the concept of necessity, as shown in Chapters 5, 7, 8 and 9, similarly started to have different meanings in different fields and sources of international law. The subsequent need to find space for coherence among the different fields and sources of international law, therefore, calls for examining the possibility for finding coherence among different meanings (interpretations) given to similar concepts found in these fields or sources of international law. This book has, in Chapters 10–12, shown that the concept of necessity is one such concept that can contribute to the process for seeking coherence among different fields or sources of international law.

Spanning from a single mention in the Trade Policy Review Mechanism to 27 mentions in the GATT 1994, the notion of necessity appears in different forms in 17 WTO agreements. These different forms include its presentation:

(a) either as an affirmative defense (as in the General and Security Exceptions of the GATT 1994 and the GATS) or as a substantive obligation (as in the TBT Agreement and the SPS Agreement);
(b) either as part of a general exception (as in Article XX of the GATT 1994 and Article XIV of the GATS) or a security exception (as in Article XXI of the GATT 1994 and Article XIV *bis* of the GATS); and
(c) with some textual definition (as in footnote 3 to Article 5.6 of the SPS Agreement) or without (such as the General and Security Exceptions of the GATT 1994 and the GATS).

It has been argued in Chapters 7–9 that the interpretation developed for the concept of necessity in the most frequently litigated provisions – the General Exceptions of the GATT 1994 and the GATS as well as those in the TBT and SPS agreements – can be adopted to concepts of necessity in other WTO agreements that are similarly worded and found in similar contexts. These similar interpretations of necessity – mainly represented in the form of the 'weighing and balancing' test including the process of examining the existence of reasonably available alternatives – are what have been identified in this book as the 'concept of necessity in WTO law'. It remains to be seen if the panels and the Appellate Body (should the latter be reinstated, or, failing that, any other body with appellate authority within the WTO system) will apply the 'weighing and balancing' test and/or the assessment of reasonably available alternatives in the concepts of necessity in other WTO agreements that have not been litigated yet. The trend of interpretation in the more than 70 disputes in which the concept of necessity has been interpreted so far (as at December 2023) shows that the panels and the Appellate Body (should the latter be reinstated, or, failing that, any other body with appellate authority within the WTO system) will probably adopt the same interpretation of necessity in the other WTO agreements as well. The book considers the analysis towards such probability as another novel contribution to the scholarship on WTO law.

The examination in Chapter 5 of the concept of necessity in eight different fields of international law showed a couple of trends in relation to the objective of this book. Firstly, the concept of necessity in CIL has influenced (can influence) the concepts of necessity in most of these fields of PIL. Secondly, some of these fields of PIL have already made use of the concept of necessity in WTO law. Given, therefore, the possibility discussed in Chapter 12 of the interoperability between the concepts of necessity in WTO law and CIL, there is a possibility for the concept of necessity in WTO law to be adopted to the concepts of necessity in these fields of PIL or influence them through its elements that can be adopted to the concept of necessity in CIL. The 2006 report on the fragmentation and coherence of international law makes frequent reference to WTO law as a field of PIL which operates within the context of such fragmentation and coherence. Although early on recognized as a 'self-contained regime', WTO law is designed, and has been interpreted, to be able to accommodate non-WTO rules owing mainly to the possibility in some WTO agreements for the direct application of non-WTO rules as well as the promise in the Dispute Settlement Understanding that the WTO Agreement shall be interpreted in accordance with customary rules of interpretation of PIL. This design may seem to have kept WTO law more on the receiving end of the interaction, i.e., a position where WTO law gets more influenced by rules and principles of other fields of international law than it influences them. Understandably, the "now extraordinarily elaborate jurisprudence of the WTO"[4] has grown with substantial utilization of rules and interpretative principles developed under the other fields of international law. However, as the number of disputes handled under the WTO Agreement increased, the visibility of WTO jurisprudence and its

4 John H. Jackson, *Sovereignty, the WTO and Changing Fundamentals of International Law* (Cambridge: Cambridge University Press, 2006), p. 60.

capacity for an outward influence also increased. Notable among such influences have been its influence on international environmental law and international investment law. The WTO Agreement in general and the GATS also have the potential to influence the international financial regime.[5]

Since the practice of international law encourages examination of interoperability between different fields of international law as well as between similar concepts that are found in different fields of international law, this book sought to include the concept of necessity within the broader trend of interoperability between WTO law and other fields of international law. The most visible and influential concept of necessity among the latter has been the concept of necessity in CIL as codified in Article 25 of the ARSIWA. Given the number of disputes that discussed necessity within WTO law and CIL and the proven potential of these two concepts of necessity to influence the concepts of necessity in other fields of international law, the concepts of necessity in WTO law and CIL were first compared along the lines of their similarities and differences. The grounds for the interoperability between these two concepts of necessity were then identified keeping in mind that the concept of necessity in WTO law is 'special' (i.e., *lex specialis*) in view of the concept of necessity in CIL. The exercise showed that there are elements that the concept of necessity in WTO law can adopt from the concept of necessity in CIL and *vice versa*. The interaction between these two most frequently litigated concepts of necessity in international law, it has been argued in this book, can contribute towards developing a more coherent concept of necessity in international law. The experience, in the ICSID, of conflicting outcomes as a

5 Notable contributions on the relationship between WTO law and the international financial regime include: Thomas Cottier, John H. Jackson and Rosa M. Lastra (eds.), *International Law in Financial Regulation and Monetary Affairs* (Oxford: Oxford University Press, 2012); Chin L. Lim and Bryan Mercurio (eds.), *International Economic Law after the Global Crisis: A Tale of Fragmented Disciplines* (Cambridge: Cambridge University Press, 2015). In September 2010, the *Journal of International Economic Law* hosted a special issue on international financial regulations wherein the link between WTO law and international financial regulation was discussed by a number of papers. Thomas Cottier and Rosa M. Lastra (special eds.), 'The Quest for International Law in Financial Regulation and Monetary Affairs', *Journal of International Economic Law*, special issue, 13(3): 2010, pp. 525–968. In the introduction to this special issue, the editors expressed their desire to open discussion on the relationship between WTO law and the international financial regime as follows (p. 528): "The papers of this Special Issue deal with general, cross-border topics and topics focusing on financial regulation on the one hand, and monetary policies and regulation on the other. Given the importance of trade regulation and World Trade Organization law, they seek to establish linkages and make comparisons wherever suitable. We hope to lay some foundations with these contributions to the Special Issue of the Journal and to encourage the much needed debate."

result of 'choosing' between the concepts of necessity in WTO law and CIL can be taken as a reminder of the call for developing a more coherent concept of necessity in international law. The book considers the analysis towards such possibility as its main contribution to the study of international law.

Since the broader context within which this book is intended to be read is the fragmentation and coherence of international law, a recommendation is made to further study whether the exercise of seeking interoperability between the concepts of necessity in WTO law and CIL can also be extended to interoperability between other rules or principles similarly contained in WTO law and other fields of international law (for example, the precautionary principle) or between rules or principles contained in different fields of international law.

Bibliography

Books

Agamben, Giorgio, *State of Exception* (translated by Kevil Attell) (Chicago: The University of Chicago Press, 2004).

Aquinas, Thomas, *Summa Theologiae*: Volume 38, Injustice (2a2æ, Questions 63–79) (Lefébure O.P., Marcus, trans., Cambridge: Cambridge University Press, 2006).

Bartels, Lorand, and Paddeu, Federica (eds.), *Exceptions in International Law* (Oxford: Oxford University Press, 2020).

Bassiouni, Cherif M., *Introduction to International Criminal Law: Second Revised Edition*, Vol. I (Leiden: Martinus Nijhoff Publishers, 2013).

Bellelli, Roberto (ed.), *International Criminal Justice: Law and Practice from the Rome Statute to it Review* (Surrey (UK) and Burlington (US): Ashgate, 2010).

Best, Geoffrey, *Humanity in Warfare: The Modern History of the International Law of Armed Conflicts* (London: Methuen, 1983).

Bowett, Derek W., *Self-Defense in International Law* (Manchester: Manchester University Press, 1958).

Brownlie, Ian, *International Law and the Use of Force by States* (2002 re-print of 1963 edn.) (Oxford: Oxford University Press, 2002).

Bücheler, Gebhard, *Proportionality in Investor-State Arbitration* (Oxford: Oxford University Press, 2015).

Cheng, Bin, *General Principles of Law as Applied by International Courts and Tribunals* (Cambridge: Cambridge University Press, 2006 edn.).

Cottier, Thomas, Jackson, John H., and Lastra, Rosa M. (eds.), *International Law in Financial Regulation and Monetary Affairs* (Oxford: Oxford University Press, 2012).

Crawford, James, *Brownlie's Principles of Public International Law* (8th ed.) (Oxford: Oxford University Press, 2012).

Crawford, James, *The International Law Commission's Articles on State Responsibility: Introduction, Text and Commentaries* (Cambridge: Cambridge University Press, 2002).

Crowe, Jonathan, and Weston-Scheuber, Kylie, *Principles of International Humanitarian Law* (Edward Elgar: Cheltenham (UK) and Northampton, MA (USA), 2013).

Cryer, Robert, *et al.*, *An Introduction to International Criminal Law and Procedure* (2nd ed.) (Cambridge: Cambridge University Press, 2010).

Davis, John A., *Naples and Napoleon: Southern Italy and the European Revolutions, 1780–1860* (Oxford: Oxford University Press, 2006).

Delimatsis, Panagiotis, *International Trade in Services and Domestic Regulations – Necessity, Transparency, and Regulatory Diversity* (Oxford: Oxford University Press, 2007).

Desierto, Diane A., *Necessity and National Emergency Clauses: Sovereignty in Modern Treaty Interpretation* (Leiden: Martinus Nijhoff Publishers, 2012).

Dinstein, Yoram, *The Conduct of Hostilities under the Law of International Armed Conflict* (1st ed.) (Cambridge: Cambridge University Press, 2004).

Dinstein, Yoram, *War, Aggression and Self-Defense* (2nd ed.) (Cambridge: Cambridge University Press, 1994).

Dinstein, Yoram, *War, Aggression and Self-Defense* (5th ed.) (Cambridge: Cambridge University Press, 2012).

Dolzer, Rudolf and Schreuer, Christoph, *Principles of International Investment Law* (2nd ed.) (Oxford: Oxford University Press, 2012).

Dordi, Claudio (ed.), *The Absence of Direct Effect of WTO Law in the EC and in Other Countries* (Turin: Giappicchelli Editore, 2010).

Dyck, Andrew Roy, *A Commentary on Cicero, De Legibus* (Ann Arbor: The University of Michigan Press, 2004).

Epps, Tracey, and Trebilcock, Michael J. (eds.), *Research Handbook on the WTO and Technical Barriers to Trade* (Cheltenham (UK) and Northampton (MA, USA): Edward Elgar Publishing Ltd., 2013).

Faust, Halley S., and Menze, Paul T., *Prevention vs. Treatment: What's the Right Balance?* (Oxford: Oxford University Press, 2012).

Fitzmaurice, Malgosia, and Tams, Christian J. (eds.), *Legacies of the Permanent Court of International Justice* (Leiden and Boston: Martinus Nijhoff Publishers, 2013).

Gardam, Judith, *Necessity, Proportionality and the Use of Force by States* (Cambridge: Cambridge University Press, 2004).

Garner, Bryan A. (ed.), *Black's Law Dictionary* (8th ed.) (St. Paul, MN: Thomson West, 2004).

GATT, *Analytical Index: Guide to GATT Law and Practice* (updated 6th ed., 1995).

Goethe, Johann Wolfgang von, *Faust: Parts 1 and 2* (Bayard Taylor trans., Dover Thrift editions) (Mineola: New York: Dover Publications, Inc., 2018).

Gourevitch, Victor (ed. and trans.), *Rousseau: The Social Contract and Other Later Political Writings* (Cambridge: Cambridge University Press, 1997).

Greig, D. W., *International Law* (2nd ed.) (London: Butterworths, 1976).

Gruszczynski, Lukasz, *Regulating Health and Environmental Risks under WTO Law: A Critical Analysis of the SPS Agreement* (Oxford: Oxford University Press, 2010).

Harris, William, *An Historical and Critical Account of the Life of Oliver Cromwell, Lord Protector of the Commonwealth of England, Scotland, and Ireland: After the Manner of Mr Bayle, Drawn from Original Writers and State Papers to Which is Added an Appendix of Original Papers, now First Published* (London: Printed for A. Millar, 1962).

Hart, H. L. A., *The Concept of Law* (3rd ed.) (Oxford: Oxford University Press, 2012).

Haugen, Hans Morten, *The Right to Food and the TRIPS Agreement: With a Particular Emphasis on Developing Countries Measures for Food Production and Distribution* (Leiden and Boston: Martinus Nijhoff Publishers, 2007).

Heller, Hermann, *Sovereignty: A Contribution to the Theory of Public and International Law* (edited and introduced by David Dyzenhaus and translated by Belinda Cooper) (Oxford: Oxford University Press, 2019).

Heller, Kevin, and Dubbe, Markus (eds.), *The Handbook of Comparative Criminal Law* (Stanford: Stanford University Press, 2011).

Hoeckman, Bernard, and Kostecki, Michael, *The Political Economy of the World Trading System: WTO and Beyond* (2nd ed.) (Oxford: Oxford University Press, 2001).

Hughes, Gerard J., *The Routledge Guidebook to Aristotle's Nicomachean Ethics* (London and New York: Routledge, 2013).

Hume, David, *The History of England: From the Invasion of Julius Caesar to the Revolution in 1688, Continued to the Death of George the Second* (compiled by Smollett, T.) (London: Joseph Ogle Robinson, 1833).

Irwin, Douglas A., *et al.*, *The Genesis of the GATT* (Cambridge: Cambridge University Press, 2008).

Jackson, John H. *Sovereignty, the WTO and Changing Fundamentals of International Law* (Cambridge: Cambridge University Press, 2006).

Jackson, John H., *The World Trading System: Law and Policy of International Economic Relations* (Cambridge, Mass.: MIT Press, 1989).

Jackson, John H., *The World Trading System: Law and Policy of International Economic Relations* (2nd ed.) (Cambridge, Mass.: MIT Press, 1997).

Jackson, John H., *World Trade and the Law of GATT* (Indianapolis: Bobbs-Merill, 1969).

Jennings, Sir Robert, and Watts, Sir Arthur (eds.), *Oppenheim's International Law* (9th ed.) Vol. I (London: Longman, 1992).

Johansen, Sigrid Redse, *The Military Commander's Necessity: The Law of Armed Conflict and its Limits* (Cambridge: Cambridge University Press, 2019).

Kant, Immanuel, *The Metaphysics of Morals: Texts in German Philosophy* (introduction, translation and notes by Gregor, Mary) (Cambridge: Cambridge University Press, 1991).

Kantorowicz, Ernst H., *The King's Two Bodies A Study in Mediaeval Political Theology* (Princeton, New Jersey: Princeton University Press, 1957).

Kiss, Alexandre, and Shelton, Dinah, *A Guide to International Environmental Law* (Leiden: Martinus Nijhoff Publishers, 2007).

Knoops, Geert-Jan Alexander, *Defenses in Contemporary International Criminal Law* (2nd ed.) (Leiden: Martinus Nijhoff Publishers, 2008).

Korman, Sharon, *The Right of Conquest: The Acquisition of Territory by Force in International Law and Practice* (Oxford: Clarendon Press Oxford, 2003 (reprint)).

Koul, Autar Krishen, *Guide to the WTO and GATT: Economics, Law and Politics* (New Delhi and Singapore: Satyam Law International and Springer, 2018).

Kurtz, Jürgen, *The World Trade Organization and International Investment Law: Converging Systems* (Cambridge: Cambridge University Press, 2016).

Lauta, Kristian Cedervall, *Disaster Law* (London and New York: Routledge, 2015).

Lazar, Nomi Claire, *States of Emergency in Liberal Democracies* (Cambridge: Cambridge University Press, 2009).

Lim, Chin L., and Mercurio, Bryan (eds.), *International Economic Law after the Global Crisis: A Tale of Fragmented Disciplines* (Cambridge: Cambridge University Press, 2015).

Lo, Chang-fa, Nakagawa, Junji, and Chen, Tsai-fang (eds.), *The Appellate Body of the WTO and Its Reform* (Singapore: Springer, 2020).

Louka, Elli, *International Environmental Law: Fairness, Effectiveness, and World Order* (Cambridge: Cambridge University Press, 2006).

Lowenfeld, Andreas, *International Economic Law* (2nd ed.) (Oxford: Oxford University Press, 2008).

MacMillan, Fiona. *WTO and the Environment* (London: Sweet & Maxwell, 2001).

Malanczuk, Peter, *Akehurst's Modern Introduction to International Law* (7th revised ed.) (New York: Routledge, 1997).

Marston, Daniel, *Seven Years' War* (Oxford: Osprey Publishing Limited, 2001).

Mattox, John Mark, *St. Augustine and the Theory of Just War* (New York: Continuum, 2006).

Mavroidis, Petros, *The General Agreement on Tariffs and Trade: A Commentary* (Vol. 1) (Oxford: Oxford University Press, 2005).

Mavroidis, Petros, *The Regulation of International Trade* (Vol. 1: GATT) (Cambridge, MA: MIT Press, 2015).

McGinness, Frederick J. (ed.), *Collected Works of Erasmus: Spiritualia and Pastoralia* (Toronto: University of Toronto Press, 2015).

Melzer, Nils, *Interpretive Guidance on the Notion of Direct Participation in Hostilities under International Humanitarian Law* (Geneva: ICRC, 2009).

Mills, J. Saxon, *The Genoa Conference* (London: Hutchinson & Co., 1925).

Mitchell, Andrew D., *Legal Principles in WTO Disputes* (Cambridge: Cambridge University Press, 2008).

Noortmann, Math, *Enforcing International Law: From Self-help to Self-contained Regimes* (London and New York: Routledge, 2016).

Ohlin, Jens David, and May, Larry, *Necessity in International Law* (New York: Oxford University Press, 2016).

Oppenheim, Lassa (ed.), *The Collected Papers of John Westlake on Public International Law* (Cambridge: Cambridge University Press, 1914).

Paddeu, Federica, *Justification and Excuse in International Law: Concept and Theory of General Defenses* (Cambridge: Cambridge University Press, 2018).

Pakaluk, Michael, *Aristotle's Nicomachean Ethics: An Introduction* (New York: Cambridge University Press, 2005).

Palmeter, David, and Mavroidis, Petros C., *Dispute Settlement in the World Trade Organization: Practice and Procedure* (Cambridge: Cambridge University Press, 2004).

Paparinskis, Martins, *The International Minimum Standard and Fair and Equitable Treatment* (Oxford: Oxford University Press, 2013).

Pauwelyn, Joost, *Conflict of Norms in Public International Law: How WTO Law Relates to Other Rules of International Law* (Cambridge: Cambridge University Press, 2003).

Post, Gaines, *Studies in Medieval Legal Thought: Public Law and the State 1100–1322* (Clark: The Law Exchange, Ltd., 3rd print, 2008).

Raimondo, Fabián O., *General Principles of Law in the Decisions of International Criminal Courts and Tribunals* (Leiden and Boston: Martinus Nijhoff Publishers, 2008).

Rao, P. K., *The World Trade Organization and the Environment* (London: Macmillan Press Ltd., 2000).

Redman, Herbert J., *Frederick the Great and the Seven Years' War, 1756–1763* (Jefferson, North Carolina: McFarland & Company, 2015).

Rodick, Burleigh Cushing, *The Doctrine of Necessity in International Law* (New York: Columbia University Press, 1928).

Rodrigues, Jr., Edson Beas, *The General Exceptions Clauses of the TRIPS Agreement: Promoting Sustainable Development* (Cambridge: Cambridge University Press, 2012).

Rogan, Eugene, *The Fall of the Ottomans: The Great War in the Middle East* (New York: Basic Books, 2015).

Rolland, Sonia E., *Development at the WTO* (Oxford: Oxford University Press, 2012).

Rosenne, Shabtai, *The International Law Commission's Draft Articles on State Responsibility*, Part 1, Articles 1–35 (Dordrecht: Martinus Nijhoff Publishers, 1991).

Sampson, Gary, and Whalley, John (eds.), *The WTO, Trade and the Environment: Critical Perspectives on the Global Trading System and the WTO* (Cheltenham (UK) and Northampton (MA, USA): Edward Elgar Publishing Ltd., 2005).

Sands, Philippe, *Principles of International Environmental Law* (2nd ed.) (Cambridge: Cambridge University Press, 2003).

Schabas, William A., and Bernaz, Nadia (eds.), *Routledge Handbook of International Criminal Law* (London and New York: Routledge, 2011).

Schachter, Oscar, *International Law in Theory and Practice* (Dordrecht: Martinus Nijhoff Publishers, 1991).

Schroeder, Paul W., *Metternich's Diplomacy at its Zenith, 1820–1823: Austria and the Congresses of Troppau, Laibach, and Verona* (Austin: University of Texas Press, 1962).

Scott, Joanne, *The WTO Agreement on Sanitary and Phytosanitary Measures: A Commentary* (New York: Oxford University Press, 2007).

Sharma, Urmila, and Sharma, S. K., *Western Political Thought (Vol. 1): From Plato to Burke* (New Delhi: Atlantic Publishers and Distributors, 2006).

Shaw, Malcolm N., *International Law* (4th ed.) (Cambridge: Cambridge University Press, 1997).

Shaw, Malcolm N., *International Law* (6th ed.) (Cambridge: Cambridge University Press, 2008).

Shaw, Malcolm N., *International Law* (8th ed.) (Cambridge: Cambridge University Press, 2017).

Spinoza, Benedictus de, *Tractatus Theologico-Politicus: A Critical Inquiry into the History, Purpose, and Authenticity of the Hebrew Scriptures; with the Right to Free Thought and Free Discussion Asserted and Shown to be Not Only Consistent but Necessarily Bound Up with True Piety and Good Government* (translated by Robert Willis) (London: Trübner & co., 1862).

Stein, Peter, *Roman Law in European History* (Cambridge: Cambridge University Press, 1999).

Stephens, Tim, *International Courts and Environmental Protection* (Cambridge: Cambridge University Press, 2009).

Storey, William Kelleher, *The First World War: A Concise Global History, 2nd ed.* (London: Rowman & Littlefield, 2014).

Stowell, Ellery C., *Intervention in International Law* (Washington, D.C.: John Byrne & Co., 1921).

Sweet, Alec Stone, and Mathews, Jud, *Proportionality Balancing and Constitutional Governance: A Comparative and Global Approach* (Oxford: Oxford University Press, 2019).

Szabo, Franz A. J., *The Seven Years War in Europe: 1756–1763* (London and New York: Routledge, 2013).

Szabó, Kinga Tibori, *Anticipatory Action in Self-defense: Essence and Limits under International Law* (The Hague: T.M.C. Asser Press, 2011).

Tsagourias, Nicholas, and Morrison, Alasdair, *International Humanitarian Law: Cases, Materials and Commentary* (Cambridge: Cambridge University Press, 2018).

Van Damme, Isabelle, *Treaty Interpretation by the WTO Appellate Body* (Oxford: Oxford University Press, 2009).

Van den Bossche, Peter and Zdouc, Werner, *The Law and Policy of the World Trade Organization* (4th ed.) (Cambridge: Cambridge University Press, 2017).

Vattel, Emer de, *The Law of Nations, Or, Principles of the Law of Nature, Applied to the Conduct and Affairs of Nations and Sovereigns with Three Early Essays on the Origin and Nature of Natural Law and on Luxury* (edited by Béla Kapossy & Richard

Whatimite, 2008), Book II, Chapter IV, para. 50 (online English version available at, http://oll.libertyfund.org/titles/vattel-the-law-of-nations-lf-ed).

Walzer, Michael, *Just and Unjust Wars: A Moral Argument with Historical Illustrations* (4th ed.) (New York: Basic Books, 1977).

Weiss, Edith Brown, Jackson, John H., and Bernasconi-Osterwalder, Nathalie (eds.), *Reconciling Environment and Trade* (2nd ed.) (Leiden: Martinus Nijhoff, 2008).

Whelan, Frederick G, *Hume and Machiavelli: Political Realism and Liberal Thought* (Lanham, Maryland: Lexington Books, 2004).

Winfield, P.H., *The Foundations & the Future of International Law* (Cambridge: Cambridge University Press, 1941).

Wolff, Christian, *Jus Gentium Methodo Scientifica Pertractatum*, § 3, pp. 9–10; § 273, p. 139 (Drake, Joseph H. trans., Oxford University Press, 1934) (1764), as quoted in Ohlin, Jens David, 'The Doctrine of Legitimate Defense', *International Law Studies*, 91: (2015).

Yearwood, Ronnie R. F., *The Interaction between World Trade Organisation (WTO) Law and External International Law: The Constrained Openness of WTO Law (A Prologue to a Theory)* (London and New York: Routledge, 2012).

Yerxa, Rufus, and Wilson, Bruce (eds.), *Key Issues in WTO Dispute Settlement: The First Ten Years* (Cambridge: Cambridge University Press, 2005).

Zleptnig, Stefan, *Non-Economic Objectives in WTO Law: Justification Provisions of GATT, GATS, SPS and TBT* (London and Boston: Martinus Nijhoff Publishers, 2010).

Book Chapters

Abi-Saab, Georges, 'The Appellate Body and Treaty Interpretation', in Fitzmaurice, Malgosia, Elias, Olufemi, and Merkouris, Panos (eds.), *Treaty Interpretation and the Vienna Convention on the Law of Treaties: 30 Years on*, Vol. 1 (Leiden & Boston: Martinus Nijhoff, 2010), pp. 99–109.

Alexandroff, Alan S., and Sharma, Rajeev, 'The National Security Provision-GATT Article XXI', in Macrory, Patrick F. J., Appleton, Arthur E., and Plummer, Michael G. (eds.), *The World Trade Organization: Legal, Economic and Political Analysis* (Vol. I) (New York: Springer, 2005), pp. 1571–1579.

Alvarez, José E., and Brink, Tegan, 'Revisiting the Necessity Defense: *Continental Casualty v. Argentina*', in Sauvant, Karl P. (ed.), *Yearbook on International Investment Law and Policy, 2010–2011* (Oxford: Oxford University Press, 2011), pp. 315–358.

Alvarez, José E., and Khamsi, Kathryn, 'The Argentine Crisis and Foreign Investors: A Glimpse into the Heart of the Investment Regime', in Sauvant, Karl P. (ed.), *Yearbook on International Investment Law and Policy, 2008–2009* (Oxford: Oxford University Press, 2009), pp. 379–478.

Alvarez-Jiménez, Alberto, 'The Interpretation of Necessity Clauses in Bilateral Investment Treaties after the Recent ICSID Annulment Decisions', in Sauvant, Karl P. (ed.), *Yearbook on International Investment Law and Policy, 2010–2011* (Oxford: Oxford University Press, 2011), pp. 419–450.

Andenas, Mads, and Zleptnig, Stefan, 'The Rule of Law and Proportionality in WTO Law', in Shan, Wenhua *et al.* (eds.), *Redefining Sovereignty in International Economic Law* (Oxford and Portland: Hart Publishing, 2008), pp. 171–192.

Bacchus, James, 'Not in Clinical Isolation', in Marceau, Gabrielle (ed.), *A History of Law and Lawyers in the GATT/WTO: The Development of the Rule of Law in the Multilateral Trading System* (Cambridge: Cambridge University Press, 2015), pp. 507–516.

Baroncini, Elisa, 'The EU Approach to Overcome the WTO Dispute Settlement Vacuum: Article 25 DSU Interim Appeal Arbitration as a Bridge Between Renovation and Innovation', in Lewis, Meredith Kolsky, *et al.*, *A Post-WTO International Legal Order: Utopian, Dystopian and Other Scenarios* (Cham: Springer, 2020), pp. 115–131.

Binder, Christina, 'Circumstances Precluding Wrongfulness', in Bungenberg, Marc, *et al.*, *International Investment Law* (1st ed.) (Baden-Baden, München and Oxford: Nomos, C. H. Beck and Hart, 2015), pp. 442–480.

Binder, Christina, and Reinisch, August, 'Economic Emergency Powers: A Comparative Law Perspective', in Schill, Stephan W. (ed.), *International Investment Law and Comparative Public Law* (Oxford: Oxford University Press, 2010), pp. 503–540.

Bjorklund, Andrea K., 'Economic Security Defenses in International Investment Law', in Muchlinski, Peter, Ortino, Federico, and Schreuer, Christoph (eds.), *The Oxford Handbook of International Investment Law* (Oxford: Oxford University Press, 2008), pp. 815–882.

Brand, Oliver, 'Commentary on Article 8 of the TRIPS Agreement', in Stoll, Peter-Tobias, Busche, Jan, and Arend, Katrin (eds.), *WTO – Trade-Related Aspects of Intellectual Property Rights* (*Max Planck Commentaries on World Trade Law, Vol. 7*) (Leiden and Boston: Martinus Nijhoff Publishers, 2009), pp. 188–204.

Carr, Indira, 'International Trade Rules and Environmental Effects', in Alam, Shawkat, *et al.* (eds.), *Routledge Handbook of International Environmental Law* (London and New York, Routledge 2013), pp. 547–560.

Chapters 2–4, 7–12, 19–31, in Muchlinski, Peter, Ortino, Federico, and Schreuer, Christoph (eds.), *The Oxford Handbook of International Investment Law* (Oxford: Oxford University Press, 2008), pp. 140–298, 434–882, 1193–2007 respectively.

Cohen, Marcelo G., 'The Notion of "state survival" in International Law', in de Chazournes, Laurence Boisson, and Sands, Philippe (eds.), *International Law, the International Court of Justice and Nuclear Weapons* (Cambridge: Cambridge University Press, 1999), pp. 293–314.

Cottier, Thomas, *et al.*, 'Introduction: Fragmentation and Coherence in International Trade Regulation: Analysis and Conceptual Foundations', in Cottier, Thomas, and

Delimatsis, Panagiotis (ed.), *The Prospects of International Trade Regulation: From Fragmentation to Coherence* (Cambridge: Cambridge University Press, 2011), pp. 1–56.

Crawford, James, and Olleson, Simon, 'The Nature and Forms of International Responsibility', in Evans, Malcom D. (ed.), *International Law* (3rd ed.) (Oxford: Oxford University Press, 2003), pp. 445–472.

Crawford, James, 'The International Court of Justice and the Law of State Responsibility', in Tams, Christian J., and Sloan, James (eds.), *The Development of International Law by the International Court of Justice* (Oxford: Oxford University Press, 2013), pp. 71–85.

De Aréchaga, Eduardo Jiménez, 'International Responsibility', in Sørensen, Max (ed.), *Manual of Public International Law* (London: Macmillan, 1968), pp. 531–603.

Delimatsis, Panagiotis, 'Who's Afraid of Necessity? And Why it Matters?', in Lim, Aik Hoe, and Meester, Bart De (eds.), *WTO Domestic Regulation and Services Trade: Putting Principles into Practice* (New York: Cambridge University Press, 2014), pp. 95–109.

Fitzmaurice, Malgosia, 'Necessity in International Environmental Law', in Dekker, Ige F., and Hey, E. (eds.), *Netherlands Yearbook of International Law: Necessity across International Law*, Vol. 41 (The Hague: T.M.C. Asser Press, 2010), pp. 159–192.

Frankel, Susy, 'The Applicability of GATT Jurisprudence to the Interpretation of the TRIPS Agreement', in Correa, Carlos M. (ed.), *Research Handbook on the Interpretation and Enforcement of Intellectual Property under WTO Rules: Intellectual Property in the WTO* (Vol. II) (Cheltenham: Edward Elgar, 2010), pp. 3–23.

Garcia-Rubio, Mariano, *Unilateral Measures as a Means of Enforcement of WTO Recommendations and Decisions* (The Hague: Academy of International Law, 2001).

Gazzini, Tarcisio, Werner, Wouter G., and Dekker, Ige F., 'Necessity across International Law: An Introduction', in Dekker, Ige F., and Hey, E. (eds.), *Netherlands Yearbook of International Law: Necessity across International Law* (Vol. 41) (The Hague: T.M.C. Asser Press, 2010), pp. 3–10.

Gomula, Joanna, 'Environmental disputes in the WTO', in Fitzmaurice, Malgosia, Ong, David M., and Merkouris, Panos (eds.), *Research Handbook on International Environmental Law* (Edward Elgar: Cheltenham (UK) and Northampton, MA (USA), 2010), pp. 401–422.

Gomula, Joanna. 'The Heritage of the Permanent Court of International Justice in WTO Concept', in Tams, Christian J., and Fitzmaurice, Malgosia (eds.), *Legacies of the Permanent Court of International Justice* (Leiden & Boston: Martinus Nijhoff, 2013), pp. 175–200.

Howse, Robert, and Türk, Elizabeth, 'The WTO Impact Upon Internal Regulations: A Case Study of the *Canada – EC Asbestos* Dispute', in Bermann, George, and Mavroidis, Petros (eds.), *Trade and Human Health and Safety* (Cambridge: Cambridge University Press, 2006), pp. 77–117.

Kahn, Victoria, 'Machiavelli's afterlife and reputation to the eighteenth century', in Najemy, John M. (ed.), *The Cambridge Companion to Machiavelli* (Cambridge: Cambridge University Press, 2010), pp. 239–255.

Karl, Joachim, 'International Investment Arbitration: A Threat to State Sovereignty?' in Shan, Wenhua, *et al.* (eds.), *Redefining Sovereignty in International Economic Law* (Oxford and Portland: Hart Publishing, 2008), pp. 225–245.

Karl, Wolfram, 'Treaties, Conflict Between', in Burnhardt, Rudolf (ed.), *Encyclopedia of Public International Law* (Vol. 7) (Amsterdam, New York and Oxford: Elsevier Science Publishers, 1984), pp. 467–473.

Jackson, John H., 'Sovereignty: Outdated Concept or New Approaches', in Shan, Wenhua, *et al.* (eds.), *Redefining Sovereignty in International Economic Law* (Oxford and Portland: Hart Publishing, 2008), pp. 3–25.

Jennings, Robert Y. (Sir) 'International Law', in Burnhardt, Rudolf (ed.), *Encyclopedia of Public International Law* (Vol. 7) (Amsterdam, New York and Oxford: Elsevier Science Publishers, 1984), pp. 278–297.

Ki-Jung, Kim, 'The War and US-Korean Relations', in Steinberg, John W., Menning, Bruce W., van der Oye, David Schimmelpenninck, Wolff, David, and Yokote, Shinji (eds.), *The Russo-Japanese War in Global Perspective: World War Zero* (Vol. 2) (Leiden and Boston: Brill, 2007), pp. 467–489.

Kobayashi, Tomohiko, and Fukunaga, Yuka, 'Like a Rolling Stone: Exploring Viable Options for the WTO Dispute Settlement Mechanism to Evolve Forward in the Post-WTO Era', in Lewis, Meredith Kolsky, *et al.*, *A Post-WTO International Legal Order: Utopian, Dystopian and Other Scenarios* (Cham: Springer, 2020), pp. 133–147.

Möldner, Mirka, 'Responsibility of International Organizations: Introducing the ILC's DARIO', in Bogdandy, Armin von, and Wolfrum, Rüdiger (eds.), *Max Planck Yearbook of United Nations Law*, Vol. 16 (Leiden: Koninklijke Brill N.V., 2012), pp. 281–328.

Muchlinski, Peter, 'The Framework of Investment Protection: The Content of BITS', in Sauvant, Karl P., and Sachs, Lisa E. (eds.), *The Effect of Treaties on Foreign Direct Investment: Bilateral Investment Treaties, Double Taxation Treaties, and Investment Flows* (Oxford: Oxford University Press, 2009), pp. 37–71.

Okowa, Phoebe N., 'Defenses in the Jurisprudence of International Tribunals', in Goodwin-Gill, Guy S., and Talmon, Stefan (eds.), *The Reality of International Law: Essays in Honour of Ian Brownlie* (Oxford and New York: Clarendon Press, 1999), pp. 389–411.

Pauwelyn, Joost, 'Sources of International Trade Law: Mantras and Controversies at the World Trade Organization', in Besson, Samantha, and d'Aspremont, Jean (eds.), *The Oxford Handbook of the Sources of International Law* (Oxford: Oxford University Press, 2018), pp. 1027–1047.

Prévost, Denise, and Van den Bossche, Peter, 'The Agreement on the Application of Sanitary and Phytosanitary Measures', in Macrory, Patrick F. J., Appleton, Arthur E., and Plummer, Michael G. (eds.), *The World Trade Organization: Legal, Economic and Political Analysis* (Vol. 1) (New York: Springer, 2005), pp. 230–370.

Qureshi, Asif H., 'An Appellate System in International Investment Arbitration?', in Muchlinski, Peter, Ortino, Federico, and Schreuer, Christoph (eds.), *The Oxford Handbook of International Investment Law* (Oxford: Oxford University Press, 2008), pp. 1934–1952.

Randelzhofer, Albrecht, 'Article 2(4)', in Bruno Simma (ed.), *The Charter of the United Nations: A Commentary* (Oxford: Clarendon Press, 1994), pp. 112–136.

Raymond, Gregory A., 'Military Necessity and the War against Global Terrorism', in Hensel, Howard M. (ed.), *The Law of Armed Conflict: Constraints on the Contemporary Use of Military Force* (Hampshire: Ashgate Publishing Limited, 2007), pp. 1–16.

Raymond, Gregory A., and Kegley Jr., Charles W., 'Pre-emption and Preventive War', in Hensel, Howard M. (ed.), *The Legitimate Use of Military Force: The Just War Tradition and the Customary Law of Armed Conflict* (London and New York: Routledge, 2008), pp. 99–112.

Reinisch, August, 'Investment Arbitration – The Role of Precedent in ICSID Arbitration', in Zeiler, Gerold *et al.* (eds.), *Austrian Arbitration Yearbook 2008* (Wien: Manz'sche Verlags- und Universitätsbuchhandlung, 2008), pp. 495–510.

Reinisch, August, 'Necessity in Investment Arbitration', in Dekker, Ige F., and Hey, E. (eds.), *Netherlands Yearbook of International Law: Necessity across International Law*, Vol. 41 (The Hague: T.M.C. Asser Press, 2010), pp. 137–158.

Ronzitti, Natalino, 'Use of Force, Jus Cogens and State Consent', in Cassese, Antonio. (ed.), *The Current Legal Regulation of the Use of Force* (Dordrecht: Martinus Nijhoff Publishers, 1986), pp. 147–166.

Ryngaert, Cedric, 'State Responsibility, Necessity and Human Rights', in Dekker, Ige F., and Hey, E. (eds.), *Netherlands Yearbook of International Law: Necessity across International Law*, Vol. 41 (The Hague: T.M.C. Asser Press, 2010), pp. 79–98.

Sacerdoti, Giorgio, 'The WTO Dispute Settlement System: Consolidating Success and Confronting New Challenges', in Elsig, Manfred, Hoekman, Bernard, and Pauwelyn, Joost (eds.), *Assessing the World Trade Organization: Fit for Purpose?* (Cambridge: Cambridge University Press, 2017), pp. 147–173.

Simma, Bruno, and Pulkowski, Dirk, '*Leges Speciales* and Self-Contained Regimes', in Crawford, James, Pellet, Alain, and Olleson, Simon (eds.), *The Law of International Responsibility* (Oxford: Oxford University Press, 2010), pp. 139–163.

Singh, Sahib, 'Non-proliferation law and countermeasures', in Roscini, Marco, and Joyner, Daniel (eds.), *Non-Proliferation Law As a Special Regime: A Contribution to Fragmentation Theory in International Law* (Cambridge: Cambridge University Press, 2012), pp. 196–249.

Sommario, Emanuele, 'Derogation from Human Rights Treaties in Situations of Natural or Man-Made Disasters', in Guttry, Andrea de, Gestri, Marco, and Venturini,

Gabriella (eds.), *International Disaster Response Law* (The Hague: T.M.C. Asser Press, 2010), pp. 323–350.

Tanzi, Attila, 'Necessity, State of', in Wolfrum, Rüdiger (Gen. ed.), *Max Planck Encyclopedia of International Law* (Oxford: Oxford University Press, 2013), pp. 583–588.

Thjoernelund, Marie Christine Hoelck, 'State of Necessity as an Exemption from State Responsibility for Investments', in Bogdandy, Armin von, and Wolfrum, Rüdiger (eds.), *Max Planck Yearbook of United Nations Law*, Vol. 13 (Leiden: Koninklijke Brill N.V., 2009), pp. 423–479.

Tomuschat, Christian, *International Law: Ensuring the Survival of Mankind on the Eve of a New Century: General Course on Public International Law (1999)*, *Recueil des Cours/ Collected Courses of The Hague Academy of International Law*, Vol. 281 (Cambridge, MA and The Hague: Kluwer Law International, 2001), pp. 1–438.

Tsagourias, Nicholas, 'Necessity and the Use of Force: A Special Regime', in Dekker, Ige F., and Hey, E. (eds.), *Netherlands Yearbook of International Law: Necessity across International Law*, Vol. 41 (The Hague: T.M.C. Asser Press, 2010), pp. 11–44.

Van den Bossche, Peter, 'The National Security Exception in International Trade Law Today: Can We Avoid Abuse?' (Hoofdstuk 5), in *Vereeniging 'Handelsrecht' Preadviezen 2020: Toetsing van buitenlandse investeringen in geopolitiek en juridisch perspectief* (Zutphen: Uitgeverij Paris bv, 2020), pp. 111–146.

Völker, Edmond L. M., 'The Agreement on Technical Barriers to Trade', in Bourgeois, Jacques H. J., Berrod, Frédérique, and Fournier, Eric Gippini (eds.), *The Uruguay Round Results: A European Lawyer's Perspective* (Brussels: Intereuropean University Press, 1995), pp. 281–309.

Wagner, Markus, 'Interpreting the SPS Agreement: Navigating Risk, Scientific Evidence and Regulatory Autonomy', available at, https://ssrn.com/abstract=2887361 or http://dx.doi.org/10.2139/ssrn.2887361, pp. 1–23.

Wagner, Markus, 'The Impending Demise of the WTO Appellate Body: From Centrepiece to Historical Relic?', in Lo, Chang-fa, Nakagawa, Junji, and Chen, Tsai-fang (eds.), *The Appellate Body of the WTO and Its Reform* (Singapore: Springer, 2020), pp. 67–85.

Williamson, Jr., Samuel R., 'The Origins of the War', in Strachan, Hew (ed.), *The Oxford Illustrated History of the First World War* (Oxford: Oxford University Press, 1998), pp. 9–25.

Articles

Abi-Saab, Georges, 'Fragmentation or Unification: Some Concluding Remarks', *New York University Journal of International Law and Politics*, 31(4): 1999, pp. 919–933.

Agius, Maria, 'The Invocation of Necessity in International Law', *Netherlands International Law Review*, 56(2): 2009, pp. 95–135.

Akande, Dapo, and Liefländer, Thomas, 'Clarifying Necessity, Imminence, and Proportionality in the Law of Self-Defense', *The American Journal of International Law*, 107(3): 2013, pp. 563–570.

Akande, Dapo, and Williams, Sope, 'International Adjudication on National Security Issues: What Role for the WTO?' *Virginia Journal of International Law*, 43(2): 2003, pp. 365–404.

Akehurst, Michael, 'The Hierarchy of the Sources of International Law' *British Yearbook of International Law*, 47(1): 1976, pp. 273–285.

Alford, Roger, 'The Self-Judging WTO Security Exception' *Utah Law Review*, 3: 2011, pp. 697–759.

Allhoff, Fritz, 'Torture Warrants, Self-Defense, and Necessity', *Public Affairs Quarterly*, 25(3): 2011, pp. 217–240.

Alston, Phillip, 'Resisting the Merger and Acquisition of Human Rights by Trade Law: A Reply to Petersmann', *European Journal of International Law*, 13(4): 2002, pp. 815–844.

Alvarez-Jiménez, Alberto, 'Foreign Investment Protection and Regulatory Failures as State's Contribution to the State of Necessity under Customary International Law: A New Approach Based on the Complexity of Argentina's 2001 Crisis', *Journal of International Arbitration*, 27(2): 2010, pp. 141–177.

Andemariam, Senai W., 'Can (Should) Article XX(b) GATT Be a Defense against Inconsistencies with the SPS and TBT Agreements?', *Journal of World Investment and Trade*, 7(4): 2006, pp. 519–544.

Andenas, Mads, and Zleptnig, Stefan, 'Proportionality: WTO Law in Comparative Perspective', *Texas International Law Journal*, 42(3): 2007, pp. 371–427.

Andreea Ioniţă, Liana, 'Is European Union Law a Fully Self-Contained Regime? A Theoretical Inquiry of the Functional Legal Regimes in the Context of Fragmentation of International Law', *Studia Politica: Romanian Political Science Review*, 15(1): 2015, pp. 39–59.

Anuradha, R. V., 'Petrificus Totalus: The Spell of National Security', *Asian Journal of WTO & International Health Law and Policy*, 13(2): 2018, pp. 311–328.

Arend, Anthony Clark, 'International Law and the Preemptive Use of Military Force', *The Washington Quarterly*, 26(2): 2003, pp. 89–103.

Author unknown, 'The Case of Russia against Turkey at the Hague Court of Arbitration', *American Journal of International Law*, 7(1): 1913, pp. 146–149.

Author unknown, 'The Declaration of St. Petersburg, 1868', *American Journal of International Law*, 1(2): 1907, pp. 95–96.

Baroncini, Elisa, 'Preserving the Appellate State in the WTO Dispute Settlement Mechanism: The EU and the Multi-Party Interim Appeal Arbitration Arrangement', *The Italian Yearbook of International Law*, 29(1): 2020, pp. 33–52.

Baroncini, Elisa, 'The Applicability of GATT Article XX to China's WTO Accession Protocol in the Appellate Body Report of the *China-Raw Materials* Case: Suggestions for a Different Interpretative Approach', *China-EU Law Journal*, 1: 2013, pp. 1–34.

Bartels, Lorand, 'Applicable Law in WTO Dispute Settlement Proceedings', *Journal of World Trade*, 35(3): 2001, pp. 499–519.

Benedict, Robert D., 'The Historical Position of the Rhodian Law', *Yale Law Journal*, 18(4): 1909, pp. 223–242.

Bethlehem, Daniel, 'Principles of Self-Defense – A Brief Response', *The American Journal of International Law*, 107(3): 2013, pp. 579–585.

Bethlehem, Daniel, 'Self-Defense against an Imminent or Actual Armed Attack by Nonstate Actors', *The American Journal of International Law*, 106(4): 2012, pp. 769–777.

Bhala, Raj, 'National Security and International Trade Law: What the GATT Says, and What the United States Does', *University of Pennsylvania Journal of International Economic Law*, 19(2): 1998, pp. 263–317.

Bhala, Raj, 'The Myth About Stare Decisis and International Trade Law (Part One of a Trilogy)', *American University International Law Review*, 14(4): 1999, pp. 845–956.

Bhala, Raj, 'The Power of the Past: Towards *De Jure Stare Decisis* in WTO Adjudication (Part Three of a Trilogy)', *George Washington International Law Review*, 33(3&4): 2001, pp. 873–978.

Bhala, Raj, 'The Precedent Setters: *De Facto Stare Decisis* in WTO Adjudication (Part Two of a Trilogy)', *Florida State University Journal of Transnational Law & Policy*, 9(1): 1999, pp. 1–151.

Bill, Brian J., 'The Rendulic "Rule": Military Necessity, Commander's Knowledge, and Methods of Warfare', *Yearbook of International Humanitarian Law*, 12: 2009, pp. 119–155.

Bjerg, Hans Christian, '"To Copenhagen a Fleet" The British Pre-emptive Seizure of the Danish-Norwegian Navy International', *Journal of Naval History*, 7(2): 2008.

Boed, Roman, 'State of Necessity as a Justification for Internationally Wrongful Conduct', *Yale Human Rights and Development Law Journal*, 3(1): 2000, pp. 1–45.

Boklan, Daria, and Bahri, Amrita, 'The First WTO's Ruling on National Security Exception: Balancing Interests or Opening Pandora's Box?', *World Trade Review*, 19(1): 2020, pp. 123–136.

Bonnan, Regis, 'The GATT Security Exception in a Dispute Resolution Context: Necessity or Incompatibility?', *Currents: International Trade Law Journal*, 19(1): 2010, pp. 3–12.

Bos, Maarten, 'The Hierarchy among the Recognized Manifestations ("Sources") of International Law', *Netherlands International Law Review*, 25(3): 1978, pp. 334–344.

Bowett, Derek, 'Reprisals Involving Recourse to Armed Force', *The American Journal of International Law*, 66(1): 1972, pp. 1–36.

B. S. K., 'Recent Moves to Reduce Trade Barriers', *Bulletin of International News*, 14(1): 1937, pp. 3–9.

Burke-White, William W., 'The Argentine Financial Crisis: State Liability Under BITS and the Legitimacy of The ICSID System', *Asian Journal of WTO and International Health Law and Policy*, 3(1): 2008, pp. 199–229.

Burke-White, William W., and Staden, Andreas von, 'Investment Protection in Extraordinary Times: The Interpretation and Application of Non-Precluded Measures Provisions in Bilateral Investment Treaties', *Virginia Journal of International Law*, 48(2): 2008, pp. 307–410.

Cameron, James, and Gray, Kevin R., 'Principles of International Law in the WTO Dispute Settlement Body', *International and Comparative Law Quarterly*, 50(2): 2001, pp. 248–298.

Carlone, Jonathan, 'An Added Exception to the TBT Agreement after *Clove, Tuna II,* and *COOL*', *Boston College International & Comparative Law Review*, 37(1): 2014, pp. 103–138.

Charnovitz, Steve, 'Exploring the Environmental Exceptions in GATT Article XX', *Journal of World Trade*, 25(5): 1991, pp. 37–55.

Charnovitz, Steve, 'The Field of International Economic Law', *Journal of International Economic Law*, 17(3): 2014, pp. 607–622.

Charnovitz, Steve, 'The Moral Exception in Trade Policy', *Virginia Journal of International Law*, 38: 1998, pp. 689–745.

Charnovitz, Steve, 'The WTO's Environmental Progress', *Journal of International Economic Law*, 10(3): 2007, pp. 685–706.

Charnovitz, Steve, 'What is International Economic Law?', *Journal of International Economic Law*, 14(1): 2011, pp. 3–22.

Chase, Claude, 'Norm Conflict between WTO Covered Agreements – Real, Apparent or Avoided?', *International and Comparative Law Quarterly*, 61(4): 2012, pp. 791–821.

Chigara, Ben, 'International Tribunal for the Law of the Sea and Customary International Law', *Loyola of Los Angeles International and Comparative Law Review*, 22(4): 2000, pp. 433–452.

Chubb, Kelley, 'The "State of Necessity" Defense: A Burden, Not A Blessing to the International Investment Arbitration System', *Cardozo Journal of Conflict Resolution*, 43(2): 2013, pp. 531–536.

Commission, Jeffery P., 'Precedent in Investment Treaty Arbitration: A Citation Analysis of a Developing Jurisprudence', *Journal of International Arbitration*, 24(2): 2007, pp. 129–158.

Cottier, Thomas, and Lastra, Rosa M., (special eds.), 'The Quest for International Law in Financial Regulation and Monetary Affairs', *Journal of International Economic Law*, special issue, 13(3): 2010, pp. 525–968.

Cottier, Thomas, *et al.*, 'The Principle of Proportionality in International Law: Foundations and Variations', *Journal of World Investment & Trade*, 18(4): 2017, pp. 628–672.

Creamer, Cosette D., 'Can International Law Recover? From the WTO's Crown Jewel to Its Crown of Thorns', *AJIL Unbound*, 113: 2019, pp. 51–55.

Dawar, Kamala, and Ronen, Eyal, 'How "Necessary"? A Comparison of Legal and Economic Assessments Under GATT Dispute Settlements, Article XX(b), TBT 2.2 and SPS 5.6', *Trade, Law and Development*, 8(1): 2016, pp. 1–23.

Desierto, Diane A., 'Necessity and "Supplementary Means of Interpretation" for Non-Precluded Measures in Bilateral Investment Treaties', *University of Pennsylvania Journal of International Law*, 31(3): 2014, pp. 827–934.

Desmedt, Axel, 'Proportionality in WTO Law', *Journal of International Economic Law*, 4(3): 2001, pp. 441–480.

Diebold, Nicolas F., 'The Morals and Order Exceptions in WTO Law: Balancing the Toothless Tiger and the Undermining Mole', *Journal of International Economic Law*, 11(1): 2007, pp. 43–74.

Dobos, Daniel, 'The Necessity of Precaution: The Future of Ecological Necessity and the Precautionary Principle', *Fordham Environmental Law Review*, 13(2): 2002, pp. 375–408.

Downey, William G. 'The Law of War and Military Necessity', *American Journal of International Law*, 47(2): 1953, pp. 251–262.

Draper, G. I. A. D., 'Military Necessity and Humanitarian Imperatives', *Military Law and the Law of War Review*, 27(2): 1973, pp. 129–151.

Du, Michael Ming, 'Domestic Regulatory Autonomy under the TBT Agreement: From Non-discrimination to Harmonization', *Chinese Journal of International Law*, 6(2): 2007, pp. 269–306.

Dumberry, Patrick, 'Satisfaction as a Form of Reparation for Moral Damages Suffered by Investors and Respondent States in Investor-State Arbitration Disputes', *Journal of International Dispute Settlement*, 3(1): (2012), pp. 205–242.

Dunbar, N. C. H., 'Military Necessity in War Crimes Trials', *British Year Book of International Law*, 29: 1952, pp. 442–452.

Editorial Comment of the American Society of International Law, 'The Hague Conventions and the Neutrality of Belgium and Luxemburg', *The American Journal of International Law*, 9(4): 1915, pp. 959–962.

Ehrenhaft, Peter D., Book Review of *Trade Policies for a Better Future: The 'Leutwiler Report', the GATT and the Uruguay Round* (Dordrecht: Martinus Nijhoff Publishers, 1987), *American Journal of International Law*, 84(1): 1990, pp. 334–338.

Engan, Luke, 'In Search of Necessity: Congruence, Proportionality, and the Least-Restrictive Means in Investor-State Dispute Settlement', *Georgetown Journal of International Law*, 43(2): 2012, pp. 495–521.

Eser, Albin, 'Justification and Excuse', *American Journal of Comparative Law*, 24(4): 1976, pp. 621–637.

Espa, Ilaria, 'The Appellate Body Approach to the Applicability of Article XX GATT in the Light of *China – Raw Materials:* A Missed Opportunity?', *Journal of World Trade*, 46(6): 2012, pp. 1399–1424.

Fernandes, Paulo Jorge, 'The Political History of Nineteenth Century Portugal', *e-Journal of Portuguese History*, 1(1): 2003, pp. 1–9.

Forrest, Craig J. S., 'The Doctrine of Military Necessity and the Protection of Cultural Property During Armed Conflicts', *California Western International Law Journal*, 37(2): 2007, pp. 177–219.

Franck, Susan D., 'The Legitimacy Crisis in Investment Treaty Arbitration: Privatizing Public International Law through Inconsistent Decisions', *Fordham Law Review*, 73(4): 2005, pp. 1521–1625.

Fukunaga, Yuka, 'The Appellate Body's Power to Interpret the WTO Agreements and WTO Members' Power to Disagree with the Appellate Body', *Journal of World Investment & Trade*, 29(6): 2020, pp. 792–819.

Gaeta, Paola, 'May Necessity Be Available as a Defense for Torture in the Interrogation of Suspected Terrorists?', *Journal of International Criminal Justice*, 2(3): 2004, pp. 785–794.

Galvez, Cynthia C., 'Necessity, Investor Rights, and State Sovereignty for NAFTA Investment Arbitration', *Cornell International Law Journal*, 46(1): 2013, pp. 143–163.

Gasser, Hans-Peter, 'A Look at the Declaration of St Petersburg of 1868', *International Review of the Red Cross*, 33 (297): 1993, pp. 511–516.

Ghanayim, Khalid, 'Excused Necessity in Western Legal Philosophy', *Canadian Journal of Law and Jurisprudence*, 19(31): 2006, pp. 1–34.

Gill, Judith, 'Is There a Special Role for Precedent in Investment Arbitration?', *ICSID Review – Foreign Investment Law Journal*, 25(1): 2010, pp. 87–94.

Gorecki, Danuta M. and Wajenberg, Arnold, 'Canon Law: History, Sources, and a Proposed Classification Scheme', *Law Library Journal*, 75: 1982, pp. 381–402.

Gray, Christine, 'The ICJ Advisory Opinion on Legal Consequences of the Construction of a Wall in the Occupied Palestinian Territory', *Cambridge Law Journal*, 63(3): 2004, pp. 527–532.

Gross, Oren and Aolain, Fionnuala Ni, 'Emergency, War and International Law – Another Perspective', *Nordic Journal of International Law*, 70(1): 2001, pp. 29–63.

Gruszczynski, Lukasz, 'Risk Management Policies under the WTO Agreement on the Application of Sanitary and Phytosanitary Measures', *Asian Journal of WTO and International Health Law and Policy*, 3(1): 2008, pp. 261–308.

Hafner-Burton, Emilie M., Helfer, Laurence R., and Fariss, Christopher J., 'Emergency and Escape: Explaining Derogations from Human Rights Treaties', *International Organization*, 65(4): 2011, pp. 673–707.

Harhoff, Frederik, 'Unauthorized Humanitarian Interventions – Armed Violence in the Name of Humanity?', *Nordic Journal of International Law*, 70(1): 2001, pp. 65–119.

Harris, Wilson, 'The Genoa Conference', *Journal of the British Institute of International Affairs*, 1(5): 1922, pp. 150–158.

Hartman, Joan F., 'Derogation from Human Rights Treaties in Public Emergencies- A Critique of Implementation by the European Commission and Court of Human Rights and the Human Rights Committee of the United Nations', *Harvard International Law Journal*, 22(1): 1981, pp. 1–52.

Hassemer, Winfried, 'Justification and Excuse in Criminal Law: Theses and Comments', *Brigham Young University Law Review*, 3: 1986, pp. 573–609.

Hayashi, Nobuo, 'Requirements of Military Necessity in International Humanitarian Law and International Criminal Law', *Boston University International Law Journal*, 28(1): 2010, pp. 39–140.

Higgins, Rosalyn, 'Derogations under Human Rights Treaties', *British Yearbook of International Law*, 48(1): 1976–1977, pp. 281–319.

Hilf, Meinhard, 'Power, Rules and Principles: Which Orientation for WTO/GATT Law?', *Journal of International Economic Law*, 4(1): 2001, pp. 111–130.

Hill-Cawthorne, Lawrence, 'The Role of Necessity in International Humanitarian and Human Rights Law', *Israel Law Review*, 47(2): 2014, pp. 225–251.

Hoekman, Bernard M., and Mavroidis, Petros C., 'To AB or Not to AB? Dispute Settlement in WTO Reform', *Journal of International Economic Law*, 23(3): 2020, pp. 703–722.

Hruschka, Joachim, 'Imputation', *Brigham Young University Law Review*, 3: 1986, pp. 669–710.

Hutchinson, Michael R., 'The Margin of Appreciation Doctrine in the European Court of Human Rights', *International and Comparative Law Quarterly*, 48(3): 1999, pp. 638–650.

Ion, Theodore P., 'The International Status of the Grand Duchy of Luxemburg and the Kingdom of Belgium in Relation to the Present European War', *Michigan Law Review*, 13(5): 1915, pp. 368–390.

Ishikawa, Yoshimichi, 'Plain Packaging Requirements and Article 2.2 of the TBT Agreement', *Chinese (Taiwan) Yearbook of International Law and Affairs*, 30: 2012, pp. 84–110.

Iyenaga, Toyokichi, 'Japan's Annexation of Korea', *The Journal of Race Development*, 3(2): 1912, pp. 201–223.

Jackson, John H., 'Reflections on International Economic Law', *University of Pennsylvania Journal of International Economic Law*, 17(1): 1996, pp. 17–28.

Jans, Jan H., 'Proportionality Revisited', *Legal Issues of Economic Integration*, 27(27): 2000, pp. 239–265.

Jenks, Clarence Wilfred, 'The Conflict of Law-Making Treaties', *British Yearbook of International Law*, 30: 1953, pp. 401–453.

Jennings, Robert Y. (Sir), 'The *Caroline* and *McLeod* Cases', *American Journal of International Law*, 32(1): 1938, pp. 82–99.

Johnstone, Ian, 'The Plea of Necessity in International Legal Discourse: Humanitarian Intervention and Counter-Terrorism', *Columbia Journal of Transnational Law*, 43(2): 2002, pp. 338–388.

Jones, Howard, 'The Caroline Affair', *The Historian*, 38(3): 1976, pp. 485–502.

Jones, Robert L., and Jones, Pauline, 'Occupation of Nacogdoches', *East Texas Historical Journal*, 50(2): 2012, pp. 16–37.

Kapterian, Gisele, 'A Critique of the WTO Jurisprudence on "Necessity"', *International and Comparative Law Quarterly*, 59(1): 2010, pp. 89–127.

Katō, Yōko, 'What Caused the Russo-Japanese War: Korea or Manchuria?', *Social Science Japan Journal*, 10(1): 2007, pp. 95–103.

Klabbers, Jan, 'Jurisprudence in International Trade Law: Article XX of GATT', *Journal of World Trade*, 26(2): 1992, pp. 63–94.

Kowner, Rotem, 'Becoming an Honorary Civilized Nation: Remaking Japan's Military Image During the Russo-Japanese War, 1904–1905', *Historian*, 64(1): 2001, pp. 19–38.

Kurtz, Jürgen, 'Adjudging the Exceptional at International Investment Law: Security, Public Order and Financial Crisis', *International and Comparative Law Quarterly*, 59(2): 2010, pp. 325–371.

Kuyper, Pieter. J., 'The Law of GATT as a Special Field of International Law: Ignorance, Further Refinement or Self-Contained System of International Law', *Netherlands Yearbook of International Law*, 25: 1994, pp. 227–257.

Kuijper, Pieter J., 'From the Board: The US Attack on the WTO Appellate Body', *Legal Issues of Economic Integration*, 45(1): 2018, pp. 1–12.

Lampe, Markus, 'Explaining nineteenth-century bilateralism: economic and political determinants of the Cobden-Chevalier network', *Economic History Review*, 64(2): 2011, pp. 644–668.

Lamy, Pascal, 'The Place of the WTO and its Law in the International Legal Order', *European Journal of International Law*, 17(5): 2006, pp. 969–984.

Lapaš, Davorin, 'Some Remarks on Fragmentation of International Law: Disintegration or Transformation?', *Comparative and International Law Journal of Southern Africa*, 40(1): 2007, pp. 1–29.

Laursen, Andreas, 'The Use of Force and (the State of) Necessity', *Vanderbilt Journal of Transnational Law*, 37(2): 2004, pp. 485–526.

Lee, Jaemin, 'Commercializing National Security? National Security Exceptions' Outer Parameter under GATT Article XXI', *Asian Journal of WTO & International Health Law and Policy*, 13(2): 2018, pp. 277–304.

Lester, Simon, 'Finding the Boundaries of International Economic Law', *Journal of International Economic Law*, 17(1): 2014, pp. 3–9.

Lester, Simon, and Stemberg, William, 'The GATT Origins of TBT Agreement Articles 2.1 and 2.2', *Journal of International Economic Law*, 17(1): 2014, pp. 215–232.

Letsas, George, 'Two Concepts of the Margin of Appreciation', *Oxford Journal of Legal Studies*, 26(4): 2006, pp. 705–732.

Li, Xiaoling, 'DSU Article 25 Appeal Arbitration: A Viable Interim Alternative to the WTO Appellate Body?', *Global Trade and Customs Journal*, 15(10): 2020, pp. 461–478.

Lindroos, Anja, and Mehling, Michael, 'Dispelling the Chimera of 'Self-Contained Regimes': International Law and the WTO', *European Journal of International Law*, 16(5): 2005, pp. 857–877.

Lindsay, Peter, 'The Ambiguity of GATT Article XXI: Subtle Success or Rampant Failure?', *Duke Law Journal*, 52(6): 2003, pp. 1277–1313.

Loughlin, Martin, 'The Erosion of Sovereignty', *Netherlands Journal of Legal Philosophy*, 45(2): 2016, pp. 57–81.

Lowe, Vaughan, 'Precluding Wrongfulness or Responsibility: A Plea for Excuses', *European Journal of International Law*, 10(2): 1999, pp. 405–411.

Malkawi, Bashar H., 'Anatomy of the Case of Arab Countries and the WTO', *Arab Law Quarterly*, 20(2): 2006, pp. 110–151.

Mancini, Matthew J., 'Francis Lieber, Slavery, and the "Genesis" of the Laws of War', *The Journal of Southern History*, 77(2): 2011, pp. 325–348.

Marceau, Gabrielle, and Trachtman, Joel P., 'A Map of the World Trade Organization Law of Domestic Regulation of Goods: The Technical Barriers to Trade Agreement, the Sanitary and Phytosanitary Measures Agreement, and the General Agreement on Tariffs and Trade', *Journal of World Trade*, 48 (2): 2014, pp. 351–432.

Marceau, Gabrielle, and Trachtman, Joel P., 'The Technical Barriers to Trade Agreement, the Sanitary and Phytosanitary Measures Agreement, and the General Agreement on Tariffs and Trade: A Map of the World Trade Organization Law of Domestic Regulation of Goods', *Journal of World Trade*, 36(5): 2002, pp. 811–881.

Marceau, Gabrielle, 'A Call for Coherence in International Law: Praises for the Prohibition against "Clinical Isolation" in WTO Dispute Settlement', *Journal of World Trade*, 33(5): 1999, pp. 87–152.

Marceau, Gabrielle, 'Conflicts of Norms and Conflicts of Jurisdictions: The Relationship between the WTO Agreement and MEAs and other Treaties', *Journal of World Trade*, 35(6): 2001, pp. 1081–1131.

Marceau, Gabrielle, 'The New TBT Jurisprudence in *US – Clove Cigarettes, WTO US – Tuna II,* and *US – COOL*', *Asian Journal of WTO & International Health Law and Policy*, 8(1): 2013, pp. 1–36.

Marceau, Gabrielle, 'WTO Dispute Settlement and Human Rights', *European Journal of International Law*, 13(4): 2002, pp. 753–814.

Marceau, Gabrielle, and Wyatt, Julian, 'The WTO's Efforts to Balance Economic Development and Environmental Protection: A Short Review of Appellate Body Jurisprudence', *Latin American Journal of International Trade Law*, 1(1): 2013, pp. 291–314.

Martin, Antoine, 'Investment Disputes after Argentina's Economic Crisis: Interpreting BIT Non-precluded Measures and the Doctrine of Necessity under Customary International Law', *Journal of International Arbitration*, 29(1): 2012, pp. 49–70.

Mavroidis, Petros C., 'No Outsourcing of Law? WTO Law as Practiced by WTO Courts', *American Journal of International Law*, 102(3): 2008, pp. 421–474.

Mavroidis, Petros, 'Remedies in the WTO Legal System: Between a Rock and a Hard Place', *European Journal of International Law*, 11(4): 2000, pp. 763–813.

McCoubrey, Hilaire, 'The Nature of the Modern Doctrine of Military Necessity', *Military Law and the Law of War Review*, 30(215): 1991, pp. 217–252.

McDougall, Robert, 'The Crisis in WTO Dispute Settlement: Fixing Birth Defects to Restore Balance', *Journal of World Trade*, 52(6): 2018, pp. 867–896.

McGrady, Benn, 'Necessity Exceptions in WTO Law: Retreaded Tyres, Regulatory Purpose and Cumulative Regulatory Measures', *Journal of International Economic Law*, 12(1): 2008, pp. 153–173.

McGrady, Benn, and Jones, Alexandra, 'Tobacco Control and Beyond: The Broader Implications of *United States – Clove Cigarettes* for Non-Communicable Diseases', *American Journal of Law & Medicine*, 39 (2 & 3): 2013, pp. 265–289.

McRae, Donald M., 'The Contribution of International Trade Law to the Development of International Law', *Recueil des Cours*, 260(1): 1996, pp. 109–232.

McRae, Donald, 'International Economic Law and Public International Law: The Past and the Future', *Journal of International Economic Law*, 17(3): 2014, pp. 627–638.

Melzer, Nils, 'Keeping the Balance between Military Necessity and Humanity: A Response to Four Critiques of the ICRC's Interpretive Guidance on the Notion of Direct Participation in Hostilities', *New York University Journal of International Law and Politics*, 42(3): 2010, pp. 831–916.

Middleton, R. W., 'The GATT Standards Code', *Journal of World Trade Law*, 14(3): 1980, pp. 201–219.

Milhizer, Eugene R., 'Justification and Excuse: What They Were, What They Are, and What They Ought To Be', *St. John's Law Review*, 78(3): 2012, pp. 725–895.

Mitchell, Andrew D., and, Henkels, Caroline, 'Variations on A Theme: Comparing the Concept of "Necessity" in International Investment Law and WTO Law', *Chicago Journal of International Law*, 14(1): 2013, pp. 93–164.

Mokhtar, Aly, 'Human Rights Obligations *v.* Derogations: Article 15 of the European Convention on Human Rights', *International Journal of Human Rights*, 8(1): 2004, pp. 65–87.

Najam, Adil, 'The Case Against a New International Environmental Organization', *Global Governance*, 9(3): 2003, pp. 367–384.

Neumann, Jan, and Türk, Elisabeth, 'Necessity Revisited: Proportionality in World Trade Organization Law after *Korea – Beef, EC – Asbestos* and *EC – Sardines*', *Journal of World Trade*, 37(1): 2003, pp. 199–233.

Ngangjoh-Hodu, Yenkong, 'Relationship of GATT Article XX Exceptions to Other WTO Agreements', *Nordic Journal of International Law*, 80 (2): 2011, pp. 219–234.

Nichols, Philip M., 'GATT Doctrine', *Virginia Journal of International Law*, 36(2): 1996, pp. 379–466.

O'Donnell, Thomas A., 'The Margin of Appreciation Doctrine: Standards in the Jurisprudence of the European Court of Human Rights', *Human Rights Quarterly*, 4(4): 1982, pp. 474–496.

Osiro, Deborah Akoth, 'GATT/WTO Necessity Analysis: Evolutionary Interpretation and its Impact on the Autonomy of Domestic Regulation', *Legal Issues of Economic Integration*, 29(2): 2002, pp. 123–141.

Owaydhah, Khalid A., 'Justifications and Concept of Criminal Liability in Shari'ah', *Humanities and Social Sciences Review*, 3(2): 2014, pp. 55–71.

Paddeu, Federica I., 'A Genealogy of *Force Majeure* in International Law', *British Yearbook of International Law*, 82(1): 2012, pp. 381–494.

Paine, Joshua, 'The WTO's Dispute Settlement Body as a Voice Mechanism', *Journal of World Investment & Trade*, 29(6): 2020, pp. 820–861.

Palmeter, David, and Mavroidis, Petros C., 'The WTO Legal System: Sources of Law', *American Journal of International Law*, 92(3): 1998, pp. 398–413.

Partem, Michael Greenfield, 'The Buffer System in International Relations', *The Journal of Conflict Resolution*, 27(1): 1983, pp. 3–26.

Paust, Jordan J., 'Dr. Francis Lieber and the Lieber Code', *Proceedings of the Annual Meeting (American Society of International Law)*, 95: 2001, pp. 112–115.

Pauwelyn, Joost, 'The Role of Public International law in the WTO: How Far Can We Go?' *American Journal of International Law*, 95(3): 2001, pp. 535–578.

Pauwelyn, Joost, 'The WTO Agreement on Sanitary and Phytosanitary (SPS) Measures as Applied in the First Three SPS Disputes: *EC – Hormones, Australia – Salmon* and *Japan – Varietals*', *Journal of International Economic Law*, 2(4): 1999, pp. 641–664.

Peng, Shin-yi, 'Cybersecurity Threats and the WTO National Security Exceptions', *Journal of International Economic Law*, 18(2): 2015, pp. 449–478.

Pescatore, Pierre, 'Fundamental Rights and Freedoms in the System of the European Communities', *American Journal of Comparative* Law, 18(2): 1970, pp. 343–351.

Petersmann, Ernst-Ulrich, 'How Should WTO Members React to Their WTO Crises?', *World Trade Review*, 18(3): 2019, pp. 503–525.

Petersmann, Ernst-Ulrich, 'International Trade Law and International Environmental Law: Prevention and Settlement of International Environmental Disputes in GATT', *Journal of World Trade*, 21(1): 1993, pp. 43–81.

Petersmann, Ernst-Ulrich, 'Taking Human Dignity, Poverty and Empowerment of Individuals More Seriously, Rejoinder to Alston', *European Journal of International Law*, 13(4): 2002, pp. 845–851.

Petersmann, Ernst-Ulrich, 'Time for a United Nations "Global Compact" for Integrating Human Rights into the Law of Worldwide Organizations: Lessons from European Integration', *European Journal of International Law*, 13(3): 2002, pp. 621–650.

Pinchis-Paulse, Mona, 'Trade Multilateralism and U.S. National Security: The Making of the GATT Security Exceptions', *Michigan Journal of International Law*, 41(1): 2019, pp. 109–194.

Poblador, Alexander J., 'The Defense of Necessity in International Law', *Philippine Law Journal*, 57(3): 1982, pp. 332–370.

Post, Gaines, '*Plena Potestas* and Consent in Medieval Assemblies: A Study in Romano-Canonical Procedure and the Rise of Representation, 1150–1325', *Traditio*, 1 (1943), pp. 355–408.

Prazeres, Tatiana Lacerda, 'Trade and National Security: Rising Risks for the WTO', *World Trade Review*, 19(1): 2020, pp. 137–148.

Purba, Elbinsar, 'Necessary Measure under the SPS Agreement', *Asian Journal of WTO & International Health Law and Policy*, 13(1): 2018, pp. 206–232.

Quigley, Harold S., and Colegrove, Kenneth W., 'Enforcement of Treaty Obligations by Self-help and Self-defense', *Proceedings of the American Society of International Law at its Annual Meeting* (1921–1969), 26 (April 28–30 1932), pp. 90–101.

Raby, Jean, 'The State of Necessity and the Use of Force to Protect Nationals', *Canadian Yearbook of International Law*, 26 (1988), pp. 253–272.

Regan, Donald H., 'The Meaning of "necessary" in GATT Article XX and GATS Article XIV: The Myth of Cost-Benefit Balancing', *World Trade Review*, 6(3): 2007, pp. 347–369.

Reichberg, Gregory M., 'Preventive War in Classical Just War Theory', *Journal of the History of International Law*, 9(1): 2007, pp. 5–34.

Reinisch, August, 'How Necessary is Necessity for International Organizations?', *International Organizations Law Review*, 3(2): 2006, pp. 177–183.

Reinisch, August, 'Necessity in International Investment Arbitration: An Unnecessary Split of Opinions in Recent ICSID Cases- Comments on *CMS v. Argentina* and *LG&E v. Argentina*', *Journal of World Investment & Trade*, 8(2): 2007, pp. 191–214.

Ritchie, David G., 'Contributions to the History of the Social Contract Theory', *Political Science Quarterly*, 6(4): 1891, pp. 656–676.

Roberts, Donna, 'Preliminary Assessment of the Effects of the WTO Agreement on Sanitary and Phytosanitary Trade Regulations', *Journal of International Trade Law*, 1(2): 1998, pp. 377–405.

Rogoff, Martin A., and Collins, Jr., Edward, 'The Caroline Incident and the Development of International Law', *Brooklyn Journal of International Law*, 16(3): 1990, pp. 493–527.

Romano, John-Alex, 'Combating Terrorism and Weapons of Mass Destruction: Reviving the Doctrine of a State of Necessity', *Georgetown Law Journal*, 87(4): 1999, pp. 1023–1057.

Root, Elihu, Opening Address, President, President of the American Society of International Law, 'Opening Address at the Fifteenth Annual Meeting of the American Society of International Law' (27 April 1921), *Proceedings of the American Society of International Law*, 15 (1921), Proc. 1, pp. 1–13.

Roscini, Marco, 'On the 'Inherent' Character of the Right of States to Self-defense', *Cambridge Journal of International and Comparative Law*, 4(3): 2015, pp. 634–660.

Royal Institute of International Affairs, 'The First World Economic Conference', *Bulletin of International News*, 3(10): 1927, pp. 5–7.

Royal Institute of International Affairs, 'The Geneva Conference on the Abolition of Trade Prohibitions and Restrictions', *Bulletin of International News*, 4(9): 1927, pp. 193–196.

Runciman, W. Leslie, 'The World Economic Conference at Geneva', *The Economic Journal*, 37(147): 1927, pp. 465–472.

Rytter, Jens Elo, 'Humanitarian Intervention without the Security Council: From San Francisco to Kosovo – and Beyond', *Nordic Journal of International Law*, 70(1): 2001, pp. 121–160.

Sacerdoti, Giorgio, 'BIT Protections and Economic Crises: Limits to Their Coverage, the Impact of Multilateral Financial Regulation and the Defense of Necessity', *ICSID Review – Foreign Investment Law Journal*, 28(2): 2013, pp. 351–383.

Sacerdoti, Giorgio, 'Solving the WTO Dispute Settlement System Crisis: An Introduction', *Journal of World Investment & Trade*, 29(6): 2020, pp. 785–791.

Schachter, Oscar, 'The Right of States to Use Armed Force', *Michigan Law Review*, 82 (5&6): 1984, pp. 1620–1646.

Schebesta, Hanna, and Sinopoli, Dominique, 'The Potency of the SPS Agreement's Excessivity Test: The Impact of Article 5.6 on Trade Liberalization and the Regulatory Power of WTO Members to take Sanitary and Phytosanitary Measures', *Journal of International Economic Law*, 21(1): 2018, pp. 123–149.

Schmitt, Michael N., 'Military Necessity and Humanity in International Humanitarian Law: Preserving the Delicate Balance', *Virginia Journal of International Law*, 50(4): 2010, pp. 795–839.

Schoenbaum, Thomas, 'WTO Dispute Settlement: Praises and Suggestions for Reform', *International & Comparative Law Quarterly*, 47(3): 1998, pp. 647–658.

Schreuer, Christoph, 'Derogation of Human Rights in Situations of Public Emergency: The Experience of the European Convention on Human Rights', *Yale Journal of World Public Order*, 9(1): 1982, pp. 113–132.

Sermet, Laurent, 'The Absence of a Derogation Clause from the African Charter on Human and Peoples' Rights: A Critical Discussion', *African Human Rights Law Journal*, 7(1): 2007, pp. 142–161.

Simma, Bruno, 'Self-contained regimes', *Netherlands Yearbook of International Law*, 16: 1985, pp. 111–136.

Simma, Bruno, 'The Work of the International Law Commission at its Fifty-Third Session (2001)', *Nordic Journal of International Law*, 71(1): 2002, pp. 123–187.

Simma, Bruno, and Pulkowski, Dirk, 'Of Planets and the Universe: Self-contained Regimes in International Law', *European Journal of International Law*, 17(3): 2006, pp. 483–529.

Slade, Alison, 'The Objectives and Principles of the WTO TRIPS Agreement: A Detailed Anatomy', *Osgoode Hall Law Journal*, 53(3): 2016, pp. 948–998.

Sloane, Robert D., 'On the Use and Abuse of Necessity in the Law of State Responsibility', *The American Journal of International Law*, 447 (2012), pp. 447–508.

Spiermann, Ole, 'Humanitarian Intervention as a Necessity and the Threat or Use of *Jus Cogens*', *Nordic Journal of International Law*, 71(4): 2002, pp. 523–543.

Stahn, Carsten, '"*Jus ad bellum*", "*jus in bello*" … "*jus post bellum*"? – Rethinking the Conception of the Law of Armed Force', *European Journal of International Law*, 17(5): 2007, pp. 921–943.

Subramanian, S. R., 'Too Similar or Too Different: State of Necessity as a Defense under Customary International Law and the Bilateral Investment Treaty and their Relationship', *Manchester Journal of International Economic Law*, 9(1): 2012, pp. 68–91.

Sweet, Alec Stone, and Mathews, Jud, 'Proportionality Balancing and Global Constitutionalism', *Columbia Journal of Transnational Law*, 47(1): 2008, pp. 72–164.

Sykes, Katie, 'Sealing Animal Welfare into the GATT Exceptions: The International Dimension of Animal Welfare in WTO Disputes', *World Trade Review*, 13(3): 2014, pp. 471–498.

Taulbee, J. L., 'Retaliation and Irregular Warfare in Contemporary International Law', *The International Lawyer*, 7(1): 1973, pp. 195–204.

Toye, Richard, 'Developing Multilateralism: The Havana Charter and the Fight for the International Trade Organization, 1947–1948', *The International History Review*, 25(2): 2003, pp. 282–305.

Trachtman, Joel P., 'The Domain of WTO Dispute Resolution', *Harvard Journal of International Law*, 40(2): 1999, pp. 333–377.

Trachtman, Joel, 'The International Economic Law Revolution', *University of Pennsylvania Journal of International Economic Law*, 17(1): 1996, pp. 33–61.

Trachtman, Joel, 'Trade and ... Problems, Cost-Benefit Analysis and Subsidiarity', *European Journal of International Law*, 9: 1998, pp. 32–85.

Treves, Tullio, 'Fragmentation of International Law: The Judicial Perspective', *Agenda Internacional*, Año XVI (N° 27): 2009, pp. 213–253.

Uniacke, Suzanne, 'Proportionality and Self-Defense', *Law and Philosophy*, 30(3): 2011, pp. 253–272.

Valinaki, Fay, '"Repairing the Defects" of Article 2.1 of the WTO Technical Barriers to Trade Agreement: An Amendment Proposal', *Legal Issues of Economic Integration*, 43(1): 2016, pp. 65–96.

Van Damme, Isabelle, 'Treaty Interpretation by the WTO Appellate Body', *European Journal of International Law*, 21(3): 2010, pp. 605–648.

Van den Bossche, Peter, 'Looking for Proportionality in WTO Law', *Legal Issues of Economic Integration*, 35(3): 2008, pp. 283–294.

Vasiljević, Mirko, and Jovanović, Marko, 'Necessity as a Ground for Precluding Wrongfulness in International Investment Law', *Belgrade Law Review*, Year LXIV, No. 3 (2016), pp. 5–22.

Venzke, Ingo, 'Making General Exceptions: The Spell of Precedents in Developing Article XX GATT into Standards for Domestic Regulatory Policy', *German Law Journal*, 12(5): 2011, pp. 1111–1140.

Vermeer-Künzli, Annemarieke, 'As If: The Legal Fiction in Diplomatic Protection', *European Journal of International Law*, 18(1): 2007, pp. 37–68.

Vidigal, Geraldo, 'Living Without the Appellate Body: Multilateral, Bilateral and Plurilateral Solutions to the WTO Dispute Settlement Crisis', *Journal of World Investment &Trade*, 29(6): 2020, pp. 862–890.

Voon, Tania, 'The Security Exception in WTO Law: Entering a New Era', *American Journal of International Law*, 113: 2019, pp. 45–50.

Waibel, Michael, 'Two Worlds of Necessity in ICSID Arbitration: CMS and LG&E', *Leiden Journal of International Law*, 20(3): 2007, pp. 637–648.

Wall, Andru E., 'International Law and the Bush Doctrine', *Israel Yearbook of Human Rights*, 34 (2004), pp. 193–229.

Wang, Jiangyu, 'The Rule of Law in China: A Realistic View of the Concept, The Impact of the WTO, and the Prospects for Future Development', *Singapore Journal of Legal Studies*, 2004, pp. 347–389.

Waszink, Jan, 'Lipsius and Grotius: Tacitism', *History of European Ideas*, 39(2): 2013, pp. 151–168.

Weidenbaum, Paul, 'Necessity in International Law', *Transactions of the Grotius Society*, Vol. 24, Problems of Peace and War, Papers Read before the Society in the Year 1938, pp. 105–132.

Weightman, M. A., 'Self-Defense in International Law', *Virginia Law Review*, 37(8): 1951, pp. 1095–1115.
Yamada, Takuhei, 'State of Necessity in International Law: A Study of International Judicial Cases', *Kobe-Gakuin Law and Politics Review*, 34(4): 2005, pp. 107–158.
Yoo, Ji Yeong, and Ahn, Dukgeun, 'Security Exceptions in the WTO System: Bridge or Bottle-neck for Trade and Security?', *Journal of International Economic Law*, 19(2): (2016), pp. 417–444.

Bilateral/Multilateral Agreements

Bilateral Agreements

Bulgaria-Czechoslovak Republic Trade Agreement (1933).
Convention of Saint-Germain-En-Laye Revising the General Act of Berlin, February 26, 1885, and the General Act and Declaration of Brussels, July 2, 1890 (relating to Congo River Basin), available at, https://iea.uoregon.edu/treaty-text/1919-congoriverentxt.
Economic Union of Belgium & Luxemburg-Switzerland Trade Agreement (1928).
Estonia-Lithuania Trade Agreement (1934).
France-Czechoslovakia Trade Agreement (1928).
Latvia-Lithuania Trade Agreement (1933).
Persian Empire-Republic of Czechoslovakia Trade Agreement (1929).
Romania-Turkish Republic Trade Agreement (1929).

Multilateral Agreements

Barcelona Convention and Statute on Freedom of Transit (1921), 7 L.N.T.S. (1921–1922), pp. 12–33.
Basel Convention on the Control of Transboundary Movements of Hazardous Wastes and their Disposal and Articles (1989).
Cartagena Protocol on Biosafety to the Convention on Biological Diversity (2000).
Convention for the Abolition of Import and Export Prohibitions and Restrictions (1927), available at, https://www.loc.gov/law/help/us-treaties/bevans/m-ust000002-0651.pdf.
European Convention on Human Rights (1950).
Inter-American Convention on Human Rights (1969).
International Convention Relating to the Simplification of Customs Formalities (1923), 30 L.N.T.S. (1924–1925), pp. 371–412.
Rome Statute of the International Criminal Court (1998).
The Charter for the International Criminal Tribunal for the Former Yugoslavia (1993).
The Charter of the International Military Tribunal (Nuremberg Charter) (1945).

The International Covenant on Civil and Political Rights (1966).
The Statute for the International Criminal Tribunal for Rwanda (1994).
Treaty of Peace with Germany (Versailles Peace Treaty) (1919), available at, https://www.loc.gov/law/help/us-treaties/bevans/m-ust000002-0043.pdf.
WTO Agreement: Marrakesh Agreement Establishing the World Trade Organization, 15 April 1994, 1867 U.N.T.S. 154, 33 I.L.M. 1144 (1994) (specifically the GATT 1994, the GATS, the TBT, the SPS and the TRIPS agreements).

League of Nations Documents

99 L.N.T.S. (1930).
105 L.N.T.S. (1930).
110 L.N.T.S. (1930–31).
112 L.N.T.S. (1931).
148 L.N.T.S. (1934).
League of Nations Doc. C.E.1.22. 1927 II.13.
The League of Nations Covenant (including amendments adopted to December, 1924), available at, https://avalon.law.yale.edu/20th_century/leagcov.asp.

United Nations Documents

A/CN.4/318/Add.5–7, *Addendum – Eighth Report on State Responsibility* by Roberto Ago, Special Rapporteur – the Internationally Wrongful Act of the State, Source of International Responsibility (part 1), Extract from the Yearbook of the International Law Commission (1980), p. 30, referring to A. D. McNair, *International Law Opinions* (Cambridge: Cambridge University Press, 1956), vol. II, pp. 231 *et. seq.*
A/CN.4/318 and Add.1 to 4, *Eighth Report on State Responsibility* by Mr. Roberto Ago, Special Rapporteur – the Internationally Wrongful act of the State, Source of International Responsibility, (Vol. II, Part I) (United Nations, 1979).
Ago, Roberto, 'Fifth Report on State Responsibility', U.N. Doc. A/CN.4/291 and Add.1 and 2, in *Yearbook of the International Law Commission* (Vol. II, part I) (United Nations, 1976).
Ago, Roberto, 'The Internationally Wrongful Act of the State, Source of International Responsibility', *Eighth Report on State Responsibility*, Addendum (1980), ILC, 32nd sess., UN Doc. A/CN.4/318/Add.5–7.
Arangio-Ruiz, Gaetano, 'Third Report on State Responsibility', U.N. Doc. A/CN.4/440 and Add.1, in *Yearbook of the International Law Commission* (Vol. II, part I) (United Nations, 1991).

Crawford, James, 'Fourth Report on State Responsibility, Addendum', (2001), ILC, 53rd sess., UN Doc. A/CN.4/517/Add.1.

Crawford, James, 'Fourth Report on State responsibility' (2001), ILC, 53rd sess., UN Doc. A/CN.4/517 and Add.1.

Crawford, James, 'Second Report on State Responsibility', (1999), ILC, 51st sess., UN Doc. A/CN.4/498 and Add 1–4.

Crawford, James, 'Second Report on State Responsibility', U.N. Doc. A/CN.4/498 and Add.1–4 (1999).

Crawford, James, 'Third Report on State Responsibility', UN document A/CN.4/507/Add.4 (2001).

Human Rights Committee, General Comment 29, States of Emergency (article 4), UN Doc. CCPR/C/21/Rev.1/Add.11 (2001), available at, http://hrlibrary.umn.edu/gencomm/hrc29.html.

International Law Commission, *Yearbook of the International Law Commission* (Vol. II, part II) (United Nations, 2001).

Koskenniemi, Martti, 'Fragmentation of International Law: Difficulties arising From the Diversification and Expansion of International Law', *Report of the Study Group of the International Law Commission* (2006), ILC, 58th sess., U.N. Doc. A/CN.4/L. 682.

Report of the International Law Commission (1980), ILC, 33rd sess., A/CN.4/SER.A/1980/Add.1 (Part 2).

Report of the International Law Commission (2001), ILC, 53rd sess., Supp. No. 10 (A/56/10).

Report of the International Law Commission (2001), ILC, 63rd sess., Supp. No. 10 (A/66/10).

Riphagen, Willem, 'Fourth Report on State Responsibility', U.N. Doc. A/CN.4/366 and Add.1, in *Yearbook of the International Law Commission* (Vol. II, part I) (United Nations, 1983).

Riphagen, Willem, 'Third Report on the Content, Forms and Degrees of International Responsibility', U.N. Doc. A/CN.4/354 and Corr.1 and Add.1 & 2 (United Nations, 1982).

UN General Assembly Resolution 3314 (XXIX) – Definition of Aggression (14 December 1974).

United Nations War Crimes Commission, *Law Reports of Trials of War Criminals*, Vol. XV (*Digest of Laws and Cases*) (1949), available at, https://www.loc.gov/rr/frd/Military_Law/pdf/Law-Reports_Vol-15.pdf.

United Nations War Crimes Commission, *Law Reports of Trials of War Criminals*, Vol. X (1949), available at, https://www.loc.gov/rr/frd/Military_Law/pdf/Law-Reports_Vol-10.pdf.

United Nations War Crimes Commission, *Law Reports of Trials of War Criminals*, Vol. IX (1949), available at, https://www.loc.gov/rr/frd/Military_Law/pdf/Law-Reports_Vol-9.pdf.

United Nations War Crimes Commission, *Law Reports of Trials of War Criminals*, Vol. XII (*The German High Command Trial*) (1949), available at, https://www.loc.gov/rr/frd/Military_Law/pdf/Law-Reports_Vol-12.pdf.

United Nations War Crimes Commission, *Law Reports of Trials of War Criminals*, Vol. XV (*Digest of Laws and Cases*) (1949), available at, https://www.loc.gov/rr/frd/Military_Law/pdf/Law-Reports_Vol-15.pdf.

United Nations War Crimes Commission, *Law Reports of Trials of War Criminals*, Vol. X (1949), available at, https://www.loc.gov/rr/frd/Military_Law/pdf/Law-Reports_Vol-10.pdf.

United Nations, *Summaries of Judgments, Advisory Opinions and Orders of the Permanent Court of International Justice*, ST/LEG/SER.F/1/Add.4 (New York: 2012), pp. 1–491.

Yearbook of the International Law Commission (Vol. II) (United Nations, 1958).

Yearbook of the International Law Commission (Vol. II) (United Nations, 1963).

Yearbook of the International Law Commission (Vol. II) (United Nations, 1966).

Yearbook of the International Law Commission (Vol. II) (United Nations, 1969).

Yearbook of the International Law Commission (Vol. II) (United Nations, 1970).

Yearbook of the International Law Commission (Vol. II, Part I) (United Nations, 1980).

Yearbook of the International Law Commission (Vol. II, Part II) (United Nations, 1980).

Yearbook of the International Law Commission (Vol. II, Part II) (United Nations, 1999).

Yearbook of the International Law Commission (Vol. II, Part II) (United Nations, 2001).

GATT Negotiation Documents

E/PC/T/103.

E/PC/T/135.

E/PC/T/180.

E/PC/T/186 and Corr. 1.

E/PC/T/196.

E/PC/T/33.

E/PC/T/34.

E/PC/T/A/PV/30.

E/PC/T/C.6/41.

E/PC/T/C.6/85.

E/PC/T/C.II/50.

E/PC/T/C.II/54.

E/PC/T/C.II/54/Rev.1.

E/PC/T/C.II/55.

E/PC/T/C.II/64.

E/PC/T/C.II/PRO/PV/14.
E/PC/T/C.II/PRO/W/11.
E/PC/T/W.46.
E/PC/T/W/245.
E/PC/T/W/269.
E/PC/T/W/281.
E/PC/T/W/293.

GATT Documents

Agreement on Technical Barriers to Trade, 12 April 1979, 1186 UNTS 276, GATT, BISD, 26th Supp. 8 (1980) (Standards Code).
BISD, Third Supplement (1960).
GATT/CP.5/17 (2 November 1950).
GATT/CP.6/38 (20 October 1951).
L/135 (23 September 1953).
L/189 15 (12 April 1954).
L/261/Add.1 (12 November 1954).
L/334 14 (1 March 1955).
L/3361 (25 February 1970).
MTN.GNG/NG7/W/16, GATT Negotiating Group on GATT Articles (Article XXI, Note by the Secretariat, 18 August 1987).
SR.16/3 (May 1960).
W.22/7 (12 March 1965).

WTO Documents

General Agreement on Tariffs and Trade (1994).
General Agreement on Trade in Services (1994).
Request for Consultations by Canada, *United States – Certain Measures on Steel and Aluminum Products*, WTO Doc. WT/DS/550/1, dated 6 June 2018.
Request for Consultations by China, *United States – Certain Measures on Steel and Aluminum Products*, WTO Doc. WT/DS/544/1, dated 9 April 2018.
Request for Consultations by India, *United States – Certain Measures on Steel and Aluminum Products*, WTO Doc. WT/DS/547/1, dated 23 May 2018.
Request for Consultations by the Republic of Korea, *Japan – Measures Related to the Exportation of Products and Technology to Korea*, WTO Doc. WT/DS/590/1, dated 16 September 2019.

Request for Consultations by Mexico, *United States – Certain Measures on Steel and Aluminum Products*, WTO Doc. WT/DS/551/1, dated 6 June 2018.

Request for Consultations by Norway, *United States – Certain Measures on Steel and Aluminum Products*, WTO Doc. WT/DS/552/1, dated 19 June 2018.

Request for Consultations by Qatar, *UAE – Measures Relating to Trade in Goods, Services and Trade Related Aspects of Intellectual Property Rights*, WTO Doc. WT/DS/526/1, dated 4 August 2017.

Request for Consultations by Switzerland, *United States – Certain Measures on Steel and Aluminum Products*, WTO Doc. WT/DS/556/1, dated 12 July, 2018.

Request for Consultations by the European Communities, *United States – The Cuban Liberty and Democratic Solidarity Act (Helms – Burton Act)*, WT/DS38/1, dated 13 May 1996.

Request for Consultations by the European Union, *United States – Certain Measures on Steel and Aluminum Products*, WTO Doc. WT/DS/548/1, dated 6 June 2018.

Request for Consultations by the Russian Federation, *United States – Certain Measures on Steel and Aluminum Products*, WTO Doc. WT/DS/554/1, dated 2 July 2018.

WT/GC/W/752, *Communication from the European Union, China, Canada, India, Norway, New Zealand, Switzerland, Australia, Republic of Korea, Iceland, Singapore and Mexico to the General Council*, dated 23 November 2018.

WT/GC/W/753, *Communication from the European Union, China and India to the General Council*, dated 23 November 2018.

WT/MIN(01)/DEC/1 (20 November 2001), WTO Fourth Ministerial Declaration, adopted on 14 November 2021, available at, https://www.wto.org/english/thewto_e/minist_e/min01_e/mindecl_e.htm#dispute.

WTO, *The Committee on Trade and Environment ('regular' CTE)*, available at, https://www.wto.org/english/tratop_e/envir_e/wrk_committee_e.htm.

Web-Based Sources

Agius, Maria, *The Invocation of Necessity in International Law*, available at, https://www.uppsalajuristernasalumnistiftelse.se/wp-content/uploads/2014/11/Maria-Agius.pdf.

Al-Majalla Al-Ahkam Al-Adaliyyah: The Ottoman Courts Manual (Hanafi), available at, http://legal.pipa.ps/files/server/ENG%20Ottoman%20Majalle%20(Civil%20Law).pdf.

An Introduction to the Book of Proverbs, available at, https://bible.org/article/introduction-book-proverbs.

Bacchus, James, 'Might Unmakes Right: The American Assault on the Rule of Law in World Trade', Centre for International Governance Innovation' CIGI Papers No. 173

(May 2018), available at, https://www.cigionline.org/sites/default/files/documents/Paper%20no.173.pdf.

Barani, Luca, 'Relationship of the EU legal order with WTO Law: Studying Judicial Activism', Garnet Working Paper No: 70/09 September 2009, available at, http://www2.warwick.ac.uk/fac/soc/pais/research/researchcentres/csgr/garnet/workingpapers/7009.pdf.

Beard, Rick 'The Lieber Codes', Opinionator, New York Times (24 April 2013), available at, https://opinionator.blogs.nytimes.com/2013/04/24/the-lieber-codes/.

Botero, Giovanni, *The Reason of State*: Book One, available at, http://www.nlnrac.org/critics/machiavelli/primary-source-documents/the-reason-of-state.

British-American Diplomacy: The Caroline Case, available at, http://avalon.law.yale.edu/19th_century/br-1842d.asp.

Bühler, George (translator), *The Laws of Manu* (Sacred Books of the East, Vol. 25), Chapter IX, available at, http://www.sacred-texts.com/hin/manu/manu09.htm.

Depth Study Option: Medieval Europe, available at, https://www.oup.com.au/__data/assets/pdf_file/0020/58061/03_SAL_BAH8_SB_71097_SPREADS_RGB.pdf.

Hillman, Jennifer, 'Three Approaches to Fixing the World Trade Organization's Appellate Body: The Good, the Bad and the Ugly?' (*Institute of International Economic Law, Georgetown University Law Center, December 2018*), available at, https://georgetown.app.box.com/s/966hfvosmran4m31biblgfszj42za40b.

Hobbes, Thomas, *Leviathan (or the Matter, Form, & Power of a Common-wealth Ecclesiastical and Civil)*, Chapter XXII, p. 218 (on pdf version available at, http://socserv2.socsci.mcmaster.ca/econ/ugcm/3ll3/hobbes/Leviathan.pdf).

http://avalon.law.yale.edu/18th_century/jay.asp.

http://avalon.law.yale.edu/19th_century/lieber.asp.

http://avalon.law.yale.edu/imt/imtconst.asp.

http://avalon.law.yale.edu/subject_menus/18th.asp.

http://avalon.law.yale.edu/subject_menus/19th.asp.

http://biblehub.com/commentaries/proverbs/6-30.htm.

http://droitromain.upmf-grenoble.fr/Anglica/D9_Scott.htm#IV.

http://gatt.stanford.edu/page/home.

http://www.icj-cij.org/court/index.php?p1=1&p2=1 e72.

http://www.icj-cij.org/en/case/11.

http://www.icty.org/x/file/Legal%20Library/Statute/statute_sept09_en.pdf.

http://opil.ouplaw.com/view/10.1093/law:epil/9780199231690/law-9780199231690-e72.

http://www.publications.parliament.uk/pa/ld200304/ldhansrd/vo040421/text/40421-07.htm#40421-07_head0.

https://catalog.hathitrust.org/Search/Home?lookfor=reciprocal%20trade.%20Agreement&searchtype=all&ft=&setft=false.

https://coggle.it/diagram/WglXovkZeAABLcdm/t/history-of-international-trade.

https://icsid.worldbank.org/en/Pages/cases/AdvancedSearch.aspx.

https://iea.uoregon.edu.

https://unctad.org/publications-search?f[0]=product%3A526.

https://wwi.lib.byu.edu/index.php/The_Annexation_of_Bosnia_and_Herzegovina_by_Austria-Hungary.

https://www.eccc.gov.kh/sites/default/files/legal-documents/KR_Law_as_amended_27_Oct_2004_Eng.pdf.

https://www.wto.org/english/docs_e/legal_e/46-dsenv.pdf.

https://www.wto.org/english/docs_e/legal_e/final_e.htm.

https://www.wto.org/english/docs_e/legal_e/tokyo_tbt_e.pdf.

Grotius, Hugo, *The Rights of War and Peace,* 1625 (translated by A. C. Campbell, 1901 ed.), available at, http://oll.libertyfund.org/titles/grotius-the-rights-of-war-and-peace-1901-ed.

ICRC, *What are* jus ad bellum *and* jus in bello?, available at, https://www.icrc.org/en/document/what-are-jus-ad-bellum-and-jus-bello-0.

Innocent IV, available at, https://en.wikisource.org/wiki/1911_Encyclop%C3%A6dia_Britannica/Innocent/Innocent_IV.

Japan – Measures Related to the Exportation of Products and Technology to Korea, available at, https://www.wto.org/english/tratop_e/dispu_e/cases_e/ds590_e.htm.

Lamy, Pascal, 'The Place and Role of the WTO (WTO Law) in the International Legal Order', Address before the European Society of International Law, available at, https://www.wto.org/english/news_e/sppl_e/sppl26_e.htm.

Legge, James, *The Chinese Classics: Vol. 2, The Life and Works of Mencius* (London: Trübner & Co., 57 & 59: Ludgate Hill, 1875), p. 151, available at, http://www.rosenfels.org/pll-v5/pdf/Legge_1430-02_EBk_v5.pdf.

Lester, Simon, 'Can Interim Appeal Arbitration Preserve the WTO Dispute System?', Free Trade Bulletin (1 September 2020), available at, https://www.cato.org/sites/cato.org/files/2020-08/FTB-77.pdf.

Letter dated 7 October 2001 from the Permanent Representative of the United States of America to the United Nations addressed to the President of the Security Council, S/2001/946, p. 1, available at, http://www.hamamoto.law.kyoto-u.ac.jp/kogi/2005kiko/s-2001-946e.pdf.

Lex Rhodia: The Ancient Ancestor of Maritime Law – 800 BC, available at, http://www.duhaime.org/LawMuseum/LawArticle-383/Lex-Rhodia-The-Ancient-Ancestor-of-Maritime-Law--800-BC.aspx.

Middle Ages, available at, https://www.encyclopedia.com/history/modern-europe/ancient-history-middle-ages-and-feudalism/middle-ages.

Middle Ages, available at, https://www.britannica.com/event/Middle-Ages.

Niccolò Machiavelli in Stanford Encyclopedia of Philosophy, available at, http://plato.stanford.edu/entries/machiavelli/.

OCED, *Fair and Equitable Treatment Standard in International Investment Law*, OECD Working Papers on International Investment, 2004/03 (OECD Publishing, 2004), available at, https://www.oecd.org/daf/inv/investment-policy/WP-2004_3.pdf.

PCA repository of cases, *Russian Claim for Interest on Indemnities* (*Russia/Turkey*), available at, https://pcacases.com/web/view/89.

Plutarch: The Parallel Lives (*The Life of Solon*), *available at*, https://penelope.uchicago.edu/Thayer/E/Roman/Texts/Plutarch/Lives/Solon*.html.

Proverbs 6 Bible Commentary, available at, http://www.christianity.com/bible/commentary.php?com=mh&b=20&c=6.

Quimbee.com, *Rainbow Warrior* (*New Zealand v. France*), available at, https://www.quimbee.com/cases/rainbow-warrior-new-zealand-v-france.

Reed, Lucy, *Scorecard of Investment Treaty Cases Against Argentina Since 2001*, available at, http://kluwerarbitrationblog.com/2009/03/02/scorecard-of-investment-treaty-cases-against-argentina-since-2001/.http://legal.un.org/avl/pdf/ha/ictr_EF.pdf.

Repertory of Appellate Body Reports, *Interpretation*, available at, https://www.wto.org/english/tratop_e/dispu_e/repertory_e/i3_e.htm#I.3.13.

Repertory of Appellate Body Reports, *Principles and Concepts of General Public International Law*, available at, https://www.wto.org/english/tratop_e/dispu_e/repertory_e/p3_e.htm#P.3.1.

Report of the High-level Panel on Threats, Challenges and Change: A More Secure World: Our Shared Responsibility, A/59/565, available at, https://www.un.org/ruleoflaw/files/gaA.59.565_En.pdf.

Russia – Measures Concerning Traffic in Transit (2019), available at, https://www.wto.org/english/tratop_e/dispu_e/cases_e/ds512_e.htm.

Samuel, Alan E., *Plutarch's Account of Solon's Reforms*, f.n. 5, available at, https://grbs.library.duke.edu/article/viewFile/12021/4037.

Secretary-General presents his annual report to General Assembly, Press Release SG/SM/7136, GA/9596, available at, https://www.un.org/press/en/1999/19990920.sgsm7136.html.

Terrell, David G., '*Pope Innocent IV and Emperor Frederick II:* Auctoritias *and* Potestas in Conflict', available at, https://www.scribd.com/document/31886312/terrell-dg-first-council-of-lyons-scribd.

The 1864 Geneva Convention, available at, https://www.icrc.org/eng/resources/documents/treaty/geneva-convention-1864.htm.

The Prince: Machiavelli, Critical Essays: Reason of State, available at, https://www.cliffsnotes.com/literature/p/the-prince/critical-essays/reason-of-state.

The Rape (*abduction*) *of the Sabine Women*, available at, https://mcvittys-classroom.wikispaces.com/file/view/Sec6-RapeSabineWomen.pdf.

The White House, *The National Security Strategy of the United States of America*, September 2002, available at, https://2009-2017.state.gov/documents/organization/63562.pdf.

The White House, *The National Security Strategy of the United States of America*, March 2006, available at, https://www.comw.org/qdr/fulltext/nss2006.pdf.

UAE – *Measures Relating to Trade in Goods, Services and Trade Related Aspects of Intellectual Property Rights*, available at, https://www.wto.org/english/tratop_e/dispu_e/cases_e/ds526_e.htm.

UNCTAD, *Bilateral Investment Treaties (1959–1999)* (2000), available at, http://unctad.org/en/Docs/poiteiiad2.en.pdf.

UNCTAD, *Bilateral Investment Treaties (1995–2006): Trends in Investment Rulemaking*, available at, http://unctad.org/en/docs/iteiia20065_en.pdf.

UNCTAD, *International Investment Agreements Navigator*, available at, https://investmentpolicy.unctad.org/international-investment-agreements.

United States Trade Representative, *The President's 2018 Trade Policy Agenda*, available at, https://ustr.gov/sites/default/files/files/Press/Reports/2018/AR/2018%20Annual%20Report%20I.pdf, pp. 22–28.

Who Drinks the Water?, available at, http://www.jewishtreats.org/2010/05/who-drinks-water.html.

WTO, *Current Status of Disputes*, available at, https://www.wto.org/english/tratop_e/dispu_e/dispu_current_status_e.htm.

WTO, *DS590: Japan – Measures Related to the Exportation of Products and Technology to Korea*, available at, www.wto.org/english/news_e/news20_e/dsb29jun20_e.htm.

WTO, *Negotiations to Improve Dispute Settlement Procedures*, available at, https://www.wto.org/english/tratop_e/dispu_e/dispu_negs_e.htm.

WTO, *Principles of the Trading System*, available at, https://www.wto.org/english/thewto_e/whatis_e/tif_e/fact2_e.htm.

Cases

Cases Brought before the PCA

PCA, *Russian Claim for Interest on Indemnities (Damages Claimed by Russia for Delay in Payment of Compensation Owed to Russians Injured during the War of 1877–1878) (Russia v. Turkey)*, Award of the Tribunal, 11 November 1912, available at, https://pcacases.com/web/sendAttach/643.

Cases Brought before the PCIJ

Case Concerning the Payment of Various Serbian Loans Issued in France (France v. Kingdom of the Serbs, Croats and Slovenes), Judgment No. 14, 12 July 1929, available at, http://www.worldcourts.com/pcij/eng/decisions/1929.07.12_payment1.htm.

Case of the S.S. Wimbledon (United Kingdom, France, Italy & Japan v. Germany), Judgment No. 1, 17 August 1923, available at, http://www.worldcourts.com/pcij/eng/decisions/1923.08.17_wimbledon.htm.

The Oscar Chinn Case (Britain v. Belgium), Judgment No. 61, 12 December 1934, available at, http://www.worldcourts.com/pcij/eng/decisions/1934.12.12_oscar_chinn.htm.

The "Société Commerciale de Belgique" (Belgium v. Greece), Judgment No. 31, 15 June 1939, available at, http://www.worldcourts.com/pcij/eng/decisions/1939.06.15_societe_commerciale.htm.

Cases Brought before the ICJ

Ambatielos Case (Greece v. United Kingdom), Preliminary Objection, Judgment (1 July 1952), pp. 28–47; Judge Hsu Mo's dissenting opinion at pp. 85–88.

Case Concerning Armed Activities on the Territory of the Congo (Congo v. Uganda), Judgment, 19 December 2005, ICJ Rep. 2005, pp. 168–283.

Case Concerning Military and Paramilitary Activities in and against Nicaragua (Nicaragua v. United States of America), Judgment, 27 June 1986, ICJ Rep. 1986, pp. 14–150.

Case Concerning Oil Platforms (Iran v. USA), Judgment, 6 November 2003, ICJ Rep. 2003, pp. 161–219.

Case Concerning Rights of Nationals of the United States of America in Morocco (France v. United States of America), ICJ, Judgment, 27 August 1952, ICJ Rep. 1952, pp. 176–214.

Case Concerning the Gabčíkovo-Nagymaros Project (Hungary v. Slovakia), Judgment, 25 September 1997, ICJ Rep. 1997, pp. 7–84.

Case Concerning United States Diplomatic and Consular Staff in Tehran (United States of America v. Iran), Judgment, 24 May 1980, ICJ Rep. 1980, pp. 3–46.

Corfu Channel case, Judgment (Merits), 9 April 1949, ICJ Rep. 1949, pp. 3–169. Dissenting opinions of Judges Krylov and Azevedo are available at, pp. 68–77 and pp. 78–114 respectively.

Fisheries Jurisdiction case (Spain v. Canada), Jurisdiction of the Court, Judgment, 4 December 1998, ICJ Rep. 1998, pp. 432–469.

Legal Consequences of the Construction of a Wall in the Occupied Palestinian Territory, Advisory Opinion, 9 July 2004, ICJ Rep. 2004, pp. 136–203.

Legality of the Threat or Use of Nuclear Weapons, Advisory Opinion, 8 July 1996, ICJ Rep. 1996, pp. 226–267.

Legality of Use of Force (*Yugoslavia v. Belgium*) (Provisional Measures), Uncorrected Translation of Oral Pleadings of Belgium, ICJ Rep. 1999, record of 10 May 1999, 3 p.m., available at, http://www.icj-cij.org/icjwww/idocket/iybe/iybeframe.htm.

Oral Proceedings, Part II for the *Case Concerning Rights of Nationals of the United States of America in Morocco*, available at, http://www.icj-cij.org/files/case-related/11/011-19520715-ORA-01-00-BI.pdf.

Cases Brought before the ICSID Tribunals

CMS Gas Transmission Company v. Argentina (ICSID Case No ARB/01/8) (Annulment Proceeding), 25 September 2007, pp. 1–44.

CMS Gas Transmission Company v. Argentina (ICSID Case No. ARB/01/8) (Award), 12 May 2005, pp. 1–140.

Continental Casualty Company v. Argentine Republic (ICSID Case No. ARB/03/9) (Award), 5 September 2008, pp. 1–140.

El Paso Energy International Company v. Argentine Republic (ICSID Case No. ARB/03/15) (Award), 31 October 2011, pp. 1–273.

Enron Creditors Recovery Corp. Ponderosa Assets, L.P. v. The Argentine Republic (ICSID Case No. ARB/01/3) (Annulment Proceeding), 30 July 2010, pp. 1–170.

Enron Creditors Recovery Corporation (*formerly Enron Corporation*) *and Ponderosa Assets, L.P. v. Argentine Republic* (ICSID Case No. ARB/01/3) (Award), 22 May 2007, pp. 1–139.

Impregilo S.p.A. v. Argentine Republic (ICSID Case No. ARB/08/14) (Award), 21 June 2011, pp. 1–86.

LG&E Energy Corp., LG&E Capital Corp. and LG&E International Inc. v. Argentine Republic (ICSID Case No. ARB/02/1) (Award), 25 July 2007, pp. 1–82.

Sempra Energy International v. Argentine Republic (ICSID Case No. ARB/02/16) (Annulment Proceeding), 29 June 2010, pp. 1–49.

Suez, Sociedad General de Aguas de Barcelona S.A. and Vivendi Universal S.A v. Argentine Republic (ICSID Case No. ARB/03/19) (Award), 9 April 2015, pp. 1–92.

Cases brought before the UNCITRAL

AWG Group Ltd. v. The Argentine Republic, UNCITRAL (Final Award), 9 April 2005, pp. 1–63.

BG Group Plc. v. The Argentine Republic, UNCITRAL (Final Award), 24 December 2007, pp. 1–139.

National Grid Plc. v. The Argentine Republic, UNCITRAL (Final Award), 3 November 2008, pp. 1–131.

Cases Brought before the ITLOS

The *M/V "Saiga"* (No. 2) *Case* (*Saint Vincent and The Grenadines v. Guinea*), ITLOS, Judgment, 1 July 1999, paras. 1–183.

Cases Brought before the ICTY

Prosecutor v. Erdemović, Case No. IT-96-22-T, Judgment, International Criminal Tribunal for the Former Yugoslavia (29 November 1996).

Prosecutor v. Galic, Case No. IT-98-29-A, Appeals Chamber, Judgment, International Criminal Tribunal for the Former Yugoslavia (30 November 2006).

Prosecutor v. Strugar, Case No. IT-01-42-T, Judgment, International Criminal Tribunal for the Former Yugoslavia (31 January 2005).

Other Cases

Case Concerning the Difference between New Zealand and France Concerning the Interpretation or Application of Two Agreements, Concluded on 9 July 1986 between the Two States and which Related to the Problems Arising from the Rainbow Warrior Affair, 30 April 1990, available at, United Nations, Reports of international Arbitral awards, Vol. XX, 2006, http://legal.un.org/riaa/cases/vol_XX/215-284.pdf, pp. 215–284.

Case of McCann and Others v. the United Kingdom (App. No. 18984/91), European Court of Human Rights, Judgment (27 September 1995).

Company General of the Orinoco Case (1905), United Nations, Reports of International Arbitral Awards (Vol. X, pp. 184–285), available at, http://legal.un.org/riaa/cases/vol_X/184-285.pdf.

French Company of Venezuelan Railroads Case (1905), United Nations, Reports of International Arbitral Awards (Vol. X, pp. 285–355), p. 353 available at, http://legal.un.org/riaa/cases/vol_X/285-355.pdf.

Harry Roberts (*United States of America*) *v. United Mexican States*, available at, http://legal.un.org/riaa/cases/vol_IV/77-81.pdf.

INA Corporation v. Iran, Iran-US Claims Tribunal, Award No. 184-161-1, 12 August 1985, available at, https://jusmundi.com/en/document/decision/en-ina-corporation-v-the-government-of-the-islamic-republic-of-iran-award-award-no-184-161-1-tuesday-13th-august-1985#decision_4872.

L. F. H. Neer and Pauline Neer (*United States of America*) *v. United Mexican States*, available at, http://legal.un.org/riaa/cases/vol_IV/60-66.pdf.

Libyan Arab Foreign Investment Company v. The Republic of Burundi (*1991*), in Yamada, Takuhei, 'State of Necessity in International Law: A Study of International Judicial Cases', *Kobe-Gakuin Law and Politics Review*, 34(4): 2005, pp. 139–143.

Rainbow Warrior case (*New Zealand* v. *France*) (1990), 20 *RIAA*, Vol. XX, pp. 215–284.

T.O.R.N. v. European Organization for Nuclear Research (*CERN*), International Labour Organization, Administrative Tribunal, 94th sess., 3 February 2003, available at, http://www.ilo.org/dyn/triblex/triblexmain.fullText?p_lang=en&p_judgment_no=2183&p_language_code=EN.

The Cyprus Case (Greece v. the United Kingdom), European Court of Human Rights (1958–59).

The Fur Seal Case (1893), Yamada, Takuhei, 'State of Necessity in International Law: A Study of International Judicial Cases', *Kobe-Gakuin Law and Politics Review*, 34(4): 2005, pp. 114–116.

The Neptune Case (1797), Yamada, Takuhei, 'State of Necessity in International Law: A Study of International Judicial Cases', *Kobe-Gakuin Law and Politics Review*, 34(4): 2005, pp. 111–114.

GATT/WTO Disputes (in Alphabetical Orders)

GATT Disputes

Disputes Not Brought before the Panels, but Discussed By the Contracting Parties

EC – Trade Measures against Yugoslavia (1991).

EC, Australia and Canada – Trade Measures against Argentina (1982).

Egypt – Boycott against Israel and Secondary Boycott (1970).

Ghana – Ban on Imports of Portuguese Goods (1961).

Prohibition of Czechoslovakian Imports by Peru (1954).

Sweden – Import Quota System for Footwear (1975).

US – Embargo on Strategic Goods (1949).

US – Embargo on Trade with Cuba (1962).

US – Imports of Sugar from Nicaragua (1982).

US – Suspension of Obligations between the US and Czechoslovakia (1951).

US – Trade Measures Affecting Nicaragua (1986).

Disputes Brought before the Panels

Short title used in the book	Full title and citation
GATT Panel Report, *Canada – FIRA* (1984)	GATT Panel Report, *Canada – Administration of the Foreign Investment Review Act*, L/5504, adopted 7 February 1984, BISD 30S/140

Short title used in the book	Full title and citation
GATT Panel Report, *Canada – Herring and Salmon (1988)*	GATT Panel Report, *Canada – Measures Affecting Exports of Unprocessed Herring and Salmon*, L/6268, adopted 22 March 1988, BISD 35S/98
GATT Panel Report, *Canada – Provincial Liquor Boards (US) (1992)*	GATT Panel Report, *Canada – Import, Distribution and Sale of Certain Alcoholic Drinks by Provincial Marketing Agencies*, DS17/R, adopted 18 February 1992, BISD 39S/27
GATT Panel Report, *EEC – Parts and Components (1990)*	GATT Panel Report, *European Economic Community – Regulation on Imports of Parts and Components*, L/6657, adopted 16 May 1990, BISD 37S/132
GATT Panel Report, *Japan – Agricultural Products I (1988)*	GATT Panel Report, *Japan – Restrictions on Imports of Certain Agricultural Products*, L/6253, adopted 2 March 1988, BISD 35S/163
GATT Panel Report, *Thailand – Cigarettes (1990)*	GATT Panel Report, *Thailand – Restrictions on Importation of and Internal Taxes on Cigarettes*, DS10/R, adopted 7 November 1990, BISD 37S/200
GATT Panel Report, *Tuna/Dolphin I (1991)*	GATT Panel Report, *United States – Prohibition of Imports of Tuna and Tuna Products from Canada*, L/5198, adopted on 22 February 1982, BISD 29S/91
GATT Panel Report, *Tuna/Dolphin II (1994)*	GATT Panel Report, *United States – Restrictions on Imports of Tuna (EEC)*, DS29/R, 16 June 1994 (unadopted)
GATT Panel Report, *US – Canadian Tuna (1982)*	GATT Panel Report, *United States – Prohibition of Imports of Tuna and Tuna Products from Canada*, L/5198, adopted on 22 February 1982, BISD 29S/91
GATT Panel Report, *US – Malt Beverages (1992)*	GATT Panel Report, *United States – Measures Affecting Alcoholic and Malt Beverages*, DS23/R, adopted 19 June 1992, BISD 39S/206
GATT Panel Report, *US – Manufacturing Clause (1984)*	GATT Panel Report, *United States – Manufacturing Clause*, L/5609, adopted 15 May 1984, BISD 31S/74

Short title used in the book	Full title and citation
GATT Panel Report, *US – Section 337 (1989)*	GATT Panel Report, *United States – Section 337 of the Tariff Act of 1930*, L/6439, adopted 7 November 1989, BISD 36S/345
GATT Panel Report, *US – Spring Assemblies (1983)*	GATT Panel Report, *United States – Imports of Certain Automotive Spring Assemblies*, L/5333, adopted on 26 May 1983, BISD 30S/107
GATT Panel Report, *US – Taxes on Automobiles (1994)*	GATT Panel Report, *United States – Taxes on Automobiles*, DS31/R, 11 October 1994, unadopted
GATT Panel Report, *US – Trade Measures Affecting Nicaragua (1986)*	GATT Panel Report, *United States – Trade Measures affecting Nicaragua*, L/6053, dated 13 October 1986, unadopted
GATT Panel Report, *US – Tuna I (Mexico) (1991)*	GATT Panel Report, *United States-Restrictions on Imports of Tuna*, DS21/R, 3 September 1991, BISD 39S/155, unadopted
GATT Panel Report, *US – Tuna II (1994)*	GATT Panel Report, *United States – Restrictions on Imports of Tuna*, DS29/R, 16 June 1994, unadopted

WTO Disputes

Panel Reports

Short title used in the book	Full title and citation
WTO Panel Report, *Argentina – Financial Services (2015)*	Panel Report, *Argentina – Measures Relating to Trade in Goods and Services*, WT/DS453/R and Add.1, adopted 9 May 2016, as modified by Appellate Body Report WT/DS453/AB/R
WTO Panel Report, *Argentina – Hides and Leather (2001)*	Panel Report, *Argentina – Measures Affecting the Export of Bovine Hides and the Import of Finished Leather*, WT/DS155/R and Corr.1, adopted 16 February 2001
WTO Panel Report, *Australia – Apples (2010)*	Panel Report, Australia – Measures Affecting the Importation of Apples from New Zealand, WT/DS367/R, adopted 17 December 2010, as modified by Appellate Body Report WT/DS367/AB/R

Short title used in the book	Full title and citation
WTO Panel Report, *Australia – Plain Packaging (2018)*	Panel Report, Australia – *Certain Measures Concerning Trademarks, Geographical Indications and other Plain Packaging Requirements Applicable To Tobacco Products and Packaging*, WT/DS435/R, Add.1 and Suppl.1 (circulated to WTO Members 28 June 2018), WT/DS441/R, Add.1 and Suppl.1 (circulated to WTO Members 28 June 2018), WT/DS458/R, Add.1 and Suppl.1, adopted 27 August 2018, WT/DS467/R, Add.1 and Suppl.1, adopted 27 August 2018
WTO Panel Report, *Australia – Salmon (1998)*	Panel Report, *Australia – Measures Affecting Importation of Salmon*, WT/DS18/R, adopted 6 November 1998, as modified by Appellate Body Report, WT/DS18/AB/R
WTO Panel Report, *Australia – Salmon (Article 21.5 – Canada) (2000)*	Panel Report, *Australia – Measures Affecting Importation of Salmon – Recourse to Article 21.5 of the DSU by Canada*, WT/DS18/RW, adopted 20 March 2000
WTO Panel Report, *Brazil – Retreaded Tyres (2007)*	Panel Report, *Brazil – Measures Affecting Imports of Retreaded Tyres*, WT/DS332/R, adopted 17 December 2007, as modified by Appellate Body Report WT/DS332/AB/R
WTO Panel Report, *Brazil – Taxation (2017)*	Panel Reports, *Brazil – Certain Measures Concerning Taxation and Charges*, WT/DS472/R, Add.1 and Corr.1 / WT/DS497/R, Add.1 and Corr.1, 11 January 2019, as modified by Appellate Body Report, WT/DS472/AB/R
WTO Panel Report, *Canada – Pharmaceutical Patents (2000)*	Panel Report, *Canada – Patent Protection of Pharmaceutical Products*, WT/DS114/R, adopted 7 April 2000
WTO Panel Report, *Canada – Wheat Exports and Grain Imports (2004)*	Panel Report, *Canada – Measures Relating to Exports of Wheat and Treatment of Imported Grain*, WT/DS276/R, adopted 27 September 2004, as modified by Appellate Body Report, WT/DS276/AB/R

Short title used in the book	Full title and citation
WTO Panel Report, *China – Auto Parts* (2009)	Panel Reports, *China – Measures Affecting Imports of Automobile Parts*, WT/DS339/R, Add.1 and Add.2, WT/DS340/R, Add.1 and Add.2, WT/DS342/R, Add.1 and Add.2, adopted 12 January 2009, upheld (WT/DS339/R) and as modified (WT/DS340/R, WT/DS342/R) by Appellate Body Reports WT/DS339/AB/R,WT/DS340/AB/R, WT/DS342/AB/R
WTO Panel Report, *China – Publications and Audiovisual Products* (2010)	Panel Report, *China – Measures Affecting Trading Rights and Distribution Services for Certain Publications and Audiovisual Entertainment Products*, WT/DS363/R and Corr.1, adopted 19 January 2010, as modified by Appellate Body Report WT/DS363/AB/R
WTO Panel Report, *China – Rare Earths* (2014)	Panel Reports, *China – Measures Related to the Exportation of Rare Earths, Tungsten, and Molybdenum*, WT/DS431/R and Add.1, WT/DS432/R and Add.1, WT/DS433/R and Add.1, adopted 29 August 2014, upheld by Appellate Body Reports WT/DS431/AB/R, WT/DS432/AB/R, WT/DS433/AB/R
WTO Panel Report, *Colombia – Ports of Entry* (2009)	Panel Report, *Colombia – Indicative Prices and Restrictions on Ports of Entry*, WT/DS366/R and Corr.1, adopted 20 May 2009
WTO Panel Report, *Colombia – Textiles* (2016)	Panel Report, *Colombia – Measures Relating to the Importation of Textiles, Apparel and Footwear*, WT/DS461/R and Add.1, adopted 22 June 2016, as modified by Appellate Body Report WT/DS461/AB/R
WTO Panel Report, *Costa Rica – Avocados (Mexico)* (2022)	Panel Report, *Costa Rica – Measures Concerning the Importation of Fresh Avocados from Mexico*, WT/DS524/R, adopted 31 May 2022
WTO Panel Report, *EC – Asbestos* (2000)	Panel Report, *European Communities – Measures Affecting Asbestos and Asbestos-Containing Products*, WT/DS135/R and Add.1, adopted 5 April 2001, as modified by Appellate Body Report WT/DS135/AB/R

Short title used in the book	Full title and citation
WTO Panel Report, *EC – Bananas III (US) (1997)*	Panel Report, *European Communities – Regime for the Importation, Sale and Distribution of Bananas, Complaint by the United States*, WT/DS27/R/USA, adopted 25 September 1997, as modified by Appellate Body Report WT/DS27/AB/R
WTO Panel Report, *EC – Biotech Products (2006)*	Panel Reports, *European Communities – Measures Affecting the Approval and Marketing of Biotech Products*, WT/DS291/R, Add.1 to Add.9 and Corr.1 / WT/DS292/R, Add.1 to Add.9 and Corr.1 / WT/DS293/R, Add.1 to Add.9 and Corr.1, adopted 21 November 2006
WTO Panel Report, *EC – Hormones (Canada) (1998)*	Panel Report, EC – *Measures Concerning Meat and Meat Products (Hormones) (Canada)*, WT/DS48/R/CAN, adopted 18 August 1997, as modified by Appellate Body Report WT/DS26/AB/R, WT/DS48/AB/R
WTO Panel Report, *EC – Hormones (US) (1998)*	Panel Report, EC – *Measures Concerning Meat and Meat Products (Hormones) (US)*, WT/DS26/R/USA, adopted 18 August 1997, as modified by Appellate Body Report WT/DS26/AB/R, WT/DS48/AB/R
WTO Panel Report, *EC – Sardines (2002)*	Panel Report, *European Communities – Trade Description of Sardines*, WT/DS231/R and Corr.1, adopted 23 October 2002, as modified by Appellate Body Report WT/DS231/AB/R
WTO Panel Report, *EC – Tariff Preferences (2004)*	Panel Report, *European Communities – Conditions for the Granting of Tariff Preferences to Developing Countries*, WT/DS246/R, adopted 20 April 2004, as modified by Appellate Body Report WT/DS246/AB/R
WTO Panel Report, *EC – Trademarks and Geographical Indications (Australia) (2005)*	Panel Report, *European Communities – Protection of Trademarks and Geographical Indications for Agricultural Products and Foodstuffs, Complaint by Australia*, WT/DS290/R, adopted 20 April 2005

Short title used in the book	Full title and citation
WTO Panel Report, *EC – Trademarks and Geographical Indications (US) (2005)*	Panel Report, *European Communities – Protection of Trademarks and Geographical Indications for Agricultural Products and Foodstuffs, Complaint by the United States*, WT/DS174/R, adopted 20 April 2005
WTO Panel Report, *EU – Energy Package (2018)*	Panel Report, *European Union and its Member States – Certain Measures Relating to the Energy Sector*, WT/DS476/R, circulated to WTO Members 10 August 2018
WTO Panel Report, *Guatemala – Cement I (1998)*	Panel Report, *Guatemala – Anti-Dumping Investigation Regarding Portland Cement from Mexico*, WT/DS60/R, adopted 25 November 1998, as reversed by Appellate Body Report WT/DS60/AB/R
WTO Panel Report, *Guatemala – Cement II (2000)*	Panel Report, *Guatemala – Definitive Anti-Dumping Measures on Grey Portland Cement from Mexico*, WT/DS156/R, adopted 17 November 2000
WTO Panel Report, *India – Agricultural Products (2015)*	Panel Report, *India – Measures Concerning the Importation of Certain Agricultural Products*, WT/DS430/R and Add.1, adopted 19 June 2015, as modified by Appellate Body Report WT/DS430/AB/R
WTO Panel Report, *India – Patents (US) (1998)*	Panel Report, *India – Patent Protection for Pharmaceutical and Agricultural Chemical Products*, Complaint by the United States, WT/DS50/R, adopted 16 January 1998, as modified by Appellate Body Report WT/DS50/AB/R,
WTO Panel Report, *India – Quantitative Restrictions (1999)*	Panel Report, *India – Quantitative Restrictions on Imports of Agricultural, Textile and Industrial Products*, WT/DS90/R, adopted 22 September 1999, upheld by Appellate Body Report WT/DS90/AB/R
WTO Panel Report, *India – Solar Cells (2016)*	Panel Report, *India – Certain Measures Relating to Solar Cells and Solar Modules*, WT/DS456/R, adopted 14 October 2016, as modified by Appellate Body Report, WT/DS456/AB/R

Short title used in the book	Full title and citation
WTO Panel Report, *Indonesia – Autos* (*1998*)	Panel Report, *Indonesia – Certain Measures Affecting the Automobile Industry*, WT/DS54/R, WT/DS55/R, WT/DS59/R, WT/DS64/R, Corr.1 and Corr.2, adopted 23 July 1998, and Corr.3 and Corr.4
WTO Panel Report, *Indonesia – Chicken* (*2017*)	*Indonesia – Measures Concerning the Importation of Chicken Meat and Chicken Products*, WT/DS484/R, adopted 22 November 2017
WTO Panel Report, *Indonesia – Raw Materials* (*2022*)	Panel Report, *Indonesia – Measures Relating to Raw Materials* (2022), WT/DS592/R, under appeal on 8 December 2022
WTO Panel Report, *Japan – Agricultural Products* (*1999*)	Panel Report, *Japan – Measures Affecting Agricultural Products*, WT/DS76/R, adopted 19 March 1999, as modified by Appellate Body Report WT/DS76/AB/R
WTO Panel Report, *Japan – Agricultural Products* (*Article 21.5 – US*) (*2005*)	Panel Report, *Japan – Measures Affecting the Importation of Apples – Recourse to Article 21.5 of the DSU by the United States*, WT/DS245/RW, adopted 20 July 2005
WTO Panel Report, *Japan – Apples* (*2003*)	Panel Report, *Japan – Measures Affecting the Importation of Apples*, WT/DS245/R, adopted 10 December 2003, upheld by Appellate Body Report WT/DS245/AB/R
WTO Panel Report, *Japan – Apples* (*Article 21.5 – US*) (*2005*)	Panel Report, *Japan – Measures Affecting The Importation of Apples – Recourse to Article 21.5 of the DSU by the United States*, WT/DS245/RW, adopted 23 June 2005
WTO Panel Report, *Korea – Alcoholic Beverages* (*1999*)	Panel Report, *Korea – Taxes on Alcoholic Beverages*, WT/DS75/R, WT/DS84/R, adopted 17 February 1999, as modified by Appellate Body Report WT/DS75/AB/R, WT/DS84/AB/R
WTO Panel Report, *Korea – Dairy* (*2000*)	Panel Report, *Korea – Definitive Safeguard Measure on Imports of Certain Dairy Products*, WT/DS98/R and Corr.1, adopted 12 January 2000, as modified by Appellate Body Report WT/DS98/AB/R

Short title used in the book	Full title and citation
WTO Panel Report, *Korea – Government Procurement* (*2000*)	Panel Report, *Korea – Measures Affecting Government Procurement*, WT/DS163/R, adopted 19 June 2000
WTO Panel Report, *Korea – Radionuclides* (*2019*)	Panel Report, *Korea – Import Bans, and Testing and Certification Requirements for Radionuclides*, WT/DS495/R and Add.1, adopted 26 April 2019, as modified by Appellate Body Report, WT/DS495/AB/R and Add.1
WTO Panel Report, *Mexico – Taxes on Soft Drinks* (*2006*)	Panel Report, *Mexico – Tax Measures on Soft Drinks and Other Beverages*, WT/DS308/R, adopted 24 March 2006, as modified by Appellate Body Report WT/DS308/AB/R
WTO Panel Report, *Russia – Traffic in Transit* (*2019*)	Panel Report, *Russia – Traffic in Transit*, WT/DS512/R, adopted 26 April 2019
WTO Panel Report, *Russia – Pigs* (*EU*) (*2017*)	Panel Report, *Russian Federation – Measures on the Importation of Live Pigs, Pork and Other Pig Products from the European Union*, WT/DS475/R and Add.1, adopted 21 March 2017, as modified by Appellate Body Report WT/DS475/AB/R
WTO Panel Report, *Russia – Railway Equipment* (*2020*)	Panel Report, *Russia – Measures Affecting the Importation of Railway Equipment and Parts Thereof*, WT/DS499/R and Add.1, adopted 5 March 2020, as modified by Appellate Body Report, WT/DS499/AB/R
WTO Panel Report, *Saudi Arabia – Measures Concerning IP Rights* (*2020*)	Panel Report, *Saudi Arabia – Measures Concerning the Protection of Intellectual Property Rights* (*2020*), WT/DS567/R, under appeal on 28 July 2020
WTO Panel Report, *Turkey – Pharmaceutical Products* (*EU*) (*2022*)	Panel Report, *Turkey – Certain Measures Concerning the Production, Importation and Marketing of Pharmaceutical Products*, WT/DS582/12, 11 November 2021, as modified by Award of the Arbitrators, WT/DS583/ARB25

Short title used in the book	Full title and citation
WTO Panel Report, *Turkey – Textiles (1999)*	Panel Report, *Turkey – Restrictions on Imports of Textile and Clothing Products*, WT/DS34/R, adopted 19 November 1999, as modified by Appellate Body Report WT/DS34/AB/R
WTO Panel Report, *US – 1916 Act* (2000)	Panel Report, *United States – Anti-Dumping Act of 1916, Complaint by the European Communities*, WT/DS136/R and Corr.1, adopted 26 September 2000, upheld by Appellate Body Report WT/DS136/AB/R, WT/DS162/AB/R
WTO Panel Report, *US – Animals* (2015)	Panel Report, *United States – Measures Affecting the Importation of Animals, Meat and Other Animal Products from Argentina*, WT/DS447/R and Add.1, adopted 31 August 2015
US – Certain Measures on Steel and Aluminum Products (China) (2022)	*United States – Certain Measures on Steel and Aluminum Products, Complaint by China*, WT/DS/544/R, under appeal on 26 January 2023
WTO Panel Report, US – Certain Measures on Steel and Aluminum Products (Norway) (2022)	*United States – Certain Measures on Steel and Aluminum Products, Complaint by Norway*, WT/DS/552/R, under appeal on 26 January 2023
US – Certain Measures on Steel and Aluminum Products (Switzerland) (2022)	*United States – Certain Measures on Steel and Aluminum Products, Complaint by Switzerland*, WT/DS/556/R, under appeal on 26 January 2023
US – Certain Measures on Steel and Aluminum Products (Türkiye) (2022)	*United States – Certain Measures on Steel and Aluminum Products, Complaint by Türkiye*, WT/DS/564/R, under appeal on 26 January 2023
WTO Panel Report, *US – Clove Cigarettes* (2012)	Panel Report, *United States – Measures Affecting the Production and Sale of Clove Cigarettes*, WT/DS406/R, adopted 24 April 2012, as modified by Appellate Body Report WT/DS406/AB/R

Short title used in the book	Full title and citation
WTO Panel Report, *US – Customs Bond Directive* (2008)	Panel Report, *United States – Customs Bond Directive for Merchandise Subject to Anti-Dumping/Countervailing Duties*, WT/DS345/R, adopted 1 August 2008, as modified by Appellate Body Report WT/DS343/AB/R, WT/DS345/AB/R
WTO Panel Report, *US – Gambling* (2005)	Panel Report, *United States – Measures Affecting the Cross-Border Supply of Gambling and Betting Services*, WT/DS285/R, adopted 20 April 2005, as modified by Appellate Body Report WT/DS285/AB/R
WTO Panel Report, *US – Line Pipe* (2002)	Panel Report, *United States – Definitive Safeguard Measures on Imports of Circular Welded Carbon Quality Line Pipe from Korea*, WT/DS202/R, adopted 8 March 2002, as modified by Appellate Body Report WT/DS202/AB/
WTO Panel Report, *US – Origin Marking Requirement* (2022)	Panel Report, *United States – Origin Marking Requirement*, WT/DS/597
WTO Panel Report, *US – Poultry (China)* (2010)	Panel Report, *United States – Certain Measures Affecting Imports of Poultry from China*, WT/DS392/R, adopted 25 October 2010
WTO Panel Report, *US – Section 211 Appropriations Act* (2002)	Panel Report, *United States – Section 211 Omnibus Appropriations Act of 1998*, WT/DS176/R, adopted 1 February 2002, as modified by Appellate Body Report WT/DS176/AB/R
WTO Panel Report, *US – Shrimp (Article 21.5 – Malaysia)* (2001)	Panel Report, *United States – Import Prohibition of Certain Shrimp and Shrimp Products – Recourse to Article 21.5 of the DSU by Malaysia*, WT/DS58/RW, 15 June 2001, as modified by Appellate Body Report, WT/DS58/AB/RW

Short title used in the book	Full title and citation
WTO Panel Report, *US – Steel Safeguards* (2003)	Panel Reports, *United States – Definitive Safeguard Measures on Imports of Certain Steel Products*, WT/DS248/R and Corr.1, WT/DS249/R and Corr.1, WT/DS251/R and Corr.1, WT/DS252/R and Corr.1, WT/DS253/R and Corr.1, WT/DS254/R and Corr.1, WT/DS258/R and Corr.1, WT/DS259/R and Corr.1, adopted 10 December 2003, as modified by Appellate Body Report WT/DS248/AB/R,WT/DS249/AB/R,WT/DS251/AB/R,WT/DS252/AB/R,WT/DS253/AB/R,WT/DS254/AB/R,WT/DS258/AB/R,WT/DS259/AB/R
WTO Panel Report, *US – Tariff Measures on Certain Goods from China* (2020)	Panel Report, *United States – Tariff Measures on Certain Goods from China*, WT/DS543, under appeal on 26 October 2020
WTO Panel Report, *US – Tuna II (Mexico)* (2012)	Panel Report, *United States – Measures Concerning the Importation, Marketing and Sale of Tuna and Tuna Products*, WT/DS381/R, adopted 13 June 2012, as modified by Appellate Body Report WT/DS381/AB/R
WTO Panel Report, *US – Wheat Gluten* (2001)	Panel Report, *United States – Definitive Safeguard Measures on Imports of Wheat Gluten from the European Communities*, WT/DS166/R, adopted 19 January 2001, as modified by Appellate Body Report WT/DS166/AB/R
WTO Panel Report, *US – Wool Shirts and Blouses* (1997)	Panel Report, *United States – Measure Affecting Imports of Woven Wool Shirts and Blouses from India*, WT/DS33/R, adopted 23 May 1997, upheld by Appellate Body Report WT/DS33/AB/R
WTO Panel Reports, *China – Raw Materials* (2012)	Panel Reports, *China – Measures Related to the Exportation of Various Raw Materials*, WT/DS394/R, WT/DS395/R, WT/DS398/R / and Corr.1, adopted 22 February 2012, as modified by Appellate Body Reports WT/DS394/AB/R, WT/DS395/AB/R, WT/DS398/AB/R

Short title used in the book	Full title and citation
WTO Panel Reports, *EC – Seal Products* (2014)	Panel Reports, *European Communities – Measures Prohibiting the Importation and Marketing of Seal Products*, WT/DS400/R and Add.1, WT/DS401/R and Add.1, adopted 18 June 2014, as modified by Appellate Body Reports WT/DS400/AB/R, WT/DS401/AB/R
WTO Panel Reports, *US – COOL* (2012)	Panel Reports, *United States – Certain Country of Origin Labelling (COOL) Requirements*, WT/DS384/R,WT/DS386/R, adopted 23 July 2012, as modified by Appellate Body Reports WT/DS384/AB/R / WT/DS386/AB/R

Appellate Body Reports

Short title used in the book	Full title and citation
Appellate Body Report, *Argentina – Footwear* (2000)	Appellate Body Report, *Argentina – Safeguard Measures on Imports of Footwear*, WT/DS121/AB/R, adopted 12 January 2000
Appellate Body Report, *Australia – Apples* (2010)	Appellate Body Report, *Australia – Measures Affecting the Importation of Apples from New Zealand*, WT/DS367/AB/R, adopted 17 December 2010
Appellate Body Report, *Australia – Salmon* (1998)	Appellate Body Report, *Australia – Measures Affecting Importation of Salmon*, WT/DS18/AB/R, adopted 6 November 1998
Appellate Body Report, *Brazil – Desiccated Coconut* (1997)	Appellate Body Report, *Brazil – Measures Affecting Desiccated Coconut*, WT/DS22/AB/R, adopted 20 March 1997
Appellate Body Report, *Brazil – Retreaded Tyres* (2007)	Appellate Body Report, *Brazil – Measures Affecting Imports of Retreaded Tyres*, WT/DS332/AB/R, adopted 17 December 2007

Short title used in the book	Full title and citation
Appellate Body Report, *Canada – Aircraft* (1999)	Appellate Body Report, *Canada – Measures Affecting the Export of Civilian Aircraft*, WT/DS70/AB/R, adopted 20 August 1999
Appellate Body Report, *Canada – Patent Term* (2000)	Appellate Body Report, *Canada – Term of Patent Protection*, WT/DS170/AB/R, adopted 12 October 2000
Appellate Body Report, *Canada – Periodicals* (1997).	Appellate Body Report, *Canada – Certain Measures Concerning Periodicals*, WT/DS31/AB/R, adopted 30 July 1997
Appellate Body Report, *China – Publications and Audiovisual Products* (2010)	Appellate Body Report, *China – Measures Affecting Trading Rights and Distribution Services for Certain Publications and Audiovisual Entertainment Products*, WT/DS363/AB/R, adopted 19 January 2010
Appellate Body Report, *China – Rare Earths* (2014)	Appellate Body Reports, *China – Measures Related to the Exportation of Rare Earths, Tungsten, and Molybdenum*, WT/DS431/AB/R, WT/DS432/AB/R, WT/DS433/AB/R, adopted 29 August 2014
Appellate Body Report, *Colombia – Textiles* (2016)	Appellate Body Report, *Colombia – Measures Relating to the Importation of Textiles, Apparel and Footwear*, WT/DS461/AB/R and Add.1, adopted 22 June 2016
Appellate Body Report, *Dominican Republic – Import and Sale of Cigarettes* (2005)	Appellate Body Report, *Dominican Republic – Measures Affecting the Importation and Internal Sale of Cigarettes*, WT/DS302/AB/R, adopted 19 May 2005
Appellate Body Report, *EC – Asbestos* (2001)	Appellate Body Report, *European Communities – Measures Affecting Asbestos and Asbestos-Containing Products*, WT/DS135/AB/R, adopted 5 April 2001
Appellate Body Report, *EC – Bananas III* (1997)	Appellate Body Report, *European Communities – Regime for the Importation, Sale and Distribution of Bananas*, WT/DS27/AB/R, adopted 25 September 1997

Short title used in the book	Full title and citation
Appellate Body Report, EC – *Computer Equipment* (*1998*)	Appellate Body Report, *European Communities – Customs Classification of Certain Computer Equipment*, WT/DS62/AB/R, WT/DS67/AB/R, WT/DS68/AB/R, adopted 22 June 1998
Appellate Body Reportc, EC – *Export Subsidies on Sugar* (*2005*)	Appellate Body Reports, *European Communities – Export Subsidies on Sugar*, WT/DS265/AB/R WT/DS266/AB/R WT/DS283/AB/R, adopted 19 May 2005
Appellate Body Report, EC – *Hormones* (*1998*)	Appellate Body Report, EC *Measures Concerning Meat and Meat Products* (*Hormones*), WT/DS26/AB/R, WT/DS48/AB/R, adopted 13 February 1998
Appellate Body Report, EC – *Poultry* (*1998*)	Appellate Body Report, *European Communities – Measures Affecting the Importation of Certain Poultry Products*, WT/DS69/AB/R, adopted 23 July 1998
Appellate Body Report, EC – *Sardines* (*2002*)	Appellate Body Report, *European Communities – Trade Description of Sardines*, WT/DS231/AB/R, adopted 23 October 2002
Appellate Body Report, EC *and certain member States – Large Civil Aircraft* (*2011*)	Appellate Body Report, *European Communities and Certain Member States – Measures Affecting Trade in Large Civil Aircraft*, WT/DS316/AB/R, adopted 1 June 2011
Appellate Body Report, EC – *Tariff Preferences* (*2004*)	Appellate Body Report, *European Communities – Conditions for the Granting of Tariff Preferences to Developing Countries*, WT/DS246/AB/R, adopted 20 April 2004
Appellate Body Report, *Guatemala – Cement I* (*1998*)	Appellate Body Report, *Guatemala – Anti-Dumping Investigation Regarding Portland Cement from Mexico*, WT/DS60/AB/R, adopted 25 November 1998
Appellate Body Report, *India – Agricultural Products* (*2015*)	Appellate Body Report, *India – Measures Concerning the Importation of Certain Agricultural Products*, WT/DS430/AB/R, adopted 19 June 2015
Appellate Body Report, *India – Patents* (*1998*)	Appellate Body Report, *India – Patent Protection for Pharmaceutical and Agricultural Chemical Products*, WT/DS50/AB/R, adopted 16 January 1998

Short title used in the book	Full title and citation
Appellate Body Report, *India – Patents (US) (1998)*	Appellate Body Report, *India – Patent Protection for Pharmaceutical and Agricultural Chemical Products*, WT/DS50/AB/R, adopted 16 January 1998, DSR 1998
Appellate Body Report, *India – Solar Cells (2016)*	Appellate Body Report, *India – Certain Measures Relating to Solar Cells and Solar Modules*, WT/DS456/AB/R and Add.1
Appellate Body Report, *Indonesia – Import Licensing Regimes (2017)*	Appellate Body Report, *Indonesia – Importation Of Horticultural Products, Animals And Animal Products*, WT/DS477/AB/R, WT/DS478/AB/R, adopted 22 November 2017
Appellate Body Report, *Japan – Agricultural Products (Varietals) (1999)*	Appellate Body Report, *Japan – Measures Affecting Agricultural Products*, WT/DS76/AB/R, adopted 19 March 1999
Appellate Body Report, *Japan – Alcoholic Beverages II (1996)*	Appellate Body Report, *Japan – Taxes on Alcoholic Beverages*, WT/DS8/AB/R, WT/DS10/AB/R, WT/DS11/AB/R, adopted 1 November 1996
Appellate Body Report, *Japan – Apples (2003)*	Appellate Body Report, *Japan – Measures Affecting the Importation of Apples*, WT/DS245/AB/R, adopted 10 December 2003
Appellate Body Report, *Korea – Dairy (2000)*	Appellate Body Report, *Korea – Definitive Safeguard Measure on Imports of Certain Dairy Products*, WT/DS98/AB/R, adopted 12 January 2000
Appellate Body Report, *Korea – Radionuclides (2019)*	Appellate Body Report, *Korea – Import Bans, and Testing and Certification Requirements for Radionuclides*, WT/DS495/AB/R and Add.1, adopted 26 April 2019
Appellate Body Report, *Korea – Various Measures on Beef (2001)*	Appellate Body Report, *Korea – Measures Affecting Imports of Fresh, Chilled and Frozen Beef*, WT/DS161/AB/R, WT/DS169/AB/R, adopted 10 January 2001
Appellate Body Report, *Mexico – Taxes on Soft Drinks (2006)*	Appellate Body Report, *Mexico – Tax Measures on Soft Drinks and Other Beverages*, WT/DS308/AB/R, adopted 24 March 2006
Appellate Body Report, *Peru – Agricultural Products (2015)*	Appellate Body Report, *Peru – Additional Duty on Imports of Certain Agricultural Products*, WT/DS457/AB/R and Add.1, adopted 31 July 2015

Short title used in the book	Full title and citation
Appellate Body Report, *Russia – Railway Equipment* (2020)	Appellate Body Report, *Russia – Measures Affecting the Importation of Railway Equipment and Parts Thereof*, WT/DS499/AB/R/, adopted 5 March 2020
Appellate Body Report, *Thailand – Cigarettes (Philippines)* (2011)	Appellate Body Report, *Thailand – Customs and Fiscal Measures on Cigarettes from the Philippines*, WT/DS371/AB/R, adopted 15 July 2011
Appellate Body Report, *US – Anti-Dumping and Countervailing Duties (China)* (2011)	Appellate Body Report, *United States – Definitive Anti-Dumping and Countervailing Duties on Certain Products from China*, WT/DS379/AB/R, adopted 25 March 2011
Appellate Body Report, *US – Clove Cigarettes* (2012)	Appellate Body Report, *United States – Measures Affecting the Production and Sale of Clove Cigarettes*, WT/DS406/AB/R, adopted 24 April 2012
Appellate Body Report, *US – Cotton Yarn* (2001)	Appellate Body Report, *United States – Transitional Safeguard Measure on Combed Cotton Yarn from Pakistan*, WT/DS192/AB/R, adopted 5 November 2001
Appellate Body Report, *US – FSC* (2000)	Appellate Body Report, *United States – Tax Treatment for "Foreign Sales Corporations"*, WT/DS108/AB/R, adopted 20 March 2000
Appellate Body Report, *US – Gambling* (2005)	Appellate Body Report, *United States – Measures Affecting the Cross-Border Supply of Gambling and Betting Services*, WT/DS285/AB/R, adopted 20 April 2005, and Corr.1
Appellate Body Report, *US – Gasoline* (1996)	Appellate Body Report, *United States – Standards for Reformulated and Conventional Gasoline*, WT/DS2/AB/R, adopted 20 May 1996
Appellate Body Report, *US – Hot-Rolled Steel* (2001)	Appellate Body Report, *United States – Anti-Dumping Measures on Certain Hot-Rolled Steel Products from Japan*, WT/DS184/AB/R, adopted 23 August 2001
Appellate Body Report, *US – Large Civil Aircraft (2nd complaint)*	Appellate Body Report, *United States – Measures Affecting Trade in Large Civil Aircraft (Second Complaint)*, WT/DS353/AB/R, adopted 23 March 2012

Short title used in the book	Full title and citation
Appellate Body Report, *US – Section 211 Appropriations Act* (2002)	Appellate Body Report, *United States – Section 211 Omnibus Appropriations Act of 1998*, WT/DS176/AB/R, adopted 1 February 2002
Appellate Body Report, *US – Shrimp* (1998)	Appellate Body Report, *United States – Import Prohibition of Certain Shrimp and Shrimp Products*, WT/DS58/AB/R, adopted 6 November 1998
Appellate Body Report, *US – Softwood Lumber V (Article 21.5 – Canada)* (2006)	Appellate Body Report, *United States – Final Dumping Determination on Softwood Lumber from Canada – Recourse to Article 21.5 of the DSU by Canada*, WT/DS264/AB/RW, mutually agreed solution on implementation notified 12 October 2006
Appellate Body Report, *US – Tuna II (Mexico)* (2012)	Appellate Body Report, *United States – Measures Concerning the Importation, Marketing and Sale of Tuna and Tuna Products*, WT/DS381/AB/R, adopted 13 June 2012
Appellate Body Report, *US – Tuna II (Mexico) (Article 21.5 II)* (2019)	Appellate Body Report, *United States – Measures Concerning the Importation, Marketing and Sale of Tuna and Tuna Products, Second Recourse to Article 21.5 of the DSU by Mexico*, WT/DS381/AB/RW/USA, WT/DS381/AB/RW2, adopted 11 January 2019
Appellate Body Report, *US – Upland Cotton* (2005)	Appellate Body Report, *United States – Subsidies on Upland Cotton*, WT/DS267/AB/R, adopted 21 March 2005
Appellate Body Report, *US – Wool Shirts and Blouses* (1997)	Appellate Body Report, *United States – Measure Affecting Imports of Woven Wool Shirts and Blouses from India*, WT/DS33/AB/R, adopted 23 May 1997, and Corr.1,
Appellate Body Report, *US – Zeroing (Japan)* (2007)	Appellate Body Report, *United States – Measures Relating to Zeroing and Sunset Reviews*, WT/DS322/AB/R, adopted 23 January 2007
Appellate Body Reports, *China – Raw Materials* (2012)	Appellate Body Reports, *China – Measures Related to the Exportation of Various Raw Materials*, WT/DS394/AB/R, WT/DS395/AB/R, WT/DS398/AB/R, adopted 22 February 2012

Short title used in the book	Full title and citation
Appellate Body Reports, *EC – Seal Products* (2014)	Appellate Body Reports, *European Communities – Measures Prohibiting the Importation and Marketing of Seal Products*, WT/DS400/AB/R, WT/DS401/AB/R, adopted 18 June 2014
Appellate Body Reports, *US – COOL* (2012)	Appellate Body Reports, *United States – Certain Country of Origin Labelling (COOL) Requirements*, WT/DS384/AB/R, WT/DS386/AB/R, adopted 23 July 2012
Appellate Body Reports, *US – COOL (Article 21.5 – Canada and Mexico)* (2015)	Appellate Body Reports, *United States – Certain Country of Origin Labelling (COOL) Requirements – Recourse to Article 21.5 of the DSU by Canada and Mexico*, WT/DS384/AB/RW, WT/DS386/AB/RW, adopted 29 May 2015
Appellate Body Reports, *US/Canada – Continued Suspension* (2008)	Appellate Body Report, *United States – Continued Suspension of Obligations in the EC – Hormones Dispute*, WT/DS320/AB/R, adopted 14 November 2008 and Appellate Body Report, *Canada – Continued Suspension of Obligations in the EC – Hormones Dispute*, WT/DS321/AB/R, adopted 14 November 2008

Reports of Arbitrators

Short title used in the book	Full title and citation
Decision by the Arbitrator, *Brazil – Aircraft (Article 22.6 – Brazil)* (2000)	Decision by the Arbitrator, *Brazil – Export Financing Programme for Aircraft – Recourse to Arbitration by Brazil under Article 22.6 of the DSU and Article 4.11 of the SCM Agreement*, WT/DS46/ARB, 28 August 2000

Short title used in the book	Full title and citation
Decision by the Arbitrator, *EC – Hormones (US) (Article 22.6 – EC) (1999)*	Decision by the Arbitrator, *European Communities – Measures Concerning Meat and Meat Products (Hormones), Original Complaint by the United States – Recourse to Arbitration by the European Communities under Article 22.6 of the DSU*, WT/DS26/ARB, 12 July 1999
Award of the Arbitrators, *Turkey – Pharmaceutical Products* (2022)	Award of the Arbitrators, *Turkey – Certain Measures Concerning the Production, Importation and Marketing of Pharmaceutical Products*, WT/DS583/ARB25, 25 July 2022

Theses

Al-Muntari, Mansour A., *Necessity in Islamic Law*, Thesis submitted to the University of Geneva for PhD in Law (Edinburgh: 1997).

Bogliolo, Luís Paulo, *Rethinking Military Necessity in the Law of Armed Conflict* (unpublished LL.M. Thesis, London School of Economics) (London: 2012) available at, http://ssrn.com/abstract=2201129.

Heathcote, Sarah, *State of Necessity and International Law*, Thesis no. 772, submitted to the University of Geneva for PhD in Law (Geneva: 2005).

Hoofnagle, Wendy Marie, *Creating Kings in Post-conquest England: The Fate of Charlemagne in Anglo-Norman Society*, Thesis no. 3313279, submitted to the University of Connecticut for PhD (Connecticut: 2008).

Hsiao, Fei-Chen, *Necessity Test in the Jurisprudence of the Appellate Body of the World Trade Organization*, Master's Thesis submitted to the World Trade Institute (MILE 5 Program) (Bern: 2005).

Moariaud, Paul, *De la Justification du Délit par L'état de Nécessité*, PhD Thesis submitted to the University of Geneva (Geneva: 1889), digital scan available at, https://archive.org/details/delajustificatiooomori.

Naegele, Charles J., *History and Influence of Law Code of Manu* (unpublished SJD Thesis at Golden Gate University School of Law) (San Francisco: 2008), available at, http://digitalcommons.law.ggu.edu/cgi/viewcontent.cgi?article=1004&context=theses.

Interviews

Prof. Ernst-Ulrich Petersmann, former Counsellor at the Legal Affairs Division of the GATT Secretariat (1981–89) and emeritus professor of international and European law and former Head of the Law Department of the European University Institute, 28 September 2017 (during the annual WTO Public Forum).

Dr. Werner Zdouc, former Director of the WTO Appellate Body Secretariat, 28 June 2017 (at the Faculty of Law of Maastricht University).

Other Sources

Damill, Mario, Frenkel, Roberto, and Rapetti, Martin, *The Argentinian Debt: History, Default and Restructuring*, Initiative for Policy, Columbia University, Working Paper Series, available at, http://policydialogue.org/files/publications/Argentinian_Debt_History_Default_Damill_Frenkel_Rapetti.pdf.

Holy Bible: Leviticus 24:5–9; 1st Samuel 21:2–7; Proverbs 6:30–33; Mathew 12:1–8; Luke 14:3–6.

Holy Koran: Sur. 5, v. 3 (Surah Al-Ma'idah); Sur. 6, v. 119 (Surah Al-An'am); Sur. 6, v. 145 (Surah Al-An'am); Sur. 16, v. 115 (Surah Al-Nahl); Surah Al-Baqarah (Surah 2, verse 185).

Ortino, Federico, 'From "non-discrimination" to "reasonableness": a paradigm shift in international economic law?', *Jean Monnet Working Paper 01/05* (2005).

Suggested Charter for an International Trade Organization of the United Nations, State Department Publication No. 2598, Commercial Policy Series 93 (September 1946).

Tams, *Christian* J., 'An Appealing Option? The Debate about an ICSID Appellate Structure', *Essays in Transnational Economic Law*, Working Paper No. 57, Martin-Luther-Universiät Halle-Wittenberg (2006), available at, http://tietje.jura.uni-halle.de/sites/default/files/altbestand/Heft57.pdf.

Index

www.ingramcontent.com/pod-product-compliance
Lightning Source LLC
LaVergne TN
LVHW012053011026
849162LV00018B/191